World Development Report 1992
Development and the Environment

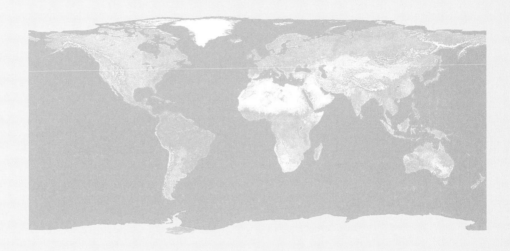

Published for the World Bank
Oxford University Press

Oxford University Press

OXFORD NEW YORK TORONTO DELHI
BOMBAY CALCUTTA MADRAS KARACHI
KUALA LUMPUR SINGAPORE HONG KONG
TOKYO NAIROBI DAR ES SALAAM
CAPE TOWN MELBOURNE AUCKLAND
and associated companies in
BERLIN IBADAN

Published by Oxford University Press, Inc.
200 Madison Avenue, New York, N.Y. 10016

Oxford is a registered trademark of Oxford University Press.

Manufactured in the United States of America
First printing May 1992

The maps that accompany the text have been prepared solely for the
convenience of the reader; the designations and presentation of material in
them do not imply the expression of any opinion whatsoever on the part of
the World Bank, its affiliates, or its Board or member countries concerning
the legal status of any country, territory, city, or area, or of the authorities
thereof, or concerning the delimitation of its boundaries or its national
affiliation.

The composite satellite photograph on the front cover
is reproduced with the permission of
The GeoSphere Project, Tom Van Sant, Inc.
146 Entrada Drive, Santa Monica, Calif. 90402 U.S.A.

ISBN 0-19-520877-3 clothbound HC
ISBN 0-19-520876-5 paperback 59.7
ISSN 0163-5085 W659
1992

Text printed on recycled paper that conforms to
the American National Standard for Permanence of Paper
for Printed Library Materials, Z39.48-1984

Foreword

World Development Report 1992, the fifteenth in this annual series, explores the links between economic development and the environment. The 1990 report on poverty, last year's report on development strategies, and this Report constitute a trilogy on the goals and means of development.

The main message of the Report is the need to integrate environmental considerations into development policymaking. The value of the environment has been underestimated for too long, resulting in damage to human health, reduced productivity, and the undermining of future development prospects. The Report argues that continued, and even accelerated, economic and human development *is* sustainable and can be consistent with *improving* environmental conditions, but that this will require major policy, program, and institutional shifts. A twofold strategy is required. First, the positive ("win-win") links between efficient income growth and the environment need to be aggressively exploited. This calls, for example, for the removal of distortionary policies (such as subsidies for energy, chemical inputs, water, and logging) that encourage the overuse of natural resources; for expanded emphasis on population programs, female education, agricultural extension and research, and sanitation and clean water; for more local participation in the design and implementation of development programs; and for open trade and investment policies, which encourage technological innovation and transfer. Second, strong policies and institutions need to be put in place which cause decisionmakers—corporations, households, farmers, and governments—to adopt less-damaging forms of behavior. Both types of policy are essential.

Where tradeoffs exist between income growth and environmental quality, the Report argues for a careful assessment of the costs and benefits of alternative policies, taking account of uncertainties and irreversibilities that may be associated with ecological processes. Some would prefer a more absolute approach to protection, but for policymakers with scarce resources seeking to raise the well-being of their citizens in an environmentally responsible manner, it is essential that tradeoffs be clarified in a rational manner and cost-effective policies designed. The Report demonstrates that much damage takes place with little or no benefit in the form of increased income and that a careful assessment of benefits and costs will result in much less environmental damage.

In emphasizing the essential consistency between sound development and environmental policies, the Report follows in the tradition of earlier analyses, including the seminal work of the World Commission on Environment and Development (*Our Common Future*, 1987). It also draws on research and experience in many parts of the World Bank and builds on the foundations laid by the Bank's Environment Department and regional environment divisions, set up in 1987. The discussion and research involved in the preparation of this Report have encouraged our economists, sector specialists, and environment staff to think more clearly and constructively about the links between environment and development and about the design of policies and programs for development that is sustainable. The lasting result is that environmental considerations will become more deeply embedded in every aspect of the Bank's work.

Like its predecessors, *World Development Report 1992* includes the World Development Indicators, which offer selected social and economic statistics on 125 countries. The Report is a study by the Bank's staff, and the judgments made herein do not necessarily reflect the views of the Board of Directors or the governments they represent.

Lewis T. Preston
President
The World Bank

March 31, 1992

This Report has been prepared by a team led by Andrew Steer and comprising Dennis Anderson, Patricia Annez, John Briscoe, John A. Dixon, Gordon Hughes, Maritta Koch-Weser, William Magrath, Stephen Mink, Kenneth Piddington, Nemat Shafik, and Sudhir Shetty. Major papers and valuable advice were contributed by Jock Anderson, Wilfred Beckerman, Nancy Birdsall, Ravi Kanbur, Theodore Panayotou, David Pearce, Anwar Shah, and David Wheeler. The team was assisted by Lara Akinbami, Ifediora Amobi, Wendy Ayres, Sushenjit Bandyopadhyay, William Cavendish, Nathalie Johnson, Andrew Parker, and Salenna Wong-Prince. The work was carried out under the general direction of Lawrence H. Summers.

Many others in and outside the Bank provided helpful comments and contributions (see the bibliographical note). Mohamed T. El-Ashry provided advice and coordinated inputs from the Bank's Environment Department. The International Economics Department prepared the data and projections presented in Chapter 1 and the environmental data appendix. It is also responsible for the World Development Indicators. The production staff of the Report included Ann Beasley, Kathryn Kline Dahl, Stephanie Gerard, Jeffrey N. Lecksell, Nancy Levine, Hugh Nees, Carol Rosen, Kathy Rosen, Walton Rosenquist, and Brian J. Svikhart. The support staff was headed by Rhoda Blade-Charest and included Laitan Alli, Trinidad S. Angeles, Kathleen Freeman, Denise M. George, Jajuk Kadarmanto, and Lucy Kimani. Frances Cairncross was the principal editor.

Contents

Text figures

Statistical appendix tables

Acronyms and initials

BOD   Biological oxygen demand

CFC   Chlorofluorocarbon

CGIAR   Consultative Group on International Agricultural Research

CITES   Convention on International Trade in Endangered Species of Fauna and Flora

EC   European Community (Belgium, Denmark, France, Germany, Greece, Ireland, Italy, Luxembourg, Netherlands, Portugal, Spain, and United Kingdom)

FAO   Food and Agriculture Organization of the United Nations

GATT   General Agreement on Tariffs and Trade

GDP   Gross domestic product

GEF   Global Environment Facility

GEMS   Global Environment Monitoring System

GHG   Greenhouse gas

GNP   Gross national product

G-7   Group of Seven (Canada, France, Germany, Italy, Japan, United Kingdom, and United States)

IBRD   International Bank for Reconstruction and Development

IDA   International Development Association

IEA   International Energy Agency

IFC   International Finance Corporation

IMF   International Monetary Fund

IPCC   Intergovernmental Panel on Climate Change

IUCN   International Union for the Conservation of Nature and Natural Resources (now World Conservation Union)

NGO   Nongovernmental organization

OECD   Organization for Economic Cooperation and Development (Australia, Austria, Belgium, Canada, Denmark, Finland, France, Germany, Greece, Iceland, Ireland, Italy, Japan, Luxembourg, Netherlands, New Zealand, Norway, Portugal, Spain, Sweden, Switzerland, Turkey, United Kingdom, and United States)

R&D   Research and development

SPM   Suspended particulate matter

UNCED   United Nations Conference on Environment and Development

UNCLOS   United Nations Convention on the Law of the Sea

UNDP   United Nations Development Programme

UNEP   United Nations Environment Programme

UNIDO   United Nations Industrial Development Organization

UNSO   United Nations Statistical Office

USAID   U.S. Agency for International Development

VOC   Volatile organic compounds

WHO   World Health Organization

Definitions and data notes

Country groups

For operational and analytical purposes the World Bank's main criterion for classifying economies is gross national product (GNP) per capita. Every economy is classified as low-income, middle-income (subdivided into lower-middle and upper-middle), or high-income. Other analytical groups, based on regions, exports, and levels of external debt, are also used.

In this edition of the *World Development Report* and its statistical annex, the World Development Indicators (WDI), the Europe, Middle East, and North Africa group has been separated into two groups, (a) Europe and (b) Middle East and North Africa. As in previous editions, this Report uses the latest GNP per capita estimates to classify countries. The country composition of each income group may therefore change from one edition to the next. Once the classification is fixed for any edition, all the historical data presented are based on the same country grouping. The country groups used in this Report are defined as follows.

• *Low-income economies* are those with a GNP per capita of $610 or less in 1990.

• *Middle-income economies* are those with a GNP per capita of more than $610 but less than $7,620 in 1990. A further division, at GNP per capita of $2,465 in 1990, is made between lower-middle-income and upper-middle-income economies.

• *High-income economies* are those with a GNP per capita of $7,620 or more in 1990.

Low-income and middle-income economies are sometimes referred to as developing economies. The use of the term is convenient; it is not intended to imply that all economies in the group are experiencing similar development or that other economies have reached a preferred or final stage of development. Classification by income does not necessarily reflect development status. (In the World Development Indicators, high-income economies classified as developing by the United Nations or regarded as developing by their authorities are identified by the symbol †.) The use of the term "countries" to refer to economies implies no judgment by the Bank about the legal or other status of a territory.

• *Other economies* are Cuba, Democratic People's Republic of Korea, and the former Union of Soviet Socialist Republics (U.S.S.R.). In the main tables of the World Development Indicators, only aggregates are shown for this group, but Box A.2 in the technical notes to the WDI contains selected indicators reported for each of these economies.

• *World* comprises all economies, including economies with less than 1 million population, which are not shown separately in the main tables. See the technical notes to the WDI for the aggregation methods used to retain the same country group across time.

Analytical groups

For analytical purposes, other overlapping classifications based predominantly on exports or external debt are used in addition to geographic country groups. Listed below are the economies in these groups that have populations of more than 1 million. Countries with less than 1 million population, although not shown separately, are included in group aggregates.

• *Fuel exporters* are countries for which exports and reexports of petroleum and gas account for at least 50 percent of exports in the period 1987–89. They are Algeria, Angola, Congo, Islamic Republic of Iran, Iraq, Libya, Nigeria, Oman, Saudi Arabia, Trinidad and Tobago, United Arab Emirates, and Venezuela. Although the former U.S.S.R. meets the established criterion, it is excluded from this group measure because of data limitations.

• *Severely indebted middle-income countries* (abbreviated to "Severely indebted" in the World Development Indicators) are fifteen countries that are deemed to have encountered severe debt-servicing difficulties. These are defined as countries in which, averaged over 1988–90, three of four key ratios are above critical levels: debt to GNP (50 percent), debt to exports of goods and all services (275 percent), accrued debt service to exports (30 percent), and accrued interest to exports (20 percent). The fifteen countries are Algeria, Argentina, Bolivia, Brazil, Bulgaria, Congo, Côte d'Ivoire, Ecuador, Mexico, Morocco, Nicaragua, Peru, Poland, Syrian Arab Republic, and Venezuela.

• In the World Development Indicators and the Environmental data appendix, *OECD members*, a subgroup of ''High-income economies,'' comprises the members of the Organization for Economic Cooperation and Development except for Greece, Portugal, and Turkey, which are included among the middle-income economies. In the main text of the *World Development Report*, the term ''OECD countries'' includes all OECD members unless otherwise stated.

Geographic regions (low-income and middle-income economies)

• *Sub-Saharan Africa* comprises all countries south of the Sahara except South Africa.

• *East Asia and the Pacific* comprises all the low- and middle-income economies of East and Southeast Asia and the Pacific, east of and including China and Thailand.

• *South Asia* comprises Bangladesh, Bhutan, India, Maldives, Myanmar, Nepal, Pakistan, and Sri Lanka.

• *Europe* comprises the middle-income European countries of Albania, Bulgaria, Czechoslovakia, Greece, Hungary, Poland, Portugal, Romania, Turkey, and Yugoslavia. Some analyses in the *World Development Report* use the categories ''Eastern Europe'' (the countries listed above except for Greece, Portugal, and Turkey) or ''Eastern Europe and former U.S.S.R.''

• *Middle East and North Africa* comprises the low- and middle-income economies of Afghanistan, Algeria, Egypt, Iran, Iraq, Jordan, Lebanon, Libya, Morocco, Oman, Saudi Arabia,

Syrian Arab Republic, Tunisia, and Republic of Yemen.

• *Latin America and the Caribbean* comprises all American and Caribbean economies south of the United States.

Data notes

• *Billion* is 1,000 million.

• *Trillion* is 1,000 billion.

• *Tons* are metric tons, equal to 1,000 kilograms, or 2,204.6 pounds.

• *Dollars* are current U.S. dollars unless otherwise specified.

• *Growth rates* are based on constant price data and, unless otherwise noted, have been computed with the use of the least-squares method. See the technical notes to the World Development Indicators for details of this method.

• *The symbol* / in dates, as in ''1988/89,'' means that the period of time may be less than two years but straddles two calendar years and refers to a crop year, a survey year, or a fiscal year.

• *The symbol* .. in tables means not available.

• *The symbol* — in tables means not applicable.

• *The number* 0 or 0.0 in tables and figures means zero or a quantity less than half the unit shown and not known more precisely.

The cutoff date for all data in the World Development Indicators is March 31, 1992.

Historical data in this Report may differ from those in previous editions because of continuous updating as better data become available, because of a change to a new base year for constant price data, and because of changes in country composition in income and analytical groups.

Economic and demographic terms are defined in the technical notes to the World Development Indicators.

Overview

The achievement of sustained and equitable development remains the greatest challenge facing the human race. Despite good progress over the past generation, more than 1 billion people still live in acute poverty and suffer grossly inadequate access to the resources—education, health services, infrastructure, land, and credit—required to give them a chance for a better life. The essential task of development is to provide opportunities so that these people, and the hundreds of millions not much better off, can reach their potential.

But although the desirability of development is universally recognized, recent years have witnessed rising concern about whether environmental constraints will limit development and whether development will cause serious environmental damage—in turn impairing the quality of life of this and future generations. This concern is overdue. A number of environmental problems are already very serious and require urgent attention. Humanity's stake in environmental protection is enormous, and environmental values have been neglected too often in the past.

This Report explores the two-way relationship between development and the environment. It describes how environmental problems can and do undermine the goals of development. There are two ways in which this can happen. First, environmental quality—water that is safe and plentiful and air that is healthy—is itself part of the improvement in welfare that development attempts to bring. If the benefits from rising incomes are offset by the costs imposed on health and the quality of life by pollution, this cannot be called development. Second, environmental damage can undermine future productivity. Soils that are degraded, aquifers that are depleted, and ecosystems that are destroyed in the name of raising incomes today can jeopardize the prospects for earning income tomorrow.

The Report also explores the impact—for good and bad—of economic growth on the environment. It identifies the conditions under which policies for efficient income growth can complement those for environmental protection and identifies tradeoffs. Its message is positive. There are strong ''win-win'' opportunities that remain unex-

ploited. The most important of these relates to poverty reduction: not only is attacking poverty a moral imperative, but it is also essential for environmental stewardship. Moreover, policies that are justified on economic grounds alone can deliver substantial environmental benefits. Eliminating subsidies for the use of fossil fuels and water, giving poor farmers property rights on the land they farm, making heavily polluting state-owned companies more competitive, and eliminating rules that reward with property rights those who clear forests are examples of policies that improve both economic efficiency and the environment. Similarly, investing in better sanitation and water and in improved research and extension services can both improve the environment *and* raise incomes.

But these policies are not enough to ensure environmental quality; strong public institutions and policies for environmental protection are also essential. The world has learned over the past two decades to rely more on markets and less on governments to promote development. But environmental protection is one area in which government must maintain a central role. Private markets provide little or no incentive for curbing pollution. Whether it be air pollution in urban centers, the dumping of unsanitary wastes in public waters, or the overuse of land whose ownership is unclear, there is a compelling case for public action. Here there may be tradeoffs between income growth and environmental protection, requiring a careful assessment of the benefits and costs of alternative policies as they affect both today's population and future generations. The evidence indicates that the gains from protecting the environment are often high and that the costs in forgone income are modest if appropriate policies are adopted. Experience suggests that policies are most effective when they aim at underlying causes rather than symptoms, concentrate on addressing those problems for which the benefits of reform are greatest, use incentives rather than regulations where possible, and recognize administrative constraints.

Strong environmental policies complement and reinforce development. It is often the poorest who suffer most from the consequences of pollution

Box 1   Development and the environment: key messages of this Report

The protection of the environment is an essential part of development. Without adequate environmental protection, development is undermined; without development, resources will be inadequate for needed investments, and environmental protection will fail.

The coming generation presents unprecedented challenges and opportunities. Between 1990 and 2030, as the world's population grows by 3.7 billion, food production will need to double, and industrial output and energy use will probably triple worldwide and increase fivefold in developing countries. This growth brings with it the risk of appalling environmental damage. Alternatively, it could bring with it better environmental protection, cleaner air and water, and the virtual elimination of acute poverty. Policy choices will make the difference.

Priorities for action

Inadequate attention has been given to the environmental problems that damage the health and productivity of the largest number of people, especially the poor. Priority should be given to:

- The one-third of the world's population that has inadequate sanitation and the 1 billion without safe water
- The 1.3 billion people who are exposed to unsafe conditions caused by soot and smoke
- The 300 million to 700 million women and children who suffer from severe indoor air pollution from cooking fires
- The hundreds of millions of farmers, forest dwellers, and indigenous people who rely on the land

and whose livelihoods depend on good environmental stewardship.

Addressing the environmental problems faced by these people will require better progress in reducing poverty and raising productivity. It is imperative that the current moment of opportunity be seized to bring about an *acceleration* of human and economic development that is sustained and equitable.

Policies for sustained development

Two types of policies are required: those that build on the positive links between development and the environment, and those that break the negative links.

Building on the positive links

The scope for actions that promote income growth, poverty alleviation, and environmental improvement is very large, especially in developing countries. Such ''win-win'' policies include:

- Removing subsidies that encourage excessive use of fossil fuels, irrigation water, and pesticides and excessive logging
- Clarifying rights to manage and own land, forests, and fisheries
- Accelerating provision of sanitation and clean water, education (especially for girls), family planning services, and agricultural extension, credit, and research
- Taking measures to empower, educate, and involve farmers, local communities, indigenous people, and women so that they can make decisions and investments in their own long-term interests.

and environmental degradation. Unlike the rich, the poor cannot afford to protect themselves from contaminated water; in cities they are more likely to spend much of their time on the streets, breathing polluted air; in rural areas they are more likely to cook on open fires of wood or dung, inhaling dangerous fumes; their lands are most likely to suffer from soil erosion. The poor may also draw a large part of their livelihood from unmarketed environmental resources: common grazing lands, for example, or forests where food, fuel, and building materials have traditionally been gathered. The loss of such resources may particularly harm the poorest. Sound environmental policies are thus likely to be powerfully redistributive.

Making decisions about some environmental problems is complicated by uncertainties about physical and ecological processes, by the long-term nature of their effects, and by the possibility

of thresholds beyond which unexpected or irreversible change may occur. New evidence that the impact of chlorofluorocarbons (CFCs) on stratospheric ozone depletion is greater than earlier thought is a timely reminder of how little we know. Such uncertainties call for much greater attention to research and to designing flexible precautionary policies.

Because this Report is about development and the environment, it focuses primarily on the welfare of developing countries. The most immediate environmental problems facing these countries—unsafe water, inadequate sanitation, soil depletion, indoor smoke from cooking fires and outdoor smoke from coal burning—are different from and more immediately life-threatening than those associated with the affluence of rich countries, such as carbon dioxide emissions, depletion of stratospheric ozone, photochemical smogs, acid rain,

Targeted environmental policies

But these "win-win" policies will not be enough. Also essential are strong policies and institutions targeted at specific environmental problems. Lessons for effective policymaking include the following:

• Tradeoffs between income and environmental quality need to be carefully assessed, taking long-term, uncertain, and irreversible impacts into account. Carefully balancing costs and benefits is especially important for developing countries, where resources are scarce and where basic needs still must be met.

• Standards and policies need to be realistic and consistent with the monitoring and enforcement capacity and the administrative traditions of the country.

• Blunter and more self-enforcing policies are likely to be attractive in developing countries. Policies need to work with the grain of the market rather than against it, using incentives rather than regulations where possible.

• Governments need to build constituencies for change—to curb the power of vested interests, to hold institutions accountable, and to increase willingness to pay the costs of protection. Local participation in setting and implementing environmental policies and investments will yield high returns.

The costs of a better environment

The costs of protecting and improving the environment are high in absolute terms, but they are modest in comparison with their benefits and with the potential gains from economic growth. Improving the environment for development may make it necessary to raise invest-

ment rates in developing countries by 2–3 percent of GDP by the end of this decade. This would enable stabilization of soil conditions, increased protection of forests and natural habitats, improved air and water quality, a doubling of family planning expenditures, sharply improved school enrollment rates for girls, and universal access to sanitation and clean water by 2030. The costs of addressing global atmospheric issues would be additional.

Partnership for solutions

Finding, implementing, and financing solutions will require a partnership of effort among nations. Specifically:

• Improved know-how, new technologies, and increased investment are essential. Open trade and capital markets, the restoration of creditworthiness through policy reform and selective debt relief, and robust, environmentally responsible growth in the world economy will all be needed.

• The close link between poverty and environmental problems makes a compelling case for increasing assistance to reduce poverty and slow population growth and for addressing environmental damage that hurts the poor.

• High-income countries must play a major role in financing the protection of natural habitats in developing countries from which the whole world benefits. They must also assume the primary responsibility for addressing worldwide problems of which they are the primary cause (greenhouse warming and depletion of stratospheric ozone).

and hazardous wastes. Industrial countries need to solve their own problems, but they also have a crucial role to play in helping to improve the environments of developing countries.

• First, developing countries need to have access to less-polluting technologies and to learn from the successes and failures of industrial countries' environmental policies.

• Second, some of the benefits from environmental policies in developing countries—the protection of tropical forests and of biodiversity, for example—accrue to rich countries, which ought therefore to bear an equivalent part of the costs.

• Third, some of the potential problems facing developing countries—global warming and ozone depletion, in particular—stem from high consumption levels in rich countries; thus, the burden of finding and implementing solutions should be on the rich countries.

• Fourth, the strong and growing evidence of the links between poverty reduction and environmental goals makes a compelling case for greater support for programs to reduce poverty and population growth.

• Fifth, the capacity of developing countries to enjoy sustained income growth will depend on industrial countries' economic policies; improved access to trade and capital markets, policies to increase savings and lower world interest rates, and policies that promote robust, environmentally responsible growth in industrial countries, will all help.

Policy reforms and institutional changes are required to bring about accelerated development and better environmental management. The obstacles are great. Nevertheless, the present time is unprecedented in its potential for change. The growing recognition of the importance of environmental concerns, the rapid introduction of economic reform programs around the world, and the trend toward democratization and participation in the development process all point in the right direction. The United Nations Conference on Environment and Development (UNCED)—the "Earth Summit"—in June 1992 has provided an opportunity for the world's nations to commit themselves to an agenda of reform. It is essential that the energies that have been unleashed by UNCED not be dissipated but rather be channeled toward addressing those environmental problems that most urgently threaten development.

Focusing on the right problems

This Report makes no attempt to be comprehensive in its discussion of environmental problems. Rather, it seeks to identify the most serious challenges and suggests strategies for addressing them. Not every problem can be a priority for every country. Taking the view that the highest environmental priorities are those that directly affect the welfare of large numbers of people, the Report concludes that the current environmental debate has paid too little attention to the problems of sanitation and clean water, urban air pollution, indoor air pollution, and severe land degradation.

Damage to the environment has three potential costs to present and future human welfare. Human health may be harmed. Economic productivity may be reduced. And the pleasure or satisfaction obtained from an unspoiled environment, often referred to as its "amenity" value, may be lost. All are difficult to measure, but the third is especially so. "Amenity" includes values that range from those associated with recreation to those associated with deeply held spiritual views about the intrinsic worth of the natural world. The difficulty in measuring it argues for much more public involvement in setting priorities. Table 1 outlines the potential consequences for health and productivity of different forms of environmental mismanagement. Since environmental problems vary across countries and with the stage of industrialization, each country needs to assess its own priorities carefully.

Table 1 Principal health and productivity consequences of environmental mismanagement

Environmental problem	Effect on health	Effect on productivity
Water pollution and water scarcity	More than 2 million deaths and billions of illnesses a year attributable to pollution; poor household hygiene and added health risks caused by water scarcity	Declining fisheries; rural household time and municipal costs of providing safe water; aquifer depletion leading to irreversible compaction; constraint on economic activity because of water shortages
Air pollution	Many acute and chronic health impacts: excessive urban particulate matter levels are responsible for 300,000–700,000 premature deaths annually and for half of childhood chronic coughing; 400 million–700 million people, mainly women and children in poor rural areas, affected by smoky indoor air	Restrictions on vehicle and industrial activity during critical episodes; effect of acid rain on forests and water bodies
Solid and hazardous wastes	Diseases spread by rotting garbage and blocked drains. Risks from hazardous wastes typically local but often acute	Pollution of groundwater resources
Soil degradation	Reduced nutrition for poor farmers on depleted soils; greater susceptibility to drought	Field productivity losses in range of 0.5–1.5 percent of gross national product (GNP) common on tropical soils; offsite siltation of reservoirs, river-transport channels, and other hydrologic investments
Deforestation	Localized flooding, leading to death and disease	Loss of sustainable logging potential and of erosion prevention, watershed stability, and carbon sequestration provided by forests
Loss of biodiversity	Potential loss of new drugs	Reduction of ecosystem adaptability and loss of genetic resources
Atmospheric changes	Possible shifts in vector-borne diseases; risks from climatic natural disasters; diseases attributable to ozone depletion (perhaps 300,000 additional cases of skin cancer a year worldwide; 1.7 million cases of cataracts)	Sea-rise damage to coastal investments; regional changes in agricultural productivity; disruption of marine food chain

Clean water and sanitation

For the 1 billion people in developing countries who do not have access to clean water and the 1.7 billion who lack access to sanitation, these are the most important environmental problems of all. Their effects on health are shocking: they are major contributors to the 900 million cases of diarrheal diseases every year, which cause the deaths of more than 3 million children; 2 million of these deaths could be prevented if adequate sanitation and clean water were available. At any time 200 million are suffering from schistosomiasis or bilharzia and 900 million from hookworm. Cholera, typhoid, and paratyphoid also continue to wreak havoc with human welfare. Providing access to sanitation and clean water would not eradicate all these diseases, but it would be the single most effective means of alleviating human distress.

The economic costs of inadequate provision are also high. Many women in Africa spend more than two hours a day fetching water. In Jakarta an amount equivalent to 1 percent of the city's gross domestic product (GDP) is spent each year on boiling water, and in Bangkok, Mexico City, and Jakarta excessive pumping of groundwater has led to subsidence, structural damage, and flooding.

Clean air

Emissions from industry and transport and from domestic energy consumption impose serious costs for health and productivity. Three specific problems stand out for their effect on human suffering.

SUSPENDED PARTICULATE MATTER. In the second half of the 1980s about 1.3 billion people worldwide lived in urban areas that did not meet the standards for particulate matter (airborne dust and smoke) set by the World Health Organization (WHO). They thus faced the threat of serious respiratory disorders and cancers (see Figure 1). If emissions could be reduced so that the WHO standards were met everywhere, an estimated 300,000 to 700,000 lives could be saved each year, and many more people would be spared the suffering caused by chronic respiratory difficulties.

LEAD. High levels of lead, primarily from vehicle emissions, have been identified as the greatest environmental danger in a number of large cities in the developing world. Estimates for Bangkok suggest that the average child has lost four or more

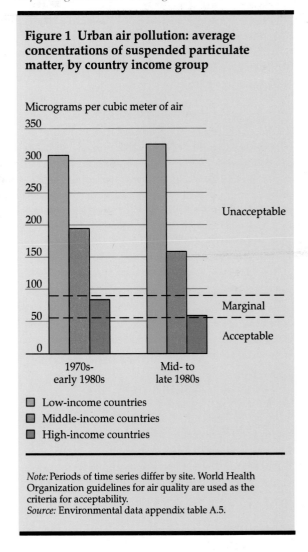

Figure 1 Urban air pollution: average concentrations of suspended particulate matter, by country income group

Micrograms per cubic meter of air

Unacceptable

Marginal

Acceptable

| 1970s-
early 1980s | Mid- to
late 1980s |

☐ Low-income countries
◼ Middle-income countries
◼ High-income countries

Note: Periods of time series differ by site. World Health Organization guidelines for air quality are used as the criteria for acceptability.
Source: Environmental data appendix table A.5.

IQ points by the age of seven because of elevated exposure to lead, with enduring implications for adult productivity. In adults the consequences include risks of higher blood pressure and higher risks of heart attacks, strokes, and death. In Mexico City lead exposure may contribute to as much as 20 percent of the incidence of hypertension.

INDOOR AIR POLLUTION. For hundreds of millions of the world's poorer citizens, smoke and fumes from indoor use of biomass fuel (such as wood, straw, and dung) pose much greater health risks than any outdoor pollution. Women and children suffer most from this form of pollution, and its effects on health are often equivalent to those of smoking several packs of cigarettes a day.

OTHER FORMS OF POLLUTION. An estimated 1 billion people live in cities that exceed WHO standards for sulfur dioxide. Nitrogen oxides and volatile organic compounds are a problem in a smaller but growing number of rapidly industrializing and heavily motorized cities.

Soil, water, and agricultural productivity

The loss of productive potential in rural areas is a more widespread and important problem, although less dramatic, than that evoked by images of advancing deserts. Soil degradation, in particular, is the cause of stagnating or declining yields in parts of many countries, especially on fragile lands from which the poorest farmers attempt to wrest a living. Erosion is the most visible symptom of this degradation. Data on soil conditions are of low quality, but crude estimates suggest that in some countries the losses in productive potential attributable to soil depletion may amount to 0.5–1.5 percent of GDP annually. Erosion can also damage economic infrastructure, such as dams, downstream. Even when erosion is insignificant, soils may suffer from nutrient, physical, and biological depletion.

Waterlogging and salinization are serious problems in some irrigated areas and are often the result of policies and infrastructure that inadequately recognize the growing scarcity of water. The increasing conflicts over the use of water mean that in the future, additional growth in agricultural productivity will have to make do with more efficient irrigation and, in some regions, less water overall.

Agricultural intensification will continue as it becomes harder to expand the area of cultivation. High levels of inputs and changes in land use will cause problems for farm communities and other parts of the economy. These problems, once confined mainly to the highly intensive agricultural systems of Europe and North America, are now increasing in such areas as the Punjab, Java, and parts of China.

Natural habitats and loss of biodiversity

Forests (especially moist tropical forests), coastal and inland wetlands, coral reefs, and other ecosystems are being converted or degraded at rates that are high by historical standards. Tropical forests have declined by one-fifth in this century, and the rate has accelerated. As Figure 2 shows, in the 1980s tropical deforestation occurred at a rate of 0.9 percent a year, with Asia's rate slightly higher

Tropical forests declined at an unprecedented rate in the 1980s

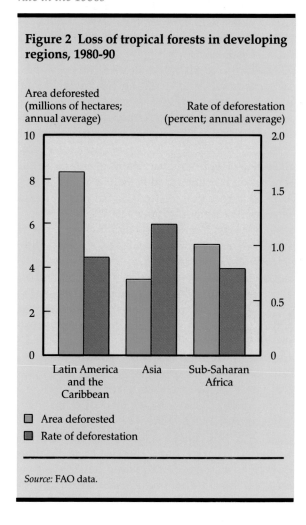

Figure 2 Loss of tropical forests in developing regions, 1980-90

Area deforested (millions of hectares; annual average)

Rate of deforestation (percent; annual average)

☐ Area deforested
■ Rate of deforestation

Source: FAO data.

(1.2 percent) and Sub-Saharan Africa's lower (0.8 percent). The loss of forests has severe ecological and economic costs—lost watershed protection, local climate change, lost coastal protection and fishing grounds—and affects people's lives. African women have to walk farther for fuelwood, indigenous forest dwellers in the Amazon have succumbed to settlers' diseases, and 5,000 villagers in the Philippines were recently killed by flooding caused in part by the deforestation of hillsides.

Extinction of species is occurring at rates that are high by historical standards, and many more species are threatened because their habitats are being lost. Models that link species extinction to habitat loss suggest that rapid rises in the rate of extinction to levels approaching those of prehistoric mass extinctions may be difficult to avoid in the next century unless current rates of deforestation and other habitat loss are sharply reduced.

Greenhouse warming

The buildup of carbon dioxide and other greenhouse gases will raise average temperatures on earth. The size of the effect remains unclear, but the best estimate of the International Panel on Climate Change (IPCC) is that average world temperatures may rise by 3° Celsius by the end of the next century under their "business as usual" scenario, with a range of uncertainty of from less than 2° Celsius to more than 5° Celsius. There is even more uncertainty about the consequences than about the extent of global warming. Although recent research has reduced fears that icecaps might melt or that the sea level might rise precipitously, there are still grounds for concern. Low-lying nations are at risk, and forests and ecosystems may not adapt easily to shifts in climatic zones. The consequences will depend both on whether policies are adopted to reduce emissions and on how effective economies are in adapting to rising temperatures. The best estimates, still extremely crude and largely based on studies in industrial countries, are that the economic costs are likely to be modest in comparison with the welfare gains brought about by higher incomes. But these costs will not be evenly distributed: climate changes will not be uniform, countries will differ in their capacity to respond to change, and the importance of agriculture, the most climate-sensitive part of the economy, differs among countries. Research is beginning on a modest scale into the potential effects on tropical agriculture; more needs to be done.

Development, the environment, and the long-term prospect

The environmental problems that countries face vary with their stage of development, the structure of their economies, and their environmental policies. Some problems are associated with the *lack* of economic development; inadequate sanitation and clean water, indoor air pollution from biomass burning, and many types of land degradation in developing countries have poverty as their root cause. Here the challenge is to accelerate equitable income growth and promote access to the necessary resources and technologies. But many other problems are exacerbated by the *growth* of economic activity. Industrial and energy-related pollution (local and global), deforestation caused by commercial logging, and overuse of water are the result of economic expansion that fails to take account of the value of the environment. Here the challenge is to build the recognition of environ-

mental scarcity into decisionmaking (Box 2). With or without development, rapid population growth may make it more difficult to address many environmental problems.

The importance of population and poverty programs

The world's population is now growing by about 1.7 percent a year. Although the rate is down from its peak of 2.1 percent in the late 1960s, absolute growth—almost 100 million a year—has never been higher. During the period 1990–2030 the world's population is likely to grow by 3.7 billion— an increase much greater than in any previous generation and probably much greater than in any succeeding one. Ninety percent of this increase will occur in developing countries. Over the next four decades Sub-Saharan Africa's population is expected to rise from 500 million to 1.5 billion, Asia's from 3.1 billion to 5.1 billion, and Latin America's from 450 million to 750 million.

Rapid population growth often contributes to environmental damage. Traditional land and resource management systems may be unable to adapt fast enough to prevent overuse, and governments may be unable to keep up with the infrastructural and human needs of a growing population. In addition, the sheer density of population will pose challenges for environmental management. Today, for example, apart from small islands and city states, only Bangladesh, the Republic of Korea, the Netherlands, and the island of Java, Indonesia, have densities exceeding 400 per square kilometer. By the middle of the next century, however, one-third of the world's population will probably live in countries with these population densities. Virtually all South Asia would have such densities (Bangladesh's would rise to 1,700 per square kilometer), as would a substantial number of African countries, the Philippines, and Viet Nam.

Rapid population growth can exacerbate the mutually reinforcing effects of poverty and environmental damage. The poor are both victims and agents of environmental damage. Because they lack resources and technology, land-hungry farmers resort to cultivating erosion-prone hillsides and moving into tropical forest areas where crop yields on cleared fields usually drop sharply after just a few years. Poor families often have to meet urgent short-term needs, prompting them to "mine" natural capital through, for example, excessive cutting of trees for firewood and failure to replace soil nutrients.

Agricultural stagnation in Sub-Saharan Africa is

Box 2 Sustainable development

The term "sustainable development" was brought into common use by the World Commission on Environment and Development (the Brundtland Commission) in its seminal 1987 report *Our Common Future*. The idea of sustaining the earth has proved a powerful metaphor in raising public awareness and focusing on the need for better environmental stewardship.

The Brundtland Commission's definition of the term—"meeting the needs of the present generation without compromising the needs of future generations"—is strongly endorsed by this Report. We also believe, with the Brundtland Commission, that meeting the needs of the poor in this generation is an essential aspect of sustainably meeting the needs of subsequent generations. There is no difference between the goals of development policy and appropriate environmental protection. Both must be designed to improve welfare.

Making the concept of sustainability precise, however, has proved difficult. It is not plausible to argue that all natural resources should be preserved. Successful development will inevitably involve some amount of land clearing, oil drilling, river damming, and swamp draining. Some have argued that natural capital should be preserved in some aggregate sense, with losses in one area replenished elsewhere. This approach has helpfully focused attention on the need to estimate the value of environmental resources and on the importance of protecting certain essential ecological systems.

This Report supports efforts to assess values but goes further. Societies may choose to accumulate human capital (through education and technological advance) or man-made physical capital in exchange, for

example, for running down their mineral reserves or converting one form of land use to another. What matters is that the overall productivity of the accumulated capital—including its impact on human health and aesthetic pleasure, as well as on incomes—more than compensates for any loss from depletion of natural capital. In the past the benefits from human activity have often been exaggerated, and the costs of environmental loss have been ignored. These costs must be built into decisionmaking, and all short- and long-term impacts must be carefully explored. This cannot be done without taking account of the uncertainties and irreversibilities associated with some environmental processes, recognizing that some environmental benefits come in intangible forms and that some impacts occur far into the future. Not all environmental resources can or should be assigned monetary values, but tradeoffs should be made as explicit as possible.

It is sometimes argued that the benefits from human investment are temporary, while the benefits of an undisturbed environment last forever. This has prompted some to advocate using a lower discount rate in project analysis. But this may lead to *more* damage (through encouraging investment) rather than less. The answer lies not in artificially lowered discount rates but in ensuring that the benefits from an expanding economy are reinvested.

Basing developmental and environmental policies on a comparison of benefits and costs and on careful macroeconomic analysis will strengthen environmental protection and lead to rising and sustainable levels of welfare. When this Report uses "sustainable development" and "environmentally responsible development," it refers to this narrower definition.

---

a particularly clear example of the mutually reinforcing nexus of poverty, population growth, and environmental damage. The slowly evolving intensification that occurred in the first half of this century was disrupted by the sharp acceleration of population growth in the past four decades. Low agricultural productivity, caused mainly by poor incentives and poor provision of services, has delayed the demographic transition and encouraged land degradation and deforestation, which in turn lowered productivity. Africa's forest declined by 8 percent in the 1980s; 80 percent of Africa's pasture and range areas show signs of damage; and in such countries as Burundi, Kenya, Lesotho, Liberia, Mauritania, and Rwanda fallow periods are often insufficient to restore soil fertility.

Ninety percent of the increase in the world's population will occur in urban areas. Indeed, only

in Sub-Saharan Africa, the Middle East and North Africa, and Central America are rural populations expected to be still increasing through the next generation. Urbanization will help reduce pressure on the rural environment, but it brings with it a different set of challenges associated with industrial growth, emissions, and wastes.

The only lasting solution to the diverse problems caused by rapid population growth lies in policies that will improve human skills, increase productivity, and so raise incomes. Improving education for girls may be the most important long-term environmental policy in Africa and in other parts of the developing world. Education is a powerful cause of reduced fertility; a recent cross-country study found that, on average, a secondary education reduces from seven to three the number of children a woman has. Access to family planning services also must be increased. The rate of contraceptive use in developing countries rose from 40 percent in 1980 to 49 percent in 1990. The population projections given above assume that the rate will rise to 56 percent by 2000 and to 61 percent by 2010. This will require expenditures on family planning programs to rise from $5 billion to $8 billion during the 1990s.

Economic growth and the environment

What pressures will economic growth place on the natural environment in the coming years? To assess this question, the Report explores a long-term projection of economic output. Under present productivity trends, and given projected population increases, developing country output would rise by 4–5 percent a year between 1990 and 2030 and by the end of the period would be about five times what it is today. Industrial country output would rise more slowly but would still triple over the period. World output by 2030 would be 3.5 times what it is today, or roughly $69 trillion (in 1990 prices).

If environmental pollution and degradation were to rise in step with such a rise in output, the result would be appalling environmental pollution and damage. Tens of millions more people would become sick or die each year from environmental causes. Water shortages would be intolerable, and tropical forests and other natural habitats would decline to a fraction of their current size. Fortunately, such an outcome need not occur, nor will it if sound policies and strong institutional arrangements are put in place.

The earth's "sources" are limited, and so is the absorptive capacity of its "sinks." Whether these limitations will place bounds on the growth of human activity will depend on the scope for substitution, technical progress, and structural change. Forcing decisionmakers to respect the scarcity and limits of natural resources has a powerful effect on their actions. For example, whereas fears that the world would run out of metals and other minerals were fashionable even fifteen years ago, the potential supply of these resources is now outstripping demand. Prices of minerals have shown a fairly consistent downward trend over the past hundred years. They fell sharply in the 1980s, leading to gluts that threatened to impoverish countries dependent on commodity exports.

With some other natural resources, by contrast, demand often exceeds supply. This is true of the demand for water, not only in the arid areas of the Middle East but also in northern China, east Java, and parts of India (see Figure 3). Aquifers are be-

Water is critically scarce in some areas but plentiful overall

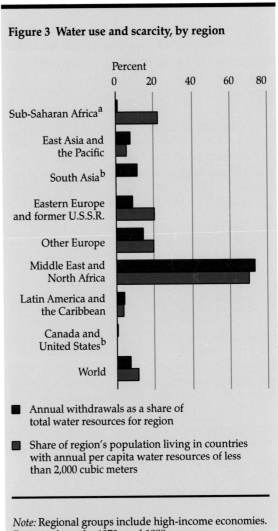

Figure 3 Water use and scarcity, by region

- ■ Annual withdrawals as a share of total water resources for region
- ■ Share of region's population living in countries with annual per capita water resources of less than 2,000 cubic meters

Note: Regional groups include high-income economies. Data are from the 1970s and 1980s.
a. Includes South Africa.
b. No countries have annual per capita water resources of less than 2,000 cubic meters.
Sources: Environmental data appendix table A.3; World Bank data.

ing depleted, sometimes irreversibly, and the extraction from rivers is often so great that their ecological functions are impaired and further expansion of irrigation is becoming severely limited.

The reason some resources—water, forests, and clean air—are under siege while others—metals, minerals, and energy—are not is that the scarcity of the latter is reflected in market prices and so the forces of substitution, technical progress, and structural change are strong. The first group is

9

characterized by open access, meaning that there are no incentives to use them sparingly. Policies and institutions are therefore necessary to force decisionmakers—corporations, farmers, households, and governments—to take account of the social value of these resources in their actions. This is not easy. The evidence suggests, however, that when environmental policies are publicly supported and firmly enforced, the positive forces of substitution, technical progress, and structural change can be just as powerful as for marketed inputs such as metals and minerals. This explains why the environmental debate has rightly shifted away from concern about *physical limits* to growth toward concern about incentives for *human behavior* and policies that can overcome *market and policy failures*.

Figure 4 illustrates how rising economic activity can cause environmental problems but can also, with the right policies and institutions, help address them. Three patterns emerge:

• Some problems decline as income increases. This is because increasing income provides the resources for public services such as sanitation and rural electricity. When individuals no longer have to worry about day-to-day survival, they can devote resources to profitable investments in conservation. These positive synergies between economic growth and environmental quality must not be underestimated.

• Some problems initially worsen but then improve as incomes rise. Most forms of air and water pollution fit into this category, as do some types of deforestation and encroachment on natural habitats. There is nothing automatic about this improvement; it occurs only when countries deliberately introduce policies to ensure that additional resources are devoted to dealing with environmental problems.

• Some indicators of environmental stress worsen as incomes increase. Emissions of carbon and of nitrogen oxides and municipal wastes are current examples. In these cases abatement is relatively expensive and the costs associated with the emissions and wastes are not yet perceived as high—often because they are borne by someone else. The key is, once again, policy. In most countries individuals and firms have few incentives to cut back on wastes and emissions, and until such incentives are put into place—through regulation, charges, or other means—damage will continue to increase. The experience with the turnarounds achieved in other forms of pollution, however, shows what may be possible once a policy commitment is made.

Figure 4 does not imply an inevitable relationship between income levels and particular environmental problems; countries can choose policies that result in much better (or worse) environmental conditions than those in other countries at similar income levels. Nor does it imply a static picture; as a result of technological progress, some of these curves have shifted downward over recent decades, providing an opportunity for countries to develop in a less damaging manner than was possible earlier.

Policies for development and the environment

Two broad sets of policies are needed to attack the underlying causes of environmental damage. Both are necessary. Neither will be sufficient on its own.

• Policies that seek to harness the positive links between development and the environment by correcting or preventing policy failures, improving access to resources and technology, and promoting equitable income growth

• Policies targeted at specific environmental problems: regulations and incentives that are required to force the recognition of environmental values in decisionmaking.

Building on the positive links

Fortunately, many policies that are good for efficiency are also good for the environment. Policies that encourage efficiency lead to less waste, less consumption of raw materials, and more technological innovation.

World Development Report 1991 described a set of "market-friendly" policies for development. These included investing in people through education, health, nutrition, and family planning; creating the right climate for enterprise by ensuring competitive markets, removing market rigidities, clarifying legal structures, and providing infrastructure; fostering integration with the global economy through promotion of open trade and capital flows; and ensuring macroeconomic stability.

All these policies can *enable* better environmental management. For example, improved education is essential for the widespread adoption of environmentally sound agricultural technologies, which are more knowledge-intensive than conventional approaches. And freedom of international capital flows can facilitate the transfer of new and cleaner technologies. Two elements of this package are especially important: the removal of distortions that encourage too much resource use, and the clarification of property rights.

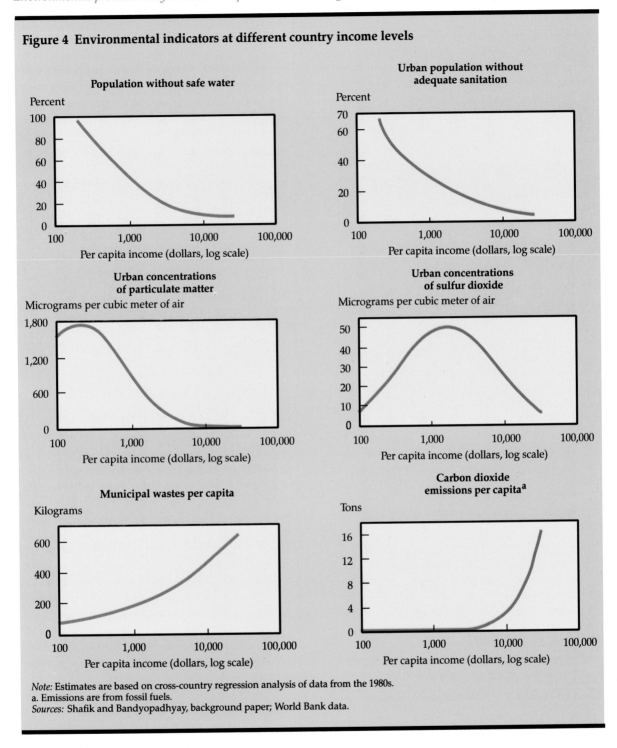

Figure 4 Environmental indicators at different country income levels

Population without safe water

Urban population without adequate sanitation

Urban concentrations of particulate matter

Urban concentrations of sulfur dioxide

Municipal wastes per capita

Carbon dioxide emissions per capita[a]

Note: Estimates are based on cross-country regression analysis of data from the 1980s.
a. Emissions are from fossil fuels.
Sources: Shafik and Bandyopadhyay, background paper; World Bank data.

REMOVING DISTORTIONS. Some government policies are downright harmful to the environment. Notable here are distorted prices in general and subsidized input prices in particular. Subsidies for energy, for example, cost developing country governments more than $230 billion a year—more than four times the total world volume of official development assistance. The former U.S.S.R. and Eastern Europe account for the bulk of this amount ($180 billion); estimates suggest that more than

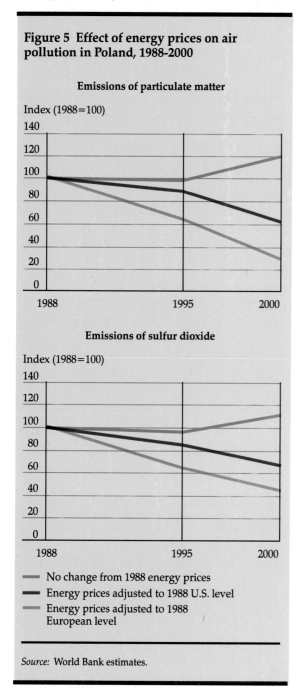

Figure 5 Effect of energy prices on air pollution in Poland, 1988-2000

Emissions of particulate matter

Index (1988=100)

— No change from 1988 energy prices
— Energy prices adjusted to 1988 U.S. level
— Energy prices adjusted to 1988 European level

Emissions of sulfur dioxide

Index (1988=100)

Source: World Bank estimates.

in a sample of five African countries ranged from 1 to 33 percent of the costs of replanting. Irrigation charges in most Asian countries covered less than 20 percent of the costs of supplying the water. And pesticide subsidies in a sample of seven countries in Latin America, Africa, and Asia ranged from 19 to 83 percent of costs.

Distorted incentives are often particularly evident in the behavior of state-owned enterprises. This is important because many sectors in which state enterprises are prominent—power generation, cement, steel, and mining—are heavy polluters; the "commanding heights" are also the "polluting heights." Thus, the environment can benefit if the managers of state enterprises are made more accountable and are exposed to the same competition as is the private sector.

CLARIFYING PROPERTY RIGHTS. When people have open access to forests, pastureland, or fishing grounds, they tend to overuse them. Providing land titles to farmers in Thailand has helped to reduce damage to forests. The assignment of property titles to slum dwellers in Bandung, Indonesia, has tripled household investment in sanitation facilities. Providing security of tenure to hill farmers in Kenya has reduced soil erosion. Formalizing community rights to land in Burkina Faso is sharply improving land management. And allocating transferable rights to fishery resources has checked the tendency to overfish in New Zealand.

The most serious mistake that governments make in seeking to eliminate open access is to nationalize resources in the name of conservation. Nationalization has often reflected the failure of policymakers and aid agencies to distinguish between traditional common-property systems, which promote sound management of natural resources, and open-access systems that result in excessive exploitation. When land and water have been nationalized and traditional management arrangements abandoned, the environmental consequences have often been severe, as they were in the forests of Nepal.

Targeted policies to change behavior

The policies described above are important, but they are not enough. Eliminating fuel subsidies will not be sufficient to end air pollution in Beijing or Mexico City. And it simply is not practical to find property-rights solutions for most of those environmental problems that adversely affect a large number of people "offsite"—air and water pollution, watershed destruction, loss of biodiversity,

half of their air pollution is attributable to these distortions (see Figure 5). The removal of all energy subsidies—including those on coal in industrial countries—would not only produce large gains in efficiency and in fiscal balances but would sharply reduce local pollution and cut worldwide carbon emissions from energy use by 10 percent. Other distortionary incentives have also had serious environmental consequences. Logging fees

and the like. For these situations specific policies are required to induce or require resource users to take account of the spillover effects that their actions have on the rest of society.

Policies designed to change behavior are of two broad types: those based on incentives ("market-based" policies), which tax or charge polluters according to the amount of damage they do, and those based on quantitative restrictions ("command-and-control" policies), which provide no such flexibility.

Market-based instruments are best in principle and often in practice. They encourage those polluters with the lowest costs of control to take the most remedial action, and they thus impose less of a burden on the economy. A survey of six studies of air pollution control in the United States found that least-cost policies could reduce the costs of control by 45–95 percent in comparison with the actual policies implemented. Economic incentives have been used for years in indirect, or blunt, forms such as fuel and vehicle taxes (most OECD countries), congestion charges (Singapore), and surcharges on potentially damaging inputs such as pesticides and plastics (Denmark and Sweden). More specific charges, such as the newly introduced carbon taxes in some European countries, tradable permits for air pollution (in the United States), deposit-refund schemes for bottles and batteries (in several European countries), hazardous waste charges and performance bonds, which are under consideration in Bangkok, and surcharges on stumpage fees to pay for replanting, as in Indonesia, are growing in importance. Industrial countries have been slow to adopt market-based strategies, in part because environmentalists contended that degrading the environment was unacceptable at any price, but more importantly because corporations feared that they would have to adopt emissions standards *and also* pay charges on the remaining emissions. Most now agree that market-based instruments have been underutilized. They are particularly promising for developing countries, which cannot afford to incur the unnecessary extra costs of less-flexible instruments that have been borne by OECD countries.

Quantitative command-and-control instruments, such as specific regulations on what abatement technologies must be used in specific industries, have acquired a bad name in recent years for their high costs and for stifling innovation. But in some situations they may be the best instruments available. Where there are a few large polluters, as was the case in the industrial city of Cubatão in Brazil, direct regulation may be the quickest and most effective instrument. Management of land use in frontier areas is another example of situations that may require direct controls.

The appropriate choice among instruments will depend on circumstances. Conserving scarce administrative capacity is an important consideration. For many developing countries blunt instruments that avoid the need for detailed monitoring will be attractive. These may involve taxes or charges on polluting inputs rather than on the pollution itself. Also attractive will be policies that provide self-enforcing incentives, such as deposit-refund and performance-bond schemes.

Several lessons can be drawn from recent experience:

• *Standards should be realistic and enforceable.* Many developing countries have set unrealistically tight standards—often those of OECD countries—and have enforced them only selectively. This has wasted resources, facilitated corruption, and undermined the credibility of all environmental policies. Laws on the books and zoning charts on the walls of government offices are often a genuine indication of concern, but unless policies are implemented, they can give a false sense that serious problems are under control. Better to have fewer and more realistic standards that are truly implemented.

• *Controls must be consistent with the overall policy framework.* Many well-intentioned policies have been thwarted by other policies that pull in the opposite direction. Both China and Poland have had pollution taxes for years, but to no effect; state-owned enterprises were not interested in profitability. Land-use planning in Sub-Saharan Africa has usually failed in the face of policies that did not encourage intensification and off-farm employment. Brazil's concern about overfishing off the Bahia coast was undermined in the early 1980s by government subsidies for new nylon nets.

• *A combination of policies will often be required.* Because environmental damage is frequently caused by different actors and for different reasons, a single policy change may not be enough. Reducing air pollution from vehicles in Mexico City, for example, will require mandated emissions and engine standards, fuel improvements, and gasoline taxes.

Reviewing public expenditures

Public expenditures can have a remarkable effect on the environment—for bad or for good. It is now clear that numerous public investments—often supported by development agencies, including the World Bank—have caused damage by failing to take environmental considerations into account or to judge the magnitude of the impacts. Indonesia's transmigration program, Sri Lanka's Mahaweli scheme, and Brazil's Polonoreste projects are examples of large programs that caused unanticipated damage in earlier years. But equally important are design issues relating to individual project components—road alignments, the design of water systems, and the provision of access to forests and wetlands.

Beginning with analysis in the 1950s and 1960s of hydroelectric projects in the United States, considerable progress has been made in applying cost-benefit techniques to environmental concerns. Such analyses have tripled estimated returns for some forestry projects and halved returns on some hydroelectric and road projects, making the latter unattractive.

Most countries and aid agencies have recently introduced environmental assessment procedures. These are still early days for such arrangements; technical skills need to be developed, and lessons are being learned about the difficulties of incorporating assessment results, which are often nonquantitative, into decisionmaking. Making the process transparent has been found to be an important way of improving its quality and impact. Listening to local views has also proved essential; some lessons from World Bank experience are that information must be shared with local people early in the life of the project and that comments from affected communities must be incorporated into project design.

Removing impediments to action

Even when straightforward ways of tackling environmental problems exist, governments have often found it difficult to translate them into effective policy. The reasons for the gap between intentions and performance include political pressures, an absence of data and knowledge, weak institutions, and inadequate participation of local people in finding solutions.

Counteracting political pressures

Stopping environmental damage often involves taking rights away from people who may be politically powerful. Industrialists, farmers, loggers, and fishermen fiercely defend their rights to pollute or to exploit resources. Examples of the results include modification of proposed carbon taxes in Europe to assist energy-intensive industries, delay in the introduction of transferable fishing rights in Chile because of pressure from powerful fishing

interests, and lack of progress almost everywhere in introducing irrigation charges. Those who are hurt when the environment is degraded, and who stand to gain most from sound policies, are often the poor and the weak. They may be less potent politically than the polluters whom governments must challenge.

A second reason for disappointing performance has to do with the inability of governments to regulate themselves. The problem arises partly because state bodies have conflicting social and economic objectives, which allow them to use resources less efficiently, and partly because of the inherent contradictions of being both gamekeeper and poacher. In the United States, for example, publicly owned municipal wastewater treatment plants are the most persistent violators of effluent discharge standards.

While private and public polluters may obstruct policy, other influences may persuade governments to set the wrong priorities. International pressures may favor issues of interest to donors rather than to developing countries. And there is always a tendency to focus on dramatic problems rather than chronic ones; few pressure groups, for example, lobby for improved sanitation or for reduced indoor air pollution. Moreover, governments may be pressed to address problems such as air pollution that affect everybody, including the rich, rather than problems such as fecal coliforms in rivers from which the rich can insulate themselves.

Improving information

Ignorance is a serious impediment to finding solutions. Governments often make decisions in the absence of even rudimentary information. International initiatives are urgently needed to overcome a grave lack of knowledge in some areas, including soil depletion (especially in Africa), land productivity in and around tropical forests, and global atmospheric issues. Countries can reap large returns from investments in basic environmental data on exposure to emissions and unsanitary conditions, soil and water depletion, land capability, and loss of forests and natural habitat.

Understanding the causes and effects of environmental damage and the costs and benefits of action is the next stage. Following a careful analysis, authorities in Bangkok found that attacking lead and particulate emissions deserved the highest priority. The U.S. Environmental Protection Agency estimated that, as a measure for avoiding deaths, placing controls on unvented indoor heaters was 1,000 times more cost-effective than further tightening certain hazardous wastes standards. A study in southern Poland discovered that the benefits from reducing emissions of particulates would greatly exceed costs but that this would not be true of controls on sulfur dioxide.

Independent commissions have proved a useful way for governments to draw on technical expertise; a growing number of developing countries, including Hungary, Nigeria, and Thailand, are finding that ad hoc commissions can bring professional objectivity to highly charged issues. In Africa, national environmental action plans, which have already been completed for Lesotho, Madagascar, and Mauritius and are under preparation for seventeen other countries, are bringing technical experts and citizens' groups into the process of setting priorities and policies.

Enhancing institutional arrangements

Governments around the world are actively seeking to strengthen their institutional capacity for environmental management. In addition to the clear needs for better technical skills, adequate finance, and a clarification of environmental regulations, experience suggests four priorities.

• *Clarify objectives and ensure accountability.* The public agencies that implement programs for the environment—forest and land departments, irrigation and water supply authorities, public works departments, and agricultural extension services—need to be held accountable for the environmental impact of their activities. The same applies to donors and aid agencies.

• *Establish the capacity to set priorities and monitor progress.* No ideal blueprint exists for environmental institutions, but a formal high-level agency for setting policies and ensuring implementation across sectors has sharply improved environmental management in Brazil, China, and Nigeria.

• *Ensure areawide coordination.* Where intersectoral decisions need to be made—the management of water within a river basin, the citywide management of pollution and wastes, the protection of a large populated forest area—coordination is required to ensure consistency and cost-effectiveness. Areawide organizations responsible for *implementation* of intersectoral plans have generally failed. Mechanisms for *coordination*, however, are essential: the recently established regional pollution units in Santiago and Mexico City are promising examples.

• *Regulate at arm's length.* Implementing agencies should be held accountable for the effects of their actions and should be kept separate from regulatory and monitoring bodies.

Involving local people

Making choices between economic and social benefits and environmental costs often requires subjective judgments and detailed local knowledge. Neither governments nor aid agencies are equipped to make judgments about how local people value their environment. A participatory process is essential. Local participation also yields high economic and environmental returns in implementing programs of afforestation, soil management, park protection, water management, and sanitation, drainage, and flood control.

Development projects that have not built on the strengths of existing practices have often failed. Haiti's top-down reforestation program was unsuccessful until small farmers and community groups were allowed to choose what kinds of trees should be planted, and where. Then, instead of the target of 3 million trees on 6,000 family farms, 20 million trees were planted on 75,000 farms. A large irrigation project in Bali, Indonesia, that failed to recognize the advantages of traditional approaches to pest management had disastrous results. A follow-up project that built on indigenous strengths succeeded.

Involving people can be expensive and in some instances can paralyze decisionmaking, hold public investments hostage to unproductive NIMBY ("not-in-my-backyard") activism, and reinforce local power structures. Experience suggests that success is greatest when tasks are devolved selectively and on the basis of actual performance. Increasing responsibilities for local governments is an important part of this process. Public agencies need training in participatory approaches and a clear indication from senior management of the importance of participation.

Putting policies to work

How can these principles be applied in practice? This Report organizes the discussion around four themes: water and sanitation, emissions from energy and industry, rural environmental challenges, and environmental challenges that cross national borders.

Water and sanitation

Investments in providing clean water and sanitation have some of the highest economic, social, and environmental returns anywhere. The 1980s witnessed progress in coverage, but the costs of inadequate provision remain enormous. In India no water supply system reliably provides water twenty-four hours a day. In rural Pakistan only 10 percent of public handpumps were functioning ten years after their installation. In the first ten weeks of the recent cholera epidemic in Peru, losses in agricultural exports and revenues from tourism were more than three times the amount that the country had invested in sanitation and water supply in the 1980s. There is growing recognition that current approaches will not meet the needs of the coming years. Changes are needed in four areas:

IMPROVING MANAGEMENT OF WATER RESOURCES. Domestic water use in developing countries will need to rise sixfold over the coming four decades. The bulk of demand will come from urban areas, where populations will triple. This increase will place severe strains on surface and groundwater supplies and will call for much more efficient allocation within river basins.

Irrigation accounts for more than 90 percent of withdrawals in low-income countries and for 70 percent in middle-income countries but for only 39 percent in high-income countries. Since domestic use almost always has a much higher private and social value than does irrigation, it is from the latter that water will need to be redirected. Governments around the world are grappling, often unsuccessfully, with the complex legal and cultural obstacles to reallocating water. Taking rights from rural areas may be impossible for legal or political reasons or undesirable for equity reasons. One solution is for urban areas to compensate farmers for the loss of irrigation water. This need not be prohibitively expensive; the current inefficiencies in use of irrigation water are so great that substantial reductions in use are often possible with only modest reductions in agricultural output.

Urban water must also be used more efficiently. Unaccounted-for water, much of it unused, constitutes 58 percent of piped water supply in Manila and about 40 percent in most Latin American countries. The reclamation of wastewater is helping conserve water in a growing number of cities, including Mexico City and Singapore, and will continue to expand.

RESPONDING TO CUSTOMER DEMANDS. The most effective means of encouraging the efficient use of water is to raise and enforce charges. On average, households in developing countries pay only 35 percent of the cost of supplying water. The vast majority of urban residents want in-house supplies of water and are willing to pay the full cost. Most countries, however, have assumed that people cannot afford to pay the full costs, and they

have therefore used limited public funds to provide a poor service to restricted numbers of people. A vicious cycle of low-level and low-reliability service and correspondingly low willingness to pay ensues. The poor suffer the most from the very policies that were supposed to help them. Excluded from the formal system, they typically pay water vendors ten times as much for a liter of water as the full cost of the same amount of piped water. But it is possible to break this pattern. First, provide those willing to pay with a good commercial service. Second, explore ways of bringing services to those unable to pay (who are much less numerous than was once thought)—by allowing longer payoff periods for capital costs, setting carefully targeted "social tariffs," or both. Third, offer people with different incomes a broader menu of options.

INCREASING INVESTMENTS IN SANITATION. Aggregate investments in water and sanitation were inadequate in the 1980s (public investment accounted for about 0.5 percent of GDP), but investments in sanitation were especially low. Most investments have been for sewage collection, with almost nothing for treatment. For example, today only 2 percent of sewage in Latin America is treated. Evidence is accumulating in countries such as Brazil, Burkina Faso, Ghana, and Pakistan that willingness to pay for household sanitation at all income levels is much higher than had been thought and is roughly equivalent to what people will pay for water and for electricity. This suggests a variety of ways of financing services if facilities can be tailored to incomes. That task may be helped by important innovations now occurring in sanitation.

RETHINKING INSTITUTIONAL ARRANGEMENTS. A recent review of forty years of World Bank experience in the water and sanitation sector identified institutional failure as the most frequent and persistent cause of poor performance. The number of employees per 1,000 water connections is two to three in Western Europe but ten to twenty in Latin America. Even so, in cities such as Caracas and Mexico City 30 percent of connections are not registered. Two conditions for better performance are essential: utilities need to be made more autonomous and more accountable for their performance, and they need to be placed on a sounder financial footing through better pricing policies. The private sector must also play a greater role. Côte d'Ivoire was a pioneer in privatizing water supply; the

Abidjan utility is one of the best run in Africa. When Guinea began franchising water supply, collection rates rose from 15 to 70 percent in eighteen months. Santiago, which contracts out many components of its water services to the private sector, has the highest staff productivity in the sector in Latin America. What holds for water supply is even more relevant to the management of solid wastes.

Privatization is not a panacea. Regulation issues are complex, and in some countries no private firms bid on contracts. Nonetheless, it is certain that the trend toward privatization will accelerate in the 1990s.

Emissions from energy and industry

The costs of pollution from industry, energy, and transport are already high and will grow exponentially if these problems are neglected. Encouraging energy conservation is a helpful first step in tackling pollution. But it cannot solve the problem alone. The effects of rising populations and incomes will soon swamp any reductions in demand per person. It is thus absolutely essential to reduce emissions per unit of production. This requires investment in new equipment and the development of new technologies.

REDUCING HOUSEHOLD ENERGY POLLUTION. Household energy use creates both indoor and outdoor air pollution. Indoor pollution is very serious in Africa and South Asia, where biomass is burned for cooking in unventilated rooms. Outdoor pollution is a great problem where low-quality coal is burned, as in China, India, and Eastern Europe.

Progress in dealing with indoor air pollution has been disappointing. Higher incomes and improved distribution systems for commercial fuels and electricity will bring about a switch away from biomass, which now accounts for 35 percent of energy use in developing countries. In the meantime, improved biomass stoves, which increase efficiency and reduce emissions, can make an important contribution and merit greater donor support.

Reduction in outdoor air pollution from household use of coal will turn (as it did in the industrial countries in the 1950s and 1960s) on two developments: policies that favor the adoption of clean coals (such as anthracite) and a transition to oil, gas, electricity, and, sometimes, district heating as household energy sources.

REDUCING POLLUTION FROM GENERATION OF ELECTRIC POWER. Because electric power generation accounts for 30 percent of all fossil fuel consumption

and 50 percent of all coal consumption worldwide, the gains from reduced pollution are substantial. Shifting to natural gas and using clean coal technologies can reduce emissions of particulates and carbon monoxide by 99.9 percent and emissions of sulfur dioxide and nitrogen oxides by more than 90 percent. Curbing emissions of particulates should be the first point of attack. It is cheap—1 to 2 percent of the total capital costs of electric power supply, on average—and, as noted earlier, it is important for human health. All new power plants should have equipment for control of particulate matter. Most new ones do, but the equipment is often not well maintained. The costs of reducing sulfur dioxide and nitrogen oxides are higher (unless natural gas is available), at 5 to 10 percent of capital costs. The effects on health of reducing these emissions are usually much lower than for particulates, and the impacts on forests, agriculture, and buildings vary greatly by area. The case for setting tough standards will depend on circumstances.

Box 3 shows how reducing pollution from electric power production requires both improvements in efficiency and investment in abatement. On average, prices today cover less than half of supply costs in developing countries, and losses in transmission are often three or four times those in industrial countries. Improved management and pricing will conserve resources and facilitate investments in abatement technologies. For example, cutting transmission losses by only one-tenth in Asia would reduce the need for investment in generating capacity during the 1990s by about $8 billion—almost enough to pay for controls to reduce particulate emissions for every new power plant to be built in the entire developing world during the 1990s.

PROMOTING USE OF RENEWABLE ENERGY. Nonfossil energy sources, especially renewable sources, offer great promise. Solar energy may have the best long-term prospects, especially if strong action is needed on carbon emissions (see below). Each year the earth receives about ten times as much energy from the sun as is stored in all fossil fuel and uranium reserves—the equivalent of 15,000 times the world's primary energy demand. The unit costs of production of photovoltaics and solar-thermal systems have fallen 95 percent in twenty years. The market for photovoltaics grew tenfold in the 1980s and, although still small, is growing at 20 percent a year. Applications include village electrification, irrigation

Box 3   Air pollution in developing countries: three scenarios

This Report shows, for a number of environmental problems, three possible paths for future development. The first, the ''unchanged practices'' scenario, assumes that current policies and patterns of resource use remain the same as in 1990. The second shows what would happen under policy and managerial reforms that would encourage more efficient use of resources. The third shows the effect of introducing both efficiency reforms and cleaner technologies and practices.

These scenarios have been quantified for the cases of pollution from energy and transport, for the use of renewable energy as a long-term means of addressing the problem of global warming, and for sanitation and water supply (see Chapters 5, 6, and 8). As an example, the top panel of Box figure 3 illustrates the case of emissions of particulates from electric power plants. The amount of electric power generated from fossil fuels doubles every five to ten years in developing countries—and so would pollution, in the absence of controls (the top curve in the figure). Raising electricity prices gradually to cost-reflecting levels (the middle curve) would reduce unnecessary waste in consumption, lower the rate of growth of pollution, and put utilities in a financially better position to invest in cleaner technologies. The bottom curve shows the effect of efficiency reforms plus pollution controls. Controls on particulate matter in coal-fired plants can reduce pollution per unit of output by 99.9 percent over the long term (see Chapter 6 for details). The investment costs for such controls are modest and are dwarfed by the efficiency gains from removing subsidies by a factor of ten to one.

Taxes on vehicle fuels are low in developing countries (and in the United States), and congestion pricing is not much used. The economic reform scenario (middle curve in the bottom panel) illustrates the potential effects on emissions (with no change in fuels) of gradually adjusting taxes to European levels and introducing a ''Singapore'' model of congestion prices in large cities. This step would have large economic benefits (see Chapters 6 and 8) and would also help to reduce pollution. Even so, emissions from vehicles in developing countries would still quadruple by 2030. The introduction of cleaner fuels and technologies is thus essential, as is illustrated for the case of lead in the bottom panel. Malaysia, Singapore, and now Mexico are phasing in lead-free fuel, using both market incentives (differential fuel and vehicle taxes) and regulations (mandatory catalytic converters and mandated emissions standards). Targeted policies of this kind would have a dramatic effect on pollution abatement (the bottom curve), and the costs would be a small fraction of the economic gains and health benefits.

Box figure 3   Selected air pollutants in developing countries: three scenarios

Emissions of particulates from electric power generation

Index (1990=100)

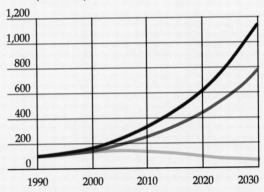

Lead emissions from vehicles

Index (1990=100)

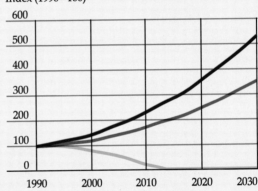

— "Unchanged practices" scenario
— Scenario with efficiency reforms
— Scenario with efficiency reforms and pollution abatement measures

Source: Anderson and Cavendish, background paper.

pumping, and power for rural health clinics. Less dramatic, but still important, progress has been made in reducing the costs of and utilizing biomass and wind power technologies. Continued rapid reductions in unit costs that can make these energy sources replicable on a very large scale will require help from industrial countries. Currently, only 6 percent of public research funds for energy is allocated to renewable sources (60 percent goes for nuclear energy and 15 percent for fossil fuels). Priorities need to be reordered.

REDUCING POLLUTION FROM TRANSPORT. Vehicles account for one-half of oil consumption in most developing countries and sometimes account for 90 to 95 percent of lead and carbon monoxide emissions. The problems are exacerbated because vehicles are often in poor condition, vehicle use is concentrated (in Mexico and Thailand half the fleet operates in the capital city), and pedestrians spend much more time in the open air than in industrial countries. Lead is the main problem. It is being tackled effectively and relatively cheaply in some countries; concentrations have gone down 85 percent in the United States and 50 percent in Europe over the past two decades. Box 3 describes how lead emissions from vehicles in developing countries could rise fivefold over the coming few decades or could fall to negligible levels. Policy choices account for the difference.

REDUCING INDUSTRIAL POLLUTION. In attacking industrial pollution and wastes, it is necessary to distinguish between large plants, which can be individually monitored and regulated, and the many thousands of small plants, which cannot. The former dominate the heavy, pollution-intensive industries (chemicals, metallurgy, cement, mining, and paper and pulp). The worst problems include emissions of heavy metals from smelters and manufacturing plants (particularly in Eastern Europe) and toxic emissions from chemical and fertilizer plants, especially in Latin America, Asia, and Eastern Europe. Water pollution that takes oxygen from rivers and kills river life is a problem everywhere. Technologies for dealing with these problems already exist and need not be expensive except for the heaviest polluters. Capital spending on controls cost 5 percent of total industrial investment in Germany, Japan, and the United States in the 1980s.

A pragmatic approach to big polluters is required. The common practice of adopting industrial country standards and then negotiating with individual firms about their enforcement has not worked. It has led to inequities and in some cases, as in Chile's copper-mining industry, is inducing foreign-owned companies to argue for tight standards that are equitably applied. Incentive-based instruments must be more widely used. Effluent charges will be especially important, and some countries, including Thailand, are considering innovative approaches such as the use of performance bonds for the management of hazardous wastes. Revenues from such charges can be used for treatment facilities and to defray the administrative costs associated with environmental audits and enforcement.

Controlling emissions from smaller plants is more difficult and calls for indirect instruments. Taxation of inputs—energy, chemicals, and technologies—can help, and deposit-refund schemes are potentially powerful. Leather tanning and small-scale gold mining pose particular problems because of their toxic emissions into rivers.

Rural environmental challenges

Two important environmental and natural resource challenges face rural people and policymakers:

• Preventing the resource degradation that can result from rapidly growing demands for food, fuel, and fiber and from poor stewardship due to poverty, ignorance, and corruption

• Preserving valuable natural forests, wetlands, coastal areas, and grasslands from being taken over for relatively low-value uses that are artificially encouraged by bad policies, imperfect markets, and flawed institutions.

PROBLEMS ON AND AROUND FARMS. Ninety percent of the doubling in food production over the past quarter century came from higher yields and only 10 percent from cultivating more land. Intensification, which will account for most future increases in production, will create environmental problems. The right policies are of two types: those that enable farmers to do what is in their own interests, such as managing soils better, and those that provide incentives to stop behavior which primarily hurts others.

Protecting soils from erosion and nutrient depletion—an urgent priority in many parts of the world—falls mainly into the first category. Many options are available, including contour-based operations, intercropping, agroforestry, and changes in fertilizer application and animal husbandry.

These improvements can sharply reduce erosion and raise yields and incomes. Why, then, are they not universally undertaken? The reasons include lack of access to credit markets and lack of knowledge of costs and benefits. Sometimes government failures may be the cause; artificially low farmgate prices may undermine profitability, or fertilizers may be rationed because of subsidies or poor distribution channels. In all such cases policies for development and policies for environmental protection are just different aspects of the same agenda. Reforming agricultural policies can be politically difficult. Strengthening local research, extension, and credit systems to enable farmers to make appropriate investments requires a long-term commitment and more support from donors. There is, however, no alternative if agriculture is to be put on a sustainable footing.

The overuse of pesticides is causing two problems: declining effectiveness through the emergence of resistance, and localized health problems caused by runoff. Governments are responding in three ways. First, subsidies on pesticides are being removed and taxes are being imposed. Second, research efforts are yielding pesticides with shorter toxic lives and plants that are less susceptible to pests. Finally, integrated pest management—a technique that uses small, carefully timed applications—is being introduced in numerous countries; it is financially attractive to farmers but requires careful training and follow-up.

COMMUNAL MANAGEMENT OF RESOURCES. Many natural resources in the developing world are managed communally. Often, this results in prudent stewardship. But sometimes management systems collapse as a result of population pressure, technical innovation, or commercialization. Problems include the overgrazing of pastoral rangelands, depletion of village woodlands due to fuelwood collection, deterioration of small-scale irrigation systems, and the overfishing of lakes and near-shore waters.

Where problems are serious, policymakers can seek to strengthen either *communal* rights and management responsibilities or those of *individuals* within the group. Which is appropriate will depend on societal factors and on administrative and legal systems. Strengthening existing institutions should be the first line of action. Experience with pastoral associations in West Africa and elsewhere suggests that successful groups are those characterized by adequate legal protection, clear leadership, and the authority to raise funds. Govern-

ments and nongovernmental groups can help overcome constraints in these areas. Interventions that are too heavy-handed, however, such as the group ranching schemes in Kenya, can erode social cohesion and make individual ownership of property the only option. Nationalization of resources is almost never a good response.

RESOURCES MANAGED BY GOVERNMENTS. In many countries governments own most of the land and natural resources and need to make environmentally responsible decisions on allocating their use.

One demand for land comes from settlers. Much of the 4.5 million hectares brought under cultivation each year are vulnerable lands, and new settlement for agriculture accounts for 60 percent of tropical deforestation. Too often, encroachers deplete resources in a manner that is neither economically nor environmentally viable. Promoting alternative income opportunities, through both off-farm employment and the intensification of agriculture, is the only long-run solution to these pressures—a further argument for adopting sound agricultural policies and human development programs. A study in Thailand found that providing educational opportunities was the single most powerful long-term policy for reducing deforestation.

In an effort to promote the right kind of settlement, some governments have sponsored official settlement programs, with mixed results. A recent World Bank review of its own experience concluded that such programs, which cost an average of $10,000 per family, were too often driven by targets and plans, tended to select settlers on the wrong criteria, often failed to do adequate soil and hydrologic surveys, and employed inappropriate mechanized land-clearing equipment. Evidence from Colombia and Indonesia indicates that, where property rights are clear, spontaneous settlers can be better resource managers than those who are officially sponsored, because they consider costs and risks. Nonetheless, settlement needs to be guided and serviced. Viable settlement areas need to be identified through better surveys than in the past, titles to land need to be provided to those settlers who demonstrate a capacity for sound resource management, and research and extension on sustainable agricultural techniques is required. Land-use zoning, which has usually failed to achieve its objectives, must be supplemented by the provision of services, by titling, and by penalties for noncompliance. Innovative approaches to integrated land management that allocate land to settlers, loggers, and extractive reserves while ensuring the rights of indigenous people are under way in the Amazon, West Africa, and Malaysia.

Areas that have particularly important ecological or habitat functions need special protection. Traditional reliance on guards and patrols is now being supplemented by integrated conservation and development projects, which build on the principle that local communities must be involved in devising and implementing protection. Nepal and Zimbabwe have pioneered buffer zones around some conservation areas; these zones are intensively managed by local people to generate incomes and establish rules of access that limit future encroachment.

Although logging directly accounts for only 20 percent of deforestation in developing countries, its impact is larger; it establishes access, encouraging farmers and ranchers to follow. Logging practices have been notoriously damaging in the past, and a recent review by the International Tropical Timber Organization found that less than 1 percent of tropical forests subject to logging is sustainably managed. Commercial logging must be limited to areas in which proper management is possible and demonstrated. Priority should be given to the preservation of intact tropical forests and to reforestation of degraded areas. In most places, stumpage fees and concession rents need to be increased to reflect the opportunity costs of cutting down trees. Felling leases or licenses and logging rights can be allocated by competitive bidding that is open to the private sector, local communities, and nongovernmental organizations (NGOs).

International environmental challenges

Institutional mechanisms for dealing with international resource and environmental problems, whether regional or global, are less developed than those available for national decisionmaking. Nonetheless, experience is accumulating from past negotiations, including those on the Law of the Sea, various fishing agreements, international river agreements, conventions on transporting hazardous wastes, and the Montreal Protocol on ozone depletion. Some lessons are that agreements are most effective when they are based on reciprocity and strong national interests; that international agreements often follow catalytic unilateral or regional action; that the lack of capacity to enforce agreements has been an important constraint on their effectiveness; and that financial

and technical assistance may be crucial to a successful outcome.

GREENHOUSE WARMING. Enough is known to discern a threat of climate change from increasing concentrations of greenhouse gases but not enough to predict how much will occur or how fast, the regional distribution of change, or the implications for human societies. A threefold strategy is suggested here.

First, measures should be taken that can be justified mainly by their benefits for efficiency and their effects on local pollution. Removing energy subsidies should be the starting point. Adjusting taxes on energy is the next step. Energy taxation in industrial countries is often skewed in favor of the most carbon-intensive fuels—especially coal. Carbon taxes have been introduced in Finland, the Netherlands, Norway, and Sweden. The nations of the European Community (EC) are considering a proposal for a carbon-cum-energy tax. A number of other measures are also desirable, mainly because of their benefits in other areas. For example, afforestation programs in watersheds and on farms (in the form of agroforestry) often have good returns because of their role in protecting watersheds and soils and, in developing countries, because they are a source of fuelwood. The fact that they sequester carbon makes them even more attractive.

Second, research is urgently needed both on the magnitude of the problem, especially as it may affect developing countries, and on potential solutions. Reducing uncertainty about potential costs and benefits is essential for designing an effective policy response, but it will require a large effort. A high priority should be given to research on energy conservation and renewable energy sources.

Third, pilot programs and innovative approaches to finding lasting solutions in developing countries need to be financed by industrial countries. A coordinated international effort is desirable to minimize duplication of effort and ensure that initiatives are consistent with overall development policies. The Global Environment Facility (GEF) has broken new ground by making finance available for pilot projects to identify the scope for widespread replication and cost reduction of technologies and practices that will lower net greenhouse gas emissions. Its priorities include slowing deforestation and encouraging afforestation; developing renewable sources such as biomass, solar energy, and microhydropower; improving efficiency in end uses; and reducing methane emis-

Box 4   For national policymakers: seven suggestions to guide action

1. *Build the environment into policymaking*

Environmental considerations need to be intrinsic to policymaking, not added on as afterthoughts. Environmental impact statements are already important in project analysis. They need to be extended to policy reforms. Where economic policies bring environmental benefits, those should add support to reform; where they carry possible adverse environmental costs, the adjustment program should include targeted environmental policies to offset them.

2. *Make population a priority*

For the sake of both development and the environment, population issues need more attention. Educating girls, enabling women to earn cash incomes and to participate fully in decisionmaking, and investing in better-equipped and better-financed family planning programs all allow women to determine their own reproductive behavior. It takes time for the environmental effects of these policies to be felt—all the more reason to take action now.

3. *Act first on local damage*

Many people are killed or made ill in developing countries by dirty water, lack of sanitation, fumes from cooking with wood, and dust and lead in city air. Soils impoverished by erosion or poisoned with badly used chemicals make it harder for developing countries to feed their people. Solving these environmental problems brings the biggest gains to health and wealth.

4. *Economize on administrative capacity*

Implementing environmental policy uses scarce money and manpower. To keep down administrative costs, countries need to set realistic goals and then enforce them; to work where possible with the grain of the market, not against it; to give preference to "self-enforcing" instruments such as deposit-refund schemes; and to harness popular support through local participation.

5. *Assess tradeoffs—and minimize them*

Governments need to be able to assess the costs of environmental damage and the least costly ways of protecting the environment. Policies should be made on the basis of explicit comparisons of cost and benefits. Citizens need to know what is being given up in the name of economic growth and what is being given up in the name of environmental protection.

6. *Research, inform, train*

Research should concentrate on appropriate technologies: low-cost chimneys to vent fumes from burning biomass, cheap sanitation systems to provide service to poor neighborhoods. Good information pays big dividends by helping to set sensible policy priorities. Better skills can solve environmental problems such as inappropriate use of pesticides and mishandling of toxic wastes.

7. *Remember: prevention is cheaper than cure*

Building pollution prevention into new investments is cheaper than adding them on later. New technology is less polluting than old. Developing countries with open markets will be able to gain from importing clean technologies already in use in industrial countries.

---

sions from mining, gas transmission, and waste disposal.

It is essential that the world community position itself to take rapid, concerted action should the balance of scientific evidence shift toward indicating that stronger concerted action is required. Current discussions concerning a convention on climate change can be important in facilitating such a response.

PROTECTING BIODIVERSITY. Most of the world's species reside in developing countries, but most spending on protection is in industrial countries. Because of the common international concern for biological resources, there is a strong case for more international efforts to provide funding and technical assistance to developing countries.

Effective conservation requires a twofold strat-egy by host governments and donors. First, complementarities between the goals of development and protection should be exploited. Policies that encourage sound agriculture, off-farm employment, and sustainable logging will also discourage encroachment into natural habitats. Ecotourism, sustainable fishing, and genetic prospecting will be good for development and for biological diversity. Second, specific measures to protect habitats should be adopted, with financial support from industrial countries. Such funding should not be regarded as aid and should not be diverted from aid budgets.

As international funding expands, two concerns will need to be addressed. First, improved coordination among donors is required. The Brazilian Tropical Rainforest Fund, a joint initiative by the Brazilian government and the Group of Seven

(G-7) countries with first-phase financing of $250 million, is an effort to ensure a coordinated approach. Second, recurrent cost financing will be required for continuous protection, where it does not pay for itself. That the pilot program launched under the GEF cannot easily handle costs of this nature highlights the need for a more durable funding arrangement.

The costs of a better environment

Policies and programs for accelerating environmentally responsible development will not happen by themselves. It is therefore important to seize the current moment of opportunity to bring about real change. The starting point should be policy changes that will promote rising incomes and better environmental stewardship (see Box 4). Some of these changes have little or no financial cost, but their political toll may be high. Subsidies and other interferences with markets are typically supported by powerful interests. The private beneficiaries of subsidies and other market interferences—and those officials who enjoy the patronage of handing them out—will fight to preserve them. Governments thus need to build constituencies of support—by, for instance, publicizing the positive economic and environmental impacts of reforms.

A second set of policies will involve financial costs. Environmental institutions will need to be strengthened, public investments in social and physical infrastructure and protection will increase, and the private sector will spend more money on abatement. The Report makes broad estimates of costs for key sectors. The additional costs of local environmental programs—many of which would add to employment and income growth—could amount to 2–3 percent of the GDP of developing countries by the end of the 1990s. These expenditures would cover pollution control in energy, industry, and transport and expanded programs of sanitation and water supply, soil conservation, agricultural extension and research, forest protection, family planning, and female education. Although the sums required are high in an absolute sense, they are modest in relation to the benefits they will bring and to the resources provided by economic growth.

Financing the program

The bulk of these investments will be paid for by the customers of the private and public enterprises responsible for the damage and by the beneficiaries of improved environmental conditions. Even so, financing for investment will still be required. In addition, governments will have to spend more on monitoring and enforcement, on research and development, on education, training, and extension, and on protection of natural habitats. Financing for these expenditures will come primarily from increased domestic savings—but international finance will also have a crucial role (Box 5).

Box 5   Complementary guidelines for the international community

1. *Adjust aid portfolios*

The composition and level of aid programs need to reflect the costs to health and productivity of a damaged environment. Preventing pollution and preserving natural resources are proper goals of aid programs. The strong links between poverty, population, and environmental damage call for higher overall allocations.

2. *Invest in research and technological development*

Gaps in fundamental knowledge must be filled. Among the priorities for international collaboration are the scale and causes of soil degradation (especially in Africa), the potential of tropical forests for sustainable production, the potential effect of climate change, and technologies for renewable energy.

3. *Ensure open trade and investment*

Providing free access to industrial country markets is needed to help developing countries industrialize and grow (both of which are essential for reducing pressure on natural resources) and to enable them to take advantage of less-polluting technologies. An immediate successful Uruguay Round agreement would increase foreign exchange earnings of developing countries by more than the costs of environmental protection.

4. *Pay for environmental services*

When industrial countries want developing countries to provide environmental benefits (preserving biodiversity, restraining greenhouse gas emissions, and the like), they should be willing to pay compensation. Such funding should be treated as equivalent to payments for imports, not as aid.

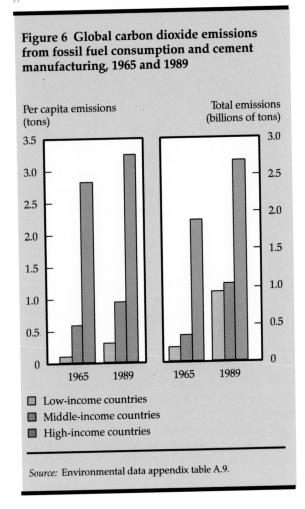

Figure 6 Global carbon dioxide emissions from fossil fuel consumption and cement manufacturing, 1965 and 1989

Per capita emissions (tons)

Total emissions (billions of tons)

☐ Low-income countries
■ Middle-income countries
■ High-income countries

Source: Environmental data appendix table A.9.

INTERNATIONAL FINANCE FOR LOCAL PROBLEMS. Access to commercial financial markets—coupled with expanded foreign investment—will be essential to facilitate the technology transfers embodied in capital imports. The encouraging restoration of commercial flows to such countries as Chile, Mexico, and Venezuela over the past two years must be extended to a much wider range of countries. This will require more consistent policies on the part of borrowing countries, which should be supported by debt relief in a number of countries.

Local environmental challenges deserve additional development assistance. Such assistance should not be viewed as separate from ongoing development needs; rather, it should be embedded in official assistance programs. Development agencies and governments need to place more emphasis on the close link between environmental quality and the reduction of poverty. This warrants additional concessional assistance, particularly in extension, credit, and education programs and in the provision of sanitation services and water supplies to squatter settlements and rural areas. Population programs must be given higher priority; assistance should double in real terms during the 1990s. The close link between the efficiency of resource use and sound environmental policymaking warrants continued support to countries that are undertaking adjustment programs.

FINANCING GLOBAL CHALLENGES. Industrial countries must bear most of the costs of addressing global problems, especially when the required investments are not in the narrow interests of developing countries. Industrial countries account for most emissions of greenhouse gases and CFCs (see Figure 6) and will benefit, along with developing countries, from the protection of natural habitats and biodiversity. It is clearly desirable to create arrangements that make it possible for rich countries to support poor ones in undertaking necessary changes. Such arrangements have the potential to make all countries better off if the world's willingness to pay for policy changes exceeds the cost of the changes. It is imperative that payments under such arrangements not be treated as development assistance or be financed from funds that would otherwise be available for development assistance. They have much more the character of imports—payment for services rendered—and are quite different from aid transfers to developing countries. As a global response to a global challenge, the allocation of such funds should be based on effectiveness in raising global welfare, rather than on meeting national needs.

The agenda for reform is a large one. Accepting the challenge to accelerate development in an environmentally responsible manner will involve substantial shifts in policies and priorities and will be costly. Failing to accept it will be more costly still.

1 Development and the environment: a false dichotomy

Economic development and sound environmental management are complementary aspects of the same agenda. Without adequate environmental protection, development will be undermined; without development, environmental protection will fail.

More than 1 billion people today live in abject poverty. The next generation will see the world's population rise by 3.7 billion, even if progress in reducing population growth accelerates. Most of these people will be born into poor families. Alleviating poverty is both morally imperative and essential for environmental sustainability.

Economic growth is essential for sustained poverty reduction. But growth has often caused serious environmental damage. Fortunately, such adverse effects can be sharply reduced, and with effective policies and institutions, income growth will provide the resources for improved environmental management.

The environmental mistakes of the past do not have to be repeated. Today, countries have more choices. They can choose policies and investments that encourage more efficient use of resources, substitution away from scarce resources, and the adoption of technologies and practices that do less environmental harm. Such changes will ensure that the improvements in human welfare which development brings are lasting.

More people today live longer, healthier, and more productive lives than at any time in history. But the gains have been inadequate and uneven. More than 1 billion people still live in abject poverty. To reduce poverty, sustained and equitable economic growth is essential. But past economic growth has often been associated with severe degradation of the natural world. On the surface, there appears to be a tradeoff between meeting people's needs—the central goal of development—and protecting the environment. This Report will argue that in every realm of economic activity, development can become more sustainable. The key is not to produce less, but to produce differently. This chapter explores the relationship between economic activity and the environment, emphasizing the concerns of developing countries.

The context: population, poverty, and economic growth

Population growth

The second half of the twentieth century has been a demographic watershed. By midcentury the rate of population growth in developing countries had risen to unprecedented levels as mortality declined and life expectancy increased. These gains were the result of progress in living standards, sanitary conditions, and public health practices, particularly the introduction of antibiotics, the increased use of vaccinations, and antimalarial spraying. World population growth peaked at 2.1 percent a year in 1965–70, the most rapid rate of increase in history. Population growth has now slowed to 1.7 percent as more countries have begun a transition toward lower fertility. Even so, world population now stands at 5.3 billion and is increasing by 93 million a year.

To project future trends in fertility—the largest factor in determining population growth—judgments have to be made about two key questions: when will a country begin its demographic transition, and how fast will fertility decline once the transition begins? Figure 1.1 illustrates three alternative paths for world population. Under the World Bank's base case projections, world population growth would decline slowly, from 1.7 percent a year in 1990 to about 1 percent a year by 2030. World population would more than double from current levels and would stabilize at about

might happen if fertility transitions are delayed in many countries.

This tremendous range of possible long-term population trends depends largely on what happens in Africa and in the Middle East. Together, these regions account for 85 to 90 percent of the differences between the alternative scenarios and the base case. Sub-Saharan Africa alone contributes more than two-thirds of the difference under the slow fertility decline scenario. Total fertility rates (measured as births per woman) in Sub-Saharan Africa as a whole have remained unchanged at about 6.5 for the past twenty-five years—a level much higher than in other parts of the world that have similar levels of income, life expectancy, and female education.

Recent statistics provide encouraging indications that a number of African countries are at or near a critical turning point. Total fertility rates have already fallen in Botswana (6.9 in 1965 to 4.7 in 1990), Zimbabwe (8.0 in 1965 to 4.9 in 1990), and Kenya (8.0 in 1965 to 6.5 in 1990) and are beginning to decline in Ghana, Sudan, and Togo. The base case projections, which assume that these positive trends will continue, imply that Sub-Saharan Africa's population will rise from 500 million at present to about 1.5 billion by 2030 and almost 3 billion by 2100. Apart from its terrible effects on health and welfare, the AIDS virus could reduce African population growth rates by as much as 0.5–1.0 percentage points in the early decades of the next century. But because increased mortality from AIDS may delay fertility declines, the overall impact of the disease is ambiguous.

POPULATION GROWTH AND THE ENVIRONMENT. Population growth increases the demand for goods and services, and, if practices remain unchanged, implies increased environmental damage. Population growth also increases the need for employment and livelihoods, which—especially in crowded rural areas—exerts additional direct pressure on natural resources. More people also produce more wastes, threatening local health conditions and implying additional stress on the earth's assimilative capacity.

Countries with higher population growth rates have experienced faster conversion of land to agricultural uses, putting additional pressures on land and natural habitat. An econometric study of twenty-three Latin American countries found that expansion of agricultural area continues to be positively related to population growth, after controlling for such factors as agricultural trade, yield in-

Figure 1.1 World population projections under different fertility trends, 1985-2160

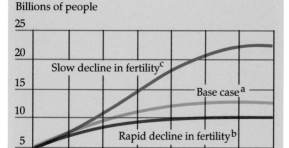

Billions of people

a. Countries with high and nondeclining fertility levels begin the transition toward lower fertility by the year 2005 and undergo a substantial decline - by more than half in many cases - over the next forty years. All countries reach replacement fertility levels by 2060.
b. Countries not yet in transition toward lower fertility begin the transition immediately. For countries already in transition, total fertility declines at twice the rate for the base case.
c. Transition toward lower fertility (triggered when life expectancy reaches 53 years) begins after 2020 in most low-income countries. For countries in transition, declines are half the rate for the base case.
Source: World Bank data.

12.5 billion around the middle of the twenty-second century. Two-thirds of the increase would occur by 2050, and 95 percent of population growth would take place in developing countries.

Alternative paths are possible. The scenario of rapid fertility decline illustrated in Figure 1.1 is comparable to the historical experience of, for example, Costa Rica, Hong Kong, Jamaica, Mexico, and Thailand. The scenario of slow fertility decline is consistent with the experience of such countries as Paraguay, Sri Lanka, Suriname, and Turkey. The stable population of 10.1 billion in the rapid fertility decline scenario is about 2.4 billion less than that in the base case, but it is still almost double the present size. In stark contrast, with a slow decline of fertility, population increases more than fourfold, to about 23 billion, and stabilizes only toward the end of the twenty-second century. Few demographers expect world population to reach 23 billion, but the projection shows what

Box 1.1 The population-agriculture-environment nexus in Sub-Saharan Africa

Rapid population growth, agricultural stagnation, and environmental degradation have been common to most Sub-Saharan countries in recent decades. These three factors have been mutually reinforcing. The World Bank recently completed a study of this "nexus" with the purpose of better understanding causal links and identifying remedies. Its preliminary findings are summarized here.

The equilibrium upset

Shifting cultivation and grazing have been appropriate traditional responses to abundant land, scarce capital, and limited technology. As population densities grew slowly in the first half of this century, these extensive systems evolved into more intensive systems, as in Rwanda, Burundi, the Kenyan highlands, and the Kivu Plateau in Zaire. This slowly evolving system has, however, proved unable to adapt to sharply accelerated population growth over the past four decades. Traditional uses of land and fuel have depleted soil and forests and contributed to agricultural stagnation. Stagnant incomes and the absence of improvements in human welfare have impeded the demographic transition. A combination of high population densities and low investment has caused arable land per person to decline from 0.5 hectare in 1965 to 0.3 hectare in 1987. As a result, in many parts of Burundi, Kenya, Lesotho, Liberia, Mauritania, and Rwanda fallow periods are no longer sufficient to restore fertility.

Population growth drives some people to cultivate land not previously used for farming—in semiarid areas and in tropical forests where soil and climatic conditions are poorly suited for annual cropping or for the practices employed by the new migrants. These problems are most severe in parts of the Sahel, in parts of mountainous East Africa, and in the dry belt stretching from Namibia through Botswana, Lesotho, and southern Mozambique. There is strong evidence that economic stagnation is delaying declines in fertility; family size may be higher (to provide additional labor) where land damage is greatest and fuelwood supplies are depleted. An integrated approach to the problem is needed.

Toward solutions

The traditional development approach, which emphasized supplying services and technologies, must be complemented by a strategy of promoting demand—for appropriate agricultural practices and inputs, for fewer children, and for resource conservation. Demand for these things can be promoted by:

• Removing subsidies that distort prices and incentives—to promote more efficient use of resources
• Improving land use planning—to promote intensification and protect valuable natural ecosystems
• Clarifying resource ownership and land tenure, giving legal recognition to traditional common-property management and private ownership, and reducing state ownership—to encourage investment
• Expanding educational programs for girls and employment opportunities for women and improving information on health and nutrition, in all cases through the use of community groups, NGOs, and the private sector—to promote demand for smaller families
• Expanding investment in and maintenance of rural infrastructure, especially roads, water supply, and sanitation—to improve production incentives, productivity, and health.

---

creases, and availability of land. A study of six Sub-Saharan African countries indicates that technological innovations are not keeping up with the demands of rapidly rising rural populations. As a consequence, in many places—Ethiopia, southern Malawi, eastern Nigeria, and Sierra Leone—farming is being intensified through shorter fallow periods rather than through the use of better inputs or techniques. Rapid population growth in these areas has led to the mining of soil resources and to stagnating or declining yields. In some circumstances, especially in rural Africa, population growth has been so rapid that traditional land management has been unable to adapt to prevent degradation. The result is overgrazing, deforestation, depletion of water resources, and loss of natural habitat (Box 1.1).

The distribution of people between countryside and towns also has important implications for the types of stress placed on the environment. In 1990 most people lived in rural areas. By 2030 the opposite will be true: urban populations will be twice the size of rural populations. Developing country cities as a group will grow by 160 percent over this period, whereas rural populations will grow by only 10 percent. By 2000 there will be twenty-one cities in the world with more than 10 million inhabitants, and seventeen of them will be in developing countries.

The pattern will vary substantially among regions. Over the next thirty years urban population growth will average 1.6 percent a year in Latin America, 4.6 percent in Sub-Saharan Africa, and 3 percent in Asia. Rural populations are expected to

Figure 1.2 Rural and urban population in developing regions and high-income countries, 1960-2025

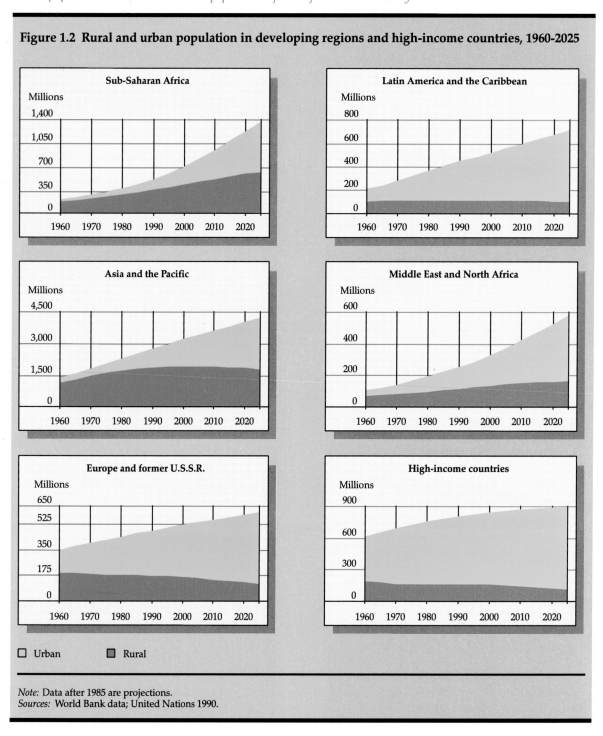

□ Urban   ■ Rural

Note: Data after 1985 are projections.
Sources: World Bank data; United Nations 1990.

decline in absolute terms within a generation in all regions except Sub-Saharan Africa, the Middle East and North Africa, and Central America (Figure 1.2). Asia's rural population will continue to increase until the turn of the century but is expected to fall back to current levels by about 2015.

In high-income countries and in Eastern Europe and the former U.S.S.R. the numbers living in rural areas have been declining steadily, and in most South American countries, too, urbanization has brought about some decline in rural populations.

The pace of urbanization poses huge environmental challenges for the cities. That is why much of this Report is devoted to the problems of sanitation, clean water, and pollution from industry, energy, and transport. But urbanization will also affect the nature of rural environmental challenges. Successful urbanization and the associated income growth should ease the pressures caused by encroachment on natural habitats—largely driven by the need for income and employment—but will increase the pressures stemming from market demand for food, water, and timber. In much of Sub-Saharan Africa, the Middle East and North Africa, and Central America rural populations are likely to increase by about 50 percent over the next generation, and direct pressure on natural resources, particularly by poor subsistence farmers, will intensify.

POLICIES FOR REDUCING POPULATION GROWTH. The declining fertility rates associated with the base case projections should not be taken for granted. They are rapid by historical standards and will require solid progress on four fronts: incomes of poor households must rise, child mortality must decline, educational and employment opportunities (especially for women) must expand, and access to family planning services must be increased.

Investments in female education have some of the highest returns for development and for the environment. Evidence from a cross-section of countries shows that where no women are enrolled in secondary education, the average woman has seven children, but where 40 percent of all women have had a secondary education, the average drops to three children, even after controlling for factors such as income. Better-educated mothers also raise healthier families, have fewer and better-educated children, and are more productive at home and at work. Investments in schools, teachers, and materials are essential. But so too are policies to encourage enrollment, such as scholarship programs. In Bangladesh a scholarship program has succeeded in almost doubling female secondary enrollment, as well as promoting higher labor force participation, later marriage, and lower fertility rates.

Efforts to expand family planning programs have contributed to significant progress; the rate of contraceptive use in developing countries rose from 40 percent in 1980 to 49 percent in 1990. But for the base case projections to be realized, the rate would need to increase by another 7 percentage points by 2000 and by yet another 5 percentage points by 2010. Unmet demand for contraceptives is large—it ranges from about 15 percent of couples in Brazil, Colombia, Indonesia, and Sri Lanka to more than 35 percent in Bolivia, Ghana, Kenya, and Togo. Meeting this demand is essential for reaching even the base case projections and will require that total annual expenditure on family planning increase from about $5 billion to about $8 billion (in 1990 prices) by 2000. An additional $3 billion would be required to achieve the rapid fertility decline scenario. Choices about family planning and education policies today will determine world population levels, and the consequent pressures on the environment, in the next century.

The persistence of poverty

The primary task of development is to eliminate poverty. Substantial progress has been achieved over the past twenty-five years. Average consumption per capita in developing countries has increased by 70 percent in real terms; average life expectancy has risen from 51 to 63 years; and primary school enrollment rates have reached 89 percent. If these gains were evenly spread, much of the world's poverty would be eliminated. Instead, more than one-fifth of humanity still lives in acute poverty.

New estimates prepared for this Report reveal a negligible reduction in the incidence of poverty in developing countries during the second half of the 1980s (Table 1.1). The numbers of poor have increased at almost the rate of population growth over the period—from slightly more than 1 billion in 1985 to more than 1.1 billion by 1990.

Asia, with its rapid income growth, continues to be the most successful at alleviating poverty. China was an exception in the second half of the 1980s; although its incidence of poverty remains, for its income, very low, the new estimates reflect some adverse changes for the poorest in that country as a result of a more uneven distribution of income. In most other East Asian countries poverty continued to decline. South Asia, including India, has maintained a steady but undramatic decline in poverty. The experience in other developing regions has been markedly different from that in Asia. All poverty measures worsened in Sub-Saharan Africa, the Middle East and North Africa, and Latin America and the Caribbean.

What are the prospects for poverty alleviation to the end of this century? The estimates presented in Table 1.1 are based on the projections of income

Table 1.1 Poverty in the developing world, 1985–2000

Region	Percentage of population below the poverty line			Number of poor (millions)		
	1985	1990	2000	1985	1990	2000
All developing countries	30.5	29.7	24.1	1,051	1,133	1,107
South Asia	51.8	49.0	36.9	532	562	511
East Asia	13.2	11.3	4.2	182	169	73
Sub-Saharan Africa	47.6	47.8	49.7	184	216	304
Middle East and North Africa	30.6	33.1	30.6	60	73	89
Eastern Europe[a]	7.1	7.1	5.8	5	5	4
Latin America and the Caribbean	22.4	25.5	24.9	87	108	126

Note: The poverty line used here—$370 annual income per capita in 1985 purchasing power parity dollars—is based on estimates of poverty lines from a number of countries with low average incomes. In 1990 prices, the poverty line would be approximately $420 annual income per capita. The estimates for 1985 have been updated from those in *World Development Report 1990* to incorporate new data and to ensure comparability across years.
a. Does not include the former U.S.S.R.
Source: Ravallion, Datt, and Chen 1992.

growth presented below (see Table 1.2) and assume that the distribution of income within countries remains constant. Under these assumptions, the number of poor in Asia would continue to decline, and the adverse poverty trends in Latin America and Eastern Europe would be reversed with economic recovery in those regions. Sub-Saharan Africa is the only region in which the situation is expected to deteriorate; with increases in the proportion of the population in poverty, the number of poor would rise by about 9 million a year, on average. By the end of the decade about one-half of the world's poor will live in Asia and one-quarter will live in Sub-Saharan Africa.

It is sobering to compare these estimates with those in *World Development Report 1990*. That report identified a path of poverty reduction that would reduce the absolute number of poor in the world by 300 million between 1985 and 2000. The path was presented to illustrate what could be accomplished with sound policies in both developing and industrial countries. Sadly, that target appears no longer feasible, partly as a result of the severity of the current recession and the disappointing progress in the 1985–90 period. Even under fairly hopeful assumptions about economic recovery in the rest of the decade, the absolute number of poor in the world at the turn of the century will probably be higher than in 1985.

POVERTY AND THE ENVIRONMENT Alleviating poverty is both a moral imperative and a prerequisite for environmental sustainability. The poor are both victims and agents of environmental damage. About half of the world's poor live in rural areas that are environmentally fragile, and they rely on natural resources over which they have little legal control. Land-hungry farmers resort to cultivating unsuitable areas—steeply sloped, erosion-prone hillsides; semiarid land where soil degradation is rapid; and tropical forests where crop yields on cleared fields frequently drop sharply after just a few years. Poor people in crowded squatter settlements frequently endure inadequate access to safe water and sanitation, as well as flooding and landslides, industrial accidents and emissions, and transport-related air pollution. The poor are often exposed to the greatest environmental health risks, and they tend to be the most vulnerable to those risks because of their poverty. The impact of environmental degradation on the poor will be described in Chapter 2.

Poor families often lack the resources to avoid degrading their environment. The very poor, struggling at the edge of subsistence, are preoccupied with day-to-day survival. It is not that the poor have inherently short horizons; poor communities often have a strong ethic of stewardship in managing their traditional lands. But their fragile and limited resources, their often poorly defined property rights, and their limited access to credit and insurance markets prevent them from investing as much as they should in environmental protection (Box 1.2). When they do make investments, they need quick results. Studies in India, for example, found implicit discount rates among poor farmers of 30–40 percent, meaning that they were willing to make an investment only if it would treble its value in three years. Similarly, efforts to introduce soil conservation and water-harvesting techniques in Burkina Faso showed that the practices most likely to be adopted were those that could deliver an increase in yields within two or three years. In many countries ef-

Box 1.2   Droughts, poverty, and the environment

Agriculture is a risky business everywhere, but perhaps the most debilitating risk is that of drought in semiarid tropical areas. Households in the poor rural societies that inhabit many of these regions have little to fall back on. The combination of poverty and drought can also have serious environmental consequences that threaten future agricultural productivity and the conservation of natural resources. For example, poor people are induced to scavenge more intensively during droughts, seeking out wood and other organic fuels, wildlife, and edible plants, both to eat and to sell. But because the plants, trees, and wildlife are already under stress from drought, such scavenging aggravates deforestation and damage to watersheds and soil. Livestock farmers tend to concentrate their animals near water holes during droughts, and the consequent overgrazing may cause long-term damage to the soil.

Many farming practices in semiarid areas have the potential to worsen the harm that droughts cause to natural resources. For example, arable cropping, by increasing soil exposure, makes the soil more vulnerable to wind and rain erosion and to loss of moisture and nutrients. These effects can be pronounced even in normal years but are particularly severe in droughts. Since farmers cannot predict droughts, they typically clear and plant the land in preparation for a normal season. When the crops subsequently fail, the land is left exposed to the full rigors of sun, wind, and rain.

The ways in which farmers try to reduce risk, although perfectly rational from their own point of view, can sometimes impose environmental costs on local communities. For example, a household may farm more than one separate parcel of land in order to exploit local variations in conditions and thus reduce production risks. But because farmers have smaller land parcels at any one location, the environmental costs (such as soil erosion and water runoff) associated with their farming practices are less likely to be felt on their own farms and more likely to be borne by their neighbors. Individual farmers have little incentive to address the problem. Even when they do, a solution may be difficult because it can require organizing neighboring farmers to undertake a joint investment (such as contouring or terracing).

A similar problem can arise in common-property pastoral farming if farmers carry extra cattle as insurance against drought. Because farmers are likely to defer as long as possible selling their cattle, this simple form of insurance often leads to overgrazing in drought years, increasing the likelihood of permanent damage to the pasture.

Markets are also inadequate for spreading risks in drought-prone regions because so many people are affected at once. Although credit markets can sustain consumption over the course of normal variations in family incomes, they may not be able to provide the huge amounts of credit required in drought years, when large numbers of people need to borrow at the same time. Governments must therefore provide relief employment and targeted food assistance in drought years, and effective drought insurance schemes may be needed.

---

forts to encourage rural communities to plant woodlots have failed when people had to wait until the trees reached maturity to realize a return but have succeeded when products such as building poles and fodder could be harvested more quickly.

In many parts of the world women play a central part in resource management and yet enjoy much less access to education, credit, extension services, and technology than do men. In Sub-Saharan Africa women provide an estimated 50–80 percent of all agricultural and agroprocessing labor. Despite such high levels of economic activity, women in many countries have no or only limited rights of tenure to land and cultivated trees. This constrains their access to credit for investments in new technologies. Women are also frequently neglected by agricultural and forestry extension services. When women have been given equal opportunities (as in combating soil erosion in Cameroon), they have

shown effective leadership in managing natural resources.

Substantial synergies exist between alleviating poverty and protecting the environment. Since the poor are less able than the rich to "buy out of" environmental problems, they will often benefit the most from environmental improvements. In addition, the economic activities stimulated by environmental policies—such as the use of agroforestry and windbreaks to slow soil erosion and the construction of infrastructure for water supply and sanitation—are often labor-intensive and thus can provide employment. Targeted social safety nets make it less necessary for the poor to "mine" natural resources in times of crisis. Extension and credit programs and the allocation of land rights to squatters increase the ability of the poor to make environmental investments and manage risks. Investments in water and sanitation and in pollution abatement will also benefit the poor by improving their health and productivity. But it is equitable economic growth, coupled with education and health services, that is most urgently needed. This will enable the poor to make environmental investments that are in their own long-term interest. It will also be essential for accelerating the demographic transition; better-off and better-educated couples have fewer children.

Economic growth—long-term trends and prospects

Average per capita incomes in developing countries rose 2.7 percent a year between 1950 and 1990—the highest sustained rate of increase in history. But the pace of economic growth has differed greatly among regions. Asian countries, which account for 65 percent of the population of the developing world, grew at an average rate of 5.2 percent a year in the 1970s and 7.3 percent in the 1980s, while growth in the non-Asian developing countries decelerated from 5.6 percent in the 1970s to 2.8 percent in the 1980s. Asia was the only developing region to achieve sustained per capita income growth during the 1980s.

RECENT ECONOMIC DEVELOPMENTS. The 1990s started badly for developing countries. In both 1990 and 1991 per capita income in developing countries as a whole fell, after rising every year since 1965. The setback was caused largely by extraordinary events—the war in the Middle East, and economic contraction in Eastern Europe and in the former U.S.S.R. Recession in several high-income countries also contributed to the stagnation of export growth in developing countries. The

projections presented in Table 1.2 assume that industrial countries will grow more slowly in the 1990s than in the 1980s. This context provides all the more reason to accelerate policy reform in developing countries. Experience has shown that, on average, the effect of domestic policies on long-run growth is about twice as large as the effects attributable to changes in external conditions.

With continued progress on economic reform in developing countries, GDP growth is projected to increase to about 5 percent a year for the decade as a whole—significantly higher than the 3.4 percent achieved in the 1980s. Growth in Asia is expected to slow from the high levels of the 1980s but will remain well above the average for developing countries. Latin America, Eastern Europe, and the Middle East and North Africa are all expected to grow more rapidly during the remainder of the 1990s. Sub-Saharan Africa's growth performance will improve in comparison with the 1980s, but the gains will be small.

LONGER-TERM PROSPECTS. Because many environmental issues evolve slowly, this Report takes a longer view than usual, giving special attention to the next four decades. About 3.7 billion people will be added to the world's population during this period—many more than in any previous generation, and probably more than in any succeeding one. Economic projections over this length of time are, of course, subject to great uncertainty. They are presented in Figure 1.3 not as predictions but as indicators of what historical experience suggests is likely to occur.

World GDP could rise from about $20 trillion in 1990 to $69 trillion in 2030 in real terms. For the

Table 1.2 Growth of real per capita income in industrial and developing countries, 1960–2000
(average annual percentage change)

Country group	1960–70	1970–80	1980–90	1990	1991[a]	1990–2000[a]
High-income countries	4.1	2.4	2.4	2.1	0.7	2.1
Developing countries	3.3	3.0	1.2	−0.2	−0.2	2.9
Sub-Saharan Africa	0.6	0.9	−0.9	−2.0	−1.0	0.3
Asia and the Pacific	2.5	3.1	5.1	3.9	4.2	4.8
East Asia	3.6	4.6	6.3	4.6	5.6	5.7
South Asia	1.4	1.1	3.1	2.6	1.5	3.1
Middle East and North Africa	6.0	3.1	−2.5	−1.9	−4.6	1.6
Latin America and the Caribbean	2.5	3.1	−0.5	−2.4	0.6	2.2
Europe	4.9	4.4	1.2	−3.8	−8.6	1.9
Eastern Europe	5.2	5.4	0.9	−8.3	−14.2	1.6
Memorandum:						
Developing countries weighted by population	3.9	3.7	2.2	1.7	2.2	3.6

Note: Totals do not include the former U.S.S.R.
a. Estimates.
Source: World Bank 1992.

Figure 1.3 GDP and GDP per capita in developing regions and high-income countries, 1990 and 2030

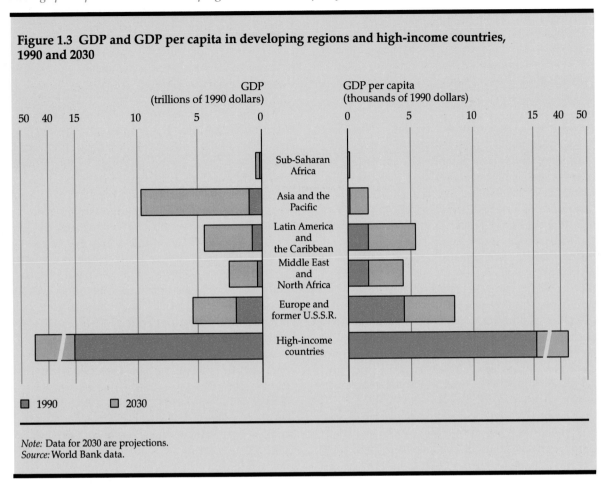

Note: Data for 2030 are projections.
Source: World Bank data.

developing countries as a whole, average incomes could more than triple in real terms, from an average of $750 today (the level of Côte d'Ivoire) to about $2,500 in 2030, roughly the income per capita of Mexico today. Substantial regional differences would persist, although in the aggregate the gap between income levels in developing and industrial countries would narrow. By the middle of the next century developing countries' share of world income would have risen from less than one-quarter to almost one-half, and if trends continued, it would rise to more than three-quarters by 2100. The most rapid growth rates are expected in Asia, particularly in East Asia, where per capita incomes would be more than $3,300 in 2030. Although growth rates in South Asia will be robust, the tripling of average incomes during the next generation would still leave them at only about $1,000 per capita. Average per capita incomes in Latin America and in the Middle East and North

Africa could exceed $5,000 and $4,000, respectively—well above the average for developing countries. Economic recovery in Eastern Europe would raise average per capita incomes to more than $9,000 by 2030, while those in the former U.S.S.R. could rise to more than $8,000. Projections for Sub-Saharan Africa are the most sobering; under present productivity trends and population projections trends in total output would rise fourfold, but per capita incomes would still reach only $400.

Sustaining development

In terms of incomes and output, the world will be a much richer place in the next century. But will the environment be much poorer? Will future generations be worse off as a result of environmental degradation that results from economic decisions made today? Will increases in the scale of economic activity be sustainable in the face of increasing pressure on natural resources? Prospective changes of the size described above raise fundamental questions about the kind of world we will bequeath to our children and about the nature and goals of development.

What is development?

Development is about improving the well-being of people. Raising living standards and improving education, health, and equality of opportunity are all essential components of economic development. Ensuring political and civil rights is a broader development goal. Economic growth is an essential means for enabling development, but in itself it is a highly imperfect proxy for progress.

The first step in improving social choices is to measure progress correctly. It has long been recognized that measures of, for example, educational opportunity, infant mortality, and nutritional status are essential complements to GDP or GNP. Some have even tried to merge these indices to capture progress in development. The human development index constructed by the United Nations Development Programme (UNDP) is such an effort.

The fact that environmental damage hurts people—both today and in the future—provides additional grounds for rethinking our measurement of progress. Indeed it raises special concerns, for unlike education, health, nutrition, and life expectancy, which tend to be improved by economic growth, the environment is sometimes damaged by that growth. Furthermore, the people suffering from the damage may be different from those enjoying the benefits of growth. They may, for example, be today's poor, or they may be future generations who inherit a degraded environment. For these reasons it is essential to assess the costs to human welfare of environmental damage—a central theme of this Report—and to take account of the distributional impacts of policies, particularly for the poor.

What is sustainable?

Sustainable development is development that lasts. A specific concern is that those who enjoy the fruits of economic development today may be making future generations worse off by excessively degrading the earth's resources and polluting the earth's environment. The general principle of sustainable development adopted by the World Commission on Environment and Development

(*Our Common Future,* 1987)—that current generations should "meet their needs without compromising the ability of future generations to meet their own needs"—has become widely accepted and is strongly supported in this Report.

Turning the concept of sustainability into policy raises fundamental questions about how to assess the well-being of present and future generations. What should we leave to our children and grandchildren to maximize the chances that they will be no worse off than ourselves? The issue is the more complicated because our children do not just inherit our pollution and resource depletion but also enjoy the fruits of our labor in the form of education, skills, and knowledge (human capital), as well as physical capital. They may also benefit from investments in natural resources—improvement in soil fertility and reforestation, for example. Thus, in considering what we pass on to future generations, we must take account of the full range of physical, human, and natural capital that will determine their welfare and their bequests to their successors.

Intergenerational choices of this kind are reflected in the discount rate used to assess investments. The discount rate is the mechanism through which present and future costs and benefits are compared. The lower the discount rate, the more it is worth investing today to make future gains. It is sometimes claimed that a lower discount rate—even a zero discount rate—should be used in order to give appropriate weight to the long-term consequences of environmental change. This argument is erroneous. Provided that the environmental effects of projects are fully taken into account—which they often are not—it is always best to choose the investments which generate the highest net rate of return. Encouraging investments that yield a lower net rate of return is wasteful; it implies a loss of welfare and of income that might have been devoted to environmental objectives.

Weighing costs and benefits

Addressing environmental problems requires not that discount rates be artificially lowered but rather that the value of the environment be factored into decisionmaking. Values that are difficult to measure are often implicit in decisionmaking, but the tradeoffs are not well thought through. There is a clear need to make such costs and benefits as explicit as possible so as to better inform policymakers and citizens. This does not imply that it is possible, or even desirable, to put mone-

Box 1.3 Natural resource and environmental accounting

The limitations of conventional measures of economic activity, such as GNP and national income, as indicators of social welfare have been well known for decades. Recently, the perception has grown that these indicators, which are based on the United Nations System of National Accounts (SNA), do not accurately reflect environmental degradation and the consumption of natural resources. Several alternative approaches have been developed. Early work in this area was conducted by some OECD countries, notably Norway and France. Recent attempts to apply natural resource accounting to developing countries have been made by UNEP, the United Nations Statistical Office (UNSO), the World Bank, and the World Resources Institute. These methods differ in both comprehensiveness and objectives.

Broadly, there are two criticisms of the SNA framework. First, aggregates such as GNP may be inadequate measures of economic activity when environmental damage occurs. The depreciation of some forms of capital, such as machinery, is taken into account, but investments in human capital and depletion of environmental capital, including nonrenewable natural resources, are not measured.

Second, it is argued, by neglecting the services provided by natural resources, the SNA limits the information available to policymakers. Leaving out these services ignores the impact of economic activity on the environment in its role both as a "sink" for wastes and a "source" of inputs. It is argued that ignoring these services and their effects on economic activity makes the national income accounts misleading for formulating economic policies, particularly in economies that are heavily dependent on natural resources.

The various approaches to natural resource and environmental accounting have divergent aims. Each responds to a different problem with the SNA framework. The simplest approaches attempt to measure more accurately the responses to environmental degradation and protection that are already imperfectly measured in the national income accounts. Examples include work in Germany, the Netherlands, and the United States on estimating pollution abatement expenditures. A second approach responds to the inconsistent treatment of natural capital in the SNA and attempts to account explicitly for the depletion of natural resources; estimates of depletion are applied to conventionally measured income to derive a measure of net income. This approach has been applied in Indonesia for forests, petroleum, and soils, in Costa Rica for fisheries and forests, and in China for minerals. Finally, the physical accounting method used by Norway and the effort to integrate environmental and resource use with economic activity being developed by the UNSO both attempt to improve the information available for environmental management. The Norwegian system focuses primarily on the country's main natural resources—petroleum, timber, fisheries, and hydropower. The more ambitious UNSO approach, currently being applied to Mexico and Papua New Guinea in collaboration with their governments and the World Bank, aims at developing a system of "satellite" national accounts that explicitly incorporate the links between economic activity and the use of natural and environmental resources.

tary values on all types of environmental resources. But it is desirable to know how much environmental quality is being given up in the name of development, and how much development is being given up in the name of environmental protection. This Report argues that too much environmental quality is now being given up. There is, however, a danger that too much income growth may be given up in the future because of failure to clarify and minimize tradeoffs and to take advantage of policies that are good for both economic development and the environment.

To clarify these tradeoffs at the national level, efforts are under way in a number of countries to amend the national accounts. Such exercises can be valuable for two reasons. First, they can help indicate how growth of GDP may bring with it environmental costs for today's citizens. For example, the costs of pollution to health and produc-

tivity should be taken into account in the same way that other measures of welfare need to be considered. Second, it can help give a more realistic measure of the capacity of an economy to produce. To this end, investment has to be adjusted to take account of depreciation of physical and natural capital. But the accumulation of human capital and the benefits of technical change must also be taken into account to provide an overall picture of an economy's productive capacity.

A number of approaches to measuring environmental costs have been tried in different countries (Box 1.3). A recent pilot study of Mexico's national accounts indicates the potential magnitudes of the adjustments required. When an adjustment was made for the depletion of oil, forests, and groundwater, Mexico's net national product was almost 7 percent lower. A further adjustment for the costs of avoiding environmental degradation, particularly air and water pollution and soil erosion, brought the national product down another 7 percent. These estimates are preliminary and are only intended to illustrate a methodology. Of more value than these aggregate numbers are sectoral calculations. In the livestock sector, for example, adjustments for the costs of soil erosion sharply reduced the sector's net value added. These calculations in themselves give no indication to policymakers as to whether Mexico's use of natural capital has been in the country's best interest, but they can be useful in reminding policymakers of potential tradeoffs and can assist in setting sectoral priorities.

Economic activity and the environment: key links

This Report will argue that the adverse impact of economic growth on environmental degradation can be greatly reduced. Poor management of natural resources is already constraining development in some areas, and the growing scale of economic activity will pose serious challenges for environmental management. But rising incomes combined with sound environmental policies and institutions can form the basis for tackling both environmental and development problems. The key to growing sustainably is not to produce less but to produce differently. In some situations, such as protection of forests or control of emissions, good environmental policies may cause short-term growth to fall, even as welfare may rise. In other cases—for example, improved soil conservation practices or investments in water supply—the effect on output and incomes is likely to be positive. In still other areas the impacts are unclear. What is clear, however, is that failure to address environmental challenges will reduce the capacity for long-term development.

UNDERSTANDING THE PROBLEM. All economic activity involves transforming the natural world. Why does economic activity sometimes lead to excessive environmental degradation? One reason is that many natural resources are shared and the true value of many environmental goods and services is not paid for by those who use them. Some natural resources are shared because there is no mechanism for enforcing property rights, as with frontier land, and others are shared because, as with the atmosphere, property rights are impossible to enforce. Unless an explicit agreement among users emerges, shared resources will be degraded over time, particularly as the scale of population and economic activity increases. In some cases government policies that subsidize environmental degradation can induce more damage than might otherwise occur. In other cases the poor, with few assets on which to draw, may have no choice but to excessively degrade natural resources.

The most pressing environmental problems are associated with resources that are regenerative but are undervalued and are therefore in danger of exhaustion. Air and water are renewable resources, but they have a finite capacity to assimilate emissions and wastes. If pollution exceeds this capacity, ecosystems can deteriorate rapidly. When fisheries or forests are excessively depleted to meet human needs, critical thresholds may be passed, resulting in the loss of ecosystems and species. Shortages of nonrenewable resources, such as metals, minerals, and energy, the possible exhaustion of which preoccupied early environmental debate, are of less concern. The evidence suggests that when the true value of such nonrenewable resources is reflected in the marketplace, there is no sign of excessive scarcity (Box 1.4).

Water provides an example of an undervalued renewable resource that is showing signs of shortage. By the end of the 1990s six East African countries and all the North African countries will have annual renewable water supplies below the level at which societies generally experience water shortage. In China fifty cities face acute water shortages as groundwater levels drop 1 to 2 meters a year. In Mexico City groundwater is being pumped at rates 40 percent faster than natural recharge. These shortages emerge when water is lost or wasted because its true scarcity value is not recognized. In such cities as Cairo, Jakarta, Lima, Manila, and Mexico City more than half of urban water supplies cannot be accounted for. In many countries scarce water is used for low-value agricultural crops, and farmers pay nothing for the water they use. The misuse of water in the Aral Sea in Central Asia is an extreme example of failure to recognize the value of a natural resource (Box 1.5).

Assessment of whether the regenerative capacity of a natural resource has been exceeded is complicated by uncertainty about the effect of economic activity on the environment. In the cases of soil erosion, atmospheric pollution, and loss of biodiversity, there is often substantial scientific uncertainty about the extent of environmental degradation. Controversy also surrounds the consequences of degradation. What are the health

Box 1.4 The dismal science—economics and scarcity of natural resources

The debate about whether the world is running out of nonrenewable resources is as old as economics. The writings of Malthus and Ricardo, which predicted rapidly growing populations and increasing scarcity of resources, earned economics the name "the dismal science." For natural resources that are nonrenewable, increases in consumption necessarily imply a reduction in the available stock. The evidence, however, gives no support to the hypothesis that marketed nonrenewable resources such as metals, minerals, and energy are becoming scarcer in an economic sense. This is because potential or actual shortages are reflected in rising market prices, which in turn have induced new discoveries, improvements in efficiency, possibilities for substitution, and technological innovations.

The rise in the prices of energy and metals in the 1970s encouraged efficiency gains and substitutions that ultimately reduced the growth of demand. Examples of such technological changes include fiber optics, which replaced copper in telecommunications, the use of thinner coatings of tin, nickel, and zinc in a number of industries, the development of synthetic substitutes, and the recycling of aluminum and other materials. Similar efficiency gains were achieved in the energy sector. The use of metals and of energy per unit of output has declined steadily in industrial countries, although it is generally rising in developing countries. Current consumption as a proportion of reserves has declined for several mineral and energy resources (Box

table 1.4). Declining price trends also indicate that many nonrenewables have become more, rather than less, abundant (Box figure 1.4).

The world is not running out of marketed nonrenewable energy and raw materials, but the unmarketed side effects associated with their extraction and consumption have become serious concerns. In the case of fossil fuels, the real issue is not a potential shortage but the environmental effects associated with their use, particularly local air pollution and carbon dioxide emissions. Similarly, the problems with minerals extraction are pollution and destruction of natural habitat. Because 95 percent of the total material removed from the earth is waste that often contain heavy metals such as copper, iron, tin, and mercury, these commonly find their way into rivers, groundwater, and soils.

Box table 1.4 Energy and mineral reserves and consumption, 1970 and 1988

	Index of commercial reserves, 1988 (1970 = 100)	Annual consumption as a percentage of reserves 1970	Annual consumption as a percentage of reserves 1988
Energy resources			
Crude oil	163	2.7	2.2
Gas	265	2.1	1.5
Mineral resources			
Bauxite	373	0.2	0.1
Copper	131	2.6	3.1
Iron ore	74	0.5	0.8
Lead	75	4.7	8.1
Nickel	72	0.8	1.7
Tin	150	5.4	3.7
Zinc	176	0.3	0.2

Source: World Bank data.

Box figure 1.4 Long-run prices for nonferrous metals, 1900-91

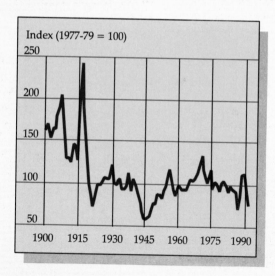

Note: The index is based on the real prices of aluminum, copper, lead, tin, and zinc, weighted by the value of developing country exports in 1979-81.
Source: World Bank data.

effects of certain pollutants? What will climate change do to the ecosystem? Can tropical forests be regenerated? The solutions are likewise often unclear. How quickly can the atmosphere restore itself? When will certain cleaner technologies be-

come available and cost-effective? Uncertainty is an inherent part of environmental problems. To reduce it, decisionmakers need better information about environmental processes and social preferences.

Box 1.5   The Aral Sea: lessons from an ecological disaster

The Aral Sea is dying. Because of the huge diversions of water that have taken place during the past thirty years, particularly for irrigation, the volume of the sea has been reduced by two-thirds. The sea's surface has been sharply diminished, the water in the sea and in surrounding aquifers has become increasingly saline, and the water supplies and health of almost 50 million people in the Aral Sea basin are threatened. Vast areas of salty flatlands have been exposed as the sea has receded, and salt from these areas is being blown across the plains onto neighboring cropland and pastures, causing ecological damage. The frost-free period in the delta of the Amu Darya River, which feeds the Aral Sea, has fallen to less than 180 days—below the minimum required for growing cotton, the region's main cash crop. The changes in the sea have effectively killed a substantial fishing industry, and the variety of fauna in the region has declined drastically. If current trends continued unchecked, the sea would eventually shrink to a saline lake one-sixth of its 1960 size.

This ecological disaster is the consequence of excessive abstraction of water for irrigation purposes from the Amu Darya and Syr Darya rivers, which feed the Aral Sea. Total river runoff into the sea fell from an average 55 cubic kilometers a year in the 1950s to zero in the early 1980s. The irrigation schemes have been a mixed blessing for the populations of the Central Asian republics—Kazakhstan, Kyrghyzstan, Tajikistan, Turkmenistan, and Uzbekistan—which they serve. The diversion of water has provided livelihoods for the region's farmers, but at considerable environmental cost. Soils have been poisoned with salt, overwatering has

turned pastureland into bogs, water supplies have become polluted by pesticide and fertilizer residues, and the deteriorating quality of drinking water and sanitation is taking a heavy toll on human health. While it is easy to see how the problem of the Aral Sea might have been avoided, solutions are difficult. A combination of better technical management and appropriate incentives is clearly essential: charging for water or allocating it to the most valuable uses could prompt shifts in cropping patterns and make more water available to industry and households.

But the changes needed are vast, and there is little room for maneuver. The Central Asian republics (excluding Kazakhstan) are poor: their incomes are 65 percent of the average in the former U.S.S.R. In the past, transfers from the central government exceeded 20 percent of national income in Kyrghyzstan and Tajikistan and 12 percent in Uzbekistan. These transfers are no longer available. The regional population of 35 million is growing rapidly, at 2.7 percent a year, and infant mortality is high. The states have become dependent on a specialized but unsustainable pattern of agriculture. Irrigated production of cotton, grapes, fruit, and vegetables accounts for the bulk of export earnings. Any rapid reduction in the use of irrigation water will reduce living standards still further unless these economies receive assistance to help them diversify away from irrigated agriculture. Meanwhile, salinization and dust storms erode the existing land under irrigation. This is one of the starkest examples of the need to combine development with sound environmental policy.

EFFICIENCY, TECHNOLOGY, AND SUBSTITUTION. The view that greater economic activity inevitably hurts the environment is based on static assumptions about technology, tastes, and environmental investments. According to this view, as populations and incomes rise, a growing economy will require more inputs (thus depleting the earth's "sources") and will produce more emissions and wastes (overburdening the earth's "sinks"). As the scale of economic activity increases, the earth's "carrying capacity" will be exceeded. In reality, of course, the relationships between inputs and outputs and the overall effects of economic activity on the environment are continually changing. Figure 1.4 illustrates that the scale of the economy is only one of the factors that will determine environmental quality. The key question is whether the factors that tend to reduce environmental damage per unit of activity can more than compensate for any

negative consequences of the overall growth in scale. Factors that can play a particularly important role are:

• *Structure:* the goods and services produced in the economy
• *Efficiency:* inputs used per unit of output in the economy
• *Substitution:* the ability to substitute away from resources that are becoming scarce
• *Clean technologies and management practices:* the ability to reduce environmental damage per unit of input or output.

Economic policies, environmental policies, and environmental investments all have a role in ensuring that individual behavior takes account of the true value of environmental resources. Economic policies affect the scale, composition, and efficiency of production, which can result in posi-

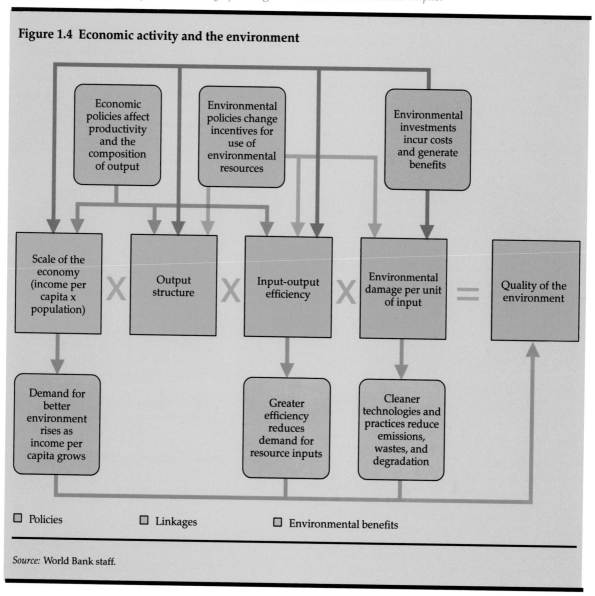

Figure 1.4 Economic activity and the environment

Source: World Bank staff.

tive or negative effects on the environment. Efficiency gains from economic policies will often reduce the demand for natural resource inputs. Environmental policies can reinforce efficiency in resource use and provide incentives for adopting less-damaging technologies and practices. The investments that are induced by environmental policies will change the way in which goods and services are produced and may result in lower output but will also generate benefits that can increase human welfare.

As incomes rise, the demand for improvements in environmental quality will increase, as will the resources available for investment. Without incen-

tives to use scarce resources sparingly, the pressure to reduce environmental damage will be weaker, and the adverse effects of economic growth are likely to dominate. But where the scarcity of natural resources is accurately reflected in decisions about their use, the positive forces of substitution, efficiency gains, innovation, and structural change will be powerful. In industrial countries these positive forces contributed significantly to improving environmental quality while maintaining economic growth (Box 1.6).

The environmental problems facing poor countries differ from those facing the better-off (see Figure 4 in the Overview). In some cases environmen-

Box 1.6   Delinking growth and pollution: lessons from industrial countries

Industrial countries have achieved substantial improvements in environmental quality along with continued economic growth. A recent report by the OECD described some of the achievements since 1970. Access to clean water, adequate sanitation, and municipal waste disposal is now virtually universal. Air quality in OECD countries is vastly improved; particulate emissions have declined by 60 percent and sulfur oxides by 38 percent. Lead emissions have fallen by 85 percent in North America and by 50 percent in most European cities. Japan, which has spent substantial amounts on pollution abatement, has achieved the largest improvement in air quality. Emissions of sulfur oxides, particulates, and nitrogen oxides as a share of GDP in Japan are less than one-quarter of OECD averages. Persistent pollutants such as DDT, polychlorinated biphenyls (PCBs), and mercury compounds have also been reduced in OECD countries, as has the frequency of large shipping accidents and oil spills. Forested areas and protected lands and habitats have increased in almost all countries. These improvements have been achieved as a result of annual expenditures on antipollution policies equivalent to 0.8–1.5 percent of GDP since the 1970s. About half of these expenditures were incurred by the public sector and half by the private sector.

These improvements in environmental quality are even more remarkable when it is recalled that the economies of the OECD grew by about 80 percent over the same period. In many cases economic growth is being "delinked" from pollution as environmentally nondamaging practices are incorporated into the capital stock (Box figure 1.6).

The OECD report, however, also identified a large "unfinished agenda" of environmental problems, as well as emerging issues, that remain to be addressed. Nitrogen oxides, which are emitted largely by transport sources, have increased by 12 percent since 1970 in the OECD countries (except Japan), reflecting the failure of policies and technology to keep up with increases in transport. Municipal wastes grew by 26 percent between 1975 and 1990 and carbon dioxide emissions by 15 percent over the past decade. Human exposure to toxic pollutants, such as cadmium, benzene, radon, and asbestos, remains a concern. Groundwater is increasingly polluted as a result of salinization, fertilizer and pesticide runoff, and contamination from urban and industrial areas. Soil degradation persists in some areas, and encroachment on coastal regions, wetlands, and other natural habitats is still a concern. A number of plant and animal species are endangered; even larger numbers are threatened.

What does the OECD's experience imply for the environmental agendas of developing countries? First, there are many policy lessons—such as the fact that it is often cheaper to prevent environmental degradation than to attempt to "cure" it later. The costly cleanup of hazardous waste sites in several OECD countries gives an indication of what environmental neglect might mean for other countries in the future. Second, many of the environmentally nondamaging technologies and practices developed in OECD countries can be adapted to the needs of developing countries. Cleaner technologies and practices can be acquired through trade and foreign direct investment, as well as through international cooperation. Third, to the extent that environmental degradation in the OECD countries affects developing countries, as in the case of climate change and ozone depletion, polluters should pay and victims should be compensated.

Box figure 1.6   Breaking the link between growth in GDP and pollution

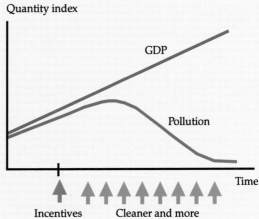

The theory

Quantity index

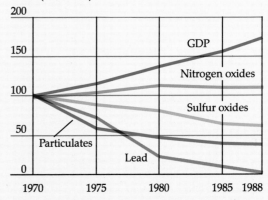

The practice: GDP and emissions in OECD countries

Index (1970=100)

Note: GDP, emissions of nitrogen oxides, and emissions of sulfur oxides are OECD averages. Emissions of particulates are estimated from the average for Germany, Italy, Netherlands, United Kingdom, and United States. Lead emissions are for United States.
Sources: OECD 1991; U.S. Environmental Protection Agency 1991.

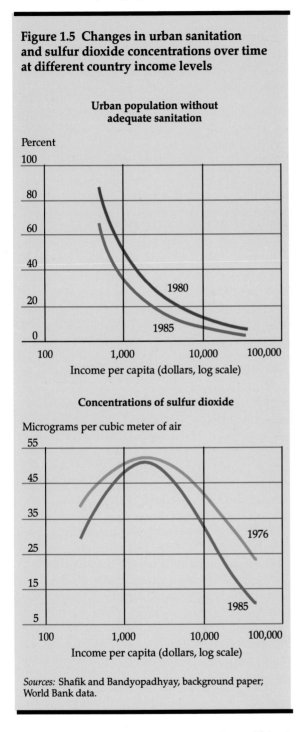

Figure 1.5 Changes in urban sanitation and sulfur dioxide concentrations over time at different country income levels

Urban population without adequate sanitation

Percent

1980

1985

Income per capita (dollars, log scale)

Concentrations of sulfur dioxide

Micrograms per cubic meter of air

1976

1985

Income per capita (dollars, log scale)

Sources: Shafik and Bandyopadhyay, background paper; World Bank data.

comes rise. Carbon dioxide emissions and municipal wastes are indicators of environmental stress that appear to keep rising with income. But this is because no incentives yet exist to change behavior. The costs of abatement in these cases are relatively high, and the benefits of changing behavior are perceived to be low—partly because (in the case of carbon dioxide) they would accrue mainly to other countries. When societies have decided to enforce a change in behavior—through regulations, charges, or other means—environmental quality has improved. Progress in reducing water pollution and emissions of particulates, lead, and sulfur dioxide are examples of how higher-income countries have been able to break the link between growth and environmental degradation. This is not easy—it requires strong institutions and effective policies—but it can be done. It explains why so many environmental indicators show an initial deterioration followed by an improvement. As incomes grow, the ability and the willingness to invest in a better environment rise.

Past patterns of environmental degradation are not inevitable. Individual countries can choose policies that lead to much better (or worse) environmental conditions than those in other countries at similar income levels. In addition, technological change, coupled with improved understanding of the links between economic activity and environmental damage, is enabling countries to grow more rapidly with less environmental impact than was possible earlier. Figure 1.5 illustrates this for a cross-section of countries. At any given income level, a higher proportion of people in any country is likely to have access to sanitation today than in the past. The same can be true of progress in reducing air pollution. Concentrations of sulfur dioxide are lower today than in the past, so that someone living in a country with a per capita income level of $500 is more likely to breathe cleaner air than in previous decades. The adoption of environmental policies and the investment and technological innovations induced by such policies imply that the environmental mistakes of the past do not have to be repeated.

The nature of the challenge

During the working lifetime of children born today, the population of the world will almost double. By the middle of the next century almost one-third of the world's population will live in countries with a population density of more than 400 per square kilometer—equivalent to the den-

tal quality improves as income rises. This is because increased income allows societies to provide public goods such as sanitation services and because once individuals no longer have to worry about day-to-day survival, they can afford profitable investments in conservation.

Some problems are observed to get worse as insity of the Netherlands or the Republic of Korea today. The next generation will also see the size of the world economy triple. Under simple extrapolation of current practices, this growth would lead to severe environmental degradation. Yet in virtually every economic sector, environmentally less damaging practices are available and are in use in a number of countries. For almost every challenge—in water supply and sanitation, or energy and industrial output, or food production—there are possibilities for growing more sustainably.

The challenge for water supply and sanitation will be to respond to the backlog of demand while meeting the needs of growing populations. Making clean water available to everyone in the next generation will require that service be extended to an additional 3.7 billion people living in urban areas and about 1.2 billion rural inhabitants. Since only about 1.5 billion urban residents currently have access to clean water, the magnitude of the task is apparent. For sanitation the problem is even larger; the number of urban dwellers currently served is little more than 1 billion. For a country like Nigeria, providing access to clean water for the entire population by 2030 will imply increasing the number of urban connections by four times and the number of rural connections by almost nine times. To prevent the number of people without access to adequate sanitation from rising, the population covered will have to increase to 6.5 times the current number. Policies to meet these challenges are discussed in Chapter 5.

The challenge for energy and industry will be to meet the projected growth in demand while controlling pollution. Total manufacturing output in developing countries will increase to about six times current levels by 2030. Average emissions of air pollutants per unit of electric power generated would have to be reduced by 90 percent to avoid an increase in total emissions from this activity. Emissions from heavily polluting industries—chemicals, metallurgy, paper, and building materials—will also require large reductions in discharges of air and water pollutants and in wastes produced if a worsening of industrial pollution is to be prevented. In the Philippines, for example, manufacturing output is likely to grow to nine or ten times the current level, and demand for electric power will rise even more rapidly. This means that many industries will have to reduce emissions per unit of output by between 90 and 95 percent to avoid worsening pollution.

The technologies for achieving such reductions in pollution from energy and industry already ex-

ist in most instances. Many possibilities also exist for dramatic improvements in pollution prevention—switching to cleaner-burning fuels or recycling industrial wastewater, for example. Cleaner processes often yield productivity gains and cost reductions as well because they use materials more frugally. The scope for pollution abatement and prevention in industry and energy, and the policies for inducing these new technologies, are discussed in Chapter 6.

The challenge for agriculture will be to meet developing countries' expected demand for food. Total world consumption of cereals will have to almost double by 2030. To protect fragile soils and natural habitats, almost all of this increase will have to be achieved by raising yields on existing cropland rather than by extending the area under cultivation. There is little doubt that cultivated soils have the capacity to meet future increases in world agricultural demand so long as they are well managed. But intensification of production will involve the application of much higher levels of fertilizers and pesticides, as well as significant improvements in the allocation of water for agricultural use. Doubling food production in India by 2030 can be achieved by maintaining past rates of crop yields but will require a fourfold increase in fertilizer application. By 2030 average yields in India would have to reach the level of those in China today.

Such gains in food production increase the risk of soil degradation, misuse of pesticides, spillovers from chemical applications, and excessive drawdown of water. Techniques such as integrated pest management, minimum tillage, agroforestry, integrated crop and livestock management, and soil-enriching crop rotations will be needed to reduce land degradation and increase yields. This will often require better-educated farmers, and sometimes social changes as well. When governments are committed to allocating resources to research and extension services and to providing undistorted incentives, many farmers are quick to adopt these less-damaging practices. Policies for improving the management of natural resources, especially of agricultural land, will be discussed in Chapter 7.

Policies and institutions

Without technologies and practices that can be applied at reasonable cost, environmental improvement is difficult. But without the backing of appropriate policies, even the most environmentally helpful technologies and practices will not necessarily be applied, unless (as is often the case in industry) they are more productive than existing methods. The principles of sound environmental policy (described in Chapter 3) are well understood. But they are difficult for national governments to introduce and are even more difficult to translate into international agreements. National governments may be reluctant to challenge those who cause environmental damage; they are likely to be the rich and influential, while those who suffer most are often the poor and powerless. The institutional obstacles to sustainable development are discussed in Chapter 4.

If institutional obstacles to addressing national environmental problems are large, they are even greater for international problems such as greenhouse warming and the preservation of biodiversity. It may be difficult to reach agreement among many different countries, each of which may perceive its national interest differently. If countries do not think that the benefits of agreement are worth more to them than the costs of refusing to cooperate, they may be willing to join only if other countries are willing to compensate them for doing so. The complications of addressing global environmental problems are analyzed in Chapter 8.

A strategy for sustaining development

The challenges facing this generation are formidable. Many countries have not yet achieved acceptable living standards for their people. Economic growth that improves human welfare is urgently needed. Protecting the environment will be an important part of improving the well-being of people today, as well as the well-being of their children and grandchildren. This Report suggests a threefold strategy for meeting the challenge of sustainable development.

* *Build on the positive links.* Policies for growth promote efficient use of resources, technology transfer, and better-working markets—all of which can help in finding solutions to environmental challenges. Rising incomes can pay for investments in environmental improvement. Policies that are effective in reducing poverty will help reduce population growth and will provide the resources and knowledge to enable the poor to take a longer-term view.

* *Break the negative links.* Rising incomes and technological advances make sustainable development possible, but they do not guarantee it. Usually, additional incentives that capture the true value of the environment will be required to induce less-damaging behavior. Effective environmental policies and institutions are essential.

* *Clarify and manage the uncertain links.* Many relationships between human activity and the environment remain poorly understood, and there will always be surprises. The response should be investment in information and research and the adoption of precautionary measures, such as safe minimum standards, where uncertainties are great and there is a potential for irreversible damage or high costs in the long run.

2 Environmental priorities for development

Setting environmental priorities inevitably involves choices. Developing countries should give priority to addressing the risks to health and economic productivity associated with dirty water, inadequate sanitation, air pollution, and land degradation, which cause illness and death on an enormous scale.

In poor countries:

*   *Diarrheal diseases that result from contaminated water kill about 2 million children and cause about 900 million episodes of illness each year.*
*   *Indoor air pollution from burning wood, charcoal, and dung endangers the health of 400 million to 700 million people.*
*   *Dust and soot in city air cause between 300,000 and 700,000 premature deaths a year.*
*   *Soil erosion can cause annual economic losses ranging from 0.5 to 1.5 percent of GNP.*
*   *A quarter of all irrigated land suffers from salinization.*
*   *Tropical forests—the primary source of livelihood for about 140 million people—are being lost at a rate of 0.9 percent annually.*

Concern over ozone depletion continues to grow. The consequences of loss of biodiversity and of greenhouse warming are less certain but are likely to extend far into the future and to be effectively irreversible.

Environmental degradation has three damaging effects. It harms human health, reduces economic productivity, and leads to the loss of "amenities," a term that describes the many other ways in which people benefit from the existence of an unspoiled environment. Amenities are harder to measure than costs to health and productivity but may be valued just as highly (see Box 2.1). The subject of this chapter is priorities for environmental policy: in which cases are the benefits for developing countries most likely to exceed the costs of action? Chapter 3 goes on to discuss ways to contain the costs of action by making sure that environmental policies are as cost-effective as possible, and later chapters look at such policies in greater detail.

The health of hundreds of millions of people is threatened by contaminated drinking water, particulates in city air, and smoky indoor air caused by use of such cooking fuels as dung and wood. Productivity of natural resources is being lost in many parts of the world because of the overuse and pollution of renewable resources—soils, water, forests, and the like. Amenities provided by the natural world, such as the enjoyment of an

unpolluted vista or satisfaction that a species is being protected from extinction, are being lost as habitats are degraded or converted to other uses. Because the interaction of various pollutants with other human and natural factors may be hard to predict, some environmental problems may entail losses in all three areas: health, productivity, and amenity.

Policymakers need to set priorities for environmental policies. In both developing and industrial countries governments rightly give greatest urgency to environmental damage that harms human health or productive potential. The priorities that developing countries set for their own environments will not necessarily be those that people in richer countries might want them to adopt. Thus, although some cultures in poor countries may value their natural heritage strongly, most developing country governments are likely to give lower priority to amenity damage as long as basic human needs remain unmet.

National priorities will vary. In Sub-Saharan Africa, for example, contaminated drinking water and poor sanitation contribute to infectious and parasitic diseases that account for more than 62 percent of all deaths—twice the level found in Latin America and twelve times the level in industrial countries. Higher-income countries have virtually eliminated these waterborne health risks, but they face other health threats because of emissions from transport and industry. The importance that societies give to different environmental problems evolves, often rapidly, in response to gains in standards of living and to other social changes. For instance, as populations age in Latin America, the share in total mortality of adult chronic and degenerative diseases will more than double and the share of infectious childhood diseases will diminish. Some of the increase in adult mortality will be a delayed response to exposure to pollution today, and in many cases preventive action now will be cheaper than remedial measures in the future.

Water

Access to safe water remains an urgent human need in many countries. Part of the problem is contamination; tremendous human suffering is caused by diseases that are largely conquered when adequate water supply and sewerage sys-tems are installed. The problem is compounded in some places by growing water scarcity, which makes it difficult to meet increasing demand except at escalating cost.

The most widespread contamination of water is from disease-bearing human wastes, usually detected by measuring fecal coliform levels. Human wastes pose great health risks for the many people who are compelled to drink and wash in untreated water from rivers and ponds. Data from UNEP's Global Environment Monitoring System (GEMS) demonstrate the enormous problem of such contamination, with poor and deteriorating surface water quality in many countries. Water pollution from human wastes matters less in countries that can afford to treat all water supplies, and it can in principle be reversed with adequate investment in treatment systems. But water quality has continued to deteriorate even in some high-income countries.

The capacity of rivers to support aquatic life is decreased when the decomposition of pollutants lowers the amount of oxygen dissolved in the water. Unlike fecal contamination, oxygen loss does not threaten health directly, but its effects on fish-

Box 2.1 Environmental damage—why does it matter?

Values to people

The costs of environmental damage to humans—which may be borne immediately or at some point in the future—are principally losses in health, productivity, and amenity. There are practical methods for evaluating such costs, but not for evaluating the fundamentally ethical issue of costs of human activity to other species.

Health. Human welfare is reduced by ill health and premature mortality caused by degradation of air and water quality and by other environmental risks. Pollutants can cause health problems through direct exposure or indirectly through changes in the physical environment—the effects of which range from increased solar radiation to lower nutrition. The links between pollutants and health have begun to be identified through epidemiological studies undertaken primarily in high-income countries; the effects are expected to be more pronounced in lower-income countries where people are less healthy and less well nourished.

Productivity. Impaired health may lower human productivity, and environmental degradation reduces the productivity of many resources used directly by people. Water pollution damages fisheries, and waterlog-ging and salinization of the soil lowers crop yields. Some productivity declines result from damage to environmental assets that people use indirectly: if forested watersheds are heavily logged, economic losses from increased downstream flooding may ensue.

Amenity. A clear vista or a clean and quiet neighborhood adds to the quality of life. Environmental assets are often valued even by people who never enjoy them directly but who cherish the thought that they exist and the prospect that future generations will enjoy them too. Such values may increase when environmental resources are unique or endangered.

Intrinsic value

Many people believe that other living things in the natural world have "intrinsic" value separate from their value to human beings. This belief is certainly not confined to the rich; many indigenous groups strongly hold such views. No measurement of intrinsic value is possible; the best that can be done is to measure people's opinions regarding such values. Thus, intrinsic values can be captured only imperfectly and partially under the notion of amenity values.

Figure 2.1 Dissolved oxygen in rivers: levels and trends across country income groups

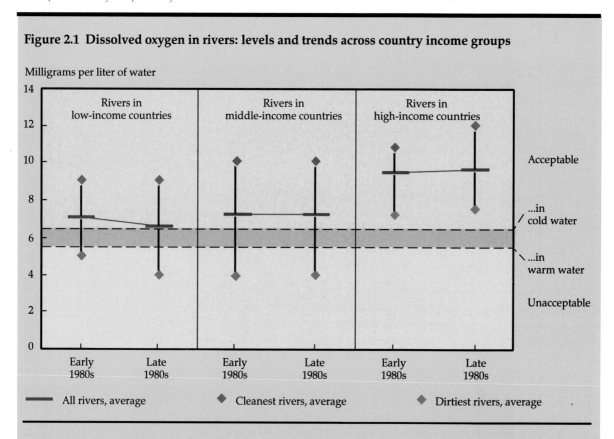

Milligrams per liter of water

Note: Data are for twenty sites in low-income countries, thirty-one sites in middle-income countries, and seventeen sites in high-income countries. "Cleanest rivers" and "dirtiest rivers" are the first and last quartiles of sites when ranked by water quality. Periods of time series differ somewhat by site. U.S. Environmental Protection Agency water standards for supporting aquatic life are used as the criteria for acceptability.
Source: Environmental data appendix table A.4.

eries may be economically important. Human sewage and agroindustrial effluent are the main causes of this problem; nutrient runoff in agricultural areas with intensive fertilizer use is another contributor. Although inadequate levels of dissolved oxygen tend to affect shorter lengths of rivers than does fecal contamination, a sample of GEMS monitoring sites in the mid-1980s found that 12 percent had dissolved oxygen levels low enough to endanger fish populations. The problem was worst where rivers passed through larger cities or industrial centers. In China, only five of fifteen river stretches sampled near large cities were capable of supporting fish. High-income countries have seen some improvement over the past decade. Middle-income countries have, on average, shown no change, and low-income ones show continued deterioration (see Figure 2.1).

Where industry, mining, and the use of agricultural chemicals are expanding, rivers become contaminated with toxic chemicals and with heavy metals such as lead and mercury. These pollutants are hard to remove from drinking water with standard purification facilities. They may accumulate in shellfish and fish, which may be eaten by people who do not realize that the food is contaminated. In a sample of fish and shellfish caught in Jakarta Bay, Indonesia, 44 percent exceeded WHO guidelines for lead, 38 percent those for mercury, and 76 percent those for cadmium. After Malaysia found that lead levels in twelve rivers frequently exceeded the national standard for safe drinking water, the country began monitoring rivers for heavy metals. During the 1980s lead also worsened or became a problem for the first time in some rivers in Brazil (Paraíba and Guandu), Korea (Han), and Turkey (Sakarya).

As surface water near towns and cities becomes increasingly polluted and costly to purify, public water utilities and other urban water users have turned to groundwater as a potential source of a cheaper and safer supply. Monitoring of groundwater for contamination has lagged behind monitoring of surface water, but that is beginning to change as in many places groundwater, too, is becoming polluted. It is often more important to prevent contamination of groundwater than of surface water. Aquifers do not have the self-cleansing capacity of rivers and, once polluted, are difficult and costly to clean.

One of the principal origins of groundwater pollution is seepage from the improper use and disposal of heavy metals, synthetic chemicals, and other hazardous wastes. In Latin America, for instance, the quantity of such compounds reaching groundwater from waste dumps appears to be doubling every fifteen years. Sometimes industrial effluents are discharged directly into groundwater. In coastal areas overpumping causes salt water to infiltrate freshwater aquifers. In some towns contamination occurs because of lack of sewerage systems or poor maintenance of septic tanks. Where intensive agriculture relies on chemical inputs combined with irrigation, the chemicals often leach into groundwater.

Water quality has continued to deteriorate despite substantial progress in bringing sanitation services to the world's population. Little has been done to extend the treatment of human sewage. The replacement of septic tank systems with piped sewerage systems greatly reduces the risks of groundwater pollution but leads to increased pollution of surface water unless the sewage is treated. Yet in Latin America as little as 2 percent of sewage receives any treatment. Moreover, despite the expansion of sanitation services, the absolute number of people in urban areas without access to these services is thought to have grown by more than 70 million in the 1980s, and more than 1.7 billion people worldwide are without access (Figure 2.2).

Access to uncontaminated water has barely kept pace with population growth. Official WHO figures suggest that between 1980 and 1990 more than 1.6 billion additional people were provided with access to water of reasonable quality. In fact, however, many of those who officially have access still drink polluted water. At least 170 million people in urban areas still lack a source of potable water near their homes, and in rural areas, although access has increased rapidly in the past decade, more than 855 million are still without safe water (see Figure 2.2).

It is the poor—the woman in Niamey drawing water from an open sewage channel or the Ban-

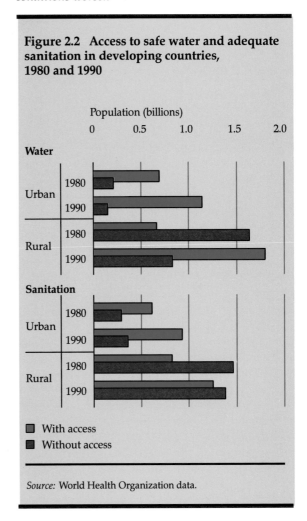

More people have safe water, but urban sanitary conditions worsen

Figure 2.2 Access to safe water and adequate sanitation in developing countries, 1980 and 1990

Source: World Health Organization data.

gladeshi child washing household utensils in a pool also used as a latrine—who bear the brunt of risks from contaminated water. The differences in access to safe water by income exist both within and across countries. The gap in access between lower- and higher-income countries has narrowed only slightly, and within countries inequities continue to be striking. For example, a family in the top fifth income group in Peru, the Dominican Republic, or Ghana is, respectively, three, six, and twelve times more likely to have a house connection than a family in the bottom fifth income group in those countries. The rural poor are more likely to rely directly on rivers, lakes, and unprotected shallow wells for their water needs and are least able to bear the cost of simple preventive measures such as boiling water to make it safe for drinking. In many cities in developing countries poor households in neighborhoods unserved by the munici-

Table 2.1 Availability of water by region

| Region[a] | Annual internal renewable water resources | | Percentage of population living in countries with scarce annual per capita resources | |
	Total (thousands of cubic kilometers)	Per capita (thousands of cubic meters)	Less than 1,000 cubic meters	1,000–2,000 cubic meters
Sub-Saharan Africa	3.8	7.1	8	16
East Asia and the Pacific	9.3	5.3	<1	6
South Asia	4.9	4.2	0	0
Eastern Europe and former U.S.S.R.	4.7	11.4	3	19
Other Europe	2.0	4.6	6	15
Middle East and North Africa	0.3	1.0	53	18
Latin America and the Caribbean	10.6	23.9	<1	4
Canada and United States	5.4	19.4	0	0
World	40.9	7.7	4	8

a. Regional groups include high-income economies. Sub-Saharan Africa includes South Africa.
Sources: World Resources Institute data; World Bank data.

pal water system buy water from private vendors, typically at prices several times greater than the charges for households with municipal hookups.

Water scarcity

Globally, fresh water is abundant. Each year an average of more than 7,000 cubic meters per capita enters rivers and aquifers. It does not always arrive where and when it is needed. Twenty-two countries already have renewable water resources of less than 1,000 cubic meters per capita—a level commonly taken to indicate that water scarcity is a severe constraint. An additional eighteen countries have less than 2,000 cubic meters per capita on average, dangerously little in years of short rainfall. Most of the countries with limited renewable water resources are in the Middle East, North Africa, and Sub-Saharan Africa, the regions where populations are growing fastest (Table 2.1). Elsewhere, water scarcity is less of a problem at the national level, but it is nevertheless severe in certain watersheds of northern China, west and south India, and Mexico.

Water scarcity is often a regional problem. More than 200 river systems, draining over half of the planet's land area, are shared by two or more countries. Overpumping of groundwater aquifers that stretch under political borders also injects international politics into the management of water scarcity.

When water is scarce, countries may sometimes have to make awkward choices between quantity and quality. As river flows decline, effluents are less diluted. In countries with inadequate effluent treatment, water quality can often be improved only if supplies from dams are used to maintain flows for dilution rather than for other economic uses. Often, the disparate agencies involved in water management cannot agree on tradeoffs between quantity and quality.

In many countries water scarcity is becoming an increasing constraint not just on household provision but on economic activity in general. Downstream cities can become so short of water as it is drawn off upstream that their industries are seasonally forced to curtail operations. That, indeed, has become routine during dry months in the Indonesian regional capital of Surabaya. As industry, irrigation, and population expand, so do the economic and environmental costs of investing in additional water supply. There is growing awareness of the need to integrate the management of water demand from the different sectors of the economy.

Health effects

The use of polluted waters for drinking and bathing is one of the principal pathways for infection by diseases that kill millions and sicken more than a billion people each year. Diseases such as typhoid and cholera are carried in infected drinking water; others are spread when people wash themselves in contaminated water. Because of their effect on human welfare and economic growth, deficient water supplies and sanitation pose the most serious environmental problems that face developing countries today. Consider first the consequences for health.

The direct impact of waterborne diseases is huge, especially for children and the poor (who are most at risk). Unsafe water is implicated in many cases of diarrheal diseases, which, as a group, kill more than 3 million people, mostly children, and cause about 900 million episodes of illness each year. At any one time more than 900 million people are afflicted with roundworm infection and 200 million with schistosomiasis. Many of these conditions have large indirect health effects—frequent diarrhea, for instance, can leave a child vulnerable to illness and death from other causes.

A key question is what the reduction in this burden of disease and death would be if water and sanitation were improved. This is not a simple question to answer, or one on which all epidemiologists agree. Too little is known about how risks and diseases are distributed and interact with each other, and uncertainty remains over the extent to which modest changes in infrastructure account for long-run health improvements. But some impression can be gained from a recent comprehensive review by the U.S. Agency for International Development (USAID), which summarized the findings from about 100 studies of the health impact of improvements in water supplies and sanitation (Table 2.2). Most of the interventions studied were improvements in the quality or availability of water or in the disposal of excreta. The review showed that the effects of these improvements are large, with median reductions ranging

Table 2.2 Effects of improved water and sanitation on sickness

Disease	Millions of people affected by illness	Median reduction attributable to improvement (percent)
Diarrhea	900[a]	22
Roundworm	900	28
Guinea worm	4	76
Schistosomiasis	200	73

a. Refers to number of cases per year.
Source: Esrey and others 1990.

from 22 percent for diarrhea to 76 percent for guinea worm. It also showed that environmental improvements have a greater impact on mortality than on illness, with median reductions of 60 percent in deaths from diarrheal diseases. A companion WHO analysis of the largest group of health impact studies—those on the effect of water and sanitation on diarrheal diseases—suggests that the effects of making several kinds of improvements at the same time (say, in the quality and availability of water) are roughly additive (Table 2.3). Project experience shows that the gains are reinforced by educating mothers and improving hygiene.

Taking these studies as a guideline, it is possible to make a rough estimate of the effects of providing access to safe water and adequate sanitation to all who currently lack it. If the health risks of these people were reduced by the levels shown in Table 2.2, then there would be:

- 2 million fewer deaths from diarrhea each year among children under five years of age (as an indication of magnitudes, about 10 million infants die each year in developing countries from all causes)
- 200 million fewer episodes of diarrheal illness annually
- 300 million fewer people with roundworm infection
- 150 million fewer people with schistosomiasis
- 2 million fewer people infected with guinea worm.

Other effects

The costs of water pollution include the damage it does to fisheries, which provide the main source of protein in many countries, and to the livelihoods of many rural people. For instance, pollution of coastal waters in northern China is implicated, along with overfishing, in a sharp drop in prawn and shellfish harvests. Heavy silt loads aggravated by land development and logging are reducing coastal coral and the fish populations that feed and breed in it, as in Bacuit Bay in Palawan, the Philippines. Fish are often contaminated by sewage and toxic substances that make them unfit for human consumption. Sewage contamination of seafood is thought responsible for a serious outbreak of hepatitis A in Shanghai and for the recent spread of cholera in Peru.

Excessive water withdrawal contributes to other environmental problems. In addition to displacing people and flooding farmland, damming rivers for reservoirs alters the mix of fresh and salt water in

Table 2.3 Effects of water supply and sanitation improvements on morbidity from diarrhea

Type of improvement	Median reduction in morbidity (percent)
Quality of water	16
Availability of water	25
Quality and availability of water	37
Disposal of excreta	22

Source: Esrey, Feachem, and Hughes 1985.

estuaries, influences coastal stability by affecting sedimentation, and transforms fisheries by changing spawning grounds and river hydrology. When groundwater is drawn off at a rate faster than the rate of natural recharge, the water table falls. In China's northern provinces, where ten large cities rely on groundwater for their basic water supply, water tables have been dropping—by as much as a meter a year in wells serving Beijing, Xian, and Tianjin. In the southern Indian state of Tamil Nadu a decade of heavy pumping has brought about a drop of more than 25 meters in the water table. The costs are often substantial and go beyond the additional costs of pumping from greater depths and replacing shallow wells with deep tubewells. Coastal aquifers can become saline, and land subsidence can compact underground aquifers and permanently reduce their capacity to recharge themselves. Sewers and roads may also be harmed, as has happened in Mexico City and Bangkok.

Air pollution

Although consistent monitoring of ambient air pollution in the world's cities has been going on for only slightly more than a decade, it has already shown that several pollutants frequently exceed the levels considered safe for health. The most serious health risks arise from exposure to suspended particulate matter (SPM), indoor air pollution, and lead. Large numbers of people are also exposed to the somewhat less health-threatening effects of sulfur dioxide.

Air pollution has three principal man-made sources—energy use, vehicular emissions, and industrial production—all of which tend to expand with economic growth unless adequate pollution abatement measures are put in place. The rates of urbanization and of energy consumption per capita are rising rapidly in developing regions. Without aggressive abatement policies, air pollution will intensify in the coming years. If the projected growth in demand for vehicular transport and electricity were to be met with the technologies currently in use, emissions of the main pollutants deriving from these sources would increase fivefold and elevenfold, respectively, by about 2030. As discussed in Chapter 6, most of this potential increase could be eliminated through improvements in efficiency and investment in abatement technologies.

In those developing countries now in the throes of industrialization, city air pollution is far worse than in today's industrial countries. In the early 1980s cities such as Bangkok, Beijing, Calcutta, New Delhi, and Tehran exceeded on more than 200 days a year the SPM concentrations that WHO guidelines indicate should not be exceeded more than seven days a year (Box 2.2). Where adequate data exist, it appears that cities in low-income countries have SPM levels much higher than those in more developed countries. Indeed, pollution levels for even the worst quartile of high-income

---

Box 2.2   Setting pollution guidelines

Ideally, environmental guidelines should be based on a comparison of the costs and the benefits of mitigating damage from pollution. Guidelines for air quality should ensure that the benefits of reducing exposure to air pollution at least equal the costs of pollution control. But with few exceptions (for example, U.S. regulations on lead in gasoline) countries have rarely based their standards on such explicit analyses, usually because of the difficulties of estimating benefits accurately. Instead, many developing countries have established national standards by adapting OECD or WHO guidelines.

The WHO exposure guidelines used in this Report are determined by the pollution levels at which the probability of adverse effects (for example, health risks) starts to increase from low levels. This is a stricter approach than establishing guidelines according to the level at which the health benefits gained from reducing environmental health risks exceed the costs. The WHO guidelines are unlikely to be met in the near future for many countries unless stringent restrictions are placed on emissions, and some countries have left the guidelines as long-range objectives while defining intermediate targets.

Pollution guidelines, particularly for air pollution, often recognize the differing impacts of high but short-duration pollution (peak guidelines) and persistent lower levels (annual guidelines). The former type of pollution particularly affects people whose health is already delicate, including asthmatics, the elderly, and children. The latter leads to degeneration of health for the broader population.

Figure 2.3 Urban air pollution levels and trends: concentrations of suspended particulate matter across country income groups

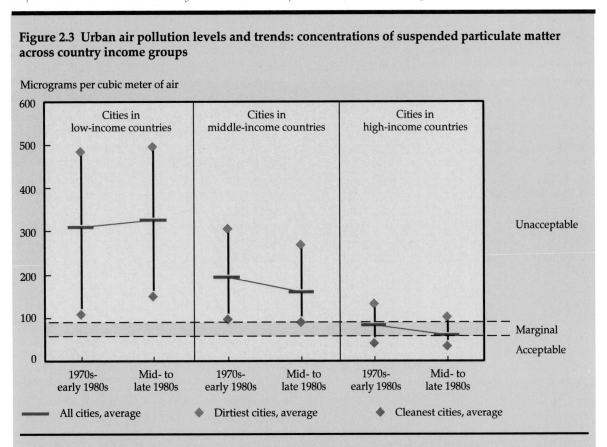

Micrograms per cubic meter of air

Note: Data are for twenty urban sites in low-income countries, fifteen urban sites in middle-income countries, and thirty urban sites in high-income countries. "Cleanest cities" and "dirtiest cities" are the first and last quartiles of sites when ranked by air quality. Periods of time series differ somewhat by site. World Health Organization guidelines for air quality are used as the criteria for acceptability.
Source: Environmental data appendix table A.5.

cities are better than for the best quartile of low-income cities. The gap widened marginally over the past decade; high-income countries took measures to manage emissions, while pollution levels deteriorated in low-income countries (Figure 2.3).

Combining indicators of ambient air pollution with the numbers of people exposed to such levels shows the severity of unhealthy urban air. An extrapolation from GEMS data on airborne particulates for a sample of about fifty cities indicates that in the mid-1980s about 1.3 billion people—mostly in developing countries—lived in towns or cities (of more than 250,000 population) which did not meet WHO standards for SPM (see Figure 2.4).

What are the health consequences for the one-fifth of humanity exposed to unsafe levels of urban air pollution? The evidence increasingly indicates

that the sickness and death linked to SPM are the most important health consequences of city air pollution. Estimates of environmental health risks in developing countries still rely on cautious extrapolation from dose-response evidence in industrial countries. Poor health and nutrition in developing countries are likely to make their populations more susceptible to the effects of pollution. Even the lower levels of SPM typically experienced in richer countries cause respiratory problems. Studies also show a pattern of increased mortality at higher particulate concentrations, particularly among old people with chronic obstructive pulmonary diseases, pneumonia, and heart diseases, because such pollution is particularly stressful for individuals whose health is already poor.

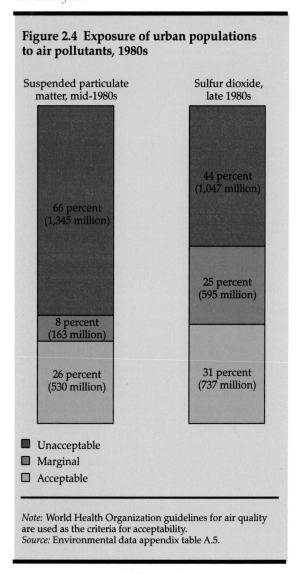

Figure 2.4 Exposure of urban populations to air pollutants, 1980s

Suspended particulate matter, mid-1980s

Sulfur dioxide, late 1980s

66 percent (1,345 million)

8 percent (163 million)

26 percent (530 million)

44 percent (1,047 million)

25 percent (595 million)

31 percent (737 million)

■ Unacceptable
▨ Marginal
□ Acceptable

Note: World Health Organization guidelines for air quality are used as the criteria for acceptability.
Source: Environmental data appendix table A.5.

Rough estimates indicate that if unhealthy levels of SPM were brought down to the annual average level that WHO considers safe, between 300,000 and 700,000 premature deaths a year could be averted in developing countries. This is equivalent to 2–5 percent of all the deaths in urban areas that have excessive levels of particulates. Many of these averted deaths would be in China and India. In addition to reduced mortality, chronic coughing in urban children under the age of fourteen could be reduced by half (or about 50 million cases annually), reducing the chance that these children will face permanent respiratory damage. Excessive particulate pollution also results in lost productivity: in urban areas with average SPM levels

above the WHO guideline at least 0.6 and perhaps 2.1 working days a year are lost to respiratory illness for every adult in the labor force.

In many developing countries indoor air pollution ranks not far behind poor urban air quality as a cause of respiratory ill health. Somewhat fewer people, mostly women and children, are exposed to indoor than to outdoor air risks—400 million to 700 million people according to rough estimates by WHO—but exposure levels are often many times higher. In high-income countries the main indoor air risks are emissions from synthetic materials and resins and from radon gas. In developing countries the problem arises when households cook with or heat their homes with biomass (wood, straw, or dung). For poor households, mostly in rural areas, these are often the only fuels available or affordable.

Studies that have measured biomass smoke in household kitchens in poor rural areas have found SPM levels that routinely exceed by several orders of magnitude the safe levels of WHO guidelines (Table 2.4). Meal preparation can expose those doing the cooking to such levels for several hours a day. Some other components of kitchen smoke to which women and children are exposed are broadly the same as for outdoor air pollution. Exposure to indoor pollution is thus important to take into account in determining overall health risks from air pollutants. Biomass burning is also often linked to deforestation, which is a separate source of environmental damage.

The health impact of exposure to indoor air pollution from biomass burning began to receive some attention only in the past decade, but scattered studies indicate its gravity. The smoke contributes to acute respiratory infections that cause an estimated 4 million deaths annually among infants and children. Recurrent episodes of such infections lead to permanent lung damage that shows up in adults as chronic bronchitis and emphysema, eventually contributing to heart failure. Studies in Nepal and India of nonsmoking women who are exposed to biomass smoke have found abnormally high levels of chronic respiratory disease, with mortality from this condition occurring at far earlier ages than in other populations and at rates comparable to those of male heavy smokers. Emissions of carbon monoxide can cause ambient levels that interfere with normal respiratory absorption of oxygen.

Lead stands out among heavy metals that pose localized health risks because of its prevalence at harmful levels. Unlike some other pollutants, lead

Table 2.4 Indoor air pollution from biomass combustion in developing countries

Location and year of study	Measurement period	Concentrations of suspended particulate matter as multiple of WHO peak guideline[a]
China, 1987	Cooking	11
Gambia, The, 1988	Average over full day	4–11
India, 1987–88	Cooking	16–91
Kenya		
1987	Average over full day	5–8
1972	Overnight (space heating)	12–34
Nepal, 1986	Cooking	9–38
Papua New Guinea, 1975	Overnight (space heating)	1–39

Note: The studies are not completely comparable because of different measurement methods.
a. The WHO peak (98th percentile) guideline recommends that a concentration of 230 micrograms per cubic meter not be surpassed more than 2 percent (seven days) of a year.
Source: Smith 1988.

can affect health through several pathways, including ingestion and inhalation. One of the most important sources is vehicular emissions in countries where lead is still used as a fuel additive. The problem is particularly acute in towns and cities where the number of motor vehicles is growing rapidly. Most OECD countries are successfully addressing this problem by setting increasingly strict standards that limit lead in gas (an approach recently copied in Malaysia, Mexico, and Thailand), but many developing countries have yet to come to grips with this issue.

Blood lead levels have fallen dramatically in countries that have reduced the lead content of fuels. In the United States and Japan average blood lead concentrations are now only a third of the levels of the mid-1970s. In developing countries, as direct monitoring of blood lead becomes more common, evidence from scattered samples clearly reveals levels that are likely to jeopardize health. High levels in children are linked with hindered neurological development, including lower IQ and agility. Rough estimates for Bangkok suggest that children lose an average of four or more IQ points by the age of seven because of elevated exposure to lead, with enduring implications for their productivity as adults. In the Mexico City Metropolitan Area, where 95 percent of automotive gasoline is still leaded, 29 percent of all children have unhealthy blood lead levels. In adults the consequences include risks of higher blood pressure, particularly in men, and higher risks of heart attacks, strokes, and death. In Mexico City exposure to lead may contribute to as much as 20 percent of the incidence of hypertension, while in Bangkok excessive exposure causes 200,000–500,000 cases of hypertension, resulting in up to 400 deaths a year. Elevated blood lead

levels have also been recorded in the neighborhoods of antiquated smelters in several Eastern European countries.

Sulfur dioxide concentrations are also serious in countries that rely on high-sulfur fuels. In the late 1970s concentrations in lower-income countries were, on average, below those in richer countries. Over the past decade concentrations have risen in poor countries but have declined in many middle- and high-income countries (Figure 2.5). As a result, sulfur dioxide pollution is now worst in low- and middle-income countries, with more than 1 billion people exposed to unhealthy levels (see Figure 2.4). Nonetheless, there are encouraging exceptions, suggesting that a country's income level need not be a constraint in tackling air pollution. A number of cities in low- and middle-income countries—Beijing and Caracas, for example—have reversed worsening trends in sulfur dioxide concentrations within the past decade, at much earlier stages of economic development than cities in developed countries managed to do.

Solid and hazardous wastes

Many cities generate more solid wastes than they can collect or dispose of. The volume increases with income. In low- and middle-income countries municipal waste services often swallow between a fifth and a half of city budgets, yet much solid waste is not removed. About 30 percent of solid wastes generated in Jakarta, four-fifths of refuse in Dar es Salaam, and more than two-thirds of solid wastes in Karachi go uncollected. Much better service is achieved in various cities in South America; collection averages between 91 and 99 percent in Caracas, Santiago, Buenos Aires, São Paulo, and Rio de Janeiro. Poor neighborhoods generate

Figure 2.5 Urban air pollution levels and trends: concentrations of sulfur dioxide across country income groups

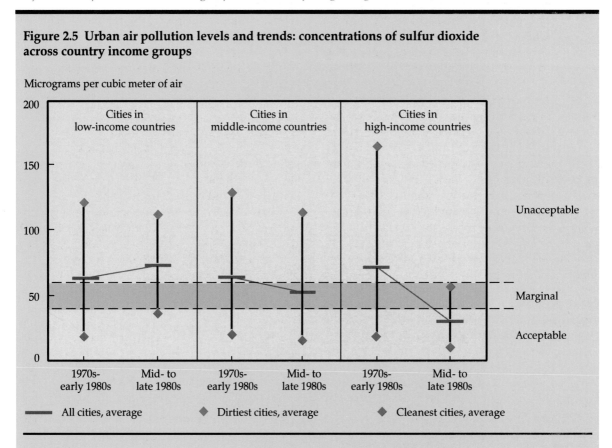

Micrograms per cubic meter of air

Note: Data are for seventeen urban sites in low-income countries, nineteen urban sites in middle-income countries, and forty-two urban sites in high-income countries. "Cleanest cities" and "dirtiest cities" are the first and last quartiles of sites when ranked by air quality. Periods of time series differ somewhat by site. World Health Organization guidelines for air quality are used as the criteria for acceptability.
Source: Environmental data appendix table A.5.

lower amounts of solid wastes per capita but typically receive the least service, often because roads are so congested that conventional collection methods are nearly impossible.

Even when municipal budgets are adequate for collection, safe disposal of collected wastes often remains a problem. Open dumping and uncontrolled landfilling remain the main disposal methods in many developing countries; sanitary landfills are becoming the norm in only a handful of cities.

Inadequate collection and unmanaged disposal present a number of problems for human health and productivity. Uncollected refuse dumped in public areas or into waterways contributes to the spread of disease. In low-income neighborhoods that lack sanitation facilities, trash heaps become mixed with human excreta. Municipal solid waste sites often receive industrial and hazardous

wastes, which may then seep into water supplies. More localized problems—air pollution from burning, gaseous emissions, and even explosions—occur around improperly managed disposal sites.

Generation of hazardous materials and wastes is increasing, but the amounts vary enormously among countries. Industrial economies typically produce about 5,000 tons for every billion dollars of GDP, while for many developing countries the total amount may be only a few hundred tons. Singapore and Hong Kong combined generate more toxic heavy metals as a by-product of industry than all of Sub-Saharan Africa (excluding South Africa). Although toxic wastes are not yet a widespread problem, industrial growth can increase the volume produced. Thailand, for example, had only about 500 factories in 1969, and roughly half of them produced hazardous wastes. Now more than 26,000 factories produce hazardous wastes, and their number could almost triple in a decade. On present trends, the volume of toxic heavy metals generated in countries as diverse as China, India, Korea, and Turkey will reach levels comparable with those of present-day France and the United Kingdom within fifteen years.

But the risks of exposure to hazardous materials cannot easily be extrapolated from the quantities produced. Their potential for causing harm differs tremendously across countries and depends mainly on how they are handled. Although management of hazardous wastes is improving in some countries, in many others wastes are dumped into water or on land sites with minimal safeguards. Severe exposure to hazardous materials can be caused by industrial accidents and by surreptitious trade in and dumping of wastes, sometimes across national boundaries. People in some occupations—for example, scavengers in dump sites in many poor cities—are particularly vulnerable.

Although exposure to pollution from toxic wastes may be serious locally, it is rarely as widespread as exposure to the other water and air pollutants discussed above, except where contamination of surface water or groundwater is involved. Nevertheless, it is usually cheaper to minimize the generation of hazardous wastes and restrict dangerous dumping practices than it is to clean up dumps.

The health effects of contamination of the air, water, and soil with hazardous wastes are in some instances known to be serious, and new compounds, perhaps with untested potential effects on environmental health, are constantly being developed. Sometimes it is difficult to distinguish the carcinogenic consequences of hazardous wastes, at the low doses that are most common, from those of naturally occurring carcinogens, particularly when the consequences are likely to become evident only after many years. Indeed, other threats to health may be more important. In the United States epidemiological evidence on the 2–3 percent of all cancers associated with environmental pollution suggests that exposure to hazardous wastes is a less important risk than exposure to indoor radon and to pesticide residues on foodstuffs.

Land and habitat

Soils

Estimates of land damaged or lost for agricultural use through soil degradation range from moderate to apocalyptic. The types of degradation are as diverse as the land pressures in rural areas. The expanding populations of poor, land-hungry farmers eking out a bare living on the highland slopes of Ecuador, Nepal, and Indonesia are hard pressed to keep their crops from washing away with the hillsides. In the Sahel expansion of cropping, with ever-shorter fallow periods, into areas with marginal rainfall exposes the soil to wind erosion. Three aspects of soil degradation—desertification, erosion, and salinization or waterlogging—receive the most attention, although desertification does not have as large and pervasive an effect on productivity as do the others. Ways of reducing these problems are addressed in Chapter 7.

Desertification in the form of advancing frontiers of sand that engulf pastures and agricultural land, as often shown in the media, is not the most serious problem in dryland areas, although it occurs locally. Definitions of desertification, however, are usually broader and include losses of vegetative cover and plant diversity that are attributable in some part to human activity, as well as the element of irreversibility. Desertification in this sense is difficult to measure. It is clearly affecting some dryland regions, but truly irreversible damage is probably less widespread than is commonly believed. Satellite imagery of the Sahel region of Sub-Saharan Africa shows that vegetation advanced and retreated by up to 200 kilometers between wet and dry years during the 1980s but does not show any underlying trend.

More widespread than desertification, if less dramatic, is the gradual deterioration of agricultural soils, particularly in dryland areas. Results of a global assessment of soil degradation sponsord by UNEP (see Oldeman, Hakkeling, and Sombroek 1990) show that 1.2 billion hectares—almost 11 percent of the earth's vegetated surface—have undergone moderate or worse soil degradation over the past forty-five years because of human activity. Responding to the productivity consequences of this degradation is difficult for most farmers and herders. As a result of this deterioration, yields and total harvests of important food crops are declining in a number of countries, particularly in Sub-Saharan Africa, counter to the global trend of increasing yields (Figure 2.6). Erosion is one of the key components of soil degradation. Its irreversibility and its potential offsite effects distinguish it from the other critical elements of soil deterioration—loss of plant nutrients, organic matter, and microorganisms.

The few comprehensive analyses of soil erosion that have been done in temperate areas indicate that the consequences are not large for aggregate

Figure 2.6 Change in crop yields in selected countries, 1970-90

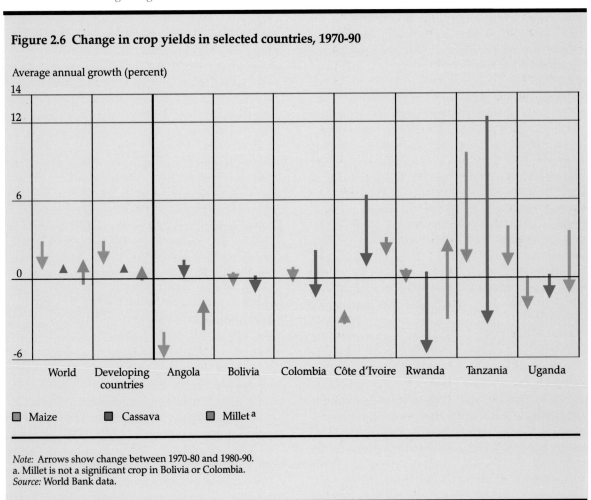

Average annual growth (percent)

Note: Arrows show change between 1970-80 and 1980-90.
a. Millet is not a significant crop in Bolivia or Colombia.
Source: World Bank data.

agricultural productivity, although they are a concern locally for susceptible soils. Several studies have concluded that erosion in the United States may cause cereal yields to be 3–10 percent less at the end of the next century than what would otherwise be achieved. The problem is substantially greater in tropical developing countries, where soils, rainfall, and agricultural practices are more conducive to erosion and where many reports have found rates of soil loss well above the natural rate of soil formation. Several country studies that extrapolate from test-plot measurements of gross soil loss to effects on agricultural productivity indicate substantial national economic losses. These are estimated at about 0.5–1.5 percent of GDP annually for countries such as Costa Rica, Malawi, Mali, and Mexico, and they offset a significant part of economic growth as conventionally measured.

A full account of erosion costs, unlike these esti-

mates, would capture the offsite effects of erosion. Although such an accounting is seldom available, the existing partial estimates may be a broadly accurate reflection of the full economic costs, since some of the spillover effects offset each other. First, soil erosion may harm productivity by depositing silt in dams, irrigation systems, and river transport channels and by damaging fisheries. Partial costings done for Java and Costa Rica show these offsite impacts to be significant but considerably less important economically than the onfarm productivity losses. Second, standard measurements of gross soil erosion from test plots typically overestimate the consequences for productivity, since the eroded soil can remain for decades elsewhere in the farming landscape before it is delivered to the oceans. Thus, a portion of onsite erosion represents a transfer of assets rather than a complete loss from the standpoint of agricultural productivity. But geographic shifts in productivity do have potentially important distributional consequences; it is no solace to Nepal that Bangladesh gains agricultural land and soil fertility from deposition of Himalayan sediment in its river deltas.

Agronomic research and project experience are revealing that erosion is best prevented through balanced management of soil moisture, nutrients, and organic matter. Low-cost techniques for soil conservation, designed to improve soil moisture levels, can increase yields sufficiently within the first several years to make the interventions profitable in their own right, regardless of the long-run benefits from soil conservation. Compared with traditional cropping methods, practices such as mulching, manuring, low tillage, contour cultivation, and agroforestry can frequently reduce surface runoff of water, sediment loss, and erosion by 50 percent and more. These techniques are not yet widely used. They will contribute to the control of soil degradation only if practical constraints such as shortages of cash and labor and the use of dung and mulching materials as household fuel are first alleviated.

Hard on the heels of rapid expansion of irrigation over the past forty years have come growing problems with salinization and waterlogging that are eating away at the productivity of irrigation investments. Irrigated land is deteriorating in parts of many countries, including China, Egypt, India, Mexico, Pakistan, the Central Asian republics, and the western United States.

Salinization of irrigated land is part of a much larger problem of managing the productivity of soils affected by salts. Globally, perhaps about 950 million hectares, or nearly one-third of arable land, are affected by elevated salt concentrations. Most of this salinization occurs naturally. But about 60 million hectares, or some 24 percent of all irrigated land, suffer from salinization caused by bad irrigation practices. Severe declines in productivity affect, according to some estimates, about 24 million hectares, or about one-tenth of irrigated land. Despite awareness of the problems, and despite several decades of reclamation efforts, new areas are being degraded faster than other soils are being rehabilitated. Prevention and reclamation may continue to be hampered by the cost and managerial complexity involved.

Forests

Pollution and soil degradation harm mainly those who live in the regions where they arise. Other kinds of environmental damage touch people in many other countries, sometimes by directly affecting health or economic productivity, but often through loss of amenity—the value that many people derive from knowing that a particular environmental resource exists. Deforestation straddles both categories. It causes productivity loss (often grossly underestimated) in individual countries, and it leads to loss of biodiversity and ecosystems that local people and foreigners may value in their own right.

The forests that occupy more than a quarter of the world's land area are of three broad types—tropical moist and dry forests, temperate forests, and degraded forest land. The main concern is with tropical moist forests, which are disappearing at a rate that threatens the economic and ecological functions they provide. These forests, which still cover more than 1.5 billion hectares, are the richest ecosystems, in biomass and biodiversity, on land. About two-thirds are located in Latin America, primarily in the Amazon basin, with the remainder split between Africa and Asia. Tropical dry forests also total some 1.5 billion hectares, with three-quarters located in Africa. These forests consist mainly of open woodlands and the secondary growth that grows up following shifting cultivation. Temperate forests total about 1.6 billion hectares, with about three-fourths found in industrial countries.

Forests are not just a source of timber; they perform a wide range of social and ecological functions. They provide a livelihood and cultural integrity for forest dwellers and a habitat for a wealth of plants and animals. They protect and enrich soils, provide natural regulation of the hydrologic cycle, affect local and regional climate through evaporation, influence watershed flows of surface and groundwater, and help to stabilize the global climate by sequestering carbon as they grow. Many forests have a deeper spiritual importance, for those who live in them and for those who may never visit them but still cherish the thought of their existence. When trees are indiscriminately cut, most or all of these services are lost. In temperate forests strict management practices that include highly selective cutting or replanting make it possible to pursue commercial logging without sacrificing all these forest services. But in tropical moist forests comparable techniques are rarely practiced, and sustainable timber production, let alone maintenance of ecological services, is not being achieved. Even when reforestation or selective logging is attempted in tropical moist forests, many services provided by forests are still at risk.

All types of forest serve to varying degrees as

carbon sinks and play a role in local hydrology, but they differ in their contribution to other services. Tropical moist forests are particularly rich in species. Although they cover only 7 percent of the earth's land mass, they provide habitat for about half of all known species. They are also the primary source of livelihood for about 140 million people who live within them or on their margins, and they supply about 15 percent of the world's commercial timber. But the land underneath them often cannot support alternative land uses. Tropical dry forests are not as species-rich as tropical moist forests, but they provide important protection against soil erosion. Their main economic uses are for livestock grazing and fuelwood collection by rural people. Temperate forests are the least biodiverse of the three, although they shelter many unique species. They are the main source of industrial wood, and they are also used extensively for recreation.

The rapid deforestation currently occurring in developing countries recalls an earlier epoch in industrial countries, when one-third of the world's temperate forests were cleared for agriculture, construction materials, and fuelwood. Net deforestation has stabilized in most industrial countries, and for temperate areas as a whole, forest area is increasing. Deforestation in developing countries is more recent, with tropical forests declining by nearly one-fifth so far in this century. The first authoritative estimate of global losses of tropical forests to conversion, extrapolated from partial data, concluded that 11.4 million hectares were disappearing each year in the early 1980s. Subsequent country studies and the increasing use of satellite imagery backed by site checks have pushed up estimates for the late 1980s to 17 million–20 million hectares a year. The latest statistics on deforestation suggest that for tropical forests the overall rate in the 1980s was 0.9 percent a year. This is also the rate in Latin America, with Asia's rate somewhat higher (1.2) and Africa's lower (0.8).

Deforestation is caused by farmers, ranchers, logging and mining companies, and fuelwood collectors, each pursuing private interests that are frequently distorted by perverse government policies. Rarely is only one source of disturbance responsible. Indeed, the first intruders may do relatively little damage, but they make it easier for others to follow. Tree felling for firewood accounts for the largest share of wood use in developing countries, but it is concentrated in tropical dry forests and nonforest wooded areas around dense human settlements in Africa and South Asia.

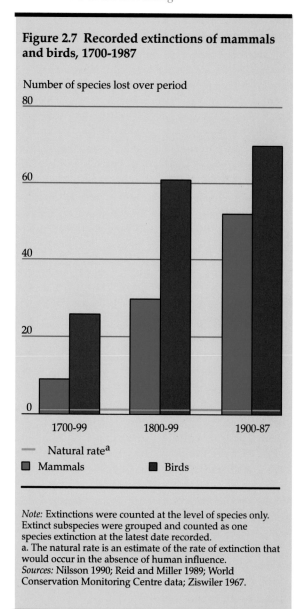

Extinctions are occurring much faster than the natural rate and are increasing

Figure 2.7 Recorded extinctions of mammals and birds, 1700-1987

Number of species lost over period

Note: Extinctions were counted at the level of species only. Extinct subspecies were grouped and counted as one species extinction at the latest date recorded.
a. The natural rate is an estimate of the rate of extinction that would occur in the absence of human influence.
Sources: Nilsson 1990; Reid and Miller 1989; World Conservation Monitoring Centre data; Ziswiler 1967.

Tropical moist forests are mostly being lost to agricultural settlement (roughly 60 percent of annual clearing), with the remainder divided about equally among logging and other uses. Small-scale farmers in land-scarce countries of Central America, Central and East Africa, and South Asia are often involved in such conversion. But in much of the Amazon region most forest destruction can be traced to livestock ranchers, who typically burn the tree cover. In East Asia tropical moist forest has mainly been exploited for its timber by logging companies.

Incentives to cut trees will remain strong.

Growth of population and income leads to a rising demand for fuelwood. Falling demand for labor in settled agricultural areas—whether the result of mechanization, consolidation of landownership, or economic stagnation—has in some countries released a flood of migrants who seek new livelihoods on forest frontiers. These frontiers have become increasingly attractive and accessible in countries such as Brazil, Ecuador, and Indonesia, thanks to mining, oil exploration, the building of roads and railways, and control of diseases. Often, such settlement has been actively encouraged by governments (with backing from the World Bank and other donors) through cheap credit, land and resettlement grants, provision of infrastructure, and low stumpage fees. Some governments are starting to reverse such policies.

Biodiversity

Biological diversity—a composite of genetic information, species, and ecosystems—provides material wealth in the form of food, fiber, medicine, and inputs into industrial processes. It supplies the raw material that may assist human communities to adapt to future and unforeseen environmental stresses. Furthermore, many people value sharing the earth with numerous other forms of life and want to bequeath this heritage to future generations. These aesthetic rewards are already threatened by the loss of biological diversity. By comparison, demonstration of immediate risks of harm to health or productivity is difficult and is constrained by the current paucity of knowledge. These risks, however, could increase and become more evident. Although we live in perhaps the richest geologic era in terms of biological diversity, this wealth risks being squandered through irreversible losses of species and destruction of ecosystems, with consequences that are among the least predictable of environmental changes.

When species become extinct, an irreversible loss occurs. Extinction is an important—albeit imperfect—measure of the severe and growing pressure on the survival of wildlife in its natural habitat. Recorded extinctions continue to increase steadily (Figure 2.7). But decreases in populations and local disappearances are also important. Attempts to project extinction of both known and estimated species on the basis of habitat loss indicate that if recent rates of habitat conversion were to continue through the next century, extinction levels comparable in magnitude to earlier episodes of mass extinction would occur. Such projections remain an inexact science, and the uncertainties are great. In any event, avoidance of mass extinction is not the only concern. The complex web of interactions that maintains the vitality of ecosystems can unravel even if only a small number of key species disappear. It is increasingly understood that the elimination of single species of carnivores, pollinating birds and insects, large herbivores, and important food plants can fundamentally and unpredictably alter the balance of particular ecosystems (Box 2.3).

Box 2.3   Key species: big and small

"Key" species have a more profound impact on their ecosystems than other species. They are organisms that, in many interconnected ways, are essential for the existence of other species. If they disappear, the dependent species may also vanish. Often, the importance of key species is not appreciated or understood until another part of the ecological system breaks down.

Key species can be as small as a bat or as big as an elephant. In Malaysia in the 1970s supplies of a popular fruit, the durian, mysteriously began to decline, threatening a $100 million a year fruit industry. The durian trees were intact and apparently healthy, but they were bearing less fruit. The mystery was solved when it was discovered by chance that the flower of the durian tree was pollinated by a single species of bat whose population was in severe decline. Although the bats pollinated the durian trees, their primary source of food was flowering trees in mangrove swamps, and development of shrimp farming was converting the swamps. In addition, the limestone caves in which the bats roosted were being blasted by a local cement factory. Conservation efforts to protect the limestone hills and the caves led to the closing of the cement factory. The bats and the durian industry then recovered.

In the Hluhluwe Game Reserve in South Africa, since the removal of the elephant population a century ago, three species of antelope have become locally extinct, and the numbers of open-country grazers such as wildebeest and waterbuck have declined. Large browsing and grazing mammals such as elephants have a considerable effect on the vegetative landscape of their habitat. By trampling and browsing saplings, they prevent open forest glades from forming canopies, shrubland from becoming forested, and grassland mosaics from becoming tall grassland. This maintains habitats in which smaller herbivores can thrive. The removal of large herbivores can cause vegetation cover to close up, thus restricting or eliminating the habitat of smaller herbivores.

Table 2.5 Estimated number and scarcity of species worldwide

Group	Number of species identified	Estimated total species	Number identified as percentage of estimated total	Number of scarce species[a]	Number of scarce species as percentage of species identified[a]
Mammals, reptiles, and amphibians	14,484	15,210	95	728	5
Birds	9,040	9,225	98	683	8
Fish	19,056	21,000	90	472	3
Plants	322,311	480,000[b]	67	..	..
Insects	751,000	30,000,000	3	895	<1
Other invertebrates and microorganisms	276,594	3,000,000[b]	9	530	<1
Total[c]	1,392,485	33,525,435	4	..	..

a. Scarce species are those classified by the IUCN as endangered, vulnerable, or rare, or as indeterminate among these categories. In some taxa few species have been evaluated.
b. Figures are taken from World Resources Institute 1989, p. 93.
c. Because these figures are sensitive to the estimated number of insect species, about which there is much debate and uncertainty, they should be considered only rough estimates.
Sources: Wilson and Peter 1988; Wolf 1987; IUCN 1990.

Table 2.6 Reduction of wildlife habitat in two regions

Type of vegetation	Original area (thousands of square kilometers)	Percentage remaining, 1986	Percentage in protected areas
Indomalayan realm[a]			
Dry forests	3,414	28	11
Moist forests	3,362	37	8
Savannah/grassland	46	36	21
Scrub/desert	816	15	21
Wetland/marsh	414	39	10
Mangroves	95	42	8
Afrotropical realm[b]			
Dry forests	8,217	42	15
Moist forests	4,700	40	7
Savannah/grassland	6,955	41	11
Wetland/marsh	177	98	10
Mangroves	88	45	3

a. South and Southeast Asia, Taiwan (China), and southern China.
b. Sub-Saharan Africa.
Source: World Resources Institute 1990.

Monitoring of identified species illuminates but a part of the threat to biodiversity, since in many ecosystems only some species have been cataloged. It is difficult to be precise about species loss because for some categories of organisms there is only a vague notion of the total in existence. Cataloging is the most complete for vertebrates—probably about 90–98 percent of mammals, reptiles, fishes, birds, and amphibians are known, and of these about 4 percent are scarce (see Table 2.5). About ten times more plants than vertebrates have been identified, but the known species may still represent only two-thirds of all plant species in existence. Least is known about insects, of which perhaps only 3 percent have been identified. Most of the unrecorded species are in tropical moist forests.

Unlike any previous species extinction, the present bout is caused principally by human activity. Loss and fragmentation of habitat because of human use is the main threat, although the link is not simple, and overexploitation, species introduction, and pollution play important secondary roles. The greatest attention has been paid to the loss of tropical forests, since they have the most intense concentrations of species and have shrunk at unprecedented rates. But other habitats—coastal and freshwater wetlands and coral reefs—are also suffering serious degradation and loss. The work of establishing the basis for global estimates of ecosystem loss has begun only recently, using vegetation mapping, land-use data, and newer tools of satellite imagery. Studies conducted in the mid-1980s by the International Union for the Conservation of Nature and Natural Resources (IUCN) and UNEP indicated that 65 percent of original wildlife habitat in tropical Africa and 68 percent in tropical South and East Asian countries have been converted to other uses (see Table 2.6). The lack of comparable estimates for other regions leaves a large gap in our knowledge, since habitat conversion is known to be important in these areas as well.

Species extinction is occurring even though increasingly large habitat areas are nominally protected. Worldwide, the area under national protection systems tripled between 1972 and 1990, from 1.6 to 4.8 percent of total land area. But because funds for management are inadequate, incentives for encroachment are strong, and preservation laws are ineffectively enforced, these areas have rarely been adequately protected. Chapter 7 discusses the prospects for improving the management of natural habitat.

Atmospheric changes

Whereas many of the consequences of pollution and loss of biodiversity are evident today, some environmental threats will have their main effects in the future. That creates special problems for policymakers with limited resources who must decide how much to devote to addressing known threats to present populations and how much to uncertain and irreversible hazards to future generations. Two examples are greenhouse warming and ozone depletion.

Greenhouse warming

The atmospheric concentrations of the gases that cause greenhouse warming—the greenhouse gases (GHGs)—are rising. Carbon dioxide, the principal GHG, has increased by more than 12 percent in the past thirty years. The change in GHG concentrations is mainly the result of human activities. Emissions of carbon dioxide from these activities have more than doubled over the period (Box 2.4).

Future trends in GHG concentrations depend on a number of factors—economic growth, the energy intensity of production, and the chemistry of the atmosphere, biosphere, and ocean—not all of which are fully understood. Nonetheless, as the recent scientific assessment by the Intergovernmental Panel on Climate Change (IPCC) empha-

---

Box 2.4 What is the greenhouse effect?

The earth's climate is driven by solar radiation. In the long term the energy absorbed from the sun must be balanced by outgoing radiation from the earth and the atmosphere. Part of this outgoing energy is absorbed and re-emitted by radiative atmospheric gases ("greenhouse gases"), thereby reducing net emission of energy to space. To maintain the global energy balances, both the atmosphere and the surface will warm until the outgoing energy equals the incoming energy. This is the greenhouse effect.

The main natural greenhouse gases are water vapor

Box table 2.4 Key greenhouse gases affected by human activity
(percent)

Effect	Carbon dioxide	Methane	Chlorofluoro-carbons[a]	Nitrous oxides
Increase in atmospheric concentrations				
Preindustrial to 1990	26	115	*	8
1990 to 2025[b]	23	51	—[c]	10
Contribution to the change in heat trapping				
Preindustrial to 1990	61	23	12	4
1990 to 2025[b]	68	17	10	5

* No preindustrial presence in the atmosphere.
Note: Ozone is not included because precise data are lacking.
a. Includes hydrochlorofluorocarbons.
b. Projections are based on IPCC "business as usual" assumptions.
c. The 1990–2025 increase is 73 percent for CFC-11 and 86 percent for CFC-12; the total is not available.
Source: Houghton and others 1990.

(the largest contributor to the greenhouse effect), carbon dioxide, methane, nitrous oxide, and ozone. There are also purely man-made greenhouse gases, including many ozone-depleting substances such as CFCs, which are controlled under the Montreal Protocol. The main greenhouse gases shown in Box table 2.4 differ in the intensity of their heat trapping (or "radiative forcing") and atmospheric lifetimes and thus in their ability to affect the radiative balance of the earth. CFCs and nitrous oxide are many times more potent than the same quantity of carbon dioxide or methane.

The additional carbon dioxide that human activities put into the atmosphere between 1980 and 1989 came principally from fossil fuels. Additions from changes in land use, such as deforestation, are estimated to have been one-fifth to one-half as large. All these net additions from human activity are dwarfed by the natural exchanges of carbon between the earth and the atmosphere.

The largest sources of methane in the atmosphere are natural wetlands, rice paddies, and livestock. Natural gas production (drilling, venting, and transmission), biomass burning, termites, landfills, and coal mining also release methane. Nitrous oxide is released by the oceans and soil, but human activities such as biomass burning and the use of fertilizers play a role that is not yet fully understood or quantified. Much uncertainty surrounds the total size of the sources of both methane and nitrous oxide.

sized, the direction is clear. Sometime in the next century, heat trapping (or "radiative forcing") from increases in greenhouse gases is likely to reach a level equivalent to a doubling of carbon dioxide concentrations over their preindustrial level. Chapter 8 discusses possible responses to the threats of greenhouse warming.

The direct effects on heat trapping of the expected increases in the atmospheric concentrations of greenhouse gases are known with reasonable certainty—within a range of about 20 percent. The direct temperature effects of doubling atmospheric carbon dioxide are estimated to be an increase of about 1.2° Celsius. But the ultimate effects on warming of changes in GHG concentrations depend on the secondary effects of those changes on the earth and oceans—effects that feed back in ways that will reinforce or counteract temperature change. Relatively little is known about these feedbacks, but the best understood is that of water vapor, which probably adds another 0.7° Celsius to the direct warming effect. Other important feedbacks, some of which would moderate warming, include the effects of clouds, ice, and snow. In addition, the ocean plays a large role in determining the timing and geographic location of warming. Climate models that attempt to capture these feedbacks vary considerably in their predictions of equilibrium temperature change following a doubling of carbon dioxide concentrations—from about 1.5° to 4.5° Celsius. Over the past century average global temperatures have increased between 0.3° and 0.6° Celsius, which is consistent with a wide range of long-term temperature responses to increased GHG concentrations.

The complex dynamic models being developed to examine those direct and indirect interactions stretch the capacity of even the most sophisticated computers to their limits. As stylized representations of global climate, they involve simplifications, reflecting both the gaps in our understanding of important physical processes affecting climate and the need to keep the calculations manageable. All models indicate that GHG accumulations will have large implications for climate; important questions remain about the magnitude, patterns, and timing of change, as well as its ultimate effects.

• *How fast?* Most climate models examine only the equilibrium response to a one-time change in GHG concentrations. Increasing attention is now being given to the pace at which climate would move toward equilibrium as GHG concentrations rise. Lags in adjustment mean that climate change could take decades, possibly centuries, to reach equilibrium. How much more time is still unknown but is the subject of intensive research.

• *Where?* Climate changes will vary across the globe. For individual countries and regions, this geographic distribution is of more interest than mean global temperature. These predictions stretch modeling capacity even more than does modeling global temperature change. Both the directions and the magnitudes of predicted climate changes for regions vary considerably across models, and the models have great difficulty in replicating the historical paths of regional climate.

• *How much will it matter?* There is considerable certainty that warming will occur, even if it is difficult to predict its speed and extent. It is much harder to know the extent and rate of warming that would cause serious effects for human societies. Potentially significant effects are more likely to result from related changes in soil moisture, storms, and sea level than from temperature as such, and these changes are more difficult to predict. There is some agreement that climate change induced by greenhouse warming may cause drier soils in midcontinental areas and lead to a substantial rise in sea levels. The plausible argument that tropical storms will become more frequent and intense remains to be convincingly demonstrated. It is still not possible either to rule out costly climatic effects of greenhouse gas accumulations or to demonstrate compellingly that they are likely to occur. Indeed, because it is so hard to narrow the range of possible answers to these questions, very different policy inferences can be drawn from the evidence.

Ozone depletion

In 1985 the appearance of a dramatic spring ozone reduction over Antarctica was confirmed. Ozone depletion is mainly the result of increasing atmospheric concentrations of chlorine originating from CFCs. In the Montreal Protocol (see Chapter 8) countries agreed to phase out production of CFCs—a decision supported by subsequent rapid improvements in scientific understanding. The decrease in the protective ozone layer has occurred more quickly than anticipated and will continue for at least a decade before it can be reversed. The long-term consequences will be harmful for health and for the productivity of marine and terrestrial systems.

Atmospheric levels of CFCs are expected to peak around 2000. In the meantime the rate, geographic scale, and seasonal peaks of the ozone layer's erosion continue to expand. The largest ozone impact is over Antarctica, where the maximum depletion—about 50 percent compared with earlier levels—was as deep and as extensive in area in 1991 as at any time since measurement began. The most recent evidence compiled by the UNEP Scientific Assessment Panel also confirms smaller ozone decreases of 5–10 percent during the past decade in the upper atmosphere over much of the middle and high latitudes in both hemispheres; so far there is no evidence that tropical latitudes are affected. Losses over the next decade may be of the same magnitude, although the possible impacts of clouds, chemical particles, and ground-level pollutants remain poorly understood. Recovery of the protective ozone layer is expected to occur slowly after 2000, with atmospheric chlorine concentrations projected to return to the levels of the late 1970s about midcentury.

An important consequence of ozone depletion is an increase in solar ultraviolet (UV) radiation received at the earth's surface. Biologically damaging UV has more than doubled during episodes of ozone depletion in Antarctica. The threat from penetration of UV radiation to ground level is certain to worsen, although various factors, including increased ozone pollution of the lower atmosphere, have made it difficult to detect longer-term changes associated with ozone depletion in the upper atmosphere. The effects of increases in UV are likely to appear first in the Southern Hemisphere.

In the absence of changes in human behavior to protect against exposure to the sun's rays, a sustained ozone decrease of 10 percent, as is now anticipated for the middle latitudes, would mean an increase in nonmelanoma skin cancers—which primarily affect fair-skinned individuals—of about 25 percent (300,000 additional cases a year) within several decades and an increase in eye damage from cataracts of about 7 percent (1.7 million cases a year). The health risks could be reduced if people would avoid unnecessary exposure by making small changes in their behavior. In countries with good health care, the severity of health consequences from these diseases has declined steadily with dramatic improvements in treatment. A greater worry is raised by preliminary evidence that exposure to increased levels of UV radiation can suppress the immune system in people of all skin colors; that would have much wider detrimental health effects.

Concern about the impact of increased UV radiation on plant productivity has spurred research, but the results are not yet sufficient to predict the consequences for agriculture, forestry, and natural ecosystems. Fluctuations over long periods of time in atmospheric ozone and in UV radiation of the earth's surface have occurred before, and many organisms have evolved protective coping mechanisms. Studies of agricultural crops have demonstrated some inhibition of growth and photosynthesis when plants are exposed to increased UV radiation. But some plants, including cultivars of rice, show considerable capacity for adaption and repair. What is of concern is whether the pace of recent and expected change is so rapid and large as to overwhelm natural defenses. There will be some scope for dealing with increased UV radiation through plant breeding. Damage to marine systems caused by reduced productivity of vegetative plankton is a more immediate concern, particularly because of the important place of these organisms in aquatic food chains that begin in the highly productive waters of Antarctica. Recent studies show that increased UV radiation in Antarctica during the peak of the ozone hole is sufficient to cause some seasonal decline (6–12 percent) in the production of vegetative plankton. The larger impact on marine productivity and ecosystems is not yet understood.

Conclusion

This chapter has tried to demonstrate why developing countries, just as much as industrial countries, should care about environmental degradation. Indeed, the imperative is even greater in poor countries. Filthy air and polluted water now harm or kill far more people in developing countries than were affected when today's industrial countries passed through their own period of Victorian grime. Moreover, some types of environmental damage are growing worse and will continue, under present policies, to worsen as populations expand and economies become more industrialized. Because natural systems work in complicated and interrelated ways that are still poorly understood, some of the effects of today's environmental neglect may turn out to have more serious consequences for health, productivity, and the quality of life than is yet apparent.

But environmental degradation can be checked. There are policies that will allow developing countries to improve the efficiency with which their economies work while at the same time addressing many of the types of environmental damage described in this chapter. Developing countries need to give priority to the kinds of damage that most immediately threaten the quality of their citizens' lives. The following chapters describe which policies are likely to be most effective.

3 Markets, governments, and the environment

Improved environmental management requires that businesses, households, farmers, and governments change the way they behave. Two sets of policies are required.

First, policies should build on the positive links between development and environment. Policies that are bad for both growth and the environment should be eliminated: subsidies to energy, pesticides, water, and logging should be removed; rights to manage and own land, forests, and fisheries should be clarified; and public enterprises should be held accountable. Other development policies, such as promoting macroeconomic stability, improving the access of the poor to education and family planning services, and liberalizing trade and investment, will facilitate environmental protection.

Second, targeted policies are needed to ensure that environmental values are properly reflected in economic activity by both the private and public sectors. The interventions that work best are those that combine incentive and regulatory policies, recognize administrative constraints, and are tailored to specific problems.

The purpose of development policies, and of environmental policies, is to improve welfare. Chapter 1 argued that the increased welfare from rising incomes need not sacrifice environmental improvement. But as Chapter 2 pointed out, human activity has often caused environmental damage and imposed considerable costs. Failure to take account of these costs can lead to bad decisions, and as a consequence, the welfare gains from income growth may be outweighed by the losses from environmental damage. Furthermore, the beneficiaries of higher incomes are often different from those who suffer the costs of environmental degradation. This chapter discusses the policies necessary to ensure that decisions better reflect the value of the environment. The next chapter looks at why such policies are politically so difficult to adopt.

Environmental damage: diverse problems, common causes

Environmental degradation, whether tropical deforestation in Africa or air pollution in Eastern Europe, occurs when those who make decisions about using these resources ignore or underestimate the costs of environmental damage to society. The reasons for this divergence in interests fall into two main categories.

Market failure

Markets frequently do not accurately reflect the social value of the environment, for several reasons:

- No market exists because it is difficult to demarcate or enforce the rights to own or use the environment—as with air quality. Thus, prices do not reflect the adverse effects of pollutants, and the result is too much air pollution.
- Some uses for a resource are marketed but others are not—as with tropical rainforests, where timber is marketed but watershed protection is not. The nonmarketed benefits are frequently ignored, while other uses of the resource are overexploited.
- Open access to resources allows them to be exploited by all—as with rainforests in the Amazon

and sardines off the coast of Costa Rica. In these instances, environmental effects are not recognized by users (and so become externalities). The results are deforestation and overfishing.

• Individuals and societies lack information about environmental impacts or about low-cost ways to avoid damage—as with the link between CFCs and ozone depletion, which is only now fully appreciated. Private firms may not provide better information because they find it difficult to capture the benefits.

Policy failure

Sometimes government actions encourage inefficiencies that in turn cause environmental damage. Examples include subsidies for agricultural and energy inputs and for logging and cattle ranching, nonaccountability of public sector polluters, provision of services such as electricity, water, and sanitation at subsidized prices, and ineffective management of public lands and forests.

These failures of government policy may aggravate the environmental damage caused by market failures, as happened in the Brazilian Amazon. Land clearance for ranching since 1970 in Mato Grosso and Para has reflected a combination of open access and tax incentives for ranching.

Contributing factors

The damage due to these primary causes is frequently exacerbated by poverty and by economic instability. Poor people may care more about extracting what they can today from environmental resources than about conserving them for tomorrow: the result is often the very opposite of sustainability, with excessive exploitation of forests and soils. Economic (or political) uncertainty also encourages short-term behavior.

Environmental damage may also be worsened by population growth and migration. The immediate causes of deforestation in the Philippine uplands are open access to public forests and low concession fees. But rapid population growth hastens deforestation by adding to the demands for agricultural land and for wood for fuel and building materials.

Even if environmental policies address all the main causes of damage, some degradation will still occur. It is too costly for societies to eliminate air pollution completely or to preserve all forests. The right mix of uses for the environment balances the costs and benefits of alternative uses—including

conservation—at the margin. When this balance is not struck, either environmental damage or conservation can be excessive.

Adopting good development policies

Poverty, uncertainty, and ignorance are the allies of environmental degradation. Addressing them is therefore the first requirement of effective environmental policies. *World Development Report 1991* identified four elements of a market-friendly approach to development: an improved climate for enterprise; integration into the global economy; investments in people; and maintenance of macroeconomic stability. These policies will also make environmental protection easier. With prudent macroeconomic policies that provide price stability and external balance, market signals are communicated more clearly, uncertainty is reduced, and it is easier to attract foreign investment. The environmental policies described below will then be more effective. Expanding the access of poor people to health and family planning will help reduce population growth. And better-educated people can more readily adopt environmentally sound but complicated techniques, such as integrated pest management.

Broadly, there are two sets of development policies that help protect the environment. One set, illustrated by the blue area in Figure 3.1, includes measures that require investment, such as improving the education of women and the supply of water. But not only do these measures yield economic dividends (represented by the blue curve in the figure); they are even more beneficial when environmental benefits are considered.

Other development policies that are good for the environment—sometimes termed "win-win" policies—are illustrated by the light red area in the figure. These improve economic efficiency and reduce environmental damage at no net financial cost to governments. Examples include ending subsidies for resource use by the private and public sectors and clarifying property rights, all discussed below. Finally, the green area in the figure shows policies that supplement those development policies. These additional measures, discussed in the next section, are targeted specifically at resolving environmental problems. As the figure shows, they are justified only because their environmental benefits outweigh their costs.

Sometimes, though, the requirements of sound economic policy may appear to jeopardize environmental goals. An example is liberalized policies

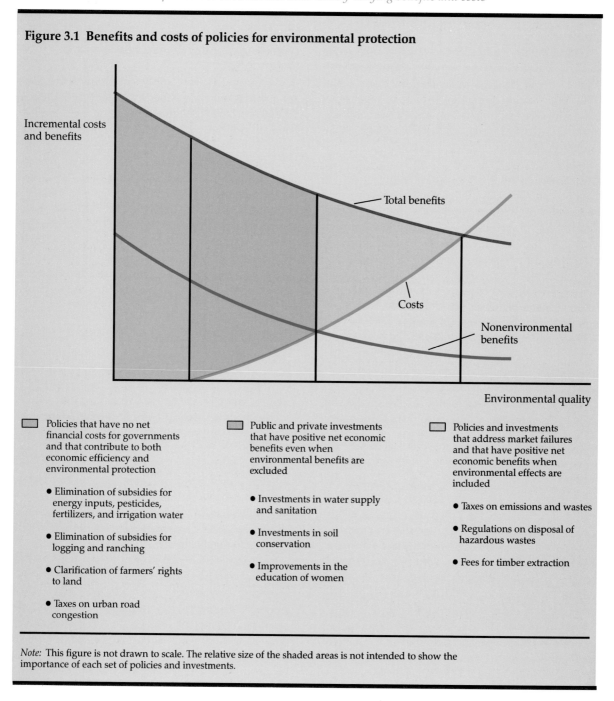

Figure 3.1 Benefits and costs of policies for environmental protection

Incremental costs and benefits

Total benefits

Costs

Nonenvironmental benefits

Environmental quality

Policies that have no net financial costs for governments and that contribute to both economic efficiency and environmental protection

- Elimination of subsidies for energy inputs, pesticides, fertilizers, and irrigation water

- Elimination of subsidies for logging and ranching

- Clarification of farmers' rights to land

- Taxes on urban road congestion

Public and private investments that have positive net economic benefits even when environmental benefits are excluded

- Investments in water supply and sanitation

- Investments in soil conservation

- Improvements in the education of women

Policies and investments that address market failures and that have positive net economic benefits when environmental effects are included

- Taxes on emissions and wastes

- Regulations on disposal of hazardous wastes

- Fees for timber extraction

Note: This figure is not drawn to scale. The relative size of the shaded areas is not intended to show the importance of each set of policies and investments.

for trade and investment, which often bring environmental improvement through greater economic efficiency but can sometimes lead to environmentally harmful changes in the structure of economic activity. In the latter case, it is usually more appropriate to introduce better policies for environmental protection than to sacrifice economic gains by restricting trade.

Open trade and investment policies

Trade policy crystallizes the scope for potential clashes between economic and environmental goals. By promoting specialization and competition and encouraging technological progress, open trade and investment policies raise productivity and improve efficiency—including efficient use of

66

Box 3.1 Trade policy and the environment: a summary of the issues

The links between trade and the environment raise three main questions.

• *What are the environmental effects of trade liberalization?* The fear that these effects are generally negative has led to calls for amending trade policies to take explicit account of environmental goals. Recent controversies have concerned the negative effects of the proposed North American Free Trade Agreement on air and water quality in Mexico and the southwestern United States, of liberalized cassava exports to the EC on soil erosion in Thailand, and of exchange rate depreciation on deforestation in Ghana. But using trade restrictions to address environmental problems is inefficient and usually ineffective. Liberalized trade fosters greater efficiency and higher productivity and may actually reduce pollution by encouraging the growth of less-polluting industries and the adoption and diffusion of cleaner technologies.

In these and other examples, the primary cause of environmental problems is not liberalized trade but the failure of markets and governments to price the environment appropriately. Trade policies are a blunt and uncertain tool for environmental management because they influence the use of environmental resources only indirectly. Indeed, modifying trade policies to deal with environmental problems may worsen degradation. Thus, restricting the export of logs, as in Indonesia, raises returns to the domestic wood-processing industry and may contribute to inefficient and high-cost production that could worsen deforestation. Usually, more direct instruments than trade policies are available for combating deforestation, soil erosion, or industrial pollution. Trade liberalization should be accompanied by better use of these targeted policies.

• *Should trade policies be used to influence environmental standards in other countries?* It has been proposed, for example, that the General Agreement on Tariffs and Trade (GATT) be amended to allow countries to neutralize international differences in pollution control expenditures and environmental standards by imposing countervailing duties. The arguments noted above apply here as well and are strengthened by another consideration: some variation in environmental standards across regions and countries is justified by differences in priorities and in capacities to assimilate pollutants or cope with resource degradation. When countries (typically, the bigger and richer ones) use trade policy to impose their environmental standards, the effect is to protect domestic producers from foreign competition. Applying the same standards to domestic production and imports may be justified when, as with cars or pesticides, consumption leads to environmental damage. But even there, environmental concerns do not warrant uniformity across countries.

Evidence shows that developing countries do not compete for foreign investment in "dirty" industries by lowering their environmental standards (see Dean, background paper, and GATT 1992). The main reason is that environmental costs are a small share of output value—about 0.5 percent, on average, for all U.S. industries in 1988 and only 3 percent for the most-polluting industry (for details see Low forthcoming). So foreign investment flows do not shift dramatically toward locations with lax environmental standards (so-called pollution havens). Rather, anecdotal data from Chile and elsewhere suggest the opposite: because it is cheaper for multinational corporations to use the same technologies as they do in industrial countries, these firms can be potent sources of environmental improvement.

• *Should trade policies be used to enforce or implement international environmental agreements?* An example of their use as an enforcement mechanism would be threats of trade sanctions against countries that do not honor prior commitments under agreements on biodiversity protection or greenhouse gas emissions. But if those countries are willing signatories to the agreement, the threat of trade sanctions will rarely need to be used.

Trade measures to implement environmental agreements include the Montreal Protocol, which phases out ozone-depleting chemicals; the Basel Convention (which entered into force in May 1992) for controlling the transboundary movement and the disposal of hazardous wastes; and the Convention on International Trade in Endangered Species (CITES), which supports the embargo on ivory trade. The use of trade instruments could be justified in some of these cases. For instance, restricting trade in hazardous and toxic wastes, as under the Basel Convention, is appropriate if the capacities of many countries to monitor and dispose of these wastes are in doubt. But in most countries the scale of such trade is small in comparison with the volume of hazardous wastes being generated domestically. Therefore, the concern should be to minimize the production of these wastes and to devise ways of ensuring their safe disposal. A total ban on all trade in hazardous and toxic wastes would be counterproductive because it would prevent the development of collective arrangements for treatment and disposal even where individual countries, as in Western Europe, can specialize in safe and low-cost disposal.

The ban on trade in ivory to protect the African elephant also involves difficult tradeoffs. Available evidence shows that ivory prices have fallen and poaching has declined since the ban became effective. But countries such as Botswana, South Africa, and Zimbabwe have argued that the ivory ban, by raising prices in the long run, will simply make poaching more lucrative. (Work by the London Environmental Economics Center supports this assertion.) These countries also claim that the ban discriminates against their efforts to manage their elephant herds sustainably by using revenue from hunting and tourism to enrich local people and finance law enforcement.

environmental resources. The pattern of adoption of thermomechanical pulping processes in the paper and pulp industry illustrates this point (see Box 6.3). That technology was developed in the 1970s and was used initially in the United States and Western Europe in response to environmental regulation. Thermomechanical pulping was not only less polluting than the earlier chemical-based technology but also cut average manufacturing costs in half. Its initial adoption and later diffusion have been significantly quicker in developing countries with fewer trade restrictions. As late as 1989, not a single pulp producer in Eastern Europe had adopted this technology.

But because greater openness also makes export production more profitable, it can exacerbate environmental pressures. Where there is open access, liberalizing trade may encourage more intensive exploitation. For instance, in Malaysia liberalizing trade in logs and timber products would worsen deforestation if stumpage fees are too low and concession agreements too short to encourage sustainable logging. Similarly, by making it more profitable to clear land to grow cocoa in Ghana or cotton in Nigeria, exchange rate depreciations have intensified pressures for deforestation where ownership of forests is not well defined. But these examples usually argue not for trade restrictions but rather for other measures to address the environmental problems that may be exacerbated (see Box 3.1). In some cases, as with hazardous wastes, trade restrictions are appropriate because more targeted measures are infeasible.

Elimination of subsidies for resource use

As Figure 3.2 shows, subsidies that cause environmental damage by encouraging resource use are common. Both economic and environmental benefits will be achieved by removing subsidies that encourage the use of coal, electricity, pesticides, and irrigation water and promote expansion of grazing and timber extraction on public lands. These reforms will require considerable political will because the subsidies typically benefit the politically influential or are intended to serve such goals as food self-sufficiency and rapid industrialization.

Recognizing the environmental cost of such subsidies will provide a powerful additional reason for removing them. Frequently, the same goals can be met in cheaper ways. It was estimated that in Poland removing energy subsidies would by itself reduce emissions of particulates and sulfur oxides

by more than 30 percent between 1989 and 1995. In Indonesia pesticide subsidies were more than 80 percent of the retail price in 1985 but had been eliminated entirely by late 1988. This step reduced excessive pesticide use (in favor of a successful integrated pest management program) and generated budgetary savings of more than $120 million annually. In Brazil discontinuing the fiscal and credit incentives extended to ranching has saved about $300 million annually while easing (although not eliminating) pressures for deforestation.

Subsidies to public industrial firms in many countries—through preferential access to the public treasury, as in Eastern Europe, or through protection from domestic and foreign competition—must be eliminated. The inefficiencies that these subsidies encourage have worsened pollution in countries where public ownership has been concentrated in capital-intensive and highly polluting industries.

Public enterprises must be given greater autonomy and be exposed to competition. If managers of public utilities are made accountable for their performance, they are more likely to set charges at levels that improve cost recovery and to compare the costs and benefits of investments systematically. Private investment should also be encouraged, particularly where private benefits are high—in irrigation and water supply, in particular—but also for collection of solid wastes and treatment of industrial wastewater. In many Latin American cities, including Caracas, Santiago, and São Paulo, private solid waste collection services are already successful.

Clarification and enforcement of property rights

Clarifying rights of ownership and use would improve environmental outcomes, especially where those who invest in environmental protection would also benefit the most. In Thailand the recent assignment of ownership titles and tenurial rights to land in recent years has made it more profitable for farmers to invest in soil conservation and land improvement, thus reducing soil erosion. Strengthening individual and communal rights would also help in many cases where governments have responded to concerns about overuse of natural resources by taking over responsibility for resource management. In the 1950s Nepal instituted state ownership of forests in place of community-based arrangements that had regulated use effectively. But as deforestation there and

Figure 3.2 Ratio of price to production cost, selected energy and agricultural inputs

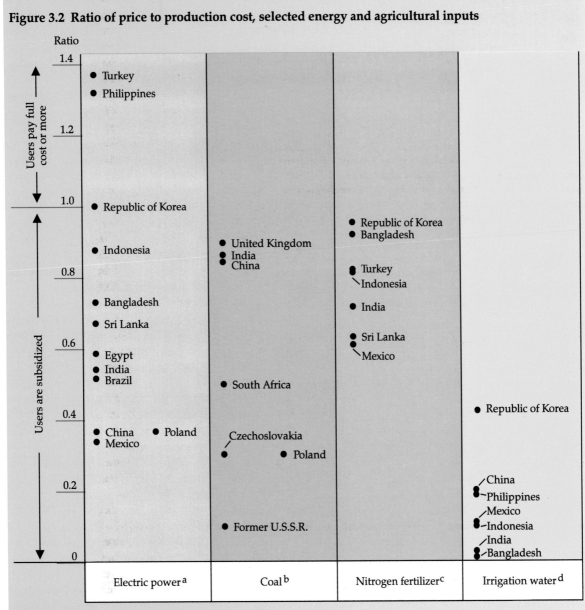

a. Average electricity tariff as a proportion of the incremental cost of system expansion (1987; Egypt, 1991).
b. Domestic price as a proportion of border price or long-run marginal cost (various years, 1987-91, except South Africa, 1982).
c. Farmgate price of urea as a proportion of the average production cost of urea (average of various years, 1980-88).
d. Direct water charge as a proportion of operating and maintenance costs plus midrange estimate of annualized capital cost (various years, 1985-88).
Sources: World Bank data; FAO various years; Shah and Larsen, background paper (b).

overgrazing on public lands in many other parts of the world show, public ownership and management have often led to overexploitation.

Even for natural resources other than land—minerals, trees, and fish—if private property rights are clearly defined, the self-interested decisions of private owners will produce more desirable environmental outcomes than will open access. Private loggers on plantation forests, for instance, will weigh the returns from cutting trees today (includ-

Box 3.2 Natural resources, open access, and property rights

When property rights to natural resources are non-existent or unenforced—when there is open access—no individual bears the full cost of environmental degradation, and there is no mechanism for regulating the use of the resources. The result is overexploitation—what Garrett Hardin termed the "tragedy of the commons." Overfishing, overgrazing, excessive extraction of groundwater, and overuse of the "global commons" are examples.

Two policy options are to create private property rights or to assert state control over the resource. Private property conveys rights, which are transferable and are enforced by the state, to exclude others from exploiting the resource. When a resource is state property, as with public forests, governments make decisions on its use. Political pressures then often lead to overexploitation and misuse. A third option is for a resource to be held and exploited by a group, in the form of common or communal property. The group excludes outsiders from using the resource and regulates use by its members. Examples of common-property management of natural resources abound. Some have argued that even the medieval English commons (which Hardin used to make his case) was actually subject to communal management, with access restricted to certain members of the village and limits on the number of animals that could be grazed. In fact, this commons system lasted for hundreds of years—hardly a tragedy! Similar communal management systems are used for forests in Japan, pastures in the Swiss Alps,

the Himalayas, and the Andes, fisheries in Turkey, and irrigation water in southern India. In each case users have developed mechanisms for restricting access by outsiders, allocating use rights among those in the group, and monitoring and enforcing these allocations.

Private property and common property can and do coexist. In Japan forests, meadows, and irrigation works were held as communal property while agricultural land was held privately. In the Swiss Alps private property governs agriculture, but forests and summer meadows are under common-property management. Property regimes can also change between seasons or over time. Communal land rights in Ghana, Kenya, and Rwanda have generally moved toward greater individualization in response to population pressure, the growth of commercial agriculture, and technological change.

Hostile government policies can lead to the deterioration of common-property regimes. For instance, long-standing cooperative fishing agreements in southern Bahia, Brazil, were undermined when subsidies from the government fisheries agency encouraged outsiders and some fishermen within the group to use nylon nets instead of traditional equipment. In addition, because Brazilian law does not recognize exclusive rights to coastal fishing areas, any registered Brazilian fishing vessel could legally enter the local fishing grounds, making it impossible for the cooperatives to exclude outsiders.

ing the accrued interest from investing these revenues) against future revenues, looking at price trends and the expected growth of timber yields. Extending the length and increasing the security of concessions in Southeast Asian forests encourages more sustainable logging practices.

But as the controversies about excessive logging even in privately owned forests in the United States and elsewhere illustrate, such measures are no panacea. Clear property rights may induce private users to adopt the "correct" pattern of timber extraction, taking into consideration the current and future benefits from logging, but give no incentive to take into account the costs of deforestation to those living outside the forests—for example, increased soil erosion and lost biodiversity. In such cases additional environmental controls are often needed.

Common-property systems—whereby communities establish rules for controlling access and

use—are capable of regulating the use of rangelands, forests, irrigation systems, and fisheries. Because such community-based arrangements are difficult to restore once they break down, governments should not undermine them by enacting laws that make encroachment by outsiders easier, as happened with the coastal fisheries in northeastern Brazil (Box 3.2).

Using targeted environmental policies

Removing policy distortions will frequently enhance both environmental quality and economic growth (even as conventionally measured). Some environmental resources, however, will remain susceptible to overexploitation. Because markets fail to reflect environmental costs accurately in a variety of cases, governments must consider going beyond removing policy distortions. Well-chosen public policies and investments that respond to

Box 3.3 Costing environmental damage

An essential step in determining what should be done about environmental damage is to value it and compare it with the costs of preventing the damage. Measurement is essential, since tradeoffs are inescapable. There are many practical problems in deriving credible estimates of economic value. But four broad approaches can be used in setting priorities for policy.

Market prices

Market prices are used in valuation when environmental damage leads to losses in productivity or to adverse health effects. Common applications include valuation of damages due to soil erosion, deforestation, and air and water pollution. In applying this approach, the physical or ecological relationship between environmental damage and its impacts on output or health—the dose-response function—is estimated and combined with prices to derive monetary values. For environmentally related health risks, income forgone because of illness or premature death is sometimes used to measure welfare losses. Such estimates are partial and controversial because they rely solely on income losses and use causal links that are difficult to quantify or to extrapolate from studies in high-income countries.

Costs of replacement

People and firms can respond to environmental degradation by making expenditures to avert damage or compensate for possible consequences. Although some effects of degradation are not accounted for, these expenditures can provide an estimate of environmental damage. For example, when water supplies are polluted, factories can invest in a private tubewell, and households can buy water from vendors. Losses of soil fertility caused by erosion can be approximated by the cost of using purchased fertilizers to replace nutrients.

Surrogate markets

Environmental degradation can sometimes be valued through its effect on other markets—especially on property values and wages. For example, clean air is implicitly traded in property markets, since buyers will consider environmental attributes as characteristics of property. Similarly, environmental risks associated with different jobs are traded in labor markets, and wage levels for higher-risk jobs will include larger risk premiums. This technique is difficult to apply when property owners or workers are unaware of environmental problems or are constrained in responding to them.

Surveys

Direct questioning can determine what value people place on environmental change. This approach is particularly relevant where markets are nonexistent or where people value an environmental resource that they do not use. Such surveys have become more sophisticated to minimize the biases that may enter into responses to hypothetical questions. They are increasingly employed to determine the amenity value of species or landmarks. In developing countries their use is rare but increasing; examples include surveys to determine willingness to pay for better access to clean water in Brazil and for improved sanitation in Ghana, and to assess tourists' valuation of elephants in Kenya.

---

market failures can often raise welfare. This section looks at how these policies should be designed.

The role of valuation

Environmental damage imposes costs on societies that are often not reflected by markets. Comparing these benefits of environmental protection with the costs of remedial action helps policymakers make better-informed decisions. In making choices about environmental priorities, standards, and policies, governments implicitly place values on different kinds of damage. It is better that these choices be guided by comparisons of the costs and benefits of environmental improvements. As analytical tools, data, and scientific knowledge im-

prove, environmental valuation is being extended into new areas of policymaking. Its use, however, remains controversial because environmental benefits are often difficult to measure (Box 3.3). Especially when damage is irreversible or would occur far into the future, assessing tradeoffs may appear meaningless. But even here, some valuation—even if imperfect, such as assessments of risks and thresholds—is better than none.

CHOOSING PRIORITIES. Deciding which environmental problems to address inevitably requires a comparison of the costs of damage with the costs of preventing it. Such techniques are being used to a greater extent in policy analysis, as illustrated by a recent study of air pollution in the southeastern Polish town of Tarnobrzeg. The economic benefits

Figure 3.3 Total estimated benefits and costs of reducing exposure to air pollutants in Tarnobrzeg, Poland

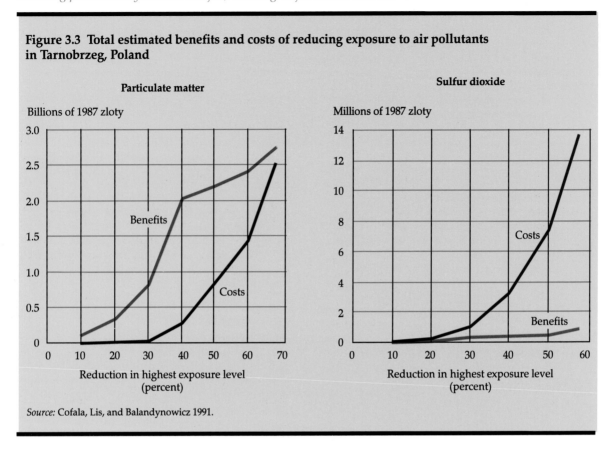

Particulate matter

Billions of 1987 zloty

Sulfur dioxide

Millions of 1987 zloty

Source: Cofala, Lis, and Balandynowicz 1991.

to the local population of reducing air pollution—decreased mortality and morbidity and less material damage and soiling—were compared with the costs of achieving reduced exposure to suspended particulate matter and to sulfur dioxide. The results were surprising: whereas the benefits of reducing sulfur dioxide were in all cases lower than the costs, the benefits of reducing particulates by up to 70 percent exceeded the costs, with net benefits greatest for a reduction of about 40 percent (Figure 3.3). Thus, from a local perspective, measures that would reduce particulates are of higher priority in this region of Poland than are those that would control sulfur dioxide.

SETTING STANDARDS. Ideally, countries should set environmental goals by comparing the benefits from environmental improvements with the costs of achieving them. The U.S. Environmental Protection Agency used this approach in setting standards for the use of lead in gasoline. The benefits of reducing lead content from 1.1 to 0.1 grams per gallon were estimated by valuing the health im-

provements in children and adults, as well as the savings from reduced misfueling, lower maintenance, and greater fuel economy. These benefits were compared with the costs to refineries of using more expensive alternatives to lead in raising octane levels. The results showed that the benefits from lowering lead concentrations were substantially greater than the costs, and the more stringent standards were adopted in 1985.

But despite the appeal of these methods, they are not always applicable because some benefits are difficult to value. Targets will therefore usually be set in response to tangible signs of damage. In these cases, it is still worth choosing cost-effective policies—those that meet specific environmental goals at lowest cost. In practice, some environmental policies impose large costs for small benefits while other measures that have more substantial payoffs are ignored. In the United States, for example, a cost-effectiveness analysis of various health and safety regulations that took account of implementation costs, mortality risks, and estimates of the number of deaths avoided found that the cost per premature death averted by the regulations varied from about $100,000 to more than $100 million.

Regulation and economic incentives

In choosing policies, regulators have to make three main related decisions, as displayed in Table 3.1. Is regulation likely to be more effective than relying on economic incentives? Should policies address the quantity or the price of pollution or resource use, or should they specify technologies? And should policies target the damaging activities directly or indirectly?

Since policies differ substantially in cost and effectiveness, and since developing countries can ill afford to waste resources, the measures they choose should be guided principally by the cost of effective implementation. The cost-effective policy mix depends, in general, on the characteristics of the environmental problem at hand as well as the capabilities of regulatory institutions. In most circumstances, a combination of policies—regulatory and market-based—is most cost-effective. Box 3.4 illustrates this for the control of air pollution from transport in Mexico City.

The behavior of polluters and resource users can be influenced in two main ways: by stipulating standards and regulations (command-and-control

policies) or by pricing additional pollution or additional resource use (incentive-based or market-based policies). Although the regulatory approach has been dominant in most countries, interest in incentive-based measures has revived. Notable examples of such measures include effluent charges on water pollution in the Netherlands and Germany; emissions charges on sulfur dioxide in Japan; charges on fuels, automobiles, pesticides, and fertilizers and deposit-refund systems for beverage containers and car batteries in Northern Europe; and emissions trading for air pollutants in the United States.

WHERE REGULATION IS APPROPRIATE. Regulatory policies, which are used extensively in both industrial and developing countries, are best suited to situations that involve a few public enterprises and noncompetitive private firms. This is particularly true when the technologies for controlling pollution or resource use are relatively uniform and can easily be specified by regulators. Cubatão, Brazil, provides a good illustration (see Box 6.4). To address serious pollution from particulates and sulfur dioxide, CETESB (the state regulatory agency) forced the larger polluters—public sector and multinational firms—to install precipitators and switch to low-sulfur oil. The result has been a dramatic improvement in air quality. This experience also

Table 3.1 Policies for changing behavior

Type of policy	Variable affected		
	Price	Quantity	Technology
Incentive			
Direct	Effluent charges (Netherlands, China) Stumpage fees (Canada, United States) Deposit-refund schemes (beverage containers, northern Europe)	Tradable emissions permits (emissions trading program, United States) Tradable fishing permits (New Zealand)	Technology taxes based on presumed emissions (water pollution control, Germany, France)
Indirect	Fuel taxes (Sweden, Netherlands) Performance bonds (hazardous wastes, Thailand)	Tradable input or production permits (lead trading program, United States)	Subsidies for R&D and fuel efficiency (catalytic converters, United States, Japan, Western Europe)
Regulation			
Direct	—	Emissions standards (United States, China) Logging quotas and bans (Thailand)	Mandated technical standards (catalytic converters, United States, Japan, Western Europe)
Indirect	—	Land zoning (Rondônia, Brazil) Bans and quotas on products and inputs (high-sulfur fuel, São Paulo, Brazil)	Efficiency standards for inputs or processes (fuel efficiency standards, United States)

Source: Eskeland and Jimenez 1991.

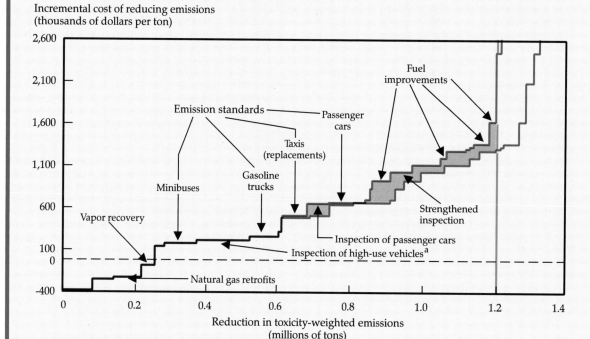
illustrates how important it is for regulators to apply environmental standards impartially to all enterprises, public and private.

Another area in which regulation may be appropriate is land use. Governments may use zoning regulations to attempt to create a land-use pattern that differs from the one that market allocations would produce. The aim of zoning laws in rural areas is typically to slow conversion of agricultural

land or to preserve ecologically sensitive habitats. Urban zoning seeks to separate land uses so as to reduce adverse effects from, for example, industrial air pollution.

ECONOMIC INCENTIVES. If effectively implemented, policies that use economic incentives such as charges will frequently be less costly in meeting environmental goals than regulatory al-

Because continuous monitoring of individual emissions from transport is obviously impossible, there is no emissions tax that can be applied easily and efficiently. Therefore indirect policies, which target proxies for emissions, have to be used. These measures reduce emissions by decreasing the overall demand for travel, by shifting travel demand toward less-polluting or less fuel-intensive modes of transport, or by reducing emissions per kilometer driven. The United States has focused almost exclusively on the third option, primarily by imposing emissions standards on all new vehicles and requiring vehicle inspections.

A combination of policies that targets all three options has advantages, however, as a recent study on Mexico City by Mexican regulatory authorities and the World Bank illustrates. Box figure 3.4 shows the incremental costs of reducing emissions from transport sources in Mexico City. The upper curve shows the costs of reducing total emissions by various amounts when only measures to reduce emissions per kilometer driven are used. The lower curve shows how the incremental control costs fall when the same measures are combined with a gasoline tax, which reduces demand and stimulates a shift toward less fuel-intensive modes of transport.

By using measures designed to decrease emissions per kilometer, Mexico City could reduce current emissions from transport by 1.2 million tons (more than 50 percent) at a cost of $560 million. Adding a gasoline tax would achieve the same reduction with a cost saving of about 20 percent (the light red area in the figure). The tax would also generate about $300 million in public revenue within the metropolitan area alone, which could be used to reduce other, more distortionary taxes.

Mexico City has already begun to implement several of the measures shown in the figure, including gas retrofits for high-use vehicles, emissions standards and inspection programs for all vehicles, and replacement of older taxis by newer catalyst-equipped models. In addition, unleaded gasoline has been introduced, and prices of leaded and unleaded gasoline have been increased by about 50 percent.

ternatives. With market-based policies, all polluters or resource users are faced with the same price and must choose their degree of control. For instance, a gasoline tax such as that proposed in Mexico City (Box 3.4) would encourage all drivers to limit vehicle use to the point at which the value of benefits forgone is the same for each driver. By contrast, the current regulations in Athens and Mexico City, which restrict driving in central urban districts according to license plates, encourage evasion and are costly because they force all drivers to give up the same proportion of trips, irrespective of the widely differing benefits they derive. With policies that rely on economic incentives, each user decides either to use fewer resources or to pay for using more. Regulations, by contrast, leave these decisions to regulators, who are rarely well informed about the relative costs and benefits faced by users.

Incentive-based policies that price environmental damage affect all polluters, in contrast to regulations, which affect only those who fail to comply. This means that incentive-based policies give the right long-term signals to resource users. The polluter or resource user has an incentive to use whichever technologies most cost-effectively reduce environmental damage. Regulations that mandate standards give polluters no reason to go further than the standard demands. Indeed, regulations that specify control technologies—that is, technology-forcing policies, which are common in the United States and Western Europe—lock in existing standards and give businesses less incentive to switch to cleaner production methods or more effective controls.

The potential savings from using economic incentives are illustrated in Table 3.2, which summarizes evidence from simulation studies of air pollution control in the United States and the United Kingdom. The studies contrast regulatory policies (such as those currently in place) with least-cost policies for the same level of pollution control. Although incentive-based measures would not, in practice, exactly mimic the least-cost outcomes, the figures show how expensive regulatory policies can be.

Policies that use economic incentives will be effective only to the extent that polluters and resource users respond to them. Responsiveness depends on three factors: ownership, competition, and differences among users. As the experiences of Poland and China with pollution charges illustrate, state-owned enterprises are particularly insensitive to policies that use economic incentives because they generally do not care much about costs. Lack of domestic and foreign competition dampens the pressures even on private businesses to minimize costs. Thus, countries such as India, Mexico, and Thailand that have state-owned petroleum refineries would gain little by using charges or tradable permits to phase out leaded gasoline. By contrast, a scheme that allowed highly competitive private refineries in the United

Table 3.2 Simulation studies of alternative policies for controlling air pollution

Pollutant	Geographic area	Ratio of costs of regulatory policies to those of least-cost policy (percent)	Study and year
Sulfates	Los Angeles, Calif.	110	Hahn and Noll (1982)
Nitrogen dioxide	Baltimore, Md.	600	Krupnick (1983)
Particulate matter	Baltimore, Md.	420	McGartland (1984)
Sulfur dioxide	Lower Delaware Valley,	180⎱	
Particulate matter	United States	2,200⎰	Spofford (1984)
Hydrocarbons	All U.S. Dupont plants	420	Maloney and Yandle (1984)
Sulfur dioxide	Five regions of the United States	190	Gollop and Roberts (1985)
Sulfur dioxide	United Kingdom	140–250	Welsch (1988)

Source: Adapted from Tietenberg 1988.

States to trade rights to use lead is estimated to have saved about $250 million in phasing out leaded gasoline in the mid-1980s.

These policies also work best when users respond to changes in prices in differing ways, as is characteristic of private firms and households. The experience with charges in controlling water pollution in the Netherlands illustrates their effectiveness as a way of influencing private firms. Charges were introduced in 1970 for all organic pollutants from industrial sources and were raised about 83 percent in real terms over the following decade. As a result, and despite a 27 percent increase in industrial output between 1970 and 1983, organic pollution fell almost 70 percent. Similarly, Malaysia uses variable license fees to charge palm oil processors for their emissions into streams and rivers. These fees were effective in reducing the processors' discharges of biological oxygen demand (BOD) by almost 90 percent between 1982 and 1987. The environmental fund for treating hazardous wastes from private firms that is being considered in Thailand will encourage businesses to minimize waste generation by charging firms and providing them rebates if less waste is generated than presumed (see Box 6.5). These advantages extend to commercial agriculture, where charges on pesticides and fertilizers, as in Austria and Sweden, may help address overuse more cost-effectively than regulation of their use.

If individuals and businesses are unable to change their behavior much—because, for example, resource use is already tightly controlled—savings from using economic incentives will be small. As Table 3.2 shows, in Los Angeles regulatory policies are not much more costly than the least-cost option because most industrial polluters already face stringent standards. By contrast, the gains from incentive-based policies would be much larger in most developing country cities, where, as

in Santiago, industry is highly differentiated and largely uncontrolled.

QUANTITY OR PRICE? Environmental degradation can be controlled either by altering the prices of environmental resources—using charges or taxes, for example—or by restricting use, as with logging permits, emissions standards, and land zoning. Policies that specify quantities of pollution or resource use fix the level of environmental damage, whereas those that alter prices fix the cost of controlling environmental damage. Quantity-based policies often take the form of regulation. But even if the overall quantity of pollution or resource use is fixed, the market can still be allowed to allocate the quantity through the use of tradable permits. Such schemes ensure that resources are used by those who value them the most.

Quantity-based policies are also appropriate when it is extremely important that certain thresholds not be exceeded, as with emissions of radioactive and toxic wastes. In these cases the costs of greater environmental damage are rightly judged to be of graver concern than the possibility that pollution control might be more expensive than expected. By contrast, the social costs of other types of environmental damage—from, say, particulates or mineral extraction—do not rise dramatically if standards are exceeded by small margins. In these cases it is more important to avoid spending too much on controlling degradation than to risk a bit more environmental damage.

So, quantity-based policies are most appropriate for pollution problems that involve threshold health impacts (for example, hazardous wastes and heavy metals) and for natural resources such as unique habitats. Similarly, enforceable zoning laws may be more reliable than differential property taxes in preserving unique habitats such as wetlands, sensitive shorelines, and coral reefs.

Costa Rica is one of many Latin American countries to use a shoreland restriction program to control commercial development.

Among incentive-based policies, the choice between charges and tradable permits depends partly on the capabilities of regulators. Although tradable permits have been used for control of air and water pollution in the United States and for fisheries in New Zealand and have been suggested for restricting emissions of greenhouse gases, they tend to be more administratively demanding than charges because the latter can typically be implemented through the existing fiscal system.

DISTRIBUTIONAL ISSUES. One obstacle to using market-based environmental policies is that businesses and individuals may be unable to invest in new technologies or pay for cleaner products. Examples include declining heavy industries in Eastern Europe and poor people who use kerosene as their principal cooking fuel. Sometimes governments have subsidized the changes, by directly financing pollution control equipment or by using environmental protection funds to finance investments. Subsidizing environmental cleanup or resource use has an obvious problem: it sends the wrong signals to resource users and conflicts with the common interpretation of the polluter-pays principle (Box 3.5). Subsidies may thus encourage a long-term increase in environmental damage, and their use should be well targeted, explicitly time-bound, and carefully monitored—as, for instance, when they are provided only for the initial installation of pollution control equipment.

Unlike regulations, incentive-based policies such as taxes raise revenues. These measures may be advantageous for governments when they replace more distortionary sources of revenue common in developing countries, such as trade tariffs and corporate taxes. Revenue generation and environmental protection are then complementary. In practice, although the potential yield from incentive-based policies is considerable—about the same as control costs for industrial pollution—revenues today are minuscule even in OECD countries.

But the corollary of those revenues is the impo-

Box 3.5 The polluter-pays principle: what it can and cannot do

The polluter-pays principle (PPP), adopted by the OECD in 1972, states that "the polluter should bear the cost of measures to reduce pollution decided upon by public authorities to ensure that the environment is in an acceptable state." The main objective is to harmonize policies among OECD members so that differential environmental regulations do not distort comparative advantage and trade flows. The principle has been widely accepted as a guide for environmental policymaking by governments and aid agencies. The polluter-pays principle is a useful starting point, but it provides little help in judging the cost-effectiveness of alternative policies. One problem is that the principle can be interpreted in two different ways: as requiring polluters to pay only the costs of pollution control and cleanup (standard PPP) or, in addition, to compensate citizens for the damages they suffer from pollution (extended PPP)—an interpretation which gives citizens an entitlement to a clean environment. Neither reading necessarily implies the use of economic incentives—charges or auctioned permits—although these are cost-effective in many instances.

Nor is the principle much help in choosing cost-effective policies when polluters or resource users are difficult to identify and monitor. For example, it is less costly and more effective to use blunter policies such as input or output taxes rather than emission charges to reduce pollution from automobiles and small-scale firms. A similar problem in identifying polluters arises in cleaning up past pollution. The United States tried to apply the polluter-pays principle through the Superfund program. Superfund aims to restore hazardous waste sites with taxes on crude oil and petrochemical feedstocks and is to be replenished by recovering cleanup costs from past polluters. This attempt has been a failure; much has been spent on litigation, little on cleanup.

Finally, where environmental effects spill over national borders and jurisdictions, it may be necessary to pay polluting or resource-using countries to cooperate in implementing cost-effective solutions. (Examples are biodiversity losses due to tropical deforestation and sulfur dioxide emissions that contribute to acid rain outside the originating country.) These inducements or side payments convert the polluter-pays principle into the victim-pays principle, but without them there may be little or no incentive to cooperate in improving environmental quality.

Thus, the polluter-pays principle should not be viewed as a guide to designing cost-effective policies. Rather, it is a specific way of distributing the costs of environmental protection among polluters or resource users and those who benefit from the improvements.

sition of costs. Emissions standards provide polluters with the right to pollute up to the specified limits; imposing charges forces them to pay for all their emissions. Similarly, if regulations on air emissions are replaced by tradable permit schemes, the overall cost of controlling air pollution falls, but businesses may still have to pay the government for the permits. That may cost businesses several times as much as meeting regulatory standards. Using economic incentives—which is often more cost-effective than regulating—may benefit society as a whole, but not individual polluters. Moreover, whereas the costs imposed by switching to economic incentives fall on relatively few polluters—who will see clearly that they are worse off and protest noisily—the gains are dispersed across large numbers of people, who may not even realize that they are better off. Not surprisingly, it is often easier politically to use regulation.

Can cost-effective policies be modified to build political support for them? Yes: revenues can be earmarked for environmental funds, or tradable permits can be given mainly to existing users ("grandfathering"). Revenues from pollution charges have been widely used to pay for cleaning up water pollution in Western Europe. Such schemes do not win support only because charges impose lower economic costs than regulation; they also win favor with those who benefit from the way the money is spent.

Grandfathering can be effective in reducing opposition to the introduction of cost-effective policies. It helped build support among businesses for incentive-based policies to eliminate leaded gasoline and reduce sulfur dioxide in the United States and to limit fishing catches in New Zealand. But policies that favor existing producers, such as subsidies from earmarked funds and grandfathering, are not costless. Because the U.S. Clean Air Act imposed more stringent standards on new pollution sources (a type of grandfathering), firms tended to postpone replacement of older, less-efficient technologies.

DIRECT OR INDIRECT POLICIES. In addition to deciding whether or not to use incentives, regulators must also choose between direct policies, which target proxies for environmental damage, such as industrial emissions or timber extraction, and blunter measures, which influence actions only indirectly related to environmental damage, such as the use of leaded gasoline or of land. Ideally, regulators would attempt to change the behavior of

resource users by means of direct policies—for instance, by taxing or regulating emissions. But these measures involve a heavy administrative burden because they target individual polluters or resource users. Blunt policies, such as taxes on polluting inputs and area-based forestry charges, are less demanding because they can be implemented through the tax system. In the United States, which primarily uses direct policies, the share of staff resources within the Environmental Protection Agency devoted to enforcing these measures rose continuously through the 1980s and by 1991 accounted for more than a quarter of the total—even though self-monitoring by large polluters is the main tool for enforcing compliance. So, in many cases it will be appropriate that developing countries use blunt policies, which require less stringent monitoring.

The difficulties involved in monitoring the actions of individual users, and thus the application of direct policies, depend on four factors. First, and most obviously, the more numerous and dispersed the sources of environmental damage, as in transport, the more costly are policies that require continuous monitoring. Second, it is almost impossible to monitor the actions of users who cannot be located, such as fuelwood gatherers in rural Africa and small-scale gold miners in the Amazon. Third, the ease of monitoring depends on the nature of the technological solutions available. After leaded fuel was phased out (as in the United States and Japan) or taxed (as in Western Europe), use of catalytic converters to control automobile emissions became easier because their operation could simply be checked during regular vehicle inspections. Last, for environmental problems that extend beyond national boundaries—such as acid rain in Europe and Asia or biodiversity in tropical forests that is valued in other countries—it may be more cost-effective for countries to coordinate the enforcement of their policy responses than to adopt policies unilaterally.

Therefore, the conditions in which direct policies (whether or not incentive-based) are most justified are best approximated for environmental problems that involve large, highly visible enterprises—notably, particulate and sulfur dioxide emissions from electric utilities, pollution from industrial and mining operations of public enterprises, and timber extraction by logging companies. The cleanup since 1985 in Cubatão (cited above) was accomplished mostly by enforcing emissions and technology standards and succeeded because the main polluters were large pub-

Figure 3.4 Policies for reducing sulfur dioxide emissions from electric power generation

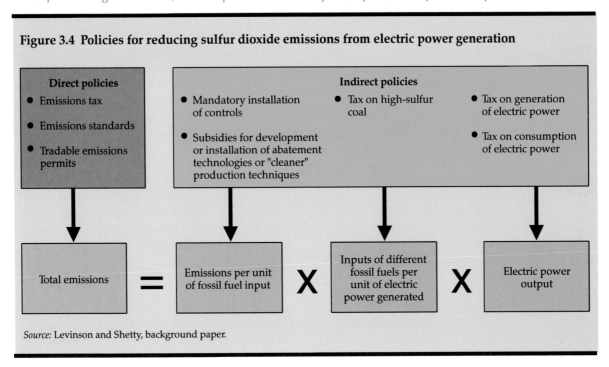

Direct policies
- Emissions tax
- Emissions standards
- Tradable emissions permits

Indirect policies
- Mandatory installation of controls
- Subsidies for development or installation of abatement technologies or "cleaner" production techniques
- Tax on high-sulfur coal
- Tax on generation of electric power
- Tax on consumption of electric power

Total emissions = Emissions per unit of fossil fuel input X Inputs of different fossil fuels per unit of electric power generated X Electric power output

Source: Levinson and Shetty, background paper.

lic or private sector firms. Similarly, the trading of sulfur dioxide emissions that will now be allowed under the U.S. Clean Air Act—a direct policy with economic incentives—applies initially only to electric utilities, which, by virtue of their size, are easier to monitor.

Indirect policies are particularly useful when the monitoring and enforcement capabilities of regulatory authorities are weak. Air pollution from automobiles and household energy use, excessive deforestation by small logging companies, pesticide and fertilizer runoff from agriculture, hazardous wastes from small enterprises, and solid wastes from households are all problems well suited to the use of blunt policies. For instance, selective zoning to create buffers around reserves—which is being discussed in Brazil—is a less direct policy for protecting reserve areas than a comprehensive land-use planning scheme. By limiting zoning to smaller areas, access to reserves can be controlled at significantly lower cost. More ambitious zoning in the Brazilian Amazon is unlikely to succeed because it cannot be enforced adequately, given the pressures for clearing land.

Because blunt policies for environmental protection can be applied at many different levels—the waste generation or resource extraction process, the pattern of resource use or conversion, or the structure of demand—many alternatives are available for addressing specific environmental problems (Figure 3.4). But because these policies often target distant proxies for emissions or extraction, a single indirect policy may not be cost-effective and, indeed, may encourage resource users to behave in ways that worsen environmental damage. Setting area-based license fees for forest concessions rather than differentiating these finely by the volume and species logged may protect a larger forested area but may lead to intensified logging of higher-value species. The costs of using many such measures have to be weighed against the administrative savings they make possible.

Improving public investments

Changing the behavior of individuals and businesses must be accompanied by steps to improve the investment decisions of government agencies and departments.

TAKING ACCOUNT OF ENVIRONMENTAL COSTS. Failure to consider environmental costs and benefits leads governments to undertake projects with adverse impacts or to neglect investments that might bring environmental gains. Understanding the environmental impacts of such public projects will require better analysis of environmental costs and benefits, using the methods described in Box 3.3. The Polonoroeste rural development and highway projects in Brazil, funded in part with a loan from the World Bank, and the Mahaweli irrigation project in Sri Lanka provide vivid illustrations of the environmental damage from ill-conceived and badly implemented development projects. Better project design and appraisal could have predicted at least some of these impacts. In the case of Polonoroeste, it should have been anticipated that building roads and other infrastructure would attract many more migrants into the project area, making already underfunded public agencies even less capable of controlling large-scale deforestation. Similarly, the appraisers of the Mahaweli scheme assumed that it would not accelerate deforestation, even though it occupied large areas of land in four wildlife sanctuaries.

Furthermore, valuing environmental benefits will make some investments more attractive. An example is a forestry project funded by the World Bank in northern Nigeria. For calculating the economic rate of return, the benefits of expanded timber production included reduced soil erosion, higher crop yields, and more fodder and forest products. These benefits (using current and estimated future market prices) increased the project's rate of return almost threefold and made it more worthwhile. Two other public investment decisions that valued environmental impacts are summarized in Box 3.6.

When it is difficult to value environmental benefits, environmental impact assessments (EIAs—also called environmental assessments, or EAs) can be useful. Although they are qualitative, they force recognition of the environmental risks of public projects. The need for these assessments is now well recognized, and their use is mandatory in many countries and by large donors. (Box 3.7 discusses the World Bank's approach.) But EIAs are often conducted too late to influence project design and approval.

Further reforms are required in the processes that governments and donors (including the World Bank) use to identify and appraise investment projects. Such reforms will be helped if the agency that implements a project also bears the cost of any environmental damage that results. They can be accomplished either by establishing geographically based development authorities (river-basin or watershed authorities) or by using mechanisms that make the managing agency responsible for the project's financial consequences. User charges should also be employed more often—in irrigation projects, for example—to reduce excess profits to some beneficiaries and thus the political pressures for public investments that have little economic justification. In Morocco the financial autonomy of the regional agricultural development office (ORMVAD), achieved through full cost recovery, was an important reason for the success of the Doukkala irrigation projects.

Project appraisal should be supplemented with

Box 3.6 Valuing environmental resources: two examples

The examples here are of two cases in which estimating environmental benefits helped improve decision-making.

Improving forest management

Market prices were used to estimate the gains from a forest development project in Nepal. The project was designed to reduce deforestation by planting trees and bushes suitable for fuelwood and fodder and so improve scrubland and timberland. Prices for milk and fertilizer—two of the increased outputs—were available, and the value of the fuelwood was estimated on the basis of the price of a substitute, cattle dung. The increased land-use values alone—even without counting the less easily quantifiable benefits from control of

soil erosion and flooding—gave the project a rate of return of about 9 percent.

Investing in water supply

When prices are not available, consumer choices can be used to value the benefits from improvements in water and sanitation and in other infrastructure. In Ukundu, Kenya, residents had three sources of water—vendors, kiosks, and wells—each with different costs in money and time. Water from door-to-door vendors cost the most but required the least collection time. A study found that the villagers were willing to pay a substantial share of their incomes—about 8 percent—in exchange for greater convenience and time saved. This finding, and similar ones in other developing countries, have been used to make the case for extending reliable public water supply even to poor communities.

Box 3.7 Integrating environmental considerations into World Bank lending

The World Bank's Operational Directive on Environmental Assessment (approved in 1989 and substantially expanded in 1991) is the principal vehicle for taking account of the environmental effects of the Bank's project lending. Fiscal 1991 was the first year in which all approved Bank projects were subject to these procedures. As noted in the Bank's latest annual report on the environment, almost half of all projects required environmental assessments. Environmental assessments (EAs) are required for all projects that could have significant adverse effects on the environment. By requiring such assessments early in project preparation, the directive helps reduce the risk of cost overruns and delays in implementation as a result of unanticipated environmental disruptions. The Bank's four regional environmental divisions are responsible for coordinating the process, but the ultimate responsibility for the EA remains with the borrower. All prospective Bank projects are now screened for potential environmental effects and are placed in one of three categories according to the effort required to mitigate adverse impacts.

For instance, all projects that could cause serious environmental damage, such as development of hydropower and thermal energy, large-scale irrigation and flood control, and forestry production, are classified in category A and require full and detailed EAs. A review of category A projects approved recently shows that several have been modified following EAs. For example, for the Lower Guayas flood control project in Ecuador, a channel was rerouted to avoid disruption to a lagoon.

To improve understanding and implementation of these procedures, an *Environmental Assessment Sourcebook* was published in 1991. It provides details on the operational directive, including a section on how the views of affected groups and NGOs are to be taken into account in preparing EAs and during project design and implementation.

It is anticipated that the current version of the directive will be reviewed and will be adapted, as it was in 1991, to the experience of the Bank and its borrowers.

---

assessments by independent evaluators who are insulated from the implementing agency. For instance, the Indira Sarovar irrigation project in India was redesigned in the late 1980s after its initial design was reviewed and criticized by several agencies, including the departments of environment and wildlife. Finally, as is discussed in Chapter 4, more attention must be given to improving knowledge about environmental impacts.

IMPROVING SERVICE PROVISION. Sometimes failure to value environmental benefits may lead not to overinvestment by the public sector but to underinvestment. This is particularly true for services such as water supply, sanitation, wastewater treatment, and irrigation. These services are likely to be undersupplied by markets, either because excluding users who do not pay is costly (stormwater drainage) or because the service is a natural monopoly and an unregulated private supplier would restrict the service in order to raise prices (water supply and wastewater treatment).

Governments frequently provide these services but artificially hold down the price charged to users. When private benefits are high, as for water supply and wastewater collection, more investment can be financed by charging realistic prices.

With other services, such as solid waste collection and wastewater treatment, the social benefits significantly exceed the benefits to users. Then it will rarely be appropriate to charge their full cost, and investments will have to be paid for partly through subsidies (see Chapter 5).

Directions for policy reform

Most countries, developing and industrial, have used direct regulations to address environmental problems. The United States is typical: its Clean Air Act mainly prescribes emissions standards or control technologies; the Clean Water Act mandates control technologies; the Resource Conservation and Recovery Act regulates the transport and disposal of hazardous wastes; and more than 28 percent of land is publicly owned and managed by various government agencies. Direct regulations are not always cost-effective. Environmental improvements—in air and water quality in industrial countries, for example—have probably been achieved at higher cost than if economic incentives had been used to a greater extent.

In developing countries this widespread preference for directly regulating polluters and resource users has also stretched administrative capabilities, particularly for monitoring and enforcement. Few policies have been enforced consistently. For instance, despite ambitious goals and regulations, air pollution remains a problem in most cities in developing countries. The inability to enforce regulations has been an important reason for the ineffectiveness of the often stringent environmental laws.

Policy reform, because of its redistributional implications, will require considerable political will. But the gains to developing countries from well-designed policies are enormous. Reform should proceed in four directions.

First, a sequence of policies will generally be required. The initial step is to remove policy distortions that damage the environment and slow growth. These measures must often be supplemented by others aimed at inducing government agencies and the private sector to recognize environmental impacts. Even here, a combination of policies will usually be required because environmental problems have several causes—deforestation, for example, results from the actions of government departments, logging companies, farmers, and fuelwood gatherers. Not every source of damage needs to be targeted, but a combination of policies, including removal of distortions, regulations (such as standards and land zoning), and economic incentives, will be needed to control even the most important sources.

Second, policies to change behavior should rely more on economic incentives such as charges, taxes, and deposit-refund schemes. Pricing environmental damage would help reduce implementation costs, encourage the faster adoption of environmentally benign technologies, and supplement public revenues. Such incentive-based policies will not be applicable to all environmental problems, particularly where only a few large firms, protected from competition or state owned, are involved. But most countries, including industrial ones, have made too little use of economic incentives in addressing environmental problems.

Third, indirect policies such as charges on inputs and products that pollute, self-enforcing deposit-refund schemes, and performance bonds should be used more frequently. Because most environmental problems in developing countries stem from the actions of numerous and dispersed resource users, it is costly and often prohibitive to enforce direct regulations. Blunt policies would simplify administration and so make enforcement more likely. Greater use of indirect policies will also typically mean that several must be used together. As in Mexico City (see Box 3.4), fuel taxes alone will not encourage vehicle owners to replace polluting engines or meet emission standards. Taxes need to be combined with regulatory measures.

Fourth, early action can reduce the costs of implementing effective environmental policies. As with air pollution from transport or hazardous solid wastes from the chemicals industry, the emergence of many environmental problems can be foreseen. It is usually possible to take steps such as setting up regulatory institutions, initiating charges, and encouraging adoption of cleaner technologies that can reduce the eventual magnitude of the problem. Countries that delay acting until problems become crises will eventually need to take extreme and costly responses, such as closing industrial plants and restricting vehicle use.

4 Making better decisions: information, institutions, and participation

The principles of sound environmental policy do not conflict with development objectives. Why, then, are wise policies frequently the exception? A principal reason is that such policies often mean the withdrawal of entrenched "rights"—to pollute or to use resources—that tend to benefit the wealthy and influential, often at the expense of the poor. Effective governmental action is also hampered by incomplete information, uncertainty, and weak regulatory powers.

In implementing change, governments must make the best use of their scarce administrative capacity. To do so requires, first, improved information and analysis to inform priority-setting and policy design; second, responsive and effective institutions suited to the administrative traditions of the particular country; and, third, greater local participation in policymaking, monitoring, and enforcement. The benefits of public participation frequently outweigh its costs.

This chapter asks why governments find it so hard to develop and implement wise environmental policies. The guidelines for environmental management discussed in Chapter 3 are easier to describe than to put into practice, so that, in both industrial and developing countries, there is a gap between policy and performance. For example, many middle- and low-income countries set environmental standards that are unrealistically high and then fail to enforce them. In some countries serious environmental problems are apparently ignored, while in others decisions are often based on the lobbying clout of industry or of environmental activists rather than on balanced analysis. Sometimes public investments proceed with little or no attention to environmental impacts, while others are thwarted by NIMBY ("not-in-my-backyard") campaigns that hamper dispassionate analysis of the benefits and costs of alternative measures.

The political economy of environmental degradation

Governments face many pressures in making environmental policy. Conflicting interest groups lobby noisily, public opinion demands action on

the most dramatic rather than the most important issues, and governments even find it difficult to curb their own damaging behavior. Building constituencies is an important part of the solution to these pressures.

Redistributing environmental rights

People benefit from being able to use environmental resources without paying for them, and removing these benefits has direct distributional consequences. Often, those who have been enjoying the benefits are the wealthiest and most politically powerful members of the society. Taking away their rights to pollute or to exploit resources can be politically painful and will often require compromises. Second-best policies are not desirable, but if well implemented, they are often preferable to unenforced "perfect" policies. Chile's new fishing law (Box 4.1) is an example.

Whereas the rich are often good at protecting their positions, the poor—whether they be slum dwellers in Manila, Lagos, or Rio de Janeiro, pastoralists in East Africa, or artisanal fishermen in Peru and Indonesia—tend to play little part in the environmental debate. Yet they usually bear the

Chile has one of the five largest fishing industries in the world. In 1990 exports of fish and fish products totaled more than $900 million, making the sector second only to mining as a foreign exchange earner. Managing the open-access fisheries has become more difficult as additional investment in the fishing sector has led to overfishing. The Chilean government has responded with a new law (*Ley de Pesca*) designed to prevent overexploitation and the collapse of any one fishery by regulating access to the different species being fished. Since any management scheme would imply some restrictions on the fish catch, the law became the subject of public debate. The evolution of the law illustrates some of the constraints on making environmental policy.

Three main regulatory systems were considered in designing the new management scheme: global quotas, individual transferable quotas (ITQs), and limits on individual boats and their gear. The final version of the law combines open access (within an overall quota), selected controls on boats, and a licensing scheme that is to be phased in gradually after the third year and is based on a percentage of the total catch.

The new law is an improvement over the previous situation of completely open access without restrictions on the catch. It was not possible, however, to implement a strict ITQ system—the preferred approach from the standpoint of both sustainable management and the economic viability of the fishermen. Fishing companies in the north opposed the inclusion of ITQs in the law. They preferred open access within overall quotas, which would allow them to switch their boats from a declining fishery to another area. Many fishermen saw any catch restriction as a zero-sum game in which they stood to lose.

The new fishery law is an important step that demonstrates that a compromise solution is frequently better than none. Its implementation will have to be monitored carefully. Chile is receiving assistance from the Nordic countries and the World Bank in strengthening its capacity to monitor and analyze the fishing industry.

brunt of environmental degradation. They may be the ones to suffer most when forests that once provided free fuel are logged or when factories pollute rivers. Unlike the better-off, they lack the means to defend themselves—by switching to other fuels, say, or by boiling polluted water. Thus, the poor generally have the most to gain from effective environmental policies. Governments must represent the interests of those without a voice, including the urban poor and ethnic minorities.

Crisis-driven policymaking

Even when environmental cause and effect are well understood by scientists, individuals may make perverse judgments about relative risks when setting priorities. People are more concerned about cancer and nuclear accidents than about many known health problems. Overreaction to environmental disasters is also common. Dramatic images of oil spills or leaking toxic wastes have captured public attention and played a powerful role in initiating policy change. Less attention has been paid to the insidious, chronic problems of exposure to high levels of particulates or to unsatisfactory drinking water—environmental problems that may put many more lives at risk.

The use of the dramatic or photogenic to garner popular support and donations is common. Many environmental activists have found these to be powerful metaphors for broader environmental concerns. The danger remains, however, that priorities can be distorted. Governments must make sober determinations of the relative importance of different environmental problems and set priorities in an informed, cost-effective manner.

Difficulties in self-regulation

In many countries the public sector owns the most-polluting industries and controls important natural resources. Instead of performing better on environmental criteria than private enterprises, state-owned enterprises tend to be less efficient, to use more resources, and to produce more wastes. The public sector is also notoriously bad at policing itself. The environmental problems of Eastern Europe and the former U.S.S.R. clearly demonstrate this. Being both poacher and gamekeeper does not work, especially when public agencies are responsible for such essential but massive tasks as wastewater treatment or solid waste disposal.

Creating a greater separation between the regulator and the regulated is one option. The establishment of semiautonomous regulatory bodies, or the use of independent commissions to regulate such natural-resource matters as interprovincial water allocation, the fish catch, or logging policies, helps depoliticize decisions and creates greater responsibility for self-regulation. Privatization with appropriate regulation can also help; in the United Kingdom when water companies were privatized, they came under tighter government scrutiny.

Building constituencies

If governments are to challenge established polluters or reallocate existing rights to resources, they need to build on and promote wider support for good environmental policies. Much evidence suggests that the basis for such support already exists, having been stimulated sometimes by particular environmental issues, sometimes by a powerful book (such as Rachel Carson's *Silent Spring*) or an expert report. As voters, protesters, and consumers, people in many countries show a similar interest in environmental causes.

''Green'' political parties have appeared in a number of countries, and increased activism by nongovernmental organizations has made governments and public institutions more accountable for their actions. Environmental causes frequently cross established political divides. Indeed, even in countries where conventional political participation is discouraged, the environment may be one area in which governments are willing to allow and respond to popular protest. It is no accident that the move toward more democratic forms of government has coincided with the worldwide increase in popular environmental awareness.

The behavior of consumers and producers is also changing. In many countries people are willing to recycle, to think about using energy and materials more efficiently, and to alter their consumption patterns. Companies often respond by using the environment as a selling point. ''Green labeling,'' increased use of recyclable and biodegradable packaging, and more energy-efficient technology are most common in industrial countries, but the same trends are appearing in some developing countries. Businesses sometimes argue that environmental measures will diminish competitiveness or lead to loss of jobs, but they are usually wrong. (As Chapter 3 noted, many environmental measures have little effect on competitiveness.) Business is increasingly realizing that it can take actions which yield both environmental and economic benefits. For example, *Changing Course* (Schmidheiny 1992), a report prepared by the Business Council for Sustainable Development in anticipation of UNCED, forcefully advances the idea that good environmental management is also good business.

Given the multitude of environmental problems and political pressures, governments must conserve their scarce administrative capacity. To develop good environmental policies, they need informed analysis based on accurate information. They also need to improve the way bureaucracies make and enforce decisions. To implement policies, they need to build popular support and encourage local participation. These are the themes of the next sections.

Improving knowledge and understanding

Ignorance is an important cause of environmental damage and a serious impediment to finding solutions. This principle holds for international negotiators and poor households alike, as is illustrated by the global damage done to the ozone layer by CFCs and the serious implications of indoor air pollution for family health. It is necessary, first, to know the facts; second, to determine values and analyze the benefits and costs of alternative measures; and, third, to ensure that information is available to inform public and private choices.

Establishing the facts

Frequently, especially in developing countries, decisions are made in the absence of environmental information. Collecting basic data can be expensive, but the rewards are usually high. Although different countries have different needs, there are some general guidelines. For example, the discussion in Chapter 2 suggests some priorities for monitoring pollution and waste problems:

• Quality and availability of drinking water and sanitation facilities
• Exposure to ambient air pollutants, especially particulate matter and lead, in urban areas
• Fecal coliform and heavy metals in rivers and lakes
• Indoor air pollution from the burning of biomass
• Hazardous wastes and pesticides in selected ''hot spots.''

Essential management information on land use and natural resources needed for improved management of these resources (see Chapter 7) includes:

• Data on soils, from surveys and experiments in each agricultural zone

Figure 4.1 Participants in the GEMS project for monitoring urban air quality

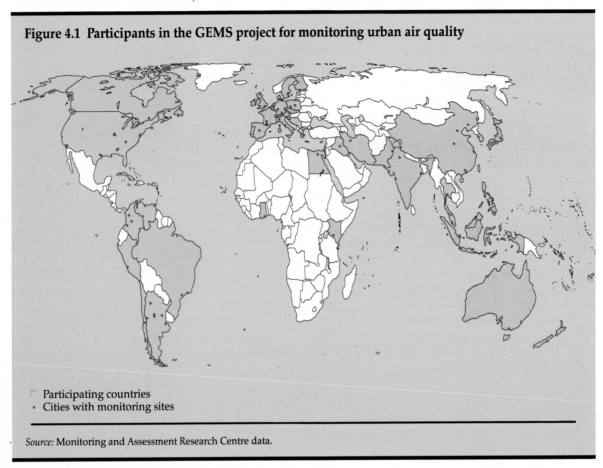

▢ Participating countries
• Cities with monitoring sites

Source: Monitoring and Assessment Research Centre data.

• Rate of depletion and quality of groundwater in threatened aquifers

• Changes in forest area and data on harvesting and replanting

• Data on fish harvest and wildlife depletion in vulnerable areas

• Damage to coastal and wetland resources.

Efforts are being made to help countries with environmental monitoring and to compile internationally comparable data. The Global Environmental Monitoring System (GEMS), managed by UNEP, has activities related to air and water quality in 142 countries. Monitoring of urban air quality began in 1974. Most of the cities shown in Figure 4.1 report on concentrations of sulfur dioxide and suspended particulate matter, both important air pollutants. Unfortunately, the amount of financial help has so far been inadequate, and thus the coverage and quality of data are weaker than is desirable.

Given limited resources, it is better to concentrate on the most significant pollutants and to limit collection points to the numbers that can be accurately monitored. In the late 1980s Poland was reported to be regularly monitoring river pollution at more than 1,000 sites. Even if all the samples collected were properly analyzed, the gain in knowledge about river quality over that attainable with a system of 100–200 monitoring points would not justify such an extensive system.

Valuing resources and analyzing benefits and costs

Ending well-entrenched but environmentally damaging practices is difficult enough for governments when the damage is readily quantifiable. When environmental damage threatens health or jeopardizes economic output, it is relatively easy to point to the benefits of changes in policy. But as previous chapters have stated, some environmental values—important to poor and rich people alike—are not only unmarketed but also intangible. The more difficult it is to quantify the benefits of preserving these values, the harder it will be for policymakers to weigh the gains from conservation against the quick profits from resource degradation or pollution. As described in Chapter 3, however, more sophisticated methodologies are now making it possible to estimate the value of less-tangible environmental benefits.

In many cases local analysis of costs and benefits can build on international experience. Researchers in Bangkok, in analyzing the health impacts of pollution, tested local data against what had been learned in other countries about the links between exposure to pollutants and health. They found that the greatest threats to health were particulate matter, lead, and microbiological diseases. Other environmental problems that traditionally receive a great deal of attention—contamination of groundwater and surface water; air pollutants such as sulfur dioxide, nitrogen dioxide, and ozone; and disposal of hazardous wastes—were much less dangerous. (In fact, the gravest threats were at least 100 times more serious than the lowest risks.) This information was used to develop cost-effective pollution control policies.

Improving information and education

Environmental education based on careful analysis can add rationality to the environmental debate. Publication of annual reports on the environment is increasingly common. When the public has a well-informed grasp of environmental issues, there is a better prospect of developing positive rather than purely defensive policies. Without such knowledge, people tend to focus on causes of death (for example, technological hazards and nuclear accidents) that are sensational and are caused by somebody else and to worry less about the probability of death from causes that are less dramatic and often under an individual's own control, such as cigarette smoking and wood fires. The work of independent research institutes—such as the Thailand Development Research Institute—can help to modify people's views.

Communities are increasingly bombarded with a variety of environmental information and need sources of information that they can trust. Independent commissions can help to depoliticize decisionmaking by analyzing thorny environmental issues and producing recommendations for policy action. Box 4.2 illustrates how some of these bodies have contributed to the development of the consensus required for policy decisions on such complex topics as global warming, pollution control, and urban planning. Independent commissions can also audit public agencies and so make them more accountable.

The most important effect of improved information and environmental education is to change behavior. Well-informed citizens are in a better position to put pressure on governments and on polluters and are more likely to accept the costs and inconveniences of environmental policies. The results can be dramatic. In Curitiba, Brazil, a combination of an energetic mayor, a committed municipal government, and an informed and involved public have led to many environmental innovations and an improved quality of urban life in this city of 2 million. Public transport is used by most of the population, green spaces have been expanded, recycling is widely practiced, and industrial location and product mix are carefully chosen to minimize pollution.

Changing institutions: making the public sector more responsive

Given that the scarcest government resource is frequently not money but administrative capacity and that political pressures make environmental policymaking particularly difficult, governments must think carefully about what they do and how they do it. The "what" of environmental management consists of setting priorities, coordinating activities and resolving conflicts, and creating responsible regulatory and enforcement institutions. The institutional response to these tasks—the "how" of the equation—includes developing legislation and administrative structures, providing needed skills, ensuring funding and donor coordination, and implementing decentralization and devolution.

Essential government functions

SETTING PRIORITIES AND FORMULATING POLICIES. Since all countries face multiple environmental problems, governments must set priorities on the basis of informed analysis so that they can make the most efficient use of scarce administrative and financial resources. Frequently, *better* environmental policy is more important than *more* environmental policy. In many developing countries top priority must be given to environmental impacts on health and productivity (see Chapter 2). Actual priorities will depend on whether a country is largely rural or urban and on the average level (and distribution) of income. In highly urbanized countries such as Argentina, Korea, and Poland,

Box 4.2 Independent commissions and improved environmental analysis

Governments have often used independent panels of experts (sometimes constituted as special commissions) to investigate contentious policy issues. In recent years environmental issues have increasingly been referred to such bodies. The procedure has a number of advantages.

- It relieves, at least temporarily, the pressure for an early decision.
- It facilitates open debate, sometimes through public submissions or hearings, without committing the government to adopt any of the recommendations that may emerge. Scientific disagreement can be clarified and the public educated.
- It allows a number of scientific disciplines and interest groups to be brought together. A consensus is more likely to emerge if the commission is chaired by an independent person rather than by a government representative.

There have been several interesting examples of the use of this approach.

On global issues. In 1990 the Enquete Commission on Preventative Measures to Protect the Earth's Atmosphere presented a comprehensive report to the German Bundestag. The commission, which was made up of scientists and representatives of the country's main political parties, made specific recommendations not only on national energy policy but also on international measures.

In the United States, Congress asked the National Academy of Sciences to review available evidence on global warming and evaluate policy options. The report, issued in 1991, recommended that even though the effect of global warming on the United States was uncertain, selected low-cost actions to reduce greenhouse gas emissions should be initiated.

On national priorities. Industrial countries have occasionally used expert panels to help prepare national environmental strategies. The United Kingdom has had a Royal Commission on Environmental Pollution since 1970. Members serve as individuals, not as representatives of organizations or professions, and are appointed for at least three years. The commission is empowered to request documents and even to visit premises. Over the years it has produced fifteen reports, most of which have influenced policy. For example, following the 1983 report on lead, the lead content of gasoline was reduced and unleaded fuel was introduced.

On specific environmental issues. Governments increasingly finance independent "think tanks," such as the Thailand Development Research Institute, which analyzes a wide range of issues, including environmental topics. Sometimes governments use interagency task forces to examine discrete issues. In Hungary a group evaluated a proposed hydropower dam on the Danube; in Mexico a task force will analyze the use of economic instruments to control pollution and manage natural resources.

---

air and water pollution in cities will be priorities. In more rural economies, as in many Sub-Saharan African countries, parts of Central America, and India and Bangladesh, land, forest, and water management may well have top priority.

The distribution of impacts is important. Wealthier city dwellers, who can protect themselves against unsafe water, may lobby governments to assign higher priority to air pollution, which affects rich and poor alike, than to ensuring a safe water supply. Yet water investments may have a much larger immediate health benefit.

National environmental action plans are proving useful tools for setting priorities. Plans are being drawn up for a number of African countries and have already been completed for Lesotho, Madagascar, and Mauritius. The experience of Burkina Faso with such a plan (Box 4.3) demonstrates the importance of building consensus and the will to act.

COORDINATING AND PLANNING. Once priorities have been determined and appropriate policies designed, implementation of policies and the resolution of conflict become important. Environmental policy often cuts across the normal bounds of bureaucratic responsibility. Whether it is watershed management to protect a new dam, allocation of a region's water resources among competing users, or the complex problem of managing a city's air quality, many different actors must be brought together. Agencies need to collaborate, and some machinery for resolving conflict is needed. Although there is a natural bureaucratic tendency for governments to respond to intersectoral conflicts by setting up regional bodies, these organizations have rarely been successful in the past because they are inevitably at odds with strongly established, sectorally organized government bureaucracies.

A common problem with environmental issues

that cross normal bureaucratic demarcation lines is the absence of an effective mechanism for coordinating the work. In São Paulo, Brazil, the metropolitan area has a planning agency, while the state has agencies with responsibilities for environmental protection, water, and sanitation. A consequence of divided responsibility is that programs for controlling industrial pollution have not been integrated with investments in wastewater treatment, and the sanitation master plan has not been sensibly implemented. (For example, treatment plants have been constructed, but not the needed interceptor and trunk line sewers.)

If regional environmental planning is to be successful, countries need flexible management frameworks that encourage the actors to "think globally, act sectorally." In rural areas resource analysis and planning should be done at the level of the individual watershed or irrigation scheme, even if line ministries take responsibility for implementation. In cities the management of air and water pollution requires a strong mechanism for intersectoral planning and coordination. For example, Santiago and Mexico City recently established special organizations for planning pollution reduction strategies to be implemented by line agencies for the wider metropolitan areas; in Mexico City the commission will include part of the state of Mexico as well as the federal capital. In Jakarta the work of several intersectoral groups has led to the relatively successful implementation of a program to protect the metropolitan area's ecologically sensitive watershed by shifting growth away from the south, where the watershed is located, and toward the east and west of the city.

REGULATING AND ENFORCING. Agencies, chronically short of money and manpower, need to devise cost-effective ways of implementing policy. One way is to give citizens more power to challenge polluters, whether public or private. For example, public environmental agencies may give local communities or voluntary organizations substantial responsibility for implementing or monitoring programs. This approach can be formalized through the legal system. In the Clean Air Act of 1970 the U.S. Congress authorized private citizens to seek injunctions (and in some cases financial penalties) against companies that violated the terms of their operating permits, thus making environmental enforcement no longer the exclusive responsibility of the government.

Enforcement may be bolstered by making more use of the private sector or of nongovernmental groups. Many governments now hire private companies and technical consultants to perform environmental assessments, collect and analyze data, undertake monitoring and inspection, and provide specialized advice. Mexico City, for example, is implementing air pollution control measures

Box 4.3 Setting priorities in Burkina Faso

Improved environmental management requires a commitment from both the government and the wider public. The recent experience of Burkina Faso in developing a national environment action plan illustrates how the process itself can be an essential component in creating awareness and building the political will needed for action.

When Burkina Faso began to develop its plan, the process was based on a series of previous national meetings synthesized by local consultants in commissioned reports. These resulted in the identification of several key program areas: developing environmental management capability at all levels, improving living conditions in rural and urban environments, focusing on environmental management at the village ("micro") level, addressing key national ("macro") resource issues, and, in support of all these, managing information on the environment.

With the aid of funding from a number of bilateral and multilateral organizations, including the World Bank, the entire process took about three years and cost about $450,000. A national seminar was held to debate the draft plan and to set priorities in preparation for approval by the Cabinet in September 1991. A meeting is planned for mid-1992 at which donors will be asked to pledge support for specific projects that make up the action plan.

The main lesson from Burkina Faso is that by working with the government and local participants, it was possible to develop a plan that incorporates the work of those who will have to implement it. Although it might have been quicker and cheaper to produce the plan using international consultants, the plan would not have been a Burkinabé product and would probably have joined other "external" products on a bookshelf instead of resulting in action.

through private vehicle-inspection stations and is considering using private laboratories to analyze air and water samples.

Community groups can play an important role in enforcement. In India an "environmental audit" procedure has been developed for the 500-megawatt Dahanu Thermal Power project, currently under construction. The authorities in charge of pollution control plan to distribute to local communities and NGOs summaries in nontechnical language of the results of environmental monitoring. Community groups can then check emissions against legal standards and seek redress in the courts if necessary.

The success of such approaches will depend partly on how freely information about polluting activities is available. Sometimes simply obliging large polluters to publish information about specific emissions will have some effect on behavior. Legislation in the United States now requires some 20,000 plants to make public information on their annual emissions of 320 potential carcinogens. Public disclosure can also help focus the attention of senior management on emissions and the opportunities for reducing them and can supplement official monitoring with public and community oversight.

The institutional response

Policymaking has frequently outpaced administrative capacity to analyze and implement policies. Laws are multiplying, and often the result is a large number of contradictory regulations that are beyond the capacity of governments to enforce. This situation, in addition to doing little for the environment, breeds skepticism about laws in general and government commitment to the environment in particular and may encourage corruption. It is essential to close the gap between making and implementing policy. That means reforming the way the machinery of government handles environmental issues.

When the World Bank expanded its lending for environmental purposes in the 1980s, it was clear that the public sector was often unable to deliver the expected results. The World Bank and member governments therefore began drawing up comprehensive country environmental action plans. These plans take into consideration both the legal and the administrative frameworks in countries as diverse as Brazil, Poland, and the Philippines (Box 4.4). Experience with the plans has shown that there are five main requirements for successful policy implementation: a clear legislative framework, an appropriate administrative structure, technical skills, adequate money, and decentralized responsibility.

ENACTING LEGISLATION. Laying the legal foundations for environmental management frequently necessitates the repeal of outdated laws and the codification of new concepts. If the laws are to be effective, detailed regulations, without which most laws are only general principles, also have to be developed. New environmental provisions need to be integrated into existing government procedures or into traditional local law. In Chile one of the first steps taken by the new National Environment Commission (CONAMA) was to review existing legislation and prepare a comprehensive environmental law. This law and a companion law implementing requirements for environmental assessments, both now under consideration, will provide a rational framework for environmental management.

BUILDING ADMINISTRATIVE STRUCTURE. Institution building is a long-term business. It depends on local conditions, political factors, and the availability of manpower and money. Frequently, it is easiest to build on existing institutions. In practice, the structure of environmental administration matters much less than the ability to get the job done. As outlined above, governments need the capacity to set priorities, coordinate and resolve conflicts, and regulate and enforce. Countries will allocate these roles differently; for instance, coordination and conflict resolution might be undertaken by an independent executive agency, by an interdepartmental committee, or by a small, politically and technically astute group in the office of the president. The key is clear statutory powers combined with the authority to resolve intragovernmental disputes and the ability to provide continuity when administrations change.

Institutional arrangements that have been found to be helpful include:

• A formal high-level agency that can provide advice on policy and monitor implementation. Examples are IBAMA in Brazil, the Federal Environmental Protection Agency (FEPA) in Nigeria, and the State Environmental Protection Commission in China.

• Environmental units in the principal line ministries that can provide the central unit with technical expertise and monitor those environmental policies that the ministries are responsible for im-

Box 4.4 The gap between policy and implementation

In a growing number of borrower countries World Bank assistance for national environment plans includes help with institution building. Here are some examples of attempts to reduce the gap between policies on paper and results on the ground.

The Brazil National Environment Project, a $117 million loan signed in mid-1990, is designed to strengthen the institutional and regulatory framework and promote better management of biological resources. In support of the first three-year phase of Brazil's National Environmental Program, the project finances the strengthening of national conservation units; improved environmental management of threatened ecosystems in the Pantanal, the Atlantic Forest, and the Brazilian coast; and reinforcement of IBAMA (Brazil's national environmental agency, the executing agency for the project) and state environmental agencies. The loan provides support for staff training, equipment, better technical information, and legal and technical assistance; improvement of regulations and technical guidelines for environmental management; and environmental education. Implementation of the project has been delayed by fiscal and management problems. The slow start highlights the need to strengthen the management capability of executing agencies before they can effectively undertake project implementation.

Building environmental institutions is a key concern in Eastern Europe. The Poland Environmental Management Project, approved in April 1990, was the third World Bank loan to Poland and the first for environmental activities. The purposes of the $18 million loan include strengthening environmental management, introducing consistent standards and enforcement, improving monitoring, and regionalizing environmental management. The government has identified the most-polluted areas and has told the eighty worst industrial polluters to improve their environmental performance at once. At the same time, government task forces are revising the regulatory system and designing a national environmental monitoring strategy.

In the Philippines a loan and credit package totaling $224 million, approved in 1991, will promote policy reform and strengthen institutions. The loan contains provisions to help protect biodiversity in the country. Since the largest threats to biodiversity are encroachment by land-hungry farmers and illegal commercial logging, the project supports more sustainable patterns of resource use by small farmers in exchange for secure tenure rights and improves the enforcement of logging regulations, partly by strengthening the regional and local offices of the Department of Environment and Natural Resources. The loan also supports the design of a network of protected areas and provides resources to manage ten priority protected areas.

---

plementing. Oversight, from a public health perspective, of general environmental quality (especially air and water) is frequently carried out by the ministry of health, and the management and conservation of natural resources may be spread among government units responsible for agriculture, forestry, fisheries, and parks and wildlife.

• Regional and local environmental units that allow local implementation and monitoring and feed information back to the national government (see below).

CLOSING THE SKILLS GAP. The public sector in many developing countries is short of qualified staff at all levels. The necessary skills may exist but may not be attracted into the public sector because salaries are well below the market rate. Environmental agencies are therefore condemned to being outstaffed by the private firms they are charged with regulating or may be forced to rely for expertise on expensive temporary consultants. Some countries have found ways to mitigate this problem. In Latin America, for example, foundations and institutes financed by nongovernmental sources sometimes undertake both policy analysis and resource management.

Another common problem is an imbalance of professional skills. In some countries agencies are dominated by engineers and contain few natural or social scientists; in other countries the reverse is true. But environmental management requires a mix: natural or biological scientists to manage renewable resources, social scientists—economists, sociologists, and anthropologists—to identify problems and formulate policies, and engineers to design solutions.

Economic analysis is particularly important to (and frequently absent from) the dialogue between those responsible for environmental management and those in charge of the budget, planning, and economic policy. An environmental economics unit in the ministry or agency responsible for economic planning and public finance can fill this role by assessing budgetary allocations, ensuring that economic incentives are consistent with environmental objectives, and helping to strike an appropriate balance between environmental and economic goals in determining development priorities.

OBTAINING FUNDING. Environmental agencies have not yet firmly established their place in the competition for scarce government funds. Given the secondary importance usually attached to environmental management, budgetary allocations are sometimes insufficient and highly variable. When money runs out, the effect may be disproportionately damaging. For instance, if a shortage of cash means that enforcement of water pollution regulations has to be suspended, the consequent damage to groundwater and surface water can be substantial. If a national park goes unprotected during a dry season because of lack of funds, poachers may quickly undo what has taken years to achieve.

Environmental administration can often be improved even within a tight budget. But an environmental agency needs a core of skilled technical staff, as well as laboratories and other monitoring devices, to do its job properly. In some countries more money is becoming available as environmental management is accepted as an important national objective. Economic instruments—fines for polluters, charges for permits to use forests and fisheries, entrance fees for parks and protected areas, and so on—can help to pay for enforcement and administration.

Donors, including development banks and multilateral agencies, are often reluctant to finance what is needed most—improved operation and maintenance of fledgling national environmental administrations. Rather, they seek to make specific investments that tie up scarce local staff. Sometimes contributions come in the form of technical assistance and other tied aid, which does not necessarily strengthen local capabilities, and sometimes the donor community floods local officials with well-meant but unorchestrated offers of assistance. Finally, most donor-funded projects are relatively short term and small scale. What is needed most is longer-term reliable funding, especially for institution building and research.

DECENTRALIZING AND DELEGATING. Once national priorities and policies have been set, it is often cost-effective to solve problems at the local level. Many governments therefore pass day-to-day responsibility to local bodies. This approach was used successfully in Japan (Box 4.5) and is being increasingly applied in other countries. In

---

Box 4.5   Japan: curbing pollution while growing rapidly

Japan's postwar reconstruction brought about both rapid economic growth and major environmental problems. In the 1960s, when it was still a middle-income country, Japan began to invest heavily in control technology to combat severe air and water pollution, largely from industrial sources. Expenditures for pollution control by large firms peaked at more than 900 billion yen in the mid-1970s before declining to 400 billion yen or less by 1980. Japan is now enjoying the benefits of its investments: between 1970 and the late 1980s emissions of sulfur oxides decreased by 83 percent, emissions of nitrogen oxides by 29 percent, and concentrations of carbon monoxide by 60 percent. Similar advances were made in improving water quality. These results were obtained through stringent governmental regulations and negotiations between industry and communities to define solutions that could be fine-tuned to varying local requirements. An estimated 28,000 such agreements are now in force.

Three lessons from the Japanese experience may offer useful guidance to today's middle-income countries:

• *Establish a national policy framework*. The initial legal framework, established by the Diet, included the Basic Law for Environmental Pollution Control (1967), the Air Pollution Control Laws (1967 and 1970), and the Water Pollution Control Law (1970). These laws define responsibilities and divide them among government at various levels, private firms, and individuals, thereby encouraging the decentralization of environmental management.

• *Negotiate agreements at the local level*. The open negotiation of agreements between polluting industries, local authorities, and citizens' groups often led to emissions considerably lower than the minimum required by law.

• *Allow flexibility in setting emissions levels and promote self-regulation*. Since industries were often located in the middle of residential areas, firms were very sensitive to local environmental concerns. The negotiating process allowed emissions levels to be tailored to local conditions and also encouraged self-regulation by industry, thus fostering the idea of good corporate citizenship.

China, for example, the actual work of environmental protection takes place mainly at lower levels of government. The provinces are responsible for carrying out national policy set by the State Environmental Protection Commission. All provinces and municipalities and most counties now have environmental protection bureaus (EPBs) that answer to local environmental policy commissions headed by a vice governor or vice magistrate. China's network of environmental protection agencies thus consists of the central units and about 2,400 EPBs, which together employ more than 16,500 people.

In Nigeria, a federal state, most policy is implemented at the state level. Over the years the states have monitored their environmental problems through their administrative systems, which include representation from local governments. Local capacity, however, has been weak. The 1988 decree establishing Nigeria's FEPA encourages the establishment of local environmental protection bodies, but most have only limited capacity to carry out their responsibilities for environmental management. If decentralization is to work, it must be accompanied by a transfer of finance. Otherwise, a policy vacuum is created: the center sheds responsibilities, but local agencies are ill equipped to take them up.

Some countries have made specific allocations to local administrations for environmental investments. China and Colombia, for example, have passed national laws that permanently assign a percentage of the income from hydropower sales to local governments for watershed protection, environmental education, soil protection, and environmental training programs for municipal officials. In others emissions fees serve as local sources of finance. The Municipal Environmental Protection Bureau of Tianjin, China, has created an industrial pollution control fund financed by emissions fees mandated under national legislation. Revenues are used to finance investments in control and treatment at individual enterprises. Investments in decentralized treatment of industrial wastewater increased the treatment rate from 35 to 46 percent between 1985 and 1990.

Involving local people

Many environmental problems cannot be solved without the active participation of local people. Few governments can afford the costs of enforcing management programs that local people do not accept. Participation can also help with afforestation, wildlife conservation, park management, improvements in sanitation systems and drainage, and flood control. Local people can provide the manpower and knowledge for dealing with the aftermath of environmental disasters, and local knowledge of genetic diversity has led to breakthroughs in crop production.

Participatory approaches offer three main advantages: (a) they give planners a better understanding of local values, knowledge, and experience; (b) they win community backing for project objectives and community help with local implementation; and (c) they can help resolve conflicts over resource use.

Drawing on local values, knowledge, and experience

People's views of their environment strongly influence how they manage it. Even when attitudes toward the natural world do not achieve the sophistication described in Box 4.6, few cultures view natural resources as worth nothing more than their cash value in the marketplace. Only if environmental programs reflect local beliefs, values, and ideology will the community support them.

The belief that traditional knowledge of the environment is simple and static is changing rapidly. More and more development projects are taking advantage of local knowledge about how to manage the environment. For example, people in the tropical rainforests of the Amazon and Southeast Asia have accumulated a valuable understanding of local ecosystems, and African pastoralists, such as the Maasai and Samburu of Kenya, are able to exploit apparently marginal savannahs (see Box 4.6). Building on these strengths requires great care, expertise, and patience. But development projects that do not take existing practices into account often fail.

A particularly costly instance of neglecting local practices occurred in Bali, Indonesia. For centuries the traditional Balinese irrigation calendar had provided a highly efficient way of making the most of water resources and soil fertility and of controlling pests. When a large internationally financed agricultural project tried to replace traditional rice varieties with high-input imported varieties, the result was a sudden increase in insect pests, followed by declining crop yields. A subsequent project that built on the indigenous production system has been much more successful.

Sometimes local knowledge can be applied in other parts of the world. Vetiver grass has been

Box 4.6 Indigenous values and knowledge of land and the environment

Many of the world's remaining indigenous people—estimated to number over 250 million living in more than seventy countries—take a view of nature that differs strikingly from conventional attitudes. A study (Davis, background paper) commissioned for this Report analyzes the attitudes of three groups of indigenous peoples: the Quichua-speaking Amerindians in the rainforests of eastern Ecuador, the Maasai and Samburu nomadic pastoralists of Kenya, and the indigenous swidden (slash-and-burn) farmers in the upland areas of the Philippines. The study concluded that many indigenous people view land not as a commodity to be bought and sold in impersonal markets but as a substance endowed with sacred meanings, embedded in social relations, and fundamental to the understanding of the groups' existence and identity.

Tribal Filipinos see land as a symbol of their historical identity: an ancestral heritage to be defended and preserved for all future generations. According to the Episcopal Commission on Tribal Filipinos,

They believe that wherever they are born, there too shall they die and be buried, and their own graves are proof of their rightful ownership of the land. It symbolizes their tribal identity because it stands for their unity, and if the land is lost, the tribe, too, shall be lost.

Ownership of the land is seen as vested upon the community as a whole. The right to ownership is acquired through ancestral occupation and active production. To them, it is not right for anybody to sell the land because it does not belong to only one generation, but should be preserved for all future generations. (p. 68)

Like many indigenous people, the surviving tribes of the rainforests of South America draw on traditional knowledge and practices to make a living in fragile environments. The study observes,

Quichua forest management is often overlooked and unappreciated by outsiders who are unfamiliar with it, in part

because the methods that they use to alter the course of forest succession are technologically simple (consisting of axe and machete and a vast array of knowledge), and also because the forest that regrows is diverse and complex and hard to distinguish from undisturbed mature rainforest. The lowland Quichua achieve this effect by altering the mix of species that regrow in their agricultural clearings. . . . [The result is] a patchwork of habitats of different ages in different stages of succession and with a varying blend of useful resources. (p. 12)

In most countries legal recognition and practical protection of the customary land and territorial rights of indigenous people are limited or nonexistent. Pastoralists in Africa face particular problems in maintaining access to their traditional pastures. An example is the case of the Maasai and Samburu of Kenya. At one time the Kenyan government hoped to set up group ranches as a way of increasing beef exports while retaining collective management. Recently, the government has promoted the privatization of these ranches, asserting that corporate land tenure impedes rational land management. The Bank study notes that Maasai elders regard private landownership as an "alien concept" and express fears that "subdivision may lead to a disastrous change of lifestyle of the Maasai people."

The only source of income for the Maasai people is livestock. Their culture provides them with a system in which they can preserve the arid and semiarid areas . . . in such a way that certain areas are put aside in periods of drought in order to keep grazing areas in good condition. Although lately it has become more difficult to do, it still works within and among group ranchers, especially where upgraded cattle breeds are introduced. However, in the fragile (semi-)arid areas it might even become impossible to keep livestock on an individual basis on small plots; it will also irrevocably lead to soil erosion, overuse of water resources, and desertification. (pp. 37–38)

---

used for centuries in the hilly areas of Tamil Nadu and other parts of India as cattle fodder and as a hedge plant to conserve soil and moisture. Experience from the Kabbalama Watershed Development Project in 1987 prompted the World Bank to support the use of vetiver in countries as diverse as China, Madagascar, Nepal, Nigeria, the Philippines, Sri Lanka, and Zimbabwe. The costs of vetiver are one-fifteenth those of soil conservation systems that rely more heavily on engineering (see Chapter 7). However, local management prac-

tices—embedded as they are in specific cultures—are not always so transferable.

Improving project design and implementation

Projects are more successful if they are participatory in design and implementation. A review of thirty completed World Bank projects from the 1970s found an average rate of return of 18 percent for projects that were judged culturally appropriate but only 9 percent for projects that did not include mechanisms for social and cultural adaptation. A more detailed study of fifty-two USAID projects similarly found a strong correlation between participation and project success, especially when participation took place through organizations created and managed by the beneficiaries themselves.

The contrasts between environmentally beneficial projects designed on participatory principles and those that fail to include participatory designs can be striking. Haiti's top-down afforestation program, plagued by high sapling mortality rates on forest department lots and by conflicts with villagers, consistently fell short of tree-planting targets. Starting in 1981, an alternative approach was tried. NGOs helped to provide trees that were selected by farm households. The result was dramatic: instead of the 3 million trees on 6,000 family farms originally planned, 20 million seedlings were planted on the farms of 75,000 families who voluntarily joined the program.

Ideally, both local communities and the responsible agencies gain from participation, as the experience of the National Irrigation Authority (NIA) in the Philippines illustrates. Early involvement of community groups in planning construction and in finding ways to avoid the silting of channels and drains has brought about better maintenance of irrigation works and higher agricultural yields. Users have also been more willing to pay for the NIA's services.

Growing numbers of countries are devising partnerships with local people to provide municipal environmental services. In Accra sanitation services in low-income areas have improved greatly since NGOs and local entrepreneurs have been allowed to operate improved community pit latrines. Desludging and disposal are carried out by the city's central waste management department. This division of responsibility has proved more effective than attempting to operate a completely centralized sewerage system that had fallen into disrepair. In Jakarta neighborhoods organize the collection of solid wastes by collecting monthly dues that are used to buy a cart and hire a local garbage collector. At least once a month, one volunteer from each household assists in collecting garbage and cleaning the neighborhood drainage system. The wastes are taken to a transfer station. There they are picked up by municipal authorities—a task that is gradually being contracted out to private companies. This combination of community collection and centralized disposal has allowed Jakarta to achieve an 80 percent waste collection rate—high by developing country standards.

Resolving local conflicts

Properly planned participation eases resolution of the conflicts inherent in environmental decisionmaking. When mechanisms for resolving conflicts exist, people may be less likely to overuse natural resources out of fear of losing their access to them. All too often, top-down rules that govern access to natural resources appear arbitrary and unfair. Many governments are changing resource allocation rules to reduce conflicts between authorities and local communities and to set up procedures for resolving disputes among competing claimants to resources.

When large infrastructural investments—dams, irrigation facilities, roads, and ports—are planned, listening to public opinion and local NGOs at an early stage is a good way to avoid trouble later on. If this is not done, community opposition can gather momentum and delay or stop the project. A good environmental assessment should clarify potential environmental and social impacts, propose mitigative measures, and present the costs and benefits of alternatives.

A particularly difficult challenge for conflict resolution is posed by projects such as dams, highways, and some types of wildlife reservations that change land use and lead to involuntary displacement and resettlement. Rarely have local views been consulted to any extent in making such investment decisions or, until recently, in planning resettlement programs. This omission has led to inefficiency, as well as injustice; traditional resettlement has turned out to be needlessly slow and expensive. Governments and donors now broadly agree on several principles: (a) project designers should explore ways of minimizing resettlement; (b) resettlers' living standards should be as good as or better than before resettlement; (c) compensation for lost assets should be paid at replacement costs; and (d) communities should be encouraged to participate in all stages of resettlement planning and implementation. Examples from Mexico and Thailand illustrate this new approach (Box 4.7).

The limitations and costs of participation

Public participation has its drawbacks. Extensive participation, especially when information is inadequate, can delay decisionmaking. Communities with political influence sometimes reject proposals

Box 4.7 Reforming resettlement through participation: Mexico and Thailand

Resettlement of people displaced by large hydroelectric dams has typically been the extreme case of nonparticipatory planning. But experience with two recent projects in Mexico and Thailand illustrates how participation can help with issues as difficult as involuntary displacement and resettlement.

The 200-meter dam at Zimapan, central Mexico, and the 17-meter Pak Mun dam on the Mun River in Thailand are at the core of two World Bank–assisted projects designed to provide urgently needed clean energy. But the national benefits of the dams meant little to the nearly 25,000 people who would be displaced. Nor was previous experience in either country encouraging; new housing and compensation for lost assets had proved no substitute for submerged farmland and uprooted communities. It was not surprising that resettlement proposals were greeted with skepticism and opposition.

In both countries the impact of resettlement was taken into account when the dams were designed. In the case of Pak Mun a review of technical options showed that locating the dam slightly upstream and lowering its height would reduce the number of people to be resettled from approximately 20,000 to fewer than 2,000. Detailed resettlement plans that followed the World Bank's guidelines were prepared to help the affected farmers recover their lost livelihoods. Under repeated prodding by NGOs and community groups, the energy company began working with the affected communities on improving its approach to resettlement. Although problems remain, sharing information about resettlement alternatives, preparing meetings and pub-

lications to inform resettlers of their rights and entitlements, and providing farmers with good-quality replacement farmland are important steps in improving the resettlement program.

To implement the resettlement policy for Mexico's Zimapan project, the parent company set up a unit that reported directly to the company's president. The unit included anthropologists, technicians, economists, architects, and social workers, all of whom were to live in the affected villages, help identify local concerns and resettlement preferences, and provide a channel of communication between the villagers and the company. As villagers in Zimapan organized, they repudiated the local administration and elected their own much tougher council to manage the negotiations on compensation and resettlement. Farmers have been active in selecting and supervising designs for replacement housing, and the company has purchased and transferred to the resettlers functioning, productive farms that will improve their incomes and living standards.

In neither case has participation in resettlement planning led to the disappearance of opposition—that was not the purpose. Indeed, opposition remains strong, and confrontational encounters between the company and antidam organizations still occur. Nevertheless, in both projects pressure for more active participation by local people has led to significant improvements in what will always be a difficult process. Participation has allowed the people most adversely affected by the projects to be actively involved in directing the course that resettlement will take.

---

to construct facilities such as waste disposal centers on the most suitable sites because of the impact on local property values, aesthetics, or safety. Making compensatory payments for local use and giving communities control over how the project is sited and designed can help defuse opposition.

Participatory approaches tend to be expensive. Consultation requires plenty of staff and time, and government agencies, already short of funds, may cut corners. If they do, the most remote and marginal—and often the neediest—communities will be the ones to suffer.

The extra net expense of seeking participation need not be large, however. In the Philippine example described above, the additional cost for the community organization program was about $25 a hectare, but savings in construction costs—largely as a result of information provided by farmers—brought the net increase down to less than $2.50 a

hectare. The outcome was a better irrigation system with higher utilization and higher revenues. Increased participation was clearly cost-effective.

A potential disadvantage of participation is that decentralization of decisionmaking can easily reinforce the power of local elites. In these cases strong supervision is needed to overcome local conflicts.

When projects involve voluntary provision of labor, participatory approaches can widen income differentials. This often happened with community woodlot programs in India in the 1970s and early 1980s. In many of these projects, despite an approach ostensibly built on village participation, poor villagers commonly found that their time and labor were welcome but that the benefits went disproportionately to wealthier villagers who made a smaller contribution. More thought is needed on ways to ensure that participatory approaches are able to balance the claims of different groups.

How participation can be improved

How can the large benefits of participation be realized while minimizing the costs? Community organizations often require strengthening through technical assistance, management training, and gradually increased levels of responsibility. Several measures can enhance participation.

USE OF INDIGENOUS INSTITUTIONS. Indigenous institutions (such as the *subak,* or traditional groups of water users, in Bali) that are already involved in managing natural resources can be useful, particularly when decisions on land use have to be made. Where such institutions do not exist, it is often necessary to create them. All too often, however, user groups have been legislated into existence rather than built on existing social foundations. User groups can be effective only when they enjoy broadly based local support.

USE OF LOCAL VOLUNTARY ORGANIZATIONS. Among the strengths of community groups and NGOs are their ability to reach the rural poor in remote areas and to promote local participation; their effective use of low-cost technologies; and their innovativeness. They work best when they complement the public sector but may also have an important "watchdog" function, thereby influencing public policy. The disadvantages of NGOs include a generally weak financial base and administrative structure and limited technical capabilities. Many NGOs are small and by themselves cannot be expected to cover large populations. The challenge is to retain the NGOs' expertise and energy while simultaneously enlarging their financial and administrative bases.

INCREASED ACCESS TO INFORMATION. Many countries now support local involvement in environmental impact assessments. But if such consultations are to be effective, the people who are involved need to be well informed. Some ways to achieve that are (a) to share information with local communities at the early stage of identifying a project, (b) to discuss local worries with the affected communities, (c) to allow public comments on background studies, (d) to encourage public comments on the draft environmental assessment, and (e) to include hearings and comments in the final document. The World Bank expects its borrowers to arrange public discussion of environmental assessments prepared for the projects it finances.

INSTITUTIONAL REFORMS. The attitudes of bureaucracies often thwart the benefits of local participation. Forestry departments, for example, generally see as their mission protecting trees from people. Wildlife conservation agencies (sometimes justifiably) fail to distinguish local communities from game poachers. Often, the institutional units that have the best relations with local communities are themselves on the margins of their own agencies. Most technical agencies lack the skills to foster participation. High priority should therefore be given to increasing the organizational weight of units that specialize in participation, to hiring professional staff trained in the social sciences, and to providing institutional incentives for participation.

The following chapters describe particular areas of environmental concern. In each area, policies are available for mitigating the worst effects of pollution and degradation without sacrificing development. Although such policies may appear simple and logical, no one should underestimate the political difficulties entailed in implementing them. As this chapter has argued, governments can reduce those difficulties by introducing well-designed administrative structures for making and implementing environmental policy and by carefully building constituencies of support.

5 Sanitation and clean water

For many people in developing countries water supply, sanitation, and solid wastes are the most important of all environmental problems. More than 2 million deaths from diarrhea alone could be avoided each year if all people had reasonable water and sanitation services. And large economic and environmental costs are incurred in trying to compensate for poor-quality services.

This chapter argues that large gains—in environmental quality, health, equity, and direct economic returns—can be realized by adopting an approach that comprises four key elements:

- *Managing water resources better, taking account of economic efficiency and environmental sustainability*
- *Providing, at full cost, those "private" services that people want and are willing to pay for (including water supply and the collection of human excreta, wastewater, and solid wastes)*
- *Using scarce public funds only for those services (specifically, treatment and disposal of human excreta, wastewater, and solid wastes) that provide wider communal benefits*
- *Developing flexible and responsive institutional mechanisms for providing these services, with a larger role for community organizations and the private sector.*

Although the provision of clean water and sanitation is often omitted from the list of priority environmental challenges, in many parts of the developing world it ranks at the top. Two environmental issues are involved: the costs to human health and productivity of polluted water and inadequate sanitation and the stresses placed on water resources by rapidly growing human demands for water. This chapter argues that to address the first problem, the second must be tackled as well. This will require better management and more efficient use of water. It may mean that agriculture will have to do more with less water (as discussed in Chapter 7), and it will certainly demand a shift in how sanitation and water supply services are provided—the main theme of this chapter.

Water supply and sanitation as environmental priorities

Inadequate sanitation is a major cause of the degradation of the quality of groundwater and surface water described in Chapter 2. Economic growth leads to larger discharges of wastewater and solid wastes per capita. Inadequate investments in

waste collection and disposal mean that large quantities of waste enter both groundwater and surface water. Groundwater contamination is less visible but often more serious because it can take decades for polluted aquifers to cleanse themselves and because large numbers of people drink untreated groundwater.

More environmental damage occurs when people try to compensate for inadequate provision. The lack or unreliability of piped water causes households to sink their own wells, which often leads to overpumping and depletion. In cities such as Jakarta, where almost two-thirds of the population relies on groundwater, the water table has declined dramatically since the 1970s. In coastal areas this can cause saline intrusion, sometimes rendering the water permanently unfit for consumption. In, for example, Bangkok excessive pumping has also led to subsidence, cracked pavements, broken water and sewerage pipes, intrusion of seawater, and flooding.

Inadequate water supply also prompts people to boil water, thus using energy. The practice is especially common in Asia. In Jakarta more than $50 million is spent each year by households for this purpose—an amount equal to 1 percent of the city's GDP. Investments in water supply can therefore reduce fuelwood consumption and air pollution.

Effects on health

The health benefits from better water and sanitation, as noted in Chapter 2, are large. When services were improved in the industrial countries in the nineteenth and twentieth centuries, the impact on health was revolutionary. Life expectancy in French cities, for example, increased from about 32 years in 1850 to about 45 years in 1900, with the timing of changes corresponding closely to improvements in water supply and wastewater disposal (Figure 5.1). Today, adequate water and sanitation services are just as vital: diarrheal death rates are typically about 60 percent lower among children in households with adequate facilities than among those in households without such facilities. Box 5.1 describes the improvements that are critical for better health.

Effects on productivity

Improved environmental sanitation has economic benefits. Consider the case of sewage collection in Santiago, Chile. The principal justification for investments was the need to reduce the extraordi-

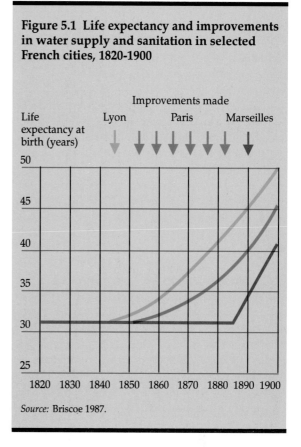

Figure 5.1 Life expectancy and improvements in water supply and sanitation in selected French cities, 1820-1900

Source: Briscoe 1987.

Box 5.1 Specific investments that matter for health

The potential health benefits from improved water and sanitation services are huge. What improvements must be made to secure these benefits?

• *Water quality.* Contrary to common belief, contamination of water in the home is relatively unimportant. What matters is whether the water coming out of the tap or pump is contaminated. In most developing countries the imperative is to get from "bad" quality (say, more than 1,000 fecal coliforms per 100 milliliters) to "moderate" quality (less than 10 fecal coliforms per 100 milliliters), not necessarily to meet the stringent quality standards of industrial countries.

• *Water availability.* As long as families have to go out of the yard to collect water, the quantities used will remain low (typically between 15 liters and 30 liters per capita per day). The use of water for personal hygiene usually increases only when availability rises to about

50 liters per capita per day and generally depends on getting the water delivered to the yard or house.

• *Excreta disposal.* It is necessary to distinguish among the effects on the household and on the neighborhood. For the household, the health impacts of improved sanitation facilities depend only on getting the excreta out of the house and are thus similar whether family members use an improved pit latrine, a cesspool overflowing into a street drain, or a conventional sewerage system. For the neighborhood, the key is the removal of excreta, a task done well by a wide range of technologies but badly by many commonly used systems (such as nightsoil collection and unemptied septic tanks). Because all the fecal-oral transmission routes are much more important when people live in close proximity to each other, the ill effects of poor environmental sanitation are greatest in high-density urban settlements.

narily high incidence of typhoid fever in the city. A secondary motive was to maintain access to the markets of industrial countries for Chile's increasingly important exports of fruit and vegetables. To ensure the sanitary quality of these exports, it was essential to stop using raw wastewater in their production. In the light of the current cholera epidemic in Latin America, this reasoning was prescient. In just the first ten weeks of the cholera epidemic in Peru, losses from reduced agricultural exports and tourism were estimated at $1 billion—more than three times the amount that the country had invested in water supply and sanitation services during the 1980s.

Improved access to water and sanitation also yields direct economic benefits. For many rural people, obtaining water is time-consuming and heavy work, taking up to 15 percent of women's time. Improvement projects have reduced the time substantially. In a village on the Mueda Plateau in Mozambique, for instance, the average time that women spent collecting water was reduced from 120 to 25 minutes a day. Family well-being was thus improved, as the time saved could be used to cultivate crops, tend a home garden, trade in the market, keep small livestock, care for children, or even rest. Because users clearly perceive these time savings, they are willing to pay substantial amounts (as discussed below) for easier access.

In the absence of formal services, people have to provide their own services, often at high cost. In Jakarta, for instance, about 800,000 households have installed septic tanks, each costing several hundred dollars (not counting the cost of the land). And in many cities and towns large numbers of people buy water from vendors. A review of vending in sixteen cities shows that the unit cost of vended water is always much higher than that of water from a piped city supply—from 4 to 100 times higher, with a median of about 12. The situation in Lima is typical; although a poor family uses only one-sixth as much water as a middle-class family, its monthly water bill is three times as large. Consequently, in the slums around many cities water costs the poor a large part of household income—18 percent in Onitsha, Nigeria, and 20 percent in Port-au-Prince, for example.

The economic costs of compensating for unreliable services—by building in-house storage facilities, sinking wells, or installing booster pumps (which can draw contaminated groundwater into the water distribution system)—are substantial. In Tegucigalpa, for example, the sum of such investments is so large that it would be enough to double

the number of deep wells providing water to the city. And the costs of compensating for poor water quality are great, too. In Bangladesh boiling drinking water would take 11 percent of the income of a family in the lowest quartile. With the outbreak of cholera in Peru the Ministry of Health has urged all residents to boil drinking water for ten minutes. The cost of doing so would amount to 29 percent of the average household income in a squatter settlement.

What needs to be done?

Investments in sanitation and water offer high economic, social, and environmental returns. Universal provision of these services should and could become a reality in the coming generation. But the next four decades will see urban populations in developing countries rise threefold and domestic demand for water increase fivefold. Current approaches will not meet these demands, and there is a real possibility that the numbers unserved could rise substantially, even while aquifers are depleted and rivers degraded. The remainder of this chapter discusses four key policy changes that need to be made.

Managing water resources better

When there was little competition for water, it was (correctly) used in large quantities for activities in which the value of a unit of water was relatively low. In many countries irrigated agriculture became the dominant "high-volume, low-value" user. Today about 73 percent of all water withdrawals (and higher proportions of consumptive use) are for irrigation. This share is even higher in low-income countries, as shown in Table 5.1. In most countries this water is provided at heavily subsidized prices, with users seldom paying more than 10 percent of operating costs.

As demand by households, industries, and farmers increases, governments find it hard to

Table 5.1 Sectoral water withdrawals, by country income group

Income group	Annual withdrawals per capita (cubic meters)	Withdrawals, by sector (percent)		
		Domestic	Industry	Agriculture
Low-income	386	4	5	91
Middle-income	453	13	18	69
High-income	1,167	14	47	39

Source: World Resources Institute 1990.

change existing arrangements. The allocation of water in all countries is a complex issue and is governed by legal and cultural traditions. Users typically have well-established rights. Reallocation is a contentious and ponderous process that generally responds to changes in demand only with long lags. Even though agricultural use of water has the lowest value per cubic meter, there is strong political opposition to diverting water from agriculture to other sectors. The result is that in many countries, industrial and developing alike, large volumes of water are used in irrigated agriculture, adding little economic value, while cities and industries, which would gladly pay more, cannot get enough.

This mismatch is most striking in the areas around large cities. In the western United States, for example, farmers in Arizona pay less than 1 cent for a cubic meter of water, while residents of the city of Phoenix pay about 25 cents. In the industrial heartland of China around Beijing and Tianjin 65 percent of water is used relatively inefficiently for low-value irrigation, while huge expenditures are contemplated to bring water from other river basins to the cities.

Paradoxically, there is good news in these distortions. Their very size indicates that urban shortages could be met with only modest reallocation. In Arizona, for instance, the purchase of the water rights from just one farm is sufficient to provide water for tens of thousands of urban dwellers. Because of the low value of water in irrigated agriculture, the loss of this marginal water has little overall effect on farm output. To help transfers, new market-driven methods for reallocation have been developed. When a recent drought dangerously reduced available water, the state of California set up a voluntary "water bank" that purchased water from farmers and sold it to urban areas. The farmers made a profit by selling the water for more than it was worth to them, while the cities got water at a cost well below that of other sources of supply.

In developing countries, too, a start is being made in applying innovative methods for managing water resources. China's State Science and Technology Commission found that the economic rate of return to a cubic meter of water used for agriculture was less than 10 percent of the return to municipal and industrial users. Once agricultural and urban users accepted that they had to look at water as an economic commodity with a price, progress—including reallocation—was possible. And Jakarta has been reasonably successful in reducing the overpumping of its aquifers by registering groundwater users (especially commercial and industrial establishments) and by introducing a groundwater levy.

The striking features of these "market-based" reallocation methods are that they are voluntary, they yield economic benefits for both buyers and sellers, they reduce the environmental problems caused by profligate use of water in irrigation, and they lessen the need for more dams.

Without effective management of water resources, the cost of supplying water to cities will continue to rise. The most dramatic examples will be in large and growing urban areas. In Mexico City, where much water is used for irrigation, the city has to contemplate pumping water over an elevation exceeding 1,000 meters into the Valley of Mexico; in Lima upstream pollution has increased treatment costs by about 30 percent; in Shanghai water intakes have already been moved upstream more than 40 kilometers at a cost of about $300 million; and in Amman the most recent works involve pumping water up 1,200 meters from a site about 40 kilometers from the city. A recent analysis of the costs of raw water for urban areas in World Bank–financed projects (Figure 5.2) shows that the unit cost of water would more than double—and in some cases more than triple—under a new water development project.

Industries and households also need to be given incentives to use water efficiently. Cities, like farmers, have tended to take demand as given and to see as their task increasing supplies to meet it. As was the case with energy twenty years ago, little attention is paid to conservation and demand management in the water sector. This is both economically and environmentally unsound. Consider the case of Washington, D.C. In the 1960s the U.S. government concluded that sixteen dams and more than $400 million were required to meet the water needs of the metropolitan area. Because of resistance from environmentalists to the construction of the dams, the plan had to be reconsidered. Eventually the number of dams was reduced to one and the total cost of the scheme to $30 million. The key changes were a revised plan for managing demand during droughts and more efficient operating rules. This illustrates once again that better economics and a better environment are compatible.

Experience in industrial and developing countries alike shows the potential for using water more cost-effectively in industry. In the United States withdrawals of fresh water by manufactur-

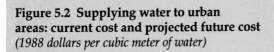

Figure 5.2 Supplying water to urban areas: current cost and projected future cost
(1988 dollars per cubic meter of water)

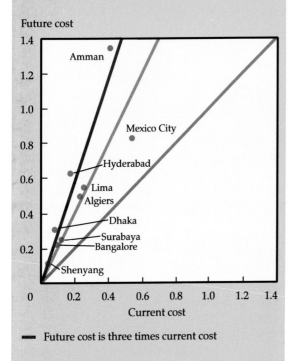

Note: Cost excludes treatment and distribution. "Current cost" refers to cost at the time data were gathered. "Future cost" is a projection of cost under a new water development project.
Source: World Bank data.

ing industries are expected to be 62 percent less in 2000 than in 1977, primarily because of the increased costs industries have to pay for disposing of industrial wastewater. In São Paulo, Brazil, the imposition of effluent charges induced three industrial plants to reduce their water demand by between 42 and 62 percent. Figure 5.3 shows how in Beijing a variety of conservation measures in industries and households could release large quantities of water at a substantially lower unit cost than the cost under the next supply augmentation project.

A particularly important conservation alternative is reclamation of wastewater. Reclamation of water for urban, industrial, and agricultural use is attractive both for improving the environment and for reducing the costs of water supply. Reclaimed wastewater has been used for many years for flushing toilets in residential and commercial buildings in Japan and Singapore. A recent reclamation scheme in the Vallejo area of Mexico City (Box 5.2) illustrates the great potential, both economic and environmental, of wastewater reuse—and, to anticipate a theme developed below, the scope for the private sector.

At present, in most countries management of water resources is fragmented (industrial users, for example, do not have to take account of the costs that their use and pollution of water imposes

---

Box 5.2 Environmental improvement, management of water resources, and the private sector in Mexico

In 1989, faced with rising water prices and potential water shortages, a group of companies in the Vallejo area of Mexico City sought an alternative to water supplied by the public agency. At about the same time, the Mexican government decided to involve the private sector in water supply and wastewater treatment.

The industrialists realized that if sewage flows could be adequately treated, this could provide a cost-effective and reliable source of industrial water (and, incidentally, could improve the environment by treating wastes and reducing the need for new water supplies). Twenty-six Vallejo companies organized a new for-profit firm, Aguas Industriales de Vallejo (AIV), to rehabilitate an old municipal wastewater treatment plant. Each shareholder company contributed equity on the basis of its water requirements, with total equity amounting to $900,000.

AIV operates the plant under a ten-year concession from the government. The plant now provides 60 liters per second to shareholders and 30 liters per second to the government as payment for the concession. The concession agreement gives AIV the right to withdraw up to 200 liters per second of wastewater from the municipal trunk sewer. AIV plans to double the plant's capacity within five years at an estimated cost of $1.5 million. The firm provides treated water to shareholder companies at a price equivalent to 75 percent of the water tariff charged by the government (currently, $0.95 per cubic meter).

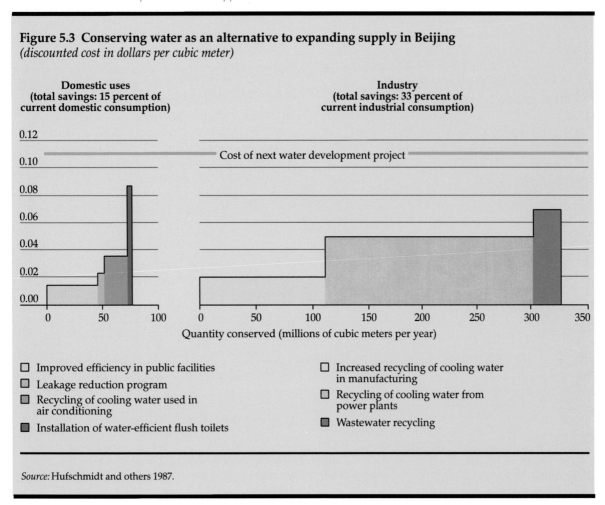

Figure 5.3 Conserving water as an alternative to expanding supply in Beijing
(discounted cost in dollars per cubic meter)

Source: Hufschmidt and others 1987.

on domestic users downstream) and is done by "command and control" (most allocations are set by administrative fiat). The challenge is to replace this system with one that recognizes the unitary nature of the resource and its economic value and that relies heavily on prices and other incentives to encourage efficient use of water.

Providing services that people want and are willing to pay for

During the United Nations Drinking Water and Sanitation Decade of the 1980s, coverage increased (see Chapter 2). But about 1 billion people still lack an adequate water supply, and about 1.7 billion people do not have adequate sanitation facilities. The quality of service often remains poor. In Latin America, for example, levels of leakage and pipe breakage are, respectively, four times and twenty

times higher than is normal in industrial countries. In Lima 70 percent of the water distribution districts provide inadequate water pressure. In Mexico 20 percent of the water supply systems have unreliable chlorination facilities.

What has been done

Developing countries cannot afford to provide all people with in-house piped water and sewerage connections. The policy has usually been to concentrate primarily on the (subsidized) provision of water, often through house connections for the better-off and standpipes or handpumps for the poor.

Consumers in most industrial countries pay all of the recurrent costs (operations, maintenance, and debt service) of both water and sewerage services. They also pay most of the capital costs of water supply and a large (typically over half) and rising portion of the capital costs of sewerage. In developing countries, by contrast, consumers pay far less. A recent review of World Bank–financed projects showed that the effective price charged for water is only about 35 percent of the average cost of supplying it. The proportion of total project financing generated by utilities points in the same direction: internal cash generation accounts for only 8 percent of project costs in Asia, 9 percent in Sub-Saharan Africa, 21 percent in Latin America and the Caribbean, and 35 percent in the Middle East and North Africa.

A new approach

In urban areas there is abundant evidence that most people want on-plot water supplies of reasonable reliability and are willing to pay the full cost of these services. In some areas this standard solution will have to be adjusted and special efforts made to accommodate poor people. In Latin America and, more recently, in Morocco utilities have helped poor families to install a connection and in-house plumbing by giving them the option of paying over several years. Another option is a ''social tariff'' whereby the better-off cross-subsi-

---

Box 5.3 Willingness to pay for water in rural areas

The World Bank, in conjunction with other agencies, recently completed a study of rural water demand in Brazil, Haiti, India, Nigeria, Pakistan, Tanzania, and Zimbabwe. The study suggests that where water demand is concerned, there are four broad categories of rural community.

Type I: willingness to pay for private connections is high and willingness to pay for public water points is low. Communities in this group offer exciting possibilities because people want and are willing to pay the full costs of reliable water service delivered by way of private metered connections into the house or yard. The availability of free public taps (for the poor) will not appreciably affect the demand for private connections. The appropriate strategy is to offer private connections and even encourage them (specifically, by amortizing connection costs in monthly water bills); to recover all costs through the tariff; and to deliver a reliable service. A striking finding from the World Bank study is that this category is larger than is commonly assumed; it probably includes many communities in Southeast Asia, South Asia, Latin America, and the Middle East and North Africa.

Type II: only a minority of households are willing to pay the full costs of private connections, but most households are willing to pay the full costs of public water points. Although overall willingness to pay for improved water service is considerable in Type II communities, users vary greatly in their willingness to pay for different levels of service. In these villages the provision of free public water points (such as standpipes, wells, or boreholes) would significantly reduce the demand for private connections. When there is heavy reliance on public water points, some charge must be levied on water from these sources in order to finance the system. Here the greatest challenge is to devise revenue collection systems that are sensitive to peoples' preferences about when they want to buy water and how they want to pay for it. Kiosks appear to be an attractive and flexible

option for many households. Those who wish to have house connections should be able to do so but must have metered connections and must pay the full cost. Many of the better-off communities in Sub-Saharan Africa and poorer communities in Asia and Latin America probably fall into this category.

Type III: households' willingness to pay for improved service is high but not high enough to pay the full costs of an improved service. This group typically includes poor communities in arid areas in South Asia and Sub-Saharan Africa. As in Type II villages, people are willing to pay a relatively large share of their income for improved water service. The distinction is that the costs of supply are so high, as a result of a combination of aridity and low population densities, that improved systems will not be built and operated without subsidies. Given the high priority that people give to improved water supply, if transfers were available from central government or from foreign donors, households would typically choose to spend the funds on an improved water supply. The primary service offered in such communities would be public taps, wells, or boreholes, although in piped systems metered yard taps should be allowed, with tariffs set to recover full costs.

Type IV: willingness to pay for any kind of improved service is low. This group typically includes poor communities in which (a) traditional water supplies are considered more or less satisfactory by the population or (b) water supply is seen as the financial responsibility of the government. In such communities self-financed improved water supplies are not feasible. Given the low priority accorded improved water supply, available subsidies could be better used in providing other, more highly valued infrastructural services. For the time being, the appropriate rural water supply policy in such cases is simply to do nothing. For the second category, once government paternalism ceases, communities may express a willingness to pay and will become Type II communities.

Users want reliable supplies

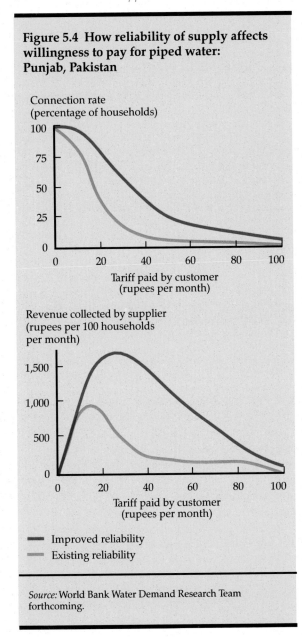

Figure 5.4 How reliability of supply affects willingness to pay for piped water: Punjab, Pakistan

Connection rate
(percentage of households)
100
75
50
25
0
0
20
40
60
80
100
Tariff paid by customer
(rupees per month)
Revenue collected by supplier
(rupees per 100 households
per month)
1,500
1,000
500
0
0
20
40
60
80
100
Tariff paid by customer
(rupees per month)
Improved reliability
Existing reliability

Source: World Bank Water Demand Research Team forthcoming.

Credit for connections is vital

Figure 5.5 How spreading connection costs over time affects willingness to pay for piped water: Kerala, India

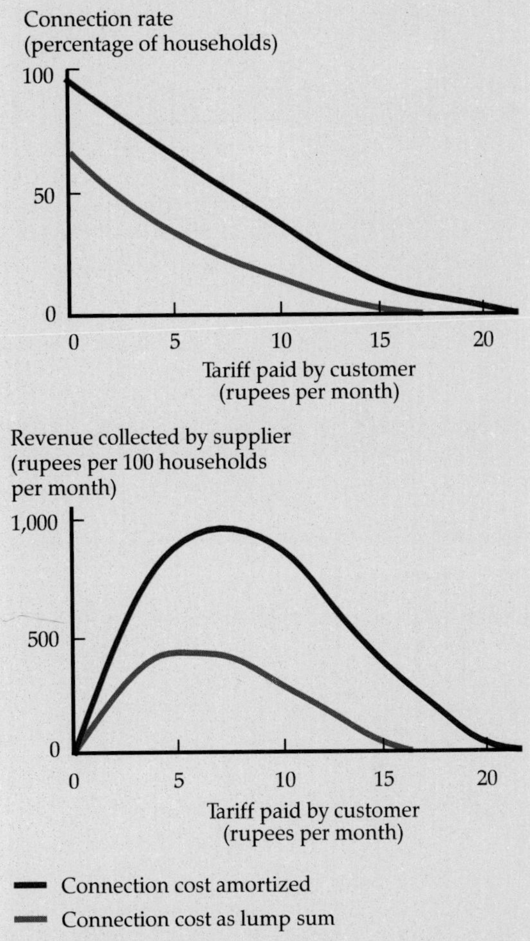

Connection rate
(percentage of households)
100
50
0
0
5
10
15
20
Tariff paid by customer
(rupees per month)
Revenue collected by supplier
(rupees per 100 households
per month)
1,000
500
0
0
5
10
15
20
Tariff paid by customer
(rupees per month)
Connection cost amortized
Connection cost as lump sum

Source: World Bank Water Demand Research Team forthcoming.

dize the poor. Properly executed, such policies are both sensible (since the poor use relatively little water) and compassionate. But there are dangers. Social tariffs can lead to a general spread of subsidies. And the assignment of noncommercial objectives to a public enterprise generally has an insidious effect on the achievement of all its objectives, commercial and noncommercial alike.

It is widely assumed that the demand situation in rural areas is quite different, that there people have only a "basic need" which can be met with a public tap or handpump. But a recent multicountry study by the World Bank of rural water demand (Box 5.3) found that most rural people want and are willing to pay for a relatively high level of service (yard taps). As shown in Figure 5.4, they will pay substantially more if that service is reliable. And, as Figure 5.5 illustrates, more people will make use of improved water supplies if innovative financing mechanisms are employed.

Twenty years of experience with the provision of water in rural Thailand (Box 5.4) shows how it is possible to break out of a "low-level equilibrium trap" (in which a low level of services is provided,

Box 5.4 Breaking out of the "low-level equilibrium trap" in northeast Thailand

A well-documented case in northeast Thailand, covering a twenty-year period, demonstrates the importance of discovering what users of rural water services want rather than making assumptions about the answers.

Since the people in the area were poor, the initial project was intended to provide protected water at the lowest possible cost. Because groundwater is abundant in the region, the technology chosen was handpumps. After five years most of the handpumps were not working, and water use habits were largely unchanged. In a follow-up phase motor pumps provided piped water at community standpipes. Again, the project failed. Five years after implementation 50 percent of the systems were not working at all, and another 25 percent operated intermittently.

As was consistent with conventional assumptions, the failures were attributed to technologies that were too complex to maintain and to the inability of the villagers to pay for improved supplies. Gradually, however, it became apparent that the main problem was not the capabilities of the villagers but the fact that the service being offered was not what they wanted. They

did not want handpumps, which were not considered an improvement over the traditional rope-and-bucket system. And standpipes, being no closer than their traditional sources, offered no obvious benefits. Only piped water to yardtaps could meet people's aspirations.

In the next project yardtaps were allowed, with the users paying the full costs of connection. Five years later the verdict was in: 90 percent of the systems were functioning reliably, 80 percent of the people were served by yardtaps, meters had been installed, and locally adapted charging systems had been developed. Not only were the systems well maintained, but because the service was so popular, many systems had extended distribution lines to previously unserved areas.

In other words, in terms of the typology discussed in Box 5.3, when these (poor) people were treated as "Type IV" cases, the result was the familiar low-level equilibrium trap. When they were treated as "Type I" communities, the cycle was broken, and a high-level equilibrium was established.

willingness to pay and thus revenues are low, and the operation consequently deteriorates) to a "high-level equilibrium" in which users get a high level of service, pay for it, and maintain the desired system.

Increasing investments in sanitation

Public investment in water supply and sanitation accounts for 10 percent of total public investment in developing countries, or about 0.6 percent of GDP. Spending on sewerage and sanitation accounts for substantially less than one-fifth of lending in World Bank–financed projects. Most of this has been for sewage collection, with little spent on treatment. An indication of the huge underinvestment in treatment is that only 2 percent of sewage in Latin America is treated. Similarly, only a small proportion (typically 5 percent in developing countries, compared with 25 percent in industrial countries) of all spending on solid wastes is directed to their safe disposal.

Taking account of demand

There is abundant evidence that urban families are willing to pay substantial amounts for the removal of excreta and wastewater from their neighbor-

hoods. People want privacy, convenience, and status; polluted water smells unpleasant and fosters mosquitos; and the installation of sewers typically increases property prices. As with water supply, so with sanitation: where public provision is absent, people pay significant amounts for privately provided services. Even in poor cities the amounts paid are considerable. In Kumasi, Ghana, for example, the use of public latrines and bucket latrines accounts for large recurrent expenditures—about 2.5 and 1 percent, respectively, of family income. In Kumasi and in Ouagadougou families are willing to pay about 2 percent of household income for an improved sanitation system. This is roughly the amount paid for water and for electricity. The examples of northeast Brazil and of Orangi, Pakistan, discussed in Boxes 5.5 and 5.6 show the willingness of households to pay for having wastewater carried out of the neighborhood (by means of a low-cost sewer).

Expanding the menu of supply options

A vital element of a demand-driven sanitation strategy is to expand the menu of services from which users can choose.

In city centers there is no alternative to costly waterborne systems. But even in relatively poor

Box 5.5 Innovative sewerage in northeast Brazil: the condominial system

The condominial system is the brainchild of José Carlos de Melo, a socially committed engineer from Recife. The name "condominial" was chosen for two reasons. First, a block of houses was treated like a horizontal apartment building—or *condominiais*, in Portuguese. Second, "Condominial" was the title of a popular Brazilian soap opera and so was associated with the best in urban life! As is evident in Box figure 5.5, the result is a layout radically different from the conventional system, with a shorter grid of smaller and shallower "feeder" sewers running through backyards and with the effects of shallower connections to the mains rippling through the system. These innovations cut construction costs to between 20 and 30 percent of those of a conventional system.

The more fundamental and radical innovation, however, is the active involvement of the population in choosing the level of service and in operating and maintaining the "feeder" infrastructure. Families can choose to continue with their current sanitation system, to connect to a conventional waterborne system (which usually means a holding tank discharging into an open street drain), or to connect to a "condominial" system.

If a family chooses to connect to a condominial system, it has to pay a connection charge (financed by the water company) of, say, X cruzados, and a monthly tariff of Y cruzados. If it wants a conventional connection, it has to pay an initial cost of about 3X cruzados and a monthly tariff of 3Y cruzados, reflecting the higher capital and operating costs of the conventional system.

Families are free to continue with their current system. In most cases, however, those families that initially choose not to connect eventually change their minds. Either they succumb to heavy pressure from their neighbors, or they find the buildup of wastewater in and around their houses intolerable once the (connected) neighbors fill in the rest of the open drain.

Individual households are responsible for maintaining the feeder sewers, with the formal agency tending only to the trunk mains. This has several related positive results. First, it increases the communities' sense of responsibility for the system. Second, the misuse of any portion of the feeder system (by, say, putting solid wastes down the toilet) soon shows up as a blockage in the neighbor's portion of the sewer. The consequence is rapid, direct, and informed feedback to the misuser. This virtually eliminates the need to "educate" the users of the system about dos and don'ts and results in fewer blockages than in conventional systems. And third, because of the greatly reduced responsibility of the utility, operating costs are much lower.

The condominial system is now providing service to hundreds of thousands of urban people in northeast Brazil. The danger is that the clever engineering may be seen as "the system." Where the community and organizational aspects have been missing, the technology has worked poorly (as in Joinville, Santa Catarina) or not at all (as in the Baixada Fluminense in Rio de Janeiro).

Box figure 5.5 Conventional and condominial sewage collection systems

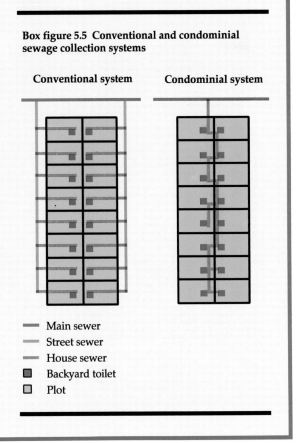

Conventional system	Condominial system

— Main sewer
— Street sewer
— House sewer
■ Backyard toilet
□ Plot

cities the difficulties are not insoluble. In Fortaleza, a poor city in northeast Brazil, developers of all high-rise buildings are required to, and do, install package sewage collection and treatment systems. The point here is not that this is a good technical solution but that even in a relatively poor city, developers can easily absorb such costs and pass them on to those who purchase units in the buildings.

Beyond the urban core, however, conventional sewerage systems (with average household costs anywhere from $300 to $1,000) are too expensive for most developing countries. In recent decades efforts have been made to develop technological alternatives. Most of this work has concerned the onsite disposal of excreta. Pour-flush latrines and ventilated improved pit (VIP) latrines are often the technologies of choice—they provide good service (privacy and few odors) at reasonable cost (typically about $100 to $200 per unit), and their installation and functioning does not depend on the municipality or other organization. At even lower cost, there are yet simpler improvements, such as the latrine slab program that proved successful in Mozambique.

For a variety of reasons—high housing densities, impermeable soils, and the need to dispose of considerable quantities of domestic wastewater—onsite solutions do not function well in many urban areas. Sewage and wastewater collect in the streets and in low-lying areas, creating serious aesthetic and health problems. And in many settings people aspire to "the real thing"—waterborne sewerage.

Current sanitation choices include a Rolls-Royce (conventional sewerage), a motorcycle (an improved latrine), and a bicycle (an unimproved latrine). What is missing is the Volkswagen—something that provides much the same service as the Rolls Royce but that many more people can afford. Several such technologies are being developed:

- Effluent sewerage is a hybrid between a septic tank and a conventional sewerage system. Its distinctive feature is a tank, located between the house sewer and the street sewer, that retains the solids, thereby allowing smaller sewers to be laid at flatter gradients and with fewer manholes. Such systems have been widely used in small towns in the United States and Australia and in Argentina, Brazil, Colombia, India, Mozambique, and Zambia. The (limited) cost data suggest that solids-free sewerage costs about 20 percent less than conventional sewerage.

- Simplified sewerage, developed in São Paulo, allows smaller, shallower, flatter sewers with fewer manholes. This simplified design works as well as conventional sewerage but costs about 30 percent less. It is now routinely used in Brazil.

- The condominial system described in Box 5.5 has been developed and applied in northeast Brazil. It comprises shallow, small-diameter backyard sewers laid at flat gradients and costs about 70 percent less than a conventional system.

- The Orangi Pilot Project in Karachi (described in Box 5.6) adapted the principles of effluent sewerage and simplified sewerage to the realities of a hilly squatter settlement in Karachi. The result—not just the result of clever engineering—was a drastic reduction in the cost of sewers, from the $1,000 per household that was standard in Karachi to less than $50 per household (excluding the cost of the trunk sewers). The achievement is extraordinary—about 600,000 people in Orangi are now served with self-financed sewers.

Investing in waste disposal

There is an important difference between "private goods" (including water supply and even wastewater and solid waste collection), in which the primary benefits accrue to individual households, and waste treatment and disposal, in which the benefits accrue to the community at large. In the first case willingness to pay is an appropriate guide to the level of service to be provided, and the main source of finance should be direct charges to the users. In the case of waste disposal, however, public financing is essential. Governments that subsidize "private" water supply and wastewater collection services are left with less money to finance treatment and disposal services.

No developing country, however, will have the luxury of collecting and treating wastewater from all households. Because the costs of meeting such goals are extremely high, even in industrial countries the full population is not served by wastewater treatment facilities; coverage is only 66 percent in Canada and 52 percent in France. In making the inevitable choices, the best ratio of benefits to costs will usually be achieved by concentrating most public funds on waste treatment in large cities, especially those that lie upstream from large populations.

In recent decades some important advances have been made in innovative sewage treatment processes. At the lower end of the spectrum is the stabilization pond, a technology that has proved robust, easy to operate, and (where land is not costly) relatively inexpensive. A promising intermediate (in both cost and operational complexity) is the upflow anaerobic sludge blanket, which has performed well in Brazil and Colombia. The point is the importance of developing technical solutions that are adapted to the climatic, economic, and managerial realities of developing countries.

Rethinking institutional arrangements

A recent comprehensive review of forty years of World Bank experience in water and sanitation pinpoints "institutional failure" as the most frequent and persistent cause of poor performance by public utilities. This section deals with the key areas for institutional reform.

Box 5.6 Innovative sewerage in a Karachi squatter settlement: the Orangi Pilot Project

In the early 1980s Akhter Hameed Khan, a world-renowned community organizer, began working in the slums of Karachi. He asked what problem he could help resolve and was told that "the streets were filled with excreta and wastewater, making movement difficult and creating enormous health hazards." What did the people want, and how did they intend to get it? he asked. What they wanted was clear—"people aspired to a traditional sewerage system. . . it would be difficult to get them to finance anything else." And how they would get it, too, was clear—they would have Dr. Khan persuade the Karachi Development Authority (KDA) to provide it free, as it did (or so the poor perceived) to the richer areas of the city.

Dr. Khan spent months going with representatives of the community to petition the KDA to provide the service. When it was clear that this would never happen, Dr. Khan was ready to work with the community to find alternatives. (He would later describe this first step as the most important thing he did in Orangi—liberating, as he put it, the people from the immobilizing myths of government promises.)

With a small amount of core external funding, the Orangi Pilot Project (OPP) was started. It was clear what services the people wanted; the task was to reduce the costs to affordable levels and to develop organizations that could provide and operate the systems. On the technical side, the achievements of the OPP architects and engineers were remarkable and innovative. Thanks partly to the elimination of corruption and the provision of labor by community members, the costs (for an in-house sanitary latrine and house sewer on the plot and underground sewers in the lanes and streets) were less than $50 per household.

The related organizational achievements are equally impressive. OPP staff members have played a catalytic role: they explain the benefits of sanitation and the technical possibilities to residents, conduct research, and provide technical assistance. The OPP staff never handle the community's money. (The total costs of the OPP's operations amounted, even in the project's early years, to less than 15 percent of the amount invested by the community.) The households' responsibilities include financing their share of the costs, participating in construction, and electing a "lane manager" who typically represents about fifteen households. Lane committees, in turn, elect members of neighborhood committees (typically representing about 600 houses), which manage the secondary sewers.

The early successes achieved by the project created a "snowball" effect, in part because of the increased value of properties with sewerage systems. As the power of the OPP-related organizations increased, they were able to put pressure on the municipality to provide funds for the construction of trunk sewers.

The Orangi Pilot Project has led to the provision of sewerage services to more than 600,000 poor people in Karachi and to recent initiatives by several municipalities in Pakistan to follow the OPP method and, according to OPP leader Arif Hasan, "have government behave like an NGO." Even in Karachi the mayor now formally accepts the principle of "internal" development by the residents and "external" development (including trunk sewers and treatment) by the municipality.

Improving the performance of public utilities

A World Bank review of more than 120 sector projects over twenty-three years concludes that only in four countries—Botswana, Korea, Singapore, and Tunisia—have public water and sewerage utilities reached acceptable levels of performance. A few examples illustrate how serious the situation is:

• In Accra only 130 connections were made to a sewerage system designed to serve 2,000 connections.
• In Caracas and Mexico City an estimated 30 percent of connections are not registered.
• Unaccounted-for water, which amounts to 8 percent in Singapore, is 58 percent in Manila and about 40 percent in most Latin American cities. For Latin America as a whole, such water losses cost between $1 billion and $1.5 billion in revenue forgone every year.
• The number of employees per 1,000 water connections is between two and three in Western Europe and about four in a well-run developing country utility (Santiago) but between ten and twenty in most Latin American utilities.

Financial performance is equally poor. A recent review of Bank projects found that borrowers often broke their financial performance covenants. A corollary is that the shortfalls have to be met through large injections of public money. In Brazil, from the mid-1970s to mid-1980s about $1 billion a year of public monies was invested in the water sector. The annual federal subsidy to Mexico City for water and sewerage services amounts to more than $1 billion a year, or 0.6 percent of national GDP.

Public utilities play a dominant role in the provision of water and sanitation services throughout the world. There are many examples of such utilities working effectively in industrial countries and, as described above, a few cases in developing countries. An essential requirement for effective performance is that both the utility and the regulatory body (essential for such natural monopolies) be free from undue political interference. In the case of the utility the vital issue is managerial autonomy, particularly as regards personnel policies; in the case of the regulatory body, it is the setting of reasonable tariffs. Although this recipe is simple and has been well tested in many industrial countries, it has been extraordinarily difficult to implement in developing countries other than those with high levels of governance. Sometimes utilities and regulators are nominally autonomous, but usually key policies (on investments, personnel policies, and tariffs, for instance) are effectively made by government and heavily influenced by short-term political considerations.

Many projects financed by external agencies have addressed the problems of public water utilities through sizable action plans, technical assistance components, and conditionality. Some of these efforts, such as that undertaken recently by Sri Lanka's National Water Supply and Drainage Board, have led to significant improvements in performance. As with public enterprises in other sectors, however, most of these efforts failed because—in the words of a recent Bank review—"public enterprises . . . are key elements of patronage systems, . . . overstaffing is often rife, and appointments to senior management positions are frequently made on the basis of political connections rather than merit." And things have been getting worse rather than better. Achievement of institutional objectives in World Bank–financed water and sanitation projects fell from about two in three projects in the late 1970s to less than one in two projects ten years later.

Improving the performance of public utilities nevertheless remains an important goal, for two reasons. First, in the medium term public utilities will continue to provide services to many. Second, improvement in the performance of public utilities is often a precondition if private operators are to be induced to participate.

Separating provision and regulation

Experience in industrial countries shows that a central problem in improving environmental quality is that the public sector acts both as supplier of water and wastewater services and as environmental regulator—it is both gamekeeper and poacher. The results of this conflict of interest are similar throughout the world. In England and Wales prosecutions of those responsible for sewage treatment were rare when the river basin authorities were responsible for water resource management, environmental protection, and services. In 1989 private companies were given responsibility for the delivery of water and sewerage services (with public agencies retaining regulatory authority). Since then, fines have been increased substantially and violators have been prosecuted. The other side of the separation of powers is that service delivery agencies are, in the process, liberated from serving multiple tasks and can pursue well-defined and specific objectives.

Expanding the role of the private sector

Increased private sector involvement is warranted in two areas. One is in services to public utilities. In industrial countries the engineering of public works is dominated by private firms, which depend for their survival on their reputation for performance and which assume legal liability for the consequences of any professional negligence. These factors provide powerful incentives for supplying cost-effective, high-quality services and concurrently furnish a stringent environment for the supervised apprenticeship training that is a required part of professional certification in these countries. By contrast, in many developing countries (particularly in Asia and Africa) the engineering of public works is dominated by large public sector bureaucracies. Employment security is total, promotion is by seniority alone, good work goes unrecognized, poor work is not subject to sanctions, and an atmosphere of lethargy prevails. The direct consequence is the construction of high-cost, low-quality facilities; the indirect effects include a weak professional labor force. The obvious answers are, first, to decrease the direct involvement of the government in public works and, second, to nurture a competitive engineering consultancy sector.

More private involvement in the operation of water, sewerage, and solid waste companies is also warranted. Many industrial countries have found it difficult to reform public enterprises, except as part of a move to privatize them. Indeed, privatization is increasingly seen as a way not only to effect performance improvements but also to lock in the gains.

In developing countries there has been some experience with private sector operation of water and sanitation utilities. Côte d'Ivoire has been a pioneer—SODECI, in Abidjan, is considered one of the best-run utilities in Africa. After Macao's water utility was privatized in 1985, performance improved dramatically; the percentage of unaccounted-for water fell by 50 percent over six years. Guinea, which recently let a lease contract for supplying water to its principal cities, experienced dramatic improvements in the financial condition of the utility in just the first eighteen months as a result of raising the efficiency of bill collection from 15 to 70 percent.

Other countries have taken more incremental approaches. EMOS, the utility serving Santiago, has used private contracts for functions such as meter reading, pipe maintenance, billing, and vehicle leasing. As a result, it has a high staff productivity rate—three to six times higher than that for other companies in the region. Many other countries, faced with persistently poor performance by their public utilities, are seriously considering greater private sector involvement, following, in general, variations of the French model. For example, in Latin America, concession contracts are currently being let for the supply of water and sewerage services in Buenos Aires and Caracas.

Private involvement in the sector is not a panacea and is never simple. In the United Kingdom water privatization is generally considered the most complex of all privatizations undertaken. In developing countries there are formidable problems. For the private operator the risk involved is typically high. In addition to the obvious political and macroeconomic risks, knowledge about the condition of the assets is usually only rudimentary, and there is uncertainty about the government's compliance with the terms of the contract. Groups such as existing agencies and labor unions that stand to lose from greater private sector involvement often strongly oppose privatization.

For the government, too, there are problems. Because of economies of scale, it is virtually impossible to have direct competition among suppliers in a specific area. Countries have tried a variety of solutions: in France, there is periodic competition for markets, and in England and Wales, economic regulators reward efficiency by comparing the relative performance of different companies (a practice that is unlikely to be applicable elsewhere). In addition, in many developing countries it is often difficult to attract private sector interest. Only a handful of firms compete internationally for such contracts.

The case for private sector involvement is stronger still in the solid waste collection business. Whereas foreign control of water supply is often perceived to involve losing sovereignty over a strategic sector, no one cares if foreigners pick up the garbage. In addition, for populations of more than about 50,000 there are no economies of scale and thus no natural monopoly. Experience in many countries—including Argentina, Brazil, Canada, Chile, Colombia, Japan, Switzerland, and the United States—has shown that the private sector almost invariably collects solid wastes more efficiently than municipalities. Unit costs for public systems are 50 to 200 percent higher, with the private sector efficiency gains apparently greatest in the developing countries listed.

Increasing community involvement

Community groups and other NGOs also have an important role to play in the supply of water and sanitation services and the collection of wastes. As the condominial (Box 5.5) and Orangi (Box 5.6) examples show, in the urban fringe the most productive relationship between community groups and the formal sector is that of partnership, with the formal sector responsible for the "external" or "trunk" infrastructure and the community paying for, providing, and managing the "internal" or "feeder" infrastructure.

Because many water and sanitation services are monopolies, consumers cannot force suppliers to be accountable by giving their business to a competitor. To give consumers a voice in the political process, consumers' associations and ratepayers' boards are vital. Paradoxically, because there is such an obvious need for oversight of the activities of a private operator of a natural monopoly, greater private sector involvement stimulates greater consumer involvement. In the United Kingdom, for example, water users have had a much greater say in running the industry since privatization.

In recent years external agencies and governments alike have become aware that in rural areas involvement of the users is essential if water supplies are to be sustained. Generally it has been assumed that support to rural communities—in the form of information, motivation, and technical assistance—will come from the government. The difficulty is that governments, especially in rural areas, are often weak, and their officials rarely have an incentive to provide support. Here the private sector (including NGOs) may be able to help.

Figure 5.6 Safe water and adequate sanitation: three scenarios, 1990-2030

Population without safe water

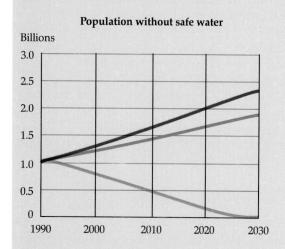

Population without adequate sanitation

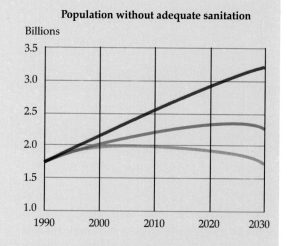

▬▬ "Business as usual" scenario

▬▬ Scenario with accelerated investment in water supply and sanitation services[a]

▬▬ Scenario with accelerated investment and efficiency reforms[b]

Note: Assumptions are as follows: growth of per capita income and population as in Chapter 1; per capita income elasticity, 0.3; price elasticity, -0.25; initial prices 60 percent of marginal costs, gradually rising to efficiency levels over a twenty-five-year period; initial supply costs 50 percent higher than with good practices (due to managerial inefficiencies), gradually being reduced in step with price efficiency reforms; and marginal costs rising at 3 percent per year.
a. Investment in water supply increases 30 percent, and investment in sanitation services increases 50 percent over the period.
b. To realize this scenario in low-income countries, efficiency reforms - and the resulting increase in investment shares - would need to be greater than average.
Source: World Bank estimates, based on Anderson and Cavendish, background paper.

Several promising examples of the involvement of small-scale private operators in developing countries have emerged:

• In rural Pakistan about 3 million families have wells fitted with pumps, many of which are motorized. The water supplies are paid for in full by the families, and all the equipment is provided and serviced by a vibrant local private sector industry.

• In Lesotho the government trained bricklayers to build improved pit latrines. Government banks also provided (unsubsidized) credit to finance the latrines. The program has been a singular success, thanks mainly to the aggressive role of the bricklayers in expanding their markets (and providing services as well).

• In West Africa a private handpump manufacturer has developed a "Sears Roebuck"–type scheme whereby purchase of a pump comes with five years of support, including training and the provision of spare parts. Later on, the community will be able to maintain the pump and will purchase the necessary spare parts from local traders. Because the private sector agent has clear incentives for providing services effectively, this arrangement may work better than government support to the communities.

Finally, women have a central role to play in these reforms. In most countries the collection of water has been considered "women's work" (except where the water is sold!). Only recently, however, have systematic efforts been made to involve women in project identification, development, maintenance, and upkeep. The results have generally been encouraging. In an urban slum in Zambia a women's organization improved drainage around public taps. Women have been trained as caretakers for handpumps in Bangladesh, India, Kenya, Lesotho, and Sudan. In Mozambique women engineers and pump mechanics perform alongside, and as effectively as, their male counterparts. In Sri Lanka women's cooperatives have been set up to assemble and maintain a locally manufactured handpump. Women's cooperatives manage communal standpipes and collect money to pay for metered supplies in Honduras, Kenya, and the Philippines. Women who are trained to manage and maintain community water systems often perform better than men because they are less likely to migrate, more accustomed to voluntary work, and better trusted to administer funds honestly.

Creating an enabling environment

This chapter has argued that massive improvements can be made in health, economic efficiency, and equity through better provision of sanitation and water. The key is firmly in the hands of governments, for the single most important factor needed is political will. Where there are long-established and deeply entrenched traditions of sound governance (as in Botswana, Korea, and Singapore), it is evident that autonomous, accountable public sector agencies can provide efficient and equitable service. For many countries, however, such levels of governance are not attainable in the short run, so that greater involvement of the private sector and NGOs will be crucial to the provision of accountable and efficient services.

To allow helpful change to occur, the government must concentrate on the things that it, and only it, can do. Its job is to define and enforce an appropriate legal, regulatory, and administrative framework. This includes tasks as fundamental and diverse as rewriting legislation so that water markets can come into existence, rewriting contract laws so that the private sector can participate with confidence, building a capacity for environmental and, where appropriate, economic regulation, developing financial mandates for utilities that encourage conservation, and setting and enforcing quality standards for equipment. The government must also create conditions under which others—the private sector, NGOs, communities, and consumers—can play their parts.

What might be accomplished

More than 1 billion people are still without access to safe water and 1.7 billion people are without access to adequate sanitation facilities. Elementary calculations show that an ''unchanged practices'' or ''business-as-usual'' scenario would lead to a rise in the number of people without service in the coming decades (the top curves in Figure 5.6). This is a result of rising unit costs, as well as unprecedented increases in population. If the shares of total investment allocated to sanitation (currently 0.6 percent of gross investment) and to water supply (currently 1.7 percent) were raised by, say, 50 and 30 percent, respectively, the numbers unserved might still rise, although not as much (the middle curves in the figure). Far more important (as shown by the bottom curves) is the combination of policy reforms and accelerated investment. By attracting financial, managerial, and skilled labor into the sector and by freeing enterprises to invest more and improve maintenance, this new approach, which is already being adopted in some countries, could bring about dramatic increases in access to sanitation and clean water within the next generation.

6 Energy and industry

Without altered policies, pollution from fossil fuel generation of electric power will rise tenfold in the next forty years, from vehicles more than fivefold, and from industrial emissions and wastes also more than fivefold as demand for industrial goods multiplies.

Low-waste and "clean" technologies and practices are capable of reducing local pollution levels appreciably as output expands. Options are also emerging for reducing carbon dioxide emissions in the long term through the use of renewable energy sources and through greater efficiency in energy production and use. To encourage the adoption of such technologies, governments need to pursue policies that improve the efficiency with which energy is used. These policies include the elimination of subsidies for power generation and, in many countries, for vehicle fuels and coal. Efficiency reforms help reduce pollution while raising a country's economic output. Policies designed to curb pollution directly, using economic incentives, laws, and regulations, are also necessary.

As developing economies grow, they will begin to catch up with the levels of energy consumption and industrial production of high-income countries. In today's industrial countries the main period of industrialization saw rapidly increasing pollution. How far can the developing countries avoid repeating that experience and benefit from the ways in which the richer countries have learned to reduce pollution from energy use and industrial production even as output expands?

At present, the omens are poor. Chapter 2 concluded that current levels of air pollution, water pollution, and hazardous wastes in developing countries pose serious threats to human health, productivity, and welfare. These types of pollution arise mainly from the use of energy and from industrial production. If growth continues at present rates or higher—as it must if poverty is to diminish—then, on present trends, increased energy use and industrial production will add enormously to pollution.

The consumption of commercial energy in developing countries is rising rapidly and will soon dominate energy markets worldwide (Figure 6.1). Despite oil price shocks and financial crises, it tri-

pled between 1970 and 1990 and now accounts for 27 percent of the world total. Even if developing countries' demand for primary energy were to grow at a rate 1 to 2 percentage points lower than the trend growth rate, demand is likely to exceed 100 million barrels a day of oil equivalent (mbdoe) by 2010 and perhaps 200 mbdoe by 2030. Yet per capita consumption in these countries would remain much lower than in industrial countries.

The production and consumption of industrial goods have also increased rapidly in developing countries. In many, the historical and current pace of industrial growth has outstripped that of industrial countries and will continue to do so as per capita incomes rise. As incomes rise, the structure of consumption will also change. Manufactures have a high income elasticity of demand, and the structural shifts brought about by development are likely to put heavy pressure on the environment. The growth of manufacturing in developing countries averaged 8.0 percent in 1965–80 and 6.0 percent in 1980–90, compared with 3.1 and 3.3 percent in the industrial countries for those periods (see World Development Indicators, Table 2). Manufacturing output will probably rise threefold in the

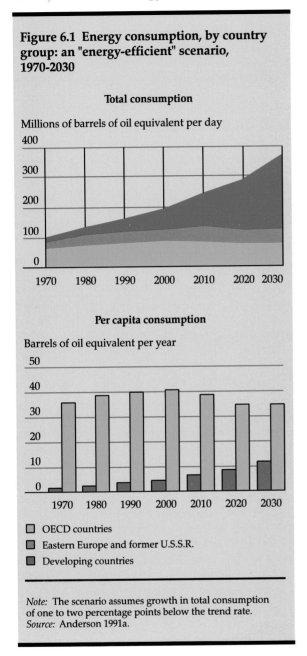

Figure 6.1 Energy consumption, by country group: an "energy-efficient" scenario, 1970-2030

Total consumption

Millions of barrels of oil equivalent per day

Per capita consumption

Barrels of oil equivalent per year

☐ OECD countries
■ Eastern Europe and former U.S.S.R.
■ Developing countries

Note: The scenario assumes growth in total consumption of one to two percentage points below the trend rate.
Source: Anderson 1991a.

generates most of these pollutants, as well as effluents and wastes, which are becoming more numerous, toxic, and exotic as industrialization proceeds. Like industrial countries, developing countries also need policies for dealing with "global pollutants" such as CFCs and greenhouse gases.

In trying to skip the most polluting stages of industrialization, developing countries have some special advantages. They are able to draw on advances in technology and management practices already made in industrial countries, under the pressure of increasingly strict pollution controls. And because they are expanding rapidly, they are generally building new generating and industrial plants rather than refitting existing ones. They should therefore be able, with investment, to go straight to low-polluting practices. Developing countries are more likely to gain from such advantages if they encourage international trade and investment and if they adopt environmental taxes, laws, and regulations that make cleaner practices profitable and polluting ones unprofitable, thus creating a commercial interest in a clean environment.

Energy

Figure 6.2 shows the main sources and uses of world energy. For developing countries, biomass, used mainly by households, is the largest source of energy, and efficiency in its use will be important in controlling air pollution. Coal, oil, and gas are the next largest sources. Hydroelectric power provides 6 percent of the energy needs of developing countries, while nuclear power provides less than 1 percent.

As Chapter 1 pointed out, fears that the world may be running out of fossil fuels are unfounded. The world's proven reserves of oil and gas in 1950 stood at 30 billion tons of oil equivalent (btoe); today they exceed 250 btoe, notwithstanding a total world consumption of 100 btoe over the forty-year period. Proven reserves of coal rose from 450 to 570 btoe in the same period. Reserves of natural gas have expanded more than fivefold since 1965 (despite a threefold increase in production during the period). They now amount to more than 100 btoe, almost as much as the world's proven oil reserves; supplies in developing countries are strong and improving. Estimates of "ultimately recoverable" fossil fuel reserves worldwide are more than 600 times the present annual rate of extraction. All told, fossil fuel resources are probably

next twenty years and fivefold in the next thirty.

In relation to energy use, the most serious problems faced by developing countries are the local effects of emissions of particulate matter (dust and smoke), the use of leaded fuels, and the indoor air pollution arising from the use of biomass fuels. In a growing number of places sulfur dioxide, nitrogen oxides, unburned hydrocarbons, and carbon monoxide also need attention. Industrial activity

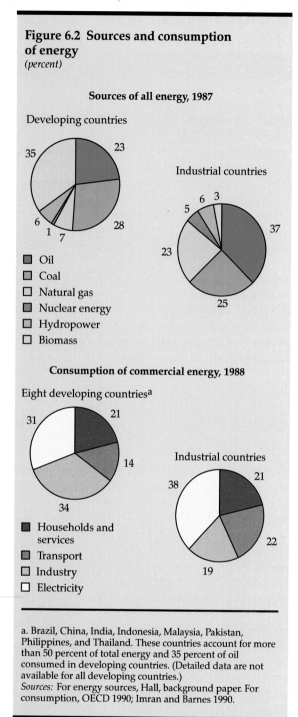

Figure 6.2 Sources and consumption of energy
(percent)

Sources of all energy, 1987

Developing countries

35 / 23 / 6 / 1 / 7 / 28

Industrial countries

6 / 3 / 5 / 37 / 23 / 25

- ■ Oil
- □ Coal
- □ Natural gas
- ■ Nuclear energy
- □ Hydropower
- □ Biomass

Consumption of commercial energy, 1988

Eight developing countries[a]

31 / 21 / 14 / 34

Industrial countries

38 / 21 / 22 / 19

- ■ Households and services
- ■ Transport
- □ Industry
- □ Electricity

a. Brazil, China, India, Indonesia, Malaysia, Pakistan, Philippines, and Thailand. These countries account for more than 50 percent of total energy and 35 percent of oil consumed in developing countries. (Detailed data are not available for all developing countries.)
Sources: For energy sources, Hall, background paper. For consumption, OECD 1990; Imran and Barnes 1990.

economic instruments and institutional reforms to encourage the more efficient use of energy. The second is either to develop technologies that reduce the polluting effects of conventional fuels or to use less-polluting substitutes. In discussing energy use for electric power generation and for transport—the two most rapidly growing categories—this chapter examines three scenarios: an ''unchanged practices'' scenario, with no environmental policies in place; a scenario that employs economic and institutional reforms to improve the efficiency with which fossil fuels are used; and a scenario that progressively adopts environmentally beneficial technologies. A combination of the second and third not only reduces local pollution appreciably but also improves economic efficiency.

But using cleaner fossil fuels and technologies and improving efficiency will not by themselves solve the long-term problem of stabilizing carbon dioxide accumulations in the atmosphere (see Chapter 8). That will require a much greater use of nuclear or of renewable energy. This chapter (which concentrates mainly on local pollution) will show that solar energy, biomass, and other renewables are developing rapidly as environmentally and commercially viable energy sources.

Electric power generation from fossil fuels

More than half the world's consumption of coal and 30 percent of fossil fuel consumption go to generate electricity. Fossil-fired power stations, in turn, account for two-thirds of the world's electric power–generating capacity, currently 2.6 million megawatts. In the 1980s electric power generation rose by 60 percent in industrial countries and by more than 110 percent in developing countries (where demand is expanding at 8 percent a year and requires roughly 50,000 megawatts of added capacity each year). Under an ''unchanged practices'' scenario, in which pollution abatement technologies are not widely deployed, emissions of pollutants will increase more than fourfold in the next twenty years and tenfold in the next forty. Good policies would make this grimy prospect avoidable.

ECONOMIC AND INSTITUTIONAL REFORM. A second scenario considered in this section looks at the possible effects of price increases and institutional reforms. At present, underpricing of electricity is the rule, not the exception, in most developing countries. Prices, on average, are barely more than one-third of supply costs and are half those in industrial countries (Figure 6.3). Whereas average

sufficient to meet world energy demands for the next century, perhaps longer.

Policies to mitigate the effect on the environment of energy production and consumption take two complementary approaches. The first uses

tariffs in the OECD countries rose by 1.4 percent a year in real terms between 1979 and 1988, they fell by 3.5 percent a year in developing countries.

Such low prices do not reflect improvements in the efficiency with which electric utilities supply their customers. On the contrary, losses during transmission and distribution, partly through theft, run at high levels: 31 percent of generation in Bangladesh, 28 percent in Pakistan, and 22 percent in Thailand and the Philippines. (In the United States only 8 percent of electricity is lost during transmission, in Japan, 7 percent.) These losses, the equivalent of about 75,000 megawatts of capacity and 300 terawatt hours (300 billion kilowatt hours) a year, represent a loss to developing countries of approximately $30 billion a year through increased supply costs. Worse, by the end of the century, on present trends, aggregate losses would double.

The reasons for persistent underpricing are largely institutional. The points made in Chapter 5 about the management of water utilities apply with equal force to electric utilities. Governments frequently intervene in the day-to-day operations of utilities, and they worry that price increases will exacerbate inflation. Utility managers and their boards may have little say in pricing or investment decisions. Lack of accountability and transparency leads to poor management, either of the utilities themselves or of the state fuel companies that frequently supply them.

Subsidizing the price of electricity has both economic costs and environmental effects. Low prices give rise to excessive demands and, by undermining the revenue base, reduce the ability of utilities to provide and maintain supplies; developing countries use about 20 percent more electricity than they would if consumers paid the true marginal cost of supply. Underpricing electricity also discourages investment in new, cleaner technologies.

Because of the need to service the borrowing incurred to build new generating capacity, some developing countries are now starting to raise electricity tariffs. Some are considering or (in a few cases) implementing privatization programs, usually in the hope of tapping capital markets to build new capacity. Price increases may be easier in countries in which parts of the energy industry are privatized, and management is also likely to be improved.

CONSERVATION. Sensible energy prices affect not just the generation of energy but also its use by industry and households. They create incentives

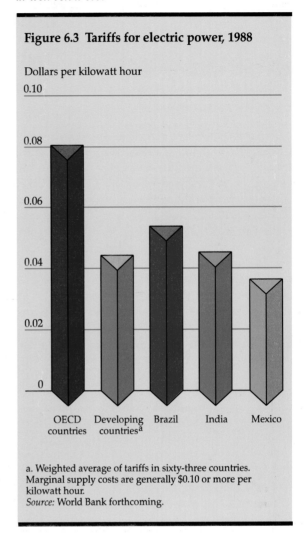

Figure 6.3 Tariffs for electric power, 1988

Dollars per kilowatt hour

a. Weighted average of tariffs in sixty-three countries. Marginal supply costs are generally $0.10 or more per kilowatt hour.
Source: World Bank forthcoming.

for industry to use waste heat—for example, through cogeneration, which combines power generation with the use of residual thermal energy for other purposes—and to improve efficiency in heating, motive power, refrigeration, and lighting.

A paradox of the energy market is that end users of electricity often appear to require much higher rates of return on the installation of more energy-efficient equipment than those that electric power producers require on new plant. This has led some countries to introduce subsidies for new types of energy-saving investments by electricity customers, paid either by the government or (as in several U.S. states) by the electric utilities themselves. Better information in the form of labeling or advisory services to help customers make more informed decisions is also required. In developing countries industrial advisory services have some-

117

times identified ways of reducing energy consumption per unit of output and other costs. Such initiatives are important for improving energy efficiency, but their success, too, will depend greatly on prices that reflect the full economic and environmental costs of energy. These will, in themselves, help to make energy-efficient technologies financially more attractive to industry and individuals.

TECHNOLOGIES. By providing strong incentives to generate and use electricity in more efficient ways, price and institutional reforms have the advantage of encouraging reductions in all polluting emissions (including carbon dioxide) per unit of output. However, low-polluting methods of generation are also required to reduce pollution significantly. The third scenario developed below therefore combines the efficiency reforms discussed above with the gradual adoption of environmentally improved technologies and practices.

Technological advance has put developing countries in a better position to reduce all forms of pollution from electric power generation than the industrial countries were in as recently as twenty years ago. In industrial countries the capital stock takes about thirty years to turn over, and retrofitting is costly. Because developing countries are making new investments, they have the opportunity to install less-polluting plant right away.

There are, broadly, four technological options for reducing harmful emissions: (a) changing the fuel by switching to low-sulfur coals, oil, and gas; (b) cleaning the coal before combustion; (c) controlling emissions; and (d) using existing fuels more efficiently, mainly by adopting advanced, high-efficiency, low-emissions technologies. Box 6.1 summarizes recent assessments and costs of these options. When coal is used, it is not unusual to find two or three approaches used in combination—for instance, to address the rather different problems posed by particulates, sulfur dioxide, and nitrogen oxides.

COAL. Coal-fired stations are currently the main source of emissions from power stations because they make up more than half of total thermal generating capacity and because of the high sulfur content of coal in many regions. Combustion efficiencies are often poor, and modern emissions control technologies are not widely deployed; this gives rise to high emission rates of particulates and sulfur dioxide. The technological developments described in Box 6.1 mean that options are now available or emerging for reducing all significant

Box 6.1 Innovations in emissions control and efficiency in power generation from fossil fuels

Smokestack pollution from power stations can be greatly reduced by clean coal- and oil-burning technologies or by using natural gas. Box table 6.1 shows typical emissions characteristics. For coal several technologies are available or emerging. The first three are in commercial use, and the others are in advanced stages of development.

• Coal-cleaning technologies to reduce nonburning mineral matter (ash). These methods can also remove the 10–30 percent of the sulfur content that is chemically bound in the inorganic form (notably, pyrites). The cleaned coal has a higher heat value and puts a lower ash load on the boiler.

• Mechanical and electrical devices for removing particulates. These devices, introduced in industrial countries over the past forty years, can remove more than 99 percent of particulate matter. Improvements in combustion technologies and thermal efficiencies have also eliminated carbon monoxide emissions, which are now rarely classified as a significant pollutant from power stations in the industrial market economies.

• Flue gas desulfurization technologies ("scrubbers"). These methods, also in commercial use, are capable of removing more than 90 percent of sulfurous emissions, albeit at some cost. Methods are also being developed for reducing emissions of nitrogen oxides by using catalysts and lowering combustion temperatures and avoiding excess air supply to the boilers.

• Fluidized bed combustion, in which crushed coal is fluidized with sand, its own ash, or limestone by supporting the particles on a strong rising current of air. The contact of the sulfur compounds with the limestone enables the sulfur to be removed from the furnace directly. Flue gas desulfurization is not needed, and sulfur dioxide abatement efficiencies are as high as 90 percent. Better control of furnace temperatures also enables nitrogen oxides to be reduced significantly, while the turbulence of the fluidized bed leads to more efficient combustion.

• Integrated coal gasification combined-cycle technologies with fluidized bed combustion. These either

pollutants from coal (other than carbon dioxide) to low levels per unit of output. The costs of the options vary, as the last column of Box table 6.1 shows, but are not so great as to compromise the ability of developing countries to meet their growing demands if they pursue rational abatement policies.

GAS. Switching to natural gas, where it is economically available, carries many environmental advantages. Its use offers reductions in particu-

gasify the coal before burning it to drive gas turbines or use the hot gases from a pressurized version of a fluidized bed combustion chamber. In both cases appreciable improvements in thermal efficiency have been obtained in pilot schemes, with further reductions of sulfur dioxide and nitrogen oxide emissions.

Box table 6.1 Controlling pollution through improved technology for electric power generation

Fuel and plant type	Emissions control	Percentage abatement in relation to base case			Thermal efficiency (percent)	Added costs as percentage of generation costs[a]
		Particulate matter	SO_2	NO_x		
Base						
Coal, conventional boiler	None	0	0	0	34.0	—
With improvements and controls						
Coal						
Conventional boiler	Mechanical cleaning (cyclone)	90	0	0	34.0	<1
Conventional boiler	Fabric ("baghouse") filters	>99	0	0	34.0	2–4
Conventional boiler	Electrostatic precipitators (ESP)	>99	0	0	34.0	2–4
Conventional boiler	ESP/coal cleaning	>99	10–30	0	34.0	4–6
Conventional boiler	ESP/SO_2 controls	>99	90	0	34.0	12–15
Conventional boiler	ESP/SO_2 and NO_x controls	>99	90	90	33.1	17–20
Fluidized bed combustion	ESP	>99	90	56	33.8	}
Pressurized fluidized bed combustion/combined cycle[b]	ESP	>99	93	50	38.9	<0–2
Integrated coal gasification/combined cycle[b]	None	>99	99	50	38.0	
Residual fuel oil						
Conventional boiler	None	97	30	12	35.2	—[c]
Conventional boiler	ESP/SO_2 controls	>99.9	93	12	35.2	10–12[d]
Combined cycle[b]	ESP/SO_2 and NO_x controls	>99.9	93	90	34.4	13–15[d]
Natural gas						
Conventional boiler	None	>99.9	>99.9	37	35.2	}
Conventional boiler	NO_x controls	>99.9	>99.9	45	35.2	<0
Combined cycle[b]	None	>99.9	>99.9	62	44.7	

Note: SO_2, sulfur dioxide; NO_x, nitrogen oxides. Figures for coal and residual fuel oil are based on 3 percent sulfur content.
a. In relation to base case. The percentages are based on generation costs of 5 cents per kilowatt hour, excluding transmission and distribution.
b. A combined cycle plant uses both gas and steam turbines to drive the generators. The gas turbines are powered by the hot gases emerging directly from the combustion chamber. Steam is also raised in the combustion chamber and by utilizing the still-hot exhaust gases from the gas turbines. The improvements in efficiency arise from the thermodynamic advantages of higher inlet temperatures to the heat engine (turbine).
c. Varies with relative costs of oil and coal.
d. In relation to conventional oil boiler without controls.
Sources: Based on OECD 1987a and 1989; Asian Development Bank 1991; Bates and Moore, background paper; Anderson 1991a.

lates and sulfur dioxide of more than 99.9 percent in relation to conventional coal-fired boilers with poor or no emissions control technologies. The use of combined-cycle gas-fired stations also brings some reductions in emissions of nitrogen oxide per unit of energy produced. Current efficiencies (the proportion of energy converted into electricity from the fuel) of combined-cycle gas units are about 45 percent and could rise to more than 50 percent—almost twice those of conventional coal-fired stations thirty-five years ago. Construction times are also short (roughly four years). For many countries gas offers the prospect of both cheaper electric power generation and less local pollution.

These developments in the efficient use of natural gas for electric power generation have coincided with a remarkable increase in proven reserves over the past twenty-five years (Figure 6.4). In addition to proven reserves, there are several "unconventional" sources of methane that are thought to be vastly greater than conventional reserves in some countries—for example, coal-bed

Figure 6.4 Proven reserves of natural gas, selected years, 1965-90

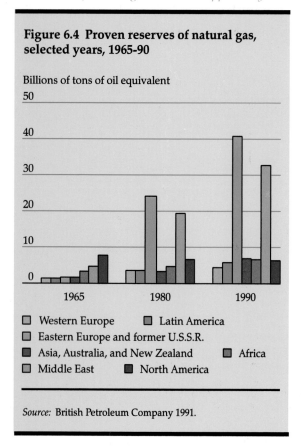

Billions of tons of oil equivalent

☐ Western Europe   ■ Latin America
☐ Eastern Europe and former U.S.S.R.
■ Asia, Australia, and New Zealand   ☐ Africa
☐ Middle East   ■ North America

Source: British Petroleum Company 1991.

methane; "tight gas" formations in which the gas is held in rocks of low permeability and rock-fracturing techniques are required to bring about useful production; and some as yet uneconomical reserves such as shale gas deposits. The costs of exploiting natural gas reserves vary according to circumstances but have generally declined. Marginal costs in developing countries range from one-quarter to three-quarters of the cost of steam coal, the cheapest imported alternative energy source.

A major barrier to development has been the high fixed costs of exploration and production and of establishing a basic pipeline network. For those countries that have a natural gas resource but have yet to exploit it, the development of gas-fired power station projects can provide the commercially justified starting point for the development of a widespread gas industry. Trade in natural gas will also be important from both commercial and environmental perspectives; there is enormous scope both for the shipment of liquefied natural gas to the main demand centers and for pipeline exports of gas from the former U.S.S.R., Europe, the Middle East, and North Africa.

FUEL OIL. Polluting emissions from the use of fuel oil for electric power generation can similarly be reduced to very low levels. Emissions of particulate matter are intrinsically much lower for oil than for coal and can be virtually eliminated by using the technologies described in Box 6.1. The use of low-sulfur fuel oil or flue gas desulfurization can reduce emissions of sulfur dioxide by more than 90 percent. Catalytic methods are also available for significantly reducing nitrogen oxides in exhaust gases. The costs of controlling emissions from oil-fired plant are lower than those for coal.

REGULATION. To encourage electric utilities to employ pollution-reducing technologies, governments generally use regulation. This has been effective (although not always cost-effective) in industrial countries because there the pollution comes from a relatively small number of easily monitored point sources. In addition, the utilities are monopolies, are already regulated, and are perhaps more responsive to regulation than to taxes. This situation may change with the growth of private ownership of power plants; pollution taxes (on, for example, sulfur emissions) would help to encourage plants to adopt more cost-effective means of abatement.

Regulation has typically involved setting abatement standards. It is fortunate that the technology for addressing one of the most serious pollution problems of electric power production—emissions of particulate matter—is relatively simple and inexpensive. Increased use of gas-fired power stations will be important in this respect. Where coal is the preferred fuel, constructing tall chimneys, siting power stations away from large population centers, and using the emissions control devices discussed in Box 6.1 all help to reduce disamenity and hazards to health from its combustion. They add less than 2 percent to total supply costs and may be associated with reductions in costs. China, for example, has numerous small coal-fired power plants that emit three to eight times more particulates per kilowatt hour generated than do large plants yet have 30 percent higher capital costs, 60 percent higher operating costs, and lower efficiencies than large plants. Given the costs to life and health of particulate matter emissions (Chapter 2) and the modest costs of reducing the emissions to low levels, the case for working toward high standards of abatement is unambiguous.

Unless natural gas is economically available, setting emissions standards for nitrogen oxides and sulfur dioxide will require a more critical examina-

Figure 6.5 Expansion of electric power in developing countries: pollution effects and investment requirement under three scenarios, 1990-2030

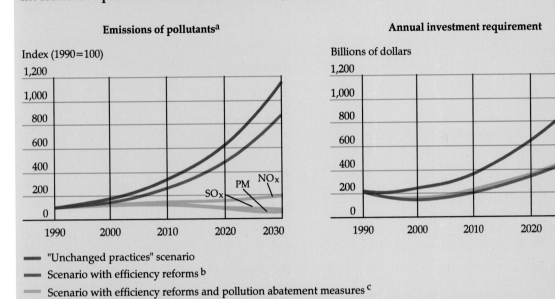

Emissions of pollutants[a]

Index (1990=100)

Annual investment requirement

Billions of dollars

— "Unchanged practices" scenario
— Scenario with efficiency reforms [b]
— Scenario with efficiency reforms and pollution abatement measures [c]

Note: NO_x, nitrogen oxides; PM, particulate matter; SO_x, sulfur oxides. Assumptions are as follows: growth of per capita income and population as in Chapter 1; per capita income elasticity, 1.5; price elasticity, -0.5; pollution abatement technologies and costs as in Box 6.1; initial average electricity prices as in Figure 6.3; and initial managerial and institutional inefficiencies that imply costs 50 percent higher than with good practices.
a. The upper two curves are indexes for all pollutants, which increase together.
b. Marginal cost pricing is phased in over twenty-five years, and losses in transmissions distribution and unused capacity are reduced to "best-practice" levels.
c. Abatement technologies are phased in over twenty years.
Source: Anderson and Cavendish, background paper.

tion of tradeoffs (as was done, for example, in Poland; see Figure 3.3). Extensive studies in Europe and North America have found that the damage from these pollutants varies greatly with region. Much can be accomplished by using coal-cleaning technologies and low-sulfur fuels. Costs can also be reduced by a proper phasing of investments. In industrial countries the costs of flue gas desulfurization are declining with experience; alternatively, it may be more cost-effective to postpone decisions until advanced coal combustion technologies or new gas deposits are fully commercialized.

The three scenarios

Figure 6.5 illustrates the three scenarios discussed in this section.
• In the "unchanged practices" scenario, envi-

ronmental policies are not in place, and rising demands for electric power are met at the cost of an exponential rise in pollution.
• In the second scenario, reforms to rectify the price inefficiencies and problems of accountability noted above are phased in gradually over twenty-five years. Pollution still rises (although more slowly), but there is less waste of capital, fuel, and operating resources in supply and less waste of energy in consumption—a clear case of good economic policies being good for the environment. The investment costs of expansion are lower (the second panel of Figure 6.5) and could even decline for a period as output expands, as a result of improved capacity utilization and reductions in losses. The net benefits of electricity supply are also higher. Efficiency in energy production and use thus reduces pollution while raising incomes and welfare.

121

• In the third scenario, in addition to energy efficiency, environmentally improved technologies and practices are gradually incorporated into the capital stock. Pollution rises initially on account of lags and difficulties in introducing new policies and practices but eventually declines as output expands. The savings in investment arising from improvements in prices and institutional arrangements far outweigh any extra costs of pollution abatement.

Renewable and nuclear energy

Fossil fuels will continue to be the predominant energy source for the next several decades, and the main task ahead will be to use them in economically and environmentally satisfactory ways. But if the threat of greenhouse warming made it necessary to restrict the use of fossil fuels, could the world's demands for commercial energy still be met? More efficient use of fossil fuels and a switch from coal to fuels lower in carbon could substantially reduce emissions of carbon dioxide per unit of output. Beyond that, the options would be nuclear energy or renewable energy (primarily solar energy, biomass, geothermal energy, hydropower, and wind).

As Figure 6.2 showed, nuclear power provides less than 1 percent of the energy used in developing countries. That share seems unlikely to rise significantly. Quite apart from the abundance of fossil fuel reserves, which will act to depress demand for all alternatives, nuclear power has two handicaps: its costs and its environmental risks. Discoveries of fossil fuel reserves and progress in production and conversion technologies have helped to hold down the prices of fossil fuels. At the same time, the costs of nuclear stations have risen for a variety of reasons: long lead times and delays in seeking approval, meeting environmental safeguards, and constructing the plants; the costs and risks of disposing of radioactive wastes; and the prospective costs of decommissioning plants. Recent estimates (OECD 1989) show that fossil fuels still have lower costs than nuclear power, except perhaps at low discount rates.

While the costs of nuclear power have increased, developments in renewable energy in the 1970s and 1980s—in solar, wind, and biomass energy, in particular—have led to remarkable cost reductions in these technologies. There is now a growing awareness that renewable energy is an abundant resource that can be harnessed.

Each year the earth's surface receives from the sun about ten times as much energy as is stored in

the whole of the world's fossil fuel and uranium reserves. This energy—the equivalent of 15,000 times the world's primary energy demand—can be captured in solar-thermal systems, which produce heat for electric power generation and for domestic and commercial uses, or with photovoltaic systems, which produce electric power directly from sunlight. Both types of scheme have been considered for the production of hydrogen, which could be used as a transport, domestic, or industrial fuel. Solar energy can also be stored by growing plants and, in the form of biomass, may be used as a feedstock for the production of commercial fuels and electric power.

In the past there have always been two commercial drawbacks to solar schemes: the amount of land they require and their costs. Both are declin-

---

Producing solar power would occupy relatively little land area

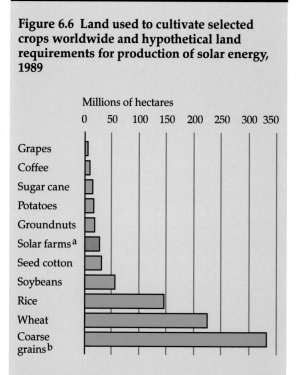

Figure 6.6 Land used to cultivate selected crops worldwide and hypothetical land requirements for production of solar energy, 1989

Millions of hectares

a. The bar shows the area that would be required in theory to meet world demand for commercial energy using only solar energy. It assumes that solar farms would be in areas with insolations of 2,000 kilowatt hours per square meter per year, the net conversion efficiency is 10 percent, primary energy demand is 8 billion tons of oil equivalent, 50 percent of primary energy goes to electricity, and conversion factors are 12,000 and 4,000 kilowatt hours per ton of oil equivalent for nonelectric and electric energy, respectively.
b. Barley, maize, millet, oats, rye, and sorghum.
Source: FAO 1990b.

ing. In developing countries solar insolation is roughly 6,500 times the annual consumption of commercial energy. At current conversion efficiencies of 15 percent, less than 0.1 percent of these countries' land area would be required to meet, in theory, the whole of their primary energy requirements. In industrial countries the fraction of land area is 0.5 percent. These areas are less than those currently occupied by hydroelectric reservoirs worldwide and are very small in relation to the area under crops (see Figure 6.6). In fact, the land intensities of solar schemes average only one-twentieth those of hydroelectric schemes and sometimes considerably less—they are less than one-hundredth that of the Aswan High Dam, for example. Moreover, the ideal locations will often be sparsely populated arid areas, and the technology is modular and allows flexibility in the choice of sites. Thus, solar schemes suffer minimally or not at all from three problems that sometimes beset hydroelectric schemes—the inundation of arable or forested lands, ecological side effects, and the displacement of people.

The costs of all commercial forms of renewable energy have declined remarkably over the past two decades (as they did in the earlier part of this century for electric power generation from fossil fuels; see Figure 6.7). The costs of solar energy

Increased efficiency has reduced costs greatly in this century

Figure 6.7 Electric power generation: cost and thermal efficiency in the United States, 1900-90

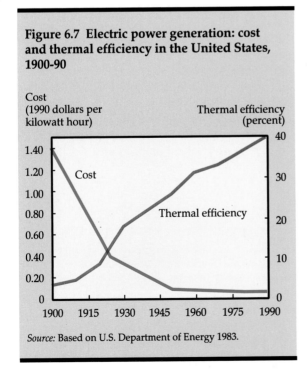

Source: Based on U.S. Department of Energy 1983.

Technological advances will make renewable energy competitive

Figure 6.8 Cost of alternative means of generating electric power in high-insolation areas, 1970-2020

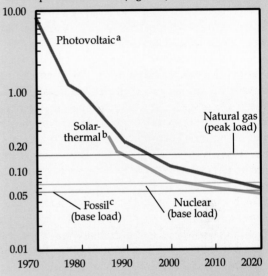

Notes: Data after 1990 are predicted. Future costs of fossil-fuel and nuclear generation are uncertain; they are affected by such factors as demand shifts, technological change, environmental concerns, and political conditions, which may act in opposite directions.
a. Excluding storage costs.
b. Including storage costs (on the basis of hybrid natural gas/solar schemes through 1990 and heat storage thereafter).
c. Natural gas and coal.
Sources: For solar sources, U.S. Department of Energy 1990; for others, *Scientific American* 1990.

may well fall further. In high-solar-insolation areas the costs of electric power from solar energy seem likely to become competitive with those of nuclear power within the next ten years or so (even ignoring their advantages in reducing environmental costs) and probably with those of fossil fuels over the long term. Figure 6.8 summarizes one set of representative but fairly conservative cost estimates.

The commercial development of renewables may thus be justified on nonenvironmental grounds. But if greenhouse warming makes it necessary to restrict the use of fossil fuels, several things could be done to promote the wider use of renewables. First, financial incentives could be put in place to encourage applications and market development. Environmental taxes (such as carbon taxes) on fossil fuels would favor renewables and encourage private research and development (R&D). Second, industrial countries, in particular, could allocate a greater share of their national energy R&D portfolios to renewables. Up to now, R&D has been heavily skewed in favor of nuclear power. The member countries of the International Energy Agency (IEA) allocate 60 percent of their R&D budgets (which totaled $7.3 billion in 1989) to nuclear power, 15 percent to coal, oil, and gas, and 19 percent to electric power transmission and other areas but only 6 percent to renewables. International collaboration on research in renewable energy also merits support. Several developing countries—including Brazil, China, India, and Thailand—already have the nucleus of good research programs. Third, applications in developing countries could be encouraged by expanding the Global Environment Facility and concessional finance (see Chapter 9).

Vehicle fuels

Pollution caused by fuels used in transport is rising rapidly in developing countries as passenger and freight traffic increases. Transport fuels account for more than 55 percent of developing countries' total oil consumption, which has grown by 50 percent since 1980, as against 10 percent in the OECD economies.

In the cities of developing countries vehicles are a significant source of airborne toxic pollutants, accounting for up to 95 percent of lead. Three factors make pollution from vehicles more serious than in industrial countries. First, many vehicles are in poor condition, and lower-quality fuels are used. Second, motor vehicles are concentrated in a few large cities. In Mexico and Thailand about half the vehicle fleet operates in the capital city, and in Brazil a quarter of the fleet operates in São Paulo. Third, a far larger percentage of the population moves and lives in the open air and is thus more exposed to automotive pollutants. The poor are usually the most affected. They and their children are more likely to walk than to ride, and they are thus exposed to noxious fumes and to lead, which is known to affect mental development and the neurological system. Lead and other pollutants also contaminate food in open-air restaurants, which are frequented by the poor.

The OECD countries have had some success in controlling the main pollutants from motor vehicles. Increasingly stringent regulations have led to changes in the design of engines, in emissions

control devices, and in the types of fuel used. Many of these developments have not yet been fully incorporated into the vehicle fleets, but the upshot has been a significant decrease in lead emissions and containment of other pollutants. Urban lead concentrations have decreased in North America, on average, by 85 percent and in large European cities by about 50 percent. Emissions of volatile organic compounds (VOCs) and nitrogen oxides, however, have generally increased, compared with the early 1970s, because motor vehicle fleets and kilometers traveled have increased much faster than the implementation of emissions controls. In developing countries leaded fuels are still widely used, and emissions standards are either nonexistent or are much slacker than in the OECD countries, as can be seen for the cases of Brazil and Mexico (Table 6.1).

Table 6.1 Emissions standards for new gasoline-powered motor vehicles in Brazil, Mexico, and the United States
(grams per kilometer)

Country and year	Carbon monoxide	Volatile organic compounds	Nitrogen oxides
Brazil, 1989	24	2.1	2.0
Mexico, 1990	24	2.9	3.2
United States			
Before controls	54	5.4	2.5
1968	32	3.7	3.1
1983	2.1	0.3	0.6

Source: Faiz and others 1990.

Three mutually reinforcing policies might be used to try to reduce vehicular pollution: improve the efficiency of fuel pricing, reduce urban congestion, and promote clean fuel and engine technologies. This section applies the three scenarios to policy options for transport (Figure 6.9). In the "unchanged practices" scenario the possibilities for improving efficiency and abating pollution are ignored, and all forms of pollution rise exponentially (as they would be bound to do) with the growth of fuel consumption. The second scenario illustrates the effect on emissions of two much-discussed possibilities for improving economic efficiency while reducing pollution: (a) lessening price inefficiencies by eliminating subsidies and increasing taxes on vehicle fuels and (b) reducing urban congestion. In the third scenario (these are the biggest effects) the additional effects of gradually introducing cleaner fuel and improved engine technologies are considered.

EFFICIENT VEHICLE FUEL PRICES AND TAXES. In Europe and Japan gasoline prices range from $3.00 to $4.00 per U.S. gallon. In the United States and in developing countries prices are less than one-third to one-half of that range; they average about $1.25 per gallon and vary from $0.40 per gallon (in Venezuela) to $2.60 per gallon (in India). Such international differences arise from differences in gasoline taxes. Smaller—although still large—differences are also found in diesel fuel taxes. Some countries have chosen high fuel taxes for several reasons: to defray the costs of road construction and maintenance, to raise revenues (because fuel taxes may have lower economic, or "deadweight," losses than some other specific taxes), and because they are relatively simple to administer.

REDUCING CONGESTION. Urban congestion is simultaneously a source of pollution, of economic inefficiency (it reduces the net economic output of urban areas), and of losses in human welfare and amenity more broadly defined. One policy approach is traffic management through such measures as segregation of motorized and non-motorized traffic, encouragement of the wider use of bicycles and development of special facilities for them, creation of vehicle-free precincts for pedestrians, incentives for greater investment in and use of public transport, incentives for higher vehicle occupancy rates, and parking controls. Schemes of this kind may reduce vehicle fuel consumption in metropolitan areas by more than 30 percent, in addition to lowering the number of accidents involving pedestrians and cyclists—a major problem in developing countries. Cities in China, Ghana, Indonesia, Japan, and the Netherlands are all considering such schemes, with a greater emphasis on nonmotorized traffic and pedestrian facilities. Traffic can also be restricted through quantity-based measures, such as the area traffic bans based on license plate numbers introduced in Athens, Mexico City, and Santiago. These, however, are only stopgap measures—and can sometimes make the situation worse, since the better-off simply purchase a second vehicle, and a market for fake license plates develops. A third possibility is some form of congestion pricing, such as area licensing, access fees to city centers, higher fees and taxes on parking during business hours, and electronic road pricing. Despite the very successful example of the Singapore Area Licensing Scheme and the benefits and practical promise of such policies, they have been more discussed than implemented.

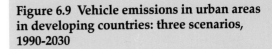

Good policies and abatement measures can dramatically reduce pollution

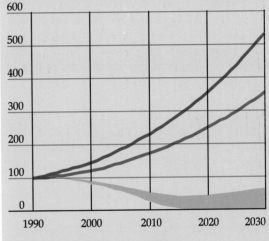

Figure 6.9 Vehicle emissions in urban areas in developing countries: three scenarios, 1990-2030

Index (1990 = 100)

— "Unchanged practices" scenario
— Scenario with efficiency reforms[a]
▨ Scenario with efficiency reforms and pollution abatement measures[b]

Note: The calculations are illustrative and are based on the following assumptions. Growth rates for per capita income and population are as in Chapter 1. Per capita income elasticity of demand for vehicle fuels equals 1.2, and fuel price and congestion price elasticities equal -0.5 and -0.6 respectively. The average life of vehicles is fifteen years. Gasoline and diesel fuels each account for about half of total consumption.
a. Efficiency reforms include congestion charges (based on data from the Singapore Area Licensing Scheme) and higher fuel taxes (assumed to rise over a twenty-five-year period to levels now found in Europe).
b. Pollution abatement measures include emission controls and the gradual introduction of cleaner fuels over a twenty-year period. Under this scenario, lead emissions gradually drop to the bottom of the yellow band; emission levels of particulate matter, hydrocarbons, and sulfuric oxides fall within the band, and nitrogen oxides are at the top.
Sources: For emission coefficients for vehicles, OECD 1987a and 1988; Faiz and Carbajo 1991. For detailed methodology, see Anderson and Cavendish, background paper.

CLEANER FUELS AND IMPROVED TECHNOLOGIES. Differential taxation can be used to promote the use of cleaner fuels. Fuel tax revenues, in turn, may be used to finance the costs of inspecting vehicles and monitoring pollution. Examples are differential taxation of leaded and unleaded gasoline, fuel price surcharges based on the sulfur content of diesel fuel, and lower taxes on "clean" fuels such as compressed natural gas. Some empirical evidence from the United States and the recent experience of the United Kingdom with tax exemptions on unleaded fuels shows that the choice of fuel is highly sensitive to price. The same would probably be true of tax incentives for the adoption of emissions control devices—for example, catalytic converters on gasoline engines and the particulate "traps" being developed for diesels. Experience suggests, however, that for a policy to be effective, any tax incentives would need to be complemented by regulations regarding standards and emissions testing (see Box 3.4).

Household energy

About half of the world's people cook all or some of their meals with biomass fuels. Until the twentieth century such fuels—mainly firewood—provided most of the world's energy. Today biomass in all its forms (wood, agricultural and forestry residues, and dung) meets about 14 percent of the world's energy demands. More than 80 percent is consumed in developing countries (see Figure 6.2), where it still accounts for 35 percent of energy supplies—more than is met by coal, oil, gas, or hydropower. Biomass is used not only for cooking but also in small-scale service industries, agricultural processing, and the manufacture of bricks, tiles, cement, and fertilizers. Such uses can be substantial, especially in and around towns and cities.

The use of biomass fuels for cooking gives rise to high levels of indoor air pollution (Chapter 2). It is also a source of ecological damage: the use of dung and crop residues depletes soil productivity, and deforestation often causes soil erosion. Finally, the poor thermal efficiency of biomass helps to explain the relatively high energy intensities of many low-income developing countries and their high carbon dioxide and particulate emissions in relation to energy use.

Making the transition from reliance on biomass to commercial fuels will be slow and difficult, and there is no obvious way of hastening the process. Some countries subsidize kerosene; this leads to some extra substitution, but people also buy excess amounts and retail it as a (very polluting) substitute for diesel fuels. Haiti, in contrast, taxes kerosene, which has discouraged its use. Substitution is further handicapped by poor infrastructure, dispersed populations, and poor delivery services in many regions, notably in Africa.

One promising strategy is to devise less-polluting ways of burning biomass. Several countries have developed and disseminated improved biomass stoves over the past two decades, although with mixed success. Much has been learned, however, and continued support for these efforts will be important (Box 6.2). The installation of chimneys has increased the popularity of the stoves—for example, in China, where 100 million improved stoves have been introduced.

When the transition is from biomass to coal or lignite, as in China and Turkey, it introduces outdoor pollution on a scale just as serious as that encountered, for example, by Sheffield, Pittsburgh, the Ruhr, and many other industrial areas fifty years ago. The histories of these places show that the reduction of outdoor pollution from household fuels depends on two developments. The first is a shift toward oil, gas, electricity, and district heating; for many cities this will take several decades. The second is the use of cleaner coals, such as anthracite, for which particulate emissions are roughly one-twentieth those of raw bituminous coal. China, where residential and commercial consumption of coal totals more than 200 million tons a year and nearly doubled in the 1980s, is weighing this option. Cleaner coal-burning technologies in district heating plants and small-scale commercial enterprises will also be required and may help to reduce costs by improving efficiency.

Reducing indoor and outdoor pollution from household use of biomass fuels and coal in developing countries presents one of the more difficult problems of development and will take two or three decades to address—possibly longer. As with pollution from other forms of energy use, it cannot be solved by efficiency alone, important though this will be. It will depend above all on the growth of per capita incomes and on the successful development of commercial energy.

Industry

Three factors intensify the environmental problems associated with rapid industrial development. First, as emissions from existing activities increase, they pass the point at which they can be readily assimilated by the environment. Second, as industrial towns expand, more people are exposed to pollution. Third, within industry the structure shifts away from activities that are moderately polluting, such as textiles, wood products, and food processing, and toward others with

Box 6.2 The future for improved stoves programs

Current worldwide trade in wood fuel is about $7 billion, and about 2 million people are employed full time in producing and marketing it. Although people will eventually switch to cooking with modern fuels, many hundreds of millions will be using biomass for decades. What has been learned from efforts to promote better biomass stoves?

The potential benefits of stoves programs are considerable. In addition to the large direct benefits of fuel savings, recent research has found that the economic value of the environmental and health benefits of improved stoves amount to $25–$100 a year per stove, leading to a payback period to society of only a few months.

Improved biomass stoves are a stepping-stone between traditional stoves and modern fuels. Most of the large investments in stoves programs have come from individual countries; the participation of donors has been modest. The two largest programs in the world are in India and China, where practically all the investments have been generated internally.

Successful stoves programs have shared the following characteristics:

• They have concentrated on the users most likely to benefit. The people who first adopt improved biomass stoves are usually not the poorest but those who have limited income and are spending much of it on cooking fuel.

• The designers and producers of the stoves discuss them with each other and with the users.

• The program relies on mass-produced stoves and stove parts, which seem to be more successful than custom-built stoves.

• Subsidies go for the development of stoves rather than to consumers for purchase of the stoves.

All these features can be found in a successful stoves program in Rwanda. Potential users, producers, and retailers participated at every stage, and several models were tested by households. High charcoal prices and unregulated prices for the stoves themselves ensured profitability for the producers and a short payback period for the consumers. Government agencies were involved only in technical support. Promotion of the stoves was carried out by women who had used them.

---

much greater potential for causing environmental harm, such as metals, chemicals, and paper.

The derelict or highly polluted industrial areas and rivers to be found in all high-income countries represent both a warning and a challenge for the developing world. The challenge is to avoid passing through the "dark satanic mills" phase of industrial growth. The policy response will need to address the rather different pollution problems posed by large plants and mines and by large numbers of small industries.

A few industries dominated by large plants are responsible for a significant share of industrial pollution. In addition to energy supply, these include ferrous and nonferrous metallurgy, industrial chemicals, paper and pulp, cement, and mining. Unchecked, the pollutants discharged by these industries damage the health of local people, reduce output from local agriculture and industry, and damage infrastructure and buildings. Small and medium-scale industries, which provide much employment and productivity growth in developing countries, cause many of the same kinds of pollution as larger enterprises and are especially important sources of organic wastes in water effluents and of inadequately handled hazardous wastes.

Technological means for improving the environmental performance of many industrial activities already exist, having often developed in response to stricter environmental controls in high-income countries. To take a few examples: air pollution in several industries, such as cement and mining, is largely caused by emissions of dust and can be checked by installing appropriate dust control systems; water effluents from large chemical and pulp plants can be treated once the biodegradable and nonbiodegradable emissions have been separated; and pollution caused by the use of coal for steel production and as a boiler fuel for process heat (once major sources of energy-related pollution in industrial countries) can be reduced by switching to natural gas, by electrifying the process, or by using one of the various precombustion, combustion, and postcombustion technologies described in Box 6.1.

But the existence of better technologies does not guarantee that they will be adopted, especially by small firms, for which the costs of control in relation to output may be large. Enforcement, as noted in Chapter 4, is notoriously difficult. Because they are so numerous and diverse, smaller firms are particularly hard to regulate or tax—whether for environmental or for other purposes—and indeed,

Table 6.2 Costs of pollution abatement, United States, 1989

Sector	Total investment in new plant and equipment				Annual cost of pollution abatement			
	Millions of dollars	Share for pollution abatement (percent)	Type of abatement (percent)		Millions of dollars	As share of total value of output (percent)	Type of abatement (percent)	
			Air	Water			Air	Water
Food and beverages	8,330	3	20	70	1,056	0.3	13	63
Textiles	2,280	1	33	56	136	0.3	14	59
Paper	10,070	8	49	32	1,449	1.1	27	47
Chemicals	13,480	9	32	50	3,509	1.3	23	46
Petroleum	3,330	13	35	55	2,170	1.5	58	27
Rubber	4,570	2	64	20	403	0.4	21	25
Stone, clay, and glass	2,870	3	75	18	592	0.9	56	14
Primary metals	5,660	7	53	34	1,931	1.3	46	27
Fabricated metals	4,610	3	33	47	896	0.6	14	43
Machinery	8,050	2	59	32	572	0.2	14	30
Electrical equipment	8,660	2	35	50	729	0.4	14	42
Transport equipment	9,970	3	54	29	1,000	0.3	21	32
All manufacturing	97,190	4	42	42	15,626	0.5	30	37

Source: U.S. Bureau of the Census 1990 and 1991.

most are not even recorded in establishment surveys.

Costs and the scope for cost reductions

The technologies thus often exist, but the costs are sometimes still high, especially for small companies. For industry as a whole, capital investment in pollution abatement accounted for about 5 percent of total industrial investment in Germany, Japan, and the United States in the late 1970s and early 1980s (although it had risen to 17 percent in Japan in the early 1970s). Table 6.2 shows that in absolute terms the heaviest cost burden in the United States fell on the chemicals, petroleum, primary metals, and paper industries. (Note that expenditures are quite small in relation to the total value of output—in the range of 0.3–1.5 percent.)

These figures overstate the likely burden of abatement expenditures on industries in developing countries, at least for large plants. The earliest steps in pollution control tend to be the least expensive. Up to 60–80 percent of pollution can be eliminated with only small increases in costs. Thereafter, the additional ("marginal") cost rises sharply as the degree of abatement is increased; in contrast, the benefits of each new step in abatement are large at first and then taper off. Emissions standards in some industrial countries have reached the point at which the costs of additional abatement rise sharply while the benefits increase only slowly. Developing countries are at an earlier stage.

Emissions often can be sharply reduced at no extra cost by installing technologies already in common use in industrial countries. There, emissions from large industrial plants fell even before the main surge of investment in pollution controls that followed the passage of key legislation in the late 1960s and early 1970s—a good example of innovations leading, rather than following, laws and regulations.

Industries in developing countries have the advantage of making new investments rather than replacing old equipment. In industrial countries basic changes in production processes often cannot easily be accommodated in existing plant. As a result, industrial countries have tended to control emissions mainly by adding on technologies. Less than a quarter of capital expenditures on pollution control for German manufacturing firms during 1975–84 was devoted to changes in production processes as distinct from the installation of end-of-pipe controls. When a new plant is being built, however, it is usually more cost-effective to adopt production processes that recycle residuals or generate less waste—the so-called "low-waste" processes. These, combined with improved operating procedures that reduce leaks and spills, can achieve substantial reductions in industrial emissions. Table 6.3, based on a study of German industry, illustrates the potential for reducing hazardous wastes by means of such changes. Box 6.3 gives an example of how technological changes have brought about greater efficiency and lower emissions in the pulp and paper industry. Recent surveys by the United Nations Industrial Development Organization (UNIDO 1991) and others have shown that possibilities for reducing both wastes and costs simultaneously are widespread.

Table 6.3 Potential for waste reduction through low-waste practices, Germany

Type of waste	Amount of waste, 1983 (millions of tons)	Potential waste reduction (percent)
Sulfurous (acids, gypsum)	2.2	80
Emulsion	0.5	40–50
Dyes and paint residues	0.3	60–70
Solvents	0.3	60–70
Galvanic sludges	0.2	60–70
Salt slags	0.2	100
Other wastes	1.2	Low
Total	4.9	50–60

Source: OECD 1991, p. 197.

In developing countries end-of-pipe controls should be less important because their industrial sectors are expanding rapidly. Each new investment offers an opportunity to incorporate cost-effective pollution control. In ten years' time new plants will account for more than half of the industrial output of developing countries and in twenty years for practically all of it. Thus policies that lead to the adoption of a proper combination of low-waste processes and end-of-pipe controls should permit developing countries to reduce emissions from large industrial plants (as output expands) at a lower cost than is being incurred by industrial countries.

Policy

At the earliest stages of policy development the crucial considerations must be, first, to ensure that the initial measures are unambiguous and easily enforced and, second, to concentrate on those emissions and wastes that cause the most damage, particularly to health.

DIFFICULTIES OF ENFORCEMENT. The standards imposed by industrial countries may set reasonable long-term goals, but developing countries rarely have the means or the need to adopt them immediately. Instead, each country must determine its own priorities. Emissions standards need to be set in the light of a balance between the marginal costs of the damage caused by the main pollutants and the marginal costs of reducing such emissions.

A common practice has been to adopt emissions standards promulgated in industrial countries and then to negotiate with firms about enforcement.

Box 6.3 Benign technological change: the manufacture of wood pulp

Until the mid-1970s most (67 percent) of the world's wood pulp—the principal raw material for paper manufacture—was produced by chemical means. Mechanical processes accounted for 25 percent and combinations of the two (semichemical processes) for the remainder. Each method has technical and environmental advantages and disadvantages. Mechanical processes produce a high yield of low-strength fiber. They require relatively large inputs of energy but otherwise have little impact on the environment. Chemical processes have lower energy requirements but also lower yields. The fibers are strong and high in quality; they are, however, dark and are usually bleached with chlorine, which then presents a disposal problem. Chemical methods also generate large volumes of biological oxygen demand (BOD) and sulfur emissions unless appropriate environmental controls are installed.

The largest paper market is that for newsprint, which used to be made from a combination of 15–25 percent chemical pulp and 75–85 percent mechanical pulp. The jump in energy prices in the mid-1970s pushed up the cost of mechanical pulp, and the price of chemical pulp also rose because of stricter environmental controls and high prices for wood and chemicals. Manufacturers then turned to pulp produced by thermomechanical methods, which have yields and energy requirements similar to those of mechanical processes but produce a stronger fiber that does not have to be bleached with chlorine. The volume of BOD generated is moderate. By using thermomechanical pulp in their mix, newsprint manufacturers were able to reduce their raw material costs by 5 percent or more.

This cost advantage, and the need for new investment to meet a shortage of pulp capacity, combined to bring about a rapid increase in thermomechanical pulping plants. In 1974 there were only four thermomechanical mills in the world. By the end of 1977 there were fifty, with another thirty under construction or on order. Chemical processes still dominate the industry, but almost half of the pulping capacity added in OECD countries during the 1980s consisted of thermomechanical plants. Thermomechanical pulping offers clear advantages to developing countries—lower capital costs, less technological complexity, and less environmental impact than with chemical processes, and stronger and better-quality fiber than that produced by mechanical plants.

This places enormous stresses on the honesty of officials. Enterprises will be uncertain about the environmental standards that they are expected to meet and unhappy about perceived differences in treatment between themselves and their competitors. Indeed, uneven enforcement may turn foreign investors into supporters of tough and effective environmental standards. For example, fear of public censure has made foreign investors in Chile's copper mining industry more willing than local enterprises to invest in sophisticated environmental controls.

Whatever instruments are chosen, they must be compatible with the administrative capacities of the regulatory agencies. Unenforced standards or uncollected fines are worse than useless: they undermine confidence in environmental controls and encourage enterprises to look for ways of avoiding penalties rather than reducing pollution. Experience shows that five conditions (all institutionally demanding) are essential if policies are to have the intended effect: a local framework for negotiation between polluting and polluted parties; a clear and publicly available statement of the standards set and agreements reached; a means of monitoring and spot-checking pollution; a means of penalizing defaulters; and fair and equal application of the laws and regulations to all parties.

Scarce administrative resources should be directed first to the control of emissions from large industrial plants and mines—the most concentrated sources of pollution. Policies will be effective only with the (perhaps reluctant) cooperation of the enterprises responsible for these plants. Even the U.S. Environmental Protection Agency, which oversees the most sophisticated environmental monitoring system in the world, is forced to rely on self-reported data on emissions for the vast majority of sources and pollutants. Developing countries might thus benefit by concentrating their monitoring resources on spot checks to validate such self-reported data and on a baseline system designed to collect data in the most heavily polluted areas. Enforcement actions must be seen as one element in a dialogue between regulators and enterprises, the objective of which is to improve the environmental performance of the plants under scrutiny.

Such a dialogue is particularly difficult when both parties are government agencies. Public enterprises account for a substantial part of production in the most-polluting industries. They account for all Tanzania's fertilizer, cement, and iron and steel production and for almost 83 percent of its pulp and paper output. In India, Mexico, and Venezuela all oil refining and distribution and a large share of basic metals production are in state hands; about 94 percent of mining production in India is in the public sector. In Turkey 95 percent of mining output, about 60 percent of chemicals production, and 70 percent of basic metals production come from public enterprises. State-owned firms make up an important part of the mining, petroleum, basic metals, and chemicals sectors in Argentina and Brazil. These firms, like private sector monopolies, are often also sheltered from import competition and consequently do not face the same pressures to minimize costs as do competitive private firms. Incentive-based pollution control policies are less likely than mandated controls to be effective in inducing these firms to reduce emissions. The ineffectiveness of economic incentives in inducing public enterprises with soft budget constraints to reduce emissions is well illustrated by the case of Poland, and the effectiveness of controls by the case of Cubatão in Brazil (Box 6.4).

Community participation can help augment official enforcement. A recent survey of enterprises in Bangladesh, for example, found that riverside villages have proved surprisingly willing and able to negotiate agreements with upstream polluters on monetary compensation and first-stage effluent treatment. With better information and legal support, such local arrangements could provide cost-effective means of both supporting central regulators and holding them to account.

MARKET-BASED INCENTIVES. As environmental policies evolve, there is a good case for making more use of market-based incentives, as discussed in Chapter 3. These policies reduce the costs of compliance, are often administratively simpler than regulatory policies, and provide a financial incentive for innovation in developing pollution controls and low-waste technologies and practices. They can also be refined (without great cost) in practical and important ways. For example, under a system of nonlinear fees and fines recently introduced in Eastern Europe, the charge is increased—in Poland by ten times—if discharges exceed some specified level.

Experience in industrial countries shows that discharges of industrial wastewater into public sewers are quite sensitive to charges for the volume of emissions and effluent concentration. In the Netherlands, for example, water pollution charges succeeded in reducing emissions once the

Box 6.4 Controlling emissions from public enterprises: Brazil and Poland

In Cubatão, Brazil, and Katowice, Poland, state-owned enterprises were implicated in severe and persistent air pollution that caused extreme levels of exposure to particulates. In Cubatão the main sources were steel, fertilizer, petrochemical, and cement plants. In Katowice steel mills, nonferrous metal smelters, chemical plants, power stations, and a wide range of other industrial plants were the principal polluters.

In September 1984 an atmospheric inversion and mounting levels of particulates spurred the governor of São Paulo state to decree an unprecedented state of emergency in Cubatão. The state environmental agency promptly shut down nine industries in the district of Vila Parisi and ordered an evacuation. Police from São Paulo city were sent to assist in the evacuation and to prevent looting. The mayor of Cubatão made the soccer stadium available for displaced residents and provided food and blankets. When atmospheric conditions improved, the state of emergency was downgraded to a state of alert (the eighth that year), and people were allowed to return to their homes.

A few months later a pipe at a fertilizer plant ruptured, releasing massive amounts of ammonia gas. Six thousand residents were evacuated and more than sixty people hospitalized. The fertilizer plant was fined, but the state governor protested that the penalty was too small.

Conditions in Cubatão have improved since then (though crises still occur periodically); plants are installing pollution control equipment and are switching to less-polluting fuel, and thousands of residents are being helped to move to more suitable areas. The environmental agency has become more aggressive in using fines and temporary plant closures to deal with recalcitrant polluters, and the government has initiated public civil actions seeking restoration of damaged wetlands, waterways, and hillsides. Extensive newspaper and television coverage of the environmental fiasco in Cubatão has given the whole country an environmental education.

Throughout the 1980s the provincial government in Katowice attempted to improve the city's air quality by levying fees for emissions that exceeded permissible levels. Although the rates were double those set by the national government for the rest of Poland, they were revised infrequently during the 1980s and fell sharply in real terms as prices rose. Furthermore, because industrial plants claimed that they lacked the resources to invest in better environmental controls, emissions permits were typically set much too high to achieve reasonable ambient air quality, and enterprises were often exempted from paying fees and fines. Technically, provincial governments could close down plants for persistently violating emissions standards, but this power seems to have been exercised only once—in the case of an aluminum plant in Krakow that was due to be closed anyway.

The situation in Katowice has changed radically since 1990. Air quality has improved significantly, and enterprises are considering or actually investing in environmental controls. There are three reasons for this change: (a) some of the worst polluters have closed down permanently; (b) the level of fees and fines has been raised more than ten times in real terms, and payment is enforced under a real threat of closure; and (c) the prospect of privatization means that enterprises no longer face "soft" budget constraints and provincial authorities no longer strive to maintain industrial production at the expense of other objectives.

The moral to be drawn from these two cases is that unless public enterprises are subject to "hard" budget constraints and are accountable to the public, economic incentives for pollution control are likely to be ineffective, and direct regulation may be required.

---

charge was high enough to represent a significant element in total operating costs for the enterprises affected. Charging systems need not be complex so long as they encourage enterprises to make process innovations that reduce the total volume of effluent and discourage the discharge of highly concentrated effluent to public sewers. In general, a policy of taxing pollution (or the offending input) has the advantage of influencing large numbers of activities and has administrative—as well as environmental and economic—appeal.

REGULATORY MECHANISMS AND TOXIC WASTES. Even with pollution charges, some regulatory mechanisms are bound to be retained. This is especially true for toxic wastes, where the main priority is to define safe standards and safeguards. Pollution charges may be evaded by illegal dumping, which causes even worse problems than legal but ill-supervised hazardous waste management. The crucial issue is one of monitoring and management. Careful records must be maintained and dumping sites monitored regularly to ensure that groundwater supplies are not being infiltrated by toxic materials leaching from the sites. This implies an administrative cost that may sometimes be beyond the capacity of environmental control agencies. In such cases an alternative is to combine regulation with market-based incentives. The latter can draw on indirect policies such as taxes on polluting inputs, product charges, deposit-refund schemes, and performance bonds. The role of the regulatory authority is to compile information about sources of emissions for the pollutants being controlled and to design the mix of policies that can reduce emissions from these sources cost-effectively. A scheme that applies to hazardous wastes some of the characteristics of a deposit-refund arrangement has been proposed for Thailand (Box 6.5).

Industrial zoning is another example of regulation that cannot easily be replaced by pricing mechanisms. The key argument for zoning is that there are economies in dealing with environmental problems when plants are concentrated in one place. Furthermore, it is difficult to ensure that spatial differences in pollution charges are sufficient to achieve an efficient concentration or dispersion of plants. Although zoning is a blunt instrument, it may be the best way of handling spatial differences in the environmental damage caused by particular forms of pollution.

ADVISORY SERVICES. One effective way to influence small firms is through extension and advisory services for industries. For example, the Pollution Control Cell of the National Productivity Council in India's Ministry of Labor works on solutions that both reduce pollution and improve profits. Effective ways have been found to reduce emissions and water use in electroplating, food processing, bleaching and dyeing, mini-cement plants, pulp and paper, drugs, and tanneries. Cooperative approaches can sometimes be helpful. For example, in Hyderabad a group of forty small companies set up a common wastewater treatment plant that they operate jointly on a nonprofit basis. In Gujarat 400 small companies did the same. Such arrangements are cheaper than individual treatment facilities at each plant, and it is easier to operate, maintain, and monitor one large facility than numerous scattered small ones.

Conclusions

In considering how to reconcile the expansion of energy and industrial activities in developing countries with the goals of reducing pollution to acceptably low levels, this chapter has made four points.

• Options are available for reducing energy and industrial pollution per unit of output by factors of ten, hundreds, and sometimes more, depending on the case.

• The investment and operating costs are not so large as to compromise economic growth in developing countries. For priority areas such as particulates, lead, and industrial effluents and wastes, investment costs are low. Indeed, pollution abatement has often been accompanied by reductions in costs. Pollution control costs can be further reduced by setting standards appropriately and by choosing the instruments of policy wisely. Offsetting these costs are the many benefits of pollution abatement, including a healthier population and a better quality of life in cities, which will help to improve economic prospects.

- Response times can be long, however, even when policies are agreed on and implemented. The rapid rate of investment may, paradoxically, reduce response times (and costs) in developing countries, since less-polluting practices can more readily be incorporated into new investment.
- Greater efficiency, whether in the production and use of energy or in the production and use of manufactured goods, can make significant contributions to pollution abatement.

7 *Rural environmental policy*

As the world's population grows by two-thirds over the next forty years, demands for food, fuel, and fiber will rise enormously. Meeting these demands will require more intensive and extensive exploitation of many natural resources, especially agricultural land, forests, water, and fisheries. The more that yields can be increased by careful and sustainable management of those resources that are already in use, the easier it will be to resist pressure to draw down new resources—to drain wetlands, clear forests, and encroach on natural habitats.

Three obstacles stand in the way of sensible resource management: failure to recognize scarcity in the natural world, failure to ensure that the institutions managing natural resources are accountable, and failure to mobilize knowledge for managing environmental problems.

To overcome these obstacles, individuals must have access to knowledge and resources, (so that they can make the right investments) and incentives, (to ensure that their activities do not impose costs on others). Communally managed resources require a clear legal framework and supporting services. Governments must devolve the responsibility for managing some resources to individuals, communities, and fiscally accountable utilities. They need to make more use of pricing to allocate resources, to protect property rights, and to support research and the dissemination of knowledge of sound environmental practices.

As the world's population expands to 9 billion over the next forty years, consumption of food will nearly double worldwide and will more than double in developing countries. To match this increase, world grain output will have to grow by about 1.6 percent a year—a difficult target, but less than the 2.0 percent a year increase achieved over the past three decades. This demand for grain (which accounts for more than four-fifths of food crops consumed in developing countries) and the demand for other foods, fuel, and fiber will add enormously to pressure on natural resources—not only on agricultural land but also on stocks of water, fish, and timber.

Natural resources will have to be managed with great care. They will need protection from the inadequate stewardship that is a consequence of poverty, population pressure, ignorance, and corruption. Natural forests, wetlands, coastal areas, and grasslands—all of high ecological value—will have to be protected from overuse and degradation.

Farmers and other managers of rural resources have two options: to intensify production on area already in use or to expand into new areas. To some extent, these are tradeoffs. If more food can be grown on the same land, that will ease the pressure to cultivate new land and will permit the preservation of intact natural areas (Box 7.1). Indeed, over the past quarter century increases in yields have accounted for 92 percent of additional food production, and area expansion for only 8 percent (Table 7.1). But intensification can also produce problems. Raising yields by increasing the use of chemicals, diverting more water for irrigation, and changing land use can create problems elsewhere. Runoff of fertilizer and animal wastes can cause algal blooms and the eutrophication of lakes, coastal estuaries, and enclosed seas. Although these externalities are more common in Western Europe and North America, pollution from agricultural sources is becoming significant in Eastern Europe and other parts of the developing world; in the Punjab in India and Pakistan and in Java, Indonesia, the use of chemical inputs is almost as great as in industrial countries.

The alternative to intensification, however, is equally problematic. Already an estimated 60 percent of the deforestation in developing countries is the result of agricultural expansion, with the great-

Box 7.1 How agricultural intensification can lessen pressure on forests

The expansion of agriculture is one of the main reasons for deforestation in the humid tropics. Researchers in Brazil, Indonesia, and Peru are exploring possibilities for maintaining productivity on deforested land and so reducing pressures for additional forest conversion. Some promising results are emerging. Farm trials conducted in Yurimaguas, Peru, show that for every additional hectare with sustainable and high productivity, an estimated 5 hectares to 10 hectares a year of tropical rainforests could be saved from the ax of the shifting cultivator.

The transition from shifting to continuous cultivation in these trials begins by taking secondary forest fallows left by slash-and-burn agriculture and applying low-input methods—acid-tolerant crops, capture of nutrients in the ash, maximum nutrient recycling, no tillage (only a planting stick is used), and managed fallow to control weeds. The profit from this initial phase averages $1,100 per hectare a year, or a 120 percent return over total costs (largely labor) for small farmers. Options for subsequent phases include intensive continuous cropping, legume-based pasture, or agroforestry.

Continuous crop rotation

Following several years of the low-input system, a transition can sometimes be made to intensive, fertilizer-based, continuous cropping. Where slopes are suitable, fields can be tilled mechanically once most of the felled vegetation has decomposed. Forty crops grown continuously over seventeen years at Yurimaguas demonstrate that productivity can be maintained. But the system will be economically attractive only if roads, credit, and market infrastructure are sufficiently developed.

Legume-based pastures

The low-input system can be the first step toward establishing improved acid-tolerant pastures for production of beef and milk. The transition from income-generating food crops to pasture is achieved by planting pasture species under a rice canopy and applying fertilizers annually or every two years. Several combinations and rotations of selected grasses and legumes have sustained high weight gains in cattle over eight years of trials. Degraded pastures have been regenerated with the use of similar techniques.

Agroforestry

Low-input cropping is a good way of providing cash income and ground cover during the establishment phase of acid-tolerant tree crops, whether the trees are grown for industrial purposes (rubber, oil palm, and guarana), food production (peach palm), or alley cropping.

Table 7.1 Contribution of increases in areas and in yields to growth of cereals production in developing regions and in high-income countries, 1961–90

Country group	Current production (1988–90 average, millions of tons)	Increase since 1961–63 (percent)			Current yield (1988–90, tons per hectare)
		Total	Attributable to increased area	Attributable to increased average yields	
Developing countries	1,315	118	8	92	2.3
Sub-Saharan Africa	57	73	47	52	1.0
East Asia	499	189	6	94	3.7
South Asia	261	114	14	86	1.9
Latin America	105	111	30	71	2.1
Middle East and North Africa	41	68	23	77	1.4
Europe and former U.S.S.R.	336	76	−13	113	2.2
High-income countries	543	67	2	98	4.0
World	1,858	100	8	92	2.6

Note: South Africa is included in figures for developing countries as a group but not in regional figures.
Source: FAO data.

---

est intrusions in Latin America and Africa. This expansion may be led by poor subsistence farmers seeking a livelihood or be driven by growing market demand. While it may meet immediate needs for food and income, it is not a long-term solution if lands are fragile. The great challenge for the future is to balance intensive and extensive growth of agriculture so as to avoid the environmental damage and constraints on productivity that each can cause (Figure 7.1).

Figure 7.1 World production of cereals to feed a growing population: recent performance and the future challenge

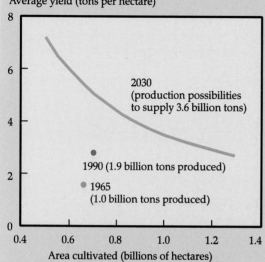

Average yield (tons per hectare)

2030 (production possibilities to supply 3.6 billion tons)

1990 (1.9 billion tons produced)

1965 (1.0 billion tons produced)

Area cultivated (billions of hectares)

Note: World population was 3.3 billion in 1965 and 5.3 billion in 1990; it is projected to be 9.0 billion in 2030 (see "base case" assumptions in Figure 1.1).
Source: World Bank data.

Policies for resource management will have to include three essential components:

• A recognition of the true value of natural resources. Failure to accept that natural resources are ultimately in finite supply, and divergences in the private and social costs of resource exploitation, are root causes of many environmental problems: erosion of deforested hill slopes, releases of carbon dioxide by land-clearing fires, and losses of biological diversity as a result of poorly controlled logging.

• Institutions that match responsibility for resource management with accountability for results. The public sector will inevitably retain responsibility for allocating some of the most sensitive natural resources; it will often own them and will sometimes manage them. Governments need to make sure that those who use natural resources bear the full costs of doing so. But when public institutions are themselves directly involved in production, that rarely happens.

• Better knowledge of the extent, quality, and potential of the resource base. At present, emerging constraints that confront resource management are often poorly understood; research is hampered by inadequate funding. In addition to developing new knowledge and techniques, there is a need to accelerate the diffusion of existing technology that can expand output in environmentally sound ways (Box 7.2).

This chapter examines ways of improving the management of natural resources. Some natural resources, as Chapter 3 noted, have no clear owner, and it is these open-access resources that are most vulnerable to overexploitation. Other resources are managed in three main ways: as private property, in common, or by the state (Figure 7.2). The pattern varies from one country (and culture) to another and is rarely clear-cut, even within a single country. For example, in most countries public authorities control surface water until it is delivered to individual farms or to canals managed by local communities. Policies for improving the management of a resource depend to a large extent on the category into which it falls.

Figure 7.2 Typical property-rights arrangements for rural resources in developing countries

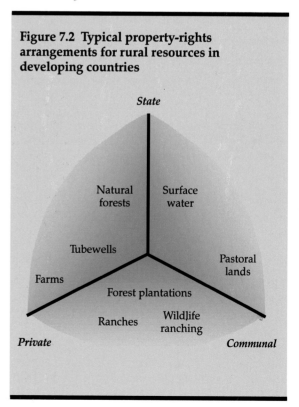

State

Natural forests

Surface water

Tubewells

Pastoral lands

Farms

Forest plantations

Ranches

Wildlife ranching

Private

Communal

Box 7.2 Increasing the knowledge base to meet growing demand for food

Meeting the doubled food demand that is anticipated by 2030 will be feasible but will require substantial productivity gains, according to a study prepared for this Report. Fundamental to meeting the challenge of increasing productivity will be better application of existing (but underused) knowledge about resource management and development of new agricultural technologies.

Among the incentives that would encourage farmers to adopt existing improved technologies and methods, none is more important than the allocation and protection of property rights. In addition, as technologies become more sophisticated, farmer education and strengthening of extension systems are essential. The spread of practices such as conservation tillage and integrated pest management demonstrates that environmentally friendly and economically attractive technologies offer practical alternatives to regulation and subsidies in controlling the environmental costs of agriculture. But even if existing knowledge is fully exploited, the availability and quality of land and irrigation water will be insufficient to meet demand. (Plant genetic resources and climate change are less immediate constraints on increasing global output.) Further expansion of cropland by perhaps 25 percent and of irrigated land by 50 percent may be possible but will have environmental costs. New knowledge will be necessary.

Experience over the past decades has demonstrated that the generation of new knowledge is the most potent and least costly avenue to improving productivity. The expansion of knowledge through research and development will need to encompass human capital, institutional innovation, and new technology. New and higher-yielding cultivars of plants will be needed, along with farming systems research that focuses on integrating livestock and crop activities and on modifying the physical environment in which plants grow— through, for example, measures that conserve soil moisture and that permit continuous cultivation on the infertile, acidic soils common in many tropical areas.

Deliberate investment in agricultural research and development has never been more important. Yet expenditures for agricultural research are stagnating. Research must address the increasing constraints posed by the environmental consequences of agricultural development. The Consultative Group on International Agricultural Research (CGIAR) is placing more emphasis on agricultural resource systems and on relatively neglected areas such as forestry, pest management, soil conservation, and irrigation, to complement the more traditional focus on commodity programs. These changes need to be reinforced and matched by commitments to strengthen national research systems in these directions.

Resource management by individuals and enterprises

Privately managed farms and woodlands produce most of the food, fiber, and fuel that people use. It is on these lands that the central issue of natural resource management will be decided: can output be increased to match demand without unacceptable environmental damage?

When land is privately owned and managed, some environmental problems are less severe. Land is less likely to be overused if its owners have a clear legal title. People who have secure rights to the land they cultivate are more likely to take the long view in managing the soil. One of the few detailed studies of the connection between greater security and improved land management, conducted in Thailand, shows a clear positive link between more secure tenure, access to formal credit, and investment in the land.

But technologies such as integrated pest management that are better for the environment are often information-intensive and require training for the farmers if they are to be effective. They may

also be too expensive for farmers, and access to credit is often inadequate. Poverty makes farmers understandably averse to new and unfamiliar risks.

Even if these constraints are overcome, private ownership may not deliver ideal results from society's point of view. As some of the instances in this section make clear, private owners do not necessarily know whether the side effects of their activities impose costs on others. Even if they do, individual farmers may not cooperate to find solutions unless the result is increased profits on their own fields. It is on privately managed farms and woodlands and the areas around them that recognition of scarcity and side effects—the first requirement of good resource management—is most important. And it is on these lands that sound agricultural policy is, most clearly, sound environmental policy.

Protecting soil fertility

Farmers are usually aware of the consequences of soil degradation and erosion for their crop yields and wish to prevent the damage. But many projects to help them have failed because they promoted only a single method of soil conservation. The greatest success is realized when farmers can select from a menu of techniques adapted to local circumstances; the profitability of a method for farmers can vary significantly, depending on the characteristics of the land, the crop mix, and the availability of labor. Experience shows that even where erosion imposes costs on others—sedimentation and siltation of dams, for example—it is important to try first to persuade farmers to do what is in their own interest. This will usually be less complex than getting farmers to be accountable for the costs borne by others and will in any case contribute toward reducing these costs.

Managing soils to maintain fertility requires achieving a balance between loss of nutrients (through crops and animal products) and replacement of nutrients through the use of manure, inorganic fertilizers, and other sources. In addition, the capability of soils to deliver nutrients and store moisture—functions of soil structure—must be maintained. Basic concerns such as the long-term viability of continuous land use in some tropical areas are poorly understood (Box 7.3). A review of more than 200 studies shows the potential effectiveness of low-cost technologies in reducing erosion and increasing yields (Table 7.2). The most

cost-effective, irrespective of land use, is contour-based cultivation. In India contour ditches have helped to quadruple the survival chances of tree seedlings and quintuple their early growth in height. Ground cover—grasses, leaf litter, and other growth—protects soil from erosion and maintains its capacity to absorb rainfall.

Successful intensification will need to combine such soil management with greater use of inputs, particularly inorganic fertilizers, which provide about 40 percent of nutrients for the world's crops. In Sub-Saharan Africa grain yields average about a third those of East Asia. Differences in land quality are part of the reason, but so too is Sub-Saharan Africa's low fertilizer use—less than one-fifth of East Asia's average (Figure 7.3). In the developing world low use rates and the consequent mining of soil nutrients are far greater problems than excessive and poorly managed fertilizer applications.

Table 7.2 Effect of low-cost soil conservation practices on erosion and crop yields

Method	Decrease in erosion (percent)	Increase in yield (percent)
Mulching	73–98	7–188
Contour cultivation	50–86	6–66
Grass contour hedges	40–70	38–73

Note: The figures are ranges derived from a review of more than 200 studies.
Source: Doolette and Smyle 1990.

Figure 7.3 Fertilizer input and cereal yields in developing regions and high-income countries, 1989

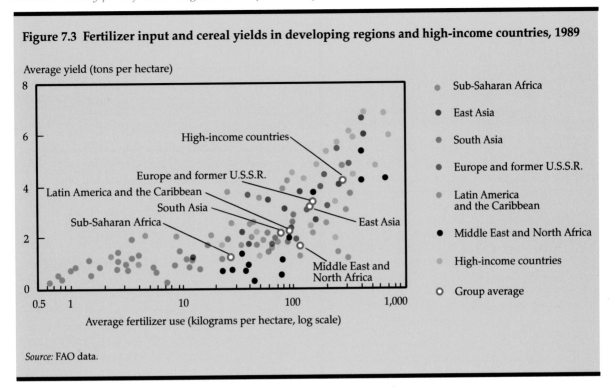

Source: FAO data.

To preserve soil fertility, better use also needs to be made of agricultural techniques such as agroforestry and integrated crop and livestock management. Agroforestry can add nutrients to the soil, reduce water runoff and evaporation from the soil's surface, supply green manure and mulch, and reduce soil erosion. It thus raises crop yields and, because the soil retains more moisture and nutrients, helps to prevent yields from declining in dry years. It provides fodder and shade for cattle and is a good source of fruit, fuelwood, and other by-products. Integrating animals into farming, in addition to providing food and income, makes use of manure to recycle nutrients, including those from otherwise low-value crop residues, grasses, and fodder trees. Smallholders will be more interested in raising livestock if markets for dairy and meat products are encouraged by government support services.

Farmer-controlled soil conservation methods can be developed and implemented at reasonable cost:

• A centuries-old practice in India is being rediscovered, adapted, and promoted. Deeply rooted, hedge-forming vetiver grass, planted in contour strips across hill slopes, slows water runoff dramatically, reduces erosion, and increases the moisture available for crop growth. Over the past six years a quiet revolution has been taking place, and today 90 percent of soil conservation efforts in India are based on such biological systems.

• In the Sahel simple technologies involving construction of rock bunds along contour lines for soil and moisture conservation have succeeded where sophisticated measures once failed. OXFAM has promoted techniques among farmers to improve water harvesting in Burkina Faso. Bunded fields yield an average of 10 percent more than traditional fields in a normal year and, in the drier years, almost 50 percent more.

• In the Central Visayas Regional Development Project in the Philippines a highly successful scheme for distributing young animals has been paired with the promotion of contour grass strips for erosion control. A farmer who establishes a 100-meter strip of napier grass is entitled to borrow a pregnant cow from the project. The farmer cares for the cow and its calf until the calf is weaned and the cow reimpregnated. The cow then goes to another farmer. Demand became so great that a lottery was needed to manage it.

• After a costly and unsuccessful attempt to reduce soil erosion on the uplands of Java, largely through construction of physical structures, Indonesia shifted to a more decentralized, farmer-oriented approach. The use of a broad range of simple agronomic and vegetative measures that farmers can control has led to a higher rate of adoption.

Pesticides, safety, and pesticide resistance

With encouragement from governments, the demand for chemical pesticides has grown enormously in the past twenty years. Pesticide use in Sub-Saharan Africa remains low, but the Asia-Pacific pesticide market had grown to $2.5 billion by the mid-1980s. Indonesia, Pakistan, the Philippines, and Sri Lanka all witnessed increases of more than 10 percent a year between 1980 and 1985.

If used judiciously and responsibly, chemical pesticides provide farmers with an important tool. But improperly used pesticides can endanger the health of users, other rural people, and consumers. They can disrupt ecosystems by polluting soil and water, accumulating in the food chain. And they can indiscriminately kill nontarget species, including natural enemies of pests, and hasten the development of resistance by pests. Many pesticides that are banned in industrial countries because of these effects remain available in the developing world. Policies for managing pesticide use will be encouraged by restrictions in importing countries on pesticide residues on food products (Box 7.4).

In most low-income agriculture, pesticide use is minimal. But its growth in intensive agriculture and for malaria control has had measurable and sometimes alarming impacts in developing countries. Breast milk samples from women in cotton-growing regions of Guatemala and Nicaragua have some of the highest levels of DDT ever recorded in humans, and the illness and mortality rates from pesticide poisoning in these areas approach those for major diseases.

Because the pesticide that one farmer uses contributes little to increased resistance by pests, no individual farmer has an incentive to use less. But increasing use of pesticides has contributed to the growth in resistant pest populations that has taken place since early in this century. From low levels, the number of resistant species has grown rapidly, giving rise to such severe outbreaks as those of the brown planthopper in Indonesia in the 1980s.

Since the effects of overusing pesticides have begun to be widely understood, several policies have been followed. Pesticides are now formulated, as far as possible, to target particular pests. Their toxic life is shorter, to reduce accumulation in the environment. Some governments are eliminating subsidies for pesticides or are even taxing them, thus signaling to farmers that pesticide use has environmental as well as financial costs.

Two technological developments—integrated pest management and bioengineering of crop varieties—offer alternatives to chemicals. Integrated pest management calls for carefully timed, selective spraying of pesticides, backed up by the encouragement of natural predators and more use of resistant varieties and crop rotation. Chemical pesticides are still used, but less often and in smaller amounts. To work, the technique requires onsite research and testing, adaptation to particular pests, and sensitivity to socioeconomic conditions. Farmers need to be well trained and to receive plenty of expert support.

One form of integrated pest management, classical biological control, uses natural predators to manage damage. The development costs can be substantial, but the results can be dramatic, as Africa's cassava mealybug program illustrates. The mealybug, inadvertently introduced from South America in the early 1970s, had cut cassava yields by two-thirds by 1983. Biologists eventually found natural enemies that would control the spread of the pest. With the help of mass-rearing and distribution techniques developed at the International Institute of Tropical Agriculture in Nigeria and the International Center for Tropical Agriculture, the natural predators are now at large in 90 percent of the cassava-growing region of Africa, bringing losses under control. This effort, which involved no chemicals and few risks to the environment, saved a crop that provides a quarter of the food energy consumed in Sub-Saharan Africa, at an estimated benefit-cost ratio of nearly 150 to 1.

Pest-resistant varieties developed through conventional plant breeding have already substantially reduced crop losses in developing countries. One of the most dramatic examples has been the genetic resistance of improved rice varieties to the brown planthopper. Although insects can overcome inbred resistance, the continuous development of new varieties, together with other techniques such as staggered planting of crop varieties with different resistance characteristics, can provide more lasting protection than chemical pesticides alone.

Governments have to enforce regulations that ban or limit the use of pesticides which pose large risks to human health and the environment. Almost all countries have the rudiments of such a regulatory system, but coverage is often incomplete and enforcement lax. The manufacture and import of pesticides is easily monitored and is thus well suited to a command-and-control approach. That approach is particularly appropriate where low levels of literacy and scientific understanding on the part of pesticide users and nonstandard repackaging by retailers create dangers of unsafe use.

Intensifying the use of private forests

Shortages of wood for domestic uses—firewood and building poles—continue to be a serious problem in many developing countries. The rural poor are particularly affected, and especially women, who have to spend time gathering and fetching heavy bundles of wood. The record of tree-planting efforts led by governments has been mixed. Successful cases indicate an important lesson: trees can be a highly profitable commercial crop—but farmers must be given the right to own, cut, and sell them, at fair market prices.

When prices and costs reflect shortages of wood and the services that trees supply, farmers plant trees. In Nepal air photographs taken in 1964 and ground surveys done in 1988 revealed that the density of tree cover on rainfed agricultural land in two remote rural districts had increased from 65 to 298 trees a hectare—not by chance but because farmers had responded to incentives by planting trees. The population in the two districts had doubled during the preceding thirty years, communal and government forests had become less accessible, and the costs of obtaining wood and forest fodder had risen.

Smallholder tree farming in Kenya shows the same responsiveness to emerging markets for wood and forest products. The afforestation efforts of the government, aid agencies, and local NGOs often assumed that farmers would be reluctant to plant trees on their land. But in the densely populated Muranga District, where wood was becoming scarce, farmers independently maintained nearly 14 percent of the area under indigenous tree cover and planted or cultivated trees on another 9 percent of the land.

High-yielding industrial plantations—mainly private but sometimes maintained with technical assistance or subsidies from the government—take pressure off natural forests and provide productive ways of using land. More than thirty years ago, Kenya, Tanzania, and Zambia began to develop plantation forestry as an alternative to exploitation of the natural forest. In Kenya in the 1950s about 90 percent of the country's industrial wood requirements were met by selectively logging natural forest areas. By the early 1970s fast-growing pine and cypress plantations made it possible to meet 80 percent of industrial requirements through sustained yields from plantations occupying 180,000 hectares—less than 10 percent of the natural forest area. This strategy slowed encroachment on the natural forest from traditional logging and allowed large parts of the natural forest to be gazetted as national parks and catchment areas. More recent problems with reforestation, recovery of costs, and control of damage caused by cypress aphids in monocultural plantations confront the Forest Department in its efforts to sustain these gains.

In Chile the government has encouraged private investment in plantation forestry through direct subsidies, increased security of tenure on forested land, and a stable macroeconomic and regulatory climate. Industrial roundwood production from plantations doubled between 1960 and 1977 and again between 1977 and 1984, making Chile one of the most successful developing countries in the international forest products market.

Resource management by communities

Many natural resources—village commons, pastures, water resources, and near-shore fisheries—are managed communally. This has often resulted in sound stewardship over many centuries. But when communal management has broken down, these areas have suffered some of the worst overexploitation. Often the forces leading to the collapse of common-property management are insurmountable, and then either private or state ownership and control are the only answers.

A compelling reason for supporting community resource management is its importance for the poor. In many parts of the world, rights to common-property resources are all that separates the landless and land-poor from destitution. In India, for instance, research by the International Crops Research Institute for the Semi-Arid Tropics showed that common-property resources accounted for between 14 and 23 percent of the income of poor households in seven states and that grazing on communally owned lands accounted for as much as 84 percent of poor people's livestock fodder. In contrast, wealthy households derived no more than 3 percent of their income and less than 38 percent of their animal grazing from common-property lands.

Pressures on community management

Population growth, technological change, difficulties in raising capital, and government interference can all make community resource management harder to sustain. The solution in these situations may lie in developing and rehabilitating collective management and decisionmaking. That will not be easy. To work, common-property management requires local responsibility, effective ways of resolving disputes, and national political support. A key to success appears to be "political entrepreneurship." The political entrepreneur motivates others, engenders trust, and demonstrates the tangible benefits of collective action. This essential ingredient is also probably the scarcest, the hardest to define, and the least substitutable in rural development. Even when it is available, deciding on whether more or less government involvement and action is appropriate remains a difficult choice. Fragile community management of land, fisheries, or woodlots can sometimes be rescued by stopping detrimental intrusions and providing supporting services.

OVERGRAZING. Millions of people in Africa and Asia raise animals on pastures and rangelands that have low carrying capacity because of poor quality or unreliable rainfall. Pastoralists and their rangelands are threatened by overgrazing, by land appropriations by governments and farmers, and by the development of water sources for competing uses.

Pastoral associations in West Africa have sought, with mixed success, to improve the productivity of commonly held livestock pastures and water sources. In addition to managing water and grazing, they procure inputs and services and sell products. Successful associations have clear leadership, adequate legal protection, and mechanisms for raising capital. Legislation has been necessary to confirm the status of the associations, the legal allocation of grazing and water points, and the enforcement duties of local authorities. Pastoral associations that have gained legal status still often have poor access to formal credit, even for short-term working capital. In Mauritania funds are currently raised by annual contributions from members; in Mali well construction is financed with payments collected from members when they water their livestock.

Government agencies and NGOs can also provide political entrepreneurship. The Aga Khan Rural Support Program in Pakistan has been successful in improving management of common grazing lands. The program has used credit and technical assistance to build village infrastructure.

OVERFISHING. Common-property regimes rely on continuing self-imposed restraints enforced by group members, which can easily be eroded. Successful self-management of a fishing village in Sri

Lanka was finally unable to cope with population growth and higher prices, and long-standing cooperative agreements among fishermen in southern Bahia, Brazil, were undermined when nylon nets were introduced under a government program (see Box 3.2).

Elsewhere, common-property management has proved more durable. In the inshore fishery at Alanya, Turkey, local fishermen came together in the 1970s to overcome problems caused by increased fishing. They developed a rotational system of spacing and assigning choice fishing spots, with mechanisms for monitoring and enforcement. The system controlled overfishing and reduced costly conflicts.

New technologies and political entrepreneurship on the part of development agencies have sometimes brought coastal communities together to improve resource management. To counter dynamite fishing, which has depleted fish stocks and destroyed coral reefs in the Philippines, the Central Visayas Regional Project established fish sanctuaries by building artificial reefs from local materials and also provided alternative employment opportunities, road construction, and village water supplies.

DEPLETING VILLAGE WOODLANDS. Rural communities in many countries have lost their traditional management responsibilities over village woodlands, and the result has often been neglect and overexploitation. Nationalization of forest resources is frequently at fault. In the 1950s Nepal nationalized forests to ''protect, manage, and conserve the forest for the benefit of the entire country.'' Analysts have documented the disruption—if not destruction—of the previous system of communal management. Because the government lacked the resources to regulate use, common property was turned, in reality, into open-access land in the name of conservation through state control. In the late 1970s Nepal reversed its policy and began to return woodlands and degraded forests to communities and villages. At first forests were formally turned over to *panchayats*—large administrative units with little previous involvement in forestry. These bodies gave the villages the most degraded lands, which required high investments for restoration and offered only delayed benefits. The World Bank is now supporting efforts to encourage management by smaller groups more closely associated with particular forest tracts and to give them responsibility for forests in good condition, as well as for degraded land.

In Niger, under the French colonial regime, forests were taken over by the state because they were being eroded by the demand for firewood. Wood harvesting was prohibited except for controlled exploitation under cutting licenses, and violators were fined. The outcome was the elimination of private and community incentives for management and replanting. Forest guards and police found that they could extract bribes from harvesters in lieu of official fines.

Prospects for community management

Many development agencies and researchers place great hope in common-property systems as a way of managing natural resources. Although, as the examples given here show, success is possible, failure and collapse into open access are more common. It is too early to say whether the benefits of common-property management outweigh the costs of rehabilitating failed community management or instituting it in new areas.

Governments need to recognize that smaller organizational units, such as villages or pastoral associations, are better equipped to manage their own resources than are large authorities and may be a more effective basis for rural development and rational resource management than institutions imposed from outside. Group action is deeply rooted in many societies—for managing land, for cooperative marketing and input supply, for running community savings and loan arrangements, and for pooling labor for urgent tasks. To succeed, cooperatives have to be voluntary and managed by group members. They can be based on customary social structures. Governments can give advice on accounting, legal rights, and technology and provide a legal framework for the creation, recognition, and dissolution of cooperatives. What is most needed is popular participation at the village level, which may usefully be fostered by NGOs and grass-roots organizations (see Chapter 4).

It is important that governments guarantee security of land tenure. Farmers with a clear title to land are more likely to have access to formal credit and to invest more in their land. Security is not synonymous with individual possession of a formal title. In Sub-Saharan Africa, in particular, greater security could be achieved by strengthening indigenous and customary land rights. The benefits extend well beyond soil conservation by individual farmers. Legal definition and enforcement of group rights have proved important for improving the management of such common property as grazing land.

Land tenure in much of Sub-Saharan Africa is evolving and is often a cross between private ownership and common access. Because of the complexity, apparent efficiency, and continuing evolution of indigenous land tenure systems, policymakers should be cautious about intervening. Unless indigenous tenure systems are weakened (by, for example, civil war or resettlement), formal land titling is unlikely to improve resource management and may lead to unnecessary landlessness. Policies for strengthening indigenous tenure systems by, for example, giving legal status to group ownership and voluntarily recording contractual arrangements related to land can be beneficial. But care must be taken to avoid introducing barriers that limit the evolution of land rights and markets.

Landownership in Sub-Saharan Africa traditionally resides with the community, but farmers are assigned rights to use specific parcels. These rights give sufficient security for growing crops and, where they can be bequeathed to children, foster a long-term interest in land management. Farmers may have limited rights to transfer land they use to others without permission from family or village elders, and other people may have supplementary use rights over the same land—to graze the land during the dry season or to collect wood or fruit. Such restrictions, however, do not appear as yet to have had significant effects on investments in land improvements or on land productivity. Moreover, as population growth and commercialization make land scarce and increasingly valuable, land is increasingly privatized. The indigenous systems of communal tenure appear flexible enough to evolve with the increasing scarcity of land and the commensurate need for greater security of land rights. At the same time, the retention of some community control over landownership helps to prevent the emergence of landlessness.

Resource management by governments

Governments play two main roles in the management of natural resources. They often own them, and they influence their allocation by setting the legal framework and through policies that affect incentives to which other resource users respond.

In many countries, particularly developing countries, economically and environmentally significant natural resources are in the hands of the government. Tropical moist forests are almost invariably publicly owned, and the infrastructure of water resources is often developed and owned by the public sector. The rationale for public management of resources is that the government is best placed to pursue multiple objectives—economic growth, regional development, environmental protection, and support of indigenous people and the cultural heritage. But government ownership and management in the pursuit of such public objectives need to be effective if they replace incentives for private gain. In practice, government stewardship of resources has shown a mixed record of successes and failures.

Part of the reason lies with the bureaucracies that manage public resources. Often, they are inefficient and overstaffed. Lack of rewards, job insecurity, and staff turnover may blunt the incentive to adopt new management techniques. Underpriced natural resources put additional pressure on resource management agencies in both industrial and developing countries. By creating enormous opportunities for corruption and gain, underpricing makes the agencies vulnerable to influence from the politically powerful. Forestry agencies come under pressure to provide low-cost materials to industry, and water authorities to build irrigation infrastructure that will serve politically important areas. Meanwhile, essential tasks with little political appeal, such as maintenance and regeneration, are overlooked.

In many cases reform will require devolving responsibility for investment and implementation from central authorities to individuals, communities, and fiscally autonomous agencies. Governments need to concentrate on generating new knowledge through research, protecting property rights, and resolving conflicts fairly.

Legal frameworks and economic incentives have often proliferated but remain confused and counterproductive. Laws and regulations need to be reviewed to ensure consistency, avoid deterring responsible private investment, and preserve the rights of local people and forest dwellers. Economic incentives that foster environmentally destructive practices need to be removed. Stable policies are essential because uncertainties encourage exploitation to obtain short-term benefits.

Deciding allocations

In theory, price is the ideal mechanism for allocating resources. In practice, it is never easy to design appropriate pricing mechanisms for natural resources, each of which presents different difficulties. But although price is not a panacea for problems of resource allocation, it is underused by many countries. The consequences, as learned from the Aral Sea, can be ecological and economic disaster (see Box 1.5). A number of developing countries are devising and using market-based mechanisms to allocate resources, with good results. When pricing is not relied on, there must be some other mechanism for bringing scarcity to bear on decisionmaking. Zoning is one such mechanism.

WATER ALLOCATION AND USE. Competition between farmers and cities for water supplies is already constraining many countries' development strategies. The problem will grow as populations increase and economies expand. The large fixed costs associated with water distribution, uncertainties about the physical availability of water from year to year, and widely held cultural and religious proscriptions against treating water as a commodity are likely to compel governments to continue to allocate water administratively.

The largest single demand for water comes from irrigation. Inefficient use of irrigation water puts pressure on other users and imposes environmental costs. Eighty-five percent of irrigated land relies on traditional surface systems based on canals and gravity flow. Their design is often too inflexible to provide water with the timeliness and predictability that farmers desire as they adopt improved crop varieties and turn to intensified and diversified cropping systems. Instead, water is delivered on arbitrary schedules and for limited periods of time, with incentives for use further distorted by subsidized prices. Farmers respond by taking as much water as possible while they can. The results are often wasted water, waterlogging, leaching of soil nutrients, and excessive runoff of agricultural chemicals with drainage water.

It is often better to improve existing systems than to build new ones. Lining canals reduces water losses, and installing drainage helps combat salinization and waterlogging. But modernizing installed designs is generally more expensive than achieving comparable gains through improved management.

Better pricing of water (and of electricity used to pump groundwater) to reflect its scarcity and the environmental costs of overuse is fundamental to better management. Governments often worry that reducing subsidies will hurt poor farmers and will be unacceptable if water delivery is unpredictable. Implementing improved pricing is difficult. Water flows are hard to measure in the open canal

systems that characterize most irrigation systems. Closed-pipe conveyance systems are best for charging by water volume, but unless there is good communication between farmers and the delivery agency, they are vulnerable to tampering and damage to volumetric gauges.

A number of countries are finding that progress is possible. In China financially semiautonomous water supply agencies sell water wholesale to water users who are grouped by village or township, partly on the basis of volume. These user groups in turn collect fees from their members, typically on the basis of the area irrigated or, less frequently, the volume of water used. Although the charges are generally set well below real costs, the link to quantities used encourages savings. Moreover, the system reinforces financial responsibility at each level because the fees collected remain in the irrigation budgets. Tighter overall budgets in other countries have prompted increases in water fees from the subsidized rates.

Additional public investment in surface irrigation must take account of increasing infrastructural costs, low commodity prices, and environmental costs. Some developments will be ruled out by the environmental consequences of reservoir inundation, water diversion, increased water pollution from nonpoint agricultural sources, and alteration of hydrologic systems.

New techniques such as drip and sprinkler systems can use water more efficiently and deliver water when farmers need it. Although they are unlikely to supplant the large surface irrigation systems for grain crops, these techniques will become more important for future expansion of irrigation, partly because they can be employed with high-value crops grown on unleveled land and permeable soils where traditional surface irrigation is impossible. They are already spreading in developing countries, especially in North Africa and the Middle East, China, and Brazil.

The spreading of these irrigation techniques will require a change in the traditional role of governments in irrigation. The new techniques work on a far smaller scale than traditional surface irrigation, and the source of water is usually a privately owned tubewell rather than a publicly managed dam. Manufacturers can be relied on to promote the systems because more marketable equipment is involved than in surface canal systems. Any price distortions that affect investment decisions by farmers must be corrected, since the farmers, rather than direct public investment, will be the main agents of expansion. Governments must also

Box 7.5 Participatory land management in Burkina Faso

Land-hungry farmers in Africa are pushing into new areas. Conflicts between agricultural and pastoral communities are common, and resource breakdown is an increasing threat. In Burkina Faso an innovative approach to the management of natural resources is using indigenous institutions and sustained local participation to resolve problems of resource allocation and environmental deterioration.

Community *terroirs* (management areas) are the basis for the approach, which is decentralized (to take into account each *terroir*'s specific features), intersectoral (embracing agriculture, forestry, and livestock), participative (respecting the goals and resources of the community), and iterative (responsive to monitored results). Several critical steps are needed to put these principles into practice.

• The community designates a natural resource management committee that includes representatives of the principal social groups of the village and of user groups such as herders, men and women farmers, and fishermen. The committee is responsible for allocating resources and dealing with neighboring communities and the government on natural resource issues.

• A resource use management plan is then drawn up with the assistance of technical advisers. The plan includes a statement of community objectives, an intersectoral environmental assessment of the *terroir*, and the choice of technologies most likely to achieve sus-

tainable output, protection of key natural resources, and generation of income for the community.

• The *terroir* management plan is agreed on by the committee and the government. The agreement stipulates the activities and expenditures needed to implement the plan. The community, for instance, may agree to measures and targets for improving pasture, planting trees, and adopting improved practices for soil conservation. In return, the government assists the community to obtain basic infrastructure and services, cofinances some investments, and provides protection from encroachment on land improvements. The agreement also conveys official recognition of the community's rights to the land and to any improvements.

• Monitoring is a key element of implementation, and along with changes in community goals, in environmental status, and in the effectiveness of chosen technologies, may lead to adjustments to the plan.

As Burkina Faso's experience shows, participation can lead to better resource management, but the parties involved must also change the basis on which resource management decisions are made. Local institutions can form a building block for the management contract, but they need to be modified and adapted to cope with the new challenges created by immigration and resource breakdown. This management strategy is currently being extended to other Sahelian countries, including Mali and Niger.

---

monitor aggregate use of groundwater and regulate tubewell pumping to prevent excessive drawdown of aquifers.

If the potential efficiency gains from these technologies are to be realized, the new methods must be integrated into a broader approach to the interactions among water, plants, soils, nutrients, and other farm inputs. Farmers will need research and extension support to acquire new management skills, credit to enable them to afford mechanical equipment, and secure legal rights to water to encourage them to invest in new technology.

CHANGING LAND USE. Zoning is used in rural areas for the same reason as in urban areas: individual decisions about land use do not necessarily produce the best results for society as a whole. Because zoning imposes constraints on land use that are contrary to the underlying incentives driving individual behavior, its effectiveness depends on whether it is enforced and to what extent those incentives can be weakened. Where economic in-

centives are the principal influence on individual behavior, land zoning alone is a weak tool for determining land use. But it can be influential if it has political support and the incentives driving individual behavior are weak. Experience with zoning in developing countries, whether to protect forests or to locate agricultural activities, has not been successful. Many countries have spent large sums on mapping and land use planning but have failed to integrate these activities into effective land management programs.

Agricultural zoning in Africa has traditionally had the primary purpose of separating crop and animal agriculture or confining the agricultural activity of particular groups to specific regions. In several countries, colonial laws that partitioned land into European and African reserves were among the first targets for change after independence. In Kenya this was followed by the registration of blocks of land with fixed boundaries for pastoralists to manage as group ranches; in several cases the lands were next to game parks. To promote the ranches, pastoralist groups were promised compensation for wildlife damage, participation in tourism revenue from the adjacent parks, upgrading of livestock, and access to credit. Results have been mixed, and the pastoralists' rangeland remains under pressure from competing uses. Some groups found that tourism receipts went elsewhere, that promised infrastructure for delivering water was ineffective, and that protected wildlife degraded ranch pastures. Lessons learned from such experiences have led to new approaches to defining resource use. Burkina Faso is relying on community-based development of resource management plans (Box 7.5). Botswana has also depended on participatory planning within districts to identify and support zoning for private and communal ranches, cropping, wildlife management, protected areas, and urban development.

Zoning of forests attempts to set forest boundaries and identify areas for various uses. Until management techniques are devised for tropical forests that enable uses which are compatible with preserving biodiversity and the natural ecosystem,

areas with high environmental value need to be set aside and protected. Similarly, areas that provide watershed protection need meaningful, enforceable boundaries. In Uganda, beginning in the 1950s, increasing population pressure led to settlement in zoned forest reserves, but the reserves were managed fairly effectively for forestry through the early 1970s. Later, the breakdown of civil order and continued population pressure brought about massive migration into the reserves. The government now faces a long and difficult process of evicting squatters from forest areas. Kenya and Nigeria have had similar experiences.

In several countries agroecological zoning is being used to prevent further encroachment into forests. Simply demarcating zones, however, is clearly not enough to prevent illegal encroachment. Zoning must be backed up by economic and financial incentives that discourage invasion. Investments must be made to intensify land use in suitable areas, develop extractive production in areas that should remain under forest cover, and protect the borders of conservation zones. (Box 7.6

Box 7.6 Land zoning in Rondônia

Growing socioeconomic problems caused by accelerating migration to the northwest frontier of Rondônia led the Brazilian government in 1980 to launch an investment program. The Integrated Development Program for Northwest Brazil (Polonoroeste) was designed to promote migration and its orderly absorption. This was done by building a highway and feeder roads, but increasing deforestation accompanied the program.

Now, agroecological zoning has distinguished areas capable of development from those with special ecological or social significance or without long-term agricultural potential. The government hopes to discourage new migration, concentrate existing populations in areas with potential for permanent agriculture, and reduce encroachment into areas that should remain under forest cover. Active intervention is needed to control the spread of itinerant agriculture. Rondônia's new constitution and the complementary laws adopt agroecological zoning as one of the basic criteria for determining legal land occupation. Zoning is ineffective if it stands alone; in Rondônia it is being supported by the following reforms:

• Public investments will be reviewed for consistency with the agroecological zones. New roads and support services will no longer be put where agriculture is not sustainable but will be concentrated in the

areas that are most suitable for population and where forest cover is already mostly cleared.

• Forest clearing will no longer be a criterion for obtaining land title. Inconsistent land regulations and laws are being regularized, and institutions for establishing property rights are being strengthened.

• Fiscal incentives for cattle ranching and deforestation have already been suspended, and credit programs are being restricted to activities that are consistent with the zoning.

• Most of the lands reserved for Amerindians—20 percent of the state's area—have been identified and demarcated, and policies and programs for improved protection are being put in place.

• A media campaign is under way to explain the zoning restrictions on use of land and discourage migration to Rondônia.

• Local NGOs are participating in consultative government bodies to represent their communities in discussions of policies and annual public investment proposals.

Agroecological zoning, strengthened government commitment, and closer community involvement are greatly improving the prospects for sustainable agricultural and extractive development, as well as environmental protection.

describes the experience in Rondônia, Brazil.) Zoning must be complemented by measures to strengthen enforcement, such as training staff and paying them properly, investing in equipment, and reinforcing the capacity of government to pursue legal action against illegal loggers and encroachers. Training for prosecutors, auditors, and judges in the handling of forestry and land use cases could be an important measure in many countries.

The settlement of new lands, which are often publicly owned, has been an important and increasingly controversial dimension of development. Settlement takes place because individuals want better lives and governments want to ease population pressures, raise agricultural output, generate employment, reinforce political control, and relocate people displaced by natural disasters and development projects. The 4.5 million hectares brought under cultivation each year is small in relation to the nearly 1.3 billion hectares of potential cropland in developing countries. But land settlement can transform the countries where it occurs. Land settlement projects have sometimes been promoted in areas that better preparation would have revealed to be unsuitable. Settlement projects are expensive—$10,000 per family in a sample of World Bank–supported projects—which has made for costly mistakes when the projects were poorly sited.

Several countries have promoted settlement by instituting fiscal incentives for investment in undeveloped areas. These incentives have encouraged uneconomic and environmentally destructive practices, such as livestock ranching in the Brazilian Amazon. From 1966 until recently, the Brazilian tax system allowed investors in approved agricultural projects in the Amazon to claim tax credits of up to 50 percent of their federal income tax liability. Investors responded enthusiastically and by the late 1980s had established cattle ranches on more than 8.4 million hectares. Subsidized agricultural credit, which was even more widely available than the tax credits, reinforced the incentive for deforestation. The elimination of such measures—in part because of environmental concerns but more for fiscal reasons—illustrates that reforms of environmental and economic policies can be complementary.

In many countries, including Colombia, Indonesia, and Senegal, willing settlers, migrating at their own initiative and expense, already play a significant role in land settlement. Their assumption of costs and risk—one test of the likely eco-

nomic viability of settlement—reduces the costs to government and the hazards of plans and targets. Spontaneous settlement can be guided by policies that provide infrastructure and social services, extension programs on viable agricultural strategies, and legal status for land occupation. In addition to creating such magnets to steer settlers toward acceptable areas, governments will still need to restrict settlement in areas where the environmental impact would be unacceptable.

Managing natural resources: industrial forestry

Many of the natural resources on which developing countries rely are and will remain public. Governments should attempt to manage resources under public ownership in ways that maximize their value to society. Such policies will yield two benefits: the resources will contribute to development, and consumers will have incentives to economize on their use, develop substitutes, and invest in sustained-yield management of privately owned resources.

Ownership of forests often remains in public hands in an attempt to ensure that multiple objectives can be achieved. In addition to wood production, these objectives include soil conservation, flood control, and protection of biodiversity. Logging often dominates because it generates money, and until recently relatively little attention was given to managing the nonwood services of forests. But that situation is changing as developing countries realize that past forest management has rarely achieved sustainability in timber harvests, let alone maintained other forest services.

In determining the future of forests, logging policy is particularly important. Although logging accounts for only about one-fifth of total deforestation in developing countries, managing it properly can help control the agriculture and ranching that often follow. And commercial logging may be the forestry subsector most amenable to policy reform.

Government efforts to rationalize industrial forestry in many countries are another instance of the advisability of using market-based approaches and the difficulties of doing so in practice. The rates (stumpage fees) charged loggers for standing timber seldom come close to the costs of replacing the volume removed with wood grown in plantations (Figure 7.4).

SUSTAINABLE MANAGEMENT TECHNIQUES. A recent review of tropical forest management by the International Tropical Timber Organization found that less than 1 percent of the tropical forest is currently under truly sustainable management. Several countries are trying to raise that total through improved harvest technologies and low-impact design of roads. In Peru the forest is harvested in long narrow strips designed to mimic the gaps created when a tree falls from natural causes. The strips to be harvested are carefully selected, and animal traction is used to avoid soil compaction. Harvesting can thus be done without serious environmental damage, and the regeneration that takes place is rapid, abundant, and diverse. This experiment is being conducted in collaboration with the Yanesha Forestry Cooperative, a group of indigenous people who own the land communally.

Much more effort is needed to find scientifically sound techniques for plantations and to learn how natural forests work. Advances in farm forestry and commercial logging have been slow, partly because of inadequate research. In Asia (excluding China) at least 5,000 scientists are working on rice research but fewer than 1,000 on forestry. In India expenditure on forestry research amounts to less than 0.01 percent of the value of forest products consumed each year.

Natural tropical forests, especially tropical moist forests, are difficult to manage even for the relatively straightforward objective of timber production. Their ecosystems are highly sensitive to intervention, often in unexpected ways. Many important tree species, for example, can mature only when the forest canopy is opened by the death or removal of older trees. At other stages in their life cycles, however, many of these same species may be dependent on light-intolerant soil microorganisms. Even selective logging alters the species and size composition of the forest and can set off a chain of changes that makes unlikely the regeneration of the original species mix. Timber extraction must be sophisticated if it is to avoid damage to the integrity of the forest as an ecosystem.

CONTROLLING PRIVATE LOGGERS. Logging in tropical forests is typically carried out by private firms, nominally under terms established by the government. These terms may stipulate the logging practices to be used, the fees to be paid, the duration of harvesting rights, and the loggers' obligation to provide for postharvest treatment of the forest. Unfortunately, these agreements are often flouted, and forestry agencies have consistently been unwilling or unable to enforce them. Forestry agencies often lack transport and good

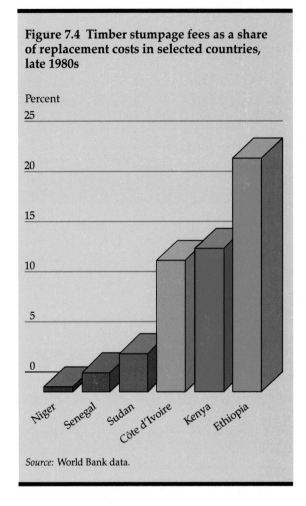

Figure 7.4 Timber stumpage fees as a share of replacement costs in selected countries, late 1980s

Source: World Bank data.

maps. They are thus unable to discover the value of the resource they are supposed to protect. Loggers, however, have incentives to be well aware of that value and to obstruct or corrupt efforts to restrict their operations. In many countries forestry officials who attempted to enforce restrictions have been assaulted and even killed. Faced with these risks, and typically underpaid, officials often ignore transgressions or accept bribes from loggers to look the other way.

One way to lessen the difficulties of enforcement is to build into timber concessions adequate incentives to ensure regeneration. Too often, the concession arrangements are too short to make concessionaire silvicultural activities after the first harvest profitable, and no provision is made for publicly financed regeneration. In Sabah, Malaysia, for example, half of all concessions are for twenty-one years, most of the remainder are for ten years, and 5 percent are for one year. Full tim-

149

ber rotation, by contrast, exceeds seventy years. Concessionaires may harvest gradually over the twenty-one-year period of the contract, but they will have little reason to undertake reforestation. Longer-term contracts or contracts with provisions for performance-based extensions, as in Canada, can force concessionaires to bear the costs that their initial harvests impose on future resource returns. They also permit concessionaires to reap the future rewards that are the necessary incentives for good harvest and regeneration practices.

Another way to reduce the difficulty of enforcement is to mobilize local communities to report illegal activities. In Indonesia private national and international firms are being recruited to monitor compliance with logging concessions. If the monitoring and enforcement capability of developing countries can be improved, efforts to redesign incentives to loggers can begin to be effective.

Managing natural resources: habitats

The most precious natural habitats are likely to be best served by remaining under some form of public ownership. But that does not necessarily mean that they should also be managed by the central government. Some successful schemes for protecting sensitive ecosystems rely on a marriage of public ownership with communal management.

Some fragile and particularly vulnerable ecosystems will always need to be protected against encroachment and degradation. The coverage of protected areas should be consistent with conservation goals. Sri Lanka is one of the few countries to devote more than 10 percent of its land area to wildlife protection, yet about 90 percent of this protected land is outside the wet zone, the country's most biologically diverse habitat, and many of the protected areas are probably too small for effective preservation. The costs of conservation programs, both financial and economic, can escalate if protected areas are not selected with care. Park consolidation and identification of underprotected habitats are thus important first steps in reorienting conservation programs.

Although 5 percent of the world's natural habitats is formally protected from development, much of this area is threatened with encroachment by farming, logging, and other activities. Not only does the level of protection in officially protected areas need to be strengthened; natural values need to be, and can be, protected in areas outside parks and reserves. Several techniques are being tested in developing countries. It is clear that involvement of and benefits to local people are the key to the viability of any scheme.

Integrated conservation and development projects build on the principle that local communities must be involved in devising ways to protect parks. When an existing park's neighbors are deriving economic benefits from encroaching on it, better alternatives must be made available; protecting parks from the local population, in addition to being ethically unjustifiable, can be prohibitively expensive. Several new schemes establish a core conservation area surrounded by multiuse buffer zones that are managed intensively by local communities to provide income and products. Agreed-on rules of access form the basis for limiting future encroachment.

One country that is reorienting its conservation strategy from the traditional pattern to this newer approach is Nepal. The Royal Chitwan Park in the fertile Terai plains is an important tourist destination, but it was generating few benefits for local communities. With control of malaria and rapid population growth on the plains, the park came under strong pressure from encroachment that was only partly kept under control by the army, at the cost of generating hostility. In contrast, in Nepal's Annapurna Conservation Area, established in 1986 as a multiple-use area rather than a national park, government collaboration with local community groups brought about the establishment and enforcement of a land-use system that increased the local benefits from tourism and provided local people with training in conservation and forest management. The project has successfully induced a skeptical local population to participate in management of the area, and the conflicts that beset Chitwan have been avoided.

Only a few developing countries have managed to establish priorities, reformulate policies, and operate protected areas effectively. Even those that have succeeded in strengthening their conservation institutions have found it hard to coordinate policy, fix the division of labor between local and central authorities, collaborate with NGOs, and devise incentives for efficient management (Box 7.7).

In Africa expanding settlements in marginal areas are reducing agricultural productivity and displacing wildlife. Conservationists and development planners are exploring ways to use wildlife resources to generate food and income. This possibility has been most seriously explored in the semiarid rangelands and particularly in southern Africa, where commercial use of wildlife is replacing livestock husbandry in many places. Zimbabwe's experience is that wildlife has significant advantages in this ecosystem: it yields greater earnings and does less damage to soils and vegetation. The scope for community-based wildlife management programs, however, depends on the economic value of the wildlife asset compared with alternative land uses.

Throughout the semiarid rangelands of Africa wildlife use could be greatly increased if a number of distortions could be removed. The most important constraint is that wildlife, albeit technically state property, is effectively an open-access resource. Access needs to be controlled, and managed culling implemented. Other distortions arise from direct and indirect subsidies to the livestock sector; quarantine and veterinary policies that restrict wildlife production; local sale and export of wild meat; and lack of accounting for environmental degradation (Box 7.8).

The establishment of extractive reserves for the harvest of nontimber forest products has emerged as a promising strategy for reconciling economic development and environmental conservation. Harvest of many nontimber forest products can take place without destroying the forest cover. The extractive reserve approach differs from traditional approaches to protection, which, by restricting access to traditionally used resources, disrupt local cultures and economies.

In 1985 a rubber tappers' union in Brazil joined with the government to establish a new way of keeping tracts of Amazonian forest under low-impact use. The creation of extractive reserves granted legal protection to forestland traditionally used by rubber tappers, Brazil-nut gatherers, and other local people. Although separate deeds were not issued, individual families retain their rights to traditional collecting territories within the reserve. The land cannot be sold or converted to nonforest uses, but subsistence crops are permitted on small plots. Twenty reserves have been proposed; the first six were established in Acre, one of the Brazilian states most threatened by deforestation.

Conclusions

A common theme in many aspects of natural resource use is the need for better research. That need will increase: as development and growth proceed, new problems will emerge. We still know little about how to protect the resource base suffi-

Box 7.8 Comparing the costs and benefits of conservation and development

The example of Korup National Park in Cameroon shows how valuation of environmental damage and conservation costs can help inform choices about how to use the environment. The park contains Africa's oldest rainforest, which is home to numerous unique and endangered species of plants and animals. Increasing pressures to convert the forest to agriculture led the government to design a conservation plan for about 126,000 hectares of the park. Economic valuation techniques were used to estimate the damage that would occur if these areas of rainforest were developed—as a measure of the benefits of conserving them—and compare the benefits with the costs of the conservation program.

Conserving the areas would provide local, national, and international benefits, but not all of these could be estimated. The measurable benefits from use of the conservation area that accrued to Cameroon included direct yields from, for example, sales of forest products (32 percent of measurable benefits) and indirect benefits such as protection of fisheries and soils (68 percent). These were set against the costs of management (88 percent) and of forgone revenues from commercial forest products (12 percent). The exercise found that (at an 8 percent discount) the measurable benefits of the conservation area for Cameroon were less than the costs.

But not all benefits were measurable. People in Cameroon and in the rest of the world derive other benefits from conservation. These include "option values" (protection against loss of future benefits—say, from medicines developed from indigenous plants) and "existence values" that arise because people value the preservation of species even when they do not expect to derive any other benefits, now or ever, from them. Since most of these nonuse values reflect benefits to people outside Cameroon, the difference between the benefits and costs of the conservation area for Cameroon—roughly $6 billion—represents the international transfers needed to justify conservation on economic grounds. The per hectare transfer would be lower than the values attributed to tropical forest conservation areas in, for example, Costa Rica. Given the diversity of species in Korup Park, making such transfers would be to the advantage of the international community. The issue then becomes whether the rest of the world is willing to pay Cameroon for the costs it would incur to protect an environmental asset that is valuable for the world as a whole.

---

ciently to feed the burgeoning world population. We know little about improving simple technologies: the design of surface irrigation and drainage systems has not changed in years, in spite of growing demands from farmers for better control of water. As countries become richer, their demands on their natural resources change but do not diminish: rising incomes in industrial countries have led to new demands—for open space, wilderness preservation, and other amenities—that could not have been foreseen fifty years ago.

Research on the conservation and use of natural resources ought to be mainly national. But some problems require international research. The CGIAR is already placing more emphasis on forestry, pest management, soil conservation, and irrigation. Countries often say they believe in the need for more agricultural research. Yet even though, as measured by rates of return, agricultural research is among the best public investments available, support for research is declining. If that trend continues, the prospects for environmentally sound agricultural intensification are poor indeed, and the implications for the protection of natural habitat from encroachment are dismal.

International environmental concerns

International environmental problems are more complicated to solve than national ones, for two reasons. First, no single authority can lay down and enforce appropriate policies. Second, solutions must accommodate large variations in the balance of benefits and costs to different countries. Some countries may have more pressing local problems and less money for solving them. To secure action, rich countries may sometimes need to pay poor ones.

Given the large uncertainties surrounding the likely effects of greenhouse warming, a wise policy would include measures that both reduce emissions and improve economic performance (for example, the elimination of subsidies for fossil fuel consumption and deforestation); investments in more information to avoid the risks of costly over- or underreaction; precautionary measures to reduce emissions now at modest costs and bring down the costs of future reductions; and financial transfers to help developing countries broaden their technological options. More pragmatic international action is needed to protect biological diversity. Individual countries can do more to manage these resources in their own interests, but additional transfers will be needed to ensure as much conservation as the rest of the world would like.

When the effects of environmental degradation cross national boundaries, an additional layer of complexity is added to the problem of devising and implementing policies. It is not possible to rely, as in an individual country, on a common legal framework, regulatory controls, economic incentives, and, if necessary, the coercive powers of a national government. Solutions to international environmental problems must be based on common principles and rules of collaboration among sovereign states, backed up by persuasion and negotiation. Setting priorities for international environmental policy is also particularly complex. The costs of doing nothing may be borne by other nations; the gains from policies may not accrue to those that take the biggest steps. Above all, the issue of how to give proper weight to the interests of the poor and politically weak lays an especially heavy burden on the world's more powerful countries.

Earlier chapters of this Report have documented the seriousness of several local environmental issues in the world's poorer countries. The common good will not be served if international issues that are mainly of concern to rich countries are allowed to divert attention and resources from these press-

ing problems. In addition, if the poor are to meet the environmental concerns of rich countries, they may reasonably expect to be paid for doing so. The right balance can be achieved, but only if the world's leaders are prepared to act responsibly and pragmatically.

Three broad classes of issues require international solutions. First, there are regional problems that arise when neighboring countries share a common resource and one country's actions therefore affect others. Into this category fall most problems of transboundary pollution, including acid rain and the management of international rivers or regional seas.

Second, the world shares certain global environmental resources such as the atmosphere and the deep oceans. Any action by one country that affects such ''global commons'' has an effect, although perhaps a rather small one, on all other countries. Into this category fall the buildup of greenhouse gases and the thinning of the ozone layer caused by the emission of CFCs. (The term ''global commons'' as used here reflects its meaning in standard writings on the environment, not necessarily its sense in international law.)

Third, there are resources that clearly belong to

Box 8.1 Enforcing international obligations: how the international legal process works

The international legal system differs from national legal systems in several respects. National systems have a central authority that establishes the law, and institutions that detect breaches and punish violators. In international law there is no central "lawmaker," no central monitoring body, and no courts with compulsory jurisdiction.

Yet international law successfully regulates many economic, technical, and social activities. Most states comply voluntarily, accepting some limitation on their sovereignty in return for similar concessions from other states. That explains, for instance, why states establish international regulations on, say, international telecommunications or gathering data on epidemics—areas in which national law is inadequate.

The rules of international law are either "customary" (based on state practice) or explicitly agreed in treaties. When states perceive cooperation to be in their interest, they negotiate a codification of their areas of agreement. States may then decide to sign legal instruments expressing their approval of the goals. But only through ratification do states take on an obligation to abide by the agreement and incorporate its provisions into national law. Once incorporated, international law benefits from the law enforcement mechanisms used within each state. Treaties may also provide machinery for international enforcement.

The international legal process provides various monitoring and enforcement mechanisms. Among them are the bodies established within the framework of the United Nations Charter, notably the Security Council; fact-finding and diplomatic missions; auditing and reporting systems (for example, those set up by the International Labour Organisation and human rights conventions); and mechanisms created by international treaties (for example, inspection of nuclear sites by the International Atomic Energy Agency). International law relies heavily on the willingness of states to subject their performance to international scrutiny.

What can be done once a breach of an international rule is detected? The International Court of Justice cannot adjudicate unless the parties to a dispute have agreed to submit to its jurisdiction. Other methods for resolving disputes include arbitration, conciliation, mediation, and negotiation. International law can use sanctions, in particular those agreed on in bodies such as the United Nations. As the recent Security Council resolutions against the Iraqi invasion of Kuwait indicate, some sanctions may include the use of force to ensure compliance. Most sanctions, however, apply economic and political pressure.

---

one country but have values for the international community which are not reflected in the market. They include tropical rainforests, other special ecological habitats, and individual species.

Some lessons from experience

Growing awareness of environmental issues has prompted institutional innovation at the international, as well as the national, level. Intergovernmental organizations such as the EC, the OECD, the Organization of African Unity, and the Organization of American States have extended their areas of cooperation to include the environment. A whole range of specialized bodies, official and nongovernmental, concern themselves with particular international environmental problems such as pollution at sea, the management of nuclear and toxic wastes, the protection of endangered species, and the conservation of ancient monuments. The UNEP plays a special coordinating role and has been the focal point for establishing legal regimes for international environmental issues.

International law: its role and limitations

Nations adhere to international agreements covering the environment because they judge such agreements to be in their own interest. The gains from cooperation can be large, but as Box 8.1 explains, the enforcement and monitoring of international agreements present several difficulties.

Building an international consensus is often slow and costly. The United Nations Convention on the Law of the Sea (UNCLOS) took more than ten years to negotiate and, a decade after the end of negotiations, still has not come into force. The time was not entirely wasted. The negotiations over the UNCLOS led to a codification of decisions to create exclusive economic zones extending 200 miles out to sea. Most countries have recognized the economic and environmental benefits of "nationalizing" what were once international waters and have therefore adopted these specific measures. There was no such consensus on the notion of creating a supranational authority with powers to ensure the equitable distribution and management of the mineral and other resources in the deep oceans.

Governments have, however, reached a number of more limited agreements on marine pollution. International conventions prohibit the dumping of radioactive and other wastes in the oceans, and there are internationally agreed procedures for handling many other wastes. Guidelines governing the maritime transport of dangerous goods have been adopted by many countries. Since the guidelines are broadly recognized as best practice, operators have strong incentives to abide by them.

Drawing on and building national capacity

The actual implementation of measures to address international environmental problems must rely on national governments, which ultimately have the capacity to make and enforce policies. The positive lesson from the establishment of 200-mile economic zones has been that when it is possible to delegate responsibility for managing resources to nations, they may do the job more effectively than international bodies. Countries now have the incentive and the legal capacity to manage their fisheries to maximize their value. Although some countries have overexploited their coastal fisheries, others have used the opportunity wisely.

Prospects for fisheries have dramatically improved in such countries as Australia, Iceland, and New Zealand.

Even when countries wish to take environmental action, they often lack the technical and administrative capacity to do so. Experience with "soft law"—nonbinding international guidelines developed by recognized experts—shows a substantial demand for technical advice on environmental issues. Already, some international agreements include provisions for financial and technical assistance with implementation—the Montreal Protocol is an instance—and the Global Environment Facility (GEF) offers help with implementing the Convention for the Prevention of Pollution from Ships (MARPOL). Such initiatives need to be strengthened.

Paying for international environmental action

The potential partners to an international environmental agreement rarely stand to gain or lose equally from it. If an agreement is to work, either it must lead to efficiency gains sufficiently large that all parties can expect to be better off (which rarely happens) or countries must be willing to negotiate transfers to assist those who will lose. Box 8.2 illustrates some of these points for the acid rain prob-

---

Box 8.2 Bargaining over acid rain in Europe

Acid rain in Europe is linked to the acidification of lakes in Scandinavia, the death of forests in Central Europe, and damage to property in many countries. One of the primary causes of acid rain is emissions of sulfur dioxide from power stations and other large combustion plants. Approximately half of all depositions of sulfur within Europe have come across national boundaries, so that international agreement is necessary to limit acid rain. In 1985 twenty-one countries signed the Helsinki Protocol to reduce their emissions of sulfur dioxide to not more than 70 percent of their 1980 levels by 1993. Another thirteen countries, including Poland, Spain, and the United Kingdom, did not sign the protocol.

Uniform targets of this kind are very inefficient because both the costs and the benefits of reducing sulfur emissions differ widely across countries. One study computed that the most cost-effective way to share a reduction of 30 percent in total sulfur emissions would be for five countries, including Hungary, the United Kingdom, and Yugoslavia, to make cuts of more than 60 percent and for ten countries, including Spain, Sweden, and the former U.S.S.R., to make reductions of less than 10 percent.

There is disagreement about whether the total benefits of controlling sulfur emissions exceed the costs because benefits are difficult to measure. Another study, which inferred these benefits from government behavior, concluded that a reduction of 39 percent in total European emissions of sulfur would be justified but that there would be large cross-country variations in abatement targets. The aggregate net benefit from reducing sulfur emissions would be large. However, three countries—Italy, Spain, and the United Kingdom—would be significant net losers. Without some form of recompense for their additional costs, they would be unwilling to cooperate to reduce emissions. Nonetheless, the net gainers would have a strong incentive to pay the net losers in order to reach an agreement, since total net losses amount to less than 10 percent of total net gains. The one obvious difficulty is that because of the prevailing wind direction, the primary net gainers are countries in Central and Eastern Europe that are much poorer than the net losers. But even if emissions reductions and payments to net losers were restricted to EC countries, all parties could be net gainers.

lem in Europe. Arranging for such transfers will not be simple. The many potential parties to an agreement may not share a common view of the urgency of the problem or of the possible solutions. It is extremely difficult to ensure that countries are paid for neither more nor less than the extra costs of meeting their international obligations. Every country has incentives to distort the costs or benefits of taking action.

Although intergovernmental transfers can be an efficient way to make international agreements work, this does not imply that individual polluters in recipient countries should be subsidized. At the national level there are more efficient ways to discourage pollution (see Chapter 3). Individual countries should be allowed to choose the policies that best fit their circumstances. Agreements should set national targets, not national policies for meeting them. To avoid biasing national policy decisions, any transfers should take the form of lump-sum payments rather than finance for specific investments.

An example of a regional problem: international river basins

For centuries countries have disagreed and negotiated over the management of international rivers. More than 200 treaties have been signed between countries on water issues, but mostly by European and North American countries; many rivers that pass through developing countries are still not covered. Over time, the need for international coordination has grown. An expanding population and rising living standards have increased demand for water; technological ability to exploit water resources has advanced; the number of nation states has grown; and people have become more concerned about the environment. A good deal is at stake. More than 200 river basins, which account for over half of the world's land area, are shared by more than one country. More than 40 percent of the world's population lives in river basins that straddle national frontiers.

The optimal solution for managing an international river is most likely to be found when all the countries that share the river basin cooperate. That rarely happens. First, river basin management has a distributional dimension—it involves the sharing of a scarce productive resource—which can make negotiations contentious or preclude them altogether. The countries upstream may see little gain in increasing the flow to those downstream. Frequently, countries need a strong incentive, such as the threat of armed conflict or the likelihood of

permanent losses for all, before they will compromise. A second obstacle is the lack of clear international law on the subject. No global convention sets out agreed law on international watercourses—indeed, there is not even a generally accepted definition of an international watercourse. But work by various international bodies and jurists has established two generally recognized basic principles: each state has a duty not to cause appreciable harm to others that share the same watercourse; and water rights should be apportioned equitably among the parties involved.

One of the most successful agreements on an international watercourse concerns the sharing of the Indus basin between India and Pakistan. After partition in 1947, Pakistan was dependent on India for much of its irrigation water. After thirteen years of disagreement had brought them to the brink of war, both countries agreed in 1960 to a division of the rivers of the Indus system. Several factors—some of them difficult to replicate—favored success. First, India and Pakistan had strong incentives to compromise: both needed adequate water for irrigation, the technical information was readily available, and neither wanted an armed conflict. Second, the agreement was reached with the help of a third party, the World Bank. Third, external donors and the World Bank provided a total of about $720 million, in addition to India's contribution of $174 million, to assist Pakistan in undertaking works to replace the flows from the river waters allocated to India. Finally, because the agreement involved allocating to each country the flows of separate rivers in the basin, the need for coordination was minimized.

There are other examples of cooperation: with the Zambezi, for instance, an agreement has been reached covering not only water flows but also other environmental aspects of river management. Another innovative case is the Lesotho Highlands Water Project, where payments between countries facilitated cooperation. Lesotho has undertaken to construct large works on the Senqu River to supply South Africa with water. In return, South Africa is underwriting and servicing the debt incurred for the project. Lesotho benefits from the water royalties that South Africa pays, while South Africa reduced the costs of ensuring its water flow because Lesotho was a better place to put the dam.

In many other cases it has been difficult to reach practicable solutions. One example is the Nile. The river flows for more than 6,800 kilometers through three climate zones and nine nations. Although coordinated management of water storage, irrigation systems, and soil erosion control for the whole river basin has the potential to benefit all countries involved, no single agreement covers the entire Nile basin. Inability to negotiate a compromise has hindered the realization of the benefits of cooperation, although the recent establishment of a coordination group of riparian countries is a promising development.

To encourage cooperation, the World Bank has drawn up guidelines to be used in projects it finances on international rivers. These require that other countries along the river be notified. The aim is to ensure that the project does not appreciably harm the interests of the other countries and is not likely to be harmed by plans they may have.

An example of a global problem: the ozone layer and the Montreal Protocol

The Montreal Protocol on Substances That Deplete the Ozone Layer, signed in 1987, is a pathbreaking international agreement dealing with an environmental "global bad." The protocol aims to control consumption, and hence emissions, of CFCs and related substances that deplete ozone (see Chapter 2). By the mid-1980s world consumption of CFCs was about 1 million tons a year, 80 percent of it in industrial countries.

HOW AGREEMENT WAS REACHED. The first evidence that CFCs might not be benign emerged in the early 1970s. In 1977 the U.S. Congress banned CFCs in aerosols. The ban stimulated development of alternative technologies at lower costs than predicted, allaying fears that a phaseout of CFCs would be impossible or prohibitively costly. Evidence of ozone depletion continued to accumulate, and, although uncertainties remained, during the late 1980s progressively more ambitious agreements were reached, culminating in 1990 with a binding agreement to phase out consumption of CFCs and related chemicals in industrial countries by 2000.

Under the Montreal Protocol and subsequent revisions, developing country consumption of CFCs may rise to specified ceilings and will be frozen in 1996, after which it must be phased out by 2010. A ban was agreed on trade between parties and non-parties to the protocol in the substances controlled by the protocol, products made with them, and products containing them. Even so, chlorine concentrations in the atmosphere are unlikely to return to their pre-CFC level until the end of the next century. The agreement also includes two important new provisions: an Interim Multilateral Fund

to help developing countries adopt replacements for CFCs if they cost more than what is being replaced, and clauses on technological transfer that urge the parties to ensure the transfer of the best technology "under fair and most favorable conditions." The fund was established on a pilot basis for three years. During that time the extra burden of phasing out CFC use for all countries expected to qualify for assistance was estimated at $240 million.

ISSUES FOR THE FUTURE. The Montreal Protocol, together with the funding and technical assistance arrangements, is a pilot program. When the program comes up for review, some of the key issues will be the following:

• *Ensuring that the program is not biased against efficient policies to phase out the use of controlled substances.* Countries have a number of policy options. One is for the government to try to identify and invest in alternative technologies. This approach involves governments in a task to which they are generally ill suited: picking good investments. But financing specific investments has the advantage of making the use of funds more transparent to donors and local industries. An alternative is the use of market-oriented mechanisms—for example, the allocation of some import quotas by tender in Singapore. Such policies provide incentives to the private sector to adopt least-cost methods of substitution while encouraging consumers to switch to less CFC-intensive products, but it may be harder to calculate the additional costs entailed.

• *Total costs.* The Interim Fund provides funding only for the first three years of the program. The ultimate costs may be much larger, and an expansion of the fund may be necessary.

• *The grace period.* Developing countries have been given longer than industrial countries to phase out CFCs. If this grace period were only used to delay action, however, it would not achieve its purpose, which is to minimize the burden on developing countries. Current arrangements offer no incentives for a more rapid phaseout than that prescribed under the agreement, although the benefits of greater speed are now commonly agreed to exceed the costs. In spite of this, some developing countries are planning to phase out CFC use more rapidly than required, and private industry in many countries is pressing forward in the search for substitutes.

The Montreal Protocol is often viewed as an example of what can be achieved through international cooperation. Actually, the Montreal Protocol may prove more a special case than a model for action on more complex and costly global issues, such as greenhouse warming and biological diversity. A number of factors made it easier. For example:

• Action was easier once ozone depletion was observed rather than merely postulated by scientists.

• A small group of products was involved, for which substitutes appear to be technically possible, although more expensive.

• The fact that there are only a few producers worldwide and that the main CFC manufacturers also make the main substitutes makes effective implementation more likely.

Most of the parties to the Montreal Protocol therefore perceived that the gains from cooperating would exceed the costs of not doing so. The negotiations carry a number of other important lessons:

• Even for a problem that is relatively inexpensive to address, negotiations can be quite involved.

• Incorporating payments to defray the costs of phasing out CFCs explicitly in the formal agreement helped to bring on board some of the key parties.

• Making payments to countries eligible for assistance has proved cumbersome. As of late 1991 payments into the fund were behind schedule (less than half of what was due had been paid), and there was not yet a smoothly functioning mechanism for disbursing the funds.

Responding to the threat of greenhouse warming

The greenhouse effect is a global issue because all emissions of greenhouse gases, regardless of their origin, affect climate. However, the costs and benefits of measures to mitigate the greenhouse effect may be spread very unevenly across countries. As a result, the negotiations leading up to any international agreement on greenhouse warming will be difficult and lengthy.

Among the factors that must be taken into account are the following:

• Climate change will differ across countries. Regional climate predictions are highly uncertain. The evidence suggests that climate changes will be smaller but more rapid in equatorial areas than in the temperate zones.

• The damage will differ across countries. Some countries may find their climate improving and may gain, while others may find that such effects

as modest declines in rainfall cause substantial losses. Even when the pattern of climate change is similar, it may affect countries differently because of differences in ecology, economic activity, or the values placed on natural habitats and other environmental resources.

• Countries are responsible for different amounts of greenhouse gas emissions. The richer countries have been emitting large amounts for many years and have thus contributed a disproportionate share of accumulated gases in the atmosphere (about 60 percent of carbon dioxide from fossil fuels). On the other hand, emissions from low-income countries, starting from a lower base, are growing more rapidly and will become more important in the future.

• Measures to reduce emissions are one response to the threat of climate change—they seek to prevent the problem. Another response is to seek to adapt, by investing in assets that will mitigate the impact of any climate change on economic and social activities. The relative costs and benefits of these two approaches will differ across countries.

• Some countries are heavily dependent on exports of fossil fuels and are likely to suffer from policies that would reduce world demand. They might respond by reducing prices to stimulate demand.

Despite these difficulties, there are various measures that can be adopted at a national or an international level to reduce current emissions of greenhouse gases and to leave the world better placed to address the problem. In important respects, such measures overlap with policies to promote the efficient production and use of energy and the development of clean energy technologies that have been identified in Chapter 6.

Uncertainty and the range of policy alternatives

Setting aside the problems of reaching agreement on a global strategy, there are two fundamental reasons why it is extraordinarily difficult to formulate an appropriate response to greenhouse warming.

First, the lags between action and effect will inevitably be long. Even adopting stringent measures to reduce output of long-lived greenhouse gases immediately will not stop their atmospheric concentration from rising until late into the next century. This means that some climate change will certainly occur and will probably require investments to mitigate its impact, whatever policies are followed.

Box 8.3 How knowledge of greenhouse gases and climate has evolved

For decades scientists have studied the climatic effects of greenhouse gases (GHGs). In 1827 Fourier conceived the theory of the greenhouse effect. Arrhenius published in 1896 an analysis of possible climate change caused by industrial emissions of radiatively active gases. Early in the twentieth century there was a lively scientific debate on whether atmospheric carbon dioxide would increase and lead to warming, or decline and lead to cooling. Major advances in measurement of greenhouse gas concentrations and physical calculations of the greenhouse effect were made in the 1950s and 1960s. Carbon dioxide accumulations were first raised as a national concern in the United States in a 1965 report of the President's Science Advisory Committee.

In the 1970s attention switched from greenhouse warming to the possibility of global cooling, motivated in part by a cooling trend that began about 1940. By the early 1980s fears of global warming had revived, again partly because temperatures indicated an end to the cooling trend. By the middle of the 1980s a number of national and international scientific panels had issued reports suggesting that mean global temperature would rise between 1.5° and 4.5° Celsius (and possibly higher) by some time in the twenty-first century (Carbon Dioxide Assessment Committee 1983; Bolin and others 1986).

What has been learned

• Perhaps the main lesson of recent scientific research on global warming is the importance of transient change (the path of change over time, given the lags in the climate system), as opposed to equilibrium change (the change that would occur once all the lags had worked through the system, which may take decades or centuries). Unfortunately, transient climate change can be only crudely simulated.

• More sophisticated analyses of the historical temperature record suggest that the temperature sensitivity to greenhouse gases may be in the lower range of climate model predictions.

• In the early 1980s a rise of several meters in the sea level was considered a possibility. By 1990 the estimated range was 0.2 meters to 0.7 meters by the year 2070 (Houghton, Jenkins, and Ephraums 1990).

What might be learned

Improvements in computing capabilities will allow more refined simulations of the path of climate change and better understanding of key climate processes such as cloud and ocean feedback. Improvements in the collection and analysis of temperature data would enable scientists to verify the results from climate models. Finally, more detailed analysis of impacts, coupled with better estimates of the timing and regional distribution of change, could help in assessing the costs and benefits of alternative policies.

Second, there is great uncertainty about the links between atmospheric concentrations of the gases and climate change and about the economic and social consequences of greenhouse warming (see Chapter 2). Much has been learned from research over the past thirty years (Box 8.3) but critical relationships are still poorly understood, and the range of possible outcomes is still very broad. Some scientists worry about the possibility of irreversible change in ecosystems or of thresholds above which climate change accelerates rapidly. Some suggest that such uncertainty highlights the need for immediate, stringent action, while others conclude that such a response is unwarranted without better evidence.

The range of possible policy responses can be divided into three broad categories:

• *Do nothing*. Finance additional research but incur no other costs until the extent and implications of warming become clearer.

• *Take out an insurance policy*. Adopt precautionary measures that entail modest costs now but will reduce the costs of a stronger response in the fu-

ture should it become necessary. The more weight is put on the worst possible consequences of climate change, even if they have a very low chance of occurring, the more costs should be incurred for such precautionary actions.

• *Take immediate action to stabilize or reduce total output of greenhouse gases*.

The choice among these options depends on an assessment of the relative costs and benefits of mitigating greenhouse warming. In all three cases it is desirable to adopt any policy, such as eliminating energy subsidies, that simultaneously improves economic performance and reduces output of greenhouse gases.

THE BENEFITS OF MITIGATING GREENHOUSE WARMING. The climate change that might arise from the increases in greenhouse gas concentrations predicted for the next century could have widespread effects.

• Agriculture and livestock would be affected, although it is uncertain whether global agricultural potential would increase or decrease. The effects may be severe in some regions, especially those that are marginal today. The evidence is not complete enough to suggest a systematic pattern of gains or losses for developing countries.

- Forests and other natural ecosystems could be threatened. Some species or ecosystems may be lost as a result; others may flourish as areas hospitable to them increase.

- Human settlements, especially in areas that are already vulnerable to flooding, droughts, landslides, and severe windstorms, could be severely affected. A rise in the sea level could flood agricultural land in heavily populated coastal lowlands. Vector-borne and viral diseases could shift to higher latitudes, putting new populations at risk. However, climatic conditions for human settlements could also improve in some areas.

Any complex and poorly understood system can spring surprises. This applies to the climate and its impact on human societies and natural ecosystems. A rise in global temperatures might cause some radical changes, although their magnitude and their probability cannot yet be analyzed. It is not yet possible to rule them in—or out—and it is impossible to estimate the associated damage without a clearer idea of how such changes might arise and what they would imply.

Detailed estimates of the damage that climate change may cause have so far been attempted only for the industrial countries, mainly the United States. The very partial evidence so far available suggests that the damage is likely to be relatively modest. One study (IPCC 1990) estimates the costs of protection against inundation from a rise of 1 meter in the sea level at 0.04 percent of world GDP. For some countries, however, such as the small island states, the costs would be much larger. Studies for the United States have estimated the total costs of adapting to climate change induced by the equivalent of doubling carbon dioxide concentrations at about 1 percent of GDP (Cline 1991; Nordhaus 1990, 1991, 1992; and National Academy of Sciences forthcoming). For longer-term warming over the next 250 years, the costs might amount to 6 percent of GDP in the United States (Cline 1991). As emphasized above, there is a high degree of uncertainty associated with these estimates. Some costs may not be quantifiable and are not included in the analyses, particularly damage to natural ecosystems, including species loss. Also, some of the gains from climate change in certain areas may have been missed. Changes in the structure of the world economy over the next century will also affect these cost estimates considerably.

THE COSTS OF PREVENTING CLIMATE CHANGE. The costs of preventing climate change rise with the extent and the speed of the reduction in the output of greenhouse gases. For carbon dioxide, modest reductions could be achieved at zero or minimal cost by eliminating subsidies for energy use and deforestation and by disseminating information about efficient energy-saving technologies. A second set of measures would involve low costs because they draw on the synergy between reducing greenhouse gas emissions and achieving other local objectives, environmental and economic. For example, policies to reduce the use of coal might be justified partly because they reduce local air pollution from particulates. Thereafter, the marginal cost of reducing emissions rises rapidly as higher taxes or other controls affect the efficiency of resource allocation, output, and future growth. These costs may be lowered by phasing in emissions reductions and encouraging the development of alternative technologies. The costs of reducing methane emissions have received less attention. The largest sources of methane associated with human activity are agriculture and animal husbandry. On current knowledge, it would be necessary to reduce output of some agricultural products to reduce methane emissions substantially. This would imply extra costs for producing alternative foodstuffs.

Numerous studies have estimated the costs of reducing the output of greenhouse gases. The range is wide, reflecting different assumptions about growth, capital mobility, the costs of substitute technologies, and the underlying rate of decline in energy per unit of output. Several studies suggest that stabilizing emissions of greenhouse gases at present levels appears to mean a reduction of global GDP of between 3 and 7 percent by the end of the next century (Hoeller, Dean, and Nicolaisen 1990). For developing countries the costs may well be higher. Two global studies which include one or more developing countries suggest that they may face costs in relation to GDP which are almost twice as high as the world average (Manne and Richels forthcoming; Whalley and Wigle 1991). The high costs for these countries reflect a number of factors that make adjustment more difficult—limited ability to use less energy in industry, low capital mobility, shortage of funds for investment, and heavy reliance on low-cost but high-carbon energy supplies.

Choosing among the policy options

Bringing together the various estimates of economic costs and benefits leads to a simple conclusion: the balance of the evidence does not support a case for doing nothing, but neither does it support stringent measures to reduce emissions now—the costs are too high in relation to the prospective benefits. This conclusion applies particularly to the developing countries, which face high costs of reducing greenhouse gas output. Indeed, the evidence implies that investments with real rates of return as low as 5 percent could do more for future generations than investments in large reductions of greenhouse gas emissions. The effects of climate change, however, could fall heavily on the poor and on particularly vulnerable countries. In that event, these countries should receive financial assistance to cover their losses. The income growth made possible by the additional general investment would be more than sufficient to cover such help.

The wisest course is to make modest immediate reductions in emissions of greenhouse gases and investments designed to lower the cost of achieving larger reductions should this become necessary in the future. Such an insurance policy, which would go further than economic efficiency alone would dictate, is justified by uncertainty about the physical and economic effects of climate change and by the lags between action and response.

A precautionary policy

INFORMATION AND RESEARCH. The case for choosing the insurance option is based on current knowledge of greenhouse warming combined with estimates of the costs and benefits of reducing emissions. As noted above, the returns to reducing the substantial uncertainty about the economic, social, and environmental effects of climate change will be high. So a crucial part of any insurance strategy will be to collect additional information and fund scientific research. Financing will be needed for work related to the developing countries (see Chapter 9). Governments should also prepare to act if evidence emerges that (a) more stringent reductions in greenhouse emissions will be required or (b) their citizens and economies need protection from the effects of climate change.

ENERGY SUBSIDIES AND TAXES. As Chapter 6 noted, many developing countries subsidize consumption of commercial energy. Eliminating such subsidies would reduce carbon dioxide emissions while yielding substantial economic gains. Table 8.1 provides rough estimates of the effect that reducing subsidies would have on carbon dioxide emissions (conventionally expressed as tons of carbon). These estimates represent an upper bound

in that world energy prices are assumed to remain constant; the projected reductions in demand could lead to lower world prices, which would tend to increase energy consumption above the predicted levels.

Energy taxes can play an important role in a precautionary strategy. In many European countries, coal, the fuel with the highest carbon content, is the least taxed. Simply on the grounds of raising tax revenue in the least distortionary manner and improving local air quality, this bias in favor of coal should be removed. Well-designed carbon taxes would give market signals for efficient energy use and provide incentives for developing new technologies (Box 8.4). The EC is considering a carbon tax, but it may allow exemptions for heavy industry, which would blunt the incentive for reducing carbon dioxide emissions and make energy taxation more rather than less distortionary.

DEVELOPING RENEWABLE ENERGY. Any long-term strategy to stabilize atmospheric concentrations of greenhouse gases must uncouple economic growth from growth in carbon dioxide emissions. Reducing the amount of energy used per unit of GDP will be one element in such a strategy, but a shift away from fossil fuels will also be essential.

Table 8.1 Effects of eliminating subsidies on commercial energy in Eastern Europe and the former U.S.S.R. and in developing countries

Effect	Eastern Europe and former U.S.S.R.	Developing countries
Reduction in emissions, 1995		
Amount (millions of tons of carbon)	446	234
As share of projected regional emissions (percent)	29	11
As share of projected global emissions (percent)	7	4
Cumulative reduction, 1991–2000		
Amount (millions of tons of carbon)	3,796	2,318
As share of projected cumulative regional emissions (percent)	24	11
As share of projected cumulative global emissions (percent)	6	4

Note: The base case is derived from World Bank projections of energy demand. In this scenario, worldwide carbon dioxide emissions increase by about 20 percent between 1990 and 2000.
Sources: World Bank staff estimates using Bates and Moore, background paper; Imran and Barnes 1990; Marland and others 1989; Hughes 1991.

Box 8.4 Carbon taxes, energy prices, and tax reform

Energy is relatively easy to tax, and many countries rely on energy taxes as a source of revenue. Even so, the structure of energy prices is often not what would be desirable on economic or environmental grounds. Because energy use has a variety of environmental effects, a tax on any one pollutant will not necessarily meet all the objectives of energy taxation equally well.

The key issues are the overall level of energy taxation and the extent of differentiation between fuels. At the very least, no fuel should be subsidized. Taxes on the carbon content of fuels are targeted specifically at emissions of carbon dioxide. By altering the relative prices of different energy sources, they will induce substitution away from carbon-rich fuels. Use of coal emits the most carbon and is also the most serious source of energy-related local pollution. A carbon tax may therefore improve welfare indirectly by reducing emissions of particulates. Petroleum is the second most carbon-intensive of the primary sources of energy. Taxing gasoline and diesel fuel is a substitute for more direct measures for dealing with traffic pollution and urban congestion, so that a carbon tax may have secondary benefits through its effect on vehicle use.

A study commissioned for this Report (Shah and Larsen, background paper [a]) found that in the absence of efficient taxes on local pollution, a higher carbon tax might be justified on local environmental grounds alone. The health benefits associated with the reduction of nitrogen oxides and sulfur dioxide as a result of imposing a $10 a ton carbon tax would be large in countries with low energy taxes, such as Indonesia and the United States.

Revenue generation

Eliminating subsidies for energy consumption would raise more than $230 billion worldwide (Shah and Larsen, background paper [b]). Beyond that, introducing even a modest carbon tax of $10 a ton could raise about $55 billion. In countries whose 1987 GDP per capita was less than $900, such a tax would yield revenues worth an average of more than 1 percent of GDP and 5.7 percent of government revenue.

Welfare costs

A carbon tax may be less distortionary than other significant sources of tax revenue. Shifting the tax burden from inefficient taxes to a carbon tax may improve welfare. But since broadly based taxes such as sales, value added, and income taxes incur lower welfare costs per unit of revenue raised than do fuel taxes (see Hughes forthcoming), fuel taxes should be regarded primarily as instruments for achieving environmental objectives.

Stabilizing carbon emissions requires a switch to renewables

Figure 8.1 How increasing alternative energy sources affects carbon emissions, 1990-2050

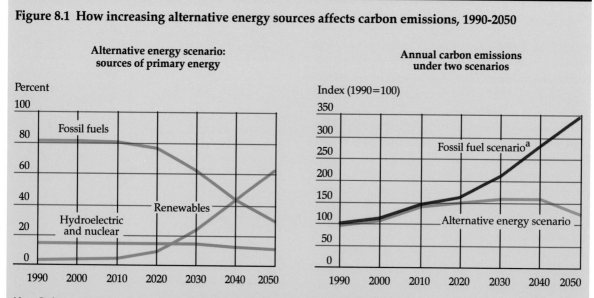

Note: Carbon emissions in 1990 are about 6 billion tons. All data after 1990 are projections.
a. The share of renewables in primary energy sources remains at its 1990 level in this scenario.
Sources: World Bank staff estimates; Anderson and Bird 1992.

Figure 8.1 illustrates two scenarios for the evolution of total carbon dioxide emissions based on the projections for world energy demand presented in Chapter 6. Continued reliance on fossil fuels leads to a tripling of emissions by 2050, whereas with a shift toward renewable energy sources the increase would be only 25 percent. The renewable energy scenario demonstrates the magnitude of the shift from fossil to renewable sources that would be required to stabilize carbon dioxide emissions. Even if the share of renewable sources were to rise from less than 10 percent of total primary energy demand in 2000 to 60 percent in 2050—an unprecedentedly rapid shift—a significant increase in carbon dioxide emissions would still occur.

The shift toward renewable energy can be promoted by appropriate government policies. The key is energy prices, as discussed above, since these provide the incentive for the development and installation of new technologies. In addition, renewable energy should receive larger shares of national expenditures on energy research and development. New technologies should also be supported by financing the dissemination of information and the establishment of pilot projects in developing countries (see Chapter 9).

OTHER MEASURES. Many afforestation projects are justified on economic and local environmental grounds. Growing extra trees can slow the increase in net emissions by fixing carbon. But because afforesting large areas solely to fix carbon would be extremely costly, afforestation cannot be relied on to ''solve'' the problem of carbon dioxide emissions (Box 8.5).

Long-term considerations

As knowledge of climate change improves, the evidence may warrant stronger action to reduce emissions. The costs could be substantial. It will therefore be essential to adopt policies that involve the least loss of welfare and to consider their impact on equity.

SETTING EFFICIENT TARGETS. Considerable gains can be made by reducing emissions in efficient ways. Uniform targets impose greater adjustment costs on some countries than on others. Giving individual countries different targets could lower the aggregate cost of meeting a global target. Adopting targets for annual reductions, rather than setting cumulative targets, will also impose significant extra costs. The scale of warming is a function of the stock of greenhouse gases, not of annual emissions. Countries should therefore be allowed to choose the speed at which they reduce their emissions if the cumulative addition of greenhouse gases does not exceed a safe level. Fixing annual percentage targets would add an unnecessary constraint. So would fixing separate emission targets for each gas rather than allowing tradeoffs among gases on the basis of their climatic effect.

The examples of Egypt and India illustrate this point (Box 8.6). Substantial burdens can be reduced to more manageable levels with few or no differential climatic effects if efficient adjustment targets are set. Making backstop technologies available eventually reduces the costs even more. But allowing flexibility in phasing emissions reductions poses an important problem. The optimal path might be to delay most reductions for a con-

---

Box 8.5 Afforestation: not a panacea for preventing climate change

As trees decay or are burned, carbon dioxide is released. As trees grow, they capture carbon dioxide. But afforestation reduces net emissions only as long as forests are growing. Once a forest is mature, the emissions from decay just offset the carbon fixing from new growth. If a forest is cut down and the wood used, its carbon will eventually be returned to the atmosphere. Offsetting emissions from fossil fuels would require continual additions to the forest stock.

Temperate forests sequester about 2.7 tons of carbon per hectare a year for the first eighty years of their lives. In temperate areas about 400 million hectares of growing forests would be required to sequester 1 billion of the 3 billion–4 billion tons of carbon that accumulate in the atmosphere each year—more than the current forested area of the United States, which is about 300 million hectares. In the tropics, where less carbon is sequestered per hectare (Houghton 1990), locking up 1 billion tons of carbon a year would require about 600 million hectares of growing forest, the equivalent of about 75 percent of the area of the Amazon basin. Intensive forest management that reduced the rotation period could increase the sequestration rate per hectare, but only at substantial additional cost.

These calculations show that afforestation is no panacea for greenhouse warming. Nonetheless, afforestation projects that are justified on other environmental and economic grounds can also help to reduce net carbon emissions.

Box 8.6 Greenhouse policy alternatives in developing countries: the cases of Egypt and India

If, eventually, targets for substantial reductions in global greenhouse gas emissions are adopted, developing countries could face the prospect of curbing the growth of their emissions. Background papers by Blitzer and others commissioned for this Report explored how the design of emission targets would affect the welfare costs of these adjustments for two countries. Scenarios for Egypt and India were examined using dynamic optimization models for the period to 2030. The models take account of features that will be important to individual countries, such as industrial structure and consumption of different sources of energy.

Egypt: flexibility in timing

Controlling concentrations of greenhouse gases involves managing cumulative net emissions. A simple approach is to stipulate annual reductions. But there are alternatives that allow for flexibility tailored to the possibilities and preferences of individual countries while reducing cumulative emissions by the same amount. The high cost of the simple approach is shown in Box figure 8.6a. If a cumulative target is phased in at an optimal pace rather than reached through a fixed annual reduction, the welfare costs decline substantially. These gains, however, are achieved only by accepting that emissions reductions eventually have to be

Box figure 8.6a Limiting carbon dioxide emissions in Egypt: cumulative and annual targets

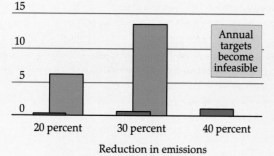

Reduction in welfare (percent)

- ■ Cumulative emissions target
- ■ Annual emissions targets

Note: Welfare is measured as the utility of discounted consumption over the time period of the model. Reductions in welfare and emissions are relative to a base case with no limits on emissions.
Source: Blitzer and others, background paper (a).

Box figure 8.6b General and specific targets for greenhouse gas emissions in India

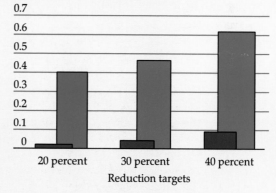

Index of policy inefficiency [a]

- ■ General target for addition to warming effect
- ■ Specific targets for annual emissions of carbon dioxide and of methane

a. Ratio of percentage decline in welfare to percentage reduction in warming effect, both relative to a base case with no limits on emissions. Welfare is measured as the utility of discounted consumption over the time period of the model.
Source: Blitzer and others, background paper (b).

made. The shock is cushioned by planning in advance, not just putting off a decision.

India: taking into account more than one greenhouse gas

Carbon dioxide accounts for a large share—more than 50 percent—of the warming effect attributable to human activities. But other gases play a role. Of these, methane is probably the most important for developing countries. Since irrigated rice production and animal husbandry give rise to these emissions, controlling them would affect critical sectors in developing economies. The case of India is illustrative because of the importance of its agricultural sector.

The technological options for reducing methane emissions in agriculture are more limited than for carbon dioxide, and the burden of methane reductions is correspondingly greater. Adding the same annual constraints on methane as on carbon dioxide roughly quadruples total welfare losses. The possibilities for reducing methane emissions while maintaining agricultural output are limited. The economy must therefore contract much more to meet a separate methane constraint than if the country can choose between gases to achieve the same climatic effect (see Box figure 8.6b).

siderable period. Eventually, countries would have to live up to commitments made long ago, and it could be difficult to make them stick. Some safeguards will be needed to ensure that countries actually adhere to a long-term strategy.

DISTRIBUTIONAL ISSUES. The way that targets for emissions reductions are set has important implications for equity. Steps to limit emissions allocate a global common resource: atmospheric carrying capacity. An agreement to a uniform percentage reduction in emissions would implicitly allocate those rights according to current emissions, favoring the world's richer populations, whose per capita emissions are high. For example, the per capita carbon dioxide emissions of the United States are almost ten times those of China. If the approach that every human has an equal right to the atmospheric resource were taken, rights to future use could be allocated according to population. Another option is to allocate rights according to some measure of output, such as GDP. That would promote energy efficiency but not equity. Any allocation of future emission rights ought to take some account of cumulative past emissions, since greenhouse gases emitted decades ago continue to contribute to warming.

What might the alternatives for allocating atmospheric carrying capacity look like? Figure 8.2 assumes, for purely illustrative purposes, that the warming effect of greenhouse gases is stabilized at the equivalent of doubling the preindustrial level of carbon dioxide in the atmosphere. It then shows how rights to use this fixed amount of atmospheric carrying capacity might be shared.

• Allocating rights according to population leaves developing countries with substantial capacity to continue emitting gases, while the high-income countries would have a net deficit equivalent to about the amount that they emitted in 1980–88. Thus, on this formula the cumulative past emissions of the richer countries exceed their future share of the atmospheric carrying capacity; they have exhausted their right to emit.

• Allocating rights according to income, which leaves all country groups with the potential to emit more greenhouse gases in the future, looks more feasible. The richest countries, however, take the lion's share of this potentially valuable resource.

TRADING EMISSION RIGHTS. These schemes show how rights to emit might be allocated, but the allocation need not translate directly into emissions targets. Countries could profitably trade their rights to use a share of atmospheric carrying ca-

Trades between rich and poor countries would facilitate allocating rights by population rather than income

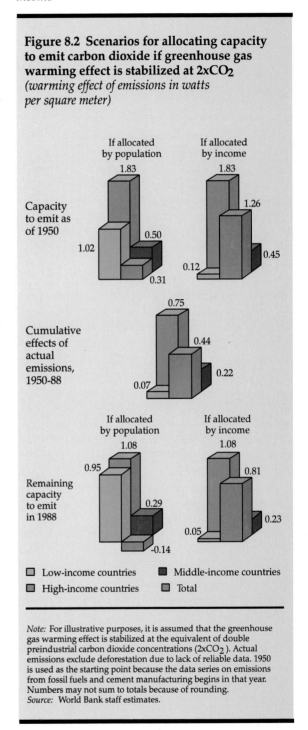

Figure 8.2 Scenarios for allocating capacity to emit carbon dioxide if greenhouse gas warming effect is stabilized at 2xCO₂
(warming effect of emissions in watts per square meter)

Note: For illustrative purposes, it is assumed that the greenhouse gas warming effect is stabilized at the equivalent of double preindustrial carbon dioxide concentrations (2xCO₂). Actual emissions exclude deforestation due to lack of reliable data. 1950 is used as the starting point because the data series on emissions from fossil fuels and cement manufacturing begins in that year. Numbers may not sum to totals because of rounding.
Source: World Bank staff estimates.

pacity, although the practical difficulties of making such a market work are substantial. For instance, if rights were allocated on the basis of population, the industrial world would purchase rights from the world's poorer countries. The outcome of such a hypothetical trade is difficult to predict, but the magnitudes could be large. If rights to emit were sold at $25 per ton of carbon, the industrial world would have to pay developing countries about $70 billion to afford one year's emissions at 1988 levels. Such a sum roughly matches total official development finance in 1989.

Biological diversity: an approach to common concerns

Humans have a lot of company on the earth. Millions of species of plants, animals, and other organisms enrich our environment. Awareness of the importance of this biological diversity has grown in recent years along with concern that more effective action is needed to preserve it. There is a particular sense of urgency because destruction of ecosystems and species extinctions entail irreversible losses.

Priorities for international action

Biological diversity is a matter of international concern, but it is not global common property. The habitats supporting biological diversity, other than those in international waters, belong to individual countries that have an interest in managing a valuable national resource well. At the same time, protecting biological diversity is of international concern because its benefits accrue not only to the local population but also—sometimes in rather different ways—to people all over the world. Some of those benefits have to do with personal values or preferences and consequently are difficult to define objectively and to quantify.

The tangible economic and health benefits are reflected directly in the use of plants, animals, and services from natural ecosystems (see Chapters 2 and 7). Benefits of this kind can to some extent be captured by the use of appropriate charging mechanisms. In addition, because of their individual preferences or moral views, many people attach value to the existence of species and habitats that they may never see or use. They may wish to save natural ecosystems intact for future generations. Or they may simply feel an ethical responsibility to avoid destruction of the variety of life forms that have evolved on earth. Growing voluntary contributions to conservation organizations bear witness to these values, as does the criticism in industrial countries of developing countries' conservation policies. But the market will not reflect the spiritual and emotional pleasure that people draw from

biological diversity, since people do not have to pay to derive these benefits. As a consequence, countries acting on their own will tend to protect their biological diversity less than if they took its global value into account.

Two questions need to be addressed:

• How can developing countries manage their resources in their own best interests?
• How should the world at large contribute to the protection of resources that people value but do not own?

Efficient management of natural resources is essential from both perspectives, and Chapter 7 describes a broad range of measures needed to achieve it. In preserving biological diversity, the starting point—as in other areas of environmental protection—should be policies that both promote development and relieve excessive pressure on natural resources (Box 8.7). In the absence of strong efforts to exploit these "win-win" oppor-

---

Box 8.7 Protecting biological diversity: key complementarities with local development activities

Programs that raise economic output in other sectors and, as a by-product, reduce pressures on wildlife and natural habitats include:

• Measures that raise yields in agriculture and reduce the need for area expansion—efficiency in agricultural pricing and marketing policies; removal of subsidies for land clearance and mechanization; good soil management practices; agroforestry programs; and human resource development in rural areas
• Policies that increase nonfarm employment opportunities, such as efficient development policies for trade, agriculture, and industry
• Sustainable forestry practices that remove subsidies for logging and other activities that cause deforestation and encourage sustainable afforestation projects in ecologically less sensitive areas.

Programs designed to capture the value of biological diversity for the local population include:

• Development of options for sustainable use of resources in areas of rich biological diversity
• Programs to add value to biological resources (for example, genetic prospecting)
• Development of ecotourism.

tunities, policies for direct protection are likely to fail.

The more developing countries can profit from the true value of their resources, the smaller will be the divergence between national and international concerns. Beyond that, if the international community wants to ensure a higher level of protection than would be chosen by nations acting on their own, policymakers in the world's richer countries must translate the concerns of their citizens into financial flows to developing countries. They must be prepared to pay the full costs of the additional conservation. That implies a transfer of additional resources, not merely a restructuring of existing aid.

Many developing countries are uncomfortable about accepting funding to manage their resources because of the implied loss of autonomy. Contributing countries may also worry that they are paying for programs that recipient countries should undertake anyway. To address these problems, developing countries should make sure that their resource use is consistent with their own development objectives when accepting international support. Even so, the problem of moral hazard will be hard to avoid altogether.

The full economic costs of preserving biological diversity will typically be much larger than the direct expenditures on protection. If certain uses of natural habitats are prohibited or reduced, the forgone revenue is part of the cost and should be covered by the assistance provided to encourage preservation. These opportunity costs will change over time, since they are closely linked to the value of land in alternative uses. Thus, increasing pressure on land resources will raise the opportunity costs of keeping out of production segments of natural habitat suitable for agricultural use. Financial arrangements to support countries that protect species and habitats will break down if they fail to take account of such changes.

Some domestic policies, in addition to being economically inefficient, may encourage the destruction of natural habitats and species. In such cases, the international community may reasonably choose not to support conservation programs, on the grounds that effectiveness would be undermined by the overall policy framework.

In the longer term there needs to be some agreement on priorities so as to ensure the best use of limited funds. Work is under way to analyze this question more systematically; it will be important for the future. In the meantime, scientists have attempted to establish criteria to guide action now.

A number of options are under consideration; there is no consensus on which is best. All agree that developing countries should have a high priority, largely because tropical ecosystems are so rich but also because industrial countries now retain so little of their own habitats in pristine state. The geographic distribution of various priority areas is shown in Figure 8.3.

These priority areas rarely lie in the countries that can afford to spend the most on conservation. Satisfactory figures are difficult to obtain, since spending on conservation appears under a wide range of categories. Many countries raise some revenues from their national parks, so net outlays may be less. One can, however, estimate a rough order of magnitude of spending on biological diversity using information on budgetary allocations for national parks management. Table 8.2 shows

Table 8.2 Conservation spending in selected countries

Country and year	As share of government spending (percent)	As share of GDP (percent)	Total spending (millions of dollars)
Botswana, 1984	0.32	0.11	1.3
Denmark, 1989	0.11	0.04	45.0
Indonesia, 1988	0.04	0.01	6.0
Malaysia, 1988	0.05	0.01	5.0
Sri Lanka, 1988	0.03	0.01	0.6
Tanzania, 1983	0.17	0.05	2.9
United States, 1988	0.15	0.04	1,702.3

Sources: For conservation spending in Botswana and Tanzania, national data; for Denmark and Finland, UNEP 1990; for the United States, U.S. Department of the Interior 1991; for Indonesia, Malaysia, and Sri Lanka, World Bank data. For GDP, World Bank data; for exchange rates and government expenditures, IMF data.

these estimates for a few countries. The figures suggest that spending on conservation-related activities may amount to between 0.01 and 0.05 percent of GDP in developing countries and about 0.04 percent in industrial countries, implying a total of about $6 billion–$8 billion a year. Estimates of international transfers for conservation activities, equally hard to come by, are roughly $200 million a year, or about 3 percent of world spending on conservation activities (excluding lending from multilateral development banks, which is growing rapidly). Most of the spending is in the richer countries. Modest increases in the amount of funds transferred by the international community could allow a significant increase in spending on conservation in developing countries. Chapter 9 discusses further the costs and financing of a program to protect biological diversity.

Figure 8.3 Priority areas for conservation: three approaches

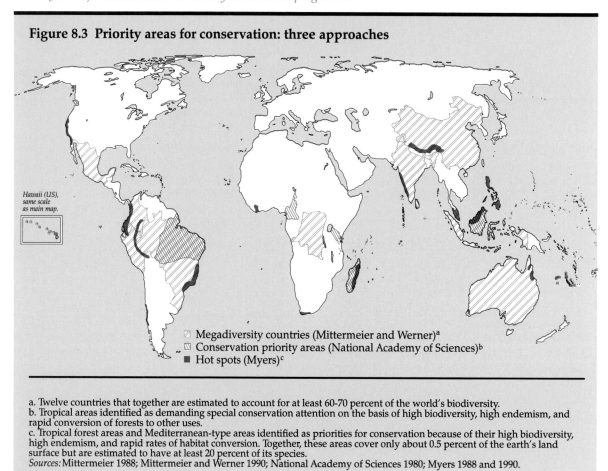

Hawaii (US), same scale as main map.

▨ Megadiversity countries (Mittermeier and Werner)[a]
▧ Conservation priority areas (National Academy of Sciences)[b]
■ Hot spots (Myers)[c]

a. Twelve countries that together are estimated to account for at least 60-70 percent of the world's biodiversity.
b. Tropical areas identified as demanding special conservation attention on the basis of high biodiversity, high endemism, and rapid conversion of forests to other uses.
c. Tropical forest areas and Mediterranean-type areas identified as priorities for conservation because of their high biodiversity, high endemism, and rapid rates of habitat conversion. Together, these areas cover only about 0.5 percent of the earth's land surface but are estimated to have at least 20 percent of its species.
Sources: Mittermeier 1988; Mittermeier and Werner 1990; National Academy of Sciences 1980; Myers 1988 and 1990.

Mobilizing resources

The international community should transfer additional funds to developing countries to achieve a level of spending that reflects its desire to protect species and habitats there. Innovative financing mechanisms such as debt-for-nature swaps may play a useful role. But debt-for-nature swaps cannot substitute for a concerted effort by the international community to make the necessary transfers (Box 8.8). There are three key elements in any strategy for making international transfers more effective.

• First, if increased spending is to be used efficiently to improve protection, it is important to develop programs rather than fund discrete projects. The receiving countries themselves should take the initiative in designing programs for international financing to ensure that these take into account their own priorities and what is feasible for them.

• Second, better coordination is needed to capitalize on the growing interest of private and public donors in supporting developing countries' efforts. International donors recognize that there is growing competition for good projects. Receiving countries spend much time and effort working separately with a number of donors. Recipient countries and donors would benefit from a process akin to the aid group mechanism that matches country program requirements with a variety of donor capacities and interests. The Brazilian Tropical Rainforest Fund is a promising example of this approach (see Box 9.4).

• Third, finance for conservation efforts needs to be sustained. Unlike traditional investment projects, most conservation activities will never become self-financing. Even new mechanisms

Box 8.8 Debt-for-nature swaps: innovative but limited

Debt-for-nature swaps were developed to transform commercial debt of developing countries into finance for the environment. The transactions have appeal in principle because they can meet two objectives: financing worthwhile environmental activities with substantial leverage for donor funds, while helping to manage developing country debt. In practice, the transactions are complex, and the instances in which both objectives can best be served with a single instrument are few.

Since the first debt-for-nature swap was completed (for Bolivia, in 1987), a further sixteen swaps in eight countries have retired nearly $100 million in external debt, using original donations of $16 million. Although this represents only a small fraction of the commercial debt of these countries, it paid for significant conservation efforts, in some cases vastly expanding existing expenditures.

For NGOs, swaps demanded a new financial expertise. NGOs have also had to build up relationships with local NGOs and government agencies. For the recipient government, the conversion of external to local-currency obligations has several implications for economic and debt management. First, debt-for-nature swaps imply greater domestic spending by the debtor government. To avoid stimulating inflation, most such swaps have been not for cash but for government bonds, with payments spread out over a number of years. Second, many severely indebted countries have serious budgetary problems that may preclude converting a foreign debt into a domestic obligation.

A recurring issue is the amount of local-currency bonds the government issues in exchange for the external debt. If the new bonds are close to the face value of old debt, the financial leverage of the donor is maximized, but so too is the financial obligation of the local government. In three-quarters of the swaps the new "conservation bonds" have a value of about 90 percent or more of the original debts.

Debt-for-nature swaps financed by NGOs are likely to be small in relation to both the overall needs of environmental funding and to foreign debts. National aid agencies in a number of countries, notably the Netherlands, Sweden, and the United States, have made grants available to buy some outstanding debt. These debt-for-nature swaps have been valuable for some countries, but their effect has been more to reallocate aid than to generate additional resources. Some official debts are now eligible for swaps. Part of eligible Paris Club debts can now be exchanged for local-currency funding of agreed environmental activities. The U.S. Enterprise for the Americas Initiative provides for local-currency payments on reduced official debt, to be used to fund eligible environmental projects in Latin America and the Caribbean.

such as the GEF do not provide long-term financing. If recurrent costs are to be financed over the long term, it is essential to find the right balance between the need to provide incentives for program development and the donors' requirements for accountability. If developing countries devote scarce managerial and institutional capacity to conservation programs for the benefit of the world at large, adjusting to wavering levels of commitment from the international community could come at high cost. Recipient countries should have assurance that funding will be provided to maintain the programs or at least to wind them down in an orderly fashion should that become necessary. Most donors, however, find it difficult to make binding financial commitments for long periods because of their budget cycles and because they need assurances that programs will be managed well as long as finance is provided.

The costs of a better environment

The costs of protecting and improving the environment appear at first sight to be large. Yet such investments must and can be afforded. With good policies, the costs are modest in comparison with the potential gains from improved efficiency and economic growth.

Most investments will pay for themselves. But increased international support will be essential. Local environmental concerns need to be better embedded in official assistance programs, and the close link between environmental quality and poverty reduction warrants additional aid. Concessional funding for global problems is required, but this should not be taken from aid budgets. Access to trade and capital markets in industrial countries will be essential for a sustainable future.

This final chapter examines the costs of the policies and programs discussed in earlier chapters. It concludes that the costs of addressing the main environmental priorities are affordable—some because of the improvements in economic efficiency they bring, others because of their environmental benefits. Yet even those that appear costless in economic terms may carry a political price. Most pollution and resource degradation occurs because people have enjoyed something for nothing. When that entitlement is threatened, polluters will resist. In considering the aggregate financial cost of environmental investments, such political costs also need to be borne in mind.

Finance and the local environment

Can countries afford to protect the quality of their environments? For many countries, the proper question is the opposite one: can they afford not to? Environmental damage has real and sometimes crippling costs. A recurring theme of this Report has been that good environmental policies often bring good economic returns. They are thus no more or less affordable than other desirable investments in industry, agriculture, public services, or human resources.

The costs of environmental policies can also be reduced, as the preceding chapters have shown, by (a) choosing standards appropriately and concentrating on those options with the highest net benefits; (b) choosing instruments that encourage producers and consumers to respond flexibly and cost-effectively; (c) preventing damage from the outset and avoiding heavy cleanup costs later; and (d) building pollution prevention into new equipment rather than adding it on later. Individual developing countries are already working out solutions to their own environmental problems (Box 9.1).

Investment requirements: an estimate

Fortunately, many investments will begin to pay for themselves within a few years—either through improved productivity, as with soil conservation, or through improved health and welfare, as with investments in sanitation and water supply and in several forms of industrial pollution control. Others, such as protecting forests and addressing carbon emissions, will have uncertain but potentially high returns to future generations. Nevertheless, substantial spending will be needed. Even low-cost investments need careful maintenance by skilled workers and involve recurrent spending.

In preparing this Report, rough estimates of the costs of environmentally responsible growth in developing countries have been made (in 1990 prices) for selected sectors. Of course, costs will depend on the standards chosen, the time path for reaching them, and the policy instruments used. Clearly, not all countries should invest in the cleanest technologies immediately. The following figures, which should be treated as orders of magnitude only, assume that new technologies and management practices are phased in over a generation. It is assumed, for example, that by 2030 emissions controls embodied in the capital stock in developing countries should be roughly equivalent to the best practices emerging in OECD countries today.

WATER AND SANITATION. Achieving universal coverage means not just supplying the 1 billion people currently without safe water supplies and the 1.7 billion without sanitation but matching population growth as well. Annual investment is currently in the range of $15 billion–$20 billion a year—about 2.3 percent of gross investment in developing countries. If that share remains constant over the next fifteen to twenty years, economic growth will allow investment to double in real terms, to $30 billion–$40 billion a year. Yet without changes in prices and institutional arrangements, the goal of universal provision will still recede. The scenarios discussed in Chapter 5 postulated that investment would gradually rise to 3 percent of gross investment, or from 0.6 to 0.8 percent of GDP. The shares will probably have to be higher in low-income countries if universal provision is to be achieved in the next forty years, even allowing for the effects of price and institutional reforms.

ELECTRIC POWER. Under the worst scenario, emissions of pollutants will rise tenfold by 2030 from their already unacceptable levels. The alternatives described in Chapter 6 show how unnecessary this is. The projections assume that reasonable improvements in efficiency and pricing policies are achieved over the next twenty-five years, while the best control technologies in current use are applied to all new investments. With such reforms, the investments required to meet the growth of demand, which are already more than $120 billion a year (roughly 15 percent of gross domestic investment, or 4 percent of GDP), will rise to an average of more than $200 billion a year in the 1990s. Controlling emissions of particulates will raise investment costs by about 1 per-

---

Box 9.1 Innovative approaches to environmental policy

Many developing countries have begun in recent years to develop policies and institutions for addressing environmental problems. Because they often start from scratch, and because their problems are so pressing, they have sometimes considered solutions that are untried or little used in the industrial world. Several examples of such innovative approaches appear in this Report.

• *Controlling pollution in Mexico City.* To control pollution from transport in Mexico City, regulators have chosen to use a combination of regulation and incentives (Box 3.4). These measures are less costly than regulation alone because they discourage driving, whereas most industrial countries merely encourage the use of cleaner engines and fuels. In Mexico City measures such as gasoline taxes are being used to reduce demand and shift travel toward less-polluting modes of transport.

• *Treating hazardous wastes in Thailand.* An Industrial Environment Fund has been proposed to finance the treatment of hazardous wastes from industrial sources (Box 6.5). The fund would be financed from charges on waste generation, and its proceeds would be used to establish and operate central treatment and disposal facilities.

• *Protecting natural habitats in Costa Rica.* In response to increased pressure on protected areas and weak management of parks and reserves, a new national system of conservation areas was created in 1986 (Box 7.7). Regional "megaparks," with greater decisionmaking authority and financial autonomy, were created, and each is being supported by a different set of international donors.

• *Improving sanitation in Ghana.* In low-income areas in Accra voluntary organizations and local entrepreneurs operate community latrines, and the municipal authority is responsible for desludging and disposing of wastes (Chapter 4).

• *Setting priorities in Poland.* Benefit-cost analysis provides a basis for setting and implementing environmental standards. As described in Chapter 3, a study of air pollution in southeastern Poland found the net benefits to be highest if stricter controls on emissions of suspended particulate matter, rather than on emissions of both particulates and sulfur dioxide, were enforced.

cent, or by 0.04 percent of GDP. In regions where acid deposition is serious enough for controls on sulfur dioxide and nitrogen oxides to be justified, a further 5–15 percent of capital costs (amounting to about 0.5 percent of the regions' GDPs) would be incurred if low-sulfur coals or natural gas were not available. For this investment, developing countries would be able in 2030 to produce ten times as much electric power as they do today, with lower emissions of particulates and of pollutants that cause acid rain.

ROAD TRANSPORT. The "unchanged practices" scenario described in Chapter 6 envisages that the demand for vehicle fuels in developing countries will grow from 425 million tons of oil equivalent a year today to 2.3 billion tons by 2030. Phasing in fuel taxes at levels found in Western Europe today and introducing congestion management schemes would reduce this consumption to 1.5 billion tons. Investments in cleaner and more-efficient fuels and engine technologies would bring the main emissions from urban vehicle traffic to much lower levels than today.

Such investments would be tiny in comparison with other costs of motoring. The extra costs of introducing unleaded gasoline range from 2 cents to 10 cents a gallon in OECD countries and average about 4 cents a gallon. They would add approximately $2 billion a year to developing country expenditures on gasoline; this is equivalent to 0.06 percent of today's GDP and less than 1 percent of expenditures on vehicles and fuels. Reducing nitrogen oxides, unburned hydrocarbons, and carbon monoxide by using catalytic converters may raise costs by an additional 15 cents a gallon. (This estimate corresponds broadly to the annualized capital costs of the controls divided by average fuel consumption.) For diesel vehicles, recently developed devices for removing particulates (the largest pollutant), nitrogen oxides, and sulfur have similar costs. Much can also be accomplished (and at low cost) by improving the quality of diesel fuels and, especially, vehicle maintenance. Assuming that the cleaner fuels and emissions control practices are phased in over twenty years, the costs of moving toward the low-polluting scenario discussed in Chapter 6 would rise to $10 billion a year, or 0.2 percent of GDP, by 2000 and to $35 billion a year, or 0.5 percent of GDP, by 2010.

INDUSTRIAL EMISSIONS AND WASTES. In this area the two elements in costs are explicit investments in end-of-pipe controls and incremental expenditures on "cleanliness-in-the-process" or in-plant measures. The latter often cannot be estimated, as they are embodied in the overall plant design or process and cannot easily be distinguished from expenditures on general investment. Some low-waste, in-plant measures now being adopted actually reduce costs and improve profits.

The cost of end-of-pipe and in-plant controls to reduce industrial emissions and effluents varies among sectors and with the standards set. In the 1970s identifiable expenditures on reducing pollution in industrial countries typically amounted to 2.0–2.5 percent of investment costs. As standards have been tightened, these expenditures have risen to 5 percent in Germany and Japan and 4 percent in the United States. Better policies would enable developing countries to spend a smaller amount than this. If spending on pollution control by manufacturers were to approach 2–3 percent of investment, developing countries could appreciably reduce industrial pollution and avoid the costs of cleanup later. The extra costs would amount to about $10 billion–$15 billion a year by the end of the decade, or 0.2–0.3 percent of GDP.

AGRICULTURE. It is not possible to estimate the costs of making agriculture sustainable. Even the land area under stress is not reliably known. But the costs of preventing soil erosion and degradation are comparatively small, while the costs of rehabilitating degraded areas can be large. The capital costs of prevention vary with the farming system, the methods used, and topography: expenditures of $50–$150 per hectare (sometimes less) for such measures as farm forestry and contouring with vetiver grass or other vegetative barriers are typical; $200–$500 may be required per hectare for "structural" measures (terracing, land leveling, earth banks, and the like) on undegraded lands. Rehabilitation, in contrast, may cost from $500 to several thousand dollars per hectare, depending on the severity of the problem. The main priority must therefore be prevention. Thanks to the favorable effects of these practices on farm output, payback periods can be short (five to ten years or less), provided—and this is an important qualification—that the programs achieve high levels of participation. Public expenditure will be needed for research, extension, training, education (including the costs of encouraging community participation in the programs), and support for infrastructure and afforestation. By far the greatest commitment of time and resources, however, will have to come from the farmers themselves.

Not all agricultural lands will need additional investment in preventive measures. But enough is known about the situation in many regions, and about measures for preventing soil erosion and degradation, for a significant program to be mounted immediately. For example, investments of $10 billion–$15 billion a year (0.2–0.3 percent of GDP) in the 1990s, including the costs borne by the farmers themselves, would probably be sufficient to extend the coverage of improved soil management practices by up to 100 million hectares each year. (Currently, 1.1 billion hectares are under crops in developing countries, and 2.5 billion hectares are under permanent pasture.) Allowing for the need to complement agricultural programs with reforestation projects in some watersheds may raise investment costs by a further $2 billion–$3 billion a year (unit costs vary between $500 and $1,500 a hectare). The main limits would be the capacity of the institutions to implement the programs and the circumstances—such as tenurial arrangements, crop prices, and education—that affect farmers' responses.

There is an urgent need to improve knowledge of the links between agriculture and environmental damage and to survey environmental conditions in rural areas. Given the increasing complexity of rural environmental problems and the need to raise agricultural yields, more money is needed for agricultural research, particularly on the effects of crop practices on soil loss and fertility (see Boxes 7.2 and 7.3). Current national R&D expenditures by developing countries are approaching $5 billion a year, and international expenditures are about $350 million. For the reasons discussed in Chapter 7, both need to be expanded by 30–50 percent in relation to projected levels. In addition, a commensurate increase in finance is required for training and for disseminating the findings of R&D. Expenditures on extension are presently about $4.5 billion a year in developing countries, or $1.5 for every hectare under crops and permanent pasture. To help put agricultural practices on a sustainable footing, the extension message will need to be broadened from the present emphasis on production technologies to include soil conservation, integrated pest management, the management of pastures, and, more generally, issues of resource custody.

POPULATION. Total spending on family planning in developing countries amounts to $4.7 billion a year, of which 80 percent is borne by developing countries and 20 percent comes from external assistance. Family planning programs have never received more than 2 percent of official development assistance. To achieve the base case projections of stabilization at 12.5 billion population discussed in Chapter 1 would mean increasing spending to $8 billion by 2000. To arrive at the lower-fertility projections, an extra $3 billion a year would be required, giving a total of $11 billion a year by 2000, or 0.2 percent of developing country GDP. (It will, of course, also require better progress on reducing poverty and increasing access to education.)

FEMALE EDUCATION. Improving education for girls may be the most important long-term environmental policy in the developing world. Educated women have smaller families, and their children tend to be healthier and better educated. Furthermore, women are often the principal managers of natural resources; they gather wood and water and undertake much agricultural labor. Better education will help them to use natural resources more productively and to depend less on natural resources for income. Educated women will have more opportunities for productive off-farm employment—a vital source of income as the average sizes of farms shrink. Raising the primary school enrollment rate for girls to equal that for boys in low-income countries would mean educating an additional 25 million girls each year, at a total annual cost of approximately $950 million. Raising the secondary school enrollment of girls to equal the rate for boys would mean educating an additional 21 million girls at a total cost of $1.4 billion a year. Eliminating educational discrimination in low-income countries would thus cost a total of $2.4 billion a year, or about 0.25 percent of these countries' GDP.

Putting costs in perspective: the case for reform

The additional costs of the investments listed above would add $75 billion a year by the end of the decade, or about 1.4 percent of the combined GDPs of developing countries (Table 9.1). Costs will be higher if an allowance is made for items not costed above, such as forest protection, the rehabilitation of environmentally degraded areas, and cleanup. And costs may rise over time, even as a share of GDP, as standards are tightened. Overall incremental costs in the range of 2–3 percent of GDP by 2000 would appear appropriate and sufficient. The estimates are, of course, approximate and are not all-embracing; even less are they a financial plan, since such plans can only be developed through careful assessments of each country's priorities and circumstances. They are indicative and are intended solely to place costs in context.

Table 9.1 Estimated costs and long-term benefits of selected environmental programs in developing countries

Program	Additional investment in 2000			Long-term benefits
	Billions of dollars a year	As a percentage of GDP in 2000[a]	As a percentage of GDP growth, 1990–2000[a]	
Increased investment in water and sanitation	10.0	0.2	0.5	Over 2 billion more people provided with service. Major labor savings and health and productivity benefits. Child mortality reduced by more than 3 million a year.
Controlling particulate matter (PM) emissions from coal-fired power stations	2.0	0.04	0.1	PM emissions virtually eliminated. Large reductions in respiratory illnesses and acid deposition, and improvements in amenity.
Reducing acid deposition from new coal-fired stations[b]	5.0	0.1	0.25	
Changing to unleaded fuels; controls on the main pollutants from vehicles[b]	10.0	0.2	0.5	Elimination of pollution from lead; more than 90 percent reductions in other pollutants, with improvements in health and amenity.
Reducing emissions, effluents, and wastes from industry	10.0–15.0	0.2–0.3	0.5–0.7	Appreciable reductions in levels of ambient pollution, and improvements in health and amenity, despite rapid industrial growth. Low-waste processes often a source of cost savings for industry.
Soil conservation and afforestation, including extension and training	15.0–20.0	0.3–0.4	0.7–1.0	Improvements in yields and productivity of agriculture and forests, which increase the economic returns to investment. Lower pressures on natural forests. All areas eventually brought under sustainable forms of cultivation and pasture.
Additional resources for agricultural and forestry research, in relation to projected levels, and for resource surveys	5.0	0.1	0.2	
Family planning (incremental costs of an expanded program)[c]	7.0	0.1	0.3	Long-term world population stabilizes at 10 billion instead of 12.5 billion.
Increasing primary and secondary education for girls[c]	2.5	0.05	0.1	Primary education for girls extended to 25 million more girls, and secondary education to 21 million more. Discrimination in education substantially reduced.

a. The GDP of developing countries in 1990 was $3.4 trillion, and it is projected to rise to $5.4 trillion by 2000 (in 1990 prices). The projected GDP growth rate is 4.7 percent a year.
b. Costs may eventually be lowered by the use of new combustion technologies and other measures discussed in Chapter 6.
c. Recurrent expenditures on these items are counted as investments in human resources.

These costs, although high in absolute terms, are small in relation to the additional incomes generated by good economic management. For example, *World Development Report 1991* found that countries with good economic policies had average growth rates fully 2.5 percentage points higher than those with middling and poor policies and nearly 1 percentage point higher than the average projected growth rate for the 1990s. Over a fifteen-year period, the total real income of countries with good policies should rise by 125 percent—more than twice the amount in other countries—and by twenty to twenty-five times the costs of a full-blown environmental program. Because their incomes will be higher, these countries will also be able to afford more environmental protection.

Financing environmental expenditures

A substantial share of the investment and maintenance expenditures related to the environment will be incurred by enterprises and will therefore be paid for by consumers. These extra costs will be reflected in the prices of the final product or service—as they should be under the "polluter-pays" principle. Thus, environmentally damaging practices and products will be less profitable to producers and less attractive to consumers, while environmentally desirable ones will be more profitable and attractive, so that there is a convergence of private and social interests. In this way, private investment (and the technical and managerial skills it brings with it) will be attracted to the resolution of environmental problems.

With financial and regulatory incentives for private action in place, public expenditure can be focused on such areas as:

- Environmental monitoring and research and the administration of policy
- Technological research, development, and demonstration
- Education and training
- Agricultural research and extension
- Provision of supporting public services, such as afforestation; the protection of forests, wildlife, and natural habitats; and the establishment and maintenance of national parks.

International finance for national environmental policies

The financing of environmental investments will require an increase in export earnings and an expansion of private and official capital flows to developing countries in the coming decades.

THE IMPORTANCE OF INTERNATIONAL TRADE. Some environmental investments will require imported capital equipment. By far the most important source of foreign exchange will be export earnings. Developing countries are currently hampered by import restrictions, which in some industrial countries have become tighter in recent years. A successful conclusion to the Uruguay Round of trade negotiations that reduced by one-half the tariff and nontariff barriers in the main industrial countries would generate additional annual export earnings in developing countries of $65 billion by the end of the decade—an amount only slightly lower than the entire incremental investment program described above. Robust, environmentally responsible growth in industrial countries can also help. An increase in OECD growth by 1 percentage point over a four-year period would generate

---

Box 9.2   Private finance and the environment

The International Finance Corporation (IFC) recently undertook nine country studies to determine market potential and opportunities for private investment in environmental goods and services. The studies—which looked at Chile, Hungary, Indonesia, Malaysia, Mexico, Pakistan, Poland, Thailand, and Turkey—considered opportunities in waste management, technology for control of industrial pollution, and related services. In developing countries the market for environmental goods and services is still small but is likely to expand rapidly during the next decade.

Market growth is driven by several factors, including the severity of environmental problems, increasing public awareness of environmental issues, growing political support, and international pressure on developing countries to harmonize and enforce environmental laws and regulations. As governments respond with environmental legislation, strengthened environmental protection institutions, and increased enforcement, opportunities are being generated for private investments in environmental goods and services. The constraints on public resources in providing traditional public services such as wastewater treatment and management of solid wastes are also creating opportunities for the private sector to provide such services. The studies identified more than 200 potential opportunities of this kind.

---

more than $80 billion in annual foreign exchange earnings by developing countries.

RESTORING ACCESS TO CAPITAL MARKETS. Access to commercial finance, coupled with expanded foreign investment, will make it easier to import clean technologies embodied in capital imports. There is no reason why additional spending on pollution control should not be financed through commercial markets and, indeed, be profitable for the companies that undertake it (Box 9.2). The encouraging restoration of commercial flows to such countries as Chile, Mexico, and Venezuela over the past two years must be extended to a much wider range of countries. This will require more consistent policies on the part of borrowing countries and would be facilitated by policies to raise savings rates—especially in the public sector. Debt relief will be required in a number of countries.

OFFICIAL ASSISTANCE. It is essential that new international financing for global environmental problems (discussed below) not detract from the

The GEF has established principles and priorities to guide project design.

Principles

- More technologies are needed to offer options for reducing emissions at least cost.
- GEF funding should encourage promising but unproven technologies when the technology, economics, or market conditions are not yet "right."
- Successful technologies will be those that show potential for widespread use and could eventually attract investment from conventional sources.

Priorities for support

I. End-use efficiency
- Reducing energy intensity of basic materials processing
- Efficient motors and drives
- Irrigation pumpsets
- Lighting and water heating
- Vehicle fuel use

II. Reduction in the emissions intensity of energy production
- Renewables such as photovoltaics, solar-thermal, and wind power
- Biomass gasifiers/gas turbines
- Sustainable biomass production to replace fossil fuels
- Advanced, efficient gas turbine cycles
- Microhydropower
- Fuel switching to natural gas

III. Non-carbon-dioxide emissions reductions
- Urban and rural waste treatment
- Reduction of flaring and venting of natural gas
- Reduction of releases associated with coal mining

IV. Generic areas
- More efficient production, transmission, and distribution of energy
- Slowing deforestation
- Sequestering carbon dioxide (for example, afforestation)

---

urgent needs of developing countries for development assistance in general. The elimination of poverty and the achievement of economic stability and growth remain the main priorities for development and, as discussed in this Report, will be fundamental if environmental problems are to be successfully addressed. At the same time, additional development assistance will be needed to tackle local environmental problems. Such assistance should not be viewed as separate from development needs but, rather, should be embedded in official programs. Three distinct changes are needed. First, development agencies need to assess thoroughly the environmental impact of all their lending, especially for infrastructural projects. That will require the further development of environmental impact assessment techniques. Second, a shift is needed in the balance of aid portfolios. Development agencies and governments need to consider how their traditional programs might deliver environmental improvements. Third, assistance will be needed for new kinds of projects that offer environmental rather than purely economic gains.

Finance and the global environment

Funds will be required to enable developing countries to meet the additional costs of addressing global environmental problems and to facilitate the implementation of international agreements. These transfers should not be thought of as development assistance, since they should be allocated in ways that offset the unequal distribution of gains and costs across countries.

GREENHOUSE WARMING. Finance is required now to assist developing countries in meeting the immediate costs involved in implementing the precautionary policy discussed in Chapter 8.

Increased knowledge is an immediate need. Studies of the vulnerabilities of individual countries to climate change would be in the interest of the world at large, and so developing countries should be helped to undertake them.

Although developing countries should adopt those measures that best promote economic efficiency and improve their local environment, it is unrealistic to expect them to do more without further incentives. Additional measures in the interests of the world at large will require further assistance, such as that already available in pilot form under the GEF. For now, the objectives of such funding should be to broaden the scope for low-cost reductions in emissions through technological innovation. That means supporting those projects that hold out the most hope for future cost declines, for future reductions in greenhouse gas emissions, and for learning by doing. Under the

GEF, work is under way to identify promising areas for investment. Box 9.3 lists some of them.

Many of the most promising areas for support are in electric power generation and related end-use technologies. In particular, investments in the application of renewable energy would sharply reduce the costs of an accelerated response to greenhouse warming, if this were to prove necessary. A shift in the emphasis of research and development, now heavily concentrated on nuclear energy and fossil fuels, should be coupled with more international collaboration. A long-term government commitment to the development and application of renewable energy would encourage manufacturers to expand their own development from its current small base. Expenditures building up to $3 billion–$4 billion a year by the end of the century—a commitment much less than industrial country R&D budgets for nuclear power—would make it possible to mount a major program of research, development, and demonstration projects.

BIODIVERSITY. Estimates of the likely direct costs of achieving a satisfactory level of protection for biological diversity range from millions to billions of dollars a year over the next decade. The wide variation is not surprising. The work of setting national priorities and analyzing what is needed is only beginning. Novel approaches to conservation may lower direct financial outlays considerably. Reducing subsidies for habitat destruction could

have an important effect in some areas, as could many of the ''win-win'' options discussed in Chapters 7 and 8.

It is not possible to estimate precisely how much is needed to conserve the world's biodiversity, but estimates for high-priority programs can be made. Much biodiversity can be conserved in protected areas, which form the mainstay of almost every conservation strategy. The costs would not be prohibitive. At present 4.8 million square kilometers of terrestrial and marine areas are under protection in developing countries, but neither the level of protection nor the areas already gazetted are sufficient. It is estimated that to make the protection of the areas already gazetted effective and to increase the total area of protected areas by 50 percent over the next decade would require some $2.5 billion a year. By comparison, the United States spends $2 billion a year on national parks.

From the perspective of the developing countries, however, official assistance for protecting biodiversity is affordable only if it is not at the expense of other concessional aid. Considering that disbursements by the International Development Association (IDA), which cover a wide range of development activities, have been about $4 billion a year over the past few years, diverting even a fraction of the funding for conservation from concessional aid flows would be highly undesirable. The Brazilian Tropical Rainforest Fund (Box 9.4) illustrates what can be achieved when donor

---

Box 9.4   The Brazilian Tropical Rainforest Fund: international cooperation to protect the Amazon

The Brazilian Amazon has long been recognized as a unique repository of natural resources of value to the world at large. Many groups in the industrial world fear that these resources are threatened, and economists have argued that there is an international willingness to pay to avert their loss. An agreement, reached in December 1991, to provide $250 million to finance the first phase of a pilot program to conserve the rainforest in Brazil promises to translate these concerns into action. A number of industrial countries led by the Group of Seven have pledged to contribute.

The pilot program is to be the start of a comprehensive effort to maximize the environmental benefits of Brazil's rainforests that is consistent with Brazil's development goals. The formulation of this plan brought together several federal agencies, the nine state governments of the Amazon region, and numerous local and national NGOs. The specific objectives of the projects in the pilot phase are (a) conserving biological di-

versity and indigenous areas, (b) consolidating policy changes and strengthening implementing institutions, and (c) developing scientific knowledge and applied technologies for environmentally benign development in the Amazon and building support for their adoption.

This innovative program results from two important developments. First, over the past few years the Brazilian government has embarked on extensive policy and institutional changes to improve environmental management. For the Amazon, this involves trying to improve the standard of living of local people while protecting the resources in the rainforest. Second, in July 1990 heads of state of the Group of Seven requested the World Bank and the EC Commission to cooperate with the Brazilian government in drawing up a pilot program and to coordinate funding. This was a quick and effective way to mobilize help for conservation.

and recipient countries cooperate to tackle the most urgent problems of preserving biodiversity.

Development in the twenty-first century

This Report has highlighted the growing consensus that policies for economic efficiency and for environmental management are complementary.

Box 9.5   Agenda 21

The United Nations Conference on Environment and Development (UNCED) in Rio de Janeiro in June 1992 has provided leaders with an opportunity to agree on a strategy for environmentally responsible development in the next century. Most environmental problems will be addressed at the local and national levels, of course, but there are a number of areas in which an international commitment to change is needed. These are set out in Agenda 21—an agenda for the next century—the primary document discussed at the conference. They include:

• Allocating international aid to programs with high returns for poverty alleviation and environmental health, such as providing sanitation and clean water, reducing indoor air pollution, and meeting basic needs
• Investing in research and extension to reduce soil erosion and degradation and put agricultural practices on a sustainable footing
• Allocating more resources to family planning and to primary and secondary education, especially for girls
• Supporting governments in their attempts to remove distortions and macroeconomic imbalances that damage the environment
• Providing finance to protect natural habitat and biodiversity
• Investing in research and development of noncarbon energy alternatives to respond to climate change
• Resisting protectionist pressures and ensuring that international markets for goods and services, including finance and technology, remain open.

Good environmental policies are good economic policies and vice versa. Efficient growth need not be an enemy of the environment, and the best policies for environmental protection will help, not hurt, economic development. The United Nations Conference on Environment and Development provides an opportunity for the world's leaders to commit themselves to these principles (Box 9.5).

With international political tensions reduced and with near unanimity on the central importance of markets and human resource investments for successful development, the coming decades offer great prospects for progress. Within the next generation, widespread poverty could be eliminated. Clean water and adequate sanitation could be made available to virtually everybody on earth. This will be possible only with rising incomes, investment, education, and employment. Agricultural productivity could continue to grow at present rates or better, thus doubling food production in developing countries by 2030 in a manner that minimizes pressure on natural habitats. But this will require a commitment to research and extension and to undistorted policies. Industrial output in developing countries could rise to six times present levels, with lower total emissions and wastes. This will require rapid investment, stronger environmental institutions, and technology transfer, supported by open trade and capital flows. Such development could be powered by clean fossil fuel technologies and, increasingly, by renewable energy. Commitment on the part of both the public and private sectors to accelerate the development and use of these technologies and resources would be required. Valuable natural habitats could be much better protected than at present. The international community would need to accept this as a joint obligation with national governments.

This is not a small agenda. But it is an affordable one, and there is already considerable knowledge and experience on which to base a successful program. Were it to be incorporated into national and international policy, the world would be wealthier, and its environment would be preserved for future generations to enjoy.

Bibliographical note

This Report has drawn on a wide range of World Bank sources—including country economic, sector, and project work and research papers—and on numerous outside sources. The principal sources are noted below and are also listed in two groups: background papers commissioned for this Report and a selected bibliography. Most of the background papers are already available on request through the Report office. The views they express are not necessarily those of the World Bank or of this Report.

In addition to the sources listed below, many persons, both inside and outside the World Bank, helped with the Report. In particular, the core team wishes to thank Anil Agarwal, Jean Baneth, Carl R. Bartone, David Bloom, Rodolfo Bulatao, Leif E. Christoffersen, Anthony Churchill, Herman Daly, Partha Dasgupta, Mohamed T. El-Ashry, Gunnar Eskeland, Robert Goodland, Johan Holmberg, Ian Johnson, Josef Leitmann, Mohan Munasinghe, Robert Repetto, Ibrahim F. I. Shihata, Vinod Thomas, T. H. Tietenberg, David Turnham, and Jeremy Warford. Others who provided notes or detailed comments include Shankar N. Acharya, David Bock, José Carbajo, Armeane M. Choksi, John Clark, Gloria Davis, Shanta Devarajan, Salah El Serafy, S. Shahid Husain, Frida Johansen, Harinder Kohli, Alan Krupnick, Johannes Linn, Karl Maler, Norman Myers, Daniel Ritchie, Robert Schneider, Ediberto L. Segura, Marcelo Selowsky, Anand Seth, Piritta Sorsa, William Tyler, and Walter Vergara. Important contributions were also made by the team's summer interns: Peter Brixsen, Linda Bui, Rafaello Cervighi, Heinz Jansen, Michaela Weber, and Min Zhu. Valuable inputs and comments were received from the Secretariat of the United Nations Conference on Environment and Development, the Organization for Economic Cooperation and Development, the U.S. Environmental Protection Agency, the Business Council for Sustainable Development, the World Wide Fund for Nature, and the International Institute for Environment and Development.

The Report benefited from comments from the meetings in Senegal and New Delhi of the NGO–World Bank Committee, from seminars in a number of cities, and from more than forty seminars held in Washington, D.C. The Economic Development Institute of the World Bank (EDI) sponsored in December 1991 a seminar course at which policymakers, academics, and representatives of NGOs discussed the main findings of the Report. The Institute of Strategic and International Studies in Malaysia cosponsored,

with the Report office, a conference in Kuala Lumpur in July 1991 at which participants from Southeast Asian countries discussed the themes of the Report.

Chapter 1

This chapter draws extensively on the academic literature and the work of various international organizations. Population projections and scenarios were provided by the Population and Human Resources Department of the World Bank. The evidence on fertility transitions and unmet demand for contraception draws on Bulatao 1992. The discussion on the role of women in resource management and the link between women's education and fertility draws on suggestions from Barbara Herz and Elizabeth Morris-Hughes and from cross-country evidence supplied by Kalanidhi Subbarao. Box 1.1 is based on Cleaver and Schreiber 1991. The new estimates of poverty in the developing world were prepared by Ravallion, Datt, and Chen 1992. The sections on the relationships among population, poverty, and the environment draw heavily on Stephen Mink's background paper. Box 1.2 was prepared by Peter Hazell. The data on economic growth and future projections are based on *Global Economic Prospects and the Developing Countries*, prepared by the World Bank International Economics Department. The section on longer-term prospects to 2030 benefited from the judgment of Paul Armington and Robert Lynn. Box 1.3 is based on the work of Ernst Lutz, Salah El Serafy, Robert Repetto, and the United Nations Statistical Office. The example of national income accounting in Mexico is based on Van Tongeren and others forthcoming. The section on links between economic activity and the environment draws on the work of Dasgupta 1982 and Maler 1974. Box 1.4 draws on the background papers by Margaret Slade. Box 1.5 is based on input from Gordon Hughes and Rory O'Sullivan. The evolution of environmental indicators with respect to changes in per capita income is based on the Shafik and Bandyopadhyay background paper. The discussion of technological options in various sectors is informed by Anderson and Cavendish, background paper. Box 1.6 draws from OECD 1991. The analysis of sustainable development is based on input from Ravi Kanbur and from Dixon and Fallon 1989.

Chapter 2

This chapter draws on technical documents from the World Health Organization, the United Nations Environment Programme, and the World Bank and from the scientific literature. Joseph Leitmann provided input on urban pollution, Carl Bartone on solid wastes, the World Bank's Energy Strategy/Management Assessment Program (ESMAP) on indoor air pollution, and David Wheeler on hazardous wastes. The sections on air and water pollution rely on the background paper by Beckerman. Material on soils draws on the background paper by Crosson and Anderson and on Nelson 1990. The forestry discussion is based on World Bank 1991d. Box 2.3 is based on personal discussion with Peter Ashton and on Lewin 1987. The section on greenhouse warming, including Box 2.4, owes much to Houghton, Jenkins, and Ephraums 1990. The ozone depletion discussion is drawn from UNEP 1991 and World Meteorological Organization and others forthcoming. The chapter also benefited from constructive comments from David Grey, Agnes Kiss, Gerald D. Mahlman, and Norman Myers. Advice on environmental indicators and data quality came from Allen Hammond, Eric Rodenberg, and Dan Tunstall of the World Resources Institute.

Chapter 3

The section on trade policy and the environment (including Box 3.1) is based on material from the background papers by Dean and by Lucas, Wheeler, and Hettige and from Wheeler and Martin forthcoming, Grossman and Krueger 1991, and Low and Safadi forthcoming. Evidence on the impact of removing subsidies is from the background paper by Hughes and from World Bank reports. The discussion of common-property rights is based on the background paper by Kanbur, as is Box 3.2. The material on valuation of environmental benefits (including Box 3.3) is based on the background paper by Pearce. Box 3.4 is based on Eskeland 1992. The section on regulation and economic incentives draws on Bernstein 1991, Eskeland and Jimenez 1991, Wheeler 1992, and the background paper by Levinson and Shetty. The section on improving public investment is based on the background paper by Ascher and on material from Anderson 1987. The examples in Box 3.5 are from Dixon and others 1988 and Mu, Whittington, and Briscoe 1991. Box 3.6 draws on Fargeix 1992. Extensive comments were provided by William Ascher, Gunnar Eskeland, Antonio Estache, Emmanuel Jimenez, Ravi Kanbur, Alan Krupnick, Arik Levinson, Patrick Low, Ashoka Mody, Vinod Thomas, Tom Tietenberg, David Wheeler, and Min Zhu.

Chapter 4

This chapter draws on academic and NGO sources. Individual staff members in the World Bank's Environment Department made significant contributions. Of particular note is the paper ''Participation for Sustainable Development'' by Guggenheim and Koch-Weser, which formed the basis for the section on participation. Barbara Lausche provided material on in-

stitutional issues. Josef Leitmann contributed to the section on decentralization and coordination for improved urban management, and Glenn Morgan provided materials on remote sensing and geographic information systems. Box 4.1 is based on press reports and Chilean publications. Box 4.5 draws on material provided by Kazuhiko Takemoto and Japan Environment Agency 1988. Box 4.6 was adapted by Shelton Davis from his background paper. Box 4.7 was written by Scott Guggenheim. Among those who provided helpful comments were Carl Bartone, Jeremy Berkoff, Alice Hill, David O'Connor, William Partridge, and Michael Stevens.

Chapter 5

This chapter draws heavily on the cumulative experience of World Bank water sector staff. In particular, published and unpublished Bank studies by Joszef Buky, Michael Garn, Dale Whittington and Guillermo Yepes were extensively used. The section on environmental priorities draws from Bhatia and Falkenmark 1992. The section on health relies on the work of Briscoe 1985 and 1987, Esrey and others 1991, Feachem and others 1983, VanDerslice and Briscoe forthcoming, WHO 1984b, and Moe and others 1991. The discussion on productivity impacts draws on Bhatia and Falkenmark 1992, Briscoe and de Ferranti 1988, Cairncross and Cliff 1986, Gilman and Skillicorn 1985, Whittington and others 1991, Whittington and others 1988, and the background paper by Webb. The section on managing water resources relies on Bhatia and Falkenmark 1992, Falkenmark, Garn, and Cestti 1990, Hufschmidt and others 1987, IFC forthcoming, Kennedy 1990, McGarry 1990, Miglino 1984, Ramnarong 1991, Repetto 1986, Rogers 1984 and 1986, Smith and Vaughan 1989, and World Resources Institute 1990. The section on financing and willingness to pay draws on Altaf, Haroon, and Whittington 1992, Briscoe and others 1990, Christmas and de Rooy 1991, Churchill 1987, OECD 1987b, Singh and others forthcoming, Whittington and others 1992, World Bank 1990b and 1991a, and World Bank Water Demand Research Team forthcoming. The section on sanitation relies on Altaf and Hughes 1991, Wright and Bakalian 1990, Bartone, Bernstein, and Wright 1990, de Melo 1985, Hasan 1986 and 1990, and Okun 1988. The discussion of institutional reforms relies on Bartone and others 1991, Borcherding, Pommerrehne, and Schneider 1982, Kinnersley 1991, Lovei and Whittington 1991, Paul 1991, Triche 1990, U.S. Environmental Protection Agency 1989, World Bank 1991e, and Yepes 1990 and 1991. Box 5.1 relies on Moe and others 1991, Feachem and others 1983, VanDerslice and Briscoe forthcoming, and WHO 1984b. Box 5.2 is taken from International Finance Corporation forthcoming, Box 5.3 from World Bank Water Demand Research Team forthcoming, and Box 5.4 from Dworkin and Pillsbury 1980. Box 5.5 is drawn from de Melo 1985, and Box 5.6 from Hasan

1986 and 1990. The chapter also benefited from detailed and constructive comments from Bank staff members Janis Bernstein, Ramesh Bhatia, John Blaxall, Pauline Boerma, Arthur Bruestle, Joszef Buky, Sergio Contreras, Christopher Couzens, Antonio Estache, David Grey, Ian Johnson, Peter Koenig, Ayse Kudat, Andrew Macoun, Geoffrey Matthews, Mohan Munasinghe, Letitia Oliveira, Walter Stottman, Alain Thys, Anthony van Vugt, and Albert Wright and from external commentators, including Anjum Altaf, Charles Griffin, Stein Hansen, Arif Hasan, Richard Helmer, Daniel Okun, Peter Rogers, Sheila Webb, Dale Whittington, and James Winpenny.

Chapter 6

The chapter draws on background papers by Bates and Moore, Anderson and Cavendish, Hall, Homer, and Panayotou and on Anderson 1991a. The section on energy relies on Asian Development Bank 1991, Balzheiser and Yeager 1987, Davis 1990, Faiz and Carbajo 1991, Gamba, Caplin, and Mulckhuyse 1986, Harrison 1988, Imran and Barnes 1990, Johansson, Bodlund, and Williams 1989, OECD 1986–91, Shell Briefing Service 1991, U.S. Department of Energy 1990, Wirtschafter and Shih 1990, and World Bank 1991c and forthcoming. Box 6.1 is taken from Asian Development Bank 1991, OECD 1989, and Bates and Moore background paper. Box 6.2 is based on World Bank 1991c, which includes research by Douglas Barnes, who also provided much valuable material on woodfuels. Eric Larsen, Joan Ogden, Robert Socolow, and Robert Williams of Princeton University's Center for Energy Studies provided valuable guidance on renewable energy technologies; Johansson and others forthcoming provided a technical review. The section on industry draws on Bartone, Bernstein, and Wright 1990, Bernstein 1991 and forthcoming, Eckenfelder 1989, GATT 1971, Hirschhorn and Oldenburg 1991, Kneese and Bower 1968, Krupnick 1983, OECD 1991, Tedder and Pohland 1990, UNIDO 1991, and Wheeler and Martin forthcoming. Bernard Baratz and Kathleen Stephenson supplied extensive comments and material on industrial pollution, as did Roger Heath, John Homer, Afsaneh Mashayekhi, and Robert Saunders on energy and industry. Box 6.3 is taken from Wheeler and Martin forthcoming. The discussion on Cubatão in Box 6.4 is based on Findley 1988. Box 6.5 is drawn from the Panayotou background paper. The discussion on transport relies on Faiz and Carbajo 1991, Hau 1990, Heggie 1991, Jones 1989, and OECD 1986 and 1988. Michael Walsh provided helpful comments.

Chapter 7

The chapter benefited from background papers by Barbier and Burgess, Crosson and Anderson, and Manwan and from Murray and Hoppin forthcoming. Sanchez, Palm, and Smyth 1990 is the main source for Box 7.1. Box 7.2 is based on the background paper by Crosson and Anderson. Box 7.3 was prepared by Donald Plucknett and Kerri Wright Platais. The section on private management draws on Carter and Gilmour 1989, Dewees 1989, Doolette and Magrath 1990, Georghiou 1986, Kiss and Meerman 1991, Norgaard 1988, Pimental 1991, and Wright and Bonkoungou 1986. Box 7.4 was written by Montague Yudelman and is based on Murray and Hoppin forthcoming and on Hoppin 1991. The discussion of community management relies on Cernea 1991, Jodha 1991, Migot-Adholla and others 1991, and National Academy of Sciences 1986. The example of Burkina Faso in Box 7.5 was provided by World Bank and others 1990. The section on public management is based on Hyde, Newman, and Sedjo 1991, Kiss 1990, Repetto and Gillis 1988, Spears forthcoming, Wells, Brandon, and Hannah 1992, and World Bank 1991e and 1992b. Material for Box 7.7 was prepared by Katrina Brandon. Box 7.8 is drawn from the background paper by Pearce. Valuable comments were received from Jock Anderson, Pierre Crosson, John Dixon, John Doolette, John English, Richard Grimshaw, Peter Hazell, Heinz Jansen, Norman Myers, John O'Connor, David Pimentel, Donald Plucknett, James Smyle, John Spears, Laura Tuck, and Montague Yudelman.

Chapter 8

The section on international law draws from background papers by Mensah, Ricker, and Tschofen with guidance from Paatii Ofosu-Amaah. Ralph Osterwoldt and Franziska Tschofen contributed Box 8.1. Box 8.2 draws on Maler 1989 and 1990 and Newbery 1990. Michael Prest contributed material on international rivers, drawing on Kolars and Mitchell 1991, Rogers 1991, Smith and Al-Rawahy 1990, Vlachos 1990, and information from Raj Krishna. Michael Prest also provided material on the ozone layer and on the Montreal Protocol, drawing on Benedick 1991, Munasinghe and King 1991, and Rowland 1990 and 1991. Andrew Solow of the Woods Hole Oceanographic Institution supplied scientific advice for the section on greenhouse warming. Gerald Mahlman of the U.S. National Oceanic and Atmospheric Administration and Robert Watson of the U.S. National Aeronautics and Space Administration reviewed the greenhouse warming section. The discussion of scientific issues and the effects of climate change draws especially on Arrhenius and Waltz 1990, Ausubel 1983, Houghton, Jenkins, and Ephraums 1990, IPCC 1990, National Academy of Sciences 1991 and forthcoming, Parry 1990, Rosenberg and others 1989, and Tegart, Sheldon, and Griffiths 1990. For Figure 8.3 a carbon cycle model (Harvey and Schneider 1985) was applied to data on carbon emissions from Marland and others 1989. Radiative forcing as a function of atmospheric concentration is from Houghton, Jenkins, and Ephraums 1990. Only carbon dioxide emissions from 1950 onward are included in allocations, but the effects of earlier emissions are taken into account in aggregate. The share of other greenhouse gases in the total warming effect is held constant at its current level in the $2 \times CO_2$ scenario. The section on biological diversity draws on Barbier and others 1990, Dixon and Sherman 1990, McNeeley and others 1990, Pearce 1991, Reid and Miller 1989, Solow, Polasky, and Broadus forthcoming, Swanson 1991, and Weitzman 1992a and b. Box 8.8 was prepared by Jeffrey Katz. The estimate of international transfers for conservation draws on Abramovitz 1989 and UNEP 1990. Robert J. Anderson, Nancy Birdsall, Charles Blitzer, Jessica Einhorn, Agnes Kiss, Barbara Lausche, Paatii Ofosu-Amaah, Ralph Osterwoldt, Susan Shen, and Ibrahim Shihata commented in detail. Richard S. Eckaus provided ideas and advice on many parts of the chapter. Claudia Alderman, Erik Arrhenius, Charles Feinstein, Mudassar Imran, Robert Kaplan, Kenneth King, John Lethbridge, Eduardo Loayza, Patrick Low, Carl Gustaf Lundin, Donald Plucknett, Michael Wells, and Anders Zeijlon provided information on specific topics. Bita Hadjimichael provided research assistance.

Chapter 9

The cost estimates for electricity, transport, and water and sanitation are from the background paper by Anderson and Cavendish; for soil conservation and afforestation from Doolette and Magrath 1990; and for agricultural research and extension from Zijp 1992 and Evenson 1991. Those for family planning were based on Bulatao 1992 and on discussions with the World Bank's Population and Human Resources Department. Costs of achieving equal education for girls are reported in Summers 1991. Unit costs of conservation in protected areas are from McNeeley and others 1990. Figures in this Report benefited from discussions with Jan Post and Mario Ramos. All estimates benefited from detailed reviews by the World Bank's operational and research staff, and helpful discussions were held with UNCED.

Background papers

Anderson, Dennis. (a) "Economic Growth and the Environment."
———. (b) "Energy and the Environment."
———. (c) "Global Warming and Economic Growth."
Anderson, Dennis, and William Cavendish. "Efficiency and Substitution in Pollution Abatement: Simulation Studies in Three Sectors."
Ascher, William. "Coping with the Disappointing Rates of Return of Development Projects with Environmental Aspects."
Barbier, Edward B., and Joanne C. Burgess. "Agricultural Pricing and Environmental Degradation."
Bates, Robin W., and Edwin A. Moore. "Commercial Energy Efficiency and the Environment."
Beckerman, Wilfred. "Economic Development and the Environment: Conflict or Complementarity?"

Bilsborrow, Richard. "Rural Poverty, Migration, and the Environment in Developing Countries: Three Case Studies."
Blitzer, Charles, R. S. Eckaus, Supriya Lahiri, and Alexander Meeraus. (a) "Growth and Welfare Losses from Carbon Emissions Restrictions: A General Equilibrium Analysis for Egypt."
———. (b) "The Effects of Restrictions of Carbon Dioxide and Methane Emissions on the Indian Economy."
Butcher, David. "Deregulation, Corporatization, Privatization, and the Environment."
Crosson, Pierre R., and Jock Anderson. "Global Food—Resources and Prospects for the Major Cereals."
Davis, Shelton H. "Indigenous Views of Land and the Environment."
Dean, Judith M. "Trade and the Environment: A Survey of the Literature."
Guerami, Behrouz. "Prospects for Coal and Clean Coal Technology."
Gutman, Pablo. "Environment and Development: Perspectives from Latin America."
Hall, David O. "Biomass."
Hammond, Allen, Eric Rodenburg, and Dan Tunstall. "Environmental Indicators."
Hamrin, Robert. "Business' Critical Role in Meeting Developing and Environmental Challenge."
Homer, John B. "Natural Gas in Developing Countries: Evaluating the Benefits to the Environment."
Hughes, Gordon. "Are the Costs of Cleaning Up Eastern Europe Exaggerated? Economic Reform and the Environment."
Kanbur, Ravi. "Heterogeneity, Distribution and Cooperation in Common Property Resource Management."
Levinson, Arik, and Sudhir Shetty. "Efficient Environment Regulation: Case Studies of Urban Air Pollution."
Lucas, Robert, David Wheeler, and Hemamala Hettige. "Economic Development, Environmental Regulation, and the International Migration of Toxic Industrial Pollution: 1960–1988."
Manwan, Ibrahim. "Soil Conservation and Upland Farming Systems in Indonesia."
Mensah, Thomas. "Existing and Emerging State of International Environmental Law."
Mink, Stephen. "Poverty, Population, and the Environment."
Mody, Ashoka, and Robert Evenson. "Innovation and Diffusion of Environmentally Responsive Technologies."
NGO—World Bank Committee. "Economics, Human Development, and Sustainability."
Panayotou, Theodore. "Policy Options for Controlling Urban and Industrial Pollution."
Pearce, David. "Economic Valuation and the Natural World."
Repetto, Robert. "Key Elements of Sustainable Development."
Ricker, Margaret. "Effectiveness of International Environmental Law."
Shafik, Nemat, and Sushenjit Bandyopadhyay. "Economic Growth and Environmental Quality: Time Series and Cross-Country Evidence."
Shah, Anwar, and Bjorn Larsen. (a) "Carbon Taxes, the Greenhouse Effect, and Developing Countries."
———. (b) "World Energy Subsidies and Global Carbon Emissions."
Sinha, Chandra Shekhar. "Renewable Energy Programmes in Brazil, China, India, Philippines, and Thailand."
Slade, Margaret E. (a) "Environmental Costs of Natural-Resource Commodities: Magnitude and Incidence."
———. (b) "Do Markets Underprice Natural-Resource Commodities?"

Sorsa, Piritta. "Environment—A New Challenge to GATT?"

Steer, Andrew, and Robert Hamrin. "Promoting Sustainable Economic Development and the Role of Industry."

Tschofen, Franziska. "Legal Content of the Notion 'Global Commons.' "

Webb, Sheila, and Associates. "Waterborne Diseases in Peru."

Selected bibliography

Ablasser, Gottfried. 1987. "Issues in Settlement of New Lands." *Finance and Development* 24:45–48.

Abramovitz, Janet. 1989. *A Survey of U.S.-Based Efforts to Research and Conserve Biological Diversity in Developing Countries.* Washington, D.C.: World Resources Institute.

Ahmad, Yusuf J., Salah El Serafy, and Ernst Lutz, eds. 1989. *Environmental Accounting for Sustainable Development.* Washington, D.C.: World Bank.

Altaf, Anjum, Jamal Haroon, and Dale Whittington. 1992. "Households' Willingness to Pay for Water in Rural Areas of the Punjab, Pakistan." Program Report Series. UNDP/World Bank Water and Sanitation Program, Washington, D.C.

Altaf, M. A., and J. A. Hughes. 1991. "Willingness to Pay for Improved Sanitation in Ouagadougou, Burkina Faso: A Contingent Valuation Study." World Bank, Infrastructure and Urban Development Department, Washington, D.C.

Anderson, Dennis. 1987. *The Economics of Afforestation: A Case Study in Africa.* World Bank Occasional Paper 1. Baltimore, Md.: Johns Hopkins University Press.

————. 1990. "Environmental Policy and Public Revenue in Developing Countries." Environment Working Paper 36. World Bank, Sector Policy and Research Staff, Environment Department, Washington, D.C.

————. 1991a. *Energy and the Environment: An Economic Perspective on Recent Technical Developments and Policies.* Special Briefing Paper 1. Edinburgh: Wealth of Nations Foundation.

————. 1991b. *The Forest Industry and the Greenhouse Effect.* Edinburgh: Scottish Forestry Trust.

————. 1992. *The Energy Industry and Global Warming: New Roles for International Aid.* Overseas Development Institute, Development Policy Studies Series. London: ODI Publications.

Anderson, Dennis, and Catherine D. Bird. 1992. "Carbon Accumulations and Technical Progress—A Simulation Study of Costs." *Oxford Bulletin of Economics and Statistics* 54(1):1–29.

Anderson, Robert C., Lisa Hofmann, and Michael Rusin. 1990. "The Use of Economic Incentive Mechanisms in Environmental Management." Research Paper 51. American Petroleum Institute, Washington, D.C.

Arrhenius, Erik, and Thomas W. Waltz. 1990. *The Greenhouse Effect: Implications for Economic Development.* World Bank Discussion Paper 78. Washington, D.C.

Asian Development Bank. 1991. *Environmental Considerations in Energy Development.* Manila.

Ausubel, Jesse H. 1983. "Annex 2: Historical Note." In *Changing Climate: Report of the Carbon Dioxide Assessment Committee.* Washington, D.C.: National Academy Press.

Balzheiser, Richard E., and Kurt E. Yeager. 1987. "Coal-Fired Power Plants for the Future." *Scientific American* 257(3):100–07.

Barbier, Edward B., Joanne C. Burgess, and David W. Pearce. 1991. "Technology Substitution Options for Controlling Greenhouse Emissions." In Rudiger Dornbusch and James M. Poterba, eds., *Global Warming: Economic Policy Responses.* Cambridge, Mass.: Massachusetts Institute of Technology Press.

Barbier, Edward B., Joanne C. Burgess, Timothy Swanson, and David W. Pearce, eds. 1990. *Elephants, Economics, and Ivory.* London: Earthscan Publications.

Barker, Randolph. 1978. "Bars to Efficient Capital Investment in Agriculture." In T.W. Schultz, ed., *Distortions of Agricultural Incentives.* Bloomington: University of Indiana Press.

Barnes, Douglas F., and Liu Qian. 1991. "Urban Interfuel Substitution, Energy Use and Equity in Developing Countries: Some Preliminary Results." Prepared for the 1991 International Conference of the International Association for Energy Economics, East-West Center, Honolulu, July 8–10. World Bank, Industry and Energy Department, Washington, D.C.

Bartone, Carl, Janis Bernstein, and Frederick Wright. 1990. "Investments in Solid Waste Management: Opportunities for Environmental Improvement." PRE Working Paper 405. World Bank Infrastructure and Urban Development Department, Washington, D.C.

Benedick, Richard Elliot. 1991. *Ozone Diplomacy.* Cambridge, Mass.: Harvard University Press.

Bernstein, Janis. 1991. "Alternative Approaches to Pollution Control and Waste Management: Regulatory and Economic Instruments." Urban Management Program Discussion Paper Series 3. World Bank, Washington, D.C.

————. Forthcoming. "Priorities for Urban Waste Management and Pollution Control in Developing Countries." Urban Management Program Discussion Paper Series, World Bank, Washington, D.C.

Bhatia, Ramesh, and Malin Falkenmark. 1992. "Water Resource Policies and the Urban Poor: Innovative Approaches and Policy Imperatives." Background paper for the Working Group on Water and Sustainable Urban Development, International Conference on Water and the Environment: Development Issues for the 21st Century, Dublin, January.

Binkley, Clark S., and Jeffrey R. Vincent. Forthcoming. "Forest-Based Industrialization: A Dynamic Perspective." In Narendra Sharma, ed., *Where Have All the Forests Gone? Local and Global Perspectives.* Baltimore, Md.: Johns Hopkins University Press.

Binswanger, Hans. 1980. "Attitudes toward Risk: Experimental Measurement in Rural India." *American Journal of Agricultural Economics* 62(3): 395–407.

Binswanger, Hans, and Prabhu Pingali. 1988. "Technological Priorities for Farming in Sub-Saharan Africa." *World Bank Research Observer* 3(1).

Bishop, Joshua, and Jennifer Allen. 1989. "The On-Site Costs of Soil Erosion in Mali." Environment Department Working Paper 21. World Bank, Washington, D.C.

Bolin, Bert, Bo R. Doos, Jill Jager, and Richard A. Warrick, eds. 1986. "The Greenhouse Effect, Climatic Change and Ecosystems." In *SCOPE 29 Report.* New York: John Wiley and Sons.

Borcherding, T. E., W. W. Pommerrehne, and F. Schneider. 1982. "Comparing the Efficiency of Private and Public Production: The Evidence from Five Countries." In D. Bos, R. A. Musgrave, and J. Wiseman, eds., "Public Production," *Zeitschrift für Nationalekonomie* Supplement 2:127–56.

Bos, Eduard, Patience W. Stephens, and My T. Vu. Forthcoming. *World Population Projections, 1992–93 Edition.* Baltimore, Md.: Johns Hopkins University Press.

Bradley, David, Sandy Cairncross, Trudy Harpham, and Carolyn Stephens. 1991. "A Review of Environmental Health Impacts in Developing Country Cities." Urban Management Program Discussion Paper 6. World Bank, Washington, D.C.

Bressers, Hans. 1983. "The Role of Effluent Changes in Dutch Water Quality Policy." In P. B. Downing and K. Hanf, eds. *International Comparisons in Implementing Pollution Laws.* Boston, Mass.: Kluwer Nijhoff Publishing.

Briscoe, John. 1987. "A Role for Water Supply and Sanitation in the Child Survival Revolution." *Bulletin of the Pan American Health Organization* 21(2):92–105.

———. 1985. "Evaluating Water Supply and Other Health Programs: Short-Run versus Long-Run Mortality Effects." *Public Health* 99:142–45.

Briscoe, John, and David de Ferranti. 1988. *Water for Rural Communities: Helping People Help Themselves.* Washington, D.C.: World Bank.

Briscoe, John, Paulo Furtado de Castro, Charles Griffin, James North, and Orjan Olsen. 1990. "Toward Equitable and Sustainable Rural Water Supplies: A Contingent Valuation Study in Brazil." *World Bank Economic Review* 4(2): 115–34.

British Petroleum Company. 1991. *BP Statistical Review of World Energy.* London: BP Corporate Communications Services.

Bulatao, Rodolfo A. 1992. "Effective Family Planning Programs." World Bank, Population and Human Resources Department, Washington, D.C.

Buschbacher, Robert J. 1990. "Natural Forest Management in the Humid Tropics: Ecological, Social, and Economic Considerations." *Ambio* 19(5):253–57.

Cairncross, Frances. 1991. *Costing the Earth.* London: Business Books Ltd.

Cairncross, Sandy, and J. Cliff. 1986. "Water and Health in Mueda, Mozambique." *Transactions of the Royal Society of Tropical Medicine and Hygiene.* London

Carbajo, Jose C. 1991. "Regulations and Economic Incentives to Reduce Automotive Air Pollution." *Science of the Total Environment.* Amsterdam: Elsevier.

Carbon Dioxide Assessment Committee. 1983. *Changing Climate.* Washington, D.C.: National Academy Press.

Carmichael, J. B., and K. M. Strzepek. 1987. *Industrial Water Use and Treatment Practices.* London: Cassell Tycooly.

Carter, A. S., and D. A. Gilmour. 1989. "Increase in Tree Cover on Private Land in Central Nepal." *Mountain Research and Development* 9(4).

Cernea, Michael, ed. 1991. *Putting People First,* 2d. ed. New York: Oxford University Press.

Chen, B. H., C. J. Hong, M. R. Pandey, and K. R. Smith. 1990. "Indoor Air Pollution in Developing Countries." *World Health Statistics Quarterly* 43(3):127–38.

Chinese Research Team for Water Resources Policy and Management. 1987. "Report on Water Resources Policy and Management for Beijing-Tianjin Region of China." Beijing, Sino-U.S. Cooperative Research Project on Water Resources.

Christmas, Joseph, and Carel de Rooy. 1991. "The Decade and Beyond: At a Glance." *Water International* 16(3): 127–34.

Churchill, Anthony A. 1987. *Rural Water Supply and Sanitation: Time for a Change.* World Bank Discussion Paper 18, Washington, D.C.

Clark, John. 1991. *Democratizing Development: The Role of Voluntary Organizations.* London: Earthscan Publications.

Cleaver, Kevin, and Gotz Schreiber. 1991. "The Population, Environment and Agriculture Nexus in Sub-Saharan Africa." Africa Region Technical Paper, World Bank, Washington, D.C.

Cline, William. 1991. "Estimating the Benefits of Greenhouse Warming Abatement." Institute for International Economics, Washington, D.C.

Club of Rome. 1972. *The Limits to Growth.* Rome.

Cofala, J., T. Lis, and H. Balandynowicz. 1991. *Cost-Benefit Analysis of Regional Air Pollution Control: Case Study for Tarnobrzeg.* Warsaw: Polish Academy of Sciences.

Dasgupta, Partha. 1982. *The Control of Resources.* Cambridge, Mass.: Harvard University Press.

Davis, Ged R. 1990. "Energy for Planet Earth." *Scientific American* 263(3):55–62.

de Melo, Jose Carlos Rodrigues. 1985. "Sistemas Condominiais de Esgotos." *Engenharia Sanitaria* 24(2):237–38. Rio de Janeiro.

Dewees, Peter. 1989. "The Fuelwood Crisis Reconsidered: Observations on the Dynamics of Abundance and Scarcity." *World Development* 17(8):1159–72.

Dixon, John, Richard Carpenter, Louise Fallon, Paul Sherman, and Supachit Manipomoke. 1988. *Economic Analysis of the Environmental Impacts of Development Projects.* London: Earthscan Publications.

Dixon, John A., and Louise A. Fallon. 1989. "The Concept of Sustainability: Origins, Extensions, and Usefulness for Policy." *Society and Natural Resources* 2:73–84.

Dixon, John, and Paul E. Sherman. 1990. *Economics of Protected Areas: A New Look at Benefits and Costs.* Washington, D.C.: Island Press.

Doolette, John B., and William B. Magrath, eds. 1990. *Watershed Development in Asia: Strategies and Technologies.* World Bank Technical Paper 127. Washington, D.C.

Doolette, John B., and James W. Smyle. 1990. "Soil and Moisture Conservation Technologies: Review of Literature." In John B. Doolette and William B. Magrath, eds. *Watershed Development in Asia: Strategies and Technologies.* World Bank Technical Paper 127. Washington, D.C.

Dworkin, D. M., and B. L. K. Pillsbury. 1980. *The Potable Water Project in Rural Thailand.* Project Impact Evaluation Report 3. Washington, D.C.: U.S. Agency for International Development.

Eckenfelder, W. Wesley, Jr. 1989. *Industrial Water Pollution Control.* McGraw-Hill Series in Water Resources and Environmental Engineering. New York: McGraw-Hill.

Elliott, Philip, and Roger Booth. 1990. *Sustainable Biomass Energy.* Shell Oil Company Selected Papers Series. London: Shell International Petroleum Company.

Eskeland, Gunnar. 1992. "Demand Management in Environmental Protection: Fuel Taxes and Air Pollution in Mexico City." World Bank, Country Economics Department, Washington, D.C.

Eskeland, Gunnar, and Emmanuel Jimenez. 1991. "Choosing Policy Instruments for Pollution Control: A Review." PRE Working Paper 624. World Bank, Country Economics Department, Washington, D.C.

Esrey, Steven A., R. G. Feachem, and J. M. Hughes. 1985. "Interventions for the Control of Diarrhoeal Diseases Among Young Children." *Bulletin of the World Health Organization* 63(4):757–72.

Esrey, Steven A., James B. Potash, Leslie Roberts, and Clive Shiff. 1991. "Effects of Improved Water Supply and Sanitation on Ascariasis, Diarrhoea, Dracunculiasis, Hookworm Infection, Schistosomiasis, and Trachoma." *Bulletin of the World Health Organization* 69(5):609–21.

———. 1990. "Health Benefits from Improvements in Water Supply and Sanitation: Survey and Analysis of the Literature of Selected Diseases." United States Agency for International Development, Water and Sanitation for Health (WASH) Technical Report 66. Washington, D.C.

Evans, J. S., T. D. Tosteson, and P. L. Kinney. 1984. "Cross-Sectional Mortality Studies and Air Pollution Risk Assessment." *Environment International* 10:55–83.

Evenson, Robert. 1991. "The Economics of Extension." In Gwyn E. Jones, ed. *Investing in Rural Extension: Strategies and Goals.* London: Elsevier Applied Science Publishers.

Faiz, Asif, and Jose Carbajo. 1991. "Automotive Air Pollution and Control: Strategic Options for Developing Countries." World Bank, Infrastructure and Urban Development Department, Washington, D.C.

Faiz, Asif, Kumares Sinha, Michael Walsh, and Amiy Varma. 1990. "Automotive Air Pollution—Issues and Options for Developing Countries." PRE Working Paper 492. World Bank, Infrastructure and Urban Development Department, Washington, D.C.

Falkenmark, Malin. 1989. "The Massive Water Scarcity Now Threatening Africa—Why Isn't It Being Addressed?" *Ambio* 18(2):112–18.

Falkenmark, Malin, Harvey Garn, and Rita Cestti. 1990. "Water Resources: A Call for New Ways of Thinking." *Ingenieria Sanitaria* 44(1–2): 66–73.

Falloux, François, and Aleki Mukendi, eds. 1988. *Desertification Control and Renewable Resource Management in the Sahelian and Sudanian Zones of West Africa*. World Bank Technical Paper 70. Washington, D.C.

FAO (Food and Agriculture Organization). Various years. *Fertilizer Yearbook*. Rome.

————. 1990a. *Forest Products Yearbook 1977–88*. Rome.

————. 1990b. *Production Yearbook 1989*. FAO Statistics Series 94. Rome.

————. 1991. Forest Resources Assessment 1990 Project. "Second Interim Report on the State of Tropical Forests." Prepared for the 10th World Forestry Conference, Paris.

Fargeix, Andre. 1992. "Financing of Pollution Control Programs." World Bank, Europe, Middle East and North Africa Region, Environment Division, Washington, D.C.

Feachem, Richard G., David J. Bradley, Hemda Garelick, and D. Duncan Mara. 1983. *Sanitation and Disease: Health Aspects of Excreta and Wastewater Management*. New York: John Wiley and Sons.

Feder, Gershon, and David Feeny. 1991. "Land Tenure and Property Rights: Theory and Implications for Development Policy." *World Bank Economic Review* 5(1): 135–53.

Feder, Gershon, Tongroj Onchan, Yongyuth Chalamwong, and Chira Hongladarom. 1988. *Land Policies and Farm Productivity in Thailand*. Baltimore, Md.: Johns Hopkins University Press.

Findley, Roger W. 1988. "Pollution Control in Brazil." *Ecology Law Quarterly* 15(1): 1–68.

Finsterbusch, Kirk, and Warren A. Van Wicklin III. 1989. "Beneficiary Participation in Development Projects: Empirical Tests of Popular Theory." *Economic Development and Cultural Change* 37 (3): 573–93.

Flavin, Christopher, and Nicholas Lenssen. 1990. *Beyond the Petroleum Age: Designing a Solar Economy*. Worldwatch Paper 100. Washington, D.C.: Worldwatch Institute.

Freeman, Harry M., ed. 1989. *Standard Handbook of Hazardous Waste Treatment and Disposal*. New York: McGraw-Hill.

Gamba, Julio, David A. Caplin, and John J. Mulckhuyse. 1986. *Industrial Energy Rationalization in Developing Countries*. Baltimore, Md.: Johns Hopkins University Press.

GATT (General Agreement on Tariffs and Trade). 1971. "Industrial Pollution Control and International Trade." GATT Studies in International Trade Series 1. Geneva, Switzerland.

————. 1992. "Trade and the Environment." In *International Trade 1990–91*. Geneva: GATT Secretariat.

Georghiou, George P. 1986. "The Magnitude of the Resistance Problem." In *Pesticide Resistance—Strategies and Tactics for Management*. Washington, D.C.: National Academy Press.

Gilman, R. H., and Paul Skillicorn. 1985. "Boiling of Drinking-Water: Can a Fuel-Scarce Community Afford It?" *Bulletin of the World Health Organization* 63(1): 157–63.

Gollop, Frank M., and Mark J. Roberts. 1985. "Cost Minimizing Regulation of Sulphur Emissions." *Review of Economics and Statistics* 67(1): 81–90.

Greene, David L. 1989. "Motor Fuel Choice: An Econometric Analysis." *Transportation Research A*, 23A(3):243–53.

Gregersen, Hans, Sydney Draper, and Dieter Elz, eds. 1989. *People and Trees: The Role of Social Forestry in Sustainable Development*. EDI Seminar Series. Washington, D.C.: World Bank.

Grossman, Gene, and Alan Krueger. 1991. "Environmental Impacts of a North American Free Trade Agreement." Princeton University, Princeton, N.J.

Grubb, Michael. 1990. "Cinderella Options: A Study of Modernized Renewable Energy Technologies: Part 1-A, Technical Assessment." and "Part 2, Political and Policy Analysis." *Energy Policy* 18:525–42, July–August, and 18: 711–25, October.

Guggenheim, Scott E., and John Spears. 1991. "Sociological and Environmental Dimensions of Social Forestry Projects." In M. M. Cernea, ed. *Putting People First*. 2d ed. New York: Oxford University Press.

Hahn, Robert, and Roger G. Noll. 1982. "Designing a Market for Tradable Emissions Permits." In Wesley A. Magat, ed. *Reform of Environmental Regulation*. Cambridge, Mass.: Ballinger.

Hahn, Robert, and Robert Stavins. 1991. "Incentive-Based Environmental Regulation: A New Era from an Old Idea?" *Ecology Law Quarterly* 18, 1:1–42.

Hall, D. O., and R. P. Overend, eds. 1987. *Biomass: Regenerable Energy*. Chichester, U.K.: John Wiley and Sons.

Hamrin, Robert A. 1991. "The Role of Monitoring and Enforcement in Pollution Control in the U.S." World Bank, Country Economics Department, Washington, D.C.

Harrison, J. S. 1988. "Innovation for the Clean Use of Coal." 1988 Robens Coal Science Lecture. British Coal, Cheltenham, U.K.

Harvey, L. D. D., and S. H. Schneider. 1985. "Transient Climate Response to External Forcing on 10^0–10^4 Year Time Scales." *Journal of Geophysical Research* 90:2191–222.

Hasan, Arif. 1986. "The Low Cost of Sanitation Programme of the Orangi Pilot Project and the Process of Change in Orangi." Orangi Pilot Project, Karachi.

————. 1990. "Community Groups and NGOs in the Urban Field in Pakistan." *Environment and Urbanization* 2:74–86.

Hau, Timothy D. 1990. "Developments in Transport Policy: Electronic Road Pricing (Developments in Hong Kong 1983–1989)." *Journal of Transport Economics and Policy* (May): 203–14.

Hazell, Peter. 1991. "Drought, Poverty and the Environment." World Bank, Agricultural Policies Division, Washington, D.C.

Heggie, Ian. 1991. "Improving Management and Charging Policies for Roads: An Agenda for Reform." INU Report 92. World Bank, Infrastructure and Urban Development Department, Washington, D.C.

Herz, Barbara, Kalanidhi Subbarao, and Laura Raney. 1991. *Letting Girls Learn: Promising Approaches in Primary and Secondary Education*. World Bank Discussion Paper 133. Washington, D.C.

Hirschhorn, Joel, and Kirsten U. Oldenburg. 1991. *Prosperity Without Pollution: The Prevention Strategy for Industry and Consumers*. New York: Van Nostrand Reinhold.

Hoeller, Peter, Andrew Dean, and Jon Nicolaisen. 1990. "A Survey of Studies of the Costs of Reducing Greenhouse Gas Emissions." Department of Economics and Statistics Working Paper 89. OECD, Paris.

Hopcraft, Peter. 1981. "Economic Institutions and Pastoral Resource Management: Considerations for a Development Strategy." In John G. Galaty, D. Aronson, P. Saltzman, and A. Chovinard, eds., *The Future of Pastoral Peoples*. Proceedings of a conference in Nairobi, August 1980. IDRC, Ottawa.

Hoppin, Polly. 1991. *Pesticide Use on Four Non-Traditional Crops in Guatemala: Program and Policy Implications*. Baltimore, Md.: Johns Hopkins University Press.

Houghton, J. T., G. J. Jenkins, and J. J. Ephraums, eds. 1990. *Climate Change: The IPPC Scientific Assessment*. Intergovernmental Panel on Climate Change, Report by Working Group 1. Cambridge, U.K.: Press Syndicate of the University of Cambridge.

Houghton, Richard A. 1990. "The Global Effects of Tropical Deforestation." *Environmental Science and Technology* 24:414–22.

Hufschmidt, Maynard M., John A. Dixon, Louise A. Fallon, and Zhongping Zhu. 1987. "Water Management Policy Options for the Beijing-Tianjin Region of China." Report by the Environment and Policy Institute North China Water Project Team, East-West Center, Honolulu.

Hughes, Gordon. 1991. "The Impact of Economic Reform in Eastern Europe on European Energy Markets." Paper presented at the conference on New Developments in the International Marketplace, Amsterdam, November 14–15. Department of Economics, Warwick University, Coventry, U.K.

————. Forthcoming. "Substitution and the Impact of Transportation on Taxation in Tunis." *World Bank Economic Review*.

Hyde, William F., David H. Newman, and Roger A. Sedjo. 1991. *Forest Economics and Policy Analysis—An Overview*. World Bank Discussion Paper 134. Washington, D.C.

International Finance Corporation. Forthcoming. *Investing in the Environment: Business Opportunities in Developing Countries*. IFC Discussion Paper. Washington, D.C.

Imran, Mudassar, and Philip Barnes. 1990. "Energy Demand in the Developing Countries: Prospects for the Future." World Bank Staff Commodity Working Paper 23. Washington, D.C.

IPCC (Intergovernmental Panel on Climate Change). 1990. *Climate Change: The IPCC Response Strategies*, World Meteorological Organization, United Nations Environment Programme, Geneva.

IUCN (World Conservation Union). 1990. *IUCN Red List of Threatened Animals*. Gland, Switzerland.

IUCN, UNEP (United Nations Environment Programme), and WWF (World Wide Fund for Nature). 1991. *Caring for the Earth, a Strategy for Sustainable Living*. Gland, Switzerland.

Japan Environment Agency. 1988. *Quality of the Environment*. Tokyo.

Jodha, N. S. 1991. *Rural Common Property Resources: A Growing Crisis*. International Institute for Environment and Development: Sustainable Agriculture Program. Gatekeeper Series SA 24. London: IIED.

Johansson, Thomas B., Birgit Bodlund, and Robert H. Williams, eds. 1989. *Electricity: Efficient End-Use and New Generation Technologies, and Their Planning Implications*. Lund, Sweden: Lund University Press.

Johansson, Thomas B., Henry Kelly, Amulya K. N. Reddy, and Robert H. Williams, eds. Forthcoming. *Renewables for Fuels and Electricity*. Washington, D.C.: Island Press.

Jones, Peter M. 1989. "The Restraint of Road Traffic in Urban Areas: Objectives, Options and Experiences." Rees Jeffrys' Discussion Paper 3. Transport and Society Research Project. Oxford University, Oxford U.K.

Jopillo, Sylvia Maria G., and Romana P. de los Reyes. 1988. *Partnership in Irrigation: Farmers and Government in Agency-Managed Systems*. Quezon City: Institute of Philippine Culture.

Kennedy, David N. 1990. "Allocating California's Water Supplies During the Current Drought—Discussion Outline." Paper presented at the International Workshop on Comprehensive Water Resource Management, June 1991. World Bank, Agriculture and Rural Development Department, Washington, D.C.

Kinnersley, David. 1991. "Privatisation and the Water Environment: A Note on Water Agencies in Britain." Paper presented at the International Workshop on Comprehensive Water Resource Management, June 1991. World Bank, Agriculture and Rural Development Department, Washington, D.C.

Kiss, Agnes, ed. 1990. *Living with Wildlife: Wildlife Resource Management with Local Participation in Africa*. World Bank Technical Paper 130. Washington, D.C.

Kiss, Agnes, and Frans Meerman. 1991. *Integrated Pest Management and African Agriculture*. World Bank Technical Paper 142. Washington, D.C.

Kneese, Allen V., and Blair T. Bower. 1968. *Managing Water Quality: Economics, Technology, Institutions*. Baltimore, Md.: Johns Hopkins University Press.

Kolars, John F., and William A. Mitchell. 1991. *The Euphrates River and the Southeast Anatolia Development Project*. Carbondale, Ill.: Southern Illinois University Press.

Korten, Frances F., and Benjamin Bagadion. 1991. "Developing Irrigators' Organizations: A Learning Process Approach." In M. M. Cernea, ed. *Putting People First*, 2d ed. New York: Oxford University Press.

Korten, Frances F., and Robert Y. Siy, Jr., eds. 1988. *Transforming a Bureaucracy: The Experience of the Philippine National Irrigation Administration*. West Hartford, Conn.: Kumarian Press.

Kotlyakov, V. M. 1991. "Aral Sea Basin: A Critical Environmental Zone." *Environment* 33:(49):36–38.

Kottak, Conrad Phillip. 1991. "When People Don't Come First: Some Sociological Lessons from Completed Projects." In M. M. Cernea, ed. *Putting People First*, 2d ed. New York: Oxford University Press.

Kreimer, Alcira, and Mohan Munasinghe, eds. 1991. "Managing Natural Disasters and the Environment." Selected Materials from Colloquium on the Environment and Natural Disaster Management, June 27–28. World Bank, Environment Department, Washington, D.C.

Krupnick, Alan J. 1983. "Costs of Alternative Policies for the Control of NO_2 in the Baltimore Region." Working Paper, Resources for the Future, Washington, D.C.

Lambert, P. M., and D. D. Reid. 1970. "Smoking, Air Pollution and Bronchitis in Britain." *Lancet* i:853–57.

Lansing, Stephen. 1991. *Priests and Programmers*. Berkeley: University of California Press.

Lave, L. B., and E. P. Seskin. 1977. *Air Pollution and Human Health*. Baltimore, Md.: Johns Hopkins University Press.

Lele, Uma, and Steven W. Stone. 1989. *Population Pressure, the Environment and Agricultural Intensification: Variations on the Boserup Hypothesis*. MADIA Discussion Paper 4. World Bank, Washington, D.C.

Lewin, Rodger. 1987. "Domino Effect Involved in Ice Age Extinctions." *Science* 238:1509–10.

Lovei, Laszlo, and Dale Whittington. 1991. "Rent-Seeking in Water Supply." Discussion Paper INU 85. World Bank, Infrastructure and Urban Development Department, Washington, D.C.

Low, Patrick. Forthcoming. "Trade Measures and Environmental Quality: The Implications for Mexico's Exports." In Patrick Low, ed. *International Trade and the Environment*. World Bank Discussion Paper, Washington, D.C.

Low, Patrick, and Raed Safadi. Forthcoming. "Trade Policy and Pollution." In Patrick Low, ed. *International Trade and the Environment*. World Bank Discussion Paper, Washington, D.C.

Lutz, Ernst, ed. Forthcoming. *Toward Improvement of Accounting for the Environment.* World Bank Symposium Paper Series. Washington, D.C.

Lutz, Ernst, and Michael Young. 1990. "Agricultural Policies in Industrial Countries and Their Environmental Impacts: Applicability to and Comparisons with Developing Nations." Environment Working Paper 25. World Bank, Environment Department. Washington, D.C.

Magrath, William. 1989. "The Challenge of the Commons: The Allocation of Nonexclusive Resources." Environment Working Paper 14. World Bank, Environment Department. Washington, D.C.

Magrath, William, and Peter Arens. 1989. "The Costs of Soil Erosion on Java: A Natural Resource Accounting Approach." Environment Working Paper 18. World Bank, Environment Department. Washington, D.C.

Maler, Karl-Goran. 1974. *Environmental Economics: A Theoretical Inquiry.* Published for Resources for the Future. Baltimore: Johns Hopkins University Press.

—————. 1989. "The Acid Rain Game." Paper presented at workshop on Economic Analysis and Environmental Toxicology, Noordwijkerhout, The Netherlands, May.

—————. 1990. "International Environmental Problems." *Oxford Review of Economic Policy* 6(1): 80–108.

Maloney, Michael T., and Bruce Yandle. 1984. "Estimation of the Cost of Air Pollution Control Regulation." *Journal of Environmental Economics and Management* 11(3): 244–63.

Manne, A. S., and R. G. Richels. Forthcoming. "Global CO_2 Emission Reductions—The Impacts of Rising Energy Costs." *Energy Journal.*

Margulis, Sergio. 1992. "Back-of-the-Envelope Estimates of Environmental Damage Costs in Mexico." Policy Research Working Paper 824. World Bank, Country Department II, Latin America and Caribbean Region, Washington, D.C.

Markandya, Anil, and David Pearce. 1991. "Development, the Environment, and the Social Rate of Discount." *World Bank Research Observer* 6(2): 137–52.

Marland, Gregg, and others. 1989. *Estimates of CO_2 Emissions from Fossil Fuel Burning and Cement Manufacturing, Based on the United Nations Energy Statistics and the U.S. Bureau of Mines Cement Manufacturing Data.* ORN/CDIAC-25 NDP030. Oak Ridge, Tenn.: Oak Ridge National Laboratory.

McGarry, Robert. 1990. "Negotiating Water Supply Management Agreements for the National Capital Region." In *Managing Water-Related Conflicts: The Engineers' Role: Proceedings of the Engineering Foundation Conference, November 1989.* New York: American Society of Civil Engineers.

McGartland, Albert M. "Marketable Permit Systems for Air Pollution Control: An Empirical Study." Ph.D. dissertation, University of Maryland, College Park.

McNeeley, J. A., and others. 1990. *Conserving the World's Biological Diversity.* Gland, Switzerland: IUCN.

Miglino, Luis C. Porto, and Joseph J. Harrington. 1984. "O Impacto da Tarifa na Geracão de Efluentes Industriais." *Revista Dae,* São Paulo, 44(138): 212–20.

Migot-Adholla, Shem, and others. 1991. "Indigenous Land Rights Systems in Sub-Saharan Africa: A Constraint on Productivity?" *World Bank Economic Review* 5, 1:155–75.

Mitchell, C. C., R. L. Westerman, J. R. Brown, and T. R. Peck. 1991. "Overview of Long-Term Agronomic Research." *Agronomy Journal* 83, 1:24–29.

Mittermaier, R. A. 1988. "Primate Diversity and the Tropical Forest: Case Studies from Brazil and Madagascar and Importance of Megadiversity Countries." In E. O. Wilson and Frances M. Peter, eds. *Biodiversity.* Washington, D.C.: National Academy Press.

Mittermaier, R. A., and T. B. Werner. 1990. "Wealth of Plants and Animals Unites 'Megadiversity' Countries." *Tropicus* 4(1):1,4–5.

Moe, C. L., M. D. Sobsey, G. P. Samsa, and V. Mesolo. 1991. "Bacterial Indicators of Risk of Diarrhoeal Disease from Drinking-Water in the Philippines." *Bulletin of the World Health Organization* 69(3):305–17.

Mu, Xinming, Dale Whittington, and John Briscoe. 1991. "Modelling Village Water Demand Behavior: A Discrete Choice Approach." *Water Resources Research* 26(4).

Munasinghe, Mohan. 1992. *Water Supply and Environmental Management.* Boulder, Colo.: Westview Press.

Munasinghe, Mohan, and Kenneth King. 1991. "Issues and Options in Implementing the Montreal Protocol in Developing Countries." Environment Working Paper 49. World Bank, Environment Department, Washington, D.C.

Murray, Douglas L., and Polly Hoppin. Forthcoming. "Recurring Contradictions in Agrarian Development: Pesticide Problems in Caribbean Basin Non-Traditional Agriculture," *World Development 1992,* 20.

Myers, Norman. 1988. "Threatened Biotas: Hotspots in Tropical Forests." *Environmentalist* 8(3):1–20.

—————. 1990. "The Biodiversity Challenge: Expanded Hot-Spot Analysis." *Environmentalist* 10(4):243–56.

National Academy of Sciences. 1980. *Research Priorities in Tropical Biology.* Washington, D.C.: National Academy Press.

—————. 1986. *Common Property Resource Management.* Washington, D.C.: National Academy Press.

—————. 1991. *Policy Implications of Greenhouse Warming.* Washington, D.C.: National Academy Press.

—————. Forthcoming. *Policy Implications of Greenhouse Warming: Report of the Adaptation Panel.* Washington, D.C.: National Academy Press.

National Research Council. 1986. *Proceedings of the Conference on Common Resource Property Management.* Washington, D.C.: National Academy Press.

Nelson, Randy, and Tom Tietenberg. Forthcoming. "Differential Environmental Regulation: Effects on Electric Utility Capital Turnover and Emissions." *Review of Economics and Statistics.*

Nelson, Ridley. 1990. *Dryland Management: The "Desertification" Problem.* World Bank Technical Paper 116. Washington, D.C.

Newbery, David M. 1990. "Acid Rain." *Economic Policy* (October) 297–346.

Nilsson, Greta. 1990. *The Endangered Species Handbook.* Washington, D.C.: Animal Welfare Institute.

Nordhaus, William. 1990. "Global Warming: Slowing the Greenhouse Express." In Henry Aarons, ed. *Setting National Priorities.* Washington, D.C.: Brookings Institution.

—————. 1991. "To Slow or Not to Slow: The Economics of the Greenhouse Effect." *Economic Journal* 101(July): 920–37.

—————. 1992. " 'Rolling the Dice': An Optimal Transition Path for Controlling Greenhouse Gases." Paper presented at the Annual Meetings of the American Association for the Advancement of Science (February).

Norgaard, R. B. 1988. "The Biological Control of Cassava Mealybug in Africa." *American Journal of Agricultural Economics* 70 (2):366–71.

OECD (Organization for Economic Cooperation and Development). 1985. *The Macro-Economic Impact of Environmental Expenditure.* Paris.

—————. 1986. *Environmental Effects of Automotive Transport: The OECD Compass Project.* Paris.

—————. 1987a. *Energy and Cleaner Air: Costs of Reducing Emissions.* Summary and Analysis of Symposium Enclair 86. Paris.

————. 1987b. *Pricing of Water Services.* Paris.

————. 1987c. *Renewable Sources of Energy.* Paris.

————. 1988. *Transport and the Environment.* Paris.

————. 1989. *Energy and the Environment: Policy Overview.* Paris.

————. 1990. *Energy Statistics of OECD Countries 1987-88.* Paris.

————. 1991. *The State of the Environment.* Annual Report. Paris.

Oil and Gas Journal. Various issues.

Okun, Daniel A. 1988. "Water Supply and Sanitation in Developing Countries: An Assessment." *American Journal of Public Health* 78:1463–67.

Oldeman, L. R., R. T. A. Hakkeling, and W. G. Sombroek. 1990. *World Map of the Status of Human-Induced Soil Degradation: An Explanatory Note.* Rev. 2d. ed. Wageningen, The Netherlands: International Soil Reference and Information Centre.

Olson, Mancur. 1965. *The Logic of Collective Action.* Cambridge, Mass.: Harvard University Press.

Opschoor, J. P., and Hans Vos. 1989. *The Application of Economic Instruments for Environmental Protection in OECD Member Countries.* Paris: OECD.

Ostro, Bart D. 1983. "The Effects of Air Pollution on Work Loss and Morbidity." *Journal of Environmental Economics and Management* 10: 371–82.

————. 1984. "A Search for a Threshold in the Relationship of Air Pollution to Mortality: A Reanalysis of Data on London Winters." *Environmental Health Perspectives* 58:397–99.

————. 1987. "Air Pollution and Morbidity Revisited: A Specification Test." *Journal of Environmental Economics and Management* 14:87–98.

————. 1989. "Estimating the Risks of Smoking, Air Pollution, and Passive Smoke on Acute Respiratory Conditions." *Risk Analysis* 9(2):189–96.

Panayotou, Theodore. 1991. "Managing Emissions and Wastes." Harvard Institute for Management, Cambridge, Mass.

Parry, Martin. 1990. *Climate Change and World Agriculture.* London: Earthscan Publications.

Paul, Samuel. 1991. "The Bank's Work on Institutional Development in Sectors—Emerging Tasks and Challenges." Country Economics Department, Public Sector Management and Private Sector Development Division Paper. World Bank, Washington, D.C.

Pearce, David. 1991. "The Global Commons." In David Pearce, ed., *Blueprint 2: The Greening of the Global Economy.* London: Earthscan Publications.

Pearce, David W., and Jeremy J. Warford. Forthcoming. *World Without End: Economics, Environment, and Sustainable Development.* New York: Oxford University Press.

Pimentel, David. 1991. "Global Warming, Population Growth, and Natural Resources for Food Production." *Society and Natural Resources* 4:347–63. October–December.

Pimentel, David, and others. 1991. "Environmental and Economic Effects of Reducing Pesticide Use." *BioScience* 41, 6:402–09.

Plucknett, Donald. 1991. "Modern Crop Production Technologies in Africa: The Conditions for Sustainability." Paper presented at Workshop on Africa's Agricultural Development in the 1990s: Can It Be Sustained? Arusha, Tanzania, May 15–17, 1991. Sasakawa African Association and the Centre for Applied Studies in International Negotiations, Geneva.

Portney, Paul R. 1990. "Air Pollution Policy." In Paul R. Portney, ed. *Public Policies for Environmental Protection.* Washington, D.C.: Resources for the Future.

Ramnarong, Vachi. 1991. "Success Story: Mitigation of Ground Water Crisis and Land Subsidence in Bangkok." Preliminary document of Global Assembly of Women and the Environment, Miami, Fla., October. WorldWIDE Network, Washington, D.C..

Ravallion, Martin, Gaurav Datt, and Dominique Van De Walle. 1991. "Quantifying Absolute Poverty in the Developing World." *Review of Income and Wealth* Series 37(4):345–61.

Ravallion, Martin, Guarav Datt, and Shaohua Chen. 1992. "New Estimates of Aggregate Poverty Measures for the Developing World, 1985–89." World Bank, Population and Human Resources Department, Washington, D.C.

Ravazzani, Carlos, Hilario Wiederkehr Filho, and Jose Paulo Fagnani, eds. 1991. *Curitiba: The Ecological Capital.* Curitiba: Edibran.

Reid, Walter V., and Kenton R. Miller. 1989. *Keeping Options Alive—The Scientific Basis for Conserving Biodiversity.* Washington, D.C.: World Resources Institute.

Repetto, Robert. 1985. *Paying the Price: Pesticide Subsidies in Developing Countries.* Research Report 2. Washington, D.C.: World Resources Institute.

————. 1986. *Skimming the Water: Rent-Seeking and the Performance of Public Irrigation Systems.* Research Report 4. Washington, D.C.: World Resources Institute.

Repetto, Robert, and Malcolm Gillis, eds. 1988. *Public Policies and the Misuse of Forest Resources,* Cambridge, U.K.: Cambridge University Press.

Rogers, Peter. 1984. "Fresh Water." In Robert Repetto, ed. *The Global Possible: Resources, Development, and the New Century.* New Haven, Conn.: Yale University Press.

————. 1986. "This Water Costs Almost Nothing—That's Why We're Running Out." *Technology Review* November/December: 31–43.

————. 1990. "Socio-Economic Development of Arid Regions: Alternative Strategies for the Aral Basin." Paper presented at the International Conference on the Aral Crisis: Causes, Consequences, and Ways of Solution, at Nukus, U.S.S.R., October. Harvard University, Cambridge, Mass.

————. 1991. "International River Basins: Pervasive Unidirectional Externalities." Paper presented at the conference on The Economics of Transnational Commons, Universita di Siena, April.

————. Forthcoming. "World Bank Comprehensive Water Resources Management Policy Paper." Policy Research Working Paper, World Bank, Infrastructure and Urban Development Department, Washington, D.C.

Romieu, Isabell, Henyk Weitzenfeld, and Jacobo Finkelman. 1990. "Urban Air Pollution in Latin America and the Caribbean: Health Perspectives." *World Health Statistics Quarterly* 43: 153–167.

Rosegrant, M. W., and P. L. Pingali. 1991. "Sustaining Rice Production Growth in Asia: A Policy Perspective." IRRI Social Science Division Papers 91-01. Manila.

Rosenberg, Norman, and others, eds. 1989. *Greenhouse Warming: Adaptation and Abatement.* Washington, D.C.: Resources for the Future.

Rowland, F. Sherwood. 1990. "The Global Commons." *Business Week* Special Supplement (June) 18, 35.

————. 1991. "Stratospheric Ozone in the 21st Century: The Chlorofluorocarbon Problem." *Environmental Science and Technology* 25(4): 624.

Russell, Clifford S. 1990. "Monitoring and Enforcement." In Paul R. Portney, ed. *Public Policies for Environmental Protection.* Washington, D.C.: Resources for the Future.

Russell, Clifford S., and N. K. Nicholson, eds. 1981. *Public Choice and Rural Development.* Washington, D.C.: Resources for the Future.

Sanchez, Pedro A., Cheryl A. Palm, and Thomas Jot Smyth. 1990. "Approaches to Mitigate Tropical Deforestation by Sustainable Soil Management Practices." In H. W. Scharpenseel, M. Schomarker, and A. Ayoub, eds. *Developments in Soil Science* 20:211–20. Amsterdam: Elsevier.

Schellinkhout, A. and J. H. C. M. Oomen. 1992. "Anaerobic Sewage Treatment in Colombia." *Land and Water International* 73:13–15.

Schmidheiny, Stephan. 1992. *Changing Course: A Global Business Perspective on Development and the Environment.* Business Council for Sustainable Development. Cambridge, Mass.: MIT Press.

Schramm, Gunter, and Jeremy J. Warford, eds. 1989. *Environmental Management and Economic Development.* Baltimore, Md.: Johns Hopkins University Press.

Scientific American. 1990. "Energy for Planet Earth," Special Issue 263(3).

Sebastian, Iona, and Adelaida Alicbusan. 1990. "Internalizing the Social Costs of Pollution: Overview of Current Issues in Air Pollution." World Bank, Environment Department Divisional Working Paper 1990–14, Washington, D.C.

Shell Briefing Service. 1987. *Synthetic Fuels and Renewable Energy.* SBS 2/PAC/222. London: Shell International Petroleum Company.

———. 1991. *Coal and the Environment.* SBS 1/PAC/233. London: Shell International Petroleum Company.

Shuhua, Gu, Huang Kun, Qiu Daxiong, and Kirk Smith. 1991. "One Hundred Million Improved Cookstoves in China: How Was It Done?" Draft ESMAP Report. World Bank, Industry and Energy Department, Washington, D.C.

Singh, Bhanwar, Radhika Ramasubban, John Briscoe, Charles Griffin, and Chongchun Kim. Forthcoming. "Rural Water Supply in Kerala, India: How to Emerge from a Low-Level Equilibrium Trap." *Water Resources Research.*

Smith, Kirk. 1988. "Air Pollution: Assessing Total Exposure in Developing Countries," *Environment* 30(10): 16–35.

Smith, Rodney T., and Roger Vaughan, eds. 1989. "Evaporating Water Markets? New Contingencies for Urban Water Use." *Water Strategist* 3(2): 11, 16.

Smith, Scott E., and Hussan M. Al-Rawahy. 1990. "The Blue Nile: Potential for Conflict and Alternatives for Meeting Future Demands." *Water International* 15(4): 217–22.

Smyle, J. W., and W. B. Magrath. 1990. *Vetiver Grass—A Hedge Against Erosion.* 3d. ed. Washington, D.C.: World Bank.

Solow, Andrew, Stephen Polasky, and James Broadus. Forthcoming. "On the Measurement of Biological Diversity." *Journal of Environmental Economics and Management.*

Southgate, Douglas. 1990. "Tropical Deforestation and Agricultural Development in Latin America." Environment Department, Divisional Working Paper. World Bank, Washington, D.C.

Spears, John. Forthcoming. *Industrial Forest Management Options in the Tropics: Environmental Implications.* World Bank, Washington, D.C.

Spofford, Walter O., Jr. 1984. "Efficiency Properties of Alternative Source Control Policies for Meeting Ambient Air Quality Standards: An Empirical Application to the Lower Delaware Valley." Discussion Paper D-118. Resources tor the Future, Washington, D.C.

Subbarao, Kalanidhi, and Laura Raney. 1992. "Social Gains from Female Education." World Bank, Population and Human Resources Department, Washington, D.C.

Summers, Lawrence H. 1991. "Investing in *All* the People." Paper prepared for the Quad-i-Azam Lecture at the Eighth Annual General Meeting of the Pakistan Society of Development Economists, Islamabad. World Bank, Office of the Vice President, Development Economics, Washington, D.C.

Summers, Robert, and Alan Heston. 1991. "The Penn World Table (Mark 5): An Expanded Set of International Comparisons 1950–1988." *Quarterly Journal of Economics* May.

Swanson, Timothy. 1991. "Conserving Biological Diversity." In David Pearce, ed. *Blueprint 2: Greening the World Economy.* London: Earthscan Publications.

Tedder, D. William, and Frederick G. Pohland, eds. 1990. *Emerging Technologies in Hazardous Waste Management.* Washington, D.C.: American Chemical Society.

Tegart, W. J. McG., G. W. Sheldon, and D. C. Griffiths. 1990. *Climate Change: The IPCC Impacts Assessment.* Canberra: Australian Government Publishing Service.

Thomas, Vinod. 1985. "Evaluating Pollution Control: The Case of São Paulo, Brazil." *Journal of Development Economics* 19:133–46.

Tietenberg, Tom. 1988. *Environmental and Natural Resource Economics.* Glenview, Ill.: Scott, Foresman and Company.

Triche, Thelma A. 1990. "Private Participation in the Delivery of Guinea's Water Supply Services." Water and Sanitation Working Paper 477. World Bank, Infrastructure and Urban Development Department, Washington, D.C.

Trieff, Norman M., ed. 1981. *Environment and Health.* Ann Arbor, Mich.: Ann Arbor Science Publishers, Inc.

Tucker, Compton J., Harold E. Dregne, and Wilber W. Newcomb. 1991. "Expansion and Contraction of the Sahara Desert from 1980 to 1990." *Science* 253 (July 19): 299–301.

UNEP (United Nations Environment Programme). 1990. "Current Multilateral, Bilateral and National Financial Support for Biological Diversity Conservation." Ad Hoc Working Group of Experts on Biological Diversity (June). UNEP/Bio.Div.3/Inf.2. New York.

———. 1991. "Environmental Effects of Ozone Depletion: 1991 Update." Panel report under the Montreal Protocol on Substances that Deplete the Ozone Layer. Nairobi.

UNEP GEMS (Global Environmental Monitoring System). 1988. *Assessment of Urban Air Quality.* Geneva.

UNEP and World Health Organization. 1988. "Global Environment Monitoring System: Assessment of Urban Air Quality." Geneva.

UNIDO (United Nations Industrial Development Organization). 1991. *1990–91 Review of Technological Options—Industry and Environment Annual Report.* Vienna.

United Nations. 1990. *World Urbanization Prospects.* New York.

UNSO (United Nations Statistical Office). Various years. *United Nations Energy Statistics Yearbook.* New York.

U.S. Agency for International Development and U.S. Environmental Protection Agency. 1990. "Ranking Environmental Health Risks in Bangkok, Thailand." Office of Housing and Urban Programs, Washington, D.C.

U.S. Bureau of the Census. 1990. *Manufacturers' Pollution Abatement Capital Expenditures and Operating Costs 1989.* Report MA200(89)-1. Washington, D.C.: Superintendent of Documents.

———. 1991. *Pollutioln Abatement Costs and Expenditures 1989.* Washington, D.C.: Government Printing Office.

U.S. Council on Environmental Quality. 1991. *Environmental Quality: 21st Annual Report.* Washington, D.C.

U.S. Department of Energy. 1983. "The Future of Electric Power in America." Washington, D.C.

———. 1990. "The Potential of Renewable Energy: An Interlaboratory White Paper." Washington, D.C.

U.S. Department of the Interior. 1991. *Fiscal Year Highlights*. Washington, D.C.: Government Printing Office.

U.S. Environmental Protection Agency. 1985. *Costs and Benefits of Reducing Lead in Gasoline: Final Regulatory Impact Analysis*. EPA-230-05-85-006. Washington, D.C.

————. 1986. "Quality Criteria for Water." EPA 440/5-86-001, May 1. Office of Water Regulation and Standards, Washington, D.C.

————. 1989. "Public-Private Partnership Case Studies: Profiles of Success in Providing Environmental Services." PM-225. Washington, D.C.

————. 1991. *National Air Pollutant Emissions Estimates 1940-1989*. Report EPA-450/4-91-004 March. Research Triangle Park, N.C.

VanDerslice, James Albert, and John Briscoe. Forthcoming. "All Pathogens Are Not Created Equal: A Comparison of the Effects of Water Source and In-house Contamination on Infantile Diarrheal Disease." *Water Resources Research*.

Van Tongeren, Jan, Stefan Schweinfest, Ernst Lutz, Maria Gomez Luna, and Guillen Martin. Forthcoming. "Integrated Environmental and Economic Accounting—A Case Study for Mexico." In Ernst Lutz, ed. *Toward Improvement of Accounting for the Environment*. World Bank Symposium Paper Series. Washington, D.C.

Vlachos, Evan. 1990. "Prologue." *Water International* 15(4): 185-88.

Walker, T. S., and John L. Pender, "Experimental Measurement of Time Preference in Rural India." Food Research Institute of Stanford and ICRISAT, Palo Alto, Calif.

Warren, D. Michael. 1991. *Using Indigenous Knowledge in Agricultural Development*. World Bank Discussion Paper 127. Washington, D.C.

Weitzman, Martin L. 1975. "Prices vs. Quantities." *Review of Economic Studies* 41, 477-91.

————. 1992a. "On Diversity." *Quarterly Journal of Economics*. In press.

————. 1992b. "What to Preserve? An Application of Diversity Theory to Crane Conservation." Harvard University, Cambridge, Mass.

Wells, Michael, and Katrina Brandon, with Lee Hannah. 1992. *People and Parks: Linking Protected Area Management with Local Communities*. Washington, D.C.: World Bank, USAID, and World Wildlife Fund-U.S.

Welsch, Heinz. 1988. "A Cost Comparison of Alternative Policies for Sulphur Dioxide Control: The Case of the British Power Plant Sector." *Energy Economics* 10(4):287-97.

Whalley, John, and Randall Wigle. 1991. "The International Incidence of Carbon Taxes." In Rudiger Dornbusch and James M. Poterba, eds. *Global Warming: Economic Policy Responses*, Cambridge, Mass.: MIT Press.

Wheeler, David. 1992. "The Economics of Industrial Pollution Control: An International Perspective." Industry Series Paper 55. World Bank, Industry and Energy Department, Washington, D.C.

Wheeler, David, and Paul Martin. Forthcoming. "Prices, Policies, and the International Diffusion of Clean Technology." World Bank, Environment Department, Washington, D.C.

Whittington, Dale, Donald T. Lauria, Daniel A. Okun, and Xinming Mu. 1988. "Water Vending and Development: Lessons from Two Countries." Water and Sanitation for Health Project. WASH Technical Report 45. USAID, Washington, D.C.

Whittington, Dale, Donald T. Lauria, and Xinming Mu. 1991. "Paying for Urban Services: A Study of Water Vending and Willingness to Pay for Water in Onitsha, Nigeria." *World Development* 19:179-98.

Whittington, Dale, Donald T. Lauria, Albert M. Wright, Kyeongae Choe, Jeffrey A. Hughes, and Venkateswarlu Swarna. 1992. "Household Demand for Improved Sanitation Services: A Case Study of Kumasi, Ghana." Program Report Series. UNDP/World Bank Water and Sanitation Program, Washington, D.C.

WHO (World Health Organization). 1984a. "Biomass Fuel Combustion and Health." Geneva.

————. 1984b. *Guidelines for Drinking-Water Quality*. Volume 1: *Recommendations*. Geneva.

————. 1989. "Health Guidelines for the Use of Wastewater in Agriculture and Aquaculture." Technical Report Series 778. Geneva.

————. 1992. "Our Planet, Our Health." WHO Commission on Health and the Environment, Geneva.

Wickremage, M. 1991. "Institutional Development: A Sri Lankan Experience." Paper presented at the Collaborative Council for Water and Sanitation, Oslo, Norway.

Wiens, Thomas. 1989. "Philippines: Environment and Natural Resource Management Study." World Bank, East Asia and Pacific Country Department, Washington, D.C.

Wilson, Edward O., and Frances M. Peter, eds. 1988. *Biodiversity*. Washington, D.C.: National Academy Press.

Wirtshafter, Robert M., and Shih, Ed. 1990. "Decentralization of China's Electricity Sector: Is Small Beautiful?" *World Development* 18:505-12.

Wolf, E. C. 1987. "On the Brink of Extinction: Conserving the Diversity of Life." Worldwatch Paper 78. Worldwatch Institute, Washington, D.C.

World Bank. 1990a. "Indonesia—Sustainable Development of Forest, Land and Water." Country Department V, Asia Regional Office, Washington, D.C.

————. 1990b. "Overview of Water and Sanitation Activities FY89." Report INU-OR4. Infrastructure and Urban Development Department, Washington, D.C.

————. 1991a. "FY91 Water and Sanitation Sector Review—Issues in Institutional Performance and 1991 Sector Activities, INUWS." Infrastructure and Urban Development Department, Washington, D.C.

————. 1991b. "FY90 Sector Review—Water Supply and Sanitation." Report INU-OR6. Infrastructure and Urban Development Department, Washington, D.C.

————. 1991c. "An Evaluation of Improved Biomass Cookstoves Program: Prospects for Success or Failure." Joint ESMAP/UNDP Report. Industry and Energy Department, Washington, D.C.

————. 1991d. *The Forest Sector*. Washington, D.C.

————. 1991e. *The Reform of Public Sector Management: Lessons from Experience*. Policy and Research Series 18. Country Economics Department, Washington, D.C.

————. 1991f. *The World Bank and the Environment: A Progress Report, Fiscal 1991*. Washington, D.C.

————. 1992a. *Global Economic Prospects and the Developing Countries*. International Economics Department, Washington, D.C.

————. 1992b. *A Strategy for Asian Forestry Development*. Washington, D.C.

————. Various years. *World Development Report*. New York: Oxford University Press.

————. Forthcoming a. "The Bank's Role in the Electric Power Sector: Policies for Effective Institutional, Regulatory, and Financial Reform." Industry and Energy Department, Washington, D.C.

————. Forthcoming b. *Water Supply and Sanitation Projects: The Bank Experience 1967-1989*. Operations Evaluation Department, Washington, D.C.

World Bank Environment Department. 1991. *Environmental Assessment Sourcebook*. Washington, D.C.

World Bank, UNDP, FAO, and Institute for Development Anthropology. 1990. *Land Settlement Review: the Experience with Land Settlement in the OCP River Basins and Strategies for Their Development*. Washington, D.C.: World Bank.

World Bank Water Demand Research Team. Forthcoming. "Towards a New Rural Water Supply Paradigm: Implications of a Multi-Country Study of Households' Willingness to Pay for Improved Water Services." *World Bank Research Observer*.

World Commission on Environment and Development. 1987. *Our Common Future*. New York: Oxford University Press.

World Energy Conference. Various years. *Survey of Energy Resources*. London: Oxford University Press.

World Meteorological Organization, UNEP, U.S. National Aeronautics and Space Administration, U.S. National Oceanic and Atmospheric Administration, and U.K. Department of Environment. Forthcoming. "Scientific Assessment of Ozone Depletion: 1991." WMO Ozone Report 25. UNEP, Nairobi.

World Resources Institute. 1990. *World Resources 1990–91*. New York: Oxford University Press.

————. 1992. *World Resources, 1992–93*. New York: Oxford University Press.

Wright, Albert M., and Alexander E. Bakalian. 1990. "Intermediate Sanitation: Cost Efficient Sewerage." *Infrastructure Notes*. W&S SW-4(July): 1–2. World Bank, Washington, D.C.

Wright, Peter, and Edouard G. Bonkoungou. 1986. "Soil and Water Conservation as a Starting Point for Rural Forestry: the OXFAM Project in Ouahigouya, Burkina Faso. *Rural Africana* 23–24:79–85.

Yepes, Guillermo. 1990. "Management and Operational Practices of Municipal and Regional Water and Sewerage Companies in Latin America and the Caribbean." Report INU-61. World Bank, Infrastructure and Urban Development Department, Washington, D.C.

————. 1991. "Water Supply and Sanitation Sector Maintenance: The Costs of Neglect and Options to Improve It." World Bank, Latin America and Caribbean Region Technical Department, Washington, D.C.

Zijp, Willem. 1992. "From Agricultural Extension to Rural Information Management." Paper presented at the Twelfth Agricultural Symposium, January. World Bank, Europe and Central Asia Regional Office, Washington, D.C.

Ziswiler, Vinzenz. 1967. *Extinct and Vanishing Animals*. New York: Springer-Verlag.

Environmental data appendix

Tables A.1 and A.2 present summary date on population and GNP; the remaining eight tables in this Appendix provide environmental and policy-related data as a supplement to the main text and to the data presented in the World Development Indicators. Readers should refer to the "Definitions and data notes" for an explanation of the country groups used in these tables. In Tables A.6 and A.7 economies are listed in the same order as in the World Development Indicators.

The data reported here are drawn from the most authoritative sources available; however, they should be used with caution. Although the data present the major differences in resources and uses among countries, true compatibility of data is limited because of variation in data collection, statistical methods, definitions, and government resources.

Table A.3 Water availability

The Département Hydrogéologie in Orléans, France, compiles water resource and withdrawal data from published documents, including national, United Nations, and professional literature. The Institute of Geography at the National Academy of Sciences in Moscow also compiles global water data on the basis of published work and, where necessary, estimates water resources and consumption from models that use other data, such as area under irrigation, livestock populations, and precipitation. These and other sources have been combined by the World Resources Institute to generate the data for this table. Data for small countries and countries in arid and semiarid zones are less reliable than are those for larger countries and those with higher rainfall.

Annual internal renewable water resources refer to the average annual flow of rivers and of aquifers generated from rainfall within the country. The regional and income group totals presented here are compiled from data that are not strictly additive, since they are based on differing sources and dates. In addition, annual country data may conceal large seasonal, year-to-year, and long-term variations.

For each region or income group, *annual with-*

drawal as a share of water resources refers to total water withdrawal as a percentage of internal renewable water resources. Withdrawals include those from nonrenewable aquifers and desalting plants but do not include evaporative losses.

Per capita figures are calculated using 1990 population estimates. Withdrawals can exceed 100 percent of renewable supplies when extractions from nonrenewable aquifers or desalting plants are considerable or if there is significant water reuse.

Sectoral withdrawal is divided into three categories: *agriculture* (irrigation and livestock), *domestic* (drinking water, private homes, commercial establishments, public services, and municipal use or provision), and *industry* (including water for cooling thermoelectric plants). The sectoral proportions are based on national reports and models that use estimates from other data and thus should be interpreted with care. Numbers may not sum to 100 percent because of rounding.

Generally, countries with an annual water availability of less than 1,000 cubic meters per capita face chronic water scarcity, while those with less than 2,000 cubic meters face water stress and major problems in drought years.

Table A.4 Selected water quality indicators for various rivers

The global water quality monitoring project (GEMS/Water) was established in 1976 as part of the Global Environment Monitoring System (GEMS). In 1990 there were a total of 488 reporting stations in 64 countries. Water quality data are available from 1979 to the present. Data shown in this table comprise two of the fifty indicators of water quality that are reported within the GEMS system and have been made available by the Canada Centre for Inland Waters, which acts as the global data center. Not all stations collect all data, and the frequency and physical accuracy of measurement vary among stations. Four-year periods are used in the table to minimize seasonal and year-to-year variability and to emphasize general trends, if any.

Dissolved oxygen is a critical factor in the health of aquatic organisms. In general, for life, growth, and reproduction, values must exceed 5.5 milligrams per liter for warm-water habitats and 6.5 milligrams per liter for cold-water habitats. Lower values of dissolved oxygen endanger stocks of fish and other oxygen-dependent organisms.

Fecal coliforms are most commonly associated with animal and human feces. This measure is used as a sentinel indicator for the presence or potential presence of many other pathogenic organisms that are more difficult to observe and measure. Water for human consumption should usually contain zero fecal coliforms per 100-milliliter sample, and bathing water and water used for irrigation should contain less than 1,000 per 100-milliliter sample.

Table A.5 Selected ambient air quality indicators for various cities

Since 1974 standardized data on concentrations of sulfur dioxide and suspended particulate matter (SPM) from selected cities worldwide have been submitted to the World Health Organization (WHO) as part of the WHO/UNEP-GEMS Urban Air Quality Monitoring Project (GEMS/Air). The project currently extends to nearly eighty cities in more than fifty countries. Most cities report data from three sites, which are classified as city center or suburban and as commercial, industrial, or residential. Data are maintained at the GEMS/Air data center at the United States Environmental Protection Agency's Atmospheric Research Exposure Assessment Laboratory in North Carolina and are made available through the Monitoring and Assessment Research Centre, London.

WHO has separate guidelines for peak (daily average) and average (annual mean) exposure of populations to air pollutants. For sulfur dioxide the daily average guideline of 100–150 micrograms per cubic meter should not be exceeded for more than seven days in one year; the annual mean guideline is 40–60 micrograms per cubic meter. For gravimetrically determined SPM the respective guidelines are 150–230 micrograms per cubic meter and 60–90 micrograms per cubic meter. It should be noted that these guidelines are generally considered to be targets; for each country the costs and benefits of achieving the targets have to be carefully assessed.

Table A.6 Changes in land use

Data on land area and use are provided to the Food and Agriculture Organization of the United Nations (FAO) by national governments in response to annual questionnaires. The FAO also compiles data from national agricultural censuses. When official information is lacking, the FAO prepares its own estimates or relies on unofficial data. Several countries use definitions of total area and land use that differ from those used in this table. (See the current edition of the FAO *Production Yearbook* for details.) The FAO often adjusts its definitions of land use categories and sometimes substantially revises earlier data. Because these changes reflect data-reporting procedures as well as actual changes in land use, apparent trends should be interpreted with caution.

Land area refers to total area, excluding the area under inland water bodies (mainly, rivers and lakes). *Agricultural land* includes both arable and permanent crop land. Arable land refers to land under temporary crops (double-cropped areas are counted only once), temporary meadows for mowing or pasture, market and kitchen gardens (including cultivation under glass), and land temporarily fallow or lying idle. Permanent crop land is occupied by crops such as cocoa, coffee, and rubber that are in place for long periods and that need not be replanted after each harvest; the category includes land under shrubs, fruit trees, nut trees, and vines but excludes land under trees grown for wood or timber. *Permanent pasture* refers to land used permanently (five years or more) for herbaceous forage crops, either cultivated or growing wild. *Forest and woodland* refers to land under natural or planted stands of trees, whether subject to harvesting or not, and includes land from which forests have been cleared but that will be reforested in the foreseeable future. *Other land* includes unused but potentially productive land, built-on areas, wasteland, parks, ornamental gardens, roads, lanes, barren land, and any other land not specifically listed in the foregoing categories.

Table A.7 Agriculture: production and yields of selected crops, fertilizer consumption, and irrigation

Most of the data in this table are supplied by national agriculture ministries in response to annual FAO questionnaires or are derived from agricultural censuses. The FAO compiles data from more than 200 country reports and from many other sources. Gaps in the data are filled by the FAO on the basis of its own estimates. As better information becomes available, the FAO corrects its estimates and recalculates the entire time-series when necessary.

Cereal crops include wheat, rice paddy, barley, maize, rye, oats, millet, and sorghum. Area and production data relate to crops harvested for dry grain only. Cereal crops harvested for hay, harvested green for food, feed, or silage, or used for grazing are excluded. Area data relate to harvested area. *Roots and tubers* include potatoes, sweet potatoes, cassava, yams, and taro. Yields are calculated by dividing total production by the area harvested.

Fertilizer consumption is calculated by dividing the total consumption of nitrogenous, phosphatic and potash fertilizers by the area of agricultural land given in table A.6.

Data on *irrigation* refer to areas purposely provided with water (including land flooded by river water) for crop production or pasture improvement, whether these areas are irrigated several times or only once during the year stated. For some African countries data on irrigation have been revised recently on the basis of new studies.

Table A.8 Nationally protected areas

Data for this table have been provided by the World Conservation Monitoring Centre in the United Kingdom, which maintains data on national parks and protected areas.

Information on protected areas combines five of the management categories originally developed by the International Union for the Conservation of Nature and Natural Resources (IUCN) in 1972. *Totally protected areas* (IUCN categories I–III) include:

• Scientific reserves and strict nature reserves that possess outstanding, representative ecosystems. Public access is prohibited or severely restricted. The reserve should be large enough to ensure the integrity of the area, meet the scientific management objectives, and provide for the protection of the reserve. In many reserves natural perturbations (for example, insect infestations and forest fires) are allowed to run their course without any direct human interference.

• National parks and provincial parks that constitute relatively large areas of national or international significance not materially altered by human beings. Visitors may use them for recreation and study.

• Natural monuments and natural landmarks that contain unique geologic formations, special animals or plants, or unusual habitats.

Partially protected areas (IUCN categories IV–V) include:

• Managed natural reserves and wildlife sanctuaries that are protected for specific purposes, such as the conservation of a significant plant or animal species. Some areas require management.

• Protected landscapes and seascapes, which may be entirely natural or may include cultural landscapes (for example, scenically attractive agricultural areas). Examples would include coastlines, lakeshores, and hilly or mountainous terrain along scenic highways.

The figures presented do not include locally or provincially protected sites, privately owned areas, or areas managed primarily for extraction of natural resources.

Table A.9 Global carbon dioxide emissions from fossil fuels and cement manufacture

The Carbon Dioxide Information Analysis Center (CDIAC) in the United States calculates world emissions from data on the net apparent consumption of fossil fuels and on world cement manufacture. Emissions are calculated from global average fuel chemistry and use.

Estimates of world emissions are probably within 10 percent of actual emissions. Individual country estimates may depart more widely from reality. The CDIAC points out that the time trends from a consistent and uniform time-series ''should be more accurate than the individual values.''

Total emissions consist of the sum of the carbon in carbon dioxide released in the consumption of solid, liquid, and gas fuels (primarily but not exclusively coals, petroleum products, and natural gas), in gas flaring (the burning off of gas released in the process of petroleum extraction—a practice that is declining), and in the production of cement (in which calcium carbonate is calcined to produce calcium oxide, with 0.136 metric tons of carbon released as carbon dioxide for each ton of cement produced).

Combustion of different fossil fuels releases carbon dioxide at different rates for the same energy production. Oil releases about 1.5 times the amount of carbon dioxide released from natural gas; coal releases about twice the carbon dioxide of natural gas.

It is assumed that approximately 1 percent of the coal used by industry and power plants is not burned and that an additional few percent are converted to nonoxidizing uses. Other oxidative reactions of coal are assumed to be of negligible importance in carbon budget modeling. Carbon emissions from gas flaring and cement production are also included. These two sources account for about 3 percent of the carbon emitted by fossil fuel combustion. Fossil fuel emissions include those released from bunker fuels in international transport and are not ascribed to particular countries.

Table A.10 Energy: consumption, production, and resources

Energy data are compiled by the United Nations Statistical Office (UNSO) and are published in the *United Nations Energy Statistics Yearbook*. The World Bank makes some modifications to these data, as explained below.

Since the difference between world consumption and production for liquid and solid fuels and for gas is small, data are only presented on the changing pattern of consumption. However, since consumption data on electricity are less reliable, production data are presented.

Under world consumption, *liquid fuels* comprise petroleum products, including feedstocks, natural gasoline, condensate, refinery gas, and the input of crude petroleum to thermal power plants; *solid fuels* include primary forms of solid fuels, net imports, and changes in stocks of secondary fuels; and *gas* includes the consumption of natural gas, net imports, and changes in gas stocks of coke-ovens and gasworks.

World production of *primary electricity* comprises electricity generated by hydroelectric, nuclear, and geothermal sources. The role of electricity is severely underestimated when a kilowatt-hour is counted at its thermal end-use equivalent of 860 kilocalories, as is often the case with UN energy data. Primary electricity substitutes for at least 2,500 kilocalories of other fuels, and the World Bank has revised UN estimates to account for this.

Fuelwood is defined as wood in the rough (from trunks and branches of trees) that is used as fuel for purposes such as cooking, heating, and power production. Wood for *charcoal*, "put kilns," and portable ovens is included, using a conversion factor (6 tons of charcoal = 1 cubic meter of fuelwood) to convert from weight to solid volume units. A further conversion factor (1 cubic meter of fuelwood = 0.222 tons of oil equivalent) has been used to obtain a rough estimate of the energy equivalent of fuelwood to show the importance of this form of energy, especially in developing countries. Data come from the FAO *Forest Products Yearbook*.

World reserves are generally taken to be those quantities that geologic and engineering information indicate with reasonable certainty can be recovered from known reservoirs under existing economic and operating conditions. Caution should be exercised when using reserve data, since estimates can vary widely from source to source. In considering reserve data, it should be borne in mind that revisions of estimates account for the greater part of the reported additions to reserves and that past increases or decreases in reserves do not necessarily mean that the volumes or economic values of reserves will continue to increase or decrease over time. Reserve data for *liquid fuels* (crude oil only) and *gas* have been compiled from the *Oil and Gas Journal*, and data for *solid fuels* (anthracite, bituminous, subbituminous, and lignite) from various editions of the World Energy Conference publication *Survey of Energy Resources*.

The *reserves/production ratio* is calculated by dividing the reserves remaining at the end of any year by the production in that year. The result is the number of years that those reserves would last if production were to continue at the same level.

The *world price* for *liquid fuels* is the average Organization of Petroleum Exporting Countries (OPEC) petroleum price, which is calculated by weighting OPEC government sales by OPEC exports. The price of *solid fuels* is for thermal coal of 12,000 British thermal units per pound, less than 1 percent sulfur, 12 percent ash, f.o.b. piers, Hampton Roads, United States. No world prices are given for gas, electricity, or fuelwood because they are not widely traded on the international market.

Table A.1 Population (midyear) and average annual growth

Country group	Population (millions)							Average annual growth (percent)				
	1965	1973	1980	1990	1991	2000[a]	2030[a]	1965–73	1973–80	1980–90	1990–2000[a]	2000–2030[a]
Low- and middle-income	2,403	2,923	3,383	4,146	4,226	4,981	7,441	2.5	2.1	2.0	1.9	1.4
Low-income	1,776	2,168	2,501	3,058	3,117	3,670	5,430	2.5	2.0	2.0	1.8	1.3
Middle-income	627	755	883	1,088	1,109	1,311	2,011	2.3	2.3	2.0	1.9	1.4
Severely indebted	258	314	370	455	464	546	794	2.5	2.3	2.1	1.8	1.3
Sub-Saharan Africa	245	302	366	495	510	668	1,346	2.7	2.8	3.1	3.0	2.4
East Asia and the Pacific	972	1,195	1,347	1,577	1,602	1,818	2,378	2.6	1.7	1.6	1.4	0.9
South Asia	645	781	919	1,148	1,170	1,377	1,978	2.4	2.4	2.2	1.8	1.1
Europe	154	167	182	200	195	217	258	1.1	1.2	1.0	0.8	0.6
Middle East and North Africa	125	154	189	256	264	341	674	2.7	3.0	3.1	2.9	2.3
Latin America and the Caribbean	243	299	352	433	441	516	731	2.6	2.4	2.1	1.8	1.2
Other economies	252	275	294	321	323	345	. .	1.1	1.0	0.9	0.7	. .
High-income	671	726	766	816	821	859	919	1.0	0.8	0.6	0.5	0.2
OECD members	649	698	733	777	781	814	863	0.9	0.7	0.6	0.5	0.2
World	3,326	3,924	4,443	5,284	5,370	6,185	8,869	2.1	1.8	1.7	1.6	1.2

a. Projections. For the assumptions used in the projections, see the technical notes for Table 26 in the World Development Indicators.

Table A.2 GNP, population, GNP per capita, and growth of GNP per capita

Country group	1990 GNP (billions of dollars)	1990 population (millions)	1990 GNP per capita (dollars)	Average annual growth of GNP per capita (percent)					
				1965–73	1973–80	1980–90	1989	1990	1991[a]
Low- and middle-income	3,479	4,146	840	4.3	2.6	1.5	0.9	0.3	. .
Low-income	1,070	3,058	350	2.4	2.7	4.0	2.3	2.4	1.3
Middle-income	2,409	1,088	2,220	5.3	2.4	0.4	0.4	-0.6	. .
Severely indebted	972	455	2,140	5.2	2.6	-0.3	-1.6	-3.5	-1.2
Sub-Saharan Africa	166	495	340	1.6	0.6	-1.1	0.1	-1.6	. .
East Asia and the Pacific	939	1,577	600	5.1	4.8	6.3	4.0	5.3	. .
South Asia	383	1,148	330	1.2	1.8	2.9	2.7	2.6	1.4
Europe	480	200	2,400	. .	. .	1.0	2.0	-3.7	. .
Middle East and North Africa	458	256	1,790	6.8	1.0	-1.5	-1.2	-1.9	. .
Latin America and the Caribbean	946	433	2,180	4.6	2.3	0.5	-1.1	-1.8	0.7
Other economies	. .	321	. .	. .	. .	. .	. .	. .	. .
High-income	15,998	816	19,590	3.7	2.1	2.4	2.7	1.5	. .
OECD members	15,672	777	21,170	3.7	2.1	2.5	2.7	1.6	. .
World	22,173	5,284	4,200	2.8	1.3	1.4	1.6	0.5	. .

a. Preliminary data.

Table A.3 Water availability

Country group	Total annual internal renewable water resources (cubic kilometers)	Total annual water withdrawal (cubic kilometers)	Annual withdrawal as a share of total water resources (percent)	Per capita annual internal renewable water resources, 1990 (cubic meters)	Per capita annual water withdrawal, year of data (cubic meters)	Sectoral withdrawal as a share of total water resources (percent)		
						Agriculture	Domestic	Industry
Low-income	14,272	1,257	9	4,649	498	91	4	5
China and India	4,650	840	18	2,345	520	90	5	6
Other low-income	9,622	417	4	8,855	460	95	3	2
Middle-income	13,730	492	4	12,597	532	69	13	18
Lower-middle-income	6,483	290	4	10,259	550	71	11	18
Upper-middle-income	7,247	202	3	15,824	508	66	16	18
Low- and middle-income	28,002	1,749	6	6,732	507	85	7	8
Sub-Saharan Africa	3,713	55	1	7,488	140	88	8	3
East Asia and the Pacific	7,915	631	8	5,009	453	86	6	8
South Asia	4,895	569	12	4,236	652	94	2	3
Europe	574	110	19	2,865	589	45	14	42
Middle East and North Africa	276	202	73	1,071	1,003	89	6	5
Latin America and the Caribbean	10,579	173	2	24,390	460	72	16	11
Other economies	4,486	375	8	13,976	1,324	66	6	28
High-income	8,368	893	11	10,528	1,217	39	14	47
OECD members	8,365	889	11	10,781	1,230	39	14	47
Other	4	4	119	186	372	67	22	12
World	40,856	3,017	7	7,744	676	69	9	22

Table A.4 Selected water quality indicators for various rivers

		Dissolved oxygen				Fecal coliform			
		Annual mean concentration (milligrams per liter)			Average annual growth rate for series (percent)	Annual mean concentration (number per 100-milliliter sample)			Average annual growth rate for series (percent)
Country	River, city	1979–82	1983–86	1987–90		1979–82	1983–86	1987–90	
Low-income									
Bangladesh	Karnaphuli	5.7	6.1	..	−1.1 (5)	..	..	..	.. (3)
Bangladesh	Meghna	6.5	7.0	..	2.6 (5)	3,133	700	..	−35.1 (5)
China	Pearl, Hong Kong	7.6	7.8	7.8	0.4 (11)	519	563	174	−14.4 (10)
China	Yangtze, Shanghai	8.3	8.3	8.2	−0.1 (11)	316	464	731	10.6 (11)
China	Yellow, Beijing	9.8	9.7	9.8	−0.1 (11)	711	1,337	1,539	9.8 (11)
India	Cauveri, d/s from KRS Reservoir	7.2	7.6	7.3	0.8 (9)	51	681	445	63.8 (9)
India	Cauveri, Satyagalam	7.0	7.3	7.5	1.1 (9)	10	684	920	121.8 (9)
India	Godavari, Dhalegaon	6.5	6.6	6.7	0.3 (9)	..	..	..	.. (0)
India	Godavari, Mancherial	8.0	8.0	7.3	−1.1 (9)	5	5	8	19.7 (7)
India	Godavari, Polavaram	7.2	7.2	6.9	0.0 (8)	4	2	4	−3.8 (7)
India	Sabarmati, Dharoi	9.4	9.1	8.9	0.0 (9)	248	222	220	−15.4 (8)
India	Subarnarekha, Jamshedpur	8.0	7.9	7.5	−0.2 (9)	659	4,513	2,800	89.0 (9)
India	Subarnarekha, Ranchi	6.7	4.0	5.3	−6.2 (9)	1,239	7,988	3,100	70.5 (9)
India	Tapti, Burhanpur	7.5	6.9	6.1	−2.3 (9)	..	110	130	−23.2 (4)
India	Tapti, Nepanagar	7.2	7.0	7.0	−0.6 (9)	..	19	163	76.0 (4)
Pakistan	Chenab, Gujra Branch	6.2	6.8	7.1	1.8 (10)	436	463	446	−1.7 (10)
Pakistan	Indus, Kotri	7.6	7.2	2.6	−13.6 (11)	105	121	78	−3.4 (11)
Pakistan	Ravi, d/s from Lahore	6.8	5.7	6.3	−1.4 (12)	378	746	555	−2.4 (10)
Pakistan	Ravi, u/s from Lahore	7.2	6.7	7.0	−0.8 (12)	275	392	249	−6.6 (10)
Sudan	Blue Nile	7.3	8.2	..	3.3 (7)	..	..	..	.. (0)
Middle-income									
Argentina	de la Plata, Buenos Aires	7.6	7.5	..	0.0 (8)	828	230	..	−23.1 (8)
Argentina	Paraná Corrientes	8.1	8.0	8.1	0.1 (10)	185	146	111	−6.6 (10)
Brazil	Guandu, Tomada d'Agua	8.1	7.8	7.7	−0.7 (11)	1,202	2,452	6	−47.0 (8)
Brazil	Paraiba, Aparecida	6.0	6.1	6.0	−0.4 (7)	13,950	9,800	6,075	−11.5 (7)
Brazil	Paraiba, Barra Mansa	7.4	7.6	7.8	0.4 (11)	8,003	8,100	8	−33.4 (7)
Chile	Maipo, el Manzano	12.9	13.2	10.8	−1.4 (10)	871	705	775	5.3 (8)
Chile	Mapocho, Los Almendros	11.8	12.1	10.0	−1.7 (10)	2	2	5	8.0 (8)
Colombia	Cauca Juanchito	..	5.2	4.8	1.0 (5)	..	10,000	10,000	0.0 (4)
Ecuador	San Pedro	7.7	7.8	..	−0.1 (5)	80,000	30,603	..	−31.5 (4)
Fiji	Waimanu	7.6	7.8	8.0	0.5 (9)	600	1,605	..	8.1 (7)
Hungary	Danube	9.4	10.4	9.9	1.7 (10)	3,419	3,075	3,750	1.2 (10)
Korea	Han	..	10.5	10.4	−0.2 (8)	..	8	12	14.4 (8)
Malaysia	Kinta	6.8	7.5	8.3	2.9 (7)	..	..	..	.. (0)
Malaysia	Klang	3.0	3.3	2.8	−1.1 (9)	..	..	..	.. (1)
Malaysia	Linggi	3.4	3.6	3.7	0.9 (10)	..	..	..	.. (0)
Malaysia	Muda	7.3	7.2	6.3	−1.3 (8)	..	..	..	.. (0)
Mexico	Atoyac	3.5	1.7	0.3	−47.5 (9)	157,500	105,000	916,667	23.9 (7)
Mexico	Balsas	7.6	6.3	6.8	−1.9 (10)	1,558	26,333	130,000	95.4 (8)
Mexico	Blanco	5.0	3.4	4.1	−3.7 (9)	21,717	39,500	12,150	1.8 (8)
Mexico	Colorado	7.9	8.7	8.2	1.4 (9)	277	58	37	−28.7 (7)
Mexico	Lerma	0.3	0.4	0.5	−18.6 (10)	192,250	165,000	67	5.7 (7)
Mexico	Panuco	7.7	8.1	8.3	0.7 (11)	110	201	..	−27.8 (6)
Panama	Aguas Claras	7.9	8.2	..	0.4 (7)	219	143	..	−14.4 (6)
Panama	San Felix	8.2	8.0	..	−1.0 (7)	850	753	..	−6.2 (6)
Philippines	Cagayan	7.8	7.9	8.1	0.3 (11)	..	..	..	.. (3)
Portugal	Tejo, Santarem	8.9	8.6	8.4	−0.7 (9)	2,252	4,163	4,225	24.6 (9)
Thailand	Chao Phrya, d/s from Nakhon Sawan	6.3	6.3	..	0.2 (8)	1,093	1,745	..	47.7 (7)
Thailand	Prasak, Kaeng Khoi	6.6	7.7	..	8.0 (5)	596	2,724	..	9.9 (8)
Turkey	Porsuk, Agackoy	9.0	9.1	9.2	0.7 (9)	..	..	..	.. (1)
Turkey	Sekarya, Adetepe	9.2	8.7	8.9	−0.3 (8)	..	..	..	.. (1)
Uruguay	de la Plata, Colonia	..	..	..	7.1 (3)	..	453	93	54.6 (4)
Uruguay	Uruguay Bella Unión	..	7.9	8.4	−1.4 (4)	..	200	1,100	66.9 (4)
High-income									
Australia	Murray	10.0	9.4	9.1	1.0 (6)	..	..	..	.. (0)
Australia	Murray, Mannum	7.1	8.2	8.6	2.4 (8)	33	103	80	15.8 (8)
Belgium	Escaut, Bleharies	5.7	6.2	5.9	1.1 (11)	76	579	867	40.8 (11)
Belgium	Meuse, Heer/Agimont	10.5	10.8	11.3	0.8 (11)	30	1,391	1,700	69.7 (11)
Belgium	Meuse, Lanaye Ternaaien	9.2	8.4	8.9	−0.7 (11)	147	5,233	7,100	78.2 (11)
Japan	Kiso, Asahi	10.0	10.6	11.7	1.7 (11)	300	400	216	−4.1 (11)
Japan	Kiso, Inuyama	10.8	10.5	10.8	−0.2 (10)	610	491	600	−2.0 (10)
Japan	Kiso, Shimo-Ochiai	11.2	11.1	11.4	0.3 (10)	546	443	353	−6.0 (10)
Japan	Shinano, Zuiun Bridge	10.1	10.3	10.3	0.2 (10)	290	346	193	−3.0 (10)
Japan	Tone, Tone-Ozeki	10.0	9.9	10.4	0.5 (10)	521	593	618	3.7 (10)
Japan	Yodo, Hirakata Bridge	8.7	8.4	8.4	−0.4 (11)	72,000	70,333	..	9.3 (7)
Netherlands	Ijssel, (arm of Rhine)	8.7	7.9	..	−3.3 (6)	9,833	2,050	..	−43.0 (5)
Netherlands	Rhine, German frontier	8.5	8.0	..	−2.6 (6)	17,633	10,500	..	−11.8 (5)
United Kingdom	Thames	9.9	10.3	9.1	0.2 (8)	..	..	..	.. (0)
United States	Delaware, Trenton, N.J.	11.1	10.6	..	−2.5 (7)	74	197	..	−4.0 (7)
United States	Hudson, Green Island, N.Y.	9.8	12.1	..	4.2 (7)	941	792	..	−7.4 (7)
United States	Mississippi, Vicksburg, Miss.	8.4	8.3	..	−0.2 (7)	435	1,473	..	40.2 (7)

Note: d/s, downstream; u/s, upstream.   a. Numbers in parentheses denote the number of years of observations. Data have been presented only when they are available for four or more years.

Table A.5 Selected ambient air quality indicators for various cities

Country group	City	Type of site	Sulfur dioxide — Annual mean concentration (micrograms per cubic meter) 1979–82	1983–86	1987–90	Sulfur dioxide — Average annual growth rate for series (percent)	Suspended particulate matter — Annual mean concentration (micrograms per cubic meter) 1979–82	1983–86	1987–90	Suspended particulate matter — Average annual growth rate for series (percent)
Low-income										
China	Beijing	CCC	77	119	107	3.5 (8)	475	500	413	-2.7 (8)
China	Beijing	CCR	132	141	115	-1.3 (8)	412	380	370	-1.6 (8)
China	Guangzhou	CCC	100	78	54	-9.0 (9)	248	198	163	-6.1 (9)
China	Guangzhou	CCR	59	107	95	7.7 (9)	146	209	234	7.4 (9)
China	Shanghai	CCC	66	59	69	2.5 (9)	224	214	253	2.5 (9)
China	Shanghai	CCR	57	84	104	9.2 (9)	240	230	290	3.8 (9)
China	Shenyang	CCC	105	100	118	2.5 (8)	409	475	435	0.3 (8)
China	Shenyang	CCR	80	127	88	1.8 (9)	471	481	465	-0.4 (9)
China	Xian	CCC	138	107	95	-4.7 (9)	399	515	555	5.7 (9)
China	Xian	CCR	116	111	100	-1.4 (9)	401	485	580	6.7 (9)
Egypt, Arab Rep.	Cairo	CCC	5	101	18	-11.0 (8)	..	..	..	.. (0)
Egypt, Arab Rep.	Cairo	SR	..	157	28	-1.2 (7)				(1)
Ghana	Accra	SI	..	..	..	.. (1)	119	109	144	2.4 (9)
Ghana	Accra	SR	..	..	..	.. (1)	108	107	137	3.5 (8)
India	Bombay	CCC	23	23	..	1.8 (4)	154	140	..	-1.1 (6)
India	Calcutta	CCC	71	54	..	4.6 (7)	410	393	..	-1.0 (13)
India	Calcutta	SR	36	36	..	8.9 (7)	468	310	..	0.5 (12)
India	Delhi	CCC	42	86	..	12.0 (6)	460	460	..	-0.3 (7)
India	Delhi	CCR	16	33	..	23.9 (6)	312	301	..	-1.3 (7)
Indonesia	Jakarta	CCR	..	..	..	.. (2)	254	271	..	2.2 (9)
Indonesia	Jakarta	SI	..	..	..	.. (2)	159	204	185	3.5 (7)
Pakistan	Lahore	SR	..	..	..	.. (1)	745	..	496	-5.1 (6)
Middle-income										
Brazil	Sao Paulo	..	78	46	41	-7.5 (12)	134	98	..	-9.1 (6)
Chile	Santiago	CCC	69	85	..	2.5 (10)	..	..	..	.. (0)
Chile	Santiago	CCR	43	46	..	-1.5 (9)	..	..	..	.. (0)
Greece	Athens	CCC	57	34	..	-4.8 (9)	224	178	..	-6.0 (9)
Greece	Athens	SI	48	27	..	-9.7 (9)	190	182	..	-4.5 (9)
Iran, Islamic Rep.	Tehran	CCC	130	115	165	6.9 (14)	226	248	261	-2.4 (14)
Iran, Islamic Rep.	Tehran	SR	114	61	64	-2.7 (14)	215	251	238	-1.3 (14)
Malaysia	Kuala Lumpur	SC	..	..	..	.. (3)	172	135	119	-3.9 (7)
Malaysia	Kuala Lumpur	SI	12	24	..	-12.4 (6)	155	139	144	-1.5 (10)
Philippines	Davao	SI	..	..	..	.. (3)	163	205	..	-2.4 (5)
Philippines	Manila	SI	73	34	..	-12.0 (9)	90	..	..	0.8 (8)
Poland	Warsaw	CCC	42	35	23	-6.4 (13)	..	..	..	.. (0)
Poland	Warsaw	CCR	31	31	18	-5.5 (13)	..	..	..	.. (0)
Poland	Wroclaw	CCC	41	53	53	2.6 (13)	..	..	..	.. (0)
Poland	Wroclaw	CCR	31	42	42	4.5 (13)	..	..	..	.. (0)
Portugal	Lisbon	CCR	32	21	27	-3.0 (10)	99	97	99	0.4 (9)
Portugal	Lisbon	SR	19	14	20	2.7 (8)	100	95	86	-2.6 (8)
Thailand	Bangkok	SI	..	..	..	.. (1)	213	247	244	0.8 (13)
Thailand	Bangkok	SR	15	15	14	-1.7 (10)	136	163	105	-2.4 (12)
Venezuela	Caracas	CCC	32	27	21	-0.5 (13)	..	..	..	.. (0)
Yugoslavia	Zagreb	CCC	79	107	92	-4.3 (19)	114	127	135	-1.7 (19)
Yugoslavia	Zagreb	SR	33	66	47	-0.9 (19)	129	117	91	-2.6 (19)
High-income										
Australia	Melbourne	CCC	7	6	..	-14.3 (10)	71	58	..	-4.5 (9)
Australia	Sydney	CCC	51	28	..	-10.9 (11)	100	114	..	2.2 (11)
Australia	Sydney	SI	31	15	..	-7.3 (11)	76	58	..	-8.5 (11)
Belgium	Brussels	CCC	74	42	..	-11.5 (11)	24	22	..	-3.3 (11)
Belgium	Brussels	SR	60	37	..	-9.1 (15)	..	..	..	.. (2)
Canada	Hamilton	CCC	..	..	..	.. (3)	102	89	89	-2.8 (13)
Canada	Hamilton	SR	32	36	..	-4.4 (9)	102	99	..	-1.9 (9)
Canada	Montreal	CCC	41	23	..	-11.0 (10)	67	55	61	-1.8 (12)
Canada	Montreal	SR	27	20	..	0.7 (11)	58	39	35	-8.3 (13)
Canada	Toronto	CCC	..	11	14	4.0 (5)	60	60	61	-0.5 (8)
Canada	Toronto	SR	18	..	..	-16.1 (7)	70	60	57	-2.2 (13)
Canada	Vancouver	CCC	21	..	..	-7.0 (5)	70	50	42	-4.5 (14)
Canada	Vancouver	CCR	18	..	..	-2.7 (11)	55	39	..	-5.2 (15)
Denmark	Copenhagen	CCC	28	30	..	-0.5 (7)	34	..	..	3.4 (6)
Denmark	Copenhagen	SI	33	27	..	-5.7 (7)	53	55	..	3.0 (9)
Finland	Helsinki	CCC	24	..	..	-2.8 (5)	72	79	81	2.0 (11)
Finland	Helsinki	SI	27	28	20	-3.8 (12)	64	68	62	0.2 (11)
Germany	Frankfurt	CCC	71	56	36	-7.2 (17)	24	39	42	0.5 (17)
Hong Kong	Hong Kong	..	..	25	64	47.3 (4)	..	99	132	14.9 (4)
Ireland	Dublin	CCI	40	34	32	-3.2 (12)	..	..	..	.. (0)
Ireland	Dublin	CCR	57	44	41	-2.9 (12)	..	..	..	.. (0)
Israel	Tel Aviv	CCC	16	30	..	-7.1 (11)	..	..	..	.. (0)
Italy	Milan	CCC	160	90	..	-14.5 (7)	..	..	..	.. (0)
Italy	Milan	CCR	259	114	..	-11.4 (7)	..	..	..	.. (0)
Japan	Osaka	CCC	37	28	28	-8.4 (14)	51	41	42	-6.3 (13)
Japan	Osaka	SR	34	26	24	-8.0 (14)	61	49	54	-4.1 (13)
Japan	Tokyo	CCC	42	23	20	-8.9 (17)	61	50	..	-4.9 (13)
Japan	Tokyo	SR	42	30	20	-5.7 (17)	54	51	..	-4.5 (14)
Netherlands	Amsterdam	CCC	33	24	..	-6.7 (15)	..	..	..	.. (0)
Netherlands	Amsterdam	SR	34	29	..	-1.8 (13)	..	..	..	.. (0)
New Zealand	Auckland	CCC	10	3	..	-17.6 (9)	..	..	..	.. (0)
New Zealand	Auckland	CCR	8	3	..	-37.2 (6)	..	..	..	.. (0)
New Zealand	Christchurch	SI	37	43	..	6.9 (9)	..	..	..	.. (0)
New Zealand	Christchurch	SR	20	18	19	-3.5 (12)	..	..	..	.. (0)
Spain	Madrid	CCC	105	54	36	-9.8 (17)	..	..	..	.. (0)
Spain	Madrid	SR	45	28	19	-8.4 (18)	..	..	..	.. (0)
United Kingdom	Glasgow	CCC	73	52	..	-8.8 (8)	..	..	..	.. (0)
United Kingdom	Glasgow	CCI	62	41	..	-9.8 (9)	..	..	..	.. (0)
United Kingdom	London	CCC	66	44	..	-11.4 (13)	..	..	..	.. (0)
United Kingdom	London	SI	56	34	..	-11.3 (13)	..	..	..	.. (0)
United States	Birmingham	CCC	..	..	..	.. (3)	83	75	..	-3.0 (11)
United States	Chicago	CCI	..	..	..	.. (2)	121	99	..	-6.2 (10)
United States	Fairfield	SI	..	..	..	.. (3)	71	53	..	-5.6 (11)
United States	Harris Co.	SR	..	..	..	.. (3)	68	54	..	-4.8 (11)
United States	Houston	CCC	..	..	..	.. (3)	82	62	..	-7.3 (10)
United States	Houston	SR	18	8	..	-32.0 (8)	93	64	..	-6.3 (11)
United States	New York City	CCR	79	60	..	-5.8 (9)	63	61	..	-2.2 (11)
United States	New York City	SR	38	31	..	-5.9 (9)	49	46	..	-2.7 (11)

Note: for type of site: CCC, city center commercial; CCI, city center industrial; CCR, city center residential; SI, suburban industrial; SR, suburban residential; SC, suburban commercial.
Numbers in parentheses denote the number of years of observations. Data have been presented only when they are available for four or more years. There are two methods for calculating concentrations of suspended particulate matter: gravimetric measurement and the smoke stain method. These methods are not comparable. Because most air monitoring stations use the former method, only data derived from this method are presented. To maximize the number of cities for which data are presented, information is given on only two site types, though more data than these may be available. Growth rates are calculated using the entire time-series available, although only part of that series may appear in the concentration data presented.

Table A.6 Changes in land use

Country group	Land area, 1989 (thousands of square kilometers)	Share of total land area, 1989 (percent)				Average annual growth rate, 1965–89 (percent)			
		Agricultural	Permanent pasture	Forest and woodland	Other	Agricultural	Permanent pasture	Forest and woodland	Other
Low-income	36,396	13	27	25	36	0.2	0.0	−0.4	0.3
China and India	12,264	22	27	16	36	0.0	0.0	−0.4	0.2
Other low-income	24,132	9	27	29	35	0.5	0.0	−0.4	0.3
Mozambique	784	4	56	18	22	0.5	0.0	−0.8	0.7
Tanzania	886	6	40	46	8	0.9	0.0	−0.3	1.3
Ethiopia	1,101	13	41	25	22	0.4	−0.1	−0.4	0.4
Somalia	627	2	69	14	15	0.5	0.0	−0.1	0.1
Nepal	137	19	15	18	48	1.6	0.9	0.0	−0.7
Chad	1,259	3	36	10	52	0.5	0.0	−0.6	0.1
Bhutan	47	3	6	55	36	1.3	0.3	0.4	−0.6
Lao PDR	231	4	3	55	37	0.4	0.0	−0.7	1.3
Malawi	94	26	20	40	15	0.8	0.0	−1.1	4.0
Bangladesh	130	71	5	15	9	0.1	0.0	−0.4	0.2
Burundi	26	52	36	3	10	1.1	1.9	1.3	−5.7
Zaire	2,268	3	7	77	13	0.5	0.0	−0.2	1.1
Uganda	200	34	9	28	29	1.6	0.0	−0.5	−0.9
Madagascar	582	5	58	27	9	1.6	0.0	−0.9	2.8
Sierra Leone	72	25	31	29	15	1.1	0.0	−0.2	−1.2
Mali	1,220	2	25	6	68	1.1	0.0	−0.4	0.0
Nigeria	911	34	44	13	8	0.3	0.0	−1.9	4.6
Niger	1,267	3	7	2	88	2.3	−0.7	−2.2	0.1
Rwanda	25	47	19	23	12	2.7	−2.8	−0.5	−0.8
Burkina Faso	274	13	37	24	26	2.1	0.0	−0.8	0.1
India	2,973	57	4	22	17	0.2	−0.8	0.3	−0.7
Benin	111	17	4	32	47	1.0	0.0	−1.4	0.9
China	9,291	10	34	13	42	−0.3	0.0	−0.8	0.4
Haiti	28	33	18	1	48	0.8	−1.2	−2.3	0.1
Kenya	570	4	67	4	25	1.0	0.0	−0.8	0.0
Pakistan	771	27	6	5	62	0.4	0.0	1.9	−0.3
Ghana	230	12	22	35	31	−0.3	0.0	−0.8	1.2
Central African Republic	623	3	5	57	34	0.5	0.0	0.0	0.0
Togo	54	27	33	30	11	0.6	0.0	−0.6	0.6
Zambia	743	7	40	39	14	0.3	0.0	−0.2	0.6
Guinea	246	3	25	60	12	0.4	0.0	−0.4	2.5
Sri Lanka	65	29	7	27	37	0.0	0.8	−0.3	0.1
Mauritania	1,025	0	38	5	57	−1.6	0.0	0.3	0.0
Lesotho	30	11	66	. .	24	−1.0	−0.4	. .	1.8
Indonesia	1,812	12	7	63	19	0.9	−0.3	−0.5	1.3
Honduras	112	16	23	30	31	0.9	0.9	−1.9	1.7
Egypt, Arab Rep.	995	3	. .	0	97	−0.6	. .	0.0	0.0
Afghanistan	652	12	46	3	39	0.1	0.0	−0.2	0.0
Cambodia	177	17	3	76	4	0.1	0.0	0.0	−0.3
Liberia	96	4	59	18	19	0.1	0.0	−1.2	1.7
Myanmar	658	15	1	49	35	−0.2	−0.1	0.0	0.0
Sudan	2,376	5	41	19	34	0.5	0.0	−0.6	0.3
Viet Nam	325	20	1	30	49	0.5	0.8	−2.3	1.6
Middle-income	40,684	10	29	33	29	0.7	0.1	−0.4	0.2
Lower-middle-income	22,141	10	31	28	31	0.6	−0.1	−0.5	0.4
Bolivia	1,084	3	25	51	21	3.1	−0.2	−0.3	0.6
Zimbabwe	387	7	13	50	30	1.1	0.0	−0.4	0.5
Senegal	193	27	30	31	12	0.7	0.0	−0.6	0.2
Côte d'Ivoire	318	12	41	24	24	1.4	0.0	−2.4	4.4
Philippines	298	27	4	35	34	0.7	2.0	−2.1	3.1
Dominican Republic	48	30	43	13	14	1.5	0.0	−0.3	−2.1
Papua New Guinea	453	1	0	84	15	0.8	0.5	−0.1	0.3
Guatemala	108	17	13	35	35	1.0	0.8	−1.3	1.1
Morocco	446	21	47	18	15	0.9	0.9	0.2	−2.8
Cameroon	465	15	18	53	14	1.0	−0.3	−0.4	1.3
Ecuador	277	10	18	40	32	0.1	4.5	−1.8	1.4
Syrian Arab Rep.	184	30	43	4	23	−0.5	0.4	0.7	−0.3
Congo	342	0	29	62	8	1.0	0.0	−0.1	0.8
El Salvador	21	35	29	5	30	0.8	0.0	−2.9	−0.3
Paraguay	397	6	52	36	6	5.0	1.6	−1.4	−2.9
Peru	1,280	3	21	54	22	1.7	0.0	−0.4	0.8
Jordan	89	4	9	1	86	0.9	0.0	1.2	−0.1
Colombia	1,039	5	39	49	7	0.3	0.7	−0.6	0.2
Thailand	511	43	2	28	27	2.4	3.5	−2.6	0.6
Tunisia	155	30	19	4	47	0.3	0.9	1.5	−0.6
Jamaica	11	25	18	17	40	0.2	−1.1	−0.5	0.5
Turkey	770	36	11	26	26	0.2	−1.2	0.0	0.4
Romania	230	45	19	28	8	0.0	0.0	0.0	−0.4
Poland	304	48	13	29	10	−0.2	−0.3	0.3	0.9

Country group	Land area, 1989 (thousands of square kilometers)	Share of total land area, 1989 (percent)				Average annual growth rate, 1965–89 (percent)			
		Agricultural	Permanent pasture	Forest and woodland	Other	Agricultural	Permanent pasture	Forest and woodland	Other
Panama	76	8	20	44	28	0.2	1.6	−1.3	1.8
Costa Rica	51	10	45	32	12	0.4	3.5	−2.8	0.1
Chile	749	6	18	12	64	0.5	1.2	0.1	−0.4
Botswana	567	2	58	19	20	1.2	0.0	−0.1	0.0
Algeria	2,382	3	13	2	82	0.5	−1.0	1.5	0.1
Mauritius	2	57	4	31	8	0.4	0.0	−0.2	−1.5
Bulgaria	111	38	18	35	9	−0.5	2.4	0.3	−2.1
Malaysia	329	15	0	58	27	0.7	0.4	−1.1	3.6
Iran, Islamic Rep.	1,636	9	27	11	53	−0.4	0.0	0.0	0.1
Argentina	2,737	13	52	22	13	0.7	−0.1	−0.1	0.0
Albania	27	26	15	38	21	1.3	−2.7	−1.0	4.4
Angola	1,247	3	23	42	31	0.2	0.0	−0.2	0.2
Lebanon	10	29	1	8	62	−0.3	0.0	−0.9	0.3
Mongolia	1,567	1	79	9	11	3.0	−0.7	−0.2	18.6
Namibia	823	1	46	22	31	0.1	0.0	−0.2	0.1
Nicaragua	119	11	45	29	15	0.3	1.1	−2.3	5.9
Yemen, Rep.	195	7	36	8	49	0.2	0.0	0.0	0.0
Upper-middle-income	18,543	9	26	38	27	1.0	0.4	−0.4	−0.1
Mexico	1,909	13	39	23	25	0.3	0.0	−1.2	1.2
South Africa	1,221	11	67	4	19	0.0	−0.1	0.5	0.4
Venezuela	882	4	20	35	41	0.5	0.4	−0.9	0.6
Uruguay	175	7	77	4	11	−0.4	−0.1	0.5	0.4
Brazil	8,457	9	20	65	5	2.1	1.1	−0.4	−1.9
Hungary	92	57	13	18	12	−0.3	−0.2	0.7	1.0
Yugoslavia	255	30	25	37	8	−0.3	0.0	0.3	0.0
Gabon	258	2	18	78	2	3.4	−0.3	0.0	0.7
Czechoslovakia	125	41	13	37	9	−0.2	−0.4	0.2	0.9
Trinidad and Tobago	5	23	2	43	31	1.0	1.0	−0.4	−0.1
Portugal	92	41	8	32	18	−0.3	0.0	0.0	0.8
Korea, Rep.	99	22	1	66	12	−0.4	6.9	−0.1	1.1
Greece	131	30	40	20	10	0.1	0.1	0.0	−0.6
Saudi Arabia	2,150	1	40	1	59	1.9	0.0	−1.9	0.0
Iraq	437	12	9	4	74	0.5	0.0	−0.1	−0.1
Libya	1,760	1	8	0	91	0.3	1.3	1.4	−0.1
Oman	212	0	5	. .	95	2.6	0.0	. .	0.0
Low- and middle-income	77,079	11	28	29	32	0.5	0.1	−0.4	0.2
Sub-Saharan Africa	22,416	7	33	30	31	0.7	0.0	−0.4	0.3
East Asia and the Pacific	15,175	11	30	25	34	0.3	−0.2	−0.7	0.8
South Asia	4,781	45	4	23	28	0.2	−0.4	0.3	−0.4
Europe	2,139	39	16	29	16	−0.1	−0.3	0.1	0.3
Middle East and North Africa	11,305	6	22	3	69	0.1	0.0	0.2	0.0
Latin America and Caribbean	20,043	9	28	48	15	1.3	0.5	−0.5	0.1
Other economies	22,502	10	17	43	30	0.1	0.0	0.2	−0.3
High-income	30,412	12	25	30	33	0.2	−0.1	−0.1	0.1
OECD members	29,870	12	26	30	32	0.2	−0.1	−0.1	0.1
Other	541	3	1	5	90	0.1	0.2	−1.0	0 1
Ireland	69	14	68	5	13	−1.9	0.5	2.2	−0.7
Israel	20	21	7	5	66	0.2	1.3	0.2	−0.2
Spain	499	41	20	31	7	−0.1	−0.8	0.7	−0.2
Singapore	1	2	. .	5	93	−7.1	. .	−0.7	1.0
Hong Kong	1	7	1	12	80	−3.0	. .	0.7	0.0
New Zealand	268	2	51	27	20	0.1	0.5	0.0	−1.1
Belgiuma	33	25	21	21	33	−0.1	0.0	−0.3	0.3
United Kingdom	242	28	46	10	16	−0.3	−0.4	1.2	1.4
Italy	294	41	17	23	20	−1.0	−0.2	0.4	3.0
Australia	7,618	6	55	14	25	0.9	−0.2	−1.5	1.4
Netherlands	34	28	32	9	32	0.0	−0.9	0.1	1.4
Austria	83	19	24	39	18	−0.5	−0.6	0.0	1.6
France	550	35	21	27	17	−0.1	−0.7	0.5	0.6
United Arab Emirates	84	0	2	0	97	7.2	0.0	5.4	0.0
Canada	9,221	5	4	39	53	0.6	2.1	0.5	−0.5
United States	9,167	21	26	32	21	0.2	−0.2	−0.2	0.5
Denmark	42	60	5	12	23	−0.2	−1.9	0.3	1.0
Germany	244	31	18	30	21	−0.1	−0.9	0.1	1.1
Norway	307	3	0	27	70	0.2	−1.9	0.5	−0.2
Sweden	412	7	1	68	24	−0.3	−0.8	0.1	0.0
Japan	377	12	2	67	19	−1.0	6.0	0.0	0.5
Finland	305	8	0	76	15	−0.5	−0.2	0.3	−0.9
Switzerland	40	10	40	26	23	0.3	−0.5	0.3	0.4
Kuwait	18	0	8	0	92	6.8	0.0	0.0	0.0
World	130,099	11	25	31	32	0.3	0.0	−0.2	0.1

a. Includes Luxembourg.

Table A.7 Agriculture: production and yields of selected crops, fertilizer consumption, and irrigation

	Production				Yields				Fertilizer consumption		Irrigation	
	Cereals		Roots and tubers		Cereals		Roots and tubers					
Country group	1989 (thousands of tons)	Growth rate, 1965–89 (percent)	1989 (thousands of tons)	Growth rate, 1965–89 (percent)	1989 (tons per hectare)	Growth rate, 1965–89 (percent)	1989 (tons per hectare)	Growth rate, 1965–89 (percent)	1989 (tons per hectare)	Growth rate, 1965–89 (percent)	Share of agricultural land, 1989 (percent)	Growth rate, 1965–89 (percent)
Low-income	779,426	3.4	297,738	1.7	2.5	3.0	11.3	1.3	94	10.3	8.9	1.7
China and India	565,269	3.5	161,841	1.2	2.9	3.4	15.1	1.9	138	10.8	14.8	1.7
Other low-income	214,156	2.9	135,897	2.5	1.9	2.1	8.8	1.1	39	9.2	4.8	1.8
Mozambique	607	−1.1	3,725	2.2	0.5	−3.0	6.3	0.7	1	−1.4	0.2	8.8
Tanzania	4,750	6.9	6,790	3.6	1.5	3.6	7.3	2.7	9	6.6	0.4	8.4
Ethiopia	6,013	1.7	1,684	2.7	1.2	2.0	3.3	−0.2	7	15.9	0.3	0.3
Somalia	654	4.3	49	3.5	0.8	2.1	10.4	0.2	3	. .	0.3	0.9
Nepal	5,673	1.8	784	3.0	1.9	−0.3	6.8	0.0	26	13.8	20.3	12.2
Chad	568	−0.8	643	4.5	0.5	−0.5	5.5	1.3	2	25.1	0.0	3.6
Bhutan	94	0.8	50	2.7	1.0	−0.8	9.6	1.1	1	0.1	8.5	4.6
Lao PDR	1,448	2.5	310	9.5	2.3	3.6	7.7	0.8	0	−0.7	7.1	12.0
Malawi	1,588	1.2	485	5.0	1.2	0.6	3.1	−1.8	23	9.7	0.5	10.9
Bangladesh	28,796	2.3	1,633	1.8	2.6	1.7	10.0	0.3	99	11.2	27.7	5.1
Burundi	265	2.9	1,523	1.0	1.2	0.8	8.1	0.0	4	13.8	3.2	6.9
Zaire	1,272	3.9	18,162	2.6	0.8	0.6	7.5	0.4	1	3.2	0.0	10.9
Uganda	1,468	−0.6	5,068	3.7	1.5	1.6	6.3	2.0	0	−14.9	0.1	4.8
Madagascar	2,542	1.2	3,128	3.3	2.0	0.2	6.4	−0.1	4	−0.8	2.4	5.3
Sierra Leone	538	0.7	158	1.5	1.4	0.2	3.3	−1.0	0	−1.5	0.9	11.7
Mali	2,157	2.7	136	3.8	0.9	1.0	8.5	0.4	5	10.2	0.6	5.6
Nigeria	13,643	2.2	47,901	2.7	1.2	3.2	12.4	1.2	12	22.2	1.2	0.3
Niger	1,849	2.5	246	1.7	0.4	−0.8	7.1	0.2	1	13.4	0.3	3.5
Rwanda	274	2.6	1,716	5.5	1.1	0.4	7.8	0.7	1	9.3	0.3	0.0
Burkina Faso	1,952	2.7	112	2.1	0.7	1.6	6.0	4.3	6	23.9	0.1	8.0
India	199,816	3.2	20,961	3.8	2.0	2.8	15.7	2.2	69	10.1	23.8	2.3
Benin	563	2.9	2,026	2.2	0.9	1.8	9.3	1.2	2	3.7	0.3	5.8
China	365,453	3.7	140,880	1.0	4.0	3.9	15.0	1.9	262	11.4	10.8	1.2
Haiti	398	−0.9	902	2.2	0.9	−0.6	4.1	−0.3	4	14.3	5.4	1.9
Kenya	3,446	0.9	1,480	2.2	1.7	1.0	8.6	0.3	48	4.9	0.1	3.9
Pakistan	21,018	4.0	649	6.2	1.8	2.8	10.1	0.1	89	12.1	63.0	1.3
Ghana	1,177	2.1	5,172	1.7	1.0	−0.3	6.2	−0.7	3	11.6	0.1	4.5
Central African Rep.	124	1.7	734	−0.7	1.0	0.9	3.5	0.7	0	−3.8	. .	. .
Togo	570	2.3	830	0.3	0.9	1.6	8.3	−2.7	8	22.9	0.2	4.2
Zambia	1,967	1.6	278	2.2	1.7	4.6	3.7	0.5	17	7.8	0.1	9.8
Guinea	740	1.7	624	0.2	0.9	−0.4	5.5	−0.6	1	−10.1	0.4	7.3
Sri Lanka	2,102	4.1	590	2.4	2.9	2.2	9.1	3.7	102	3.6	23.9	1.8
Mauritania	184	1.3	6	−0.3	1.0	4.2	1.8	0.0	12	. .	0.0	2.2
Lesotho	147	−1.5	7	3.2	0.8	0.3	14.0	0.4	14	13.6	. .	. .
Indonesia	50,921	5.0	20,054	0.8	3.8	3.9	11.6	2.3	117	13.6	22.8	2.6
Honduras	644	1.9	28	−1.5	2.1	1.6	7.6	1.6	18	2.6	2.1	1.4
Egypt, Arab Rep.	11,113	1.6	1,838	7.0	5.4	1.3	23.1	1.5	404	6.5	100.0	−0.6
Afghanistan	3,410	−0.4	300	4.3	1.3	0.8	15.0	2.3	7	12.6	7.0	0.8
Cambodia	2,550	−1.3	203	7.3	1.4	−0.5	8.1	−1.1	0	. .	2.5	−0.3
Liberia	280	3.3	404	1.4	1.2	1.3	7.2	1.0	11	3.3	0.0	0.0
Myanmar	14,261	3.5	208	8.6	2.8	3.5	8.4	4.4	9	11.2	9.8	1.4
Sudan	1,971	2.6	134	−2.4	0.4	−2.4	2.2	−1.4	4	1.5	1.7	0.9
Viet Nam	19,839	3.1	4,797	5.3	3.1	1.9	7.5	1.3	84	5.9	26.4	3.5
Middle-income	332,878	2.5	145,806	0.6	2.2	2.0	12.0	0.3	69	4.7	2.9	2.3
Lower-middle-income	183,637	2.4	104,465	1.5	1.9	1.9	11.8	0.6	60	4.8	3.2	2.3
Bolivia	811	3.0	1,221	1.6	1.3	1.0	6.0	−0.8	2	2.1	0.6	4.0
Zimbabwe	2,460	2.1	119	2.7	1.5	0.7	4.8	0.9	60	1.9	2.9	9.2
Senegal	1,067	1.8	75	−6.8	0.8	1.7	4.3	0.5	6	1.7	1.7	3.1
Philippines	13,981	3.9	2,711	4.2	1.9	2.7	6.8	1.3	67	5.0	17.6	3.6
Côte d'Ivoire	1,193	3.4	4,404	0.9	0.9	0.3	6.1	2.3	11	3.7	0.4	8.4
Dominican Rep.	608	5.1	331	−2.1	3.6	2.7	6.8	0.1	50	3.6	6.4	3.1
Papua New Guinea	3	1.0	1,283	1.9	1.7	−0.7	7.1	0.2	40	13.8	. .	. .
Guatemala	1,480	3.2	60	4.5	1.8	3.0	4.4	0.9	73	6.5	2.4	2.3
Morocco	7,429	1.9	916	6.5	1.3	1.4	16.7	3.1	34	6.6	4.2	1.8
Cameroon	991	1.1	2,048	1.3	1.3	2.0	2.6	0.8	4	6.0	0.2	8.5
Ecuador	1,450	3.2	498	−2.2	1.7	3.1	6.6	−1.1	34	5.0	7.1	0.9
Syrian Arab Rep.	1,404	3.8	371	11.0	0.3	1.0	16.4	2.1	45	13.1	5.0	1.1
Congo	22	2.4	755	1.9	0.7	−2.0	6.4	2.1	3	. .	. .	8.7
El Salvador	802	2.7	37	3.7	1.9	1.6	15.2	2.7	106	1.0	8.9	10.4
Paraguay	1,605	9.1	4,087	4.4	2.0	1.8	16.5	0.5	9	3.8	0.3	2.7
Peru	2,439	2.5	2,440	0.0	2.5	2.2	8.5	1.0	41	1.2	4.1	0.7
Jordan	77	−5.1	40	11.9	0.5	−0.8	22.3	5.2	77	8.8	4.9	2.4
Colombia	3,790	3.3	4,318	3.7	2.5	2.7	11.9	2.1	90	5.5	1.1	3.8
Thailand	25,241	3.0	24,486	11.7	2.1	0.6	15.2	0.5	37	8.6	18.5	4.1
Tunisia	635	0.2	179	5.0	0.6	0.6	11.2	2.2	23	6.6	3.6	5.9
Jamaica	3	0.5	198	3.1	1.3	1.6	12.2	1.1	116	−0.2	7.6	1.7
Turkey	23,499	2.8	4,060	4.1	1.7	2.6	21.7	2.9	64	9.6	6.1	1.6
Romania	18,379	2.0	4,420	3.1	3.0	2.4	12.6	3.0	133	6.6	23.4	10.6
Poland	26,958	1.8	34,390	−1.5	3.2	1.9	18.5	0.2	205	3.0	0.5	−5.1
Panama	328	1.6	86	2.5	1.9	2.6	9.2	0.8	54	4.5	1.5	2.7
Costa Rica	246	3.4	91	5.3	2.6	2.5	8.2	0.5	203	4.5	4.1	8.2

Country group	Production Cereals 1989 (thousands of tons)	Cereals Growth rate, 1965–89 (percent)	Roots and tubers 1989 (thousands of tons)	Roots and tubers Growth rate, 1965–89 (percent)	Yields Cereals 1989 (tons per hectare)	Cereals Growth rate, 1965–89 (percent)	Roots and tubers 1989 (tons per hectare)	Roots and tubers Growth rate, 1965–89 (percent)	Fertilizer consumption 1989 (tons per hectare)	Fertilizer Growth rate, 1965–89 (percent)	Irrigation Share of agricultural land, 1989 (percent)	Irrigation Growth rate, 1965–89 (percent)
Chile	3,148	1.7	889	1.0	4.0	2.9	14.0	2.0	80	3.8	7.0	0.5
Botswana	76	−1.0	7	2.1	0.3	−2.1	5.4	1.7	1	−5.2	0.0	3.5
Algeria	1,698	0.3	1,030	6.8	0.7	0.9	8.6	1.1	28	5.4	0.9	1.7
Bulgaria	9,527	1.4	553	0.9	4.4	1.8	13.8	−0.3	195	3.0	20.3	1.3
Mauritius	2	8.5	21	4.5	3.8	2.4	20.2	2.1	330	1.1	15.0	1.0
Malaysia	1,778	1.1	510	1.1	2.7	1.1	9.4	0.6	157	8.4	7.0	1.7
Argentina	17,407	1.8	3,210	0.3	2.1	2.4	20.4	2.9	5	4.3	1.0	1.9
Iran, Islamic Rep.	10,002	3.2	1,295	9.1	1.1	2.0	13.5	−0.8	80	15.4	9.8	0.5
Albania	1,036	4.4	88	1.8	3.0	4.0	9.1	1.6	151	7.2	38.1	2.8
Angola	289	−2.7	2,130	1.4	0.3	−4.2	4.1	1.1	7	2.5	. .	. .
Lebanon	79	−2.6	235	4.8	2.0	2.8	17.8	2.7	92	0.4	27.7	1.3
Mongolia	839	5.7	156	10.3	1.2	3.2	12.3	2.6	12	12.6	0.1	13.1
Namibia	135	2.9	265	2.1	0.6	1.1	8.8	0.0	0	. .	0.0	0.0
Nicaragua	504	2.3	91	8.8	1.6	2.8	12.1	6.4	65	4.4	1.3	6.2
Yemen, Rep.	. .	. .	. .	. .	. .	. .	. .	. .	0	35.5	3.0	1.2
Upper-middle-income	149,241	2.6	41,341	−1.0	2.6	2.2	12.5	−0.2	82	4.5	2.6	2.3
Mexico	21,308	3.0	1,091	3.1	2.2	2.8	14.7	2.0	73	7.1	5.2	2.2
South Africa	14,911	2.0	1,300	4.0	2.2	2.1	13.8	1.1	58	3.2	1.2	1.0
Venezuela	1,830	4.9	692	0.8	2.2	2.8	8.3	0.4	151	12.2	1.2	2.7
Uruguay	1,491	2.4	188	0.3	2.6	4.6	6.3	0.8	45	0.8	0.7	4.8
Brazil	43,943	3.4	26,693	−1.0	2.0	1.5	12.5	−0.6	43	8.3	1.1	6.8
Hungary	15,417	3.1	1,334	−1.9	5.5	3.8	18.6	3.5	246	5.3	2.7	−0.7
Yugoslavia	16,110	1.4	2,359	−1.0	3.8	2.5	8.0	−0.1	116	3.6	1.2	1.5
Gabon	21	4.3	371	3.4	1.4	0.4	6.2	1.1	3	23.7	. .	. .
Czechoslovakia	12,047	2.8	3,167	−2.3	4.9	3.0	18.6	1.1	321	2.7	4.6	3.6
Trinidad and Tobago	15	−2.3	9	−2.3	2.6	0.0	9.3	0.4	28	−4.3	16.8	2.8
Portugal	1,859	−0.6	1,194	−0.3	1.7	2.0	9.7	−0.6	73	2.9	14.0	0.1
Korea, Rep.	8,748	1.0	1,226	−4.5	6.0	3.2	22.7	2.0	425	3.2	61.0	0.7
Greece	5,743	3.1	1,109	3.0	4.0	3.7	20.1	2.8	175	4.3	13.0	2.8
Saudi Arabia	3,674	9.7	38	. .	4.2	5.9	15.8	. .	401	25.7	0.5	0.9
Iraq	1,497	−0.7	226	14.8	0.9	−0.3	17.5	2.7	40	16.2	27.0	1.9
Libya	322	3.9	131	12.8	0.7	3.9	7.5	2.1	37	12.9	1.6	2.2
Oman	2	−4.8	4	. .	1.4	0.4	25.3	. .	111	19.6	3.9	2.5
Low- and middle-income	1,112,303	3.1	443,544	1.3	2.4	2.7	11.6	0.9	83	7.4	5.8	1.9
Sub-Saharan Africa	58,089	2.1	113,655	2.6	1.0	1.1	7.8	1.0	9	5.8	0.6	2.2
East Asia and Pacific	490,836	3.7	197,024	1.5	3.6	3.4	13.9	1.7	186	10.1	9.9	1.6
South Asia	271,760	3.1	24,884	3.6	2.0	2.7	14.0	2.0	69	10.2	27.5	2.1
Europe	130,583	2.2	52,693	−0.9	3.1	2.5	16.7	0.6	142	4.1	8.4	3.1
Middle East and N. Africa	41,342	2.0	6,603	7.5	1.4	1.5	14.5	1.5	63	9.2	5.5	0.8
Latin America and the Caribbean	104,782	2.9	47,385	0.0	2.1	2.1	11.6	−0.1	44	6.4	2.0	2.5
Other economies	212,387	1.3	75,644	−1.0	2.0	1.6	11.9	0.3	110	6.0	3.8	3.8
High-income	545,234	2.0	68,475	−1.2	3.9	1.6	29.2	1.7	118	1.5	3.0	1.1
OECD members	542,093	2.0	67,663	−1.0	3.9	1.6	29.4	1.6	117	1.5	3.0	1.1
Other	3,141	−0.5	812	−8.0	4.2	1.5	20.6	1.3	117	1.5	3.0	1.1
Ireland	2,051	2.9	668	−4.3	5.9	2.6	25.8	−0.8	722	6.0	. .	. .
Israel	208	−0.2	231	3.5	1.9	1.2	37.8	2.8	242	3.6	36.9	1.7
Spain	19,698	3.2	5,407	0.7	2.5	2.9	19.3	2.0	101	3.2	11.0	1.7
Singapore	. .	. .	0	−16.2	. .	. .	16.8	1.1	5,600	11.7	. .	. .
Hong Kong	0	−35.1	0	−14.3	3.0	0.0	23.2	5.2	0	. .	25.0	−6.1
New Zealand	672	2.4	283	0.0	4.2	1.5	30.0	0.7	656	−0.7	2.0	5.6
Belgium[a]	2,300	0.8	1,750	0.3	6.2	2.5	40.7	1.3	502	−0.2	0.1	0.0
United Kingdom	22,725	2.8	6,262	−0.5	5.9	2.5	35.8	1.9	350	2.4	0.9	2.9
Italy	17,133	1.0	2,468	−2.1	3.7	2.1	19.7	2.3	151	4.2	18.3	1.0
Australia	22,551	3.2	1,054	2.2	1.7	1.5	29.7	2.6	23	−0.2	0.4	1.3
Netherlands	1,368	−1.3	6,856	2.1	6.8	3.0	41.5	1.2	642	0.6	27.5	2.2
Austria	5,009	3.3	845	−5.7	5.3	2.7	26.1	0.9	201	0.3	0.1	0.0
France	57,216	2.9	5,417	−1.9	6.1	2.8	28.5	2.3	319	2.3	3.8	2.2
United Arab Emirates	5	. .	5	19.1	4.8	. .	13.3	−2.2	162	5.5	2.1	0.9
Canada	48,199	1.9	2,811	1.3	2.2	1.0	24.8	1.7	47	5.2	1.1	3.6
United States	284,357	1.9	17,322	1.0	4.5	1.7	31.3	1.7	99	1.4	4.2	1.0
Denmark	8,795	1.2	1,238	1.4	5.6	1.4	36.9	2.0	250	0.9	15.5	9.7
Germany	26,113	2.1	7,948	−4.5	5.6	2.4	37.0	1.2	384	0.4	2.8	0.9
Norway	1,180	3.2	455	−3.7	3.4	1.4	24.2	0.3	242	1.2	9.6	6.6
Sweden	5,493	1.1	1,179	−0.6	4.3	1.3	35.0	1.3	127	−0.1	3.3	7.5
Japan	14,322	−1.4	5,689	−1.7	5.7	0.7	25.0	1.4	418	1.0	54.3	−0.7
Finland	3,800	1.4	981	−1.4	3.2	1.3	22.0	0.8	210	1.6	2.4	10.0
Switzerland	1,411	2.9	770	−1.3	6.8	2.5	38.5	1.3	426	1.1	1.2	0.2
Kuwait	3	44.4	1	30.4	5.5	6.4	16.7	3.6	200	. .	1.5	4.1
World	1,880,693	2.5	596,829	0.5	2.7	2.2	12.6	0.7	97	4.3	4.9	1.9

Note: Growth rates are average annual rates.   a. Includes Luxembourg

Table A.8 Nationally protected areas

Country group	All nationally protected areas (thousand square kilometers)		Number of protected areas		Protected areas as a share of total land area (percent)		Share of protected areas totally protected (percent)		Share of protected areas partially protected (percent)	
	1972	1990	1972	1990	1972	1990	1972	1990	1972	1990
Low-income	592	1,441	361	1,407	1.6	3.8	59	46	41	54
China and India	27	411	84	736	0.2	3.2	12	11	88	89
Other low-income	565	1,031	277	671	2.3	4.1	61	61	39	39
Middle-income	778	2,215	691	1,839	1.9	5.3	70	53	30	47
Lower-middle-income	623	1,316	377	975	2.7	5.8	71	65	29	35
Upper-middle income	156	899	314	864	0.8	4.8	67	35	33	65
Low- and middle-income	1,370	3,656	1,052	3,246	1.7	4.6	65	50	35	50
Sub-Saharan Africa	790	1,105	251	379	3.4	4.8	65	65	35	35
East Asia and the Pacific	58	611	150	857	0.4	3.9	38	37	62	63
South Asia	32	198	110	469	0.6	3.8	17	34	83	66
Europe	16	77	144	411	0.7	3.6	48	20	52	80
Middle East and North Africa	128	427	50	126	1.1	3.7	80	38	20	62
Latin America and the Caribbean	293	1,173	238	797	1.4	5.8	72	53	28	47
Other economies	75	247	109	231	0.3	1.1	95	97	5	3
High-income	988	3,412	1,840	3,632	2.9	10.2	49	67	51	33
OECD members	986	2,423	1,820	3,581	3.2	7.8	48	54	52	46
Other	2	989	20	51	0.1	41.5	71	100	29	0
World[a]	2,434	7,354	3,012	7,152	1.6	4.9	59	60	41	40

a. Includes countries not elsewhere specified and some economies with populations under 30,000.

Table A.9 Global carbon dioxide emissions from fossil fuels and cement manufacture

Country group	Total emissions from fossil fuels and cement manufacture (million tons of carbon)		Average annual rate of growth 1980–89 (percent)	Carbon dioxide emissions (tons of carbon)		Share of emissions from different sources 1989 (percent)			
	1965	1989		Per capita 1989	Per million dollars of GDP 1989	Solid	Liquid	Gas	Other[a]
Low-income	203	952	5.8	0.32	926	71	20	3	6
China[b]	131	652	5.9	0.59	1,547	82	12	1	4
India[b]	46	178	7.0	0.21	670	71	22	2	5
Middle-income	373	1,061	2.3	0.96	471	36	45	12	6
Lower-middle-income	176	478	2.3	0.70	551	39	42	14	5
Upper-middle-income	198	583	2.3	1.38	421	35	48	11	6
Low- and middle-income	576	2,013	3.8	0.50	614	53	33	8	6
Sub-Saharan Africa	12	61	4.9	0.13	376	19	55	4	22
East Asia and the Pacific	157	837	5.7	0.54	934	70	22	2	6
South Asia	47	201	7.0	0.18	567	64	25	6	5
Europe	191	391	1.0	2.00	809	61	25	11	4
Middle East and North Africa	37	189	4.3	0.76	516	2	66	23	9
Latin America and the Caribbean	97	258	1.2	0.61	278	9	67	17	7
Other economies	535	1,089	2.0	. .	. .	37	32	28	3
High-income	1,901	2,702	0.5	3.26	186	36	45	17	2
Germany[b]	178	175	–1.2	2.82	147	44	39	15	2
Japan[b]	106	284	1.0	2.31	99	29	58	9	4
United Kingdom[b]	171	155	0.1	2.72	185	44	35	18	2
United States[b]	948	1,329	1.0	5.34	259	38	43	19	1
World[c]	3,012	5,822	1.8	1.12	327	42	38	16	4

a. Other sources of emissions are gas flaring and cement manufacture.
b. Top six emitters of carbon dioxide; data refer to Federal Republic of Germany only.
c. Includes countries not elsewhere specified and economies with populations under 30,000.

Table A.10 Energy: consumption, production and resources

(millions of tons of oil equivalent, unless otherwise specified)

Energy resource and country group	1965	1970	1975	1980	1985	1989	Average annual growth rate (percent) 1965–80	1980–89
Liquid fuels								
World consumption	1,537	2,255	2,709	3,002	2,797	3,081	4.8	0.6
Low- and middle-income	247	400	554	719	751	872	7.7	2.2
Sub-Saharan Africa	12	17	21	26	28	31	4.9	2.0
East Asia and the Pacific	32	78	127	174	174	219	12.2	2.9
South Asia	17	26	32	42	54	69	5.7	5.6
Europe	40	71	110	136	124	137	9.0	0.5
Middle East and North Africa	39	56	75	110	142	159	7.3	3.8
Latin America and the Caribbean	101	141	175	217	212	240	5.5	0.8
Other economies	191	278	391	462	439	457	6.4	-0.2
High-income economies	1,095	1,568	1,750	1,801	1,589	1,733	3.7	0.1
World reserves	48,016	83,150	89,581	88,199	95,219	135,879	..	..
Reserves/production ratio (years)	31	36	33	28	34	44	..	..
World price (constant 1987 dollars per barrel)	5.3	4.6	21.4	37.7	34.6	15.3	16.0	-13.1
Solid fuels								
World consumption	1,367	1,495	1,553	1,794	2,094	2,321	1.9	3.2
Low- and middle-income	338	425	528	658	853	989	5.1	5.1
Sub-Saharan Africa	3	3	3	3	3	5	-0.1	6.2
East Asia and the Pacific	120	182	247	321	453	543	8.0	6.6
South Asia	35	37	47	66	91	116	4.7	6.5
Europe	143	162	179	204	222	231	2.5	1.9
Middle East and North Africa	1	1	3	2	3	3	7.0	4.6
Latin America and the Caribbean	7	8	11	15	20	24	5.1	5.5
Other economies	290	315	352	365	374	407	1.8	1.8
High-income economies	680	693	617	711	800	858	0.0	2.0
World reserves	..	328,000	504,000	517,000	468,000	935,000	..	..
Reserves/production ratio (years)	..	218	317	282	222	405	..	..
World price (constant 1987 dollars per ton)	..	..	..	53.2	60.4	38.0	..	-6.7
Gas								
World consumption	572	848	1,017	1,253	1,471	1,681	5.0	3.8
Low- and middle-income	49	80	119	173	251	323	8.9	8.1
Sub-Saharan Africa	0	0	1	1	3	4	21.8	11.1
East Asia and the Pacific	4	4	11	17	22	35	12.6	9.3
South Asia	2	3	5	8	14	19	11.0	10.1
Europe	20	34	48	67	75	82	8.2	2.3
Middle East and North Africa	3	11	18	23	75	109	15.1	22.8
Latin America and the Caribbean	20	28	37	56	63	75	6.6	3.2
Other economies	119	155	226	316	472	550	6.5	6.9
High-income economies	404	612	668	759	740	800	3.9	0.8
World reserves	26,556	40,459	56,938	67,193	88,877	107,346	..	..
Reserves/production ratio (years)	46	47	55	53	60	66	..	..
Primary electricity								
World production	236	316	458	616	855	985	6.8	5.6
Low- and middle-income	31	53	85	132	180	217	10.2	5.9
Sub-Saharan Africa	3	5	7	12	9	10	10.6	-1.5
East Asia and the Pacific	4	7	15	19	35	49	11.6	11.0
South Asia	5	8	11	16	19	20	8.5	2.9
Europe	6	9	14	23	30	39	9.1	7.0
Middle East and North Africa	1	2	4	6	5	5	11.9	-2.7
Latin America and the Caribbean	13	21	34	57	81	93	10.5	5.7
Other economies	23	35	41	68	104	123	6.7	7.7
High-income economies	181	227	331	413	567	641	6.0	5.2
Fuelwood and charcoal								
World consumption	244	263	286	329	372	399	1.8	2.2
Low- and middle income	198	228	254	281	315	343	2.2	2.3
Sub-Saharan Africa	46	53	61	71	84	95	2.9	3.2
East Asia and Pacific	60	67	75	83	91	98	2.1	1.9
South Asia	44	50	56	62	70	76	2.3	2.3
Europe	9	13	12	8	7	7	-2.8	-1.7
Middle East and North Africa	2	3	3	3	3	4	2.6	1.3
Latin America and Caribbean	37	41	46	52	58	62	2.4	2.1
Other economies	24	20	19	19	21	19	-1.5	0.5
High-income economies	22	15	13	29	36	36	-0.1	2.3

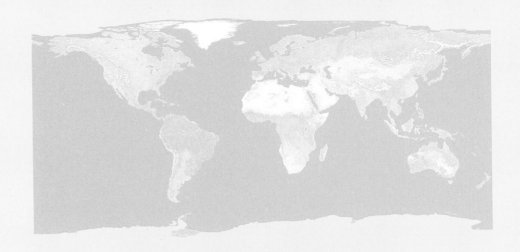

World Development Indicators

Contents

Key

In the main tables, economies are listed within their groups in ascending order of GNP per capita except those for which no GNP per capita can be calculated. These are italicized, in alphabetical order, at the end of their group. The ranking below refers to the order in the tables.

The key shows the years of the most recent census and the years of the latest demographic survey or vital registration-based estimates. This information is included to show the currentness of the sources of demographic indicators, which can be a reflection of the overall quality of a country's indicators. Beyond these years, demographic estimates may be generated by projection models, interpolation routines, or other methods. Explanations of how World Bank estimates and projections are derived from the sources, as well as more information on the sources, are given in *World Population Projections, 1992–93 Edition* (forthcoming).

Figures in colored bands in the tables are summary measures for groups of economies.

The letter *w* means weighted average; *m*, median value; *t*, total.

All growth rates are in real terms.

Data cutoff date is March 31, 1992.

The symbol . . means not available.

The figures 0 and 0.0 mean zero or less than half the unit shown.

A blank means not applicable.

Figures with asterisks indicate data that are for years or periods other than those specified.

The symbol † indicates economies classified by the United Nations or otherwise regarded by their authorities as developing.

Economy	Country ranking in tables	Population census	Life expectancy	Infant mortality	Total fertility
Afghanistan	38	1979	1979	1970	1979
Albania	78	1989	1986–87	1989	1989
Algeria	72	1987	1985	1985	1984
Angola	79	1970			1984
Argentina	76	1980	1979–81	1983	1988
Australia	111	1986	1989	1989	1989
Austria	113	1981	1990	1990	1990
Bangladesh	10	1991	1989	1989	1989
Belgium	108	1981	1990	1990	1990
Benin	22	1979	1961	1977–82	1976–80
Bhutan	7	1969			1984
Bolivia	44	1976	1989	1989	1989
Botswana	71	1981	1988	1983–88	1983–87
Brazil	89	1980	1986	1986	1986
Bulgaria	73	1985	1985	1990	1990
Burkina Faso	20	1985	1976	1971–76	1961
Burundi	11	1979	1970–71	1982–86	1981–86
Cambodia	39				1982
Cameroon	53	1987	1976–80	1973–78	1985–90
Canada	116	1986	1989	1989	1989
Central African Rep.	28	1975	1970–75	1970–75	1955–59
Chad	6	1964	1963–64	1962–64	1963–64
Chile	70	1982	1989	1989	1989
China	23	1982	1986	1986	1987
Colombia	61	1985	1990	1990	1990

Economy	Country ranking in tables	Population census	Life expectancy	Infant mortality	Total fertility
Congo	56	1984	1974	1969–74	1969–74
Costa Rica	69	1988	1990	1990	1990
Côte d'Ivoire	48	1975	1988	1978–79	1983–88
Czechoslovakia	92	1980	1989	1990	1989
Denmark	118	1981	1989	1989	1990
Dominican Rep.	49	1990	1986	1986	1986
Ecuador	54	1982	1987	1987	1987
Egypt, Arab Rep.	37	1986	1975–77	1988	1988
El Salvador	57	1971	1988	1988	1988
Ethiopia	3	1984			1988
Finland	123	1985	1990	1990	1990
France	114	1990	1989	1989	1989
Gabon	93	1981	1960–61	1960–61	1960–61
Germany	119	1987	1990	1989	1990
Ghana	27	1984	1988	1983–87	1983–87
Greece	97	1991	1985	1990	1990
Guatemala	51	1981	1987	1987	1987
Guinea	31	1983	1955	1954–55	1954–55
Haiti	24	1982	1970–71	1987	1987
Honduras	36	1988	1982	1982	1982
†Hong Kong	106	1986	1985–86	1990	1990
Hungary	90	1980	1990	1990	1990
India	21	1991	1981–83	1986	1985
Indonesia	35	1990	1971–80	1986	1988–91
Iran, Islamic Rep.	77	1986	1986	1986	1971–75
Iraq	99	1987	1974–75	1974–75	1974–75
Ireland	102	1986	1990	1989	1990
†Israel	103	1983	1990	1990	1990
Italy	110	1981	1990	1990	1990
Jamaica	64	1982	1969–71	1989	1990
Japan	122	1985	1989	1989	1989
Jordan	60	1979	1983	1983	1983
Kenya	25	1979	1977–78	1973–78	1984–89
Korea, Rep.	96	1985	1978–79	1985	
†Kuwait	125	1985	1987	1987	1987
Lao PDR	8	1985		1988	1988
Lebanon	80	1970	1971	1971	1971
Lesotho	34	1986	1977	1972–77	1972–77
Liberia	40	1984	1975	1981–86	1981–86
Libya	100	1984		1969	1971–75
Madagascar	14	1974–75	1984	1979–84	1975–80
Malawi	9	1987	1966–77	1977–82	1972–77
Malaysia	75	1980	1988	1988	1984
Mali	16	1987	1976	1982–86	1982–86
Mauritania	33	1988		1975	1987–88
Mauritius	74	1983	1989	1984–86	1985
Mexico	85	1990	1987	1987	1987
Mongolia	81	1989		1989	1985
Morocco	52	1982	1987	1987	1987
Mozambique	1	1980	1985	1975	1976–80
Myanmar	41	1983		1983	1983
Namibia	82	1970			
Nepal	5	1991	1974–76	1986	1986
Netherlands	112	1971	1990	1990	1990
New Zealand	107	1986	1988	1989	1989

Economy	Country ranking in tables	Population census	Life expectancy	Infant mortality	Total fertility
Nicaragua	83	1971	1978	1978	1978
Niger	18	1988	1978	1977–78	1959–63
Nigeria	17	1991		1985–90	1985–90
Norway	120	1980	1989	1989	1989
Oman	101		1986	1986	1986
Pakistan	26	1981	1972–81	1972–81	1985
Panama	68	1980	1970–80	1985–87	1986
Papua New Guinea	50	1990		1980	1980
Paraguay	58	1982	1982	1990	1990
Peru	59	1981	1981	1986	1986
Philippines	47	1990	1979–81	1986	1988
Poland	67	1988	1990	1990	1990
Portugal	95	1981	1988	1989	1988
Romania	66	1977	1990	1990	1990
Rwanda	19	1978	1978	1978–83	1978–83
Saudi Arabia	98	1974	1974	1974	1974
Senegal	46	1988	1978	1981–85	1981–86
Sierra Leone	15	1985		1971	1971–75
†Singapore	105	1990	1989	1989	1989
Somalia	4	1987	1976–80	1976–80	1976–80
South Africa	86	1985	1970	1980	1976–81
Spain	104	1981	1989	1989	1989
Sri Lanka	32	1981	1980–81	1988	1982–86
Sudan	42	1983	1983	1978–83	1976–80
Sweden	121	1985	1990	1990	1990
Switzerland	124	1980	1990	1990	1990
Syrian Arab Rep.	55	1981	1976–78	1976–78	1976–80
Tanzania	2	1988	1977–78	1977–80	1977–78
Thailand	62	1990	1978	1989	1987
Togo	29	1981	1988	1983–88	1983–88
Trinidad and Tobago	94	1990	1987	1987	1987
Tunisia	63	1984	1988	1988	1988
Turkey	65	1990	1988	1988	1988
Uganda	13	1991	1991	1983–88	1983–89
†United Arab Emirates	115	1985	1980	1980	1980
United Kingdom	109	1981	1990	1990	1990
United States	117	1990	1990	1990	1990
Uruguay	88	1985	1985	1985	1985
Venezuela	87	1990	1981	1981	1986
Viet Nam	43	1989		1989	1985–89
Yemen, Rep.	84	1986–88	1979	1979	1981
Yugoslavia	91	1981	1990	1990	1990
Zaire	12	1984	1955–57	1979–84	1979–84
Zambia	30	1990	1980	1979–80	1976–80
Zimbabwe	45	1982	1988	1983–88	1983–88

Note: Economies with populations of less than 1 million are included only as part of the country groups in the main tables, but are shown in greater detail in Box A.1. Other economies not listed in the main tables nor in Box A.1, but also included in the aggregates, are shown in greater detail in Box A.2. For data comparability and coverage throughout the tables, see the technical notes.

Introduction

This fifteenth edition of the World Development Indicators provides economic, social, and natural resource indicators for selected periods or years for 185 economies and various analytical and geographical groups of economies. Most of the data collected by the World Bank are on low- and middle-income economies. Because comparable data for high-income economies are readily available, these are also included. Additional information may be found in other World Bank publications, notably the *World Bank Atlas*, *World Tables*, *World Debt Tables*, and *Social Indicators of Development*. These data are now also available on diskette, in the World Bank's ☆STARS☆ retrieval system.

Although every effort has been made to standardize the data, full comparability cannot be ensured, and care must be taken in interpreting the indicators. The statistics are drawn from the sources thought to be most authoritative, but the data are subject to considerable margins of error. Variations in national statistical practices also reduce the comparability of data, which should thus be construed only as indicating trends and characterizing major differences among economies, rather than taken as precise quantitative indications of those differences.

The indicators in Table 1 give a summary profile of economies. Data in the other tables fall into the following broad areas: production, domestic absorption, fiscal and monetary accounts, core international transactions, external finance, and human and natural resources.

In this edition, Table 30, Income distribution and ICP estimates of GDP, offers more complete country coverage of ICP data by the inclusion of extrapolated and imputed data. Note also that Table 33, Forests, protected land areas, and water resources, is complemented by several environmental tables in the Environmental Data Annex to this volume.

Data on external debt are compiled directly by the Bank on the basis of reports from developing member countries through the Debtor Reporting System. Other data are drawn mainly from the United Nations and its specialized agencies, the International Monetary Fund, and country reports to the World Bank. Bank staff estimates are also used to improve currency or consistency. For most countries, national accounts estimates are obtained from member governments through World Bank economic missions. In some instances these are adjusted by Bank staff to provide conformity with international definitions and concepts, and consistency and currentness.

For ease of reference, only ratios and rates of growth are usually shown; absolute values are generally available from other World Bank publications, notably the 1991 edition of the *World Tables*. Most growth rates are calculated for two periods, 1965–80 and 1980–90, and are computed, unless otherwise noted, by using the least-squares regression method. Because this method takes into account all observations in a period, the resulting growth rates reflect general trends that are not unduly influenced by exceptional values, particularly at the end points. To exclude the effects of inflation, constant price economic indicators are used in calculating growth rates. Details of this methodology are given at the beginning of the technical notes. Data in italics indicate that they are for years or periods other than those specified—up to two years earlier for economic indicators and up to three years on either side for social indicators, since the latter tend to be collected less regularly and change less dramatically over short periods of time. All dollar figures are U.S. dollars unless otherwise stated. The various methods used for converting from national currency figures are described in the technical notes.

The Bank continually reviews methodologies in an effort to improve the international comparability and analytical significance of the indicators. Differences between data in this year's and last year's edition reflect not only updates for the countries but also revisions to historical series and changes in methodology.

In these notes the term "country" does not imply political independence but may refer to any territory whose authorities present for it separate social or economic statistics.

As in the Report itself, the main criterion used to classify economies and broadly distinguish different stages of economic development is GNP per capita. This year, the per capita income groups are: low-income, $610 or less in 1990 (43 economies); middle-income, $611 to $7,619 (54 economies); and high-income, $7,620 or more (24 economies). One new Bank member, Albania, is now included in the main tables, in the middle-income group. Economies with populations of less than 1 million are not shown separately in the main tables, but are included in the aggregates. Basic indicators for these countries and territories, and for Puerto Rico, are in a separate table in Box A.1 of the technical notes.

Further classification of economies is by geographical location, and in this edition two changes have occurred in the geographical groupings. "Europe" has been separated from last year's group "Europe, Middle East, and North Africa," and "other economies" has been moved from the bottom of the page to the low- and middle-income section. Other classifications include severely indebted middle-income economies and fuel exporters. For a list of economies in each group, see Definitions and Data Notes and the tables on Country Classification.

Data for "other economies," which includes Cuba, the Democratic People's Republic of Korea, and the former Soviet Union, are shown only as aggregates in the main tables because of paucity of data, differences in methods of computing national income, and difficulties of conversion. Some selected indicators for these countries, however, are included in Box A.2 of the technical notes. Increased World Bank data collection and analysis in the former Soviet Union will result in better coverage and reporting of these emerging economies in future editions.

The summary measures in the colored bands are totals (indicated by *t*), weighted averages (*w*), or median values (*m*) calculated for groups of economies. Countries for which individual estimates are not shown, because of size, nonreporting, or insufficient history, have been implicitly included by assuming they follow the trend of reporting countries during such periods. This gives a more consistent aggregate measure by standardizing country coverage for each period shown. Group aggregates also include countries with less than 1 million population, even though country-specific data for these countries do not appear in the tables. Where missing information accounts for a third or more of the overall estimate, however, the group measure is reported as not available. The weightings used for computing the summary measures are stated in each technical note.

Germany, recently unified, does not yet have a fully merged statistical system. Throughout the tables, data for Germany are footnoted to explain coverage; most economic data refer to the Federal Republic of Germany before unification, but demo-

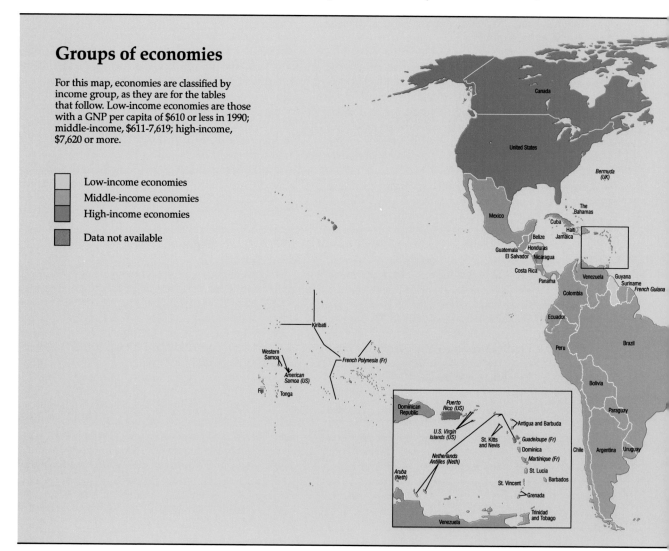

Groups of economies

For this map, economies are classified by income group, as they are for the tables that follow. Low-income economies are those with a GNP per capita of $610 or less in 1990; middle-income, $611-7,619; high-income, $7,620 or more.

- ☐ Low-income economies
- ☐ Middle-income economies
- ■ High-income economies

- ▨ Data not available

graphic and social data generally refer to the unified Germany. As in previous editions, the data for China do not include Taiwan, China, but footnotes to Tables 14, 15, 16, and 18 provide estimates of the international transactions for Taiwan, China.

The table format of this edition follows that used in previous years. In each group, economies are listed in ascending order of GNP per capita, except those for which no such figure can be calculated. These are italicized and in alphabetical order at the end of the group deemed appropriate. This order is used in all tables except Table 19, which covers only high-income OPEC and OECD countries. The alphabetical list in the key shows the reference number for each economy; here, too, italics indicate economies with no estimates of GNP per capita. Economies in the high-income group marked by the symbol † are those classified by the United Nations or otherwise regarded by their authorities as developing.

The technical notes and the footnotes to tables should be referred to in any use of the data. These notes outline the methods, concepts, definitions, and data sources used in compiling the tables. A bibliographic list at the end of the notes details the data sources, which contain comprehensive definitions and descriptions of concepts used. It should also be noted that country notes to the *World Tables* provide additional explanations of sources used, breaks in comparability, and other exceptions to standard statistical practices that Bank staff have identified in national accounts and international transactions.

Comments and questions relating to the World Development Indicators should be addressed to:

Socio-Economic Data Division
International Economics Department
The World Bank
1818 H Street, N.W.
Washington, D.C. 20433.

Population density

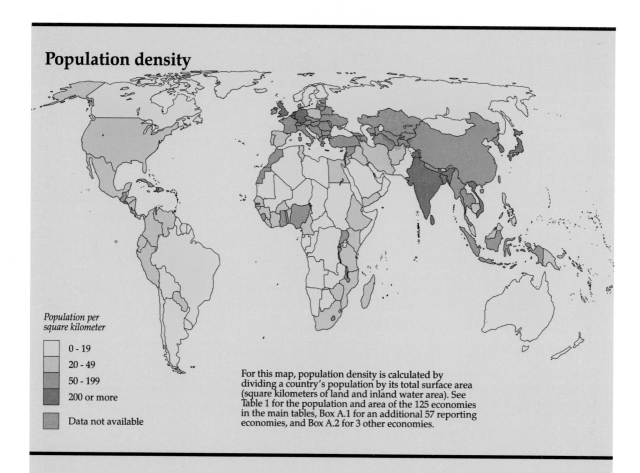

Population per
square kilometer

- 0 - 19
- 20 - 49
- 50 - 199
- 200 or more
- Data not available

For this map, population density is calculated by
dividing a country's population by its total surface area
(square kilometers of land and inland water area). See
Table 1 for the population and area of the 125 economies
in the main tables, Box A.1 for an additional 57 reporting
economies, and Box A.2 for 3 other economies.

Fertility and mortality

Total fertility

Births per woman

Infant mortality

Deaths per 1,000 live births

Life expectancy

Years

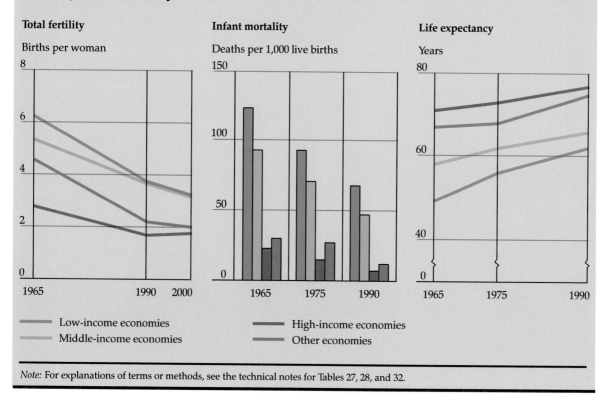

Low-income economies
Middle-income economies
High-income economies
Other economies

Note: For explanations of terms or methods, see the technical notes for Tables 27, 28, and 32.

Share of agriculture in GDP

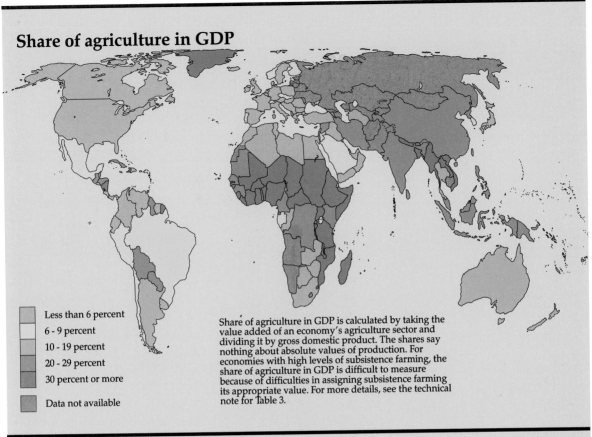

Less than 6 percent

6 - 9 percent

10 - 19 percent

20 - 29 percent

30 percent or more

Data not available

Share of agriculture in GDP is calculated by taking the value added of an economy's agriculture sector and dividing it by gross domestic product. The shares say nothing about absolute values of production. For economies with high levels of subsistence farming, the share of agriculture in GDP is difficult to measure because of difficulties in assigning subsistence farming its appropriate value. For more details, see the technical note for Table 3.

Annual renewable water resources

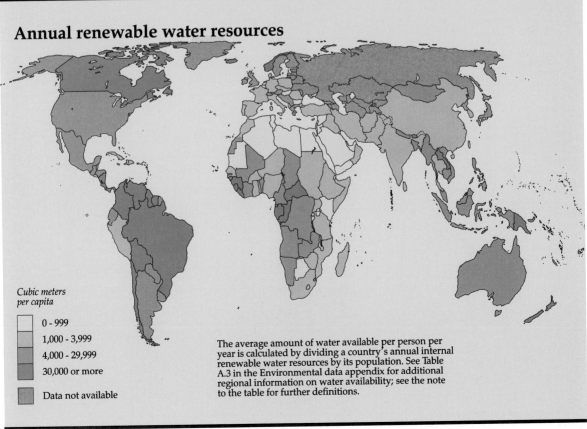

*Cubic meters
per capita*

0 - 999

1,000 - 3,999

4,000 - 29,999

30,000 or more

Data not available

The average amount of water available per person per year is calculated by dividing a country's annual internal renewable water resources by its population. See Table A.3 in the Environmental data appendix for additional regional information on water availability; see the note to the table for further definitions.

Table 1. Basic indicators

			GNP per capita[a]		Average annual rate of inflation[a] (percent)		Life expectancy birth (years)	Adult illiteracy (percent)	
	Population (millions) mid-1990	Area (thousands of square kilometers)	Dollars 1990	Average annual growth rate (percent) 1965-90	1965-80	1980-90	1990	Female 1990	Total 1990
Low-income economies	**3,058.3** *t*	**37,780** *t*	**350** *w*	**2.9** *w*	**8.0** *w*	**9.6** *w*	**62** *w*	**52** *w*	**40** *w*
China and India	**1,983.2** *t*	**12,849** *t*	**360** *w*	**3.7** *w*	**3.2** *w*	**6.8** *w*	**65** *w*	**50** *w*	**37** *w*
Other low-income	**1,075.1** *t*	**24,931** *t*	**320** *w*	**1.7** *w*	**17.3** *w*	**15.1** *w*	**55** *w*	**56** *w*	**45** *w*
1 Mozambique	15.7	802	80		. .	36.6	47	79	67
2 Tanzania[b]	24.5	945	110	-0.2	9.6	25.8	48	. .	. .
3 Ethiopia	51.2	1,222	120	-0.2	3.4	2.1	48	. .	. .
4 Somalia	7.8	638	120	-0.1	10.2	49.7	48	86	76
5 Nepal	18.9	141	170	0.5	7.8	9.1	52	87	74
6 Chad	5.7	1,284	190	-1.1	6.2	1.2	47	82	70
7 Bhutan	1.4	47	190	. .	. .	8.4	49	75	62
8 Lao PDR	4.1	237	200	. .	. .	. .	49	. .	. .
9 Malawi	8.5	118	200	0.9	7.4	14.7	46	. .	. .
10 Bangladesh	106.7	144	210	0.7	15.9	9.6	52	78	65
11 Burundi	5.4	28	210	3.4	5.0	4.2	47	60	50
12 Zaire	37.3	2,345	220	-2.2	24.7	60.9	52	39	28
13 Uganda	16.3	236	220	-2.4	21.4	107.0	47	65	52
14 Madagascar	11.7	587	230	-1.9	7.7	17.1	51	27	20
15 Sierra Leone	4.1	72	240	0.0	7.9	56.1	42	89	79
16 Mali	8.5	1,240	270	1.7	9.0	3.0	48	76	68
17 Nigeria	115.5	924	290	0.1	14.6	17.7	52	61	49
18 Niger	7.7	1,267	310	-2.4	7.5	2.9	45	83	72
19 Rwanda	7.1	26	310	1.0	12.5	3.8	48	63	50
20 Burkina Faso	9.0	274	330	1.3	6.3	4.5	48	91	82
21 India	849.5	3,288	350	1.9	7.5	7.9	59	66	52
22 Benin	4.7	113	360	-0.1	7.4	1.9	50	84	77
23 China	1,133.7	9,561	370	5.8	-0.3	5.8	70	38	27
24 Haiti	6.5	28	370	0.2	7.3	7.2	54	53	47
25 Kenya	24.2	580	370	1.9	7.2	9.2	59	42	31
26 Pakistan	112.4	796	380	2.5	10.3	6.7	56	79	65
27 Ghana	14.9	239	390	-1.4	22.9	42.5	55	49	40
28 Central African Rep.	3.0	623	390	-0.5	8.2	5.4	49	75	62
29 Togo	3.6	57	410	-0.1	7.1	4.8	54	69	57
30 Zambia	8.1	753	420	-1.9	6.3	42.2	50	35	27
31 Guinea	5.7	246	440		. .	. .	43	87	76
32 Sri Lanka	17.0	66	470	2.9	9.4	11.1	71	17	12
33 Mauritania	2.0	1,026	500	-0.6	7.6	9.0	47	79	66
34 Lesotho	1.8	30	530	4.9	6.7	12.7	56	. .	. .
35 Indonesia	178.2	1,905	570	4.5	35.5	8.4	62	32	23
36 Honduras	5.1	112	590	0.5	5.7	5.4	65	29	27
37 Egypt, Arab Rep.	52.1	1,001	600	4.1	6.4	11.8	60	66	52
38 *Afghanistan*	. .	652	. .	. .	. .	. .	42	86	71
39 *Cambodia*	8.5	181	. .	. .	. .	. .	50	78	65
40 *Liberia*	2.6	111	. .	. .	6.3	. .	54	71	61
41 *Myanmar*	41.6	677	. .	. .	. .	. .	61	28	19
42 *Sudan*	25.1	2,506	. .	. .	11.5	. .	50	88	73
43 *Viet Nam*	66.3	330	. .	. .	. .	. .	67	16	12
Middle-income economies	**1,087.5** *t*	**41,139** *t*	**2,220** *w*	**2.2** *w*	**21.1** *w*	**85.6** *w*	**66** *w*	**27** *w*	**22** *w*
Lower-middle-income	**629.1** *t*	**22,432** *t*	**1,530** *w*	**1.5** *w*	**23.6** *w*	**64.8** *w*	**65** *w*	**32** *w*	**25** *w*
44 Bolivia	7.2	1,099	630	-0.7	15.9	317.9	60	29	23
45 Zimbabwe	9.8	391	640	0.7	5.8	10.8	61	40	33
46 Senegal	7.4	197	710	-0.6	6.3	6.7	47	75	62
47 Philippines	61.5	300	730	1.3	11.4	14.9	64	11	10
48 Côte d'Ivoire	11.9	322	750	0.5	9.4	2.3	55	60	46
49 Dominican Rep.	7.1	49	830	2.3	6.7	21.8	67	18	17
50 Papua New Guinea	3.9	463	860	0.1	8.1	5.3	55	62	48
51 Guatemala	9.2	109	900	0.7	7.1	14.6	63	53	45
52 Morocco	25.1	447	950	2.3	7.0	7.2	62	62	51
53 Cameroon	11.7	475	960	3.0	9.0	5.6	57	57	46
54 Ecuador	10.3	284	980	2.8	10.9	36.6	66	16	14
55 Syrian Arab Rep.	12.4	185	1,000	2.9	7.9	14.6	66	49	36
56 Congo	2.3	342	1,010	3.1	6.8	0.5	53	56	43
57 El Salvador	5.2	21	1,110	-0.4	7.0	17.2	64	30	27
58 Paraguay	4.3	407	1,110	4.6	9.3	24.4	67	12	10
59 Peru	21.7	1,285	1,160	-0.2	20.6	233.9	63	21	15
60 Jordan[c]	3.2	89	1,240	. .	. .	. .	67	30	20
61 Colombia	32.3	1,139	1,260	2.3	17.5	24.8	69	14	13
62 Thailand	55.8	513	1,420	4.4	6.2	3.4	66	10	7
63 Tunisia	8.1	164	1,440	3.2	6.7	7.4	67	44	35
64 Jamaica	2.4	11	1,500	-1.3	12.8	18.3	73	f	f
65 Turkey	56.1	779	1,630	2.6	20.8	43.2	67	29	19
66 Romania	23.2	238	1,640	. .		1.8	70	. .	. .

Note: For economies with populations of less than 1 million, see Box A.1; for other economies, see Box A.2. For data comparability and coverage, see the technical notes. Figures in italics are for years other than those specified.

#	Country	Population (millions) mid-1990	Area (thousands of sq. km)	GNP per capita[a] Dollars 1990	GNP per capita[a] Avg. annual growth rate (%) 1965–90	Avg. annual rate of inflation[a] (%) 1965–80	Avg. annual rate of inflation[a] (%) 1980–90	Life expectancy at birth (years) 1990	Adult illiteracy Female (%) 1990	Adult illiteracy Total (%) 1990
67	Poland	38.2	313	1,690	..	..	54.3	71	..	..
68	Panama	2.4	77	1,830	1.4	5.4	2.3	73	12	12
69	Costa Rica	2.8	51	1,900	1.4	11.2	23.5	75	7	7
70	Chile	13.2	757	1,940	0.4	129.9	20.5	72	7	7
71	Botswana	1.3	582	2,040	8.4	8.4	12.0	67	35	26
72	Algeria	25.1	2,382	2,060	2.1	10.9	6.6	65	55	43
73	Bulgaria	8.8	111	2,250	..	..	2.2	73	..	..
74	Mauritius	1.1	2	2,250	3.2	11.8	8.8	70	..	..
75	Malaysia	17.9	330	2,320	4.0	4.9	1.6	70	30	22
76	Argentina	32.3	2,767	2,370	−0.3	78.4	395.2	71	5	5
77	Iran, Islamic Rep.	55.8	1,648	2,490[d]	0.1	15.5	13.5	63	57	46
78	*Albania*	3.3	29	..	..	..	..	72	..	..
79	*Angola*	10.0	1,247	..	..	..	..	46	72	58
80	*Lebanon*	..	10	..	..	..	..	65	27	20
81	*Mongolia*	2.1	1,565	..	..	..	−1.3	63	..	..
82	*Namibia*	1.8	824	..	..	..	13.4	57	..	..
83	*Nicaragua*	3.9	130	..	−3.3	8.9	432.3	65	..	..
84	*Yemen, Rep.*	11.3	528	..	..	..	..	48	74	62
	Upper-middle-income	**458.4 t**	**18,706 t**	**3,410 w**	**2.8 w**	**19.3 w**	**102.1 w**	**68 w**	**19 w**	**16 w**
85	Mexico	86.2	1,958	2,490	2.8	13.0	70.3	70	15	13
86	South Africa	35.9	1,221	2,530	1.3	10.3	14.4	62	..	..
87	Venezuela	19.7	912	2,560	−1.0	10.4	19.3	70	10	12
88	Uruguay	3.1	177	2,560	0.8	58.2	61.4	73	4	4
89	Brazil	150.4	8,512	2,680	3.3	31.3	284.3	66	20	19
90	Hungary	10.6	93	2,780	..	2.6	9.0	71	..	..
91	Yugoslavia	23.8	256	3,060	2.9	15.2	122.9	72	12	7
92	Czechoslovakia	15.7	128	3,140	..	..	1.9	72	..	..
93	Gabon	1.1	268	3,330	0.9	12.8	−1.7	53	52	39
94	Trinidad and Tobago	1.2	5	3,610	0.0	13.7	6.4	71	..	..
95	Portugal	10.4	92	4,900	3.0	11.7	18.1	75	19	15
96	Korea, Rep.	42.8	99	5,400	7.1	18.4	5.1	71	f	f
97	Greece	10.1	132	5,990	2.8	10.3	18.0	77	11	7
98	Saudi Arabia	14.9	2,150	7,050	2.6	17.9	−4.2	64	52	38
99	*Iraq*	18.9	438	..	..	..	..	63	51	40
100	*Libya*	4.5	1,760	..	−3.0	15.4	0.2	62	50	36
101	*Oman*	1.6	212	..	6.4	19.9	..	66	..	..
	Low- and middle-income	**4,145.8 t**	**78,919 t**	**840 w**	**2.5 w**	**16.7 w**	**61.8 w**	**63 w**	**46 w**	**36 w**
	Sub-Saharan Africa	**495.2 t**	**23,066 t**	**340 w**	**0.2 w**	**11.4 w**	**20.0 w**	**51 w**	**62 w**	**50 w**
	East Asia & Pacific	**1,577.2 t**	**15,572 t**	**600 w**	**5.3 w**	**9.3 w**	**6.0 w**	**68 w**	**34 w**	**24 w**
	South Asia	**1,147.7 t**	**5,158 t**	**330 w**	**1.9 w**	**8.3 w**	**8.0 w**	**58 w**	**67 w**	**53 w**
	Europe	**200.3 t**	**2,171 t**	**2,400 w**	**..**	**13.9 w**	**38.8 w**	**70 w**	**22 w**	**15 w**
	Middle East & N.Africa	**256.4 t**	**11,334 t**	**1,790 w**	**1.8 w**	**13.6 w**	**7.5 w**	**61 w**	**60 w**	**47 w**
	Latin America & Caribbean	**433.1 t**	**20,397 t**	**2,180 w**	**1.8 w**	**31.4 w**	**192.1 w**	**68 w**	**18 w**	**15 w**
	Other economies	**320.9 t**	**22,634 t**	**..**	**..**	**..**	**..**	**71 w**	**7 w**	**6 w**
	Severely indebted	**455.2 t**	**21,048 t**	**2,140 w**	**2.1 w**	**27.4 w**	**173.5 w**	**67 w**	**24 w**	**21 w**
	High-income economies	**816.4 t**	**31,790 t**	**19,590 w**	**2.4 w**	**7.7 w**	**4.5 w**	**77 w**	**5 w**	**4 w**
	OECD members	**776.8 t**	**31,243 t**	**20,170 w**	**2.4 w**	**7.6 w**	**4.2 w**	**77 w**	**5 w**	**4 w**
	†Other	**39.6 t**	**547 t**	**..**	**..**	**13.8 w**	**26.1 w**	**75 w**	**33 w**	**27 w**
102	Ireland	3.5	70	9,550	3.0	11.9	6.5	74	..	..
103	†Israel	4.7	21	10,920	2.6	25.2	101.4	76	..	..
104	Spain	39.0	505	11,020	2.4	12.3	9.2	76	7	5
105	†Singapore	3.0	1	11,160	6.5	5.1	1.7	74	..	..
106	†Hong Kong	5.8	1	11,490[e]	6.2	8.1	7.2	78	..	..
107	New Zealand	3.4	269	12,680	1.1	10.3	10.5	75	f	f
108	Belgium	10.0	31	15,540	2.6	6.6	4.4	76	f	f
109	United Kingdom	57.4	245	16,100	2.0	11.2	5.8	76	f	f
110	Italy	57.7	301	16,830	3.0	11.3	9.9	77	4	3
111	Australia	17.1	7,687	17,000	1.9	9.5	7.4	77	f	f
112	Netherlands	14.9	37	17,320	1.8	7.5	1.9	77	f	f
113	Austria	7.7	84	19,060	2.9	5.8	3.6	76	f	f
114	France	56.4	552	19,490	2.4	8.4	6.1	77	f	f
115	†United Arab Emirates	1.6	84	19,860	..	..	1.1	72	..	..
116	Canada	26.5	9,976	20,470	2.7	7.1	4.4	77	f	f
117	United States	250.0	9,373	21,790	1.7	6.5	3.7	76	f	f
118	Denmark	5.1	43	22,080	2.1	9.3	5.6	75	f	f
119	Germany[g]	79.5	357	22,320[h]	2.4[h]	5.2[h]	2.7[h]	76	f	f
120	Norway	4.2	324	23,120	3.4	7.7	5.5	77	f	f
121	Sweden	8.6	450	23,660	1.9	8.0	7.4	78	f	f
122	Japan	123.5	378	25,430	4.1	7.7	1.5	79	f	f
123	Finland	5.0	338	26,040	3.2	10.5	6.8	76	f	f
124	Switzerland	6.7	41	32,680	1.4	5.3	3.7	78	f	f
125	†Kuwait	2.1	18	..	−4.0	15.9	−2.7	74	33	27
	World	**5,283.9 t**	**133,342 t**	**4,200 w**	**1.5 w**	**9.2 w**	**14.7 w**	**66 w**	**45 w**	**35 w**
	Fuel exporters, excl. former USSR	**272.9 t**	**12,387 t**	**..**	**1.1 w**	**14.5 w**	**8.4 w**	**58 w**	**54 w**	**44 w**

† Economies classified by the United Nations or otherwise regarded by their authorities as developing.   a. See the technical notes.   b. In all tables GDP and GNP data cover mainland Tanzania only.   c. In all tables data for Jordan cover the East Bank only.   d. Reflects last-minute revisions of population estimate (previous estimate was $2,450).   e. Data refer to GDP.   f. According to Unesco, illiteracy is less than 5 percent.   g. In all tables, data refer to the unified Germany, unless otherwise specified.   h. Data refer to the Federal Republic of Germany before unification.

Table 2. Growth of production

		GDP		Agriculture		Industry		Manufacturing[a]		Services, etc.[b]	
		1965-80	*1980-90*	*1965-80*	*1980-90*	*1965-80*	*1980-90*	*1965-80*	*1980-90*	*1965-80*	*1980-90*
	Low-income economies	**4.9** *w*	**6.1** *w*	**2.6** *w*	**3.9** *w*	**7.3** *w*	**8.2** *w*	**6.7** *w*	**11.1** *w*	**6.2** *w*	**6.5** *w*
	China and India	**4.9** *w*	**7.6** *w*	**2.7** *w*	**4.6** *w*	**7.0** *w*	**10.3** *w*	**6.8** *w*	**12.0** *w*	**6.5** *w*	**7.7** *w*
	Other low-income	**4.8** *w*	**3.9** *w*	**2.4** *w*	**2.6** *w*	**8.0** *w*	**3.7** *w*	**6.4** *w*	**7.2** *w*	**5.8** *w*	**4.8** *w*
1	Mozambique	..	-0.7	..	1.3	..	-4.1	..	..	..	-3.2
2	Tanzania	3.9	2.8	1.6	4.1	4.2	0.0	5.6	-0.4	10.8	1.3
3	Ethiopia	2.7	1.8	1.2	-0.1	3.5	2.9	5.1	3.1	5.2	3.7
4	Somalia	3.5	2.4	..	3.3	..	1.0	..	-1.7	..	0.9
5	Nepal	1.9	4.6	1.1	4.8	..	..	..	..	..	..
6	Chad[c]	0.1	5.9	*-0.3*	2.7	*-0.6*	7.9	..	..	*0.2*	8.6
7	Bhutan	..	7.5	..	4.8	..	14.8	..	15.2	..	7.4
8	Lao PDR[c]	..	..	..	..	..	..	..	..	..	..
9	Malawi	5.5	2.9	*4.1*	2.0	*6.4*	3.0	..	3.6	*6.7*	3.5
10	Bangladesh[c]	1.7	4.3	0.6	2.6	1.5	4.9	2.8	2.8	3.6	5.8
11	Burundi	7.1	*3.9*	6.6	*3.1*	17.4	*4.5*	6.0	*5.5*	5.2	*5.4*
12	Zaire[c]	1.9	1.8	..	2.5	..	2.3	..	2.3	..	1.6
13	Uganda	0.6	2.8	1.2	2.5	-4.3	5.5	-3.7	5.2	1.1	3.3
14	Madagascar[c]	1.6	1.1	..	2.4	..	1.2	..	..	..	0.3
15	Sierra Leone	2.7	1.5	3.9	2.6	-0.8	-1.5	0.7	-1.6	4.3	1.4
16	Mali[c]	4.2	4.0	2.8	2.3	1.8	6.8	..	..	7.6	5.6
17	Nigeria	6.0	1.4	1.7	3.3	13.1	-1.2	14.6	-1.0	5.9	2.7
18	Niger[c]	0.3	-1.3	-3.4	..	11.4	..	..	..	0.6	..
19	Rwanda[c]	4.9	1.0	..	-1.5	..	1.2	..	1.0	..	3.9
20	Burkina Faso	..	4.3	..	3.3	..	4.4	..	2.6	..	4.9
21	India	3.6	5.3	2.5	3.1	4.2	6.6	4.5	7.1	4.4	6.5
22	Benin[c]	2.1	2.8	..	*3.6*	..	*4.8*	..	*5.8*	..	*1.8*
23	China[c]	6.8	9.5	2.8	6.1	10.0	12.5	*8.9* [d]	*14.4* [d]	11.9	9.1
24	Haiti	2.9	-0.6	..	..	..	..	..	..	..	..
25	Kenya	6.8	4.2	5.0	3.3	9.7	3.9	10.5	4.9	7.2	4.9
26	Pakistan	5.2	6.3	3.3	4.3	6.4	7.3	5.7	7.7	5.9	6.9
27	Ghana[c]	1.3	3.0	1.6	1.0	1.4	3.3	2.5	4.0	1.1	5.7
28	Central African Rep.	2.8	1.5	2.1	2.7	5.3	3.0	..	..	2.9	0.0
29	Togo[c]	4.3	1.6	1.9	5.4	6.8	0.3	..	0.7	4.7	-0.2
30	Zambia[c]	2.0	0.8	2.2	*3.7*	2.1	*0.7*	5.3	*3.5*	1.8	*0.2*
31	Guinea[c]	..	..	..	..	..	..	..	..	..	..
32	Sri Lanka	4.0	4.0	2.7	2.3	4.7	4.6	3.2	6.3	4.6	4.7
33	Mauritania	2.1	1.4	-2.0	0.7	2.2	4.9	..	..	6.5	0.8
34	Lesotho	6.8	3.1	..	-0.7	..	2.9	..	13.5	..	5.6
35	Indonesia[c]	7.0	5.5	4.3	3.2	11.9	5.6	12.0	12.5	7.3	6.7
36	Honduras	5.0	2.3	2.0	1.8	6.8	2.4	7.5	3.7	5.7	2.4
37	Egypt, Arab Rep.	7.3	5.0	2.7	2.5	6.9	4.3	..	..	13.7	6.7
38	*Afghanistan*	..	..	..	..	..	..	..	..	..	..
39	*Cambodia*	..	..	..	..	..	..	..	..	..	..
40	*Liberia*	..	..	..	..	..	..	..	..	..	..
41	*Myanmar*	..	..	..	..	..	..	..	..	..	..
42	*Sudan*	3.8	..	2.9	..	3.1	..	..	..	4.9	..
43	*Viet Nam*	..	..	..	..	..	..	..	..	..	..
	Middle-income economies	**6.3** *w*	**2.5** *w*	**3.4** *w*	**2.4** *w*	**6.7** *w*	**2.3** *w*	..	**3.5** *w*	**7.4** *w*	**2.6** *w*
	Lower-middle-income	**5.5** *w*	**2.6** *w*	**3.6** *w*	**2.5** *w*	**5.0** *w*	**2.8** *w*	..	..	**7.7** *w*	**2.5** *w*
44	Bolivia[c]	4.4	-0.1	3.8	1.9	3.7	-1.7	5.4	-0.9	5.6	-0.4
45	Zimbabwe	5.0	2.9	..	2.4	..	2.4	..	2.8	..	3.4
46	Senegal[c]	2.3	3.0	1.4	3.1	5.5	3.5	4.5	4.8	1.9	2.9
47	Philippines[c]	5.7	0.9	3.9	1.0	7.7	-0.8	6.8	0.1	5.0	2.6
48	Côte d'Ivoire	6.8	0.5	3.3	1.0	10.4	0.3	..	..	11.8	-0.1
49	Dominican Rep.[c]	8.0	2.1	6.3	1.3	10.8	2.3	8.9	0.8	7.3	2.3
50	Papua New Guinea[c]	4.1	1.9	3.1	1.7	..	2.7	..	1.9	..	1.4
51	Guatemala[c]	5.9	0.8	5.1	2.6	7.3	1.9	6.5	..	5.7	2.1
52	Morocco[c]	5.7	4.0	2.4	6.4	6.1	2.8	..	3.8	7.1	4.1
53	Cameroon[c]	5.1	2.3	4.2	1.6	7.8	3.1	7.0	10.2	4.8	2.1
54	Ecuador[c]	8.8	2.0	3.4	4.4	13.7	1.5	11.5	0.3	7.6	1.5
55	Syrian Arab Rep.[c]	9.1	*2.1*	5.9	-0.6	12.0	*6.8*	..	..	10.5	*1.6*
56	Congo[c]	6.2	3.6	3.1	3.6	9.9	4.9	..	6.8	4.7	2.3
57	El Salvador[c]	4.3	0.9	3.6	-0.7	5.3	-0.6	4.6	..	4.1	1.7
58	Paraguay[c]	7.0	2.5	4.9	3.6	9.1	-0.5	7.0	5.3	7.4	3.4
59	Peru[c]	3.9	-0.3	1.0	2.8	4.4	-1.2	3.8	-0.5	4.2	-0.4
60	Jordan	..	..	..	..	..	..	..	..	..	..
61	Colombia	5.7	3.7	4.5	3.0	5.7	5.1	6.4	3.4	6.3	2.9
62	Thailand[c]	7.3	7.6	4.6	4.1	9.5	9.0	11.2	8.9	7.4	7.8
63	Tunisia	6.5	3.6	5.5	2.3	7.4	2.6	9.9	6.0	6.4	4.5
64	Jamaica[c]	1.4	1.6	0.5	0.8	-0.1	2.2	0.4	2.4	3.1	1.1
65	Turkey	6.2	5.1	3.2	3.0	7.2	6.2	7.5	7.2	7.6	5.2
66	Romania	..	*1.2*	..	*0.1*	..	*0.7*	..	..	..	*2.4*

Note: For data comparability and coverage, see the technical notes.   Figures in italics are for years other than those specified.

		GDP		Agriculture		Industry		Manufacturing[a]		Services, etc.[b]	
		Average annual growth rate (percent)									
		1965–80	1980–90	1965–80	1980–90	1965–80	1980–90	1965–80	1980–90	1965–80	1980–90
67	Poland[c]	..	1.8	..	..	..	..	..	..	..	..
68	Panama[c]	5.5	0.2	2.4	1.9	5.9	–3.4	4.7	–1.4	6.0	0.9
69	Costa Rica[c]	6.3	3.0	4.2	3.2	8.7	2.9	..	3.1	5.9	3.1
70	Chile[c]	1.9	3.2	1.6	4.2	0.8	3.4	0.6	3.5	2.7	2.9
71	Botswana[c]	13.9	11.3	9.7	–4.0	24.0	13.0	13.5	5.3	11.5	11.9
72	Algeria[c]	..	3.1	..	4.3	..	2.9	..	3.0	..	2.9
73	Bulgaria	..	2.6	..	–2.9	..	4.6	..	..	..	1.3
74	Mauritius	5.2	6.0	..	2.6	..	9.2	..	10.8	..	5.1
75	Malaysia[c]	7.4	5.2	..	3.8	..	7.1	..	8.8	..	4.2
76	Argentina[c]	3.4	–0.4	1.4	1.1	3.3	–1.1	..	..	4.1	–0.1
77	Iran, Islamic Rep.	6.1	2.5	4.5	4.0	2.2	3.4	9.9	0.3	13.5	1.1
78	*Albania*	..	..	..	..	..	..	..	..	..	..
79	*Angola*	..	..	..	–0.5	..	12.6	..	–4.6	..	..
80	*Lebanon[c]*	..	..	..	..	..	..	..	..	..	..
81	*Mongolia*	..	5.6	..	..	..	..	..	..	..	..
82	*Namibia*	..	0.4	..	–1.0	..	–2.0	..	1.4	..	3.0
83	*Nicaragua[c]*	2.5	–2.2	3.8	–2.6	4.2	–4.4	5.1	–4.3	1.0	–1.0
84	*Yemen, Rep.[c]*	..	..	..	..	..	..	..	..	..	..
	Upper-middle-income	**7.0 w**	**2.4 w**	**3.2 w**	**2.3 w**	**7.8 w**	**2.0 w**	**8.9 w**	**3.5 w**	**7.4 w**	**2.7 w**
85	Mexico[c]	6.5	1.0	3.2	0.4	7.6	1.0	7.4	1.4	6.5	1.1
86	South Africa	3.7	1.3	3.0	2.6	3.0	0.0	5.6	–0.1	4.7	2.4
87	Venezuela[c]	3.7	1.0	3.9	3.1	1.5	1.5	5.8	4.2	5.8	0.5
88	Uruguay	2.4	0.3	1.0	0.0	2.9	–0.2	..	0.4	2.3	0.8
89	Brazil	9.0	2.7	3.8	2.8	10.1	2.1	9.8	1.7	9.4	3.4
90	Hungary[c]	5.7	1.3	2.7	1.6	6.4	–0.5	..	..	6.2	2.8
91	Yugoslavia	6.1	0.8	3.1	0.7	7.8	0.8	..	..	5.5	0.8
92	Czechoslovakia[c]	..	1.4	..	0.3	..	2.1	..	..	..	1.4
93	Gabon[c]	9.5	2.3	..	..	..	..	..	..	..	..
94	*Trinidad and Tobago*	4.8	–4.7	0.0	–6.0	5.0	–5.5	2.6	–3.0	5.3	–3.4
95	Portugal[c]	5.3	2.7	..	..	..	..	..	..	..	..
96	Korea, Rep.[c]	9.9	9.7	3.0	2.8	16.4	12.2	18.7	12.7	9.6	9.2
97	Greece	5.8	1.8	2.3	0.7	7.1	1.0	8.4	0.6	6.4	2.6
98	Saudi Arabia[c]	10.6	–1.8	4.1	14.6	11.6	–4.4	8.1	8.8	9.8	–0.3
99	*Iraq*	..	..	..	..	..	..	..	..	..	..
100	*Libya*	4.2	..	10.7	..	1.2	..	13.7	..	15.5	..
101	*Oman[c]*	13.0	12.8	..	5.1	..	13.7	..	27.0	..	10.5
	Low- and middle-income	**5.9 w**	**3.2 w**	**2.9 w**	**3.2 w**	**6.8 w**	**3.8 w**	**8.0 w**	**6.0 w**	**7.1 w**	**3.6 w**
	Sub-Saharan Africa	**4.2 w**	**2.1 w**	**2.0 w**	**2.1 w**	**7.2 w**	**2.0 w**	**..**	**3.1 w**	**4.7 w**	**2.5 w**
	East Asia & Pacific	**7.3 w**	**7.8 w**	**3.2 w**	**4.8 w**	**10.8 w**	**10.2 w**	**10.3 w**	**12.4 w**	**8.9 w**	**8.0 w**
	South Asia	**3.6 w**	**5.2 w**	**2.5 w**	**3.0 w**	**4.3 w**	**6.5 w**	**4.5 w**	**6.8 w**	**4.5 w**	**6.3 w**
	Europe	**..**	**2.1 w**	**..**	**1.0 w**	**..**	**2.7 w**	**..**	**..**	**..**	**2.7 w**
	Middle East & N.Africa	**6.7 w**	**0.5 w**	**4.3 w**	**4.3 w**	**6.3 w**	**0.7 w**	**..**	**3.4 w**	**10.9 w**	**1.9 w**
	Latin America & Caribbean	**6.0 w**	**1.6 w**	**3.1 w**	**1.9 w**	**6.6 w**	**1.2 w**	**8.3 w**	**1.7 w**	**6.6 w**	**1.7 w**
	Other economies	**..**	**..**	**..**	**..**	**..**	**..**	**..**	**..**	**..**	**..**
	Severely indebted	**6.3 w**	**1.7 w**	**3.3 w**	**1.8 w**	**6.6 w**	**1.6 w**	**8.4 w**	**1.7 w**	**6.8 w**	**1.9 w**
	High-income economies	**3.7 w**	**3.1 w**	**..**	**1.7 w**	**2.7 w**	**..**	**3.2 w**	**..**	**4.5 w**	**..**
	OECD members	**3.7 w**	**3.1 w**	**..**	**1.7 w**	**2.8 w**	**..**	**3.1 w**	**3.3 w**	**4.5 w**	**..**
	†Other	**..**	**2.3 w**	**..**	**..**	**..**	**..**	**..**	**..**	**..**	**..**
102	Ireland	4.9	3.1	..	..	..	..	..	..	..	..
103	†Israel[c]	6.8	3.2	..	..	..	..	..	..	..	..
104	Spain[c]	4.6	3.1	..	..	..	..	..	..	..	..
105	†Singapore[c]	10.0	6.4	2.8	–6.2	11.9	5.4	13.2	6.6	9.1	7.2
106	†Hong Kong	8.6	7.1	..	..	..	..	..	..	..	..
107	New Zealand[c]	2.4	1.9	..	4.7	..	1.7	..	1.3	..	1.6
108	Belgium[c]	3.9	2.0	..	2.0	..	1.9	..	2.8	..	1.6
109	United Kingdom	2.3	3.1	..	–3.1	..	1.3	..	4.8	..	3.0
110	Italy[c]	4.3	2.4	..	0.8	..	1.9	..	2.7	..	2.9
111	Australia[c]	4.0	3.4	..	3.2	..	3.2	..	1.9	..	3.7
112	Netherlands[c]	3.9	1.9	4.3[e]	3.6	2.3[e]	..	..	..	3.8[e]	1.8
113	Austria[c]	4.3	2.1	2.2	1.0	4.4	1.7	4.6	2.2	4.3	2.1
114	France[c]	4.0	2.2	..	2.0	..	0.6	..	0.2	..	2.9
115	†United Arab Emirates	..	–4.5	..	9.3	..	–8.7	..	2.7	..	3.7
116	Canada	4.8	3.4	0.7	0.2	3.5	3.2	3.8	3.4	6.4	3.5
117	United States[c]	2.7	3.4	1.0	..	1.7	..	2.6	..	3.3	..
118	Denmark	2.8	2.4	0.9	2.6	1.9	3.3	3.2	1.5	3.0	2.0
119	Germany[c,f]	3.3	2.1	1.4	1.6	2.9	0.4	3.3	0.9	3.7	2.7
120	Norway	4.4	2.9	..	..	..	..	..	..	..	..
121	Sweden	2.7	2.2	..	1.1	..	2.8	..	2.7	..	1.4
122	Japan[c]	6.4	4.1	–0.6	1.3	7.1	4.5	7.8	5.3	6.8	3.8
123	Finland	4.0	3.4	0.0	–0.7	4.3	3.0	4.9	3.3	4.7	3.4
124	Switzerland[c]	2.0	2.2	..	..	..	..	..	..	..	..
125	†Kuwait[c]	1.6	0.7	..	18.8	..	1.0	..	–0.2	..	0.6
	World	**4.0 w**	**3.2 w**	**1.7 w**	**2.7 w**	**..**	**..**	**..**	**..**	**..**	**..**
	Fuel exporters, excl. former USSR	**6.6 w**	**0.8 w**	**3.7 w**	**4.3 w**	**6.0 w**	**–1.0 w**	**8.3 w**	**3.0 w**	**9.6 w**	**1.2 w**

a. Because manufacturing is generally the most dynamic part of the industrial sector, its growth rate is shown separately.   b. Services, etc. includes unallocated items.   c. GDP and its components are at purchaser values.   d. World Bank estimate.   e. Data refer to the period 1970–1980.   f. Data refer to the Federal Republic of Germany before unification.

Table 3. Structure of production

		GDP (millions of dollars)		Distribution of gross domestic product (percent)							
				Agriculture		Industry		Manufacturing[a]		Services, etc.[b]	
		1965	1990	1965	1990	1965	1990	1965	1990	1965	1990
	Low-income economies	**168,700** *t*	**915,520** *t*	**41** *w*	**31** *w*	**26** *w*	**36** *w*	**19** *w*	**27** *w*	**32** *w*	**35** *w*
	China and India	**117,730** *t*	**619,450** *t*	**41** *w*	**29** *w*	**29** *w*	**36** *w*	**22** *w*	**30** *w*	**30** *w*	**35** *w*
	Other low-income	**49,810** *t*	**307,040** *t*	**42** *w*	**30** *w*	**20** *w*	**34** *w*	**8** *w*	. .	**38** *w*	**38** *w*
1	Mozambique	. .	1,320	. .	65	. .	15	. .	. .	. .	21
2	Tanzania	790	2,060	46	59	14	12	8	10	40	29
3	Ethiopia	1,180	5,490	58	41	14	17	7	11	28	42
4	Somalia	220	890	71	65	6	9	3	5	24	26
5	Nepal	730	2,890	65	60	11	14	3	5	23	26
6	Chad[c]	290	1,100	42	38	15	17	12	14	43	45
7	Bhutan	. .	280	. .	43	. .	27	. .	10	. .	29
8	Lao PDR[c]	. .	870	. .	. .	. .	. .	. .	. .	. .	. .
9	Malawi	220	1,660	50	33	13	20	. .	14	37	46
10	Bangladesh[c]	4,380	22,880	53	38	11	15	5	9	36	46
11	Burundi	150	1,000	. .	56	. .	15	. .	10	. .	29
12	Zaire[c]	4,040	7,540	20	30	32	33	. .	13	48	36
13	Uganda	1,100	2,820	52	67	13	7	8	4	35	26
14	Madagascar[c]	750	2,750	25	33	14	13	. .	12	61	54
15	Sierra Leone	320	840	34	32	28	13	6	6	38	55
16	Mali[c]	260	2,450	65	46	9	13	5	8	25	41
17	Nigeria	5,380	34,760	55	36	12	38	5	7	33	25
18	Niger[c]	670	2,520	68	36	3	13	2	5	29	51
19	Rwanda[c]	150	2,130	75	38	7	22	2	15	18	40
20	Burkina Faso	350	3,060	37	32	24	24	11	14	39	44
21	India	50,530	254,540	44	31	22	29	16	19	34	40
22	Benin	220	1,810	59	37	8	15	. .	. .	33	48
23	China[c]	67,200	364,900	38	27	35	42	28[d]	38[d]	27	31
24	Haiti[c]	350	2,760	. .	. .	. .	. .	. .	. .	. .	. .
25	Kenya	920	7,540	35	28	18	21	11	11	47	51
26	Pakistan	5,450	35,500	40	26	20	25	14	17	40	49
27	Ghana[c]	2,050	6,270	44	48	19	16	10	9	38	37
28	Central African Rep.	140	1,220	46	42	16	17	4	. .	38	41
29	Togo[c]	190	1,620	45	33	21	22	10	9	34	46
30	Zambia[c]	1,060	3,120	14	17	54	55	6	43	32	29
31	Guinea[c]	. .	2,820	. .	28	. .	33	. .	4	. .	39
32	Sri Lanka	1,770	7,250	28	26	21	26	17	15	51	48
33	Mauritania	160	950	32	26	36	29	4	. .	32	44
34	Lesotho	50	340	65	24	5	30	1	14	30	46
35	Indonesia[c]	5,980	107,290	51	22	13	40	8	20	36	38
36	Honduras	460	2,360	40	23	19	24	12	16	41	53
37	Egypt, Arab Rep.	4,550	33,210	29	17	27	29	. .	16	45	53
38	Afghanistan	970	. .	. .	. .	. .	. .	. .	. .	. .	. .
39	Cambodia	870	. .	. .	. .	. .	. .	. .	. .	. .	. .
40	Liberia	270	. .	27	. .	40	. .	3	. .	34	. .
41	Myanmar	. .	. .	. .	. .	. .	. .	. .	. .	. .	. .
42	Sudan	1,330	. .	54	. .	9	. .	4	. .	37	. .
43	Viet Nam	. .	. .	. .	. .	. .	. .	. .	. .	. .	. .
	Middle-income economies	**209,520** *t*	**2,437,660** *t*	**19** *w*	**12** *w*	**34** *w*	**37** *w*	**20** *w*	. .	**46** *w*	**50** *w*
	Lower-middle-income	**108,570** *t*	**930,020** *t*	**22** *w*	**17** *w*	**32** *w*	**31** *w*	**20** *w*	. .	**44** *w*	**50** *w*
44	Bolivia[c]	710	4,480	23	24	31	32	15	13	46	44
45	Zimbabwe	960	5,310	18	13	35	40	20	26	47	47
46	Senegal[c]	810	5,840	25	21	18	18	14	13	56	61
47	Philippines[c]	6,010	43,860	26	22	27	35	20	25	47	43
48	Côte d'Ivoire	760	7,610	47	47	19	27	11	. .	33	26
49	Dominican Rep.[c]	890	7,310	23	17	22	27	16	13	55	56
50	Papua New Guinea[c]	340	3,270	42	29	18	31	. .	12	41	40
51	Guatemala[c]	1,330	7,630	. .	26	. .	19	. .	. .	. .	55
52	Morocco[c]	2,950	25,220	23	16	28	33	16	18	49	51
53	Cameroon[c]	810	11,130	33	27	20	28	10	13	47	46
54	Ecuador[c]	1,150	10,880	27	13	22	42	18	23	50	45
55	Syrian Arab Rep.[c]	1,470	14,730	29	28	22	22	. .	. .	49	50
56	Congo[c]	200	2,870	19	13	19	39	. .	7	62	48
57	El Salvador[c]	800	5,400	29	11	22	21	18	19	49	67
58	Paraguay[c]	440	5,260	37	28	19	23	16	23	45	49
59	Peru[c]	5,020	36,550	18	7	30	37	17	27	53	57
60	Jordan	. .	3,330	. .	8	. .	26	. .	12	. .	66
61	Colombia	5,910	41,120	27	17	27	32	19	21	47	51
62	Thailand[c]	4,390	80,170	32	12	23	39	14	26	45	48
63	Tunisia	880	11,080	22	16	24	32	9	17	54	52
64	Jamaica[c]	970	3,970	10	5	37	46	17	20	53	49
65	Turkey	7,660	96,500	34	18	25	33	16	24	41	49
66	Romania	. .	34,730	. .	18	. .	48	. .	. .	. .	34

Note: For data comparability and coverage, see the technical notes.   Figures in italics are for years other than those specified.

		GDP (millions of dollars)		Distribution of gross domestic product (percent)							
				Agriculture		Industry		Manufacturing[a]		Services, etc.[b]	
		1965	1990	1965	1990	1965	1990	1965	1990	1965	1990
67	Poland[c]	..	63,590	..	14	..	36	..	..	..	50
68	Panama[c]	660	4,750	18	10	19	9	12	7	63	80
69	Costa Rica[c]	590	5,700	24	16	23	26	..	19	53	58
70	Chile[c]	5,880	27,790	9	..	40	..	24	..	52	..
71	Botswana[c]	50	2,700	34	3	19	57	12	6	47	40
72	Algeria[c]	..	42,150	..	13	..	47	..	12	..	41
73	Bulgaria	..	19,910	..	18	..	52	..	..	..	31
74	Mauritius	190	2,090	16	12	23	33	14	24	61	55
75	Malaysia[c]	3,130	42,400	28	..	25	..	9	..	47	..
76	Argentina[c]	19,410	93,260	17	13	42	41	33	..	42	45
77	Iran, Islamic Rep.	6,170	116,040	26	21	36	21	12	8	38	58
78	Albania	..	..	..	..	..	..	..	..	..	..
79	Angola	..	7,700	..	13	..	44	..	4	..	43
80	Lebanon[c]	1,150	..	12	..	21	..	..	..	67	..
81	Mongolia	..	..	..	17	..	34	..	..	..	49
82	Namibia	..	..	..	11	..	38	..	5	..	50
83	Nicaragua[c]	570	..	25	..	24	..	18	..	51	..
84	Yemen, Rep.[c]	..	6,690	..	20	..	28	..	8	..	47
	Upper-middle-income	**103,960 t**	**1,520,340 t**	**16 w**	**9 w**	**36 w**	**40 w**	**19 w**	**25 w**	**47 w**	**51 w**
85	Mexico[c]	21,640	237,750	14	9	27	30	20	23	59	61
86	South Africa	10,170	90,720	10	5	41	44	24	26	48	51
87	Venezuela[c]	9,930	48,270	6	6	40	50	..	20	55	45
88	Uruguay	1,810	8,220	18	11	35	34	..	28	47	55
89	Brazil	19,470	414,060	19	10	33	39	26	26	48	51
90	Hungary[c]	..	32,920	..	12	..	32	..	27	..	56
91	Yugoslavia	11,190	82,310	23	12	42	48	..	..	35	40
92	Czechoslovakia[c]	..	44,450	..	8	..	56	..	..	..	36
93	Gabon[c]	230	4,720	26	9	34	49	7	7	40	42
94	Trinidad and Tobago	690	4,750	8	3	48	48	..	13	44	49
95	Portugal[c]	3,740	56,820	..	..	25	45	18	31	37	46
96	Korea, Rep.[c]	3,000	236,400	38	9	25	45	18	31	37	46
97	Greece	5,270	57,900	24	17	26	27	16	14	49	56
98	Saudi Arabia[c]	2,300	80,890	8	8	60	45	9	9	31	48
99	Iraq	2,430	..	18	..	46	..	8	..	36	..
100	Libya	1,500	..	5	..	63	..	3	..	33	..
101	Oman[c]	60	7,700	61	3	23	80	0	4	16	18
	Low- and middle-income	**382,780 t**	**3,334,260 t**	**29 w**	**17 w**	**30 w**	**37 w**	**20 w**	**25 w**	**40 w**	**47 w**
	Sub-Saharan Africa	**27,020 t**	**162,940 t**	**40 w**	**32 w**	**20 w**	**30 w**	**7 w**	**..**	**39 w**	**40 w**
	East Asia & Pacific	**92,540 t**	**821,230 t**	**37 w**	**21 w**	**32 w**	**45 w**	**24 w**	**34 w**	**30 w**	**36 w**
	South Asia	**64,510 t**	**345,640 t**	**44 w**	**33 w**	**21 w**	**26 w**	**15 w**	**17 w**	**35 w**	**41 w**
	Europe	**..**	**489,240 t**	**..**	**..**	**..**	**31 w**	**..**	**..**	**..**	**..**
	Middle East & N.Africa	**27,960 t**	**..**	**20 w**	**..**	**38 w**	**..**	**10 w**	**..**	**40 w**	**..**
	Latin America & Caribbean	**102,480 t**	**1,015,160 t**	**16 w**	**10 w**	**33 w**	**36 w**	**23 w**	**25 w**	**50 w**	**54 w**
	Other economies	**..**	**...**	**..**	**..**	**..**	**..**	**..**	**..**	**..**	**..**
	Severely indebted	**97,440 t**	**1,025,990 t**	**16 w**	**10 w**	**34 w**	**35 w**	**23 w**	**26 w**	**49 w**	**53 w**
	High-income economies	**1,413,490 t**	**16,316,290 t**	**5 w**	**..**	**43 w**	**..**	**32 w**	**..**	**54 w**	**..**
	OECD members	**1,392,410 t**	**15,993,410 t**	**5 w**	**..**	**43 w**	**..**	**32 w**	**..**	**54 w**	**..**
	†Other	**..**	**..**	**..**	**..**	**..**	**..**	**..**	**..**	**..**	**..**
102	Ireland	2,690	42,500	..	..	..	..	..	..	..	..
103	†Israel[c]	3,590	53,200	..	..	..	..	..	..	..	..
104	Spain[c]	24,020	491,240	..	..	..	..	..	..	..	..
105	†Singapore[c]	970	34,600	3	0	24	37	15	29	74	63
106	†Hong Kong	2,150	59,670	2	0	40	26	24	18	58	73
107	New Zealand[c]	5,640	42,760	..	9	..	27	..	19	..	65
108	Belgium[c]	16,600	192,390	..	2	..	31	..	23	..	67
109	United Kingdom	100,690	975,150	3	..	46	..	34	..	51	..
110	Italy[c]	66,880	1,090,750	..	4	..	33	..	23	..	63
111	Australia[c]	24,220	296,300	9	4	39	31	26	15	51	64
112	Netherlands[c]	19,890	279,150	..	4	..	31	..	20	..	65
113	Austria[c]	9,480	157,380	9	3	46	37	33	27	45	60
114	France[c]	99,300	1,190,780	..	4	..	29	..	21	..	67
115	†United Arab Emirates	..	28,270	..	2	..	55	..	9	..	43
116	Canada	52,870	570,150	6	..	40	..	26	..	54	..
117	United States[c]	701,380	5,392,200	3	..	38	..	28	..	59	..
118	Denmark	10,180	130,960	9	5	36	28	23	19	55	67
119	Germany[c,e]	114,790	1,488,210	4	2	53	39	40	31	43	59
120	Norway	7,080	105,830	..	..	..	..	..	..	..	..
121	Sweden	21,980	228,110	..	3	..	35	..	24	..	62
122	Japan[c]	91,290	2,942,890	10	3	44	42	34	29	46	56
123	Finland	8,320	137,250	16	6	37	36	23	23	47	58
124	Switzerland[c]	13,920	224,850	..	..	..	..	..	..	..	..
125	†Kuwait[c]	2,100	23,540	0	1	70	56	3	9	29	43
	World	**2,039,890 t**	**22,298,850 t**	**10 w**	**..**	**41 w**	**..**	**30 w**	**..**	**51 w**	**..**
	Fuel exporters, excl. former USSR	**33,840 t**	**..**	**20 w**	**..**	**37 w**	**..**	**..**	**..**	**42 w**	**..**

a. Because manufacturing is generally the most dynamic part of the industrial sector, its share of GDP is shown separately.   b. Services, etc. includes unallocated items.   c. GDP and its components are at purchaser values.   d. World Bank estimate.   e. Data refer to the Federal Republic of Germany before unification.

Table 4. Agriculture and food

		Value added in agriculture (millions of current dollars)		Cereal imports (thousands of metric tons)		Food aid in cereals (thousands of metric tons)		Fertilizer consumption (hundreds of grams of plant nutrient per hectare of arable land)		Average index of food production per capita (1979–81=100)
		1970	1990	1974	1990	1974/75	1989/90	1970/71	1989/90	1988–90
Low-income economies		**84,469** *t*	**287,958** *t*	**26,538** *t*	**35,748** *t*	**6,643** *t*	**6,599** *t*	**178** *w*	**946** *w*	**119** *w*
China and India		**55,737** *t*	**178,447** *t*	**11,294** *t*	**14,166** *t*	**1,582** *t*	**540** *t*	**241** *w*	**1,383** *w*	**127** *w*
Other low-income		**28,323** *t*	**109,352** *t*	**15,243** *t*	**21,582** *t*	**5,061** *t*	**6,059** *t*	**91** *w*	**394** *w*	**105** *w*
1	Mozambique	..	854	62	416	34	493	22	8	81
2	Tanzania	483	*1,444*	431	73	148	22	31	93	88
3	Ethiopia	931	2,271	118	687	54	538	4	70	84
4	Somalia	170	585	42	194	111	90	27	26	94
5	Nepal	579	1,743	18	21	..	6	27	256	115
6	Chad[a]	142	416	37	36	20	27	7	15	85
7	Bhutan	..	119	3	11	..	6	..	8	93
8	Lao PDR[a]	..	..	53	54	8	29	2	3	114
9	Malawi	119	554	17	115	0	175	52	227	83
10	Bangladesh[a]	3,650	8,721	1,866	1,726	2,076	1,134	157	993	96
11	Burundi	159	557	7	17	6	2	5	35	92
12	Zaire[a]	721	*2,649*	343	336	1	107	6	10	97
13	Uganda	929	1,880	36	7	..	35	14	1	95
14	Madagascar[a]	243	906	114	183	7	31	61	36	88
15	Sierra Leone	108	265	72	146	10	37	17	3	89
16	Mali[a]	207	1,125	281	61	107	38	31	54	97
17	Nigeria	4,787	12,582	389	502	7	..	2	121	106
18	Niger[a]	420	*744*	155	86	73	35	1	8	71
19	Rwanda[a]	135	812	3	21	19	7	3	14	77
20	Burkina Faso	121	970	99	145	28	44	3	58	114
21	India	23,916	78,099	5,261	447	1,582	456	137	687	119
22	Benin[a]	..	..	8	126	9	13	36	18	112
23	China[a]	31,821	100,348	6,033	13,719	..	84	410	2,619	133
24	Haiti	..	..	83	236	25	179	4	41	94
25	Kenya	484	2,131	15	188	2	62	238	481	106
26	Pakistan	3,352	9,165	1,274	2,048	584	428	146	890	101
27	Ghana[a]	1,030	2,980	177	337	33	73	11	31	97
28	Central African Rep.	60	515	7	37	1	4	12	4	91
29	Togo[a]	85	533	6	111	11	11	3	83	88
30	Zambia[a]	191	521	93	100	5	3	73	166	103
31	Guinea[a]	..	776	63	210	49	25	44	11	87
32	Sri Lanka	627	1,910	951	996	271	231	555	1,015	87
33	Mauritania	58	248	115	205	48	72	11	116	85
34	Lesotho	23	..	48	97	14	30	10	144	86
35	Indonesia[a]	4,340	23,368	1,919	1,828	301	39	133	1,166	123
36	Honduras	212	546	52	162	31	134	156	185	83
37	Egypt, Arab Rep.	1,942	5,771	3,877	8,580	610	1,210	1,312	4,043	118
38	*Afghanistan*	..	..	5	322	10	145	24	69	85
39	*Cambodia*	..	..	223	20	226	11	11	..	165
40	*Liberia*	91	..	42	70	3	28	63	107	84
41	*Myanmar*	..	..	26	..	9	..	21	86	93
42	*Sudan*	757	..	125	586	46	335	28	39	71
43	*Viet Nam*	..	..	1,854	204	64	72	513	841	127
Middle-income economies		**49,480** *t*	**290,333** *t*	**39,283** *t*	**77,607** *t*	**1,284** *t*	**4,483** *t*	**363** *w*	**693** *w*	**102** *w*
Lower-middle-income		**28,936** *t*	**154,202** *t*	**21,082** *t*	**38,669** *t*	**1,013** *t*	**4,122** *t*	**300** *w*	**601** *w*	**98** *w*
44	Bolivia[a]	202	1,069	209	147	22	93	7	23	109
45	Zimbabwe	214	688	56	83	..	13	446	604	94
46	Senegal[a]	208	1,199	341	534	27	61	17	55	102
47	Philippines[a]	1,975	9,686	817	2,545	89	59	287	674	84
48	Côte d'Ivoire	462	3,554	172	502	4	26	74	113	101
49	Dominican Rep.[a]	345	1,273	252	662	16	6	334	504	90
50	Papua New Guinea[a]	240	942	71	222	..	0	58	399	103
51	Guatemala[a]	..	1,978	138	383	9	155	298	728	91
52	Morocco	789	3,963	891	1,578	75	219	117	344	128
53	Cameroon[a]	364	2,964	81	398	4	..	34	41	89
54	Ecuador[a]	401	1,435	152	474	13	38	133	338	100
55	Syrian Arab Rep.[a]	435	4,091	339	2,091	47	22	68	454	80
56	Congo[a]	49	380	34	94	2	7	525	32	94
57	El Salvador[a]	292	605	75	176	4	249	1,043	1,064	97
58	Paraguay[a]	191	1,462	71	2	10	3	98	89	116
59	Peru[a]	1,351	2,420	637	1,562	37	194	300	411	100
60	Jordan	..	252	171	1,491	79	250	87	771	100
61	Colombia	1,806	6,876	502	880	28	7	287	902	104
62	Thailand[a]	1,837	9,948	97	387	..	95	59	365	106
63	Tunisia	245	1,807	307	1,439	59	479	76	232	87
64	Jamaica[a]	93	209	340	262	1	165	873	1,156	95
65	Turkey	3,383	17,485	1,276	3,177	16	13	157	645	97
66	Romania	..	6,255	1,381	1,137	..	..	565	1,332	92

Note: For data comparability and coverage, see the technical notes.   Figures in italics are for years other than those specified.

		Value added in agriculture (millions of current dollars)		Cereal imports (thousands of metric tons)		Food aid in cereals (thousands of metric tons)		Fertilizer consumption (hundreds of grams of plant nutrient per hectare of arable land)		Average index of food production per capita (1979–81=100)
		1970	1990	1974	1990	1974/75	1989/90	1970/71	1989/90	1988–90
67	Poland	..	8,775	4,185	1,550	..	1,582	1,678	2,052	109
68	Panama[a]	149	482	63	125	3	1	387	541	90
69	Costa Rica	222	915	110	326	1	60	1,001	2,027	91
70	Chile[a]	557	..	1,737	247	323	4	322	800	113
71	Botswana[a]	28	75	21	87	5	5	15	7	75
72	Algeria[a]	492	5,288	1,816	5,185	54	11	163	283	96
73	Bulgaria[a]	..	3,486	649	475	..	..	1,411	1,946	96
74	Mauritius	30	257	160	210	22	9	2,095	3,302	100
75	Malaysia[a]	1,198	..	1,023	2,582	1	1	436	1,572	147
76	Argentina[a]	2,693	12,405	0	4	..	..	26	46	93
77	Iran, Islamic Rep.	2,120	24,484	2,076	6,250	..	22	60	797	104
78	Albania	..	..	48	148	..	..	736	1,506	92
79	Angola	..	997	149	272	..	113	33	74	81
80	Lebanon[a]	136	..	354	356	26	16	1,354	917	135
81	Mongolia[a]	..	..	28	57	..	..	22	124	86
82	Namibia	..	187				4			93
83	Nicaragua[a]	199	..	44	177	3	57	215	648	58
84	Yemen, Rep.[a]	..	1,376	306	2,001	33	..	1	11	..
	Upper-middle-income	**21,267 t**	**140,171 t**	**18,200 t**	**38,938 t**	**271 t**	**361 t**	**459 w**	**824 w**	**109 w**
85	Mexico[a]	4,462	21,074	2,881	7,648	..	341	232	728	102
86	South Africa	1,292	4,594	127	876	..	..	422	575	87
87	Venezuela[a]	835	2,671	1,270	1,603	..	..	170	1,507	96
88	Uruguay	378	893	70	55	6	..	485	454	109
89	Brazil	4,388	42,288	2,485	3,421	31	20	186	430	115
90	Hungary[a]	1,010	4,091	408	503	..	..	1,497	2,463	113
91	Yugoslavia	2,212	9,641	992	1,407	..	..	770	1,155	95
92	Czechoslovakia	..	3,979	1,296	205	..	..	2,404	3,213	119
93	Gabon[a]	60	431	24	57	..	..	..	27	84
94	Trinidad and Tobago	40	124	208	295	..	..	880	275	87
95	Portugal[a]	..	..	1,861	1,725	..	..	326	727	106
96	Korea, Rep.[a]	2,311	21,364	2,679	9,087	234	..	2,450	4,250	106
97	Greece	1,569	8,234	1,341	588	..	..	861	1,752	103
98	Saudi Arabia[a]	219	6,150	482	5,273	..	..	54	4,008	189
99	Iraq	579	..	870	2,834	..	..	34	395	92
100	Libya	93	..	612	2,290	..	..	62	367	78
101	Oman	40	..	52	338	..	..	..	1,108	..
	Low- and middle-income	**135,849 t**	**575,864 t**	**65,820 t**	**113,355 t**	**7,928 t**	**11,083 t**	**256 w**	**833 w**	**115 w**
	Sub-Saharan Africa	**13,167 t**	**51,410 t**	**4,209 t**	**7,838 t**	**910 t**	**2,677 t**	**33 w**	**89 w**	**94 w**
	East Asia & Pacific	**44,838 t**	**176,368 t**	**14,948 t**	**30,955 t**	**923 t**	**391 t**	**364 w**	**1,903 w**	**127 w**
	South Asia	**32,980 t**	**112,436 t**	**9,404 t**	**5,274 t**	**4,522 t**	**2,264 t**	**135 w**	**689 w**	**116 w**
	Europe	**.. t**	**59,446 t**	**13,564 t**	**11,030 t**	**16 t**	**1,595 t**	**878 w**	**1,424 w**	**102 w**
	Middle East & N.Africa	**7,248 t**	**58,699 t**	**11,879 t**	**38,083 t**	**993 t**	**2,373 t**	**138 w**	**646 w**	**101 w**
	Latin America & Caribbean	**19,843 t**	**104,716 t**	**13,312 t**	**21,698 t**	**563 t**	**1,783 t**	**201 w**	**468 w**	**106 w**
	Other economies	**..**	**..**	**10,484 t**	**35,922 t**	**..**	**..**	**464 w**	**1,102 w**	**113 w**
	Severely indebted	**19,194 t**	**106,991 t**	**15,765 t**	**26,512 t**	**288 t**	**2,610 t**	**321 w**	**549 w**	**106 w**
	High-income economies	**77,501 t**	**..**	**73,739 t**	**73,797 t**	**53 t**	**..**	**1,022 w**	**1,218 w**	**100 w**
	OECD members	**76,637 t**	**..**	**68,356 t**	**62,607 t**	**..**	**..**	**1,017 w**	**1,206 w**	**101 w**
	†Other	**..**	**..**	**5,383 t**	**11,190 t**	**53 t**	**..**	**2,192 w**	**4,019 w**	**80 w**
102	Ireland	559	..	640	367	..	..	3,067	7,225	109
103	†Israel[a]	295	..	1,176	1,802	53	..	1,401	2,425	95
104	Spain[a]	..	18,537	4,675	3,020	..	..	593	1,009	112
105	†Singapore[a]	44	97	682	737	..	..	2,500	5,600	69
106	†Hong Kong	62	181	657	754	..	..	..	..	80
107	New Zealand[a]	913	..	92	279	..	..	7,745	6,558	102
108	Belgium[a]	..	3,136	4,585[b]	4,597[b]	..	..	5,648	5,018	108
109	United Kingdom	2,981	10,735	7,540	3,084	..	..	2,631	3,502	105
110	Italy[a]	8,387	30,542	8,101	6,699	..	..	896	1,507	94
111	Australia[a]	2,277	..	2	41	..	..	232	226	95
112	Netherlands[a]	1,850	9,940	7,199	6,899	..	..	7,493	6,424	111
113	Austria[a]	992	3,915	164	92	..	..	2,426	2,008	106
114	France[a]	..	33,598	654	922	..	..	2,435	3,192	103
115	†United Arab Emirates	..	481	132	576	..	..	..	1,615	..
116	Canada	3,224	..	1,513	840	..	..	191	472	108
117	United States[a]	27,856	..	460	2,217	..	..	816	985	92
118	Denmark	882	4,367	462	140	..	..	2,234	2,503	126
119	Germany[a]	5,951[d]	19,207[d]	9,985	5,389	..	..	3,844	3,705	112[d]
120	Norway	624	2,551	713	379	..	..	2,443	2,420	100
121	Sweden	..	5,426	300	116	..	..	1,646	1,271	99
122	Japan[c]	12,467	74,085	19,557	27,008	..	..	3,547	4,179	101
123	Finland	1,205	6,436	222	46	..	..	1,822	2,102	105
124	Switzerland	..	..	1,458	450	..	..	3,831	4,262	101
125	†Kuwait[a]	8	238	101	427	..	..	..	2,000	..
	World	**239,431 t**	**..**	**150,043 t**	**223,074 t**	**7,981 t**	**11,083 t**	**493 w**	**974 w**	**112 w**
	Fuel exporters, excl. former USSR	**9,646 t**	**57,828 t**	**8,163 t**	**25,709 t**	**63 t**	**153 t**	**49 w**	**448 w**	**104 w**

a. Value added in agriculture data are at purchaser values.   b. Includes Luxembourg.   c. Value added in agriculture data refer to net domestic product at factor cost.   d. Data refer to the Federal Republic of Germany before unification.

Table 5. Commercial energy

| | | Average annual growth rate (percent) | | | | Energy consumption per capita (kilograms of oil equivalent) | | Energy imports as a percentage of merchandise exports | |
| | | Energy production | | Energy consumption | | | | | |
		1965-80	1980-90	1965-80	1980-90	1965	1990	1965	1990
	Low-income economies	**10.0** w	**4.7** w	**8.2** w	**5.5** w	**124** w	**339** w	**7.0** w	**4.0** w
	China and India	**9.1** w	**5.8** w	**8.8** w	**5.7** w	**146** w	**440** w	**8.0** w	**3.0** w
	Other low-income	**12.2** w	**1.7** w	**5.7** w	**4.3** w	**76** w	**153** w	**7.0** w	**6.0** w
1	Mozambique	19.8	−43.2	2.2	2.4	81	85	13.0	2.0
2	Tanzania	7.3	3.2	3.7	2.0	37	38	. .	4.0
3	Ethiopia	7.5	5.5	4.1	3.5	10	20	8.0	25.0
4	Somalia	. .	. .	16.7	2.0	11	64	9.0	8.0
5	Nepal	18.4	10.7	6.2	9.2	6	25	. .	2.0
6	Chad	. .	. .	6.6	0.3	12	17	23.0	6.0
7	Bhutan	. .	. .	. .	. .	. .	13	. .	. .
8	Lao PDR	. .	0.5	4.2	1.8	24	39	. .	. .
9	Malawi	18.2	4.4	8.0	1.0	25	41	7.0	17.0
10	Bangladesh	. .	12.1	. .	7.9	. .	57		4.0
11	Burundi	. .	7.2	6.0	7.3	5	21	11.0	1.0
12	Zaire	9.4	3.1	3.6	1.7	75	71	6.0	4.0
13	Uganda	−0.5	3.3	−0.5	4.7	36	27	1.0	0.0
14	Madagascar	3.9	7.4	3.5	1.8	34	40	8.0	2.0
15	Sierra Leone	. .	. .	0.8	−0.1	109	77	11.0	4.0
16	Mali	38.6	6.6	7.0	2.1	14	24	16.0	2.0
17	Nigeria	17.3	0.2	12.9	4.8	34	138	7.0	4.0
18	Niger	. .	11.3	12.5	2.3	8	40	9.0	2.0
19	Rwanda	8.8	4.4	15.2	3.1	8	41	10.0	2.0
20	Burkina Faso	. .	. .	10.5	1.1	7	17	11.0	2.0
21	India	5.6	7.0	5.8	5.9	100	231	8.0	24.0
22	Benin	. .	8.1	9.9	3.8	21	46	14.0	6.0
23	China	10.0	5.5	9.8	5.6	178	598	. .	3.0
24	Haiti	. .	5.9	8.4	2.0	23	53	. .	2.0
25	Kenya	13.1	6.8	4.5	1.1	110	100	20.0	4.0
26	Pakistan	6.5	6.5	3.5	6.5	135	233	7.0	21.0
27	Ghana	17.7	−5.1	7.8	−4.1	76	68	6.0	4.0
28	Central African Rep.	6.7	2.6	2.2	3.5	22	30	7.0	2.0
29	Togo	2.9	. .	10.7	0.7	27	51	6.0	12.0
30	Zambia	25.7	1.7	4.0	1.1	464	379	. .	. .
31	Guinea	16.5	4.0	2.3	1.5	64	73	. .	4.0
32	Sri Lanka	10.4	8.7	2.2	5.1	106	179	6.0	5.0
33	Mauritania	. .	. .	9.5	0.2	48	114	2.0	18.0
34	Lesotho	. .	. .	. .	. .	0	0	a	a
35	Indonesia	9.9	1.0	8.4	4.1	91	272	3.0	6.0
36	Honduras	14.0	4.7	7.6	2.1	111	198	5.0	3.0
37	Egypt, Arab Rep.	10.7	4.8	6.2	5.0	313	598	11.0	10.0
38	Afghanistan	15.7	2.4	6.6	8.3	30	90	8.0	1.0
39	Cambodia	. .	4.9	7.6	2.5	19	59	. .	. .
40	Liberia	14.6	1.8	7.9	−4.1	179	169	6.0	2.0
41	Myanmar	8.4	4.4	4.9	4.8	39	82	4.0	4.0
42	Sudan	17.8	2.1	2.0	0.7	67	58	5.0	3.0
43	Viet Nam	5.3	2.5	−2.6	2.6	97	100	. .	1.0
	Middle-income economies	**5.1** w	**1.9** w	**6.1** w	**3.6** w	**712** w	**1,357** w	**8.0** w	**14.0** w
	Lower-middle-income	**4.9** w	**4.7** w	**6.0** w	**3.6** w	**579** w	**1,025** w	**7.0** w	**23.0** w
44	Bolivia	9.5	0.5	7.7	−0.4	156	257	1.0	2.0
45	Zimbabwe	−0.7	3.8	5.2	1.2	441	525	. .	0.0
46	Senegal	. .	. .	−1.2	−0.5	342	156	8.0	10.0
47	Philippines	9.0	7.5	5.8	2.3	158	215	12.0	17.0
48	Côte d'Ivoire	11.1	−0.1	8.6	2.7	101	173	5.0	2.0
49	Dominican Rep.	10.9	4.4	11.5	2.4	127	336	7.0	13.0
50	Papua New Guinea	13.7	5.9	13.0	2.4	56	233	7.0	. .
51	Guatemala	12.5	4.9	6.8	0.6	150	171	9.0	6.0
52	Morocco	2.5	1.1	7.9	2.9	124	247	5.0	25.0
53	Cameroon	13.0	11.9	6.3	4.5	67	147	6.0	2.0
54	Ecuador	35.0	2.7	11.9	4.4	162	678	11.0	3.0
55	Syrian Arab Rep.	56.3	6.8	12.4	4.0	212	913	13.0	3.0
56	Congo	41.1	7.5	7.8	3.4	90	213	8.0	0.0
57	El Salvador	9.0	3.8	7.0	2.3	140	233	6.0	13.0
58	Paraguay	. .	13.5	9.7	5.1	84	232	14.0	26.0
59	Peru	6.6	−1.5	5.0	1.5	395	509	3.0	9.0
60	Jordan	. .	. .	9.3	5.8	393	994	42.0	49.0
61	Colombia	1.0	11.2	6.0	3.3	412	811	1.0	4.0
62	Thailand	9.0	26.2	10.1	7.2	82	352	11.0	10.0
63	Tunisia	20.4	0.1	8.5	4.6	170	520	12.0	14.0
64	Jamaica	−0.9	4.4	6.1	−1.5	703	931	12.0	24.0
65	Turkey	4.3	8.5	8.5	6.9	257	857	12.0	28.0
66	Romania	4.3	0.5	6.6	1.3	1,536	3,623	. .	. .

Note: For data comparability and coverage, see the technical notes. Figures in italics are for years other than those specified.

| | | Average annual growth rate (percent) | | | | Energy consumption per capita (kilograms of oil equivalent) | | Energy imports as a percentage of merchandise exports | |
| | | Energy production | | Energy consumption | | | | | |
		1965–80	1980–90	1965–80	1980–90	1965	1990	1965	1990
67	Poland	4.0	1.1	4.8	1.2	2,027	3,416	. .	. .
68	Panama	6.9	10.3	−1.2	0.0	3,065	1,694	61.0	54.0
69	Costa Rica	8.2	6.6	8.8	3.8	267	622	8.0	5.0
70	Chile	1.8	3.1	3.0	2.9	652	887	5.0	9.0
71	Botswana	8.8	2.6	9.5	3.1	191	425	a	a
72	Algeria	5.3	5.9	11.9	17.8	226	1,956	0.0	2.0
73	Bulgaria	1.3	3.1	6.1	1.7	1,788	4,945	. .	. .
74	Mauritius	2.1	8.5	7.2	3.5	160	394	6.0	1.0
75	Malaysia	36.9	14.4	6.7	7.8	313	974	11.0	4.0
76	Argentina	4.5	3.3	4.3	3.5	975	1,801	8.0	5.0
77	Iran, Islamic Rep.	3.6	5.8	8.9	4.5	524	1,026	0.0	3.0
78	Albania	9.4	1.7	7.1	3.1	420	1,152	. .	. .
79	Angola	19.9	12.5	5.3	2.5	114	203	2.0	1.0
80	Lebanon	2.0	−1.5	2.0	4.1	713	968	50.0	7.0
81	Mongolia	10.3	3.0	9.6	3.1	461	1,277	. .	. .
82	Namibia	. .	. .	. .	. .	. .	. .	a	a
83	Nicaragua	2.6	2.6	6.5	2.9	172	261	6.0	6.0
84	Yemen, Rep.	. .	. .	21.0	23.8	6	234	. .	10.0
	Upper-middle-income	**5.1** *w*	**0.4** *w*	**6.1** *w*	**3.6** *w*	**884** *w*	**1,818** *w*	**8.0** *w*	**12.0** *w*
85	Mexico	9.7	1.3	7.9	1.2	605	1,300	4.0	4.0
86	South Africa	5.1	4.3	4.3	3.1	1,744	2,447	10.0[a]	1.0[a]
87	Venezuela	−3.1	0.2	4.6	2.1	2,319	2,582	0.0	2.0
88	Uruguay	4.7	7.9	1.3	0.5	765	821	13.0	12.0
89	Brazil	8.6	7.9	9.9	4.9	286	915	14.0	14.0
90	Hungary	0.8	1.1	3.8	1.4	1,825	3,211	12.0	11.0
91	Yugoslavia	3.5	3.5	6.0	3.8	898	2,409	7.0	21.0
92	Czechoslovakia	1.0	0.5	3.2	0.8	3,374	5,081	. .	. .
93	Gabon	13.7	3.6	14.7	2.5	153	1,158	3.0	0.0
94	Trinidad and Tobago	3.8	−3.3	3.6	1.4	4,492	5,940	59.0	5.0
95	Portugal	3.6	3.1	6.5	2.8	506	1,507	13.0	16.0
96	Korea, Rep.	4.1	10.4	12.1	8.1	238	1,898	18.0	12.0
97	Greece	10.5	6.4	8.5	2.7	615	2,092	29.0	14.0
98	Saudi Arabia	11.5	−4.2	7.2	9.3	1,759	5,033	0.0	0.0
99	Iraq	6.2	7.5	7.4	5.3	399	774	0.0	0.0
100	Libya	0.6	−1.7	18.2	7.1	222	3,399	2.0	2.0
101	Oman	16.0	8.9	30.5	10.7	14	2,648	. .	1.0
	Low- and middle-income	**6.2** *w*	**2.8** *w*	**6.8** *w*	**4.3** *w*	**277** *w*	**605** *w*	**8.0** *w*	**10.0** *w*
	Sub-Saharan Africa	**15.5** *w*	**2.8** *w*	**5.3** *w*	**2.6** *w*	**74** *w*	**103** *w*	**7.0** *w*	**28.0** *w*
	East Asia & Pacific	**10.0** *w*	**5.4** *w*	**9.4** *w*	**5.7** *w*	**164** *w*	**553** *w*	**10.0** *w*	**8.0** *w*
	South Asia	**5.8** *w*	**7.0** *w*	**5.7** *w*	**6.0** *w*	**90** *w*	**205** *w*	**7.0** *w*	. .
	Europe	**3.3** *w*	**1.7** *w*	**5.2** *w*	**2.0** *w*	**1,372** *w*	**2,677** *w*	**12.0** *w*	**19.0** *w*
	Middle East & N. Africa	**7.1** *w*	**0.6** *w*	**8.4** *w*	**7.8** *w*	**355** *w*	**1,102** *w*	**3.0** *w*	**20.0** *w*
	Latin America & Caribbean	**1.9** *w*	**2.5** *w*	**6.2** *w*	**2.7** *w*	**579** *w*	**1,057** *w*	**8.0** *w*	**5.0** *w*
	Other economies	**4.9** *w*	**2.9** *w*	**4.6** *w*	**2.8** *w*	**2,470** *w*	**4,828** *w*	. .	. .
	Severely indebted	**2.8** *w*	**2.5** *w*	**6.5** *w*	**3.3** *w*	**714** *w*	**1,368** *w*	**5.0** *w*	**6.0** *w*
	High-income economies	**2.3** *w*	**1.7** *w*	**3.1** *w*	**1.4** *w*	**3,566** *w*	**5,158** *w*	**11.0** *w*	**10.0** *w*
	OECD members	**2.2** *w*	**1.8** *w*	**3.0** *w*	**1.5** *w*	**3,649** *w*	**5,179** *w*	**11.0** *w*	**10.0** *w*
	†Other	**3.2** *w*	**1.6** *w*	**7.0** *w*	**−0.4** *w*	**1,208** *w*	**4,292** *w*	**7.0** *w*	**10.0** *w*
102	Ireland	0.1	2.7	3.9	0.5	1,504	2,653	14.0	5.0
103	†Israel	−15.2	−8.9	4.4	2.3	1,574	2,050	13.0	10.0
104	Spain	3.6	2.8	6.5	1.5	901	2,201	31.0	19.0
105	†Singapore	. .	. .	5.7	5.8	2,214	5,685	17.0	15.0
106	†Hong Kong	. .	. .	7.5	3.9	584	1,717	6.0	6.0
107	New Zealand	4.7	6.4	3.6	5.4	2,622	4,971	7.0	6.0
108	Belgium	. .	. .	. .	. .	. .	2,807	. .	. .
109	United Kingdom	3.6	0.7	0.9	0.8	3,483	3,646	13.0	7.0
110	Italy	1.3	0.8	3.7	0.9	1,564	2,754	16.0	13.0
111	Australia	10.5	6.0	5.0	2.2	3,287	5,041	10.0	6.0
112	Netherlands	15.4	−3.5	5.0	1.3	3,134	5,123	12.0	10.0
113	Austria	0.8	−0.2	4.0	1.5	2,060	3,503	10.0	7.0
114	France	−0.9	6.9	3.7	1.1	2,468	3,845	16.0	10.0
115	†United Arab Emirates	14.7	4.0	36.6	13.9	126	10,874	. .	1.0
116	Canada	5.7	3.5	4.5	2.1	6,007	10,009	7.0	5.0
117	United States	1.1	0.8	2.3	1.5	6,535	7,822	8.0	16.0
118	Denmark	2.6	38.2	2.3	−0.1	2,911	3,618	13.0	7.0
119	Germany[b]	−0.1	0.0	3.0	0.3	2,478	3,491	8.0	6.0
120	Norway	12.4	7.6	4.1	1.9	4,650	9,083	11.0	3.0
121	Sweden	4.9	4.5	2.5	1.7	4,162	6,347	12.0	7.0
122	Japan	−0.4	4.2	6.1	2.1	1,474	3,563	19.0	16.0
123	Finland	3.8	4.8	5.1	3.0	2,233	5,650	11.0	10.0
124	Switzerland	3.7	1.1	3.1	1.5	2,501	3,902	8.0	4.0
125	†Kuwait	−1.6	1.6	−0.1	5.0	16,781	6,414	0.0	0.0
	World	**4.1** *w*	**2.4** *w*	**4.1** *w*	**2.5** *w*	**1,114** *w*	**1,567** *w*	**10.0** *w*	**10.0** *w*
	Fuel exporters, excl. former USSR	**6.0** *w*	**0.7** *w*	**7.9** *w*	**7.1** *w*	**439** *w*	**1,171** *w*	**3.0** *w*	**5.0** *w*

a. Figures for the South African Customs Union comprising South Africa, Namibia, Lesotho, Botswana, and Swaziland are included in South African data; trade among the component territories is excluded.   b. Data refer to Federal Republic of Germany before unification.

Table 6. Structure of manufacturing

| | | Value added in manufacturing (millions of current dollars) | | Distribution of manufacturing value added (percent; current prices) | | | | | | | | | |
| | | | | Food, beverages, and tobacco | | Textiles and clothing | | Machinery and transport equipment | | Chemicals | | Other[a] | |
		1970	1989	1970	1989	1970	1989	1970	1989	1970	1989	1970	1989
	Low-income economies	**43,345** *t*	**243,089** *t*										
	China and India	**35,483** *t*	**190,090** *t*										
	Other low-income	**7,264** *t*	..										
1	Mozambique	..	..	51	..	13	..	5	..	3	..	28	..
2	Tanzania	118	212	36	..	28	..	5	..	4	..	26	..
3	Ethiopia	149	594	46	48	31	19	0	2	2	4	21	28
4	Somalia	27	47	88	..	6	..	0	..	1	..	6	..
5	Nepal	32	151	..	35	..	25	..	2	..	8	..	30
6	Chad[b]	51	178	..	..	..	..	..	..	..	..	..	..
7	Bhutan	..	19	..	..	..	..	..	..	..	..	..	..
8	Lao PDR[b]	..	..	..	..	..	..	..	..	..	..	..	..
9	Malawi	..	182	51	..	17	..	3	..	10	..	20	..
10	Bangladesh[b]	527	1,730	30	23	47	36	3	5	11	18	10	18
11	Burundi	16	102	*53*	..	*25*	..	*0*	..	*6*	..	*16*	..
12	Zaire[b]	..	986	*38*	..	*16*	..	*7*	..	*10*	..	*29*	..
13	Uganda	158	123	*40*	..	*20*	..	*2*	..	*4*	..	*34*	..
14	Madagascar[b]	..	..	36	..	28	..	6	..	7	..	23	..
15	Sierra Leone	22	60	..	..	..	..	..	..	..	..	..	..
16	Mali[b]	25	153	36	..	40	..	4	..	5	..	14	..
17	Nigeria	426	2,365	36	..	26	..	1	..	6	..	31	..
18	Niger[b]	30	124	..	..	..	..	..	..	..	..	..	..
19	Rwanda[b]	8	320	86	..	0	..	3	..	2	..	8	..
20	Burkina Faso	65	360	69	..	9	..	2	..	1	..	19	..
21	India	7,928	44,445	13	11	21	12	20	26	14	17	32	33
22	Benin[b]	..	..	..	..	..	..	..	..	..	..	..	..
23	China[b]	27,555[c]	145,646[c]	..	*12*	..	*14*	..	*26*	..	*12*	..	*36*
24	Haiti[b]	..	..	..	..	..	..	..	..	..	..	..	..
25	Kenya	174	832	33	41	9	10	16	11	9	9	33	29
26	Pakistan	1,462	5,923	24	*30*	38	*19*	6	8	9	*16*	23	27
27	Ghana[b]	252	525	34	..	16	..	4	..	4	..	41	..
28	Central African Rep.	12	..	..	..	..	..	..	..	..	..	..	..
29	Togo[b]	25	114	..	..	..	..	..	..	..	..	..	..
30	Zambia[b]	181	1,588	49	40	9	13	5	8	10	11	27	28
31	Guinea[b]	..	108	..	..	..	..	..	..	..	..	..	..
32	Sri Lanka	369	969	26	*52*	19	20	10	*2*	11	*3*	33	23
33	Mauritania	10	..	..	..	..	..	..	..	..	..	..	..
34	Lesotho	3	*49*	..	..	..	..	..	..	..	..	..	..
35	Indonesia[b]	994	17,272	65	..	14	..	2	..	6	..	13	..
36	Honduras	91	461	58	49	10	7	1	3	4	5	28	36
37	Egypt, Arab Rep.	..	..	17	31	35	16	9	9	12	8	27	35
38	*Afghanistan*	..	..	..	..	..	..	..	..	..	..	..	..
39	*Cambodia*	..	..	..	..	..	..	..	..	..	..	..	..
40	Liberia	15	..	..	..	..	..	..	..	..	..	..	..
41	*Myanmar*	..	..	..	..	..	..	..	..	..	..	..	..
42	*Sudan*	140	..	39	..	34	..	3	..	5	..	19	..
43	*Viet Nam*	..	..	..	..	..	..	..	..	..	..	..	..
	Middle-income economies	**67,652** *t*	**573,015** *t*										
	Lower-middle-income	**28,385** *t*	..										
44	Bolivia[b]	135	585	33	37	34	8	1	1	6	6	26	47
45	Zimbabwe	293	1,384	24	31	16	16	9	10	11	11	40	32
46	Senegal[b]	141	609	51	..	19	..	2	..	6	..	22	..
47	Philippines[b]	1,665	10,728	39	41	8	8	8	9	13	10	32	32
48	Côte d'Ivoire	149	..	27	..	16	..	10	..	5	..	42	..
49	Dominican Rep.[b]	275	925	74	..	5	..	1	..	6	..	14	..
50	Papua New Guinea[b]	35	392	23	..	1	..	35	..	4	..	37	..
51	Guatemala[b]	..	..	42	43	*14*	9	4	*3*	*12*	16	27	28
52	Morocco[b]	641	3,932	..	..	..	..	..	..	..	..	..	..
53	Cameroon[b]	119	1,447	50	..	15	..	4	..	3	..	27	..
54	Ecuador[b]	305	2,298	43	33	14	13	3	7	8	9	32	39
55	Syrian Arab Rep.[b]	..	..	37	32	40	22	3	5	2	5	20	36
56	Congo[b]	..	173	65	..	4	..	1	..	8	..	22	..
57	El Salvador[b]	194	1,042	40	..	30	..	3	..	8	..	18	..
58	Paraguay[b]	99	933	56	..	16	..	1	..	5	..	21	..
59	Peru[b]	1,430	7,730	25	*28*	14	*14*	7	*11*	7	*9*	47	*38*
60	Jordan	..	443	21	*22*	14	*4*	7	*2*	6	*11*	52	*61*
61	Colombia	1,487	8,177	31	32	20	15	8	10	11	13	29	30
62	Thailand[b]	1,130	17,635	43	*29*	13	*18*	9	*13*	6	7	29	*33*
63	Tunisia	121	1,460	29	17	18	21	4	5	13	9	36	49
64	Jamaica[b]	221	783	46	..	7	..	11	..	5	..	30	..
65	Turkey	1,930	18,030	26	17	15	15	8	14	7	14	45	41
66	Romania	..	..	..	14	..	21	..	23	..	4	..	38

Note: For data comparability and coverage, see the technical notes.   Figures in italics are for years other than those specified.

		Value added in manufacturing (millions of current dollars)		Distribution of manufacturing value added (percent; current prices)									
				Food, beverages, and tobacco		Textiles and clothing		Machinery and transport equipment		Chemicals		Other[a]	
		1970	1989	1970	1989	1970	1989	1970	1989	1970	1989	1970	1989
67	Poland[b]	..	..	20	16	19	16	24	27	8	6	28	35
68	Panama[b]	127	352	41	54	9	6	1	2	5	8	44	30
69	Costa Rica[b]	203	1,065	48	45	12	8	6	7	7	9	28	31
70	Chile[b]	2,088	..	17	24	12	7	11	4	5	8	55	57
71	Botswana[b]	5	155	..	..	..	..	..	..	..	..	..	..
72	Algeria[b]	682	4,598	32	20	20	17	9	13	4	3	35	47
73	Bulgaria	..	..	..	..	..	..	..	..	..	..	..	..
74	Mauritius	26	417	75	23	6	51	5	3	3	5	12	18
75	Malaysia[b]	500	..	26	18	3	7	8	23	9	14	54	39
76	Argentina[b]	5,523	..	18	20	17	10	17	13	8	12	40	44
77	Iran, Islamic Rep.	1,501	10,209	30	23	20	19	18	12	6	7	26	37
78	Albania	..	..	..	..	..	..	..	..	..	..	..	..
79	Angola	..	308										
80	Lebanon[b]	..	..	27	..	19	..	1	..	3	..	49	..
81	Mongolia	..	..	..	..	..	..	..	..	..	..	..	..
82	Namibia	..	80	..	..	..	..			..	..	..	..
83	Nicaragua[b]	159	..	53	..	14	..	2	..	8	..	23	..
84	Yemen, Rep.[b]	..	601	20	..	50	..	..	..	1	..	28	..
	Upper-middle-income	**39,180** t	**382,108** t										
85	Mexico[b]	8,449	51,138	28	20	15	11	13	14	11	14	34	42
86	South Africa	3,892	19,937	15	13	13	8	17	18	10	11	45	49
87	Venezuela[b]	2,163	9,064	30	19	13	6	9	7	8	10	39	57
88	Uruguay	619	2,202	34	32	21	18	7	9	6	10	32	31
89	Brazil	10,421	120,845	16	12	13	12	22	24	10	12	39	40
90	Hungary[b]	..	8,724	12	10	13	9	28	29	8	13	39	40
91	Yugoslavia	..	..	10	16	15	19	23	24	7	8	45	31
92	Czechoslovakia[b]	..	..	9	9	12	11	34	34	6	7	39	38
93	Gabon[b]	22	279	37	..	7	..	6	..	6	..	44	..
94	Trinidad and Tobago	198	540	18	46	3	4	7	8	2	3	70	39
95	Portugal[b]	..	..	18	17	19	20	13	14	10	10	39	39
96	Korea, Rep.[b]	1,880	66,215	26	12	17	14	11	30	11	9	36	36
97	Greece	1,642	8,291	20	22	20	24	13	10	7	8	40	36
98	Saudi Arabia[b]	372	7,292	..	..	..	..	..	..	..	..	..	..
99	Iraq	325	..	26	..	14	..	7	..	3	..	50	..
100	Libya	81	..	64	..	5	..	0	..	12	..	20	..
101	Oman[b]	0	319	..	..	..	..	..	..	..	..	..	..
	Low- and middle-income	**112,550** t	**815,003** t										
	Sub-Saharan Africa	**3,013** t											
	East Asia & Pacific	**34,582** t	**274,680** t										
	South Asia	**10,545** t	**54,788** t										
	Europe	..	..										
	Middle East & N.Africa	**4,813** t	**38,858** t										
	Latin America & Caribbean	**35,817** t	**258,271** t										
	Other economies	..	..										
	Severely indebted	**35,199** t	**272,336** t										
	High-income economies	**635,108** t	..										
	OECD members	**627,996** t	..										
	†Other	..	..										
102	Ireland	786	..	31	28	19	4	13	30	7	15	30	24
103	†Israel[b]	..	..	15	16	14	8	23	28	7	10	41	38
104	Spain[b]	..	102,313	13	17	15	8	16	25	11	11	45	39
105	†Singapore[b]	379	8,463	12	5	5	4	28	53	4	11	51	28
106	†Hong Kong	1,013	11,034	4	6	41	38	16	22	2	2	36	32
107	New Zealand[b]	1,809	7,845	24	26	13	9	15	14	4	6	43	45
108	Belgium[b]	..	35,612	17	20	12	7	22	23	9	14	40	37
109	United Kingdom	35,489	..	13	12	9	5	31	32	10	12	37	38
110	Italy[b]	29,093	200,937	10	8	13	13	24	33	13	10	40	36
111	Australia[b]	9,551	44,505	16	18	9	7	24	20	7	8	43	47
112	Netherlands[b]	8,652	45,135	17	19	8	3	27	25	13	13	36	39
113	Austria[b]	4,873	33,748	17	15	12	7	19	26	6	7	45	44
114	France[b]	..	204,445	12	13	10	7	26	31	8	9	44	41
115	†United Arab Emirates	..	2,507	..	..	..	..	..	..	..	..	..	..
116	Canada	16,711	..	16	13	8	5	23	25	7	10	46	46
117	United States[b]	254,115	..	12	12	8	5	31	32	10	11	39	40
118	Denmark	2,929	16,741	20	22	8	5	24	22	8	11	40	40
119	Germany[b,d]	70,888	369,689	13	9	8	4	32	41	9	13	38	33
120	Norway	2,416	13,064	15	20	7	2	23	22	7	8	49	47
121	Sweden	..	39,815	10	9	6	2	30	34	5	8	49	46
122	Japan[b]	73,339	829,238	8	9	8	5	34	39	11	10	40	37
123	Finland	2,588	23,477	13	12	10	4	20	22	6	8	51	54
124	Switzerland[b]	..	..	10	..	7	..	31	..	9	..	42	..
125	†Kuwait[b]	120	2,032	5	..	4	..	1	..	4	..	86	..
	World	**848,690** t	..										
	Fuel exporters, excl. former USSR	**6,004** t	**41,523** t										

a. Includes unallocable data; see the technical notes.   b. Value added in manufacturing data are at purchasers values.   c. World Bank estimates.   d. Data refer to the Federal Republic of Germany before unification.

Table 7. Manufacturing earnings and output

		Earnings per employee Growth rate		Earnings per employee Index (1980=100)			Total earnings as a percentage of value added				Gross output per employee (1980=100)			
		1970-80	1980-89	1987	1988	1989	1970	1987	1988	1989	1970	1987	1988	1989
Low-income economies														
China and India														
Other low-income														
1	Mozambique	..	..	..	..	..	29	..	..	..	..	..	..	..
2	Tanzania	..	-12.7	..	..	..	42	..	..	..	122	..	..	..
3	Ethiopia	-4.6	0.1	106	102	94	24	20	20	19	61	115	115	116
4	Somalia	-5.1	..	..	..	..	28	..	..	..	..	..	..	..
5	Nepal	..	..	..	..	..	..	25	26	..	..	..	..	..
6	Chad	..	..	..	..	..	..	..	..	..	..	..	..	..
7	Bhutan	..	..	..	..	..	..	..	..	..	..	..	..	..
8	Lao PDR													
9	Malawi	..	-0.8	..	..	..	37	..	..	..	126	..	..	..
10	Bangladesh	-3.0	0.9	101	100	100	26	32	30	31	151	112	117	120
11	Burundi	-7.5	..	..	..	..	..	..	..	..	..	..	..	..
12	Zaire													
13	Uganda													
14	Madagascar	-0.8	-8.3	..	..	..	36	..	..	..	106	..	..	..
15	Sierra Leone													
16	Mali	..	..	..	..	..	46	..	..	..	..	..	..	..
17	Nigeria	-0.8	..	..	..	..	18	..	..	..	105	..	..	..
18	Niger	..	0.4	68	..	..	..	7	6	..	..	..	..	..
19	Rwanda	..	..	..	..	..	22	10	..	..	..	..	..	..
20	Burkina Faso	..	..	..	..	..	..	..	..	..	..	..	..	..
21	India	0.4	3.0	123	124	127	47	49	48	48	83	166	171	169
22	Benin													
23	China	..	4.2	..	..	..	..	..	..	..	..	..	..	..
24	Haiti	-3.3	4.6	153	157	..	..	..	..	..	..	..	..	..
25	Kenya	-3.4	0.1	102	104	104	50	44	44	44	42	186	193	203
26	Pakistan	3.4	6.1	152	155	..	21	21	21	..	51	157	164	..
27	Ghana	..	7.8	170	..	..	23	..	..	..	193	..	..	..
28	Central African Rep.	..	..	..	..	..	..	..	..	..	..	..	..	..
29	Togo													
30	Zambia	-3.2	6.5	170	172	150	34	27	27	27	109	117	128	93
31	Guinea													
32	Sri Lanka	..	2.1	106	106	..	..	17	17	..	70	130	137	..
33	Mauritania	..	..	..	..	..	..	..	..	..	..	..	..	..
34	Lesotho													
35	Indonesia	5.0	5.9	..	..	..	26	..	..	..	42	..	..	..
36	Honduras	..	1.5	..	..	..	..	41	40	38	..	..	..	..
37	Egypt, Arab Rep.	4.1	-2.1	99	94	90	54	52	37	35	89	194	205	223
38	*Afghanistan*	..	..	..	..	..	..	..	..	..	..	..	..	..
39	*Cambodia*	..	..	..	..	..	..	..	..	..	..	..	..	..
40	*Liberia*	..	1.7	..	..	..	..	..	..	..	..	..	..	..
41	*Myanmar*	..	..	..	..	..	..	..	..	..	..	..	..	..
42	*Sudan*	..	..	..	..	..	31	..	..	..	..	..	..	..
43	*Viet Nam*	..	..	..	..	..	..	..	..	..	..	..	..	..
Middle-income economies														
Lower-middle-income														
44	Bolivia	0.0	-4.8	64	64	69	43	26	27	27	65	44	41	59
45	Zimbabwe	1.6	0.0	101	106	110	43	38	37	37	98	134	140	139
46	Senegal	-4.9	..	..	..	..	..	44	..	..	..	..	..	..
47	Philippines	-3.7	6.4	145	168	182	21	26	26	25	104	110	123	139
48	Côte d'Ivoire	-0.9	..	..	..	..	27	..	..	..	52	..	..	..
49	Dominican Rep.	-1.1	-4.4	..	..	..	35	..	..	..	63	..	..	..
50	Papua New Guinea	2.9	-1.9	..	..	..	40	..	..	..	..	..	..	..
51	Guatemala	-3.2	-1.9	89	89	100	..	19	19	20	..	..	..	..
52	Morocco	..	-3.6	80	..	..	..	..	..	..	..	95	87	..
53	Cameroon	3.2	..	..	..	..	30	..	..	..	80	..	..	..
54	Ecuador	3.3	-0.2	98	95	108	27	38	33	36	83	113	114	103
55	Syrian Arab Rep.	2.6	-5.6	70	64	66	33	32	27	21	70	217	277	336
56	Congo	..	..	..	..	..	34	..	..	..	..	..	..	..
57	El Salvador	2.4	-9.4	..	..	..	28	..	..	..	71	..	..	..
58	Paraguay													
59	Peru	..	-3.0	95	..	..	..	18	..	..	82	70	..	..
60	Jordan	..	-1.0	99	101	..	37	25	23	..	..	..	..	..
61	Colombia	-0.2	1.7	116	114	114	25	17	15	15	86	146	148	154
62	Thailand	1.0	6.5	..	..	..	25	24	24	24	68	135	..	..
63	Tunisia	4.2	..	..	..	..	44	..	..	..	95	..	..	..
64	Jamaica	-0.2	-0.8	104	101	..	43	..	..	..	99	81	78	..
65	Turkey	6.1	-3.1	86	80	82	26	17	15	15	108	169	167	184
66	Romania	..	..	..	..	..	..	..	..	..	..	..	..	..

Note: For data comparability and coverage, see the technical notes.   Figures in italics are for years other than those specified.

		Earnings per employee					Total earnings as a percentage of value added				Gross output per employee (1980=100)			
		Growth rate		Index (1980=100)										
		1970-80	1980-89	1987	1988	1989	1970	1987	1988	1989	1970	1987	1988	1989
67	Poland	..	..	..	..	..	24	22	23	..	67	88	81	79
68	Panama	0.2	2.1	124	123	125	32	32	37	38				
69	Costa Rica	..	..	..	..	..	41	33	31	..	..	..	..	..
70	Chile	8.1	-1.0	99	105	111	19	17	17	17	60	..	..	..
71	Botswana	2.6	-5.7	..	..	..	..	..	..	..	..	..	..	..
72	Algeria	-1.0	..	..	..	..	45	..	..	..	120	..	..	..
73	Bulgaria	..	..	..	..	..	..	..	..	..	..	..	..	..
74	Mauritius	1.8	-0.6	93	98	97	34	43	45	45	139	69	69	71
75	Malaysia	2.0	3.2	10	126	132	29	29	27	28	96	..	..	..
76	Argentina	-2.1	-0.8	99	94	75	28	22	20	16	78	60	56	54
77	Iran, Islamic Rep.	..	-8.2	47	..	..	25	47	..	..	84	81	..	..
78	Albania	..	..	..	..	..	..	..	..	..	..	..	..	..
79	Angola	..	..	..	..	..	..	..	..	..	..	..	..	..
80	Lebanon	..	..	..	..	..	..	..	..	..	..	..	..	..
81	Mongolia	..	..	..	..	..	..	..	..	..	..	..	..	..
82	Namibia	..	..	..	..	..	..	..	..	..	..	..	..	..
83	Nicaragua	..	-10.0	..	..	..	16	..	..	..	210	..	..	..
84	Yemen, Rep.	..	..	..	..	..	..	..	..	..	..	..	..	..
	Upper-middle-income													
85	Mexico	1.2	-3.9	74	73	76	44	20	20	20	77	112	113	128
86	South Africa	2.7	0.0	101	100	104	46	49	49	48	..	..	..	..
87	Venezuela	3.8	-2.9	102	98	77	31	25	28	21	118	132	139	121
88	Uruguay	..	0.8	116	112	111	..	26	26	26	..	110	109	110
89	Brazil	4.0	7.1	166	161	164	22	21	20	21	71	119	123	125
90	Hungary	3.6	2.6	112	125	127	28	33	39	36	41	112	105	103
91	Yugoslavia	1.3	-0.7	93	88	102	39	30	26	26	59	89	97	75
92	Czechoslovakia	..	..	..	..	..	49	41	40	39	..	..	..	..
93	Gabon	..	..	..	..	..	..	..	..	..	..	..	..	..
94	Trinidad and Tobago	..	-0.7	..	..	..	..	72	70	..	..	..	..	..
95	Portugal	2.5	0.3	100	102	103	34	36	36	36	..	..	..	..
96	Korea, Rep.	10.0	6.3	145	161	163	25	27	28	28	40	166	185	187
97	Greece	4.9	-0.5	95	98	100	32	39	39	39	56	104	108	110
98	Saudi Arabia	..	..	..	..	..	..	..	..	..	..	..	..	..
99	Iraq	..	..	..	..	..	36	25	..	..	..	..	..	..
100	Libya	..	..	..	..	..	37	..	..	..	45	..	..	..
101	Oman	..	..	..	..	..	..	..	..	..	..	..	..	..

Low- and middle-income
   Sub-Saharan Africa
   East Asia & Pacific
   South Asia
   Europe
   Middle East & N.Africa
   Latin America & Caribbean
Other economies

Severely indebted

High-income economies
   OECD members
   †Other

		1970-80	1980-89	1987	1988	1989	1970	1987	1988	1989	1970	1987	1988	1989
102	Ireland	4.1	1.8	108	111	..	49	31	29	..	..	..	..	..
103	†Israel	8.8	-3.4	93	95	73	36	63	62	38	..	..	..	..
104	Spain	4.4	0.8	101	106	110	52	37	38	38	..	112	..	..
105	†Singapore	3.0	5.0	146	148	164	36	29	28	30	73	121	122	130
106	†Hong Kong	6.4	4.4	135	137	137	..	57	56	56	..	..	..	..
107	New Zealand	1.1	-0.5	95	94	96	62	58	55	57	..	136	140	..
108	Belgium	4.6	-0.1	99	104	..	46	46	46	..	..	122	130	..
109	United Kingdom	1.7	2.8	119	123	125	52	41	40	40	93	135	..	..
110	Italy	4.1	1.1	103	109	112	41	41	41	41	50	130	139	145
111	Australia	2.9	0.0	103	103	101	53	47	47	45	..	120	121	121
112	Netherlands	2.5	0.8	104	106	106	52	47	47	46	68	107	110	..
113	Austria	3.4	1.9	113	114	120	47	56	54	54	65	114	117	124
114	France	..	2.0	112	117	121	..	64	63	63	72	109	116	122
115	†United Arab Emirates	..	..	..	..	..	..	..	..	..	..	..	..	..
116	Canada	1.8	0.1	101	101	101	53	44	43	43	69	112	..	..
117	United States	0.1	0.9	107	107	106	47	37	36	35	63	125	..	..
118	Denmark	2.5	0.6	103	105	104	56	53	52	51	64	98	103	108
119	Germany[a]	3.5	1.8	110	113	114	46	43	42	60	60	103	107	113
120	Norway	2.6	1.6	109	110	110	50	59	56	54	74	116	118	127
121	Sweden	0.4	0.9	102	103	107	52	35	34	34	..	119	125	130
122	Japan	3.1	2.0	113	117	120	32	35	34	33	48	110	120	129
123	Finland	2.6	2.7	118	122	126	47	46	44	43	73	127	132	142
124	Switzerland	..	..	..	..	..	..	..	..	..	..	..	..	..
125	†Kuwait	..	3.8	..	..	..	12	..	..	..	..	..	..	..

World
   Fuel exporters, excl. former USSR

a. Data refer to the Federal Republic of Germany before unification.

Table 8. Growth of consumption and investment

		Average annual growth rate (percent)					
		General government consumption		Private consumption, etc.		Gross domestic investment	
		1965–80	1980–90	1965–80	1980–90	1965–80	1980–90
	Low-income economies	**5.8** w	**6.4** w	**4.2** w	**4.6** w	**7.6** w	**7.4** w
	China and India	**5.3** w	**8.5** w	**4.2** w	**6.0** w	**7.0** w	**10.1** w
	Other low-income	**6.5** w	**3.3** w	**4.3** w	**2.5** w	**8.8** w	**1.3** w
1	Mozambique	. .	–0.9	. .	0.8	. .	1.8
2	Tanzania	a	8.4	4.5	3.3	6.2	0.3
3	Ethiopia	6.4	. .	3.0	. .	–0.1	. .
4	Somalia	12.7	7.0	2.7	1.4	12.1	–2.6
5	Nepal	. .	. .	. .	. .	. .	. .
6	Chad	. .	. .	. .	. .	. .	. .
7	Bhutan	. .	. .	. .	. .	. .	. .
8	Lao PDR	. .	. .	. .	. .	. .	. .
9	Malawi	5.7	6.2	3.5	2.2	9.0	–2.4
10	Bangladesh	a	a	2.0	3.7	0.0	–0.6
11	Burundi	7.3	4.4	7.6	4.0	9.0	3.2
12	Zaire	0.7	0.3	1.4	2.8	6.6	–1.7
13	Uganda	a	. .	1.4	. .	–5.7	. .
14	Madagascar	2.0	0.9	1.2	–0.9	1.5	4.8
15	Sierra Leone	a	–0.1	4.1	–0.3	–1.0	–1.0
16	Mali	1.9	2.8	5.3	2.7	1.8	9.8
17	Nigeria	13.9	–3.6	6.2	–3.3	14.7	–10.2
18	Niger	2.9	1.8	–1.4	–0.9	6.3	–6.0
19	Rwanda	6.2	6.3	4.6	0.1	9.0	1.7
20	Burkina Faso	8.7	7.1	2.8	2.4	8.5	10.3
21	India	4.7	7.8	3.1	5.3	4.3	5.0
22	Benin	0.7	0.1	2.7	0.2	10.4	–4.4
23	China	6.2	9.5	6.0	6.8	10.7	13.7
24	Haiti	1.9	–1.4	2.4	0.3	14.8	–3.4
25	Kenya	10.6	2.6	5.4	5.3	7.2	0.6
26	Pakistan	4.7	10.3	4.5	4.7	2.4	5.7
27	Ghana	3.8	–0.9	1.2	3.6	–1.3	7.7
28	Central African Rep.	–1.1	–3.6	4.8	2.3	–5.4	6.6
29	Togo	9.5	2.2	1.2	5.1	9.0	–1.9
30	Zambia	5.1	–4.1	–2.7	7.8	–3.6	–3.6
31	Guinea	. .	. .	. .	. .	. .	. .
32	Sri Lanka	1.1	8.3	4.1	4.0	11.5	0.4
33	Mauritania	10.0	–4.7	1.3	3.7	19.2	–5.4
34	Lesotho	12.4	2.2	9.9	1.7	17.8	5.6
35	Indonesia	11.4	4.6	5.2	4.5	16.1	7.1
36	Honduras	6.9	4.3	4.8	2.4	6.8	–0.7
37	Egypt, Arab Rep.	a	2.2	6.7	3.4	11.3	0.2
38	*Afghanistan*	. .	. .	. .	. .	. .	. .
39	*Cambodia*	. .	. .	. .	. .	. .	. .
40	*Liberia*	3.4	. .	3.2	. .	6.4	. .
41	*Myanmar*	. .	. .	. .	. .	. .	. .
42	*Sudan*	0.2	. .	4.4	. .	6.4	. .
43	*Viet Nam*	. .	. .	. .	. .	. .	. .
	Middle-income economies	**7.4** w	**2.5** w	**5.9** w	**2.6** w	**8.6** w	**–0.1** w
	Lower-middle-income	**9.3** w	**0.7** w	**4.7** w	**3.0** w	**8.1** w	**–0.4** w
44	Bolivia	8.2	–1.9	3.1	2.3	4.4	–10.7
45	Zimbabwe	10.6	8.9	5.1	2.6	0.9	–0.8
46	Senegal	2.9	3.2	2.0	2.3	3.9	2.8
47	Philippines	7.7	0.4	5.2	2.4	7.6	–2.5
48	Côte d'Ivoire	13.2	–3.7	6.6	2.5	10.7	–11.6
49	Dominican Rep.	0.2	1.7	8.3	0.8	13.5	4.3
50	Papua New Guinea	0.1	–0.3	5.3	1.0	1.4	–1.7
51	Guatemala	6.2	2.6	5.1	0.9	7.4	–2.1
52	Morocco	10.9	5.8	5.2	3.4	10.6	2.6
53	Cameroon	5.0	6.9	4.1	2.8	9.9	–3.5
54	Ecuador	12.2	–1.5	7.2	2.0	9.5	–2.9
55	Syrian Arab Rep.	. .	–2.2	. .	3.9	. .	–6.8
56	Congo	5.5	3.8	2.2	3.1	4.5	–11.7
57	El Salvador	7.0	2.7	4.2	0.5	6.6	2.2
58	Paraguay	5.1	0.9	6.6	1.9	13.9	–1.4
59	Peru	6.3	–2.3	4.9	0.9	0.3	–5.0
60	Jordan	. .	. .	. .	. .	. .	. .
61	Colombia	6.7	4.1	5.8	2.9	5.8	0.6
62	Thailand	9.5	4.3	6.4	6.5	8.0	8.7
63	Tunisia	7.2	3.8	8.9	3.7	4.6	–3.1
64	Jamaica	9.7	0.1	2.9	1.4	–3.1	4.1
65	Turkey	6.1	3.1	5.4	5.9	8.8	3.8
66	Romania	. .	. .	. .	. .	. .	–1.2

Note: For data comparability and coverage, see the technical notes.   Figures in italics are for years other than those specified.

		General government consumption		Private consumption, etc.		Gross domestic investment	
	Average annual growth rate (percent)						
		1965–80	1980–90	1965–80	1980–90	1965–80	1980–90
67	Poland		1.0		1.3		1.0
68	Panama	7.4	0.5	4.6	1.4	5.9	-12.8
69	Costa Rica	6.8	1.2	5.1	3.2	9.4	5.2
70	Chile	4.0	-0.1	0.9	1.7	0.5	4.3
71	Botswana	12.0	12.5	10.2	6.8	21.0	*0.4*
72	Algeria	8.6	3.7	4.4	2.5	15.9	-1.2
73	Bulgaria		3.5		3.5		1.8
74	Mauritius	7.1	3.1	6.1	5.7	8.3	10.0
75	Malaysia	8.5	2.7	6.2	4.2	10.4	2.9
76	Argentina	3.2	*-4.0*	2.9	*-0.3*	4.6	*-8.3*
77	Iran, Islamic Rep.	14.6	-4.3	5.4	5.5	11.5	-2.0
78	*Albania*	..	..	..	..	..	..
79	*Angola*	..	..	..	..	..	..
80	*Lebanon*	..	..	..	..	..	..
81	*Mongolia*	..	..	..	..	..	..
82	*Namibia*	..	*4.3*	..	*1.1*	..	-7.0
83	*Nicaragua*	6.1	1.9	2.2	-1.9	..	-4.5
84	*Yemen, Rep.*	..	..	..	..	..	..
Upper-middle-income		**5.9 w**	**4.1 w**	**7.1 w**	**2.3 w**	**9.0 w**	**0.2 w**
85	Mexico	8.5	1.9	5.9	1.1	8.5	-3.4
86	South Africa	5.7	3.4	4.0	1.7	4.7	-4.3
87	Venezuela	..	2.1	..	1.4	..	-5.4
88	Uruguay	3.2	1.9	0.9	1.0	8.2	-8.2
89	Brazil	6.8	8.8	8.7	1.7	11.3	0.2
90	Hungary	..	2.1	..	0.8	9.1	-0.8
91	Yugoslavia	3.6	0.3	10.1	-1.1	6.5	-3.3
92	Czechoslovakia	..	2.6	..	1.8	..	0.1
93	Gabon	10.7	*3.3*	7.5	-0.2	14.1	-7.5
94	Trinidad and Tobago	8.9	1.5	4.2	-8.0	12.1	-7.5
95	Portugal	8.1	2.5	6.6	*5.0*	4.6	-2.7
96	Korea, Rep.	7.7	6.0	8.0	8.0	15.9	12.5
97	Greece	6.6	2.8	5.1	3.4	5.3	-1.9
98	Saudi Arabia	..	..	..	..	..	..
99	*Iraq*	..	..	..	..	..	..
100	*Libya*	19.7	..	19.1	..	7.3	..
101	*Oman*	..	..	..	..	..	..
Low- and middle-income		**7.0 w**	**3.5 w**	**5.4 w**	**3.2 w**	**8.3 w**	**2.3 w**
Sub-Saharan Africa		**6.8 w**	**1.0 w**	**4.2 w**	**0.8 w**	**8.7 w**	**-4.3 w**
East Asia & Pacific		**7.5 w**	**6.2 w**	**6.2 w**	**6.1 w**	**11.1 w**	**10.6 w**
South Asia		**4.6 w**	**8.5 w**	**3.1 w**	**5.1 w**	**4.1 w**	**4.6 w**
Europe		..	**1.8 w**	..	**2.7 w**	..	**-0.1 w**
Middle East & N.Africa		..	..	..	..	**8.2 w**	**-2.0 w**
Latin America & Caribbean		**6.5 w**	**4.2 w**	**5.9 w**	**1.2 w**	..	..
Other economies		..	..	..	..	..	..
Severely indebted		**7.2 w**	**3.9 w**	**6.2 w**	**1.4 w**	**9.3 w**	**-1.8 w**
High-income economies		**2.9 w**	**2.5 w**	**4.0 w**	**3.1 w**	**3.3 w**	**4.2 w**
OECD members		**2.8 w**	**2.5 w**	**4.0 w**	**3.1 w**	**3.2 w**	**4.3 w**
†Other		..	**0.6 w**	..	**3.7 w**	..	**-0.7 w**
102	Ireland	6.6	-0.4	4.0	1.8	6.3	-0.5
103	†Israel	8.8	0.4	5.9	5.0	5.9	1.7
104	Spain	5.1	5.1	4.9	3.0	3.6	5.7
105	†Singapore	10.2	6.6	7.8	5.9	13.3	3.6
106	†Hong Kong	7.7	5.3	9.0	6.8	8.6	3.6
107	New Zealand	3.3	1.3	2.4	2.3	0.8	4.4
108	Belgium	4.4	0.4	4.3	1.7	3.0	3.3
109	United Kingdom	2.3	1.1	2.2	4.0	1.2	6.4
110	Italy	3.3	2.7	4.8	3.0	3.2	2.0
111	Australia	5.0	3.4	4.1	3.5	2.7	3.0
112	Netherlands	3.1	1.0	4.5	1.6	1.6	2.3
113	Austria	3.6	1.3	4.4	2.4	4.5	2.8
114	France	3.6	2.2	4.1	2.4	3.3	2.6
115	†United Arab Emirates	..	-3.9	..	-5.0	..	-8.7
116	Canada	4.8	2.3	5.0	3.6	4.7	4.9
117	United States	1.3	3.3	3.3	3.4	2.1	4.4
118	Denmark	4.8	0.9	2.4	1.9	1.2	3.7
119	Germany[b]	3.6	1.4	4.1	1.9	1.8	2.4
120	Norway	5.5	3.0	3.8	1.6	4.4	0.6
121	Sweden	4.0	1.5	2.5	2.1	0.9	4.2
122	Japan	5.3	2.4	6.2	3.7	6.9	5.7
123	Finland	5.3	3.6	3.8	4.6	2.9	3.3
124	Switzerland	2.7	2.9	2.3	1.7	0.8	4.9
125	†Kuwait	a	0.5	5.9	*0.7*	11.9	*-5.1*
World		**3.2 w**	**2.6 w**	**4.2 w**	**3.2 w**	**4.0 w**	**3.8 w**
Fuel exporters, excl. former USSR		..	..	..	..	..	..

a. General government consumption figures are not available separately; they are included in private consumption, etc. b. Data refer to the Federal Republic of Germany before unification.

Table 9. Structure of demand

		General government consumption		Private consumption, etc.		Gross domestic investment		Gross domestic savings		Exports of goods and nonfactor services		Resource balance	
		1965	1990	1965	1990	1965	1990	1965	1990	1965	1990	1965	1990
	Low-income economies	**9 w**	**11 w**	**74 w**	**61 w**	**19 w**	**31 w**	**18 w**	**28 w**	**8 w**	**18 w**	**−2 w**	**−1 w**
	China and India	**8 w**	**10 w**	**71 w**	**57 w**	**21 w**	**32 w**	**20 w**	**33 w**	**4 w**	**14 w**	**0 w**	**1 w**
	Other low-income	**11 w**	**13 w**	**76 w**	**67 w**	**15 w**	**27 w**	**13 w**	**20 w**	**16 w**	**24 w**	**−2 w**	**−5 w**
1	Mozambique	..	20	..	92	..	37	..	−12	..	16	..	−49
2	Tanzania	10	_10_	74	95	15	_25_	16	−6	26	_18_	1	_−31_
3	Ethiopia	11	26	77	68	13	_13_	12	6	12	13	−1	−7
4	Somalia	8	a	84	78	11	16	8	22	17	10	−3	6
5	Nepal	a	12	100	80	6	18	0	8	8	12	−6	−10
6	Chad	20	23	74	92	12	10	6	−15	19	25	−6	−26
7	Bhutan	..	20	..	58	..	36	..	22	..	29	..	_−14_
8	Lao PDR	..	12	..	89	..	12	..	−2	..	10	..	−14
9	Malawi	16	15	84	75	14	19	0	10	19	24	−14	−9
10	Bangladesh	9	9	83	89	11	12	8	2	10	8	−4	−10
11	Burundi	7	15	89	84	6	19	4	1	10	8	−2	−18
12	Zaire	10	..	75	..	17	11	16	..	26	25	−1	−6
13	Uganda	10	7	78	94	11	12	12	−1	26	7	1	−13
14	Madagascar	16	9	84	83	7	17	0	8	13	15	−7	−9
15	Sierra Leone	8	10	83	85	12	11	8	5	30	17	−3	−6
16	Mali	_10_	10	_84_	80	_18_	26	5	10	_12_	18	_−13_	−16
17	Nigeria	7	11	83	59	15	15	10	29	11	39	−5	15
18	Niger	6	..	90	..	8	9	3	..	9	16	−5	−7
19	Rwanda	14	18	81	78	10	12	5	4	12	9	−5	−9
20	Burkina Faso	5	13	90	83	10	20	4	5	6	11	−6	−15
21	India	9	12	76	68	17	23	15	20	4	8	−2	−3
22	Benin	11	11	87	87	11	12	3	2	13	20	−8	−10
23	China	8	8	68	49	24	39	25	43	4	18	1	4
24	Haiti	8	9	90	90	7	11	2	1	13	12	−5	−10
25	Kenya	15	18	70	63	14	24	15	18	31	25	1	−5
26	Pakistan	11	15	76	73	21	19	13	12	8	16	−8	−7
27	Ghana	14	8	77	82	18	15	8	11	17	..	−10	−4
28	Central African Rep.	22	14	67	88	21	11	11	−2	27	17	−11	−13
29	Togo	11	19	65	70	22	22	23	11	32	41	1	−11
30	Zambia	15	15	45	68	25	14	40	17	49	32	15	3
31	Guinea	..	8	..	71	..	20	..	21	..	30	..	1
32	Sri Lanka	13	9	74	76	12	22	13	15	38	30	1	−8
33	Mauritania	19	10	54	88	14	15	27	3	42	47	13	−12
34	Lesotho	18	24	109	118	11	71	−26	−41	16	14	−38	−112
35	Indonesia	5	9	87	54	8	36	8	37	5	26	0	1
36	Honduras	10	15	75	80	15	13	15	6	27	40	0	−7
37	Egypt, Arab Rep.	19	10	67	80	18	23	14	10	18	20	−4	−13
38	_Afghanistan_	..	..	..	..	11	..	1	..	11	..	−10	..
39	_Cambodia_	16	..	71	..	13	..	12	..	12	..	−1	..
40	_Liberia_	12	..	61	..	17	..	27	..	50	..	10	..
41	_Myanmar_	..	..	..	..	..	..	..	..	..	..	..	..
42	_Sudan_	12	..	79	..	10	..	9	..	15	..	−1	..
43	_Viet Nam_	..	..	..	..	..	..	..	..	..	..	..	..
	Middle-income economies	**11 w**	**14 w**	**67 w**	**62 w**	**21 w**	**23 w**	**22 w**	**24 w**	**17 w**		**0 w**	
	Lower-middle-income	**10 w**	**12 w**	**69 w**	**65 w**	**19 w**	**23 w**	**20 w**	**23 w**	**17 w**	**28 w**	**0 w**	**0 w**
44	Bolivia	9	15	74	77	22	11	17	8	21	21	−5	−3
45	Zimbabwe	12	26	65	53	15	21	23	21	..	32	8	0
46	Senegal	17	14	75	77	12	13	8	9	24	26	−4	−4
47	Philippines	9	9	70	75	21	22	21	16	17	28	0	−6
48	Côte d'Ivoire	11	18	61	68	22	10	29	14	37	37	7	4
49	Dominican Rep.	19	7	75	82	10	15	6	11	16	28	−4	−4
50	Papua New Guinea	34	24	64	66	22	25	2	10	18	37	−20	−15
51	Guatemala	7	7	82	85	13	12	10	8	17	21	−3	−4
52	Morocco	12	16	76	65	10	26	12	20	18	25	1	−6
53	Cameroon	13	12	75	70	13	17	12	19	24	21	−1	2
54	Ecuador	9	8	80	70	14	19	11	22	16	31	−3	3
55	Syrian Arab Rep.	14	14	76	72	10	14	10	14	17	27	0	−1
56	Congo	14	19	80	51	22	16	5	31	36	49	−17	15
57	El Salvador	9	11	79	88	15	12	12	1	27	16	−2	−11
58	Paraguay	7	6	79	70	15	22	14	23	15	34	−1	1
59	Peru	10	6	59	71	34	23	31	23	16	11	−3	0
60	Jordan	..	24	..	85	..	19	..	−9	..	65	..	−27
61	Colombia	8	10	75	64	16	19	17	25	11	20	1	6
62	Thailand	10	10	72	57	20	37	19	34	16	38	−1	−3
63	Tunisia	15	16	71	64	28	27	14	19	19	42	−13	−7
64	Jamaica	8	15	69	56	27	30	23	30	33	59	−4	0
65	Turkey	12	14	74	68	15	23	13	18	6	19	−1	−5
66	Romania	..	5	..	68	..	34	..	27	..	..	..	−7

Note: For data comparability and coverage, see the technical notes.   Figures in italics are for years other than those specified.

		Distribution of gross domestic product (percent)											
		General government consumption		Private consumption, etc.		Gross domestic investment		Gross domestic savings		Exports of goods and nonfactor services		Resource balance	
		1965	1990	1965	1990	1965	1990	1965	1990	1965	1990	1965	1990
67	Poland	..	7	..	54	..	31	..	39	..	26	..	8
68	Panama	11	22	73	62	18	16	16	16	36	38	-2	0
69	Costa Rica	13	18	78	60	20	29	9	22	23	34	-10	-8
70	Chile	11	10	73	67	15	20	16	23	14	37	1	3
71	Botswana	24	..	89	..	6	..	-13	..	32	..	-19	..
72	Algeria	15	18	66	44	22	33	19	38	22	25	-3	5
73	Bulgaria	..	18	..	54	..	29	..	28	..	40	..	-2
74	Mauritius	13	12	74	66	17	30	13	21	36	67	-4	-9
75	Malaysia	15	13	61	54	20	34	24	33	42	79	4	-1
76	Argentina	8	5	69	79	19	9	22	16	8	14	3	7
77	Iran, Islamic Rep.	13	11	63	69	17	21	24	20	20	15	6	-1
78	Albania	..	..	..	..	..	..	..	..	..	..	..	..
79	Angola	..	..	..	..	..	..	..	..	..	..	..	..
80	Lebanon	10	..	81	..	22	..	9	..	36	..	-13	..
81	Mongolia	..	24	..	73	..	30	..	3	..	23	..	-27
82	Namibia	..	..	74	73	21	20	18	-2	29	23	-3	-23
83	Nicaragua	8	29	..	66	..	15	..	8	..	23	..	-8
84	Yemen, Rep.	..	26	..	..	..	..	..	..	..	..	..	..
	Upper-middle-income	**11 w**	**16 w**	**64 w**	**61 w**	**23 w**	**24 w**	**25 w**	**23 w**	**19 w**	**..**	**0 w**	**..**
85	Mexico	6	11	75	70	20	20	19	19	8	16	-2	0
86	South Africa	11	19	63	56	27	19	26	25	27	26	-1	6
87	Venezuela	10	9	56	62	25	9	34	29	26	39	9	20
88	Uruguay	14	13	65	67	14	12	21	19	18	27	7	8
89	Brazil	11	16	67	61	20	22	22	23	8	7	2	2
90	Hungary	a	11	75	62	26	23	..	27	..	33	..	4
91	Yugoslavia	18	7	52	72	30	21	30	21	22	24	0	-1
92	Czechoslovakia	..	21	..	51	..	30	..	28	..	33	..	-2
93	Gabon	11	20	52	43	31	19	37	37	43	56	6	18
94	Trinidad and Tobago	12	16	67	52	26	17	21	33	65	46	-5	16
95	Portugal	12	13	68	66	25	32	20	21	27	35	-5	-10
96	Korea, Rep.	9	a	83	63	15	37	8	37	9	32	-7	-1
97	Greece	12	21	73	71	26	19	15	8	9	22	-11	-11
98	Saudi Arabia	18	..	34	..	14	..	48	..	60	..	34	..
99	Iraq	20	..	50	..	16	..	31	..	38	..	15	..
100	Libya	14	..	36	..	29	..	50	..	53	..	21	..
101	Oman	..	..	..	..	..	..	..	..	..	..	..	..
	Low- and middle-income	**10 w**	**13 w**	**70 w**	**63 w**	**20 w**	**26 w**	**20 w**	**24 w**	**13 w**	**24 w**	**-1 w**	**0 w**
	Sub-Saharan Africa	**11 w**	**15 w**	**77 w**	**68 w**	**15 w**	**16 w**	**13 w**	**16 w**	**22 w**	**29 w**	**-3 w**	**-1 w**
	East Asia & Pacific	**8 w**	**10 w**	**69 w**	**55 w**	**22 w**	**37 w**	**22 w**	**35 w**	**8 w**	**31 w**	**0 w**	**0 w**
	South Asia	**9 w**	**12 w**	**77 w**	**69 w**	**17 w**	**21 w**	**14 w**	**19 w**	**6 w**	**9 w**	**-3 w**	**-4 w**
	Europe	**..**	**14 w**	**..**	**65 w**	**..**	**25 w**	**..**	**21 w**	**..**	**29 w**	**..**	**-3 w**
	Middle East & N.Africa	**15 w**	**..**	**63 w**	**..**	**17 w**	**..**	**22 w**	**..**	**26 w**	**..**	**3 w**	**..**
	Latin America & Caribbean	**9 w**	**12 w**	**69 w**	**66 w**	**20 w**	**19 w**	**22 w**	**22 w**	**13 w**	**15 w**	**0 w**	**2 w**
	Other economies	**..**	**..**	**..**	**..**	**..**	**..**	**..**	**..**	**..**	**..**	**..**	**..**
	Severely indebted	**9 w**	**13 w**	**68 w**	**64 w**	**21 w**	**20 w**	**23 w**	**23 w**	**13 w**	**15 w**	**2 w**	**3 w**
	High-income economies	**15 w**	**17 w**	**61 w**	**61 w**	**23 w**	**22 w**	**24 w**	**22 w**	**12 w**	**20 w**	**0 w**	**0 w**
	OECD members	**15 w**	**17 w**	**61 w**	**61 w**	**23 w**	**22 w**	**24 w**	**22 w**	**12 w**	**19 w**	**0 w**	**0 w**
	†Other	**..**	**..**	**..**	**..**	**..**	**..**	**..**	**..**	**..**	**..**	**..**	**..**
102	Ireland	14	16	72	55	24	21	15	29	35	62	-9	8
103	†Israel	20	29	65	59	29	18	15	12	19	32	-13	-6
104	Spain	8	15	67	62	28	26	24	22	10	17	-3	-3
105	†Singapore	10	11	80	45	22	39	10	45	123	190	-12	6
106	†Hong Kong	7	8	64	59	36	28	29	33	71	137	-7	5
107	New Zealand	12	17	61	63	28	22	26	21	21	28	-2	-2
108	Belgium	13	14	64	62	23	21	23	24	43	74	0	3
109	United Kingdom	17	20	64	63	20	19	19	17	19	25	-1	-2
110	Italy	14	17	60	62	23	21	25	21	15	21	2	0
111	Australia	13	18	61	61	28	21	25	21	14	17	-2	0
112	Netherlands	15	15	59	59	27	21	26	26	43	57	-1	5
113	Austria	13	18	59	55	28	25	27	27	25	41	-1	1
114	France	14	18	59	60	26	22	27	22	13	23	1	0
115	†United Arab Emirates	..	..	..	..	..	..	..	..	..	..	..	..
116	Canada	14	20	60	59	26	21	26	21	19	25	0	0
117	United States	17	18	63	67	20	16	21	15	5	10	1	-1
118	Denmark	16	25	59	52	26	17	25	23	29	35	-2	5
119	Germany(b)	15	18	56	54	28	22	29	28	18	32	0	6
120	Norway	15	21	56	50	30	21	29	29	41	44	-1	7
121	Sweden	18	27	56	52	27	21	26	21	22	30	-1	0
122	Japan	8	9	59	57	32	33	33	34	11	11	1	1
123	Finland	14	21	60	53	28	27	27	26	20	23	-2	-1
124	Switzerland	10	13	60	57	30	29	30	30	29	37	-1	0
125	†Kuwait	13	..	26	..	16	..	60	..	68	..	45	..
	World	**14 w**	**16 w**	**63 w**	**62 w**	**23 w**	**23 w**	**23 w**	**23 w**	**11 w**	**20 w**	**0 w**	**0 w**
	Fuel exporters, excl. former USSR	**12 w**	**..**	**60 w**	**..**	**20 w**	**..**	**28 w**	**..**	**29 w**	**..**	**8 w**	**..**

a. General government consumption figures are not available separately; they are included in private consumption, etc. b. Data refer to the Federal Republic of Germany before unification.

Table 10. Structure of consumption

		Food		Clothing and footwear	Gross rents, fuel and power		Medical care	Education	Transport and communication		Other consumption	
		Total	Cereals and tubers		Total	Fuel and power			Total	Automobiles	Total	Other consumer durables
	Low-income economies											
	China and India											
	Other low-income											
1	Mozambique	..	..	..	..	..	..	..	..	..	..	..
2	Tanzania	64	32	10	8	3	3	3	2	0	10	3
3	Ethiopia	50	24	6	14	7	3	2	8	1	17	2
4	Somalia	..	..	..	..	..	..	..	..	..	..	..
5	Nepal	57	38	12	14	6	3	1	1	0	13	2
6	Chad	..	..	..	..	..	..	..	..	..	..	..
7	Bhutan	..	..	..	..	..	..	..	..	..	..	..
8	Lao PDR	..	..	..	..	..	..	..	..	..	..	..
9	Malawi	55	28	5	12	2	3	4	7	2	15	3
10	Bangladesh	59	36	8	17	7	2	1	3	0	10	3
11	Burundi	..	..	..	..	..	..	..	..	..	..	..
12	Zaire	55	15	10	11	3	3	1	6	0	14	3
13	Uganda	..	..	..	..	..	..	..	..	..	..	..
14	Madagascar	59	26	6	12	6	2	4	4	1	14	1
15	Sierra Leone	56	22	4	15	6	2	3	12	..	9	1
16	Mali	57	22	6	8	6	2	4	10	1	13	1
17	Nigeria	52	18	7	10	2	3	4	4	1	20	6
18	Niger	..	..	..	..	..	..	..	..	..	..	..
19	Rwanda	30	11	11	16	6	3	4	9	..	28	9
20	Burkina Faso	..	..	..	..	..	..	..	..	..	..	..
21	India	52	18	11	10	3	3	4	7	0	13	3
22	Benin	37	12	14	12	2	5	4	14	2	15	5
23	China	61[b]	..	13	8	3	1	1	1	..	15	..
24	Haiti	..	..	..	..	..	..	..	..	..	15	..
25	Kenya	39	16	7	12	2	3	9	8	1	22	6
26	Pakistan	54	17	9	15	6	3	3	1	0	15	5
27	Ghana	50	..	13	11	..	3	5[c]	3	..	15	..
28	Central African Rep.	..	..	..	..	..	..	..	..	..	..	..
29	Togo	..	..	..	..	..	..	..	..	..	..	..
30	Zambia	37	8	10	11	5	7	13	5	1	16	1
31	Guinea	..	..	..	..	..	..	..	..	..	..	..
32	Sri Lanka	43	18	7	6	3	2	3	15	1	25	5
33	Mauritania	..	..	..	..	..	..	..	..	..	..	..
34	Lesotho	..	..	..	..	..	..	..	..	..	..	..
35	Indonesia	48	21	7	13	7	2	4	4	0	22	5
36	Honduras	39	..	9	21	..	8	5[c]	3	..	15	..
37	Egypt, Arab Rep.	50	10	11	9	3	3	6	4	1	18	3
38	*Afghanistan*	..	..	..	..	..	..	..	..	..	..	..
39	*Cambodia*	..	..	..	..	..	..	..	..	..	..	..
40	*Liberia*	..	..	..	..	..	..	..	..	..	..	..
41	*Myanmar*	..	..	..	..	..	..	..	..	..	..	..
42	*Sudan*	*60*	..	*5*	*15*	*4*	*5*	*3*	*2*	..	*11*	..
43	*Viet Nam*	..	..	..	..	..	..	..	..	..	..	..
	Middle-income economies											
	Lower-middle-income											
44	Bolivia	*33*	..	9	*12*	*1*	5	7	*12*	..	22	..
45	Zimbabwe	40	9	11	13	5	4	7	6	1	20	3
46	Senegal	50	15	11	12	4	2	5	6	0	14	2
47	Philippines	51	20	4	19	5	2	4	4	2	16	2
48	Côte d'Ivoire	40	14	10	5	1	9	4	10	..	23	3
49	Dominican Rep.	46	13	3	15	5	8	3	4	0	21	8
50	Papua New Guinea	..	..	..	..	..	..	..	..	..	..	..
51	Guatemala	36	10	10	14	5	13	4	3	0	20	5
52	Morocco	40	12	11	9	2	4	6	8	1	22	5
53	Cameroon	24	8	7	17	3	11	9	12	1	21	3
54	Ecuador	30	..	10	7[d]	1[d]	5	6[c]	12[e]	..	30	..
55	Syrian Arab Rep.	..	..	..	..	..	..	..	..	..	..	..
56	Congo	42	19	6	11	4	3	1	17	1	20	4
57	El Salvador	33	12	9	7	2	8	5	10	1	28	7
58	Paraguay	30	6	12	21	4	2	3	10	1	22	3
59	Peru	35	8	7	15	3	4	6	10	0	24	7
60	Jordan	35	..	5	6	..	5	8	6	..	35	..
61	Colombia	29	..	6	12	2	7	6	13	..	27	..
62	Thailand	30	7	16	7	3	5	5	13	0	24	5
63	Tunisia	37	7	10	13	4	6	9	7	1	18	5
64	Jamaica	39	..	4	15	7	3[f]	..	17	..	22	..
65	Turkey	40	8	15	13	7	4	1	5	..	22	..
66	Romania	..	..	..	..	..	..	..	..	..	..	..

Note: For data comparability and coverage, see the technical notes. Figures in italics are for years other than those specified.

Percentage share of total household consumption[a]

		Food Total	Food Cereals and tubers	Clothing and footwear	Gross rents, fuel and power Total	Fuel and power	Medical care	Education	Transport and communication Total	Automobiles	Other consumption Total	Other consumer durables
67	Poland	29	..	9	7	2	6	7	8	2	34	9
68	Panama	38	7	3	11	3	8	9	7	0	24	6
69	Costa Rica	33	8	8	9	1	7	8	8	0	28	9
70	Chile	29	7	8	13	2	5	6	11	0	29	5
71	Botswana	35	13	8	15	5	4	9	8	2	22	7
72	Algeria	..	..	..	..	..	..	..	..	..	..	..
73	Bulgaria	..	..	..	..	..	..	..	..	..	..	..
74	Mauritius	24	7	5	19	3	5	7	11	1	29	4
75	Malaysia	23	..	4	9	..	5	7	19	..	33	..
76	Argentina	35	4	6	9	2	4	6	13	0	26	6
77	Iran, Islamic Rep.	37	10	9	23	2	6	5	6	1	14	5
78	Albania	..	..	..	..	..	..	..	..	..	..	..
79	Angola	..	..	..	..	..	..	..	..	..	..	..
80	Lebanon	..	..	..	..	..	..	..	..	..	..	..
81	Mongolia	..	..	..	..	..	..	..	..	..	..	..
82	Namibia	..	..	..	..	..	..	..	..	..	..	..
83	Nicaragua	..	..	..	..	..	..	..	..	..	..	..
84	Yemen, Rep.	..	..	..	..	..	..	..	..	..	..	..
Upper-middle-income												
85	Mexico	35[b]	..	10	8	..	5	5	12	..	25	..
86	South Africa	34	..	7	12	..	5[f]	..	17	..	26	..
87	Venezuela	23	..	7	10	..	8	5[c]	11	..	36	..
88	Uruguay	31	7	7	12	2	6	4	13	0	27	5
89	Brazil	35	9	10	11	2	6	5	8	1	27	8
90	Hungary	25	..	9	10	5	5	7	9	2	35	8
91	Yugoslavia	27	..	10	9	4	6	5	11	2	32	9
92	Czechoslovakia	..	..	..	..	..	..	..	..	..	..	..
93	Gabon	..	..	..	..	..	..	..	..	..	..	..
94	Trinidad and Tobago	..	..	..	..	..	..	..	..	..	..	..
95	Portugal	34	..	10	8	3	6	5	13	3	24	7
96	Korea, Rep.	35	14	6	11	5	5	9	9	..	25	5
97	Greece	30	..	8	12	3	6	5	13	2	26	5
98	Saudi Arabia	..	..	..	..	..	..	..	..	..	..	..
99	Iraq	..	..	..	..	..	..	..	..	..	..	..
100	Libya	..	..	..	..	..	..	..	..	..	..	..
101	Oman	..	..	..	..	..	..	..	..	..	..	..
Low- and middle-income												
Sub-Saharan Africa												
East Asia												
South Asia												
Europe												
Middle East and N. Africa												
Latin America & Caribbean												
Other economies												
Severely indebted												
High-income economies												
OECD members												
†Other												
102	Ireland	22	4	5	11	5	10	7	11	3	33	5
103	†Israel	21	..	5	20	2	9	12	10	..	23	..
104	Spain	24	3	7	16	3	7	5	13	3	28	6
105	†Singapore	19	..	8	11	..	7	12	13	..	30	..
106	†Hong Kong	12	1	9	15	2	6	5	9	1	44	15
107	New Zealand	12	2	6	14	2	9	6	19	6	34	9
108	Belgium	15	2	6	17	7	10	9	11	3	31	7
109	United Kingdom	12	2	6	17	4	8	6	14	4	36	7
110	Italy	19	2	8	14	4	10	7	11	3	31	7
111	Australia	13	2	5	21	2	10	8	13	4	31	7
112	Netherlands	13	2	6	18	6	11	8	10	3	33	8
113	Austria	16	2	9	17	5	10	8	15	3	26	7
114	France	16	2	6	17	5	13	7	13	3	29	7
115	†United Arab Emirates	..	..	..	..	..	..	..	..	..	..	..
116	Canada	11	2	6	21	4	5	12	14	5	32	8
117	United States	13	2	6	18	4	14	8	14	5	27	7
118	Denmark	13	2	5	19	5	8	9	13	5	33	7
119	Germany[g]	12	2	7	18	5	13	8	13	4	31	9
120	Norway	15	2	6	14	5	10	8	14	6	32	7
121	Sweden	13	2	5	19	4	11	8	11	2	32	7
122	Japan	16	4	6	17	3	10	8	9	1	34	6
123	Finland	16	3	4	15	4	9	8	14	4	34	6
124	Switzerland	17	..	4	17	6	15	..	9	..	38	..
125	†Kuwait	..	..	..	..	..	..	..	..	..	..	..
World												
Fuel exporters, excl. former USSR												

a. Data refer to either 1980 or 1985.   b. Includes beverages and tobacco.   c. Refers to government expenditure.   d. Excludes fuel.   e. Includes fuel.   f. Excludes government expenditure.   g. Data refer to the Federal Republic of Germany before unification.

Table 11. Central government expenditure

Percentage of total expenditure

		Defense		Education		Health		Housing, amenities; social security and welfare[a]		Economic services		Other [a]		Total expenditure as a percentage of GNP		Overall surplus/deficit as a percentage of GNP	
		1972	1990	1972	1990	1972	1990	1972	1990	1972	1990	1972	1990	1972	1990	1972	1990
Low-income economies																	
China and India																	
Other low-income																	
1	Mozambique	..	..	..	..	..	..	..	..	..	..	..	..	..	..	..	..
2	Tanzania	11.9	..	17.3	..	7.2	..	2.1	..	39.0	..	22.6	..	19.7	..	−5.0	..
3	Ethiopia	14.3	..	14.4	..	5.7	..	4.4	..	22.9	..	38.3	..	13.7	..	−1.4	..
4	Somalia[b]	23.3	..	5.5	..	7.2	..	1.9	..	21.6	..	40.5	..	13.5	..	0.6	..
5	Nepal	7.2	6.0	7.2	10.9	4.7	4.8	0.7	8.4	57.2	41.2	23.0	28.6	8.5	20.4	−1.2	−8.1
6	Chad	24.6	..	14.8	..	4.4	..	1.7	..	21.8	..	32.7	..	14.9	..	−2.7	..
7	Bhutan	..	0.0	..	11.6	..	5.3	..	4.7	..	56.6	..	21.9	..	43.9	..	−7.2
8	Lao PDR	..	..	..	..	..	..	..	..	..	..	..	..	..	..	..	..
9	Malawi[b]	3.1	5.4	15.8	8.8	5.5	7.4	5.8	3.2	33.1	35.0	36.7	40.2	22.1	29.2	−6.2	−1.9
10	Bangladesh[b]	5.1	10.1	14.8	11.2	5.0	4.8	9.8	8.0	39.3	34.4	25.9	31.5	9.2	15.0	−1.9	−0.4
11	Burundi	10.3	..	23.4	..	6.0	..	2.7	..	33.9	..	23.8	..	19.9	..	0.0	..
12	Zaire	11.1	6.7	15.1	1.4	2.4	0.7	2.1	1.5	13.2	25.0	56.2	64.7	14.1	13.0	−2.7	1.9
13	Uganda	23.1	..	15.3	..	5.3	..	7.3	..	12.4	..	36.6	..	21.8	..	−8.1	..
14	Madagascar[b]	3.6	..	9.1	..	4.2	..	9.9	..	40.5	..	32.7	..	16.7	..	−2.0	..
15	Sierra Leone[b]	3.6	5.3	15.5	10.4	5.3	3.6	2.7	2.3	24.6	9.0	48.3	69.4	23.9	11.1	−4.4	−1.4
16	Mali	..	8.0	..	9.0	..	2.1	..	3.1	..	5.3	..	72.4	..	28.9	..	−4.6
17	Nigeria[b]	40.2	..	4.5	..	3.6	..	0.8	..	19.6	..	31.4	..	9.1	..	−0.8	..
18	Niger	..	..	..	..	..	..	..	..	..	..	..	..	..	..	..	..
19	Rwanda	25.6	..	22.2	..	5.7	..	2.6	..	22.0	..	21.9	..	12.5	..	−2.7	..
20	Burkina Faso	11.5	..	20.6	..	8.2	..	6.6	..	15.5	..	37.6	..	8.4	..	0.3	..
21	India	26.2	17.0	2.3	2.5	1.5	1.6	3.2	6.9	19.9	20.8	46.9	51.2	10.5	18.2	−3.2	−7.3
22	Benin	..	..	..	..	..	..	..	..	..	..	..	..	..	..	..	..
23	China	..	..	..	..	..	..	..	..	..	..	..	..	..	..	..	..
24	Haiti	..	..	..	..	..	..	..	..	..	..	..	..	14.5	..	..	..
25	Kenya[b]	6.0	7.8	21.9	19.8	7.9	5.4	3.9	3.6	30.1	26.6	30.2	36.9	21.0	31.4	−3.9	−6.8
26	Pakistan	39.9	30.9	1.2	2.0	1.1	0.7	3.2	3.1	21.4	12.4	33.2	50.9	16.9	23.6	−6.9	−7.2
27	Ghana[b]	7.9	3.2	20.1	25.7	6.3	9.0	4.1	11.9	15.1	19.2	46.6	31.1	19.5	14.0	−5.8	0.4
28	Central African Rep.	..	..	..	..	..	..	..	..	..	..	..	..	..	26.1	..	..
29	Togo	..	..	..	..	..	..	..	..	..	..	..	..	..	..	..	..
30	Zambia[b]	0.0	0.0	19.0	8.6	7.4	7.4	1.3	2.0	26.7	24.8	45.7	57.2	34.0	21.9	−13.8	−5.0
31	Guinea	..	..	..	..	..	..	..	..	..	..	..	..	..	24.9	..	−4.2
32	Sri Lanka	3.1	7.4	13.0	9.9	6.4	5.4	19.5	14.9	20.2	16.8	37.7	45.6	25.4	28.4	−5.3	−7.9
33	Mauritania	..	..	..	..	..	..	..	..	..	..	..	..	..	33.5	..	−4.2
34	Lesotho	0.0	9.9	19.5	15.2	8.0	7.4	6.5	2.4	24.5	27.4	41.5	37.6	16.6	25.1	−0.9	−2.8
35	Indonesia	18.6	8.0	7.4	8.4	1.4	2.0	0.9	1.5	30.5	27.6	41.3	52.4	15.1	20.4	−2.5	−2.1
36	Honduras	12.4	..	22.3	..	10.2	..	8.7	..	28.3	..	18.1	..	16.1	..	−2.9	..
37	Egypt, Arab Rep.	..	12.7	..	13.4	..	2.8	..	17.8	..	8.2	..	45.3	..	40.2	..	−6.9
38	*Afghanistan*	..	..	..	..	..	..	..	..	..	..	..	..	..	..	..	..
39	*Cambodia*	..	..	..	..	..	..	..	..	..	..	..	..	..	..	..	..
40	*Liberia*	5.3	9.8	15.2	11.6	9.8	5.4	3.5	1.8	25.8	29.5	40.5	41.9	16.7	..	1.1	..
41	*Myanmar*	31.6	24.7	15.0	16.8	6.1	4.6	7.5	15.4	20.1	20.5	19.7	18.1	..	..	..	..
42	*Sudan*[b]	24.1	..	9.3	..	5.4	..	1.4	..	15.8	..	44.1	..	19.2	..	−0.8	..
43	*Viet Nam*	..	..	..	..	..	..	..	..	..	..	..	..	..	..	..	..
Middle-income economies																	
Lower-middle-income																	
44	Bolivia	..	14.1	..	18.0	..	2.3	..	17.9	..	19.1	..	28.6	..	18.8	0.0	−1.9
45	Zimbabwe	..	16.5	..	23.4	..	7.6	..	3.9	..	22.4	..	26.2	..	40.5	..	−7.9
46	Senegal	..	..	..	..	..	..	..	..	..	..	..	..	17.4	..	−0.8	..
47	Philippines[b]	10.9	11.0	16.3	16.9	3.2	4.1	4.3	2.3	17.6	23.6	47.7	42.1	14.2	19.8	−2.1	−3.5
48	Côte d'Ivoire	..	..	..	..	..	..	..	..	..	..	..	..	..	..	..	..
49	Dominican Rep.	8.5	4.6	14.2	9.5	11.7	11.3	11.8	24.2	35.4	36.7	18.3	13.6	17.7	15.3	−0.2	0.0
50	Papua New Guinea[b]	..	4.7	..	15.3	..	9.4	..	3.1	..	20.8	..	46.6	..	29.0	..	−0.9
51	Guatemala	11.0	13.3	19.4	19.5	9.5	9.9	10.4	7.8	23.8	21.7	25.8	27.8	9.9	12.0	−2.2	−1.8
52	Morocco	12.3	..	19.2	..	4.8	..	8.4	..	25.6	..	29.7	..	22.8	..	−3.9	..
53	Cameroon	..	6.7	..	12.0	..	3.4	..	8.7	..	48.1	..	21.2	..	20.8	..	−3.2
54	Ecuador[b]	15.7	12.9	27.5	18.2	4.5	11.0	0.8	2.5	28.9	11.8	22.6	43.6	13.4	15.6	0.2	2.0
55	Syrian Arab Rep.	37.2	40.7	11.3	8.6	1.4	1.3	3.6	3.3	39.9	30.4	6.7	15.7	29.0	28.0	−3.5	−0.7
56	Congo	..	..	..	..	..	..	..	..	..	..	..	..	..	..	..	..
57	El Salvador[b]	6.6	24.5	21.4	16.2	10.9	7.8	7.6	5.5	14.4	16.7	39.1	29.3	12.8	9.9	−0.9	−0.1
58	Paraguay	13.8	13.3	12.1	12.7	3.5	4.3	18.3	14.8	19.6	12.8	32.7	42.1	13.1	9.3	−1.7	2.9
59	Peru[b]	14.5	11.2	23.6	16.2	5.5	5.1	1.8	0.1	30.9	..	23.6	67.4	16.1	10.0	−0.9	−5.0
60	Jordan	33.5	23.1	9.4	14.2	3.8	5.8	10.5	11.7	26.6	12.9	16.2	32.3	..	39.4	..	−6.0
61	Colombia	..	..	..	..	..	..	..	..	..	..	..	..	13.1	15.1	−2.5	−2.0
62	Thailand	20.2	17.3	19.9	20.1	3.7	6.8	7.0	5.8	25.6	22.1	23.5	28.0	16.7	15.1	−4.2	4.9
63	Tunisia	4.9	6.5	30.5	16.3	7.4	6.1	8.8	14.4	23.3	31.0	25.1	25.7	23.1	37.2	−0.9	−4.5
64	Jamaica	..	..	..	..	..	..	..	..	..	..	..	..	..	..	..	..
65	Turkey	15.5	11.7	18.1	19.2	3.2	3.6	3.1	3.6	42.0	17.8	18.1	44.2	22.7	24.6	−2.2	−4.2
66	Romania	5.4	10.3	2.9	2.7	0.5	8.7	16.2	31.5	61.8	38.3	13.1	8.6	..	34.2	..	0.9

Note: For data comparability and coverage, see the technical notes. Figures in italics are for years other than those specified.

Percentage of total expenditure

		Defense		Education		Health		Housing, amenities; social security and welfare [a]		Economic services		Other [a]		Total expenditure as a percentage of GNP		Overall surplus/deficit as a percentage of GNP	
		1972	1990	1972	1990	1972	1990	1972	1990	1972	1990	1972	1990	1972	1990	1972	1990
67	Poland	..	..	..	..	..	..	..	..	..	..	..	..	..	40.4	..	-2.4
68	Panama	0.0	7.9	20.7	18.5	15.1	17.9	10.8	24.1	24.2	7.5	29.1	24.1	27.6	31.8	-6.5	-8.2
69	Costa Rica	2.6	..	28.5	19.0	4.0	26.3	26.5	14.9	21.2	10.3	17.2	29.6	19.0	27.1	-4.5	-3.3
70	Chile	6.1	8.4	14.5	10.1	10.0	5.9	39.8	33.9	15.3	8.8	16.3	33.0	43.2	32.8	-13.0	-0.2
71	Botswana[b]	0.0	11.6	10.0	20.2	6.0	4.8	21.7	10.6	28.0	20.9	34.5	32.0	33.7	42.2	-23.8	12.6
72	Algeria	..	..	..	..	..	..	..	..	..	..	..	..	..	..	..	..
73	Bulgaria	..	6.5	..	6.0	..	4.1	..	24.0	..	47.2	..	12.1	..	76.9	..	-1.5
74	Mauritius	0.8	1.3	13.5	14.4	10.3	8.6	18.0	17.0	13.9	16.5	43.4	42.2	16.3	24.2	-1.2	-0.5
75	Malaysia	..	..	..	..	..	..	..	..	..	..	..	..	26.5	31.3	-9.4	-2.8
76	Argentina	..	8.6	..	9.3	..	2.0	..	40.9	..	20.5	..	18.7	..	15.5	0.0	-2.7
77	Iran, Islamic Rep.	24.1	13.6	10.4	22.0	3.6	8.5	6.1	18.4	30.6	14.7	25.2	22.8	30.8	16.9	-4.6	-4.0
78	Albania	..	..	..	..	..	..	..	..	..	..	..	..	..	..	..	..
79	Angola	..	..	..	..	..	..	..	..	..	..	..	..	..	..	..	..
80	Lebanon	..	..	..	..	..	..	..	..	..	..	..	..	..	..	..	..
81	Mongolia	..	..	..	..	..	..	..	..	..	..	..	..	..	..	..	..
82	Namibia	..	5.5	..	20.8	..	11.1	..	15.0	..	14.4	..	33.2	..	42.8	..	7.0
83	Nicaragua	12.3	..	16.6	..	4.0	..	16.4	..	27.2	..	23.4	..	15.8	..	-4.0	..
84	Yemen, Rep.	..	..	..	..	..	..	..	..	..	..	..	..	..	..	..	..
Upper-middle-income																	
85	Mexico	4.5	2.4	16.4	13.9	4.5	1.9	25.4	13.0	35.8	13.4	13.4	55.5	11.4	18.4	-2.9	0.8
86	South Africa	..	..	..	..	..	..	..	..	..	..	..	..	22.7	34.6	-4.4	-2.5
87	Venezuela	10.3	..	18.6	..	11.7	..	9.2	..	25.4	..	24.8	..	18.1	23.1	-0.2	-1.2
88	Uruguay	5.6	9.2	9.5	7.4	1.6	4.5	52.3	50.3	9.8	8.7	21.2	20.0	26.8	27.5	-2.7	0.4
89	Brazil	8.3	4.2	8.3	5.3	6.7	7.2	35.0	20.1	23.3	6.9	18.3	56.2	29.1	36.0	-0.3	-16.6
90	Hungary	..	3.6	..	3.3	..	7.9	..	35.3	..	22.0	..	27.9	..	54.8	..	0.8
91	Yugoslavia	20.5	53.4	..	..	24.8	..	35.6	6.0	12.0	19.6	7.0	21.0	21.1	5.2	4.0	0.3
92	Czechoslovakia	..	6.7	..	1.8	..	0.4	..	25.3	..	46.1	..	19.9	..	61.1	..	-7.1
93	Gabon[b]	..	..	..	..	..	..	..	..	..	..	..	..	37.0	..	-11.9	..
94	Trinidad and Tobago	..	..	..	..	..	..	..	..	..	..	..	..	..	..	..	..
95	Portugal	..	..	..	..	..	..	..	..	..	..	..	..	..	43.3	..	-5.0
96	Korea, Rep.	25.8	25.8	15.8	19.6	1.2	2.2	5.9	12.2	25.6	17.0	25.7	23.2	18.0	15.7	-3.9	-0.7
97	Greece	14.9	..	9.1	..	7.4	..	30.6	..	26.4	..	11.7	..	27.5	..	-1.7	..
98	Saudi Arabia	..	..	..	..	..	..	..	..	..	..	..	..	..	..	..	..
99	Iraq	..	..	..	..	..	..	..	..	..	..	..	..	..	..	..	..
100	Libya	..	..	..	..	..	..	..	..	..	..	..	..	..	..	..	..
101	Oman	39.3	41.0	3.7	10.7	5.9	4.6	3.0	9.0	24.4	9.7	23.6	25.0	62.1	48.6	-15.3	-9.9

Low- and middle-income
Sub-Saharan Africa
East Asia & Pacific
South Asia
Europe
Middle East & N.Africa
Latin America & Caribbean
Other economies

Severely indebted

High-income economies
OECD members
†Other

		Defense		Education		Health		Housing, amenities; social security and welfare [a]		Economic services		Other [a]		Total expenditure as a percentage of GNP		Overall surplus/deficit as a percentage of GNP	
		1972	1990	1972	1990	1972	1990	1972	1990	1972	1990	1972	1990	1972	1990	1972	1990
102	Ireland	..	2.8	..	11.3	..	12.1	..	28.9	..	15.6	..	29.3	33.0	54.5	-5.5	-5.3
103	†Israel	42.9	25.4	7.1	10.2	0.0	4.1	7.1	24.3	7.1	9.2	35.7	26.7	43.9	50.8	-15.7	-4.3
104	Spain	6.5	5.5	8.3	5.6	0.9	12.8	49.8	37.7	17.5	10.8	17.0	27.6	19.4	33.5	-0.5	-3.6
105	†Singapore	35.3	21.6	15.7	18.1	7.8	4.7	3.9	11.7	9.9	20.0	27.3	24.0	16.7	23.3	1.3	10.5
106	†Hong Kong	..	..	..	..	..	..	..	..	..	..	..	..	..	..	..	..
107	New Zealand[b]	5.8	4.8	16.9	12.5	14.8	12.7	25.6	33.8	16.5	9.0	20.4	27.1	29.2	47.1	-3.9	4.3
108	Belgium	6.7	..	15.5	..	1.5	..	41.0	..	18.9	..	16.4	..	39.9	49.3	-4.4	-6.4
109	United Kingdom	16.7	12.2	2.6	3.2	12.2	14.6	26.5	34.8	11.1	7.4	30.8	27.9	32.0	34.8	-2.7	0.8
110	Italy	6.3	3.6	16.1	8.3	13.5	11.3	44.8	38.6	18.4	11.5	0.9	26.6	29.5	48.5	-8.7	-10.4
111	Australia	14.2	8.5	4.2	..	7.0	12.8	20.3	29.7	14.4	7.1	39.9	35.1	18.7	25.8	0.3	1.9
112	Netherlands	6.8	5.0	15.2	10.8	12.1	11.7	38.1	42.3	9.1	7.4	18.7	22.8	41.0	52.8	0.0	-4.9
113	Austria	3.3	2.5	10.2	9.2	10.1	12.9	53.8	48.2	11.2	9.9	11.4	17.3	29.6	39.1	-0.2	-4.4
114	France	..	6.7	..	6.8	..	15.2	..	46.4	..	5.4	..	19.5	32.3	43.0	0.7	-2.2
115	†United Arab Emirates[b]	24.4	43.9	16.5	15.0	4.3	6.9	6.1	3.6	18.3	4.3	30.5	26.3	3.8	13.0	0.3	-0.6
116	Canada	7.6	7.3	3.5	2.9	7.6	5.5	35.3	37.0	19.5	10.8	26.5	36.5	20.2	23.4	-1.3	-2.9
117	United States	32.2	22.6	3.2	1.7	8.6	13.5	35.3	28.2	10.6	10.2	10.1	23.8	19.0	24.0	-1.5	-4.0
118	Denmark	7.3	5.4	16.0	9.3	10.0	1.1	41.6	38.8	11.3	7.3	13.7	38.1	32.6	41.2	2.7	-0.4
119	Germany[c]	12.4	8.3	1.5	0.6	17.5	19.3	46.9	48.2	11.3	8.0	10.4	15.5	24.2	29.4	0.7	-1.3
120	Norway	9.7	8.0	9.9	9.4	12.3	10.4	39.9	39.2	20.2	17.5	8.0	15.4	35.0	46.3	-1.5	0.7
121	Sweden	12.5	6.3	14.8	8.7	3.6	0.9	44.3	55.9	10.6	7.6	14.3	20.5	27.7	42.3	-1.2	3.2
122	Japan[b]	..	..	..	..	..	..	..	..	..	..	..	..	12.7	16.7	-1.9	-2.9
123	Finland	6.1	4.6	15.3	14.4	10.6	10.8	28.4	35.1	27.9	20.8	11.6	14.3	24.3	31.1	1.2	0.1
124	Switzerland	15.1	..	4.2	..	10.0	..	39.5	..	18.4	..	12.8	..	13.3	..	0.9	..
125	†Kuwait	8.4	19.9	15.0	14.0	5.5	7.4	14.2	20.5	16.6	14.5	40.1	23.7	34.4	31.0	17.4	-7.2

World
Fuel exporters, excl. former USSR

a. See the technical notes.　b. Data are for budgetary accounts only.　c. Data refer to the Federal Republic of Germany before unification.

Table 12. Central government current revenue

		Percentage of total current revenue												
		Tax revenue												
		Taxes on income, profit, and capital gains		Social security contributions		Domestic taxes on goods and services		Taxes on international trade and transactions		Other taxes[a]		Nontax revenue		Total current revenue as a percentage of GNP	
		1972	1990	1972	1990	1972	1990	1972	1990	1972	1990	1972	1990	1972	1990
	Low-income economies														
	China and India														
	Other low-income														
1	Mozambique	..	..	..	..	..	..	..	..	..	..	..	..	..	..
2	Tanzania	29.9	..	0.0	..	29.1	..	21.7	..	0.5	..	18.8	..	15.8	..
3	Ethiopia	23.0	..	0.0	..	29.8	..	30.4	..	5.6	..	11.1	..	10.5	..
4	Somalia[b]	10.7	..	0.0	..	24.7	..	45.3	..	5.2	..	14.0	..	13.7	..
5	Nepal	4.1	10.8	0.0	0.0	26.5	35.7	36.7	31.0	19.0	5.3	13.7	17.2	5.2	10.0
6	Chad	16.7	..	0.0	..	12.3	..	45.2	..	20.5	..	5.3	..	10.8	..
7	Bhutan	..	7.9	..	0.0	..	17.6	..	0.4	..	0.6	..	73.6	..	21.0
8	Lao PDR	..	..	..	..	..	..	..	..	..	..	..	..	..	..
9	Malawi[b]	31.4	35.0	0.0	0.0	24.2	33.2	20.0	17.7	0.5	1.2	23.8	12.9	16.0	23.7
10	Bangladesh[b]	3.7	8.6	0.0	0.0	22.4	25.8	18.0	27.3	3.8	15.2	52.2	23.0	8.4	11.4
11	Burundi	18.1	..	1.2	..	18.3	..	40.3	..	15.6	..	6.5	..	11.5	..
12	Zaire	22.5	28.9	2.3	1.4	12.1	16.5	57.8	47.3	1.6	0.8	3.6	5.2	10.2	12.0
13	Uganda	22.1	5.5	0.0	0.0	32.8	19.1	36.3	75.3	0.3	0.0	8.5	0.0	13.7	5.3
14	Madagascar	13.1	..	7.2	..	29.9	..	33.6	..	5.5	..	10.8	..	14.7	..
15	Sierra Leone[b]	32.7	26.3	0.0	0.0	14.6	25.7	42.4	44.6	0.3	0.3	9.9	3.1	19.5	8.8
16	Mali[b]	..	10.8	..	4.4	..	28.6	..	12.0	..	30.8	..	13.5	..	18.9
17	Nigeria[b]	43.0	..	0.0	..	26.3	..	17.5	..	0.2	..	13.0	..	10.3	..
18	Niger	..	..	..	..	..	..	..	..	..	..	..	..	..	..
19	Rwanda	17.9	..	4.4	..	14.1	..	41.7	..	13.8	..	8.1	..	9.8	..
20	Burkina Faso	16.8	..	0.0	..	18.0	..	51.8	..	3.2	..	10.2	..	8.6	..
21	India	21.3	15.4	0.0	0.0	44.5	35.5	20.1	28.8	0.9	0.4	13.2	19.9	10.2	14.8
22	Benin	..	..	..	..	..	..	..	..	..	..	..	..	..	..
23	China	..	..	..	..	..	..	..	..	..	..	..	..	..	..
24	Haiti	..	..	..	..	..	..	..	..	..	..	..	..	..	..
25	Kenya[b]	35.6	27.4	0.0	0.0	19.9	42.8	24.3	15.8	1.4	1.2	18.8	12.8	18.0	22.6
26	Pakistan	13.6	10.0	0.0	0.0	35.9	32.2	34.2	30.6	0.5	0.2	15.8	26.9	12.5	19.0
27	Ghana[b]	18.4	28.7	0.0	0.0	29.4	28.3	40.6	35.2	0.2	0.1	11.5	7.8	15.1	13.9
28	Central African Rep.	..	23.9	..	0.0	..	13.1	..	45.2	..	11.4	..	6.4	..	13.3
29	Togo	..	..	..	..	..	..	..	..	..	..	..	..	..	..
30	Zambia[b]	49.7	38.1	0.0	0.0	20.2	37.0	14.3	15.8	0.1	4.9	15.6	4.2	23.2	11.9
31	Guinea	..	17.1	..	..	..	74.4			..	2.4	..	6.1	..	14.6
32	Sri Lanka	19.1	10.8	0.0	0.0	34.7	46.4	35.4	28.6	2.1	4.6	8.7	9.5	20.1	21.1
33	Mauritania	..	32.3	..	0.0	..	19.4	..	36.8	..	1.4	..	10.1	..	21.8
34	Lesotho	14.3	12.4	0.0	0.0	2.0	22.8	62.9	54.5	9.5	0.2	11.3	10.2	11.7	21.2
35	Indonesia	45.5	57.5	0.0	0.0	22.8	25.1	17.6	6.0	3.5	3.0	10.6	8.3	13.4	18.3
36	Honduras	19.2	..	3.0	..	33.8	..	28.2	..	2.3	..	13.5	..	13.2	..
37	Egypt, Arab Rep.	..	15.9	..	14.2	..	11.9	..	14.0	..	8.2	..	35.8	..	35.9
38	Afghanistan	..	..	..	..	..	..	..	..	..	..	..	..	..	..
39	Cambodia	..	..	..	..	..	..	..	..	..	..	..	..	..	..
40	Liberia	40.4	33.9	0.0	0.0	20.3	25.1	31.6	34.6	3.1	2.3	4.6	4.2	17.0	17.8
41	Myanmar	28.7	9.0	0.0	0.0	34.2	30.7	13.4	14.9	0.0	0.0	23.8	45.5	..	..
42	Sudan[b]	11.8	..	0.0	..	30.4	..	40.5	..	1.5	..	15.7	..	18.0	..
43	Viet Nam	..	..	..	..	..	..	..	..	..	..	..	..	..	..
	Middle-income economies														
	Lower-middle-income														
44	Bolivia	..	4.9	..	8.8	..	31.6	..	7.3	..	2.9	..	44.5	..	15.7
45	Zimbabwe	..	44.9	..	0.0	..	26.3	..	17.5	..	1.1	..	10.1	..	35.6
46	Senegal	17.5	..	0.0	..	24.5	..	30.9	..	23.9	..	3.2	..	16.9	..
47	Philippines[b]	13.8	28.3	0.0	0.0	24.3	30.7	23.0	25.1	29.7	2.9	9.3	12.9	13.1	16.3
48	Côte d'Ivoire	..	..	..	..	..	..	..	..	..	..	..	..	..	..
49	Dominican Rep.	17.9	20.9	3.9	4.1	19.0	19.8	40.4	41.1	1.7	4.7	17.0	9.4	17.2	15.1
50	Papua New Guinea[b]	..	44.6	..	0.0	..	10.5	..	24.9	..	1.8	..	18.1	..	23.2
51	Guatemala	12.7	18.1	0.0	0.0	36.1	23.2	26.2	33.8	15.6	7.2	9.4	17.7	8.9	9.8
52	Morocco	16.4	..	5.9	..	45.7	..	13.2	..	6.1	..	12.6	..	18.5	..
53	Cameroon	..	45.2	..	6.4	..	20.2	..	14.0	..	9.1	..	5.1	..	17.7
54	Ecuador[b]	19.6	56.9	0.0	0.0	19.1	21.5	52.4	14.3	5.1	5.5	3.8	1.7	13.6	17.7
55	Syrian Arab Rep.	6.8	29.5	0.0	0.0	10.4	4.1	17.3	6.8	12.1	33.6	53.4	26.0	25.3	25.5
56	Congo	19.4	..	0.0	..	40.3	..	26.5	..	6.3	..	7.5	..	18.4	..
57	El Salvador[b]	14.7	18.8	0.0	0.0	24.9	38.4	35.0	18.5	19.6	21.5	5.8	2.8	12.0	9.9
58	Paraguay	8.8	9.3	10.4	12.9	26.1	19.5	24.8	20.1	17.0	24.8	12.9	26.2	11.5	12.2
59	Peru[b]	16.0	10.0	0.0	0.0	34.0	44.2	14.0	26.3	26.0	16.8	10.0	2.6	14.6	5.0
60	Jordan	9.4	10.0	0.0	2.0	15.6	20.7	36.2	29.7	3.1	8.4	35.6	29.2	..	22.3
61	Colombia	37.1	27.8	13.7	12.6	15.2	27.7	19.8	17.8	7.1	6.7	7.1	7.4	10.6	13.4
62	Thailand	12.1	24.2	0.0	0.1	46.3	41.4	28.7	22.1	1.8	4.3	11.2	7.9	12.5	19.9
63	Tunisia	15.9	12.9	7.1	11.1	31.6	20.1	21.8	27.9	7.8	5.1	15.7	22.8	23.6	31.8
64	Jamaica	..	..	..	..	..	..	..	..	..	..	..	..	..	..
65	Turkey	30.8	43.3	0.0	0.0	31.0	32.1	14.6	6.2	6.1	3.0	17.5	15.4	20.6	19.3
66	Romania	..	18.9	..	22.9	..	32.6	..	0.5	..	14.9	..	10.2	..	34.8

Note: For data comparability and coverage, see the technical notes.   Figures in italics are for years other than those specified.

		Tax revenue												Total current revenue as a percentage of GNP	
		Taxes on income, profit, and capital gains		Social security contributions		Domestic taxes on goods and services		Taxes on international trade and transactions		Other taxes[a]		Nontax revenue			
		1972	1990	1972	1990	1972	1990	1972	1990	1972	1990	1972	1990	1972	1990
67	Poland	..	30.4	..	21.4	..	30.4	..	6.2	..	6.5	..	5.1	..	38.7
68	Panama	23.3	14.7	22.4	27.3	13.3	17.9	16.0	8.3	7.7	3.5	17.3	28.2	21.8	24.5
69	Costa Rica	18.0	9.8	13.9	28.8	37.7	27.4	18.9	23.0	1.6	-3.5	9.8	14.4	15.3	24.3
70	Chile	14.3	23.3	28.6	6.0	28.6	37.1	14.3	9.8	0.0	-0.2	14.3	24.1	30.2	31.1
71	Botswana[b]	20.1	38.6	0.0	0.0	1.4	1.5	47.7	13.2	0.4	0.1	30.3	46.6	30.4	60.9
72	Algeria	..	..	..	..	..	..	..	..	..	..	..	..	..	..
73	Bulgaria	..	36.4	..	12.7	..	15.1	..	6.1	..	0.7	..	29.0	..	78.5
74	Mauritius	22.7	13.9	0.0	4.1	23.3	20.9	40.2	46.4	5.5	6.1	8.2	8.7	15.6	24.2
75	Malaysia	25.2	30.5	0.1	0.8	24.2	24.3	27.9	16.7	1.4	2.5	21.2	25.2	20.3	28.9
76	Argentina	..	4.3	..	43.4	..	22.4	..	11.4	..	10.3	..	8.2	..	13.3
77	Iran, Islamic Rep.	7.9	12.6	2.7	10.9	6.4	5.0	14.6	10.5	4.9	6.6	63.6	54.4	26.2	12.9
78	Albania	..	..	..	..	..	..	..	..	..	..	..	..	..	..
79	Angola	..	..	..	..	..	..	..	..	..	..	..	..	..	..
80	Lebanon	..	..	..	..	..	..	..	..	..	..	..	..	..	..
81	Mongolia	..	..	..	..	..	..	..	..	..	..	..	..	..	..
82	Namibia	..	42.7	..	0.0	..	28.5	..	16.4	..	1.1	..	11.3	..	43.6
83	Nicaragua	9.5	..	14.0	..	37.3	..	24.4	..	9.0	..	5.8	..	12.8	..
84	Yemen, Rep.	..	..	..	..	..	..	..	..	..	..	..	..	..	..

Upper-middle-income

		1972	1990	1972	1990	1972	1990	1972	1990	1972	1990	1972	1990	1972	1990
85	Mexico	37.3	36.5	18.6	13.6	32.2	56.0	13.6	4.6	-8.5	-18.3	6.8	7.7	10.1	14.9
86	South Africa	54.8	48.6	1.2	1.7	21.5	34.1	4.6	4.9	5.0	2.8	12.8	7.9	22.1	30.9
87	Venezuela	54.2	57.5	6.0	2.7	6.7	3.8	6.1	7.2	1.1	5.6	25.9	23.2	18.5	21.9
88	Uruguay	4.7	6.7	30.0	27.0	24.5	35.9	6.1	9.8	22.0	15.5	12.6	5.1	24.3	28.0
89	Brazil	..	..	..	..	..	..	..	..	..	..	..	..	..	..
90	Hungary	..	17.9	..	29.2	..	31.3	..	5.8	..	0.2	..	15.5	..	55.6
91	Yugoslavia	..	..	60.0	..	20.0	66.4	20.0	31.3	..	..	..	2.3	18.7	5.5
92	Czechoslovakia	..	21.7	..	0.0	..	34.2	..	6.0	..	21.3	..	16.8	..	54.5
93	Gabon[b]	18.2	..	6.0	..	9.5	..	44.9	..	4.2	..	17.2	..	26.1	..
94	Trinidad and Tobago	..	..	..	..	..	..	..	..	..	..	..	..	..	..
95	Portugal	..	23.8	..	25.9	..	36.9	..	2.5	..	3.2	..	7.7	..	36.6
96	Korea, Rep.	29.0	34.0	0.7	4.9	41.7	33.5	10.7	10.6	5.3	5.7	12.6	11.4	13.1	15.7
97	Greece	12.2	..	24.5	..	35.5	..	6.7	..	12.0	..	9.2	..	25.4	..
98	Saudi Arabia	..	..	..	..	..	..	..	..	..	..	..	..	..	..
99	Iraq	..	..	..	..	..	..	..	..	..	..	..	..	..	..
100	Libya	..	..	..	..	..	..	..	..	..	..	..	..	..	..
101	Oman	71.1	23.4	0.0	0.0	0.0	0.7	3.0	2.1	2.3	0.5	23.6	73.3	47.4	38.2

Low- and middle-income
  Sub-Saharan Africa
  East Asia & Pacific
  South Asia
  Europe
  Middle East & N.Africa
  Latin America & Caribbean
Other economies

Severely indebted

High-income economies
  OECD members
  †Other

		1972	1990	1972	1990	1972	1990	1972	1990	1972	1990	1972	1990	1972	1990
102	Ireland	28.3	38.0	9.0	13.6	32.1	31.0	16.7	7.7	3.2	3.2	10.6	6.6	30.3	47.1
103	†Israel	40.0	35.9	0.0	8.9	20.0	33.1	20.0	1.7	10.0	3.9	10.0	16.5	31.3	40.3
104	Spain	15.9	28.4	38.9	37.9	23.4	24.1	10.0	2.5	0.7	1.1	11.1	6.0	19.5	30.3
105	†Singapore	24.4	24.3	0.0	0.0	17.6	19.6	11.1	2.5	15.5	14.9	31.4	38.8	21.5	27.9
106	†Hong Kong	..	..	..	..	..	..	..	..	..	..	..	..	..	..
107	New Zealand[b]	61.4	53.1	0.0	0.0	19.9	27.1	4.1	2.1	4.5	3.1	10.0	14.6	28.0	45.6
108	Belgium	31.3	35.2	32.4	34.9	28.9	23.7	1.0	0.0	3.3	3.1	3.1	3.0	35.6	43.3
109	United Kingdom	39.4	40.3	15.6	17.1	27.1	30.8	1.7	0.1	5.4	2.1	10.8	9.6	32.8	35.5
110	Italy	16.6	36.6	39.2	29.0	31.7	29.1	0.4	0.0	4.3	2.2	7.7	3.1	24.9	39.0
111	Australia	58.3	65.1	0.0	0.0	21.9	21.1	5.2	4.1	2.1	0.4	12.5	9.3	20.5	27.2
112	Netherlands	32.5	30.7	36.7	35.6	22.3	22.3	0.5	0.0	3.4	2.8	4.7	8.6	43.4	47.5
113	Austria	20.7	19.0	30.0	36.7	28.3	25.5	5.4	1.5	10.2	8.7	5.5	8.6	29.7	35.2
114	France	16.8	17.3	37.0	43.9	37.9	28.3	0.3	0.0	3.0	3.3	4.9	7.2	33.4	40.8
115	†United Arab Emirates[b]	0.0	0.0	0.0	3.1	0.0	39.7	0.0	0.0	0.0	0.0	100.0	57.2	0.2	1.3
116	Canada	54.0	53.7	8.8	14.2	15.9	19.6	11.0	3.5	-0.6	0.0	10.9	9.0	21.3	20.5
117	United States	59.4	51.6	23.6	34.6	7.1	3.2	1.6	1.6	2.5	1.1	5.7	7.9	17.0	20.0
118	Denmark	40.0	38.0	5.1	3.2	42.1	41.2	3.1	0.1	2.8	3.3	6.8	14.2	35.5	40.1
119	Germany[c]	19.7	16.4	46.6	53.4	28.1	23.8	0.8	0.0	0.8	0.2	4.0	6.2	25.3	28.7
120	Norway	22.6	16.6	20.6	24.2	48.0	34.4	1.6	0.5	1.0	1.4	6.2	23.0	36.8	47.3
121	Sweden	27.0	18.1	21.6	30.5	34.0	28.9	1.5	0.5	4.7	8.9	11.3	13.2	32.2	45.3
122	Japan[b]	64.8	71.2	0.0	0.0	22.6	12.0	3.5	1.3	6.8	9.9	2.4	5.6	11.2	13.9
123	Finland	30.0	30.2	7.8	9.1	47.7	45.8	3.1	1.0	5.8	4.7	5.5	9.1	26.5	31.3
124	Switzerland	13.9	..	37.3	..	21.5	..	16.7	..	2.6	..	8.0	..	14.5	..
125	†Kuwait	68.8	0.7	0.0	0.0	19.7	0.0	1.5	2.9	0.2	0.1	9.9	96.2	55.2	23.6

World
Fuel exporters, excl. former USSR

a. See the technical notes.   b. Data are for budgetary accounts only.   c. Data refer to the Federal Republic of Germany before unification.

Table 13. Money and interest rates

| | | Monetary holdings, broadly defined | | | | | Average annual inflation (GDP deflator) | Nominal interest rates of banks (average annual percentage) | | | |
| | | Average annual nominal growth rate (percent) | | Average outstanding as a percentage of GDP | | | | Deposit rate | | Lending rate | |
		1965–80	1980–90	1965	1980	1990	1980–90	1980	1990	1980	1990
	Low-income economies										
	China and India										
	Other low-income										
1	Mozambique	..	..	..	..	..	36.5	..	..	..	..
2	Tanzania	19.7	21.5	..	37.2	..	25.7	4.0	17.0	11.5	31.0
3	Ethiopia	12.7	12.2	12.5	25.3	52.5	2.1	..	2.4	..	6.0
4	Somalia	20.4	50.0	12.7	17.8	..	49.7	4.5	25.0	7.5	..
5	Nepal	17.9	19.7	8.4	21.9	34.9	9.1	4.0	8.5	14.0	14.4
6	Chad	12.5	10.3	9.3	20.0	23.3	1.2	5.5	4.3	11.0	11.5
7	Bhutan	..	33.9	..	..	20.7	8.4	..	6.5	..	15.0
8	Lao PDR	..	..	..	..	..	..	7.2	14.0	4.8	15.0
9	Malawi	15.4	18.1	17.6	20.5	..	14.7	7.9	12.1	16.7	21.0
10	Bangladesh	..	21.6	..	16.7	28.3	9.6	8.3	12.0	11.3	16.0
11	Burundi	15.8	9.9	10.1	13.5	17.8	4.2	2.5	..	12.0	..
12	Zaire	28.2	69.1	8.6	6.4	10.7	60.9	..	..	..	..
13	Uganda	23.2	..	..	12.7	7.8	107.0	6.8	35.0	10.8	38.7
14	Madagascar	12.2	17.5	15.8	22.3	21.4	17.1	5.6	..	9.5	..
15	Sierra Leone	15.9	55.6	11.7	20.6	16.1	56.2	9.2	40.5	11.0	52.5
16	Mali	14.4	9.4	..	17.9	20.8	3.0	6.2	7.0	9.4	8.8
17	Nigeria	28.5	14.1	10.7	23.8	17.6	18.2	5.3	13.1	8.4	35.0
18	Niger	18.3	6.1	3.8	13.3	19.9	3.3	6.2	7.0	9.4	8.8
19	Rwanda	19.0	9.0	15.8	13.6	17.6	3.8	6.3	6.9	13.5	13.2
20	Burkina Faso	17.1	11.7	6.9	13.8	17.8	4.6	6.2	7.0	9.4	8.8
21	India	15.3	16.7	23.7	36.2	44.7	7.9	..	..	16.5	16.5
22	Benin	17.3	4.8	8.6	17.2	23.0	1.9	6.2	7.0	9.4	8.8
23	China	..	25.4	..	33.6	74.7	5.8	5.4	..	5.0	11.2
24	Haiti	20.3	8.6	9.9	26.1	..	7.2	10.0	..	..	..
25	Kenya	18.6	14.9	..	36.8	38.3	9.2	5.8	13.7	10.6	18.8
26	Pakistan	14.7	13.3	40.7	38.7	36.8	6.7	..	..	..	..
27	Ghana	25.9	44.8	20.3	16.2	12.5	42.7	11.5	..	19.0	..
28	Central African Rep.	12.7	5.2	13.5	18.9	17.8	5.5	5.5	7.5	10.5	12.5
29	Togo	20.3	6.5	10.9	29.0	34.6	4.8	6.2	7.0	9.4	8.8
30	Zambia	12.7	..	..	32.6	..	42.3	7.0	11.4	9.5	18.4
31	Guinea	..	..	..	..	..	..	..	..	..	..
32	Sri Lanka	15.4	15.1	32.3	35.3	32.6	11.0	14.5	19.4	19.0	13.0
33	Mauritania	20.7	11.4	5.7	20.5	24.4	8.8	..	..	..	..
34	Lesotho	..	17.8	..	..	39.8	13.0	..	13.0	11.0	20.4
35	Indonesia	54.4	25.8	..	13.2	36.2	8.4	6.0	17.3	..	20.6
36	Honduras	14.8	12.5	15.4	22.8	33.1	5.4	7.0	8.6	18.5	15.8
37	Egypt, Arab Rep.	17.7	21.9	35.3	52.2	93.2	11.9	8.3	12.0	13.3	19.0
38	*Afghanistan*	14.0	..	14.4	26.8	..	..	9.0	..	13.0	..
39	*Cambodia*	..	..	..	..	..	..	..	..	..	..
40	*Liberia*	..	..	..	..	..	..	10.3	6.8	18.4	13.8
41	*Myanmar*	11.5	11.2	..	..	..	..	1.5	1.5	8.0	8.0
42	*Sudan*	21.6	28.0	14.1	32.5	..	..	6.0	..	..	..
43	*Viet Nam*	..	..	..	..	..	..	..	..	..	..
	Middle-income economies										
	Lower-middle-income										
44	Bolivia	24.3	444.2	10.9	16.2	21.7	318.4	18.0	..	28.0	..
45	Zimbabwe	..	..	..	..	54.0	10.8	3.5	8.8	17.5	11.7
46	Senegal	15.6	6.4	15.3	26.6	22.6	6.6	6.2	7.0	9.4	8.8
47	Philippines	17.7	16.1	19.9	11.0	21.1	14.9	12.3	19.5	14.0	24.1
48	Côte d'Ivoire	20.4	4.6	21.8	25.8	31.7	2.7	6.2	7.0	9.4	8.8
49	Dominican Rep.	18.5	26.9	18.0	21.8	22.0	21.8	..	..	..	..
50	Papua New Guinea	..	8.0	..	32.9	34.0	5.3	6.9	8.7	11.2	15.5
51	Guatemala	16.3	15.7	15.2	20.5	19.1	14.6	9.0	18.2	11.0	23.3
52	Morocco	15.7	14.5	29.4	42.4	..	7.2	4.9	8.5	7.0	9.0
53	Cameroon	19.0	7.9	11.7	18.3	22.7	5.6	7.5	7.5	13.0	14.0
54	Ecuador	22.6	35.5	15.6	20.2	13.4	36.7	..	43.6	9.0	37.5
55	Syrian Arab Rep.	21.9	19.4	24.6	40.9	..	14.7	5.0	..	..	..
56	Congo	14.2	7.3	16.5	14.7	19.8	0.7	6.5	8.0	11.0	12.5
57	El Salvador	14.3	16.9	21.6	28.1	25.8	17.2	..	18.0	..	21.2
58	Paraguay	21.3	20.0	12.1	19.8	..	24.4	..	..	..	..
59	Peru	25.9	157.0	18.8	16.5	..	233.7	..	..	..	..
60	Jordan	19.1	12.9	..	..	129.8	..	..	..	..	..
61	Colombia	26.5	..	19.8	23.7	..	24.8	..	27.7	19.0	28.2
62	Thailand	17.9	18.8	23.6	37.4	71.5	3.3	12.0	12.3	18.0	15.0
63	Tunisia	17.4	15.5	30.2	42.1	..	7.4	2.5	7.4	7.3	9.9
64	Jamaica	17.2	24.1	24.3	35.4	50.2	18.3	10.3	26.0	13.0	34.2
65	Turkey	27.5	51.9	23.0	17.2	21.3	43.2	8.0	47.6	25.7	..
66	Romania	..	..	..	33.4	..	1.8	..	..	..	..

Note: For data comparability and coverage, see the technical notes.   Figures in italics are for years other than those specified.

| | | Monetary holdings, broadly defined | | | | | Average annual inflation (GDP deflator) | Nominal interest rates of banks (average annual percentage) | | | |
| | | Average annual nominal growth rate (percent) | | Average outstanding as a percentage of GDP | | | | Deposit rate | | Lending rate | |
		1965-80	1980-90	1965	1980	1990	1980-90	1980	1990	1980	1990
67	Poland	..	51.5	..	58.4	22.4	54.3	3.0	27.8	8.0	101.4
68	Panama	..	..	..	..	..	2.4	..	..	..	..
69	Costa Rica	24.6	25.6	19.3	38.8	38.1	23.5	..	21.2	..	32.6
70	Chile	..	30.3	16.3	21.0	..	20.5	37.5	40.3	47.1	48.8
71	Botswana	..	25.9	..	30.7	32.0	12.1	5.0	6.1	8.5	7.9
72	Algeria	22.3	14.3	..	58.5	82.2	6.6	..	..	..	..
73	Bulgaria	..	..	..	..	..	2.3	..	1.6	..	5.1
74	Mauritius	21.8	21.9	27.3	41.1	61.4	8.8	..	12.6	..	18.0
75	Malaysia	21.5	12.6	26.3	69.8	..	1.6	6.2	5.9	7.8	7.2
76	Argentina	86.6	368.5	18.1	22.2	7.6	395.1	79.4	1,586.0	..	..
77	Iran, Islamic Rep.	28.4	16.7	21.6	54.5	..	13.8	..	..	..	..
78	Albania	..	..	..	..	..	..	..	..	..	..
79	Angola	..	..	..	..	..	..	..	..	..	..
80	Lebanon	16.2	72.7	83.4	176.1	..	..	..	16.9	..	39.9
81	Mongolia	..	..	..	..	..	-1.3	..	..	..	..
82	Namibia	..	..	..	..	..	13.2	..	..	..	..
83	Nicaragua	15.0	..	15.4	22.1	..	432.0	7.5	..	..	..
84	Yemen, Rep.	..	18.7	..	..	..	..	9.3	..	..	..
Upper-middle-income											
85	Mexico	21.9	62.4	25.1	27.5	20.4	70.4	20.6	31.2	28.1	..
86	South Africa	14.0	16.6	58.8	50.9	56.2	14.4	5.5	18.9	9.5	21.0
87	Venezuela	22.9	17.8	17.4	43.0	33.8	19.3	..	27.8	..	28.2
88	Uruguay	65.8	65.9	26.8	32.1	45.7	61.4	50.3	97.8	66.6	174.5
89	Brazil	-22.0	..	20.6	18.4	..	284.4	115.0	9,387.5	..	..
90	Hungary	..	..	..	..	..	9.0	3.0	23.0	9.0	28.0
91	Yugoslavia	25.7	119.0	43.6	59.1	29.7	122.8	5.9	5,644.8	11.5	4,353.8
92	Czechoslovakia	..	6.1	..	..	69.2	1.9	2.7	2.8	..	..
93	Gabon	25.2	5.3	16.2	15.2	22.0	-1.7	7.5	8.8	12.5	12.5
94	Trinidad and Tobago	23.1	..	21.3	32.0	..	6.3	..	6.0	10.0	12.9
95	Portugal	19.4	15.9	77.7	95.6	71.1	18.2	19.0	13.6	18.8	21.7
96	Korea, Rep.	35.5	21.0	11.1	31.7	53.2	5.1	19.5	10.0	18.0	10.0
97	Greece	21.4	27.5	35.0	61.6	..	18.0	14.5	19.5	21.3	27.6
98	Saudi Arabia	32.1	8.4	16.4	18.6	..	-5.2	..	..	..	..
99	Iraq	..	..	19.7	..	..	..	..	..	..	..
100	Libya	29.2	2.3	14.2	34.7	75.8	0.2	5.1	..	7.0	..
101	Oman	..	11.6	..	13.8	..	..	..	8.3	..	9.7
Low- and middle-income											
Sub-Saharan Africa											
East Asia & Pacific											
South Asia											
Europe											
Middle East & N.Africa											
Latin America & Caribbean											
Other economies											
Severely indebted											
High-income economies											
OECD members											
†Other											
102	Ireland	16.1	6.5	..	58.1	44.8	6.5	12.0	6.3	16.0	11.3
103	†Israel	52.7	101.8	15.3	56.4	63.6	101.4	..	14.1	176.9	31.6
104	Spain	19.7	10.4	58.5	74.4	65.0	9.2	13.1	10.7	16.9	16.0
105	†Singapore	17.6	13.3	58.4	74.4	121.9	1.7	9.4	4.7	11.7	7.4
106	†Hong Kong	..	..	..	69.3	..	7.2	..	..	..	..
107	New Zealand	12.8	..	54.8	51.2	..	10.5	..	10.9	12.6	14.4
108	Belgium	10.4	7.1	59.2	57.0	..	4.4	7.7	6.1	..	13.0
109	United Kingdom	13.8	..	48.4	46.0	..	5.8	14.1	6.2	16.2	14.8
110	Italy	17.9	12.0	68.8	81.9	77.0	9.9	12.7	6.8	19.0	14.1
111	Australia	15.9	12.8	48.9	57.9	73.5	7.4	8.6	13.7	10.6	20.3
112	Netherlands	14.7	..	54.5	79.0	..	1.9	6.0	3.3	13.5	11.8
113	Austria	13.3	7.3	49.0	72.6	86.1	3.6	5.0	3.4	..	..
114	France	15.0	9.9	53.7	69.7	..	6.1	6.3	6.7	18.7	16.0
115	†United Arab Emirates	..	11.1	..	19.0	..	1.1	9.5	..	12.1	..
116	Canada	15.3	8.6	40.5	65.0	72.5	4.4	12.9	12.8	14.3	14.1
117	United States	9.2	8.4	63.8	58.8	66.6	3.7	..	..	15.3	10.0
118	Denmark	11.5	12.0	45.8	42.6	58.2	5.6	10.8	8.3	17.2	13.4
119	Germany[a]	10.1	6.1	46.1	60.7	66.6	2.7	8.0	7.1	12.0	11.6
120	Norway	12.8	10.8	51.9	52.9	63.6	5.5	5.0	9.7	12.6	14.2
121	Sweden	10.7	9.8	46.5	46.5	47.4	7.4	11.3	9.9	15.1	17.2
122	Japan	17.2	9.0	106.7	134.0	183.1	1.5	5.5	4.1	8.4	7.0
123	Finland	14.7	13.8	39.1	39.5	52.7	6.8	..	7.5	9.8	11.6
124	Switzerland	7.1	7.3	101.1	107.4	117.4	3.7	..	8.3	..	7.4
125	†Kuwait	17.8	5.1	28.1	33.1	..	-2.9	4.5	4.5	6.8	6.8
World											
Fuel exporters, excl. former USSR											

a. Data refer to the Federal Republic of Germany before unification.

243

Table 14. Growth of merchandise trade

		Merchandise trade (millions of dollars)		Average annual growth rate[a] (percent)				Terms of trade (1987 = 100)	
		Exports 1990	Imports 1990	Exports 1965-80	Exports 1980-90	Imports 1965-80	Imports 1980-90	1985	1990
	Low-income economies	**141,176 t**	**144,431 t**	**5.1 w**	**5.4 w**	**4.8 w**	**2.8 w**	**107 m**	**100 m**
	China and India	**80,059 t**	**77,037 t**	**4.1 w**	**9.8 w**	**4.4 w**	**8.0 w**	**103 m**	**103 m**
	Other low-income	**61,117 t**	**67,394 t**	**5.8 w**	**1.5 w**	**5.0 w**	**-1.9 w**	**107 m**	**100 m**
1	Mozambique	..	..	..	..	..	..	..	..
2	Tanzania	300	935	-4.2	-7.4	1.6	-0.5	101	108
3	Ethiopia	297	1,081	-0.5	-0.3	-0.9	4.2	117	84
4	Somalia	130	360	4.4	-3.3	4.4	-4.3	107	111
5	Nepal	162	543	..	..	..	..	98	..
6	Chad	200	450	..	..	..	..	..	..
7	Bhutan	..	..	..	..	..	..	..	..
8	Lao PDR	..	..	..	..	..	..	..	..
9	Malawi	412	576	5.1	4.3	3.3	0.7	104	93
10	Bangladesh	1,674	3,646	..	7.6	..	8.0	109	95
11	Burundi	75	235	3.3	-1.9	-0.2	5.0	133	70
12	Zaire	999	888	4.7	-11.2	-2.9	-4.0	111	163
13	Uganda	151	458	-3.4	-1.9	-5.3	3.2	143	88
14	Madagascar	335	480	0.6	-1.5	-0.4	-0.4	98	102
15	Sierra Leone	138	146	-2.4	-1.4	-4.6	-2.3	106	80
16	Mali	347	640	9.5	9.9	4.4	6.7	95	97
17	Nigeria	13,671	5,688	11.1	-1.6	14.6	-15.1	167	100
18	Niger	435	230	12.8	4.3	6.6	-8.8	126	77
19	Rwanda	112	279	7.9	0.1	5.1	11.4	116	98
20	Burkina Faso	160	480	3.6	10.1	5.7	1.0	108	100
21	India	17,967	23,692	3.0	6.5	1.2	4.2	96	96
22	Benin	93	483	..	..	..	..	..	..
23	China*	62,091	53,345	4.8	11.0	7.4	9.8	109	111
24	Haiti	138	272	4.2	-12.4	6.5	-6.2	89	97
25	Kenya	1,033	2,124	3.9	1.0	2.4	1.6	114	103
26	Pakistan	5,590	7,377	-1.8	9.0	0.4	4.0	90	95
27	Ghana	739	1,199	-2.6	3.8	-1.4	-0.1	106	75
28	Central African Rep.	130	170	-1.3	-1.3	-4.8	6.1	107	109
29	Togo	300	700	5.6	2.4	8.5	1.4	118	114
30	Zambia	..	..	..	..	..	..	..	..
31	Guinea	..	..	..	..	..	..	..	..
32	Sri Lanka	1,984	2,689	0.2	6.8	-1.2	2.1	103	90
33	Mauritania	468	248	4.0	3.8	6.3	-5.1	113	107
34	Lesotho[b]	..	..	..	..	..	..	..	..
35	Indonesia	25,553	21,837	9.6	2.8	13.0	1.4	134	111
36	Honduras	916	1,028	3.1	2.4	2.5	-0.7	111	104
37	Egypt, Arab Rep.	2,985	10,340	-0.1	2.1	3.6	-1.7	131	76
38	Afghanistan	..	..	..	..	..	..	..	..
39	Cambodia	..	..	..	..	..	..	..	..
40	Liberia	500	450	4.4	-2.7	1.5	-2.2	97	111
41	Myanmar	322	270	-2.1	-10.1	-4.4	-14.5	106	127
42	Sudan	400	600	-0.3	-0.9	2.3	-8.3	106	100
43	Viet Nam	..	..	..	..	..	..	..	..
	Middle-income economies	**491,128 t**	**485,897 t**	**3.9 w**	**3.8 w**	**6.1 w**	**0.9 w**	**110 m**	**102 m**
	Lower-middle-income	**184,340 t**	**195,680 t**	**..**	**7.2 w**	**4.7 w**	**2.1 w**	**110 m**	**99 m**
44	Bolivia	923	716	2.7	1.4	5.0	-2.4	167	97
45	Zimbabwe	..	1,851	..	..	..	..	100	..
46	Senegal	783	1,620	2.5	5.6	4.1	4.6	106	106
47	Philippines	8,681	13,080	4.6	2.5	2.9	2.3	93	93
48	Côte d'Ivoire	2,600	2,100	5.5	2.7	7.6	-1.2	110	80
49	Dominican Rep.	734	2,057	0.3	1.3	4.9	3.5	109	98
50	Papua New Guinea	1,140	1,288	13.0	6.2	1.6	2.6	111	75
51	Guatemala	1,211	1,626	4.8	-1.7	4.6	-1.4	108	102
52	Morocco	4,263	6,918	3.7	6.1	6.5	2.9	88	86
53	Cameroon	1,200	1,300	4.9	-1.3	5.6	-3.3	139	91
54	Ecuador	2,714	1,862	15.1	4.3	6.4	-3.2	153	109
55	Syrian Arab Rep.	4,173	2,400	11.4	8.7	8.5	-8.3	125	87
56	Congo	1,130	570	10.3	5.9	0.6	-3.1	145	99
57	El Salvador	550	1,200	1.0	-0.8	2.7	-0.5	126	114
58	Paraguay	959	1,113	6.5	10.7	3.7	1.5	108	110
59	Peru	3,277	3,230	1.6	0.3	-1.4	-4.0	111	78
60	Jordan	1,146	2,663	11.2	10.3	9.7	-0.5	95	112
61	Colombia	6,766	5,590	1.4	10.6	5.3	-2.3	140	92
62	Thailand	23,002	33,129	8.6	13.2	4.1	10.2	91	99
63	Tunisia	3,498	5,471	10.8	4.8	10.4	1.1	105	99
64	Jamaica	1,347	1,685	-0.4	0.6	-1.9	1.1	95	88
65	Turkey	12,959	22,300	5.5	9.1	7.7	7.0	82	98
66	Romania	..	..	..	..	..	..	..	..
*	Data for Taiwan, China, are:	67,025	54,696	18.9	12.1	15.1	10.1	103	109

Note: For data comparability and coverage, see the technical notes. Figures in italics are for years other than those specified.

		Merchandise trade (millions of dollars)		Average annual growth rate[a] (percent)				Terms of trade (1987 = 100)	
				Exports		Imports			
		Exports 1990	Imports 1990	1965–80	1980–90	1965–80	1980–90	1985	1990
67	Poland	13,627	9,781	. .	3.0	. .	1.2	94	103
68	Panama	321	1,539	–5.7	–0.3	–1.9	–3.0	130	138
69	Costa Rica	1,457	2,026	7.0	3.1	5.7	2.5	111	114
70	Chile	8,579	7,023	8.0	4.8	1.4	0.6	102	131
71	Botswana[b]	. .	. .	. .	. .	. .	. .	. .	. .
72	Algeria	15,241	10,433	1.8	5.3	13.0	–4.6	174	99
73	Bulgaria	. .	. .	. .	. .	. .	. .	. .	. .
74	Mauritius	1,182	1,616	3.1	9.6	5.2	11.2	83	114
75	Malaysia	29,409	29,251	4.6	10.3	2.2	5.6	117	94
76	Argentina	12,353	4,077	4.7	1.4	1.8	–8.4	110	112
77	Iran, Islamic Rep.	15,000	13,000	. .	21.1	. .	8.0	160	72
78	Albania	. .	. .	. .	. .	. .	. .	. .	. .
79	Angola	3,000	1,200	. .	. .	. .	. .	. .	. .
80	Lebanon	. .	. .	. .	. .	. .	. .	. .	. .
81	Mongolia	. .	. .	. .	. .	. .	. .	. .	. .
82	Namibia[b]	. .	. .	. .	. .	. .	. .	. .	. .
83	Nicaragua	379	750	2.8	–5.3	1.3	–2.8	111	110
84	Yemen, Rep.	. .	. .	. .	. .	. .	. .	. .	. .
	Upper-middle-income	**306,789** *t*	**290,217** *t*	**3.9** *w*	**1.9** *w*	**7.2** *w*	**0.1** *w*	**111** *m*	**105** *m*
85	Mexico	26,714	28,063	7.7	3.4	5.7	–1.1	133	110
86	South Africa[b]	23,612	18,258	7.8	1.7	–0.1	–3.7	105	93
87	Venezuela	17,220	6,364	–9.5	1.8	8.1	–4.6	174	164
88	Uruguay	1,696	1,415	4.6	3.2	1.2	–1.1	89	104
89	Brazil	31,243	22,459	9.3	4.0	8.2	–0.3	92	123
90	Hungary	9,588	8,646	. .	5.5	. .	1.3	104	87
91	Yugoslavia	14,365	18,911	5.6	0.1	6.6	0.6	95	121
92	Czechoslovakia	17,950	19,862	. .	. .	. .	. .	. .	. .
93	Gabon	2,471	760	8.6	1.4	9.5	–1.8	140	96
94	Trinidad and Tobago	2,080	1,262	–5.5	–3.7	–5.8	–12.8	156	110
95	Portugal	16,416	25,333	3.4	11.7	3.7	8.2	85	105
96	Korea, Rep.	64,837	69,585	27.2	12.8	15.2	10.8	103	108
97	Greece	8,053	19,701	11.9	3.8	5.2	4.3	94	105
98	Saudi Arabia	31,065	24,069	8.8	–9.7	25.9	–10.0	176	95
99	Iraq	16,809	4,314	. .	. .	. .	. .	. .	. .
100	Libya	14,285	3,976	3.3	1.8	11.7	–10.4	196	97
101	Oman	458	2,608	. .	. .	. .	. .	. .	. .
	Low- and middle-income	**632,304** *t*	**630,328** *t*	**4.1** *w*	**4.1** *w*	**5.8** *w*	**1.4** *w*	**109** *m*	**100** *m*
	Sub-Saharan Africa	**34,056** *t*	**32,377** *t*	**6.1** *w*	**0.2** *w*	**5.6** *w*	**–4.3** *w*	**110** *m*	**100** *m*
	East Asia & Pacific	**217,030** *t*	**224,021** *t*	**8.5** *w*	**9.8** *w*	**7.1** *w*	**8.0** *w*	**106** *m*	**103** *m*
	South Asia	**27,699** *t*	**38,217** *t*	**1.8** *w*	**6.8** *w*	**0.6** *w*	**4.1** *w*	**101** *m*	**95** *m*
	Europe	**94,082** *t*	**126,493** *t*	. .	. .	. .	. .	**94** *m*	**103** *m*
	Middle East & N.Africa	**112,644** *t*	**89,842** *t*	**5.7** *w*	**–1.1** *w*	**12.8** *w*	**–4.7** *w*	**130** *m*	**96** *m*
	Latin America & Caribbean	**123,181** *t*	**101,119** *t*	**–1.0** *w*	**3.0** *w*	**4.1** *w*	**–2.1** *w*	**111** *m*	**110** *m*
	Other economies	. .	. .	. .	. .	. .	. .	. .	. .
	Severely indebted	**135,856** *t*	**99,721** *t*	**–0.5** *w*	**3.4** *w*	**6.6** *w*	**–2.1** *w*	**118** *m*	**101** *m*
	High-income economies	**2,555,661** *t*	**2,725,419** *t*	**7.3** *w*	**4.3** *w*	**4.4** *w*	**5.3** *w*	**97** *m*	**100** *m*
	OECD members	**2,379,089** *t*	**2,501,753** *t*	**7.2** *w*	**4.1** *w*	**4.1** *w*	**5.2** *w*	**94** *m*	**100** *m*
	†Other	**176,573** *t*	**223,666** *t*	**8.8** *w*	**8.3** *w*	**9.8** *w*	**6.7** *w*	**100** *m*	**100** *m*
102	Ireland	23,796	20,716	10.0	7.3	4.8	3.6	97	95
103	†Israel	12,047	15,197	8.9	7.5	6.2	4.7	105	103
104	Spain	55,607	87,487	12.4	7.4	4.4	9.0	91	106
105	†Singapore	52,627	60,647	4.7	8.6	7.0	6.7	99	100
106	†Hong Kong	29,002	82,495	9.1	6.2	8.3	11.0	97	100
107	New Zealand	9,045	9,466	3.8	3.4	1.1	3.6	88	99
108	Belgium[c]	118,002	119,725	7.8	4.7	5.2	3.1	94	96
109	United Kingdom	185,891	224,914	5.1	2.7	1.4	4.9	103	105
110	Italy	168,523	176,153	7.7	3.5	3.5	4.2	84	97
111	Australia	35,973	39,740	5.4	3.9	1.0	4.7	111	115
112	Netherlands	131,479	125,909	8.0	4.4	4.4	3.5	101	102
113	Austria	41,876	49,960	8.2	6.2	6.1	5.2	87	92
114	France	209,491	232,525	8.5	3.4	4.3	3.2	96	102
115	†United Arab Emirates	. .	. .	13.3	. .	. .	. .	. .	. .
116	Canada	125,056	115,882	5.4	5.9	2.5	8.4	110	109
117	United States	371,466	515,635	6.4	3.3	5.5	7.6	100	100
118	Denmark	34,801	31,562	5.4	5.1	1.7	4.2	93	104
119	Germany[d]	397,912	341,248	7.2	4.2	5.3	3.9	82	97
120	Norway	34,072	26,889	8.2	7.2	3.0	2.5	130	91
121	Sweden	57,326	54,536	4.9	4.4	1.8	3.5	94	101
122	Japan	286,768	231,223	11.4	4.2	4.9	5.6	71	91
123	Finland	26,718	27,098	5.9	3.0	3.1	4.7	85	98
124	Switzerland	63,699	69,427	6.2	3.5	4.5	3.8	86	100
125	†Kuwait	8,300	4,800	18.5	–11.1	11.8	–5.7	175	77
	World	**3,187,965** *t*	**3,355,746** *t*	**6.6** *w*	**4.3** *w*	**4.6** *w*	**4.5** *w*	**106** *m*	**100** *m*
	Fuel exporters, excl. former USSR	**138,638** *t*	**76,773** *t*	**2.5** *w*	**–1.4** *w*	**12.1** *w*	**–7.2** *w*	**170** *m*	**98** *m*

a. See the technical notes.   b. Figures are for the South African Customs Union comprising South Africa, Namibia, Lesotho, Botswana, and Swaziland; trade among the component territories is excluded.   c. Includes Luxembourg.   d. Data refer to the Federal Republic of Germany before unification.

Table 15. Structure of merchandise imports

		Food		Fuels		Other primary commodities		Machinery and transport equipment		Other manufactures	
		1965	1990	1965	1990	1965	1990	1965	1990	1965	1990
Low-income economies		**17** w	**12** w	**5** w	**9** w	**8** w	**8** w	**33** w	**33** w	**37** w	**38** w
China and India		**15** w	**8** w	**3** w	**7** w	**12** w	**10** w	**38** w	**34** w	**31** w	**41** w
Other low-income		**18** w	**15** w	**5** w	**11** w	**5** w	**7** w	**30** w	**32** w	**42** w	**35** w
1	Mozambique	17	..	8	..	7	..	24	..	45	..
2	Tanzania	7	7	9	31	2	2	40	35	42	25
3	Ethiopia	6	17	6	10	6	3	37	44	44	26
4	Somalia	31	19	5	14	8	10	24	24	33	33
5	Nepal	..	9	..	9	..	10	..	26	..	46
6	Chad	13	14	20	14	4	3	21	29	42	40
7	Bhutan	..	..	..	..	..	..	..	..	..	..
8	Lao PDR	27	..	14	..	6	..	19	..	34	..
9	Malawi	15	7	5	13	3	3	21	29	57	47
10	Bangladesh	..	30	..	14	..	6	..	17	..	33
11	Burundi	16	18	6	9	8	7	15	29	55	37
12	Zaire	18	20	7	8	5	5	33	32	37	36
13	Uganda	6	8	2	30	3	2	34	27	55	34
14	Madagascar	19	15	5	22	2	3	25	29	48	31
15	Sierra Leone	17	20	9	20	3	3	29	25	41	32
16	Mali	20	20	6	27	5	3	23	18	47	32
17	Nigeria	9	16	6	1	3	2	34	44	48	37
18	Niger	12	21	6	15	6	6	21	26	55	32
19	Rwanda	12	9	7	16	5	6	28	35	50	35
20	Burkina Faso	23	23	4	17	14	6	19	24	40	30
21	India	22	8	5	17	14	12	37	18	22	45
22	Benin	18	16	6	5	7	10	17	22	53	47
23	China*	7	8	1	2	10	9	39	41	43	39
24	Haiti	19	23	6	13	4	4	21	20	51	40
25	Kenya	6	10	10	32	4	4	34	25	46	30
26	Pakistan	20	19	3	17	5	8	38	27	34	29
27	Ghana	12	11	4	35	3	2	33	21	48	31
28	Central African Rep.	13	20	7	2	2	4	29	34	49	41
29	Togo	14	22	4	6	5	6	32	25	45	41
30	Zambia	..	..	..	..	..	..	..	..	..	..
31	Guinea	..	..	..	..	..	..	..	..	..	..
32	Sri Lanka	41	16	8	15	4	4	12	22	34	44
33	Mauritania	9	22	4	6	1	1	56	42	30	28
34	Lesotho[a]	..	..	..	..	..	..	..	..	..	..
35	Indonesia	6	5	3	9	2	9	39	43	50	35
36	Honduras	11	13	6	16	1	3	26	25	56	44
37	Egypt, Arab Rep.	26	31	7	2	12	10	23	23	31	34
38	*Afghanistan*	17	..	4	..	1	..	8	..	69	..
39	*Cambodia*	6	..	7	..	2	..	26	..	58	..
40	*Liberia*	17	24	8	20	3	3	33	27	39	27
41	*Myanmar*	15	9	4	3	5	2	18	40	58	46
42	*Sudan*	23	18	5	19	4	4	21	22	47	37
43	*Viet Nam*	..	..	..	..	..	..	..	..	..	..
Middle-income economies		**15** w	**11** w	**10** w	**12** w	**11** w	**8** w	**30** w	**34** w	**34** w	**35** w
Lower-middle-income		**17** w	**11** w	**9** w	**10** w	**8** w	**8** w	**28** w	**34** w	**37** w	**37** w
44	Bolivia	19	11	1	1	3	3	34	45	42	41
45	Zimbabwe	7	3	0	16	4	5	41	37	47	38
46	Senegal	36	27	6	16	4	5	15	21	38	30
47	Philippines	20	10	10	13	7	7	33	20	30	50
48	Côte d'Ivoire	18	16	6	22	3	4	28	22	46	36
49	Dominican Rep.	24	12	10	35	4	3	23	23	40	27
50	Papua New Guinea	23	17	4	8	3	2	25	40	45	34
51	Guatemala	11	11	7	13	2	8	29	27	50	42
52	Morocco	36	12	5	15	10	12	18	28	31	33
53	Cameroon	11	15	5	1	4	3	28	31	51	49
54	Ecuador	10	9	9	4	4	7	33	34	44	46
55	Syrian Arab Rep.	22	17	10	18	9	7	16	26	43	32
56	Congo	15	18	6	2	1	2	34	36	44	42
57	El Salvador	15	14	5	11	4	5	28	26	48	43
58	Paraguay	14	9	14	23	2	5	37	30	33	33
59	Peru	17	38	3	4	5	5	41	22	34	31
60	Jordan	28	19	6	16	6	5	18	23	42	38
61	Colombia	8	7	1	5	10	8	45	36	35	44
62	Thailand	6	5	9	9	6	8	31	41	49	37
63	Tunisia	16	10	6	9	7	9	31	28	41	43
64	Jamaica	21	19	9	14	5	4	23	21	42	42
65	Turkey	6	7	10	21	10	11	37	31	37	30
66	Romania	..	..	..	..	..	..	..	..	..	..
*	Data for Taiwan, China, are:	13	6	5	9	25	14	29	37	29	34

Note: For data comparability and coverage, see the technical notes.   Figures in italics are for years other than those specified.

		Food		Fuels		Other primary commodities		Machinery and transport equipment		Other manufactures	
		1965	1990	1965	1990	1965	1990	1965	1990	1965	1990
67	Poland	14	12	18	13	11	11	27	33	24	32
68	Panama	11	15	21	17	2	2	21	18	45	48
69	Costa Rica	9	8	5	10	2	5	29	28	54	49
70	Chile	20	4	6	12	10	4	35	44	30	36
71	Botswana[a]	..	..	..	..	..	..	..	..	..	..
72	Algeria	27	27	0	2	6	8	15	28	52	35
73	Bulgaria	..	..	..	..	..	..	..	..	..	..
74	Mauritius	35	25	5	19	3	5	15	12	42	39
75	Malaysia	25	11	12	5	10	6	22	45	32	33
76	Argentina	6	4	10	9	21	11	25	33	38	44
77	Iran, Islamic Rep.	16	12	0	0	6	5	36	44	42	38
78	Albania	..	..	..	..	..	..	..	..	..	..
79	Angola	17	14	2	4	3	4	24	34	54	43
80	Lebanon	28	..	9	..	9	..	17	..	36	..
81	Mongolia	..	..	..	..	..	..	..	..	..	..
82	Namibia[a]	..	..	..	..	..	..	..	..	..	..
83	Nicaragua	12	12	5	18	2	2	30	27	51	40
84	Yemen, Rep.	55	..	8	..	4	..	12	..	21	..
	Upper-middle-income	**13** w	**10** w	**11** w	**13** w	**13** w	**9** w	**32** w	**33** w	**31** w	**34** w
85	Mexico	5	16	2	4	10	7	50	36	33	37
86	South Africa[a]	5	6	5	1	11	5	42	41	37	48
87	Venezuela	12	12	1	3	5	9	44	39	39	37
88	Uruguay	7	7	17	18	16	6	24	30	36	39
89	Brazil	20	9	21	23	9	11	22	27	28	30
90	Hungary	12	7	11	14	22	8	27	35	28	36
91	Yugoslavia	16	12	6	17	19	8	28	26	32	37
92	Czechoslovakia	13	6	10	30	20	11	34	32	23	20
93	Gabon	16	17	5	2	2	2	37	40	40	38
94	Trinidad and Tobago	12	19	49	11	2	7	16	23	21	39
95	Portugal	16	11	8	11	19	6	27	37	30	35
96	Korea, Rep.	15	5	7	16	26	15	13	34	38	29
97	Greece	15	15	8	8	11	7	35	31	30	40
98	Saudi Arabia	30	15	1	0	5	4	27	39	37	42
99	Iraq	24	15	0	0	7	4	25	48	44	33
100	Libya	13	16	4	1	3	3	36	37	43	43
101	Oman	1	18	4	4	2	2	17	37	75	39
	Low- and middle-income	**15** w	**11** w	**9** w	**11** w	**10** w	**8** w	**31** w	**34** w	**35** w	**36** w
	Sub-Saharan Africa	**15** w	**16** w	**6** w	**14** w	**3** w	**4** w	**30** w	**30** w	**46** w	**36** w
	East Asia & Pacific	**13** w	**7** w	**6** w	**9** w	**9** w	**10** w	**32** w	**38** w	**40** w	**35** w
	South Asia	**25** w	**13** w	**4** w	**16** w	**11** w	**10** w	**34** w	**20** w	**27** w	**41** w
	Europe	**14** w	**11** w	**12** w	**17** w	**17** w	**9** w	**32** w	**34** w	**28** w	**34** w
	Middle East & N.Africa	**24** w	**17** w	**5** w	**6** w	**7** w	**6** w	**24** w	**33** w	**40** w	**37** w
	Latin America & Caribbean	**12** w	**12** w	**13** w	**13** w	**8** w	**7** w	**32** w	**31** w	**35** w	**35** w
	Other economies	..	..	..	..	..	..	..	..	..	..
	Severely indebted	**14** w	**15** w	**9** w	**11** w	**10** w	**9** w	**32** w	**31** w	**34** w	**35** w
	High-income economies	**19** w	**9** w	**10** w	**11** w	**19** w	**7** w	**20** w	**34** w	**32** w	**39** w
	OECD members	**19** w	**9** w	**11** w	**11** w	**20** w	**8** w	**20** w	**34** w	**31** w	**39** w
	†Other	**23** w	**7** w	..	..	**15** w	**7** w	**22** w	**33** w	**42** w	**45** w
102	Ireland	18	10	8	6	10	4	25	36	39	43
103	†Israel	16	7	6	9	12	6	28	27	38	52
104	Spain	19	10	10	12	16	7	27	38	28	33
105	†Singapore	23	5	13	16	19	5	14	42	30	32
106	†Hong Kong	25	6	3	2	13	5	13	26	46	60
107	New Zealand	7	7	7	8	10	4	33	41	43	41
108	Belgium[b]	14	10	9	8	21	8	24	25	32	49
109	United Kingdom	30	10	11	6	25	7	11	37	23	40
110	Italy	24	12	16	11	24	11	15	31	21	36
111	Australia	5	5	8	5	10	4	37	42	41	44
112	Netherlands	15	12	10	10	13	6	25	30	37	42
113	Austria	14	5	7	6	13	7	31	38	35	44
114	France	19	9	15	10	18	7	20	34	27	40
115	†United Arab Emirates	..	..	..	..	..	..	..	..	..	..
116	Canada	10	6	7	6	9	4	40	50	34	33
117	United States	19	6	10	13	20	5	14	40	36	36
118	Denmark	14	12	11	7	11	6	25	31	39	45
119	Germany[c]	22	10	8	8	21	8	13	32	35	42
120	Norway	10	6	7	4	12	10	38	36	32	39
121	Sweden	12	6	11	9	12	6	30	38	36	41
122	Japan	22	14	20	25	38	16	9	16	11	30
123	Finland	10	5	10	12	12	7	35	38	34	38
124	Switzerland	16	6	6	5	11	5	24	31	43	53
125	†Kuwait	22	18	1	1	7	4	32	29	39	46
	World	**18** w	**9** w	**10** w	**11** w	**17** w	**8** w	**23** w	**34** w	**32** w	**39** w
	Fuel exporters, excl. former USSR	**16** w	**16** w	**6** w	**2** w	**5** w	**5** w	**31** w	**38** w	**42** w	**39** w

a. Figures are for the South African Customs Union comprising South Africa, Namibia, Lesotho, Botswana, and Swaziland; trade among the component territories is excluded.   b. Includes Luxembourg.   c. Data refer to the Federal Republic of Germany before unification.

Table 16. Structure of merchandise exports

		Percentage share of merchandise exports									
		Fuels, minerals, and metals		Other primary commodities		Machinery and transport equipment		Other manufactures		Textiles and clothing [a]	
		1965	1990	1965	1990	1965	1990	1965	1990	1965	1990
	Low-income economies	**17 w**	**27 w**	**52 w**	**20 w**	**3 w**	**9 w**	**28 w**	**45 w**	**17 w**	**21 w**
	China and India	**13 w**	**10 w**	**29 w**	**17 w**	**6 w**	**15 w**	**52 w**	**58 w**	**31 w**	**26 w**
	Other low-income	**21 w**	**48 w**	**69 w**	**24 w**	**1 w**	**1 w**	**10 w**	**28 w**	**6 w**	**15 w**
1	Mozambique	14	..	84	..	0	..	2	..	1	..
2	Tanzania	1	5	86	84	0	1	13	10	0	3
3	Ethiopia	0	3	100	94	0	0	0	3	0	1
4	Somalia	0	1	86	94	4	0	10	4	..	0
5	Nepal	..	0	..	25	..	0	..	74	..	57
6	Chad	5	9	92	83	0	5	3	3	0	1
7	Bhutan	..	..	..	..	..	..	..	..	..	..
8	Lao PDR	62	..	32	..	0	..	6	..	0	..
9	Malawi	0	0	99	95	0	0	1	5	0	3
10	Bangladesh	..	1	..	25	..	1	..	72	..	60
11	Burundi	0	0	94	98	0	0	6	1	0	0
12	Zaire	72	56	20	37	0	1	8	6	0	0
13	Uganda	13	3	86	97	0	..	1	0	0	0
14	Madagascar	4	8	90	85	1	2	4	6	1	3
15	Sierra Leone	25	38	14	32	0	..	60	31	0	0
16	Mali	1	0	96	98	1	..	2	2	1	2
17	Nigeria	32	97	65	2	..	0	2	0	0	0
18	Niger	0	81	95	17	1	1	4	2	1	1
19	Rwanda	40	5	60	94	0	0	1	1	..	0
20	Burkina Faso	1	0	94	89	1	4	4	6	2	2
21	India	10	8	41	19	1	7	47	66	36	23
22	Benin	1	4	94	48	2	4	3	44	0	2
23	China*	15	10	20	16	9	17	56	56	29	27
24	Haiti	17	12	57	37	..	7	26	44	4	11
25	Kenya	13	19	77	70	0	0	10	11	0	1
26	Pakistan	2	1	62	29	1	0	35	70	29	58
27	Ghana	13	35	86	64	0	0	1	1	0	0
28	Central African Rep.	1	0	45	74	0	0	54	26	0	..
29	Togo	33	53	62	38	1	1	4	7	0	0
30	Zambia	..	..	..	..	..	..	..	..	..	..
31	Guinea	..	..	..	..	..	..	..	..	..	..
32	Sri Lanka	0	6	99	47	0	1	1	47	0	34
33	Mauritania	94	81	5	13	1	5	0	1	0	0
34	Lesotho[b]	..	..	..	..	..	..	..	..	..	..
35	Indonesia	43	48	53	16	3	1	1	34	0	11
36	Honduras	6	8	90	85	0	0	4	7	1	1
37	Egypt, Arab Rep.	8	41	71	20	0	0	20	39	15	27
38	*Afghanistan*	0	..	87	..	..	..	13	..	12	..
39	*Cambodia*	0	..	99	..	0	..	0	..	0	..
40	*Liberia*	72	65	25	34	1	0	3	1	0	..
41	*Myanmar*	5	4	94	93	0	..	0	3	0	0
42	*Sudan*	1	5	99	94	..	0	0	1	0	1
43	*Viet Nam*	..	..	..	..	..	..	..	..	..	..
	Middle-income economies	**38 w**	**32 w**	**39 w**	**20 w**	**11 w**	**17 w**	**14 w**	**33 w**	**3 w**	**9 w**
	Lower-middle-income	**30 w**	**32 w**	**52 w**	**30 w**	**7 w**	**11 w**	**9 w**	**27 w**	**2 w**	**9 w**
44	Bolivia	93	69	3	27	0	0	4	5	0	1
45	Zimbabwe	24	..	47	..	6	..	23	..	6	..
46	Senegal	9	22	88	56	1	2	2	20	1	1
47	Philippines	11	12	84	26	0	10	6	52	1	7
48	Côte d'Ivoire	2	10	93	80	1	2	4	8	1	2
49	Dominican Rep.	10	0	88	76	0	4	2	19	0	0
50	Papua New Guinea	0	61	90	34	..	4	10	1	..	0
51	Guatemala	0	2	86	74	1	1	13	23	4	4
52	Morocco	40	23	55	30	0	4	5	42	1	20
53	Cameroon	17	29	77	55	3	5	2	11	0	2
54	Ecuador	2	49	96	48	0	0	2	2	1	0
55	Syrian Arab Rep.	1	45	89	17	1	1	9	37	7	25
56	Congo	4	89	45	8	2	1	49	2	0	0
57	El Salvador	2	4	82	74	1	2	16	21	6	6
58	Paraguay	0	0	92	90	0	0	8	10	0	2
59	Peru	45	55	54	29	0	2	1	14	0	8
60	Jordan	33	45	60	10	2	1	5	44	1	5
61	Colombia	18	32	75	42	0	1	6	24	2	8
62	Thailand	11	2	86	34	0	20	3	44	0	16
63	Tunisia	31	19	51	12	0	8	19	61	2	35
64	Jamaica	28	16	41	26	0	1	31	58	4	13
65	Turkey	9	7	89	25	0	7	2	61	1	37
66	Romania	..	..	..	..	..	..	..	..	..	..
*	Data for Taiwan, China, are:	2	2	57	41	4	36	37	57	15	15

Note: For data comparability and coverage, see the technical notes.   Figures in italics are for years other than those specified.

Percentage share of merchandise exports

		Fuels, minerals, and metals		Other primary commodities		Machinery and transport equipment		Other manufactures		Textiles and clothing [a]	
		1965	1990	1965	1990	1965	1990	1965	1990	1965	1990
67	Poland	20	18	9	15	36	34	25	34	6	5
68	Panama	35	2	63	78	0	0	2	19	1	7
69	Costa Rica	0	2	84	72	1	3	15	22	2	6
70	Chile	89	57	7	33	1	1	4	9	0	1
71	Botswana [b]	..	..	..	..	..	..	..	..	..	..
72	Algeria	57	96	39	0	2	2	2	2	0	0
73	Bulgaria	..	..	..	..	..	..	..	..	..	..
74	Mauritius	0	0	100	70	0	0	0	30	0	24
75	Malaysia	34	19	60	37	2	27	4	17	0	5
76	Argentina	1	6	93	59	1	7	5	29	0	3
77	Iran, Islamic Rep.	88	98	8	1	0	0	4	1	4	0
78	*Albania*	..	..	..	..	..	..	..	..	..	..
79	*Angola*	6	82	76	5	1	..	17	12	0	..
80	*Lebanon*	14	..	52	..	14	..	19	..	2	..
81	*Mongolia*	..	..	..	..	..	..	..	..	..	..
82	*Namibia* [b]	..	..	..	..	..	..	..	..	..	..
83	*Nicaragua*	4	0	90	94	0	0	6	6	0	1
84	*Yemen, Rep.*	..	..	..	..	..	..	..	..	..	..
	Upper-middle-income	**44** *w*	**32** *w*	**26** *w*	**13** *w*	**14** *w*	**20** *w*	**18** *w*	**37** *w*	**4** *w*	**9** *w*
85	Mexico	22	43	62	13	1	25	15	19	3	2
86	South Africa [b]	24	14	44	12	3	3	29	71	1	1
87	Venezuela	97	87	1	2	0	2	2	9	0	1
88	Uruguay	0	0	95	60	0	2	5	37	2	14
89	Brazil	9	16	83	31	2	18	7	35	1	3
90	Hungary	5	9	25	26	32	26	37	40	9	6
91	Yugoslavia	10	9	33	12	24	30	33	49	8	7
92	Czechoslovakia	7	4	6	6	50	54	37	36	6	6
93	Gabon	52	86	37	8	1	1	10	5	0	0
94	Trinidad and Tobago	84	68	9	6	0	2	7	25	0	0
95	Portugal	4	6	34	13	3	19	58	61	24	29
96	Korea, Rep.	15	2	25	5	3	37	56	57	27	22
97	Greece	8	14	78	32	2	4	11	50	3	27
98	Saudi Arabia	98	88	1	1	0	1	1	11	0	0
99	*Iraq*	95	35	4	41	0	0	1	24	0	0
100	*Libya*	99	100	1	0	0	0	0	0	0	0
101	*Oman*	100	14	0	18	..	41	0	27	..	6
	Low- and middle-income	**33** *w*	**31** *w*	**42** *w*	**20** *w*	**9** *w*	**15** *w*	**17** *w*	**35** *w*	**7** *w*	**12** *w*
	Sub-Saharan Africa	**23** *w*	**63** *w*	**70** *w*	**29** *w*	**0** *w*	**1** *w*	**7** *w*	**7** *w*	**0** *w*	**1** *w*
	East Asia & Pacific	**21** *w*	**13** *w*	**48** *w*	**18** *w*	**5** *w*	**22** *w*	**27** *w*	**47** *w*	**13** *w*	**19** *w*
	South Asia	**6** *w*	**6** *w*	**57** *w*	**24** *w*	**1** *w*	**5** *w*	**36** *w*	**65** *w*	**29** *w*	**33** *w*
	Europe	**10** *w*	**9** *w*	**21** *w*	**16** *w*	**33** *w*	**27** *w*	**32** *w*	**47** *w*	**8** *w*	**16** *w*
	Middle East & N.Africa	**74** *w*	**75** *w*	**24** *w*	**12** *w*	**0** *w*	**1** *w*	**4** *w*	**15** *w*	**3** *w*	**4** *w*
	Latin America & Caribbean	**45** *w*	**38** *w*	**48** *w*	**29** *w*	**1** *w*	**11** *w*	**6** *w*	**21** *w*	**1** *w*	**3** *w*
	Other economies	..	..	..	..	..	..	..	..	..	..
	Severely indebted	**39** *w*	**42** *w*	**42** *w*	**22** *w*	**8** *w*	**14** *w*	**9** *w*	**22** *w*	**2** *w*	**4** *w*
	High-income economies	**10** *w*	**8** *w*	**21** *w*	**11** *w*	**31** *w*	**42** *w*	**38** *w*	**40** *w*	**7** *w*	**5** *w*
	OECD members	**9** *w*	**7** *w*	**21** *w*	**12** *w*	**31** *w*	**42** *w*	**38** *w*	**39** *w*	**7** *w*	**4** *w*
	†Other	**39** *w*	**11** *w*	**24** *w*	**7** *w*	**5** *w*	**36** *w*	**36** *w*	**48** *w*	**16** *w*	**15** *w*
102	Ireland	3	2	63	24	5	32	29	43	7	4
103	†Israel	6	2	28	11	2	24	63	62	9	6
104	Spain	9	7	51	17	10	39	29	37	6	4
105	†Singapore	21	19	44	8	10	48	24	25	6	5
106	†Hong Kong	1	1	5	3	7	23	87	73	52	39
107	New Zealand	1	10	94	65	0	5	5	20	0	2
108	Belgium [c]	13	8	11	11	20	27	55	54	12	7
109	United Kingdom	7	11	9	8	42	40	42	41	7	4
110	Italy	8	3	14	7	30	38	47	52	15	13
111	Australia	13	34	73	29	5	6	10	30	1	1
112	Netherlands	12	12	32	24	21	22	35	41	9	4
113	Austria	8	4	17	8	20	37	55	51	12	8
114	France	8	5	21	18	26	37	45	40	10	5
115	†United Arab Emirates	99	..	1	..	0	..	..	..	1	..
116	Canada	28	19	35	18	15	37	22	26	1	1
117	United States	8	6	27	16	37	47	28	31	3	2
118	Denmark	2	5	55	31	22	26	21	38	4	4
119	Germany [d]	7	4	5	6	46	49	42	41	5	5
120	Norway	21	58	28	9	17	13	34	19	2	1
121	Sweden	9	6	23	9	35	44	33	40	2	2
122	Japan	2	1	7	1	31	66	60	32	17	2
123	Finland	3	5	40	12	12	31	45	52	2	3
124	Switzerland	3	3	7	4	30	32	60	62	10	5
125	†*Kuwait*	98	5	1	7	1	26	0	58	0	9
	World	**16** *w*	**12** *w*	**27** *w*	**13** *w*	**25** *w*	**36** *w*	**33** *w*	**39** *w*	**7** *w*	**6** *w*
	Fuel exporters, excl. former USSR	**85** *w*	**85** *w*	**14** *w*	**7** *w*	**0** *w*	**1** *w*	**2** *w*	**8** *w*	**0** *w*	**0** *w*

a. See the technical notes.   b. Figures are for the South African Customs Union comprising South Africa, Namibia, Lesotho, Botswana, and Swaziland; trade among the component territories is excluded.   c. Includes Luxembourg.   d. Data refer to the Federal Republic of Germany before unification.

Table 17. OECD imports of manufactured goods: origin and composition

		Value of imports of manufactures, by origin (millions of dollars)[a]		Composition of 1990 imports of manufactures (percent)[a]				
		1970	1990[a]	Textiles and clothing	Chemicals	Electrical machinery and electronics	Transport equipment	Others
	Low-income economies	**1,259** *t*	**59,379** *t*	**40** *w*	**5** *w*	**7** *w*	**3** *w*	**45** *w*
	China and India	**777** *t*	**43,249** *t*	**38** *w*	**6** *w*	**9** *w*	**1** *w*	**47** *w*
	Other low-income	**483** *t*	**16,130** *t*	**46** *w*	**4** *w*	**1** *w*	**8** *w*	**41** *w*
1	Mozambique	7	16	57	1	5	0	37
2	Tanzania	9	47	60	2	1	2	36
3	Ethiopia	4	74	11	7	2	4	75
4	Somalia	0	2	5	0	17	7	70
5	Nepal	1	214	92	0	1	1	7
6	Chad	0	11	1	90	0	0	8
7	Bhutan	0	1	8	1	0	0	91
8	Lao PDR	0	7	86	1	1	0	13
9	Malawi	1	14	81	0	5	1	14
10	Bangladesh	0	1,212	87	0	0	0	13
11	Burundi	0	3	36	2	1	3	57
12	Zaire	9	334	0	1	0	1	98
13	Uganda	1	2	7	9	13	30	42
14	Madagascar	7	46	59	11	0	2	28
15	Sierra Leone	2	87	1	0	0	0	99
16	Mali	2	23	3	1	5	23	68
17	Nigeria	13	269	6	16	2	1	76
18	Niger	0	280	0	82	0	0	18
19	Rwanda	0	1	2	14	12	0	72
20	Burkina Faso	0	7	7	1	8	1	83
21	India	534	9,182	44	5	1	1	49
22	Benin	0	2	12	0	5	0	82
23	China	243	34,068	36	6	11	1	46
24	Haiti	17	373	54	2	13	2	29
25	Kenya	16	111	8	2	6	4	80
26	Pakistan	207	2,878	82	1	0	0	17
27	Ghana	8	130	0	1	1	0	98
28	Central African Rep.	12	77	0	0	0	0	100
29	Togo	0	11	1	1	2	0	97
30	Zambia	4	41	27	1	0	4	68
31	Guinea	38	119	0	27	1	0	72
32	Sri Lanka	9	1,126	70	1	1	0	28
33	Mauritania	0	9	7	3	2	3	85
34	Lesotho[b]	. .	. .	. .	. .	. .	. .	. .
35	Indonesia	15	5,827	36	2	2	1	60
36	Honduras	3	175	71	2	1	2	24
37	Egypt, Arab Rep.	33	799	53	5	1	18	24
38	*Afghanistan*	9	49	93	1	1	0	6
39	*Cambodia*	1	2	41	0	5	0	55
40	*Liberia*	20	1,480	0	0	0	73	27
41	*Myanmar*	4	43	25	3	0	3	68
42	*Sudan*	1	11	7	0	2	3	87
43	*Viet Nam*	0	78	77	3	0	0	19
	Middle-income economies	**5,006** *t*	**175,503** *t*	**25** *w*	**7** *w*	**17** *w*	**7** *w*	**44** *w*
	Lower-middle-income	**1,401** *t*	**55,667** *t*	**34** *w*	**7** *w*	**17** *w*	**3** *w*	**40** *w*
44	Bolivia	1	48	16	3	0	1	80
45	Zimbabwe	0	279	19	0	1	1	78
46	Senegal	4	24	8	47	3	2	40
47	Philippines	108	5,035	36	2	29	1	33
48	Côte d'Ivoire	7	239	21	3	1	1	76
49	Dominican Rep.	10	1,498	51	1	7	0	42
50	Papua New Guinea	4	28	5	1	1	14	78
51	Guatemala	5	329	68	3	0	18	12
52	Morocco	32	2,326	67	16	7	1	10
53	Cameroon	4	57	19	0	1	2	78
54	Ecuador	3	77	16	3	4	14	64
55	Syrian Arab Rep.	2	40	66	1	1	5	28
56	Congo	4	160	0	0	0	0	99
57	El Salvador	2	142	56	1	25	0	18
58	Paraguay	5	87	20	28	0	0	52
59	Peru	12	477	51	7	3	1	38
60	Jordan	1	99	10	23	4	26	37
61	Colombia	52	1,027	26	6	0	0	68
62	Thailand	32	10,515	22	2	16	1	60
63	Tunisia	19	2,041	69	9	8	3	12
64	Jamaica	117	797	34	62	0	0	3
65	Turkey	47	6,709	70	4	5	2	20
66	Romania	188	1,729	33	5	3	1	58

Note: For data comparability and coverage, see the technical notes.   Figures in italics are for years other than those specified.

		Value of imports of manufactures, by origin (millions of dollars)[a]		Composition of 1990 imports of manufactures (percent)[a]				
		1970	1990[a]	Textiles and clothing	Chemicals	Electrical machinery and electronics	Transport equipment	Others
67	Poland	287	4,553	21	18	7	5	49
68	Panama[c]	18	893	8	2	0	58	32
69	Costa Rica	5	610	69	1	9	0	21
70	Chile	15	611	11	29	1	1	59
71	Botswana[b]	. .	. .	. .	. .	. .	. .	. .
72	Algeria	39	1,326	0	5	1	1	94
73	Bulgaria	68	489	24	18	4	6	48
74	Mauritius	1	800	82	0	0	3	15
75	Malaysia	39	9,703	15	3	53	1	28
76	Argentina	104	1,715	10	18	1	4	66
77	Iran, Islamic Rep.	133	546	93	0	0	0	7
78	Albania	1	45	40	4	1	0	56
79	Angola	2	273	0	0	0	2	98
80	Lebanon	17	144	17	6	4	4	69
81	Mongolia	0	4	64	14	1	0	22
82	Namibia[b]	. .	. .	. .	. .	. .	. .	. .
83	Nicaragua	6	6	4	19	14	8	56
84	Yemen, Rep.	0	. .	. .	. .	. .	. .	. .
Upper-middle-income		**3,605** *t*	**119,836** *t*	**21** *w*	**7** *w*	**17** *w*	**9** *w*	**46** *w*
85	Mexico	508	23,704	5	5	34	17	40
86	South Africa[b]	325	3,236	5	16	2	3	75
87	Venezuela	24	955	4	11	3	7	75
88	Uruguay	23	321	47	4	0	2	48
89	Brazil	197	11,001	7	10	5	13	65
90	Hungary	210	3,433	23	18	10	4	45
91	Yugoslavia	443	9,229	28	8	9	11	44
92	Czechoslovakia	467	3,315	16	16	5	5	58
93	Gabon	8	76	0	56	0	2	41
94	Trinidad and Tobago	39	327	1	56	0	0	43
95	Portugal	396	13,069	38	6	9	10	37
96	Korea, Rep.	524	40,773	24	3	20	6	48
97	Greece	185	4,162	59	5	4	1	31
98	Saudi Arabia	16	1,871	0	47	5	10	38
99	Iraq	4	84	1	18	3	4	73
100	Libya	5	381	0	95	0	1	4
101	Oman	0	204	16	0	15	15	53
Low- and middle-income		**6,266** *t*	**234,882** *t*	**29** *w*	**7** *w*	**14** *w*	**6** *w*	**44** *w*
Sub-Saharan Africa		**193** *t*	**5,237** *t*	**17** *w*	**8** *w*	**1** *w*	**22** *w*	**53** *w*
East Asia & Pacific		**1,077** *t*	**108,021** *t*	**29** *w*	**4** *w*	**19** *w*	**3** *w*	**46** *w*
South Asia		**755** *t*	**14,676** *t*	**58** *w*	**3** *w*	**1** *w*	**1** *w*	**38** *w*
Europe		**2,316** *t*	**47,712** *t*	**38** *w*	**9** *w*	**8** *w*	**7** *w*	**39** *w*
Middle East & N. Africa		**315** *t*	**10,103** *t*	**40** *w*	**20** *w*	**5** *w*	**5** *w*	**31** *w*
Latin America & Caribbean		**1,285** *t*	**45,896** *t*	**11** *w*	**9** *w*	**19** *w*	**14** *w*	**47** *w*
Other economies		**369** *t*	**5,618** *t*	**3** *w*	**23** *w*	**3** *w*	**10** *w*	**60** *w*
Severely indebted		**1,296** *t*	**47,115** *t*	**11** *w*	**8** *w*	**19** *w*	**13** *w*	**49** *w*
High-income economies		**120,192** *t*	**1,566,722** *t*	**6** *w*	**12** *w*	**12** *w*	**19** *w*	**52** *w*
OECD members		**117,067** *t*	**1,465,897** *t*	**5** *w*	**13** *w*	**11** *w*	**20** *w*	**52** *w*
†Other		**3,125** *t*	**100,825** *t*	**18** *w*	**4** *w*	**18** *w*	**3** *w*	**57** *w*
102	Ireland	439	15,204	7	26	11	2	55
103	†Israel	308	7,998	9	14	9	3	65
104	Spain	773	30,894	5	10	7	31	47
105	†Singapore	112	19,504	5	6	30	2	57
106	†Hong Kong	1,861	24,331	42	1	14	1	43
107	New Zealand	121	1,909	9	21	8	4	59
108	Belgium[d]	7,660	80,341	8.8	19.7	5.9	20.8	44.9
109	United Kingdom	10,457	105,934	5	17	10	12	56
110	Italy	7,726	115,210	16	7	8	11	58
111	Australia	471	6,763	3	33	4	13	46
112	Netherlands	5,678	73,069	7	28	9	10	46
113	Austria	1,637	28,723	9	8	13	6	63
114	France	9,240	133,346	6	16	9	23	47
115	†United Arab Emirates	1	841	30	21	3	8	38
116	Canada	8,088	74,359	1	8	7	40	44
117	United States	21,215	206,284	2	12	13	21	52
118	Denmark	1,413	18,267	8	14	11	4	63
119	Germany[e]	23,342	280,732	5	14	10	21	50
120	Norway	1,059	8,964	2	22	7	9	61
121	Sweden	4,143	41,476	2	9	10	19	61
122	Japan	8,851	177,815	1	3	19	30	46
123	Finland	1,170	17,028	3	8	9	5	75
124	Switzerland	3,568	49,436	5	22	9	3	61
125	†Kuwait	6	147	4	46	4	6	39
World		**127,126** *t*	**1,808,855** *t*	**9** *w*	**11** *w*	**12** *w*	**17** *w*	**51** *w*
Fuel exporters, excl. former USSR		**292** *t*	**7,773** *t*	**11** *w*	**25** *w*	**3** *w*	**5** *w*	**56** *w*

Note: Data cover high-income OECD countries only. a. Trade data is based on the UN Comtrade data base, Revision 1 SITC for 1970 and Revision 2 SITC for 1990. b. Figures are for the South African Customs Union comprising South Africa, Namibia, Lesotho, Botswana, and Swaziland; trade among the component territories is excluded. c. Excludes the Canal Zone. d. Includes Luxembourg. e. Data refer to the Federal Republic of Germany before unification.

Table 18. Balance of payments and reserves

		Current account balance (millions of dollars)				Net workers' remittances (millions of dollars)		Gross international reserves		
		After official transfers		Before official transfers				Millions of dollars		In months of import coverage
		1970	1990	1970	1990	1970	1990	1970	1990	1990
Low-income economies								**3,799 t**	**63,863 t**	**3.4 w**
China and India								**1,023 t**	**40,113 t**	**4.4 w**
Other low-income								**2,775 t**	**23,749 t**	**2.4 w**
1	Mozambique	..	−335[a]	..	−784[a]	..	45[a]	..	..	..
2	Tanzania	−36	−426	−37	−955	..	0	65	193	1.4
3	Ethiopia	−32	−146[a]	−43	−308[a]	..	..	72	55	0.6
4	Somalia	−6	−81	−18	−346	..	..	21	23	0.5
5	Nepal	−1[a]	−264[a]	−25[a]	−316[a]	..	0[a]	94	354	5.4
6	Chad	2	−79	−33	−298	−6	0	2	133	3.5
7	Bhutan	..	19	..	−38	..	0	..	86	7.4
8	Lao PDR	..	−106	..	−148	..	..	6	61	2.9
9	Malawi	−35	−80	−46	−162	−4	..	29	142	2.4
10	Bangladesh	−114[a]	−775[a]	−234[a]	−1,541[a]	0[a]	761	..	660	1.8
11	Burundi	2[a]	−56[a]	−2[a]	−205	..	..	15	112	4.3
12	Zaire	−64	−643	−141	−860	−98	..	189	261	1.0
13	Uganda	20	−255[a]	19	−434[a]	−5	..	57	44	0.7
14	Madagascar	10	−153	−42	−324	−26	−11	37	245	3.7
15	Sierra Leone	−16	−95	−20	−136	..	0	39	5	0.2
16	Mali	−2	−94	−22	−364	−1	68	1	198	2.7
17	Nigeria	−368	5,126	−412	5,027	..	−14	223	4,129	5.1
18	Niger	0	−65	−32	−247	−3	12	19	226	4.6
19	Rwanda	7	−85	−12	−224	−4	−14	8	44	1.4
20	Burkina Faso	9	−111	−21	−383	16	83	36	305	4.2
21	India	−385[a]	−9,304[a]	−591[a]	−9,828[a]	80[a]	1,947[a]	1,023	5,637	1.9
22	Benin	−3	−94[a]	−23	−153[a]	0	70[a]	16	69	1.4
23	China*	−81[a]	12,000[a]	−81[a]	11,935[a]	0[a]	108[a]	..	34,476	7.4
24	Haiti	11	−55	4	−158	13	47	4	10	0.3
25	Kenya	−49	−477	−86	−684	..	−2	220	236	0.9
26	Pakistan	−667	−1,362	−705	−1,902	86	1,947	195	1,046	1.2
27	Ghana	−68	−229	−76	−442	−9	3	43	309	2.3
28	Central African Rep.	−12	−97	−24	−260	−4	−260	1	118	3.6
29	Togo	3	−100	−14	−208	−3	5	35	358	5.3
30	Zambia	108	−343	107	−490	−48	−23	515	201	0.9
31	Guinea	..	−182	..	−283	..	..	..	..	..
32	Sri Lanka	−59	−296	−71	−474	3	401	43	447	1.7
33	Mauritania	−5	−199	−13	−199	−6	0	3	59	1.0
34	Lesotho	18[a]	97	−1[a]	−148	29[a]	391	..	72	1.2
35	Indonesia	−310	−2,369	−376	−2,430	..	153	160	8,657	3.2
36	Honduras	−64	−190	−68	−397	..	..	20	47	0.4
37	Egypt, Arab Rep.	−148	−1,425[a]	−452	−2,535[a]	29	3,744[a]	165	3,620	2.7
38	*Afghanistan*	..	−142	..	−454	..	..	49	638	10.3
39	*Cambodia*	..	..	..	..	..	..	..	..	..
40	*Liberia*	−16[a]	..	−27[a]	..	−18[a]	..	..	8	..
41	*Myanmar*	−63	−163[a]	−81	−204[a]	..	0[a]	98	410	4.7
42	*Sudan*	−42	−876[a]	−43	−1,217[a]	..	188[a]	22	11	0.1
43	*Viet Nam*	..	−213	..	−323	..	..	243	..	..
Middle-income economies								**16,301 t**	**194,139 t**	**3.4 w**
Lower-middle-income								**6,292 t**	**81,842 t**	**3.1 w**
44	Bolivia	4	−194	2	−339	..	1	46	511	4.5
45	Zimbabwe	−14[a]	−158	−26[a]	−266	..	..	59	295	1.5
46	Senegal	−16	−125	−66	−481	−16	32	22	22	0.1
47	Philippines	−48	−2,695	−138	−3,052	..	262	255	2,036	1.5
48	Côte d'Ivoire	−38	−1,104	−73	−1,210	−56	−540	119	21	0.1
49	Dominican Rep.	−102	−59	−103	−114	25	315	32	69	0.3
50	Papua New Guinea	−89[a]	−352	−239[a]	−566	..	51	..	427	2.6
51	Guatemala	−8	−279	−8	−335	..	64	79	362	2.1
52	Morocco	−124	−200	−161	−520	27	1,995	142	2,338	3.2
53	Cameroon	−30	−278[a]	−47	−278[a]	−11	3[a]	81	92	0.5
54	Ecuador	−113	−136	−122	−236	..	..	76	1,009	3.5
55	Syrian Arab Rep.	−69	1,827	−72	1,747	7	375	57	..	..
56	Congo	−45[a]	−123	−53[a]	−197	−3[a]	−41	9	21	0.2
57	El Salvador	9	−135	7	−360	..	345	64	595	4.4
58	Paraguay	−16	102[a]	−19	102[a]	..	..	18	700	4.6
59	Peru	202	−674	146	−921	..	..	339	1,891	4.3
60	Jordan	−20	−754[a]	−130	−1,147[a]	..	500[a]	258	1,139	3.3
61	Colombia	−293	391	−333	406	6	488	207	4,453	5.6
62	Thailand	−250	−7,053	−296	−7,235	..	74	911	14,258	4.4
63	Tunisia	−53	−500	−88	−715	20	591	60	867	1.6
64	Jamaica	−153	−271	−149	−386	29	..	139	168	0.7
65	Turkey	−44	−2,616	−57	−3,778	273	3,246	440	7,626	3.1
66	Romania	−23	−3,254	−23	−3,254	..	..	..	1,374	1.7
*	Data for Taiwan, China, are:	1	10,769	2	10,774	..	..	627	77,653	13.4

Note: For data comparability and coverage, see the technical notes. Figures in italics are for years other than those specified.

		Current account balance (millions of dollars)				Net workers' remittances (millions of dollars)		Gross international reserves		
		After official transfers		Before official transfers				Millions of dollars		In months of import coverage
		1970	1990	1970	1990	1970	1990	1970	1990	1990
67	Poland	..	3,067	..	2,762	..	0	..	4,674	2.9
68	Panama	−64	91	−79	−27	..	..	16	406	0.9
69	Costa Rica	−74	−514	−77	−679	..	..	16	525	2.3
70	Chile	−91	−790	−95	−935	..	..	392	6,784	7.1
71	Botswana	−30[a]	137	−35[a]	−179	−9[a]	−41	..	3,385	17.0
72	Algeria	−125	1,420	−163	1,419	178	321	352	2,703	2.6
73	Bulgaria	..	−1,710	..	−1,710	..	..	..	..	
74	Mauritius	8	−119	5	−128	..	..	46	761	4.7
75	Malaysia	8	−1,672	2	−1,733	..	0	667	10,659	3.5
76	Argentina	−163	1,789	−160	1,789	..		682	6,222	5.6
77	Iran, Islamic Rep.	−507	−385	−511	−385	..	..	217	..	..
78	Albania	..	−154	..	−154	..	..	..	..	..
79	Angola	..	..	..	..	..	..	..	..	..
80	Lebanon	..	..	..	..	..	..	405	4,210	..
81	Mongolia	..	−640	..	−647	..	0	..	..	..
82	Namibia	..	..	..	..	..	..	..	..	..
83	Nicaragua	−40	−369	−43	−571	..	..	49		
84	Yemen, Rep.	..	620[a]	..	503[a]	..	1,366[a]		280	1.2
	Upper-middle-income							**10,009 t**	**112,297 t**	**3.6 w**
85	Mexico	−1,068	−5,255	−1,098	−6,521	..	2,020	756	10,217	2.4
86	South Africa	−1,215	2,253	−1,253	2,243	..	..	1,057	2,583	1.2
87	Venezuela	−104	8,198	−98	8,221	−87	−619	1,047	12,733	12.2
88	Uruguay	−45	224	−55	216	..	..	186	1,466	8.1
89	Brazil	−837	−2,983	−861	−2,983	..	..	1,190	9,200	2.8
90	Hungary	−25	230[a]	−25	230[a]	..	0[a]	..	1,186	1.2
91	Yugoslavia	−372	−2,364	−378	−2,362	441	9,360	143	6,208	2.2
92	Czechoslovakia	146	−1,227	156	−1,175	..	..	..	2,059	1.5
93	Gabon	−3	224	−15	236	−8	−141	15	40	0.2
94	Trinidad and Tobago	−109	430	−104	434	3	3	43	513	3.3
95	Portugal	−158[a]	−139	−158[a]	−1,119	504[a]	4,271	1,565	20,579	8.7
96	Korea, Rep.	−623	−2,172	−706	−2,181	..	0	610	14,916	2.2
97	Greece	−422	−3,537	−424	−6,438	333	1,775	318	4,721	2.6
98	Saudi Arabia	71	−4,107	152	294	−183	−11,637	670	13,437	3.6
99	Iraq	105	..	104	..	..	..	472	..	..
100	Libya	645	2,203	758	2,239	−134	−446	1,596	7,225	9.2
101	Oman	..	1,095	..	1,153	..	−845	13	1,784	5.5
	Low- and middle-income							**20,100 t**	**258,002 t**	**3.4 w**
	Sub-Saharan Africa							**2,028 t**	**12,684 t**	**2.3 w**
	East Asia & Pacific							**2,885 t**	**85,907 t**	**3.4 w**
	South Asia							**1,453 t**	**8,665 t**	**3.6 w**
	Europe							**2,624 t**	**49,920 t**	**3.7 w**
	Middle East & N.Africa							**4,526 t**	**39,533 t**	**4.2 w**
	Latin America & Caribbean							**5,527 t**	**58,710 t**	**3.2 w**
	Other economies							**..**	**..**	**..**
	Severely indebted							**4,863 t**	**51,538 t**	**2.8 w**
	High-income economies							**71,917 t**	**892,347 t**	**3.1 w**
	OECD members							**69,975 t**	**846,197 t**	**3.1 w**
	†Other							**1,942 t**	**46,151 t**	**4.1 w**
102	Ireland	−198	1,433	−228	−1,249	..	..	698	5,362	2.1
103	†Israel	−562	702	−766	−3,105	..	..	452	6,598	3.4
104	Spain	79	−16,819	79	−18,023	469	1,747	1,851	57,238	6.3
105	†Singapore	−572	2,350	−585	2,445	..	..	1,012	27,748	4.8
106	†Hong Kong	225	..	225	..	..	..	..	..	..
107	New Zealand	−232	−1,594	−222	−1,555	16	259	258	4,129	3.4
108	Belgium[b]	717	4,548	904	5,967	38	−386	..	..	..
109	United Kingdom	1,970	−24,596	2,376	−16,314	..	..	2,918	43,145	1.3
110	Italy	800	−12,733	1,096	−9,487	446	1,181	5,547	88,595	4.5
111	Australia	−777	−14,823	−682	−14,725	..	..	1,709	19,319	3.3
112	Netherlands	−489	10,393	−513	12,374	−51	−298	3,362	34,401	2.5
113	Austria	−75	958	−73	1,067	−7	307	1,806	17,228	2.9
114	France	−204	−9,875	18	−3,648	−641	−1,983	5,199	68,291	2.4
115	†United Arab Emirates	90	..	100	..	..	..	..	4,891	..
116	Canada	1,008	−18,815	960	−17,955	..	..	4,733	23,530	1.6
117	United States	2,330	−92,160	4,680	−71,710	−650	−1,100	15,237	173,094	2.9
118	Denmark	−544	1,541	−510	1,551	..	..	488	11,226	2.5
119	Germany[c]	852	46,800	1,899	62,774	−1,366	−4,556	13,879	104,547	2.8
120	Norway	−242	3,783	−200	4,991	..	−66	813	15,788	4.2
121	Sweden	−265	−5,833	−160	−4,188	..	18	775	20,324	2.9
122	Japan	1,990	35,870	2,170	40,380	..	..	4,876	87,828	2.6
123	Finland	−240	−6,682	−233	−5,947	..	..	455	10,415	3.1
124	Switzerland	161	6,941	203	7,111	−313	−1,980	5,317	61,281	6.4
125	†Kuwait	853[a]	8,445	853[a]	8,656	..	−1,287	209	4,120	4.3
	World							**92,016 t**	**1,150,349 t**	**3.1 w**
	Fuel exporters, excl. former USSR							**4,693 t**	**48,426 t**	**5.4 w**

a. World Bank estimate.　b. Includes Luxembourg.　c. Data prior to July 1990 refer to the Federal Republic of Germany before unification.

Table 19. Official development assistance from OECD and OPEC members

OECD: Total net flows[a]	1965	1970	1975	1980	1985	1987	1988	1989	1990
				Millions of US dollars					
102 Ireland	0	0	8	30	39	51	57	49	57
107 New Zealand	..	14	66	72	54	87	104	87	95
108 Belgium	102	120	378	595	440	687	601	703	889
109 United Kingdom	472	500	904	1,854	1,530	1,871	2,645	2,587	2,638
110 Italy	60	147	182	683	1,098	2,615	3,193	3,613	3,395
111 Australia	119	212	552	667	749	627	1,101	1,020	955
112 Netherlands	70	196	608	1,630	1,136	2,094	2,231	2,094	2,592
113 Austria	10	11	79	178	248	201	301	283	394
114 France	752	971	2,093	4,162	3,995	6,525	6,865	7,450	9,380
116 Canada	96	337	880	1,075	1,631	1,885	2,347	2,320	2,470
117 United States	4,023	3,153	4,161	7,138	9,403	9,115	10,141	7,676	11,394
118 Denmark	13	59	205	481	440	859	922	937	1,171
119 Germany[b]	456	599	1,689	3,567	2,942	4,391	4,731	4,949	6,320
120 Norway	11	37	184	486	574	890	985	917	1,205
121 Sweden	38	117	566	962	840	1,375	1,534	1,799	2,012
122 Japan	244	458	1,148	3,353	3,797	7,342	9,134	8,965	9,069
123 Finland	2	7	48	110	211	433	608	706	846
124 Switzerland	12	30	104	253	302	547	617	558	750
Total	6,480	6,968	13,855	27,296	29,429	41,595	48,114	46,713	55,632
				As a percentage of donor GNP					
102 Ireland	0.00	0.00	0.09	0.16	0.24	0.19	0.20	0.17	0.16
107 New Zealand	..	0.23	0.52	0.33	0.25	0.26	0.27	0.22	0.23
108 Belgium	0.60	0.46	0.59	0.50	0.55	0.48	0.39	0.46	0.45
109 United Kingdom	0.47	0.41	0.39	0.35	0.33	0.28	0.32	0.31	0.27
110 Italy	0.10	0.16	0.11	0.15	0.26	0.35	0.39	0.42	0.32
111 Australia	0.53	0.59	0.65	0.48	0.48	0.34	0.46	0.38	0.34
112 Netherlands	0.36	0.61	0.75	0.97	0.91	0.98	0.98	0.94	0.94
113 Austria	0.11	0.07	0.21	0.23	0.38	0.17	0.24	0.23	0.25
114 France	0.76	0.66	0.62	0.63	0.78	0.74	0.72	0.78	0.79
116 Canada	0.19	0.41	0.54	0.43	0.49	0.47	0.50	0.44	0.44
117 United States	0.58	0.32	0.27	0.27	0.24	0.20	0.21	0.15	0.21
118 Denmark	0.13	0.38	0.58	0.74	0.80	0.88	0.89	0.93	0.93
119 Germany[b]	0.40	0.32	0.40	0.44	0.47	0.39	0.39	0.41	0.42
120 Norway	0.16	0.32	0.66	0.87	1.01	1.09	1.13	1.05	1.17
121 Sweden	0.19	0.38	0.82	0.78	0.86	0.88	0.86	0.96	0.90
122 Japan	0.27	0.23	0.23	0.32	0.29	0.31	0.32	0.31	0.31
123 Finland	0.02	0.06	0.18	0.22	0.40	0.49	0.59	0.63	0.64
124 Switzerland	0.09	0.15	0.19	0.24	0.31	0.31	0.32	0.30	0.31
				National currencies					
102 Ireland (millions of pounds)	0	0	4	15	37	35	37	34	35
107 New Zealand (millions of dollars)	..	13	55	74	109	146	158	146	160
108 Belgium (millions of francs)	5,100	6,000	13,902	17,399	26,145	25,656	22,088	27,714	29,720
109 United Kingdom (millions of pounds)	169	208	409	798	1,180	1,142	1,485	1,577	1,478
110 Italy (billions of lire)	38	92	119	585	2,097	3,390	4,156	4,958	4,068
111 Australia (millions of dollars)	106	189	402	591	966	895	1,404	1,286	1,223
112 Netherlands (millions of guilders)	253	710	1,538	3,241	3,773	4,242	4,410	4,440	4,720
113 Austria (millions of schillings)	260	286	1,376	2,303	5,132	2,542	3,722	3,737	4,477
114 France (millions of francs)	3,713	5,393	8,971	17,589	35,894	39,219	40,897	47,529	51,076
116 Canada (millions of dollars)	104	353	895	1,257	2,227	2,500	2,888	2,747	2,882
117 United States (millions of dollars)	4,023	3,153	4,161	7,138	9,403	9,115	10,141	7,676	11,394
118 Denmark (millions of kroner)	90	443	1,178	2,711	4,657	5,877	6,204	6,850	7,247
119 Germany (millions of deutsche marks)[b]	1,824	2,192	4,155	6,484	8,661	7,892	8,319	9,302	10,211
120 Norway (millions of kroner)	79	264	962	2,400	4,946	5,998	6,418	6,335	7,542
121 Sweden (millions of kronor)	197	605	2,350	4,069	7,226	8,718	9,396	11,600	11,909
122 Japan (billions of yen)	88	165	341	760	749	1,062	1,171	1,236	1,313
123 Finland (millions of markkaa)	6	29	177	414	1,308	1,902	2,542	3,031	3,236
124 Switzerland (millions of francs)	52	131	268	424	743	815	903	912	1,041

Summary

	1965	1970	1975	1980	1985	1987	1988	1989	1990
				Billions of US dollars					
ODA (current prices)	6.5	7.0	13.9	27.3	29.4	41.6	48.1	46.7	55.6
ODA (1987 prices)	28.2	25.3	29.8	36.8	39.4	41.6	44.9	43.6	47.6
GNP (current prices)	1,374.0	2,079.0	4,001.0	7,488.0	8,550.0	12,082.0	13,547.0	13,968.0	15,498.0
				Percent					
ODA as a percentage of GNP	0.47	0.34	0.35	0.36	0.34	0.34	0.36	0.33	0.36
				Index (1987 = 100)					
GDP deflator[c]	23.0	27.6	46.5	74.1	74.6	100.0	107.1	107.0	116.8

OECD: Total net bilateral flows to low-income economies[a]	1965	1970	1975	1980	1985	1986	1987	1988	1989	1990
					As a percentage of donor GNP					
102 Ireland	..	..	..	0.01	0.03	0.02	0.02	0.02	0.01	0.01
107 New Zealand	..	..	0.14	0.01	0.00	0.01	0.01	0.01	0.01	0.00
108 Belgium	0.56	0.30	0.31	0.13	0.13	0.12	0.08	0.09	0.05	0.09
109 United Kingdom	0.23	0.09	0.11	0.10	0.07	0.07	0.05	0.06	0.07	0.05
110 Italy	0.04	0.06	0.01	0.00	0.06	0.12	0.13	0.17	0.12	0.09
111 Australia	0.08	0.00	0.10	0.07	0.04	0.04	0.04	0.04	0.06	0.05
112 Netherlands	0.08	0.24	0.24	0.32	0.23	0.28	0.25	0.27	0.23	0.25
113 Austria	0.06	0.05	0.02	0.11	0.05	0.03	0.04	0.03	0.07	0.10
114 France	0.12	0.09	0.10	0.06	0.11	0.10	0.08	0.12	0.14	0.13
116 Canada	0.10	0.22	0.24	0.13	0.14	0.13	0.15	0.13	0.09	0.10
117 United States	0.26	0.14	0.08	0.06	0.06	0.04	0.03	0.03	0.02	0.05
118 Denmark	0.02	0.10	0.20	0.17	0.26	0.23	0.25	0.25	0.26	0.24
119 Germany[b]	0.14	0.10	0.12	0.07	0.13	0.10	0.07	0.08	0.08	0.10
120 Norway	0.04	0.12	0.25	0.28	0.34	0.43	0.34	0.37	0.32	0.37
121 Sweden	0.07	0.12	0.41	0.26	0.24	0.30	0.19	0.21	0.23	0.25
122 Japan	0.13	0.11	0.08	0.12	0.10	0.10	0.12	0.13	0.13	0.10
123 Finland	..	..	0.06	0.03	0.09	0.10	0.17	0.24	0.22	0.17
124 Switzerland	0.02	0.05	0.10	0.07	0.11	0.10	0.10	0.10	0.12	0.11
Total	0.20	0.13	0.11	0.08	0.08	0.08	0.08	0.09	0.08	0.09

OPEC: Total net flows[d]	1976	1980	1983	1984	1985	1986	1987	1988	1989	1990
					Millions of US dollars					
17 Nigeria	80	35	35	51	45	52	30	14	70	13
Qatar	180	277	20	10	8	18	0	4	−2	1
72 Algeria	11	81	37	52	54	114	39	13	40	7
77 Iran, Islamic Rep.	751	−72	10	52	−72	69	−10	39	−94	2
87 Venezuela	109	135	142	90	32	85	24	55	52	15
99 *Iraq*	123	864	−10	−22	−32	−21	−35	−22	21	55
100 *Libya*	98	376	144	24	57	68	66	129	86	4
98 Saudi Arabia	2,791	5,682	3,259	3,194	2,630	3,517	2,888	2,048	1,171	3,692
115 United Arab Emirates	1,028	1,118	351	88	122	87	15	−17	2	888
125 *Kuwait*	706	1,140	997	1,020	771	715	316	108	169	1,666
Total OPEC[d]	5,877	9,636	4,985	4,559	3,615	4,704	3,333	2,369	1,514	6,341
Total OAPEC[e]	4,937	9,538	4,798	4,366	3,610	4,498	3,289	2,261	..	..
					As a percentage of donor GNP					
17 Nigeria	0.19	0.04	0.04	0.06	0.06	0.13	0.12	0.05	0.28	0.06
Qatar	7.35	4.16	0.40	0.18	0.12	0.36	0.00	0.08	−0.04	0.02
72 Algeria	0.07	0.20	0.08	0.10	0.10	0.19	0.07	0.03	0.11	0.03
77 Iran, Islamic Rep.	1.16	−0.08	0.01	0.03	−0.04	0.03	0.00	0.01	−0.02	..
87 Venezuela	0.35	0.23	0.22	0.16	0.06	0.14	0.06	0.09	0.13	0.03
99 *Iraq*	0.76	2.36	−0.02	−0.05	−0.06	−0.05	−0.08	−0.04	0.04	..
100 *Libya*	0.66	1.16	0.51	0.10	0.24	0.30	0.30	0.63	0.41	0.01
98 Saudi Arabia	5.95	4.87	2.69	3.20	2.92	3.99	3.70	2.53	1.37	3.90
115 United Arab Emirates	8.95	4.06	1.26	0.32	0.45	0.41	0.07	−0.07	0.02	2.65
125 *Kuwait*	4.82	3.52	3.83	3.95	2.96	2.84	1.15	0.40	0.54	..
Total OPEC[d]	2.32	1.85	0.82	0.76	0.60	0.78	0.52	0.34	0.21	..
Total OAPEC[e]	4.23	3.22	1.70	1.60	1.39	1.80	1.10	0.86	..	..

a. Organization of Economic Cooperation and Development.   b. Data refer to the Federal Republic of Germany before unification.   c. See the technical notes.
d. Organization of Petroleum Exporting Countries.   e. Organization of Arab Petroleum Exporting Countries.

Table 20. Official development assistance: receipts

Net disbursement of ODA from all sources

	Millions of dollars							Per capita (dollars) 1990	As a percentage of GNP 1990
	1984	1985	1986	1987	1988	1989	1990		
Low-income economies	**14,476** *t*	**15,896** *t*	**18,781** *t*	**20,555** *t*	**23,722** *t*	**23,862** *t*	**29,353** *t*	**9.6** *w*	**2.8** *w*
China and India	**2,471** *t*	**2,532** *t*	**3,254** *t*	**3,300** *t*	**4,086** *t*	**4,048** *t*	**3,662** *t*	**1.8** *w*	**0.6** *w*
Other low-income	**12,006** *t*	**13,364** *t*	**15,527** *t*	**17,255** *t*	**19,636** *t*	**19,813** *t*	**25,691** *t*	**23.9** *w*	**6.9** *w*
1 Mozambique	259	300	422	651	893	772	946	60.2	65.7
2 Tanzania	558	487	681	882	982	920	1155	47.1	48.2
3 Ethiopia	364	715	636	634	970	752	888	17.4	14.6
4 Somalia	350	353	511	580	433	427	428	54.8	45.9
5 Nepal	198	236	301	347	399	493	429	22.7	13.8
6 Chad	115	182	165	198	264	241	315	55.5	28.6
7 Bhutan	18	24	40	42	42	42	47	32.7	16.5
8 Lao PDR	34	37	48	58	77	140	152	36.6	17.5
9 Malawi	158	113	198	280	366	412	479	56.3	25.7
10 Bangladesh	1,200	1,152	1,455	1,635	1,592	1,800	2,103	19.7	9.2
11 Burundi	141	142	187	202	188	196	265	48.8	24.0
12 Zaire	312	325	448	627	576	634	823	22.0	10.9
13 Uganda	163	182	198	280	363	403	557	34.1	18.4
14 Madagascar	153	188	316	321	304	321	382	32.8	12.3
15 Sierra Leone	61	66	87	68	102	100	70	16.9	7.8
16 Mali	321	380	372	366	427	454	474	56.0	19.4
17 Nigeria	33	32	59	69	120	346	234	2.0	0.7
18 Niger	161	304	307	353	371	296	358	46.7	14.2
19 Rwanda	165	181	211	245	252	232	287	40.3	13.4
20 Burkina Faso	189	198	284	281	298	272	315	34.9	9.9
21 India	1,673	1,592	2,120	1,839	2,097	1,895	1,586	1.9	0.6
22 Benin	77	95	138	138	162	263	261	55.1	. .
23 China	798	940	1,134	1462	1,989	2,153	2,076	1.8	0.6
24 Haiti	135	153	175	218	147	200	183	28.3	6.6
25 Kenya	411	438	455	572	808	967	1,000	41.4	11.4
26 Pakistan	749	801	970	879	1,408	1,129	1,152	10.3	2.9
27 Ghana	216	203	371	373	474	552	465	31.2	7.4
28 Central African Rep.	114	104	139	176	196	192	232	76.3	17.8
29 Togo	110	114	174	126	199	183	210	57.8	13.0
30 Zambia	239	328	464	430	478	392	438	54.0	14.0
31 Guinea	123	119	175	213	262	346	292	51.0	10.4
32 Sri Lanka	466	484	570	502	598	547	665	39.1	8.2
33 Mauritania	175	209	225	185	184	242	211	107.0	20.0
34 Lesotho	101	94	88	107	108	127	138	78.0	24.5
35 Indonesia	673	603	711	1,246	1,632	1,839	1,724	9.7	1.6
36 Honduras	286	272	283	258	321	242	448	87.8	16.4
37 Egypt, Arab Rep.	1,794	1,791	1,716	1,773	1,537	1,568	5,604	107.6	15.9
38 *Afghanistan*	7	17	2	45	72	167	143	7.0	. .
39 *Cambodia*	17	13	13	14	18	31	42	4.9	. .
40 *Liberia*	133	90	97	78	65	59	115	44.9	. .
41 *Myanmar*	275	356	416	367	451	184	170	4.1	0.8
42 *Sudan*	622	1,128	945	898	937	772	792	31.5	9.3
43 *Viet Nam*	109	114	147	111	148	129	190	2.9	2.1
Middle-income economies	**9,557** *t*	**9,756** *t*	**11,438** *t*	**12,607** *t*	**11,847** *t*	**12,446** *t*	**17,882** *t*	**18.7** *w*	**0.7** *w*
Lower-middle-income	**7,730** *t*	**7,851** *t*	**8,847** *t*	**9,997** *t*	**9,306** *t*	**9,652** *t*	**14,365** *t*	**26.0** *w*	**1.6** *w*
44 Bolivia	172	202	322	318	394	440	491	68.4	10.9
45 Zimbabwe	298	237	225	294	273	265	343	35.0	5.5
46 Senegal	368	295	567	641	569	650	739	99.8	12.7
47 Philippines	397	486	956	770	854	844	1,277	20.8	2.9
48 Côte d'Ivoire	128	125	186	254	439	403	689	57.9	6.9
49 Dominican Rep.	188	207	93	130	118	142	93	13.2	1.3
50 Papua New Guinea	322	259	263	322	380	339	376	96.1	11.4
51 Guatemala	65	83	135	241	235	261	199	21.6	2.6
52 Morocco	352	785	403	447	481	450	970	38.6	3.8
53 Cameroon	186	159	224	213	284	458	483	41.2	4.3
54 Ecuador	136	136	147	203	137	160	154	14.9	1.4
55 Syrian Arab Rep.	641	610	728	684	191	127	650	52.6	4.4
56 Congo	98	71	110	152	89	91	209	92.0	7.3
57 El Salvador	261	345	341	426	420	443	347	66.5	6.4
58 Paraguay	50	50	66	81	76	92	57	13.1	1.1
59 Peru	310	316	272	292	272	305	392	18.1	1.1
60 Jordan	687	538	564	577	417	273	891	282.5	22.8
61 Colombia	88	62	63	78	61	67	87	2.7	0.2
62 Thailand	475	481	496	504	563	739	805	14.4	1.0
63 Tunisia	178	163	222	274	316	234	316	39.2	2.5
64 Jamaica	170	169	178	168	193	262	280	115.7	7.1
65 Turkey	242	179	339	376	267	140	1,264	22.5	1.2
66 Romania	. .	. .	. .	. .	. .	. .	. .	. .	. .

Note: For data comparability and coverage, see the technical notes.   Figures in italics are for years other than those specified.

		Net disbursement of ODA from all sources								
		Millions of dollars							Per capita (dollars)	As a percentage of GNP
		1984	1985	1986	1987	1988	1989	1990	1990	1990
67	Poland	. .	. .	. .	. .	22	. .	92	38.2	1.9
68	Panama	72	69	52	40	187	18	228	81.0	4.0
69	Costa Rica	218	280	196	228	44	226	228	7.1	0.3
70	Chile	2	40	−5	21	151	61	94	118.2	5.5
71	Botswana	102	96	102	156		160	148	9.1	0.4
72	Algeria	122	173	165	214	171	152	227		
73	Bulgaria	. .	. .	. .	. .	59	. .	89	82.9	3.6
74	Mauritius	36	28	56	65	104	58	469	26.3	1.1
75	Malaysia	327	229	192	363	152	140	172	5.3	0.2
76	Argentina	49	39	88	99		211			
77	Iran, Islamic Rep.	13	16	27	71	82	96	69	1.2	0.1
78	Albania	. .	. .	. .	. .	159	. .	212	21.2	. .
79	Angola	95	92	131	135	141	148	134	50.0	. .
80	Lebanon	77	83	62	101	. .	119	. .	. .	. .
81	Mongolia	. .	. .	. .	. .	22	. .	57	32.0	. .
82	Namibia	0	6	15	17	213	59	324	84.0	. .
83	Nicaragua	114	102	150	141	303	225	392	34.7	5.6
84	Yemen, Rep.	326	283	257	422		358			
	Upper-middle-income	**1,827 t**	**1,905 t**	**2,591 t**	**2,610 t**	**2,541 t**	**2,794 t**	**3,517 t**	**8.5 w**	**0.1 w**
85	Mexico	83	144	252	155	173	86	140	1.6	0.1
86	South Africa	. .	. .	. .	. .	18	. .	79	4.0	0.1
87	Venezuela	14	11	16	19	41	21	47	15.1	0.2
88	Uruguay	4	5	27	18	210	38	164	1.1	0.6
89	Brazil	161	123	178	289		206			0.0
90	Hungary	. .	. .	. .	. .	44	43	48	2.0	0.1
91	Yugoslavia	3	11	19	35	106	. .	. .	. .	0.1
92	Czechoslovakia	. .	. .	. .	. .	9	133	140	123.0	3.0
93	Gabon	76	61	79	82		6	10	8.3	0.2
94	Trinidad and Tobago	5	7	19	34					
95	Portugal	97	101	139	64	102	78	67	6.5	0.1
96	Korea, Rep.	−37	−9	−18	11	10	52	52	1.2	0.0
97	Greece	13	11	19	35	35	30	35	3.5	0.1
98	Saudi Arabia	36	29	31	22	19	36	44	2.9	. .
99	Iraq	4	26	33	91	10	11	52	2.7	. .
100	Libya	5	5	11	6	6	17	20	4.4	. .
101	Oman	67	78	84	16	1	18	69	44.2	. .
	Low- and middle-income	**24,033 t**	**25,653 t**	**30,219 t**	**33,162 t**	**35,570 t**	**36,307 t**	**47,235 t**	**11.8 w**	**1.4 w**
	Sub-Saharan Africa	**7,941 t**	**9,006 t**	**11,093 t**	**12,500 t**	**14,077 t**	**14,505 t**	**16,810 t**	**33.9 w**	**9.6 w**
	East Asia & Pacific	**3,553 t**	**3,577 t**	**4,529 t**	**5,548 t**	**6,405 t**	**7,053 t**	**7,771 t**	**4.9 w**	**0.8 w**
	South Asia	**4,585 t**	**4,655 t**	**5,888 t**	**5,630 t**	**6,615 t**	**6,118 t**	**6,174 t**	**5.4 w**	**1.6 w**
	Europe	**376 t**	**348 t**	**543 t**	**522 t**	**461 t**	**285 t**	**1,420 t**	**14.1 w**	**0.4 w**
	Middle East & N.Africa	**4,506 t**	**4,668 t**	**4,405 t**	**4,745 t**	**3,743 t**	**3,622 t**	**9,680 t**	**37.8 w**	**3.4 w**
	Latin America & Caribbean	**3,072 t**	**3,400 t**	**3,761 t**	**4,217 t**	**4,269 t**	**4,724 t**	**5,380 t**	**12.3 w**	**0.4 w**
	Other economies	**12 t**	**18 t**	**18 t**	**30 t**	**20 t**	**24 t**	**33 t**	**1.0 w**	**. .**
	Severely indebted	**2,379 t**	**2,836 t**	**3,016 t**	**3,267 t**	**2,938 t**	**2,877 t**	**4,660 t**	**11.4 w**	**0.4 w**
	High-income economies	**1,525 t**	**2,232 t**	**2,306 t**	**1,746 t**	**1,655 t**	**1,667 t**	**1,802 t**	**44.7 w**	**0.8 w**
	OECD members	. .	. .	. .	. .	. .	. .	. .	. .	. .
	†Other	**1,525 t**	**2,232 t**	**2,306 t**	**1,746 t**	**1,655 t**	**1,667 t**	**1,802 t**	**44.7 w**	**0.8 w**
102	Ireland	. .	. .	. .	. .	. .	. .	. .	. .	. .
103	†Israel	1,256	1,978	1,937	1,251	1,241	1,192	1,374	295.0	2.6
104	Spain	. .	. .	. .	. .	. .	. .	. .	. .	. .
105	†Singapore	41	24	29	23	22	95	−3	−1.0	0.0
106	†Hong Kong	14	20	18	19	22	40	37	6.4	0.1
107	New Zealand	. .	. .	. .	. .	. .	. .	. .	. .	. .
108	Belgium	. .	. .	. .	. .	. .	. .	. .	. .	. .
109	United Kingdom	. .	. .	. .	. .	. .	. .	. .	. .	. .
110	Italy	. .	. .	. .	. .	. .	. .	. .	. .	. .
111	Australia	. .	. .	. .	. .	. .	. .	. .	. .	. .
112	Netherlands	. .	. .	. .	. .	. .	. .	. .	. .	. .
113	Austria	. .	. .	. .	. .	. .	. .	. .	. .	. .
114	France	. .	. .	. .	. .	. .	. .	. .	. .	. .
115	†United Arab Emirates	3	4	34	115	−12	−6	5	3.3	. .
116	Canada	. .	. .	. .	. .	. .	. .	. .	. .	. .
117	United States	. .	. .	. .	. .	. .	. .	. .	. .	. .
118	Denmark	. .	. .	. .	. .	. .	. .	. .	. .	. .
119	Germany	. .	. .	. .	. .	. .	. .	. .	. .	. .
120	Norway	. .	. .	. .	. .	. .	. .	. .	. .	. .
121	Sweden	. .	. .	. .	. .	. .	. .	. .	. .	. .
122	Japan	. .	. .	. .	. .	. .	. .	. .	. .	. .
123	Finland	. .	. .	. .	. .	. .	. .	. .	. .	. .
124	Switzerland	. .	. .	. .	. .	. .	. .	. .	. .	. .
125	†Kuwait	4	4	5	3	6	4	3	1.6	. .
	World	**25,570 t**	**27,903 t**	**32,542 t**	**34,938 t**	**37,244 t**	**37,997 t**	**49,070 t**	**12.0 w**	**1.4 w**
	Fuel exporters, excl. former USSR	**582 t**	**637 t**	**826 t**	**1,048 t**	**798 t**	**1,077 t**	**1,376 t**	**5.0 w**	**0.4 w**

Table 21. Total external debt

		Long-term debt (millions of dollars)				Use of IMF credit (millions of dollars)		Short-term debt (millions of dollars)		Total external debt (millions of dollars)	
		Public and publicly guaranteed		Private nonguaranteed							
		1970	1990	1970	1990	1970	1990	1970	1990	1970	1990
Low-income economies											
China and India											
Other low-income											
1	Mozambique	. .	4,053	0	19	0	74	. .	572	. .	4,718
2	Tanzania	180	5,294	15	12	0	140	. .	420	. .	5,866
3	Ethiopia	169	3,116	0	0	0	6	. .	128	. .	3,250
4	Somalia	77	1,922	0	0	0	159	. .	268	. .	2,350
5	Nepal	3	1,557	0	0	0	44	. .	20	. .	1,621
6	Chad	33	430	0	0	3	31	. .	31	. .	492
7	Bhutan	. .	80	0	0	0	0	. .	3	. .	83
8	Lao PDR	8	1,053	0	0	0	8	. .	2	. .	1,063
9	Malawi	122	1,366	0	3	0	115	. .	60	. .	1,544
10	Bangladesh	0	11,464	0	0	0	626	. .	156	. .	12,245
11	Burundi	7	850	0	0	8	43	. .	13	. .	906
12	Zaire	311	8,851	0	0	0	521	. .	744	. .	10,115
13	Uganda	152	2,301	0	0	0	282	. .	144	. .	2,726
14	Madagascar	89	3,677	0	0	0	144	. .	118	. .	3,938
15	Sierra Leone	59	606	0	0	0	108	. .	475	. .	1,189
16	Mali	238	2,306	0	0	9	69	. .	57	. .	2,433
17	Nigeria	452	33,709	115	391	0	0	. .	1,968	. .	36,068
18	Niger	32	1,326	0	261	0	85	. .	157	. .	1,829
19	Rwanda	2	692	0	0	3	0	. .	48	. .	741
20	Burkina Faso	21	750	0	0	0	0	. .	84	. .	834
21	India	7,838	61,097	100	1,488	0	2,623	. .	4,908	. .	70,115
22	Benin	41	1,262	0	0	0	9	. .	157	. .	1,427
23	China	. .	45,319	0	0	0	469	. .	6,766	. .	52,555
24	Haiti	40	745	0	0	3	38	. .	91	. .	874
25	Kenya	319	4,810	88	578	0	482	. .	971	. .	6,840
26	Pakistan	3,064	16,532	5	124	45	836	. .	3,191	. .	20,683
27	Ghana	511	2,670	10	33	46	745	. .	50	. .	3,498
28	Central African Rep.	24	815	0	1	0	37	. .	48	. .	901
29	Togo	40	1,096	0	0	0	87	. .	113	. .	1,296
30	Zambia	624	4,784	30	2	0	949	. .	1,488	. .	7,223
31	Guinea	312	2,230	0	0	3	52	. .	215	. .	2,497
32	Sri Lanka	317	4,911	0	136	79	410	. .	394	. .	5,851
33	Mauritania	26	1,898	0	0	0	70	. .	259	. .	2,227
34	Lesotho	8	372	0	0	0	15	. .	3	. .	390
35	Indonesia	2,497	44,974	461	9,405	139	494	. .	13,035	. .	67,908
36	Honduras	90	3,159	19	66	0	32	. .	222	. .	3,480
37	Egypt, Arab Rep.	1,517	34,242	0	1,000	49	125	. .	4,518	. .	39,885
38	*Afghanistan*	. .	. .	. .	. .	. .	. .	. .	. .	. .	. .
39	*Cambodia*	. .	. .	. .	. .	. .	. .	. .	. .	. .	. .
40	*Liberia*	158	1,127	0	0	4	322	. .	422	. .	1,870
41	*Myanmar*	106	4,447	0	0	17	0	. .	229	. .	4,675
42	*Sudan*	298	9,156	0	496	31	956	. .	4,775	. .	15,383
43	*Viet Nam*	. .	. .	. .	. .	. .	. .	. .	. .	. .	. .
Middle-income economies											
Lower-middle-income											
44	Bolivia	480	3,683	11	177	6	257	. .	159	. .	4,276
45	Zimbabwe	229	2,449	0	153	0	7	. .	591	. .	3,199
46	Senegal	115	2,954	31	60	0	314	. .	417	. .	3,745
47	Philippines	625	24,108	919	1,006	69	912	. .	4,431	. .	30,456
48	Côte d'Ivoire	256	10,050	11	4,372	0	431	. .	3,103	. .	17,956
49	Dominican Rep.	212	3,440	141	99	7	72	. .	789	. .	4,400
50	Papua New Guinea	36	1,509	173	965	0	61	. .	72	. .	2,606
51	Guatemala	106	2,179	14	127	0	67	. .	405	. .	2,777
52	Morocco	712	22,097	15	200	28	750	. .	477	. .	23,524
53	Cameroon	131	4,784	9	230	0	121	. .	888	. .	6,023
54	Ecuador	193	9,854	49	164	14	265	. .	1,823	. .	12,105
55	Syrian Arab Rep.	233	14,959	0	0	10	0	. .	1,487	. .	16,446
56	Congo	119	4,380	0	0	0	11	. .	727	. .	5,118
57	El Salvador	88	1,898	88	26	7	0	. .	209	. .	2,133
58	Paraguay	112	1,736	0	19	0	0	. .	376	. .	2,131
59	Peru	856	13,343	1,799	1,554	10	755	. .	5,453	. .	21,105
60	Jordan	120	6,486	0	0	0	94	. .	1,097	. .	7,678
61	Colombia	1,297	14,680	283	1,123	55	0	. .	1,438	. .	17,241
62	Thailand	324	12,572	402	4,973	0	1	. .	8,322	. .	25,868
63	Tunisia	541	6,506	0	218	13	176	. .	634	. .	7,534
64	Jamaica	160	3,873	822	34	0	357	. .	334	. .	4,598
65	Turkey	1,846	38,595	42	1,054	74	0	. .	9,500	. .	49,149
66	Romania	. .	19	0	0	0	0	. .	350	. .	369

Note: For data comparability and coverage, see the technical notes.   Figures in italics are for years other than those specified.

		Long-term debt (millions of dollars)				Use of IMF credit (millions of dollars)		Short-term debt (millions of dollars)		Total external debt (millions of dollars)	
		Public and publicly guaranteed		Private nonguaranteed							
		1970	1990	1970	1990	1970	1990	1970	1990	1970	1990
67	Poland	..	39,282	0	0	0	509	..	9,595	..	49,386
68	Panama	194	3,987	0	0	0	272	..	2,417	..	6,676
69	Costa Rica	134	3,077	112	304	0	11	..	380	..	3,772
70	Chile	2,067	10,339	501	4,263	2	1,157	..	3,356	..	19,114
71	Botswana	17	510	0	0	0	0	..	6	..	516
72	Algeria	945	24,316	0	0	0	670	..	1,820	..	26,806
73	Bulgaria	..	9,564	0	0	0	0	..	1,363	..	10,927
74	Mauritius	32	739	0	148	0	22	..	30	..	939
75	Malaysia	390	16,107	50	1,489	0	0	..	1,906	..	19,502
76	Argentina	1,880	46,146	3,291	1,800	0	3,083	..	10,115	..	61,144
77	Iran, Islamic Rep.	..	1,797	0	0	0	0	..	7,224	..	9,021
78	Albania	..	..	..	..	..	..	..	..	..	..
79	Angola	..	7,152	0	0	0	0	..	558	..	7,710
80	Lebanon	64	545	0	0	0	0	..	1,387	..	1,932
81	Mongolia	..	..	..	..	..	..	..	..	..	..
82	Namibia	..	..	..	..	..	..	..	..	..	..
83	Nicaragua	147	8,067	0	0	8	0	..	2,430	..	10,497
84	Yemen, Rep.	31	5,040	0	0	0	0	..	1,196	..	6,236
	Upper-middle-income										
85	Mexico	3,196	76,204	2,770	4,409	0	6,551	..	9,645	..	96,810
86	South Africa	..	..	..	..	..	..	..	..	..	..
87	Venezuela	718	24,643	236	3,650	0	3,012	..	2,000	..	33,305
88	Uruguay	269	3,044	29	110	18	101	..	452	..	3,707
89	Brazil	3,426	82,098	1,706	7,771	0	1,821	..	24,483	..	116,173
90	Hungary	..	18,046	0	0	0	330	..	2,941	..	21,316
91	Yugoslavia	1,199	13,492	854	3,860	0	467	..	2,871	..	20,690
92	Czechoslovakia	..	5,346	0	0	0	0	..	2,885	..	8,231
93	Gabon	91	2,945	0	0	0	140	..	562	..	3,647
94	Trinidad and Tobago	101	1,808	0	0	0	329	..	169	..	2,307
95	Portugal	515	14,432	268	748	0	0	..	5,233	..	20,413
96	Korea, Rep.	1,816	17,814	175	5,400	0	0	..	10,800	..	34,014
97	Greece	..	..	..	..	..	..	..	..	..	..
98	Saudi Arabia	..	..	..	..	..	..	..	..	..	..
99	Iraq	..	..	..	..	..	..	..	..	..	..
100	Libya	..	..	..	..	..	..	..	..	..	..
101	Oman	..	2,205	0	0	0	0	..	279	..	2,484

Low- and middle-income
Sub-Saharan Africa
East Asia & Pacific
South Asia
Europe
Middle East & N.Africa
Latin America & Caribbean
Other economies

Severely indebted

High-income economies
OECD members
†Other

102	Ireland
103	†Israel
104	Spain
105	†Singapore
106	†Hong Kong
107	New Zealand
108	Belgium
109	United Kingdom
110	Italy
111	Australia
112	Netherlands
113	Austria
114	France
115	†United Arab Emirates
116	Canada
117	United States
118	Denmark
119	Germany
120	Norway
121	Sweden
122	Japan
123	Finland
124	Switzerland
125	†Kuwait

World
Fuel exporters, excl. former USSR

Table 22. Flow of public and private external capital

		Disbursements (millions of dollars)				Repayment of principal (millions of dollars)				Interest payments (millions of dollars)			
		Long-term public and publicly guaranteed		Private nonguaranteed		Long-term public and publicly guaranteed		Private nonguaranteed		Long-term public and publicly guaranteed		Private nonguaranteed	
		1970	1990	1970	1990	1970	1990	1970	1990	1970	1990	1970	1990
Low-income economies													
China and India													
Other low-income													
1	Mozambique	..	153	0	20	..	8	0	12	..	8	0	0
2	Tanzania	51	299	8	0	2	53	3	0	3	46	1	0
3	Ethiopia	28	277	0	0	15	144	0	0	6	44	0	0
4	Somalia	4	42	0	0	1	3	0	0	0	4	0	0
5	Nepal	1	166	0	0	2	31	0	0	0	26	0	0
6	Chad	6	96	0	0	3	3	0	0	0	3	0	0
7	Bhutan	..	8	0	0	..	4	0	0	..	2	0	0
8	Lao PDR	6	107	0	0	1	8	0	0	0	3	0	0
9	Malawi	40	127	0	0	3	42	0	1	4	32	0	0
10	Bangladesh	0	1,121	0	0	0	275	0	0	0	159	0	0
11	Burundi	1	94	0	0	0	28	0	0	0	12	0	0
12	Zaire	32	226	0	0	28	51	0	0	9	93	0	0
13	Uganda	26	305	0	0	4	47	0	0	4	16	0	0
14	Madagascar	11	185	0	0	5	70	0	0	2	93	0	0
15	Sierra Leone	8	37	0	0	11	3	0	0	3	3	0	0
16	Mali	23	110	0	0	0	23	0	0	0	17	0	0
17	Nigeria	56	727	25	0	38	1,205	30	15	20	1,758	8	3
18	Niger	12	112	0	43	2	7	0	37	1	6	0	16
19	Rwanda	0	62	0	0	0	10	0	0	0	6	0	0
20	Burkina Faso	2	79	0	0	2	18	0	0	0	10	0	0
21	India	883	5,191	25	214	289	2,162	25	318	187	3,275	6	135
22	Benin	2	95	0	0	1	5	0	0	0	5	0	0
23	China	..	9,620	0	0	..	3,371	0	0	..	2,534	0	0
24	Haiti	4	37	0	0	3	6	0	0	0	6	0	0
25	Kenya	35	676	41	0	17	282	12	37	13	189	4	38
26	Pakistan	489	1,786	3	25	114	863	1	39	77	497	0	11
27	Ghana	42	380	0	8	14	123	0	8	12	57	0	2
28	Central African Rep.	2	121	0	0	2	6	0	0	1	9	0	0
29	Togo	5	82	0	0	2	27	0	0	1	33	0	0
30	Zambia	351	152	11	2	35	91	6	0	29	58	2	0
31	Guinea	90	150	0	0	11	37	0	0	4	16	0	0
32	Sri Lanka	66	464	0	0	30	163	0	2	12	118	0	2
33	Mauritania	5	80	0	0	3	28	0	0	0	13	0	0
34	Lesotho	0	52	0	0	0	14	0	0	0	8	0	0
35	Indonesia	441	4,615	195	5,533	59	4,140	61	977	25	2,536	21	485
36	Honduras	29	330	10	8	3	162	3	25	3	181	1	1
37	Egypt, Arab Rep.	199	2,192	0	102	227	1,715	0	183	40	1,054	0	89
38	*Afghanistan*	..	..	..	..	..	..	..	..	..	..	..	..
39	*Cambodia*	..	..	..	..	..	..	..	..	..	..	..	..
40	*Liberia*	7	0	0	0	11	0	0	0	6	0	0	0
41	*Myanmar*	22	122	0	0	20	45	0	0	3	13	0	0
42	*Sudan*	53	185	0	0	22	14	0	0	12	8	0	0
43	*Viet Nam*	..	..	..	..	..	..	..	..	..	..	..	..
Middle-income economies													
Lower-middle-income													
44	Bolivia	55	294	3	0	17	168	2	24	7	116	1	14
45	Zimbabwe	0	297	0	94	5	227	0	18	5	139	0	9
46	Senegal	19	212	1	15	7	128	3	12	2	82	0	3
47	Philippines	141	2,155	276	291	74	705	186	47	26	1,471	19	55
48	Côte d'Ivoire	78	826	4	900	29	280	2	529	12	187	0	212
49	Dominican Rep.	38	141	22	0	7	89	20	5	4	57	8	3
50	Papua New Guinea	43	275	111	205	0	174	20	199	1	86	8	90
51	Guatemala	37	140	6	7	20	87	2	3	6	76	1	10
52	Morocco	168	1,345	8	8	37	742	3	8	24	873	1	5
53	Cameroon	29	764	11	53	5	127	2	130	4	173	1	17
54	Ecuador	41	629	7	30	16	470	11	25	7	401	3	12
55	Syrian Arab Rep.	60	361	0	0	31	1,253	0	0	6	122	0	0
56	Congo	18	134	0	0	6	140	0	0	3	104	0	0
57	El Salvador	8	109	24	0	6	111	16	14	4	72	6	3
58	Paraguay	14	80	0	0	7	111	0	9	4	75	0	0
59	Peru	148	248	240	0	100	149	233	35	43	89	119	10
60	Jordan	15	381	0	0	3	349	0	0	2	272	0	0
61	Colombia	253	1,857	0	146	78	1,876	59	296	44	1,240	15	101
62	Thailand	51	1,513	169	1,149	23	2,424	107	847	16	877	17	334
63	Tunisia	89	1,021	0	30	47	909	0	37	18	399	0	10
64	Jamaica	15	264	165	0	6	300	164	8	9	224	54	3
65	Turkey	331	4,344	1	543	128	3,426	3	283	42	2,763	2	61
66	Romania	..	19	0	0	..	0	0	0	..	0	0	0

Note: For data comparability and coverage, see the technical notes.   Figures in italics are for years other than those specified.

		Disbursements (millions of dollars)				Repayment of principal (millions of dollars)				Interest payments (millions of dollars)			
		Long-term public and publicly guaranteed		Private nonguaranteed		Long-term public and publicly guaranteed		Private nonguaranteed		Long-term public and publicly guaranteed		Private nonguaranteed	
		1970	1990	1970	1990	1970	1990	1970	1990	1970	1990	1970	1990
67	Poland	..	540	0	0	..	642	0	0	..	206	0	0
68	Panama	67	6	0	0	24	51	0	0	7	90	0	0
69	Costa Rica	30	202	30	5	21	263	20	6	7	169	7	2
70	Chile	408	707	247	1,545	166	474	41	271	78	1,096	26	252
71	Botswana	6	25	0	0	0	62	0	0	0	36	0	0
72	Algeria	313	5,568	0	0	35	6,156	0	0	10	1,914	0	0
73	Bulgaria	..	437	0	0	..	828	0	0	..	456	0	0
74	Mauritius	2	93	0	57	1	43	0	16	2	35	0	6
75	Malaysia	45	1,779	12	685	47	2,220	9	470	22	1,125	3	104
76	Argentina	482	914	424	0	344	1,664	428	0	121	2,129	217	144
77	Iran, Islamic Rep.	..	139	0	0	..	225	0	0	..	28	0	0
78	*Albania*	..	..	..	..	..	..	..	..	..	..	..	..
79	*Angola*	..	628	0	0	..	133	0	0	..	89	0	0
80	*Lebanon*	12	76	0	0	2	56	0	0	1	32	0	0
81	*Mongolia*	..	..	..	..	..	..	..	..	..	..	..	..
82	*Namibia*	..	..	..	..	..	..	..	..	..	..	..	..
83	*Nicaragua*	44	445	0	0	16	4	0	0	7	5	0	0
84	*Yemen, Rep.*	6	261	0	0	0	73	0	0	0	23	0	0
	Upper-middle-income												
85	Mexico	772	7,901	603	1,484	475	2,615	542	1,046	216	5,365	67	400
86	South Africa	..	..	..	..	..	..	..	..	..	..	..	..
87	Venezuela	216	2,224	67	0	42	920	25	173	40	2,597	13	400
88	Uruguay	37	375	13	80	47	399	4	75	16	311	2	10
89	Brazil	896	2,686	900	875	256	2,718	200	1,008	135	2,223	89	460
90	Hungary	..	2,573	0	0	..	2,233	0	0	..	1,571	0	0
91	Yugoslavia	179	446	465	1,215	170	776	204	1,210	73	1,266	32	380
92	Czechoslovakia	..	1,866	0	0	..	984	0	0	..	365	0	0
93	Gabon	26	161	0	0	9	53	0	0	3	75	0	0
94	Trinidad and Tobago	8	47	0	0	10	164	0	0	6	133	0	0
95	Portugal	18	2,332	20	185	81	3,310	22	99	55	1,007	5	48
96	Korea, Rep.	444	3,198	32	1,529	198	3,539	7	2,090	71	1,267	5	507
97	Greece	..	..	..	..	..	..	..	..	..	..	..	..
98	Saudi Arabia	..	..	..	..	..	..	..	..	..	..	..	..
99	*Iraq*	..	..	..	..	..	..	..	..	..	..	..	..
100	*Libya*	..	..	..	..	..	..	..	..	..	..	..	..
101	*Oman*	0	104	0	0	0	567	0	0	0	177	0	0

Low- and middle-income
  Sub-Saharan Africa
  East Asia & Pacific
  South Asia
  Europe
  Middle East & N. Africa
  Latin America & Caribbean
Other economies

Severely indebted

High-income economies
  OECD members
  †Other

102	Ireland
103	†Israel
104	Spain
105	†Singapore
106	†Hong Kong
107	New Zealand
108	Belgium
109	United Kingdom
110	Italy
111	Australia
112	Netherlands
113	Austria
114	France
115	†United Arab Emirates
116	Canada
117	United States
118	Denmark
119	Germany
120	Norway
121	Sweden
122	Japan
123	Finland
124	Switzerland
125	†Kuwait

World
  Fuel exporters, excl. former USSR

Table 23. Aggregate net resource flows and net transfers

| | | Net flows on long-term debt (millions of dollars) | | | | | | | | | | | |
| | | Public and publicly guaranteed | | Private nonguaranteed | | Official grants | | Net foreign direct investment | | Aggregate net resource flows | | Aggregate net transfers | |
		1970	1990	1970	1990	1970	1990	1970	1990	1970	1990	1970	1990
	Low-income economies												
	China and India												
	Other low-income												
1	Mozambique	..	145	0	8	0	764	0	0	0	917	0	909
2	Tanzania	49	246	5	0	6	729	0	0	60	975	57	904
3	Ethiopia	13	133	0	0	6	590	4	0	23	723	10	678
4	Somalia	4	40	0	0	9	304	5	0	17	344	16	340
5	Nepal	−2	135	0	0	16	160	0	0	14	295	14	269
6	Chad	3	93	0	0	11	179	1	0	15	271	13	268
7	Bhutan	..	4	0	0	0	28	0	0	0	32	0	29
8	Lao PDR	4	99	0	0	28	66	0	0	33	165	32	162
9	Malawi	37	84	0	−1	7	262	9	0	52	345	41	312
10	Bangladesh	0	846	0	0	0	891	0	3	0	1,740	0	1,582
11	Burundi	1	67	0	0	7	144	0	1	8	212	8	196
12	Zaire	3	175	0	0	37	319	0	0	41	494	2	393
13	Uganda	22	258	0	0	2	260	4	0	27	519	10	503
14	Madagascar	5	116	0	0	20	360	10	0	36	476	34	383
15	Sierra Leone	−3	35	0	0	1	47	8	0	7	81	−1	78
16	Mali	23	87	0	0	12	229	0	−1	34	315	32	294
17	Nigeria	18	−479	−5	−15	40	149	205	588	259	243	−207	−1,653
18	Niger	11	105	0	6	15	224	1	0	26	334	23	312
19	Rwanda	0	53	0	0	10	159	0	8	10	220	10	207
20	Burkina Faso	0	61	0	0	13	170	0	0	13	230	11	220
21	India	594	3,029	0	−104	157	684	6	0	757	3,610	565	200
22	Benin	1	90	0	0	9	110	7	0	17	200	13	196
23	China	..	6,249	0	0	0	333	0	3,489	0	10,071	0	7,492
24	Haiti	1	31	0	0	2	88	3	8	6	128	2	114
25	Kenya	17	394	30	−37	4	942	14	26	64	1,324	−2	1,010
26	Pakistan	375	923	2	−13	79	381	23	249	479	1,540	395	978
27	Ghana	28	257	0	0	9	440	68	15	104	712	79	646
28	Central African Rep.	−1	116	0	0	6	87	1	0	7	203	5	194
29	Togo	3	54	0	0	7	97	1	0	11	152	5	98
30	Zambia	316	61	5	2	2	633	−297	0	26	696	−65	638
31	Guinea	80	113	0	0	1	106	0	0	80	219	76	203
32	Sri Lanka	36	301	0	−2	14	226	0	31	50	556	30	409
33	Mauritania	1	51	0	0	3	97	1	0	5	148	−8	136
34	Lesotho	0	38	0	0	8	69	0	17	8	124	7	103
35	Indonesia	383	476	134	4,556	84	342	83	964	683	6,337	510	1,242
36	Honduras	26	167	7	−18	0	223	8	0	41	373	17	191
37	Egypt, Arab Rep.	−29	477	0	−81	150	4,376	0	947	122	5,719	82	4,558
38	*Afghanistan*	..	..	..	..	..	..	..	..	..	..	..	..
39	*Cambodia*	..	..	..	..	..	..	..	..	..	..	..	..
40	*Liberia*	−4	0	0	0	1	49	0	0	−3	49	−9	49
41	*Myanmar*	2	77	0	0	16	75	0	0	17	152	14	139
42	*Sudan*	30	171	0	0	2	476	0	0	32	647	16	639
43	*Viet Nam*	..	..	..	..	..	..	..	..	..	..	..	..
	Middle-income economies												
	Lower-middle-income												
44	Bolivia	38	125	1	−24	0	193	−76	45	−37	340	−61	193
45	Zimbabwe	−5	71	0	76	0	210	0	0	−5	356	−9	209
46	Senegal	13	83	−2	4	16	512	5	0	32	599	15	481
47	Philippines	67	1,450	90	245	16	394	−25	530	148	2,618	80	781
48	Côte d'Ivoire	49	546	2	371	12	286	31	−48	94	1156	33	756
49	Dominican Rep.	31	52	2	−5	10	31	72	133	115	210	102	150
50	Papua New Guinea	43	101	91	7	144	277	0	0	278	385	268	209
51	Guatemala	17	53	4	4	4	67	29	0	55	124	18	38
52	Morocco	131	603	5	0	23	472	20	165	179	1,240	134	292
53	Cameroon	24	637	9	−77	21	376	16	0	70	936	61	746
54	Ecuador	26	159	−4	5	2	51	89	82	112	297	83	−241
55	Syrian Arab Rep.	29	−892	0	0	11	582	0	0	41	−311	35	−433
56	Congo	13	−6	0	0	5	51	0	0	18	46	15	−58
57	El Salvador	2	−2	8	−14	2	160	4	0	15	145	−1	70
58	Paraguay	7	−31	0	−9	2	9	4	79	13	47	5	−43
59	Peru	48	99	7	−35	20	186	−70	34	4	285	−231	169
60	Jordan	12	32	0	0	41	670	0	0	53	702	51	430
61	Colombia	174	−18	−59	−149	21	59	43	501	179	392	26	−1,991
62	Thailand	28	−911	62	302	6	219	43	2,376	139	1,985	87	468
63	Tunisia	42	112	0	−7	42	184	16	58	99	347	61	−173
64	Jamaica	9	−37	1	−8	3	129	162	0	174	84	6	−143
65	Turkey	203	918	−2	260	21	817	58	697	280	2,692	202	−293
66	Romania	0	19	0	0	0	0	0	0	0	19	0	19

Note: For data comparability and coverage, see the technical notes. Figures in italics are for years other than those specified.

| | | Net flows on long-term debt (millions of dollars) | | | | Official grants | | Net foreign direct investment | | Aggregate net resource flows | | Aggregate net transfers | |
| | | Public and publicly guaranteed | | Private nonguaranteed | | | | | | | | | |
		1970	1990	1970	1990	1970	1990	1970	1990	1970	1990	1970	1990
67	Poland	24	–102	0	0	0	0	0	89	24	–13	24	–239
68	Panama	44	–45	0	0	0	91	33	–30	77	16	51	–98
69	Costa Rica	9	–62	10	–1	4	119	26	111	49	168	31	–60
70	Chile	242	233	206	1,274	11	66	–79	595	381	2,167	172	484
71	Botswana	6	–37	0	0	9	90	0	148	15	201	14	–133
72	Algeria	279	–589	0	0	56	76	47	0	381	–513	221	–2,578
73	Bulgaria	. .	–391	0	0	0	0	0	0	0	–391	0	–847
74	Mauritius	1	50	0	41	3	27	2	41	5	160	3	96
75	Malaysia	–2	–441	3	215	4	54	94	2,902	99	2,730	–92	–417
76	Argentina	139	–749	–4	0	1	39	11	2,036	147	1,326	–264	–1,665
77	Iran, Islamic Rep.	. .	–86	0	0	0	52	28	0	28	–33	–788	–61
78	*Albania*	. .	. .	. .	. .	. .	. .	. .	. .	. .	. .	. .	. .
79	*Angola*	. .	495	0	0	0	160	0	0	0	655	0	566
80	*Lebanon*	10	20	0	0	2	95	0	0	12	114	11	83
81	*Mongolia*	. .	. .	. .	. .	. .	. .	. .	. .	. .	. .	. .	. .
82	*Namibia*	. .	. .	. .	. .	. .	. .	. .	. .	. .	. .	. .	. .
83	*Nicaragua*	28	441	0	0	2	251	15	0	45	692	15	687
84	*Yemen, Rep.*	6	187	0	0	8	273	0	0	14	460	14	437
	Upper-middle-income												
85	Mexico	297	5,286	61	438	11	64	323	2,632	692	8,420	50	1,341
86	South Africa	. .	. .	. .	. .	. .	. .	. .	. .	. .	. .	. .	. .
87	Venezuela	174	1,304	41	–173	0	9	–23	451	192	1,591	–429	–1,630
88	Uruguay	–10	–23	9	14	2	14	0	0	1	–4	–18	–325
89	Brazil	640	–32	700	–133	26	71	421	1,340	1,787	1,247	1,177	–3,816
90	Hungary	. .	340	0	0	0	0	0	0	0	340	0	–1,268
91	Yugoslavia	9	–331	261	5	0	0	0	0	270	–326	166	–1,972
92	Czechoslovakia	. .	882	0	0	0	0	0	207	0	1,089	0	724
93	Gabon	17	108	0	0	10	41	–1	–50	26	100	23	–45
94	Trinidad and Tobago	–3	–117	0	0	1	7	83	109	81	0	16	–331
95	Portugal	–63	–978	–1	86	0	14	0	2,123	–64	1,245	–124	78
96	Korea, Rep.	246	–341	25	–561	119	13	66	715	456	–174	374	–2,214
97	Greece	. .	. .	. .	. .	. .	. .	. .	. .	. .	. .	. .	. .
98	Saudi Arabia	. .	. .	. .	. .	. .	. .	. .	. .	. .	. .	. .	. .
99	*Iraq*	. .	. .	. .	. .	. .	. .	. .	. .	. .	. .	. .	. .
100	*Libya*	. .	. .	. .	. .	. .	. .	. .	. .	. .	. .	. .	. .
101	*Oman*	. .	–463	0	0	0	61	0	144	0	–259	0	–825

Low- and middle-income
 Sub-Saharan Africa
 East Asia & Pacific
 South Asia
 Europe
 Middle East & N.Africa
 Latin America & Caribbean
Other economies

Severely indebted

High-income economies
 OECD members
 †Other

102	Ireland
103	†Israel
104	Spain
105	†Singapore
106	†Hong Kong

107	New Zealand
108	Belgium
109	United Kingdom
110	Italy
111	Australia

112	Netherlands
113	Austria
114	France
115	†United Arab Emirates
116	Canada

117	United States
118	Denmark
119	Germany
120	Norway
121	Sweden

122	Japan
123	Finland
124	Switzerland
125	†*Kuwait*

World
 Fuel exporters, excl. former USSR

Table 24. Total external debt ratios

		Total external debt as a percentage of				Total debt service as a percentage of exports of goods and services		Interest payments as a percentage of exports of goods and services	
		Exports of goods and services		GNP					
		1980	1990	1980	1990	1980	1990	1980	1990
	Low-income economies	**105.1** w	**218.5** w	**16.4** w	**41.0** w	**10.3** w	**20.1** w	**5.1** w	**9.3** w
	China and India	**69.0** w	**132.3** w	**5.3** w	**19.0** w	**6.4** w	**15.3** w	**2.6** w	**7.6** w
	Other low-income	**120.4** w	**306.5** w	**33.2** w	**82.6** w	**11.9** w	**24.9** w	**6.1** w	**11.0** w
1	Mozambique	0.0	1,573.3	0.0	384.5	0.0	14.4	0.0	7.7
2	Tanzania	317.8	1,070.7	47.7	282.0	19.6	25.8	10.0	10.9
3	Ethiopia	136.2	480.3	19.5	54.2	7.6	33.0	4.7	8.1
4	Somalia	252.0	2,576.2	109.5	276.9	4.9	11.7	0.9	5.8
5	Nepal	85.5	402.6	10.4	53.0	3.2	18.2	2.1	7.4
6	Chad	305.9	207.1	30.2	44.8	8.3	5.1	0.7	2.2
7	Bhutan	. .	81.9	0.0	32.3	. .	6.8	. .	2.5
8	Lao PDR	. .	1,113.5	. .	123.3	. .	12.1	. .	3.2
9	Malawi	260.8	328.5	72.1	85.6	27.7	22.5	16.7	9.1
10	Bangladesh	345.6	448.2	31.3	53.8	23.2	25.4	6.4	7.7
11	Burundi	180.1	930.1	18.2	83.2	9.5	43.6	4.8	14.5
12	Zaire	206.4	438.0	35.3	141.0	22.6	15.4	11.0	6.6
13	Uganda	240.2	1,175.2	62.9	92.1	18.3	54.5	3.7	14.5
14	Madagascar	242.4	805.5	31.5	134.1	17.2	47.2	10.9	22.5
15	Sierra Leone	157.7	773.7	40.7	146.2	22.9	15.9	5.7	11.2
16	Mali	227.3	433.4	45.4	100.7	5.1	11.5	2.3	4.2
17	Nigeria	32.2	242.7	10.0	110.9	4.2	20.3	3.3	12.1
18	Niger	132.8	464.2	34.5	73.6	21.7	24.1	12.9	8.9
19	Rwanda	103.4	494.1	16.3	35.0	4.2	14.5	2.8	7.6
20	Burkina Faso	88.0	156.0	19.4	26.4	5.9	6.4	3.1	2.9
21	India	136.0	282.4	11.9	25.0	9.3	28.8	4.2	15.9
22	Benin	131.1	316.9	29.8	. .	6.3	3.4	4.5	1.9
23	China	21.2	77.4	1.5	14.4	4.4	10.3	1.5	4.6
24	Haiti	72.9	258.4	20.9	36.1	6.2	9.5	1.8	4.1
25	Kenya	165.1	306.3	48.3	81.2	21.4	33.8	11.3	14.8
26	Pakistan	208.8	249.6	42.4	52.1	17.9	22.8	7.6	9.8
27	Ghana	116.0	353.4	31.8	56.8	13.1	34.9	4.4	9.9
28	Central African Rep.	94.7	400.7	24.3	70.6	4.9	11.9	1.6	5.1
29	Togo	180.1	212.2	95.3	81.8	9.0	14.1	5.8	7.0
30	Zambia	201.0	500.8	90.9	261.3	25.3	12.3	8.8	4.3
31	Guinea	201.9	287.1	. .	97.6	19.8	8.3	6.0	2.4
32	Sri Lanka	123.4	209.8	46.1	73.2	12.0	13.8	5.7	6.2
33	Mauritania	306.6	449.8	125.7	226.6	17.3	13.9	7.9	5.0
34	Lesotho	19.5	41.2	11.2	39.6	1.5	2.4	0.6	0.8
35	Indonesia	94.2	229.4	28.0	66.4	13.9	30.9	6.5	13.1
36	Honduras	152.0	322.2	61.5	140.9	21.4	40.0	12.4	19.4
37	Egypt, Arab Rep.	227.7	300.8	97.8	126.5	14.8	25.7	9.2	11.0
38	*Afghanistan*	. .	. .	. .	. .	. .	. .	. .	. .
39	*Cambodia*	. .	. .	. .	. .	. .	. .	. .	. .
40	*Liberia*	111.8	. .	62.7	. .	8.7	. .	5.8	. .
41	*Myanmar*	269.9	. .	. .	. .	25.4	. .	9.4	. .
42	*Sudan*	499.4	1,829.1	77.2	. .	25.5	5.8	12.8	4.0
43	*Viet Nam*	. .	. .	. .	. .	. .	. .	. .	. .
	Middle-income economies	**135.2** w	**155.6** w	**31.9** w	**39.9** w	**24.3** w	**19.1** w	**12.5** w	**8.3** w
	Lower-middle-income	**115.2** w	**179.0** w	**31.7** w	**53.3** w	**18.8** w	**20.3** w	**9.1** w	**8.4** w
44	Bolivia	258.2	428.7	93.3	100.9	35.0	39.8	21.1	15.9
45	Zimbabwe	45.4	155.0	14.9	54.1	3.8	22.6	1.5	9.6
46	Senegal	162.7	236.8	50.5	66.5	28.7	20.4	10.5	8.1
47	Philippines	212.3	229.2	53.8	69.3	26.6	21.2	18.2	13.0
48	Côte d'Ivoire	160.7	487.4	58.8	204.8	28.3	38.6	13.0	13.3
49	Dominican Rep.	133.8	188.7	31.5	63.3	25.3	10.3	12.0	3.7
50	Papua New Guinea	66.1	168.6	29.2	83.9	13.8	36.0	6.6	11.7
51	Guatemala	62.3	175.2	14.9	37.5	7.7	13.3	3.6	6.9
52	Morocco	224.5	282.5	53.3	97.1	32.7	23.4	17.0	11.7
53	Cameroon	136.7	257.6	36.8	56.8	15.2	21.5	8.1	10.4
54	Ecuador	201.6	371.8	53.8	120.6	33.9	33.2	15.9	14.5
55	Syrian Arab Rep.	106.2	301.2	27.1	118.1	11.4	26.9	4.7	3.9
56	Congo	146.7	352.5	98.0	203.6	10.8	20.7	6.7	10.5
57	El Salvador	71.1	170.8	25.9	40.4	7.5	17.1	4.7	6.7
58	Paraguay	121.8	112.3	20.7	40.5	18.6	11.0	8.5	4.6
59	Peru	207.7	488.3	51.0	58.7	46.5	11.0	19.9	5.3
60	Jordan	79.2	249.2	. .	221.1	8.4	23.0	4.3	11.4
61	Colombia	117.1	183.4	20.9	44.5	16.0	38.9	11.6	15.8
62	Thailand	96.8	82.0	26.0	32.6	18.9	17.2	9.5	6.0
63	Tunisia	96.0	127.7	41.6	62.2	14.8	25.8	6.9	7.8
64	Jamaica	129.3	202.6	78.3	132.0	19.0	31.0	10.8	12.5
65	Turkey	332.9	195.0	34.3	46.1	28.0	28.2	14.9	13.3
66	Romania	80.3	5.5	. .	1.1	12.6	0.4	4.9	0.4

Note: For data comparability and coverage, see the technical notes.   Figures in italics are for years other than those specified.

		Total external debt as a percentage of				Total debt service as a percentage of exports of goods and services		Interest payments as a percentage of exports of goods and services	
		Exports of goods and services		GNP					
		1980	1990	1980	1990	1980	1990	1980	1990
67	Poland	54.9	251.5	16.3	82.0	17.9	4.9	5.2	1.6
68	Panama	38.4	126.5	92.3	154.7	6.3	4.3	3.3	2.0
69	Costa Rica	224.7	184.2	59.5	69.9	29.0	24.5	14.6	10.1
70	Chile	192.5	181.3	45.2	73.5	43.1	25.9	19.0	16.8
71	Botswana	17.8	22.9	16.2	20.6	1.9	4.4	1.1	1.6
72	Algeria	130.0	193.0	47.1	53.1	27.1	59.4	10.4	15.1
73	Bulgaria	2.9	135.9	1.1	56.9	0.3	16.7	0.2	6.4
74	Mauritius	80.7	53.5	41.6	37.9	9.1	8.7	5.9	2.9
75	Malaysia	44.6	55.9	28.0	48.0	6.3	11.7	4.0	4.0
76	Argentina	242.4	405.6	48.4	61.7	37.3	34.1	20.8	18.4
77	Iran, Islamic Rep.	32.0	48.2	4.9	7.6	6.8	3.5	3.1	2.3
78	*Albania*	..	..	..	..	..	..	..	..
79	*Angola*	..	..	..	..	..	..	..	..
80	*Lebanon*	..	..	..	..	..	..	..	..
81	*Mongolia*	..	..	..	..	..	..	..	..
82	*Namibia*	..	..	..	..	..	..	..	..
83	*Nicaragua*	422.2	2,728.6	112.1	..	22.3	4.1	13.4	3.0
84	*Yemen, Rep.*	..	214.2	..	97.1	..	5.4	..	2.9
	Upper-middle-income	**159.6** *w*	**132.1** *w*	**32.0** *w*	**29.8** *w*	**31.0** *w*	**17.9** *w*	**16.6** *w*	**8.2** *w*
85	Mexico	259.2	222.0	30.5	42.1	49.5	27.8	27.4	16.7
86	South Africa	..	..	..	..	..	..	..	..
87	Venezuela	131.9	158.7	42.1	71.0	27.2	20.7	13.8	15.5
88	Uruguay	104.1	155.9	17.0	46.9	18.8	41.0	10.6	15.9
89	Brazil	304.9	326.8	31.2	25.1	63.1	20.8	33.8	8.2
90	Hungary	95.9	188.6	44.8	67.8	18.9	37.9	10.8	15.2
91	Yugoslavia	103.1	67.1	25.6	23.7	20.8	13.7	7.2	6.1
92	Czechoslovakia	68.6	55.6	9.8	18.6	9.5	10.4	9.5	3.8
93	Gabon	62.2	138.4	39.2	86.2	17.7	7.6	6.3	5.0
94	Trinidad and Tobago	24.6	99.4	14.0	50.8	6.8	14.5	1.6	7.4
95	Portugal	99.5	75.4	40.5	36.5	18.3	17.8	10.5	5.3
96	Korea, Rep.	130.6	44.0	48.7	14.4	19.7	10.7	12.7	3.5
97	Greece	..	..	..	..	..	..	..	..
98	Saudi Arabia	..	..	..	..	..	..	..	..
99	*Iraq*	..	..	..	..	..	..	..	..
100	*Libya*	..	..	..	..	..	..	..	..
101	*Oman*	15.4	42.1	11.2	..	6.4	13.0	1.8	3.4
	Low- and middle-income	**127.0** *w*	**171.3** *w*	**26.2** *w*	**40.2** *w*	**20.5** *w*	**19.4** *w*	**10.5** *w*	**8.5** *w*
	Sub-Saharan Africa	**96.8** *w*	**324.3** *w*	**28.5** *w*	**109.4** *w*	**10.9** *w*	**19.3** *w*	**5.7** *w*	**8.9** *w*
	East Asia & Pacific	**88.8** *w*	**91.1** *w*	**16.8** *w*	**26.9** *w*	**13.5** *w*	**14.6** *w*	**7.7** *w*	**5.8** *w*
	South Asia	**162.9** *w*	**281.5** *w*	**17.3** *w*	**30.7** *w*	**12.2** *w*	**25.9** *w*	**5.2** *w*	**13.1** *w*
	Europe	**90.6** *w*	**125.7** *w*	**23.8** *w*	**41.0** *w*	**15.9** *w*	**16.9** *w*	**7.1** *w*	**6.8** *w*
	Middle East & N.Africa	**114.9** *w*	**180.3** *w*	**31.1** *w*	**52.6** *w*	**16.4** *w*	**24.4** *w*	**7.4** *w*	**8.1** *w*
	Latin America & Caribbean	**196.8** *w*	**257.4** *w*	**35.2** *w*	**41.6** *w*	**37.3** *w*	**25.0** *w*	**19.7** *w*	**13.3** *w*
	Other economies	..	..	..	..	..	..	..	..
	Severely indebted	**180.7** *w*	**273.8** *w*	**34.4** *w*	**46.4** *w*	**35.1** *w*	**25.3** *w*	**17.7** *w*	**11.8** *w*
	High-income economies								
	OECD members								
	†Other								
102	Ireland								
103	†Israel								
104	Spain								
105	†Singapore								
106	†Hong Kong								
107	New Zealand								
108	Belgium								
109	United Kingdom								
110	Italy								
111	Australia								
112	Netherlands								
113	Austria								
114	France								
115	†United Arab Emirates								
116	Canada								
117	United States								
118	Denmark								
119	Germany								
120	Norway								
121	Sweden								
122	Japan								
123	Finland								
124	Switzerland								
125	†Kuwait								
	World								
	Fuel exporters, excl. former USSR								

Table 25. Terms of external public borrowing

		Commitments (millions of dollars)		Average interest rate (percent)		Average maturity (years)		Average grace period (years)		Public loans with variable interest rates, as a percentage of public debt	
		1970	1990	1970	1990	1970	1990	1970	1990	1970	1990
	Low-income economies	**4,823** *t*	**36,364** *t*	**3.2** *w*	**5.4** *w*	**29** *w*	**23** *w*	**8** *w*	**7** *w*	**0.1** *w*	**19.0** *w*
	China and India	**954** *t*	**16,682** *t*	**2.5** *w*	**6.5** *w*	**34** *w*	**20** *w*	**8** *w*	**6** *w*	**0.0** *w*	**25.5** *w*
	Other low-income	**3,869** *t*	**19,682** *t*	**3.3** *w*	**4.4** *w*	**27** *w*	**26** *w*	**9** *w*	**7** *w*	**0.2** *w*	**16.0** *w*
1	Mozambique	..	163	..	1.6	..	37	..	10	..	4.2
2	Tanzania	271	603	1.0	0.8	40	37	11	10	0.0	4.5
3	Ethiopia	21	383	4.4	2.4	32	30	7	8	0.1	3.2
4	Somalia	22	72	0.0	0.8	20	42	16	11	0.0	1.0
5	Nepal	17	204	2.8	0.9	27	40	6	10	0.0	0.0
6	Chad	10	66	5.7	1.0	8	35	1	11	0.0	0.0
7	Bhutan	..	0	..	0.0	..	0	..	0	..	0.0
8	Lao PDR	12	139	3.0	0.8	28	40	4	15	0.0	0.0
9	Malawi	14	237	3.8	1.0	29	36	6	10	0.0	3.5
10	Bangladesh	0	1,325	0.0	2.0	0	34	0	9	0.0	0.0
11	Burundi	1	120	2.9	0.8	5	41	2	11	0.0	0.0
12	Zaire	258	27	6.5	1.1	12	36	4	10	0.0	15.5
13	Uganda	12	469	3.9	1.0	29	33	7	9	2.4	1.7
14	Madagascar	23	207	2.3	1.0	39	37	9	10	0.0	6.4
15	Sierra Leone	25	13	2.9	4.5	27	15	6	7	10.6	1.2
16	Mali	34	97	1.1	1.1	25	34	9	10	0.0	0.4
17	Nigeria	65	2,017	6.0	6.7	14	19	4	4	2.7	34.5
18	Niger	19	146	1.2	7.6	40	21	8	9	0.0	9.1
19	Rwanda	9	72	0.8	1.4	50	34	10	9	0.0	0.0
20	Burkina Faso	9	76	2.3	2.2	36	29	8	9	0.0	0.3
21	India	954	6,896	2.5	4.8	34	25	8	8	0.0	17.5
22	Benin	7	47	1.8	0.8	32	48	7	10	0.0	1.7
23	China	..	9,786	..	7.6	..	17	..	4	..	36.4
24	Haiti	5	104	4.8	1.4	10	39	1	12	0.0	0.7
25	Kenya	50	582	2.6	4.4	37	23	8	6	0.1	3.5
26	Pakistan	951	2,997	2.8	5.5	32	21	12	6	0.0	12.6
27	Ghana	51	526	2.0	2.4	37	34	10	9	0.0	0.8
28	Central African Rep.	7	175	2.0	1.0	36	38	8	10	0.0	0.0
29	Togo	3	97	4.5	0.8	17	41	4	10	0.0	3.4
30	Zambia	557	52	4.2	9.0	27	6	9	2	0.0	13.8
31	Guinea	68	174	2.9	0.7	13	40	5	10	0.0	8.0
32	Sri Lanka	81	789	3.0	1.9	27	34	5	9	0.0	2.6
33	Mauritania	7	146	6.0	3.9	11	29	3	8	0.0	5.6
34	Lesotho	0	13	5.5	3.0	20	37	2	8	0.0	0.0
35	Indonesia	530	6,071	2.6	6.0	34	22	9	6	0.0	28.4
36	Honduras	23	287	4.1	6.3	30	22	7	6	0.0	18.2
37	Egypt, Arab Rep.	528	800	4.1	5.3	17	27	5	8	0.0	11.3
38	*Afghanistan*	..	..	..	..	..	..	..	..	..	..
39	*Cambodia*	..	..	..	..	..	..	..	..	..	..
40	*Liberia*	12	0	6.7	0.0	19	0	5	0	0.0	10.9
41	*Myanmar*	48	0	4.1	0.0	16	0	5	0	0.0	0.0
42	*Sudan*	98	0	1.8	0.0	17	0	9	0	0.0	16.1
43	*Viet Nam*	..	..	..	..	..	..	..	..	..	..
	Middle-income economies	**7,300** *t*	**56,313** *t*	**6.3** *w*	**7.8** *w*	**16** *w*	**14** *w*	**4** *w*	**5** *w*	**2.9** *w*	**47.6** *w*
	Lower-middle-income	**3,752** *t*	**31,372** *t*	**5.6** *w*	**7.2** *w*	**18** *w*	**16** *w*	**4** *w*	**5** *w*	**0.6** *w*	**43.7** *w*
44	Bolivia	24	495	1.9	4.1	48	30	4	8	0.0	19.9
45	Zimbabwe	0	399	0.0	7.0	0	16	0	4	0.0	21.0
46	Senegal	7	376	3.9	1.8	23	33	7	9	0.0	2.7
47	Philippines	171	3,249	7.3	6.0	11	22	2	7	0.8	40.2
48	Côte d'Ivoire	71	1,066	5.8	3.7	19	19	5	6	9.0	50.6
49	Dominican Rep.	20	193	2.4	5.9	28	25	5	6	0.0	29.3
50	Papua New Guinea	91	200	6.4	6.4	22	15	8	5	0.0	27.1
51	Guatemala	50	62	5.5	6.0	26	21	6	6	10.3	11.9
52	Morocco	187	1,503	4.6	6.3	20	21	3	7	0.0	45.1
53	Cameroon	42	451	4.7	6.9	29	16	8	5	0.0	11.9
54	Ecuador	78	643	6.2	7.2	20	15	4	4	0.0	61.6
55	Syrian Arab Rep.	14	375	4.4	5.8	9	21	2	5	0.0	0.0
56	Congo	31	158	2.8	4.7	18	17	6	7	0.0	29.1
57	El Salvador	12	131	4.7	4.6	23	30	6	7	0.0	8.8
58	Paraguay	14	98	5.7	2.6	25	33	6	10	0.0	16.6
59	Peru	125	195	7.4	6.7	14	8	4	2	0.0	31.6
60	Jordan	36	175	3.7	8.2	16	17	5	5	0.0	24.4
61	Colombia	363	1,268	6.0	8.2	21	16	5	5	0.0	45.4
62	Thailand	106	1,721	6.8	5.5	19	21	4	7	0.0	24.5
63	Tunisia	144	649	3.5	5.6	28	20	6	6	0.0	19.3
64	Jamaica	24	315	6.0	8.0	16	17	3	4	0.0	25.0
65	Turkey	489	3,654	3.6	8.9	19	10	5	5	0.9	32.4
66	Romania	..	19	..	3.0	..	26	..	10	..	0.0

Note: For data comparability and coverage, see the technical notes. Figures in italics are for years other than those specified.

		Commitments (millions of dollars)		Average interest rate (percent)		Average maturity (years)		Average grace period (years)		Public loans with variable interest rates, as a percentage of public debt	
		1970	1990	1970	1990	1970	1990	1970	1990	1970	1990
67	Poland	..	1,474	..	8.3	..	14	..	5	..	67.0
68	Panama	111	0	6.9	0.0	15	0	4	0	0.0	58.1
69	Costa Rica	58	220	5.6	6.9	28	15	6	4	7.5	24.6
70	Chile	361	1,041	6.8	7.8	12	17	3	4	0.0	65.6
71	Botswana	38	47	0.6	6.7	39	22	10	6	0.0	14.3
72	Algeria	378	6,753	5.7	8.7	12	9	3	2	2.8	37.8
73	Bulgaria	..	88	..	8.8	..	2	..	2	..	73.7
74	Mauritius	14	136	0.0	6.2	24	18	2	6	6.0	18.1
75	Malaysia	84	2,270	6.1	7.4	19	14	5	5	0.0	48.8
76	Argentina	494	459	7.3	8.5	12	9	3	2	0.0	80.3
77	Iran, Islamic Rep.	..	585	..	7.7	..	9	..	4	..	70.9
78	*Albania*	..	..	..	..	..	..	..	..	..	..
79	*Angola*	..	196	..	7.0	..	17	..	3	..	6.7
80	*Lebanon*	7	60	2.9	7.1	21	25	1	3	0.0	9.6
81	*Mongolia*	..	..	..	..	..	..	..	..	..	..
82	*Namibia*	..	..	..	..	..	..	..	..	..	..
83	*Nicaragua*	23	304	7.1	5.8	18	9	4	1	0.0	23.2
84	*Yemen, Rep.*	72	134	0.5	1.5	19	34	10	9	0.0	1.6
	Upper-middle-income	**3,548 t**	**24,941 t**	**7.0 w**	**8.5 w**	**14 w**	**13 w**	**4 w**	**5 w**	**5.9 w**	**53.3 w**
85	Mexico	858	8,004	7.9	8.6	12	13	3	4	5.7	46.3
86	South Africa	..	..	..	..	..	..	..	..	..	..
87	Venezuela	188	2,976	7.6	8.3	8	14	2	6	2.6	56.0
88	Uruguay	71	358	7.9	9.2	12	11	3	2	0.7	74.0
89	Brazil	1,439	1,862	7.0	8.5	14	12	3	5	11.8	69.2
90	Hungary[a]	..	3,285	..	8.9	..	8	..	5	..	59.5
91	Yugoslavia	199	991	7.0	8.7	17	15	6	5	3.3	66.0
92	Czechoslovakia	..	1,270	..	8.9	..	5	..	3	..	27.0
93	Gabon	33	25	5.1	7.4	11	21	1	6	0.0	10.0
94	Trinidad and Tobago	3	157	7.4	8.0	10	17	1	5	0.0	47.4
95	Portugal	59	3,573	4.3	8.3	17	16	4	5	0.0	29.0
96	Korea, Rep.	691	2,027	5.8	7.1	19	13	6	7	1.2	22.7
97	Greece	..	..	..	..	..	..	..	..	..	..
98	Saudi Arabia	..	..	..	..	..	..	..	..	..	..
99	*Iraq*	..	..	..	..	..	..	..	..	..	..
100	*Libya*	..	..	..	..	..	..	..	..	..	..
101	Oman	..	395	..	7.7	..	13	..	4	..	54.3
	Low- and middle-income	**12,123 t**	**92,677 t**	**5.0 w**	**6.8 w**	**21 w**	**18 w**	**6 w**	**5 w**	**1.7 w**	**37.8 w**
	Sub-Saharan Africa	**1,890 t**	**9,577 t**	**3.6 w**	**3.9 w**	**26 w**	**26 w**	**8 w**	**7 w**	**0.9 w**	**18.2 w**
	East Asia & Pacific	**1,689 t**	**25,581 t**	**5.0 w**	**6.8 w**	**23 w**	**19 w**	**6 w**	**6 w**	**0.5 w**	**33.1 w**
	South Asia	**2,052 t**	**12,223 t**	**2.7 w**	**4.4 w**	**32 w**	**26 w**	**10 w**	**8 w**	**0.0 w**	**12.9 w**
	Europe	**755 t**	**14,366 t**	**4.6 w**	**8.7 w**	**19 w**	**12 w**	**5 w**	**5 w**	**1.5 w**	**51.2 w**
	Middle East & N.Africa	**1,366 t**	**11,429 t**	**4.3 w**	**7.7 w**	**17 w**	**13 w**	**5 w**	**4 w**	**0.6 w**	**24.1 w**
	Latin America & Caribbean	**4,372 t**	**19,501 t**	**7.0 w**	**8.0 w**	**14 w**	**15 w**	**4 w**	**5 w**	**4.0 w**	**55.9 w**
	Other economies	..	..	..	..	..	..	..	..	..	..
	Severely indebted	**3,910 t**	**26,354 t**	**6.9 w**	**8.0 w**	**14 w**	**13 w**	**3 w**	**4 w**	**5.0 w**	**55.2 w**

High-income economies
  OECD members
  †Other

102	Ireland
103	†Israel
104	Spain
105	†Singapore
106	†Hong Kong
107	New Zealand
108	Belgium
109	United Kingdom
110	Italy
111	Australia
112	Netherlands
113	Austria
114	France
115	†United Arab Emirates
116	Canada
117	United States
118	Denmark
119	Germany
120	Norway
121	Sweden
122	Japan
123	Finland
124	Switzerland
125	†*Kuwait*

World
Fuel exporters, excl. former USSR

a. Includes debt in convertible currencies only.

Table 26. Population growth and projections

		Average annual growth of population (percent)			Population (millions)			Hypothetical size of stationary population (millions)	Age structure of population (percent)			
									0–14 years		15–64 years	
		1965–80	1980–90	1989–2000[a]	1990	2000[a]	2025[a]		1990	2025[a]	1990	2025[a]
Low-income economies		**2.3** *w*	**2.0** *w*	**1.8** *w*	**3,058** *t*	**3,670** *t*	**5,154** *t*		**35.2** *w*	**26.3** *w*	**60.3** *w*	**65.6** *w*
China and India		**2.2** *w*	**1.7** *w*	**1.5** *w*	**1,983** *t*	**2,300** *t*	**2,945** *t*		**31.2** *w*	**22.2** *w*	**63.6** *w*	**67.4** *w*
Other low-income		**2.5** *w*	**2.6** *w*	**2.5** *w*	**1,075** *t*	**1,370** *t*	**2,209** *t*		**42.5** *w*	**31.8** *w*	**54.2** *w*	**63.3** *w*
1	Mozambique	2.5	2.6	3.0	16	21	42	97	44.1	40.4	52.7	56.9
2	Tanzania	2.9	3.1	3.1	25	33	64	146	46.7	40.2	50.3	57.2
3	Ethiopia	2.7	3.1	3.4	51	71	156	420	47.0	43.1	50.2	54.4
4	Somalia	2.9	3.1	3.1	8	11	21	47	46.0	39.4	51.0	57.4
5	Nepal	2.4	2.6	2.5	19	24	37	59	42.0	28.7	54.9	66.2
6	Chad	2.0	2.4	2.7	6	7	14	28	41.9	37.0	54.5	58.9
7	Bhutan	1.6	2.1	2.4	1	2	3	5	39.9	32.7	56.8	63.1
8	Lao PDR	1.9	2.7	3.2	4	6	10	21	44.8	37.0	53.3	59.5
9	Malawi	2.9	3.4	3.4	9	12	24	63	46.7	42.3	50.7	55.2
10	Bangladesh	2.6	2.3	1.8	107	128	176	257	42.9	25.7	54.0	68.9
11	Burundi	1.9	2.8	3.1	5	7	14	32	45.6	40.7	51.4	56.7
12	Zaire	3.1	3.2	3.0	37	50	89	172	46.4	35.5	51.0	61.0
13	Uganda	3.0	2.5	3.3	16	23	42	92	48.7	39.7	48.5	58.3
14	Madagascar	2.5	3.0	2.8	12	15	26	46	45.5	32.6	51.5	63.7
15	Sierra Leone	2.0	2.4	2.6	4	5	10	23	43.4	40.4	53.5	56.3
16	Mali	2.1	2.5	3.0	8	11	23	58	46.6	40.8	50.2	56.7
17	Nigeria	2.5	3.2	2.8	115	153	255	453	46.4	32.1	51.0	63.9
18	Niger	2.6	3.3	3.3	8	11	24	72	47.2	44.7	50.2	52.9
19	Rwanda	3.3	3.3	3.9	7	10	23	65	48.0	44.1	49.5	53.3
20	Burkina Faso	2.1	2.6	2.9	9	12	22	48	45.5	38.4	51.4	58.9
21	India	2.3	2.1	1.7	850	1,006	1,348	1862	36.9	24.0	58.7	68.4
22	Benin	2.7	3.2	2.9	5	6	10	19	47.6	33.5	49.7	63.4
23	China	2.2	1.4	1.3	1134	1,294	1,597	1890	27.0	20.8	67.2	66.5
24	Haiti	1.7	1.9	1.9	6	8	11	20	40.0	31.2	55.9	64.2
25	Kenya	3.6	3.8	3.5	24	34	64	125	49.9	35.2	47.3	61.6
26	Pakistan	3.1	3.1	2.7	112	147	240	399	44.2	30.4	53.0	65.1
27	Ghana	2.2	3.4	3.0	15	20	34	62	46.8	32.9	50.3	63.3
28	Central African Rep.	1.8	2.7	2.5	3	4	6	11	42.1	33.9	54.9	62.8
29	Togo	3.0	3.5	3.2	4	5	9	18	48.1	35.4	48.8	61.4
30	Zambia	3.0	3.7	3.1	8	11	20	42	49.3	38.6	48.5	59.2
31	Guinea	1.5	2.5	2.8	6	8	15	33	46.1	40.2	51.3	57.0
32	Sri Lanka	1.8	1.4	1.1	17	19	24	28	32.3	21.0	62.7	66.0
33	Mauritania	2.4	2.4	2.8	2	3	5	14	44.6	42.4	52.1	55.0
34	Lesotho	2.3	2.7	2.6	2	2	4	6	43.4	29.5	53.1	65.7
35	Indonesia	2.4	1.8	1.6	178	209	275	360	35.8	23.0	60.3	68.3
36	Honduras	3.2	3.4	2.9	5	7	11	18	44.8	28.1	52.1	66.9
37	Egypt, Arab Rep.	2.1	2.4	1.8	52	62	86	120	39.2	24.4	56.6	67.6
38	*Afghanistan*	2.4	. .	. .	. .	. .	. .	. .				
39	*Cambodia*	0.3	2.6	1.9	8	10	14	20	34.8	26.1	62.3	66.6
40	*Liberia*	3.0	3.1	3.0	3	3	6	11	44.9	32.2	52.0	63.6
41	*Myanmar*	2.3	2.1	2.0	42	51	70	96	37.1	24.0	58.8	68.5
42	*Sudan*	3.0	2.7	2.8	25	33	55	102	45.2	33.6	52.2	62.5
43	*Viet Nam*	2.3	2.1	2.1	66	82	116	159	39.6	24.1	55.9	68.8
Middle-income economies		**2.3** *w*	**2.0** *w*	**1.9** *w*	**1,088** *t*	**1,311** *t*	**1,878** *t*		**35.8** *w*	**26.8** *w*	**58.1** *w*	**64.7** *w*
Lower-middle-income		**2.4** *w*	**2.2** *w*	**2.0** *w*	**629** *t*	**771** *t*	**1,163** *t*		**37.6** *w*	**28.3** *w*	**57.8** *w*	**64.2** *w*
44	Bolivia	2.5	2.5	2.5	7	9	14	21	42.5	26.2	54.1	68.1
45	Zimbabwe	3.1	3.4	2.4	10	12	18	28	45.5	26.8	52.0	68.1
46	Senegal	2.9	2.9	3.1	7	10	19	44	46.7	40.0	50.6	57.6
47	Philippines	2.8	2.4	1.8	61	74	101	137	39.9	23.9	56.8	68.4
48	Côte d'Ivoire	4.1	3.8	3.5	12	17	31	64	47.4	36.2	50.1	60.5
49	Dominican Rep.	2.7	2.2	1.6	7	8	11	14	37.3	22.9	59.3	68.0
50	Papua New Guinea	2.4	2.5	2.3	4	5	7	11	41.1	27.6	56.2	67.8
51	Guatemala	2.8	2.9	2.8	9	12	20	33	45.2	28.7	51.8	66.4
52	Morocco	2.5	2.6	2.4	25	32	47	70	40.8	25.7	55.6	68.0
53	Cameroon	2.7	3.0	2.9	12	16	28	53	46.3	33.7	49.9	62.4
54	Ecuador	3.1	2.4	2.0	10	13	18	24	39.5	23.7	56.9	68.5
55	Syrian Arab Rep.	3.4	3.6	3.6	12	18	35	66	48.2	34.3	49.1	61.8
56	Congo	2.8	3.4	3.3	2	3	6	14	45.2	38.9	50.9	58.1
57	El Salvador	2.8	1.4	1.8	5	6	9	13	43.7	25.0	52.7	69.4
58	Paraguay	2.8	3.2	2.8	4	6	10	16	41.1	30.2	55.4	63.7
59	Peru	2.8	2.3	2.0	22	27	37	50	38.0	23.9	58.3	68.4
60	Jordan[b]	4.3	3.7	3.8	3	5	10	28	45.4	39.7	52.1	56.8
61	Colombia	2.4	2.0	1.5	32	38	50	63	35.4	22.0	60.6	68.0
62	Thailand	2.9	1.8	1.4	56	64	84	105	33.9	21.9	63.1	68.0
63	Tunisia	2.1	2.3	1.9	8	10	14	18	37.8	23.4	58.1	68.5
64	Jamaica	1.3	1.3	0.7	2	3	3	4	34.2	21.7	59.3	67.6
65	Turkey	2.4	2.4	1.9	56	68	91	120	34.8	23.1	60.9	67.6
66	Romania	1.1	0.4	0.4	23	24	27	31	23.8	20.3	65.9	64.1

Note: For data comparability and coverage, see the technical notes.   Figures in italics are for years other than those specified.

		Average annual growth of population (percent)			Population (millions)			Hypothetical size of stationary population (millions)	Age structure of population (percent)			
									0-14 years		15-64 years	
		1965-80	1980-90	1989-2000[a]	1990	2000[a]	2025[a]		1990	2025[a]	1990	2025[a]
67	Poland	0.8	0.7	0.4	38	40	44	50	25.1	19.9	64.9	62.3
68	Panama	2.6	2.1	1.6	2	3	4	5	34.9	21.9	60.4	67.2
69	Costa Rica	2.7	2.4	1.9	3	3	5	6	36.1	22.1	59.7	66.2
70	Chile	1.7	1.7	1.3	13	15	19	23	30.5	21.3	63.6	65.7
71	Botswana	3.6	3.3	2.5	1	2	2	4	47.4	25.5	49.2	69.0
72	Algeria	3.1	3.0	2.8	25	33	52	78	43.6	25.7	52.7	68.5
73	Bulgaria	0.5	0.0	-0.2	9	9	9	9	19.9	17.9	66.6	60.9
74	Mauritius	1.6	1.0	0.9	1	1	1	2	29.4	19.0	65.2	67.0
75	Malaysia	2.5	2.6	2.3	18	22	32	44	38.3	23.9	58.1	67.4
76	Argentina	1.6	1.3	1.0	32	36	44	54	29.8	21.5	61.1	65.0
77	Iran, Islamic Rep.	3.1	3.6	3.4	56	78	166	492	44.4	40.0	52.6	55.9
78	*Albania*	2.4	2.0	1.5	3	4	5	6	33.5	22.1	61.2	66.3
79	*Angola*	2.8	2.6	3.0	10	13	27	62	44.8	39.9	52.1	56.9
80	*Lebanon*	1.7	..	..	..	..	..	..	..	..	..	..
81	*Mongolia*	2.6	2.8	2.5	2	3	4	6	40.7	25.9	55.7	67.9
82	*Namibia*	2.4	3.2	3.0	2	2	4	7	45.8	31.2	51.1	64.5
83	*Nicaragua*	3.1	3.4	3.0	4	5	9	14	45.9	28.4	51.5	66.4
84	*Yemen, Rep.*	2.3	3.1	3.7	11	16	37	110	48.7	44.2	48.2	54.1
	Upper-middle-income	**2.2** w	**1.7** w	**1.7** w	458 t	541 t	715 t		**33.8** w	**24.3** w	**60.9** w	**65.7** w
85	Mexico	3.1	2.0	1.8	86	103	142	184	37.3	22.9	59.0	68.3
86	South Africa	2.4	2.4	2.2	36	45	65	96	38.2	25.6	57.8	67.0
87	Venezuela	3.5	2.7	2.1	20	24	34	45	38.3	23.3	58.2	67.5
88	Uruguay	0.4	0.6	0.6	3	3	4	4	25.8	20.0	62.8	63.9
89	Brazil	2.4	2.2	1.7	150	178	237	305	35.4	22.8	60.2	66.9
90	Hungary	0.4	-0.2	-0.4	11	10	10	10	19.5	17.5	67.0	61.1
91	Yugoslavia	0.9	0.7	0.6	24	25	28	30	22.7	18.6	67.8	62.1
92	Czechoslovakia	0.5	0.3	0.3	16	16	17	19	23.2	19.1	65.0	62.8
93	Gabon	3.6	3.6	2.8	1	1	3	6	39.1	38.0	56.0	57.6
94	Trinidad and Tobago	1.2	1.3	1.0	1	1	2	2	33.9	22.3	60.6	65.7
95	Portugal	0.4	0.6	0.4	10	11	11	11	20.7	16.4	66.3	63.5
96	Korea, Rep.	2.0	1.1	0.9	43	47	54	56	25.1	18.1	69.4	66.0
97	Greece	0.7	0.4	0.2	10	10	10	9	19.0	15.5	66.9	60.7
98	Saudi Arabia	4.6	4.7	3.7	15	21	43	89	45.5	36.3	51.9	59.1
99	*Iraq*	3.4	3.6	3.4	19	26	48	85	46.5	32.0	50.8	63.6
100	*Libya*	4.3	4.1	3.6	5	6	14	36	46.0	39.5	51.6	56.7
101	*Oman*	3.6	4.7	3.9	2	2	5	10	46.3	36.8	51.3	58.5
	Low- and middle-income	**2.3** w	**2.0** w	**1.9** w	4,146 t	4,981 t	7,032 t		**35.3** w	**26.5** w	**59.7** w	**65.4** w
	Sub-Saharan Africa	**2.7** w	**3.1** w	**3.0** w	495 t	668 t	1,229 t		**46.4** w	**36.9** w	**50.8** w	**59.8** w
	East Asia & Pacific	**2.2** w	**1.6** w	**1.4** w	1,577 t	1,818 t	2,276 t		**29.2** w	**21.6** w	**64.3** w	**67.0** w
	South Asia	**2.4** w	**2.2** w	**1.8** w	1,148 t	1,377 t	1,896 t		**38.2** w	**25.0** w	**57.7** w	**68.0** w
	Europe	**1.1** w	**0.1** w	**0.8** w	200 t	217 t	252 t		**26.3** w	**20.4** w	**64.6** w	**64.4** w
	Middle East & N.Africa	**2.8** w	**3.1** w	**2.9** w	256 t	341 t	615 t		**43.3** w	**34.1** w	**53.4** w	**61.1** w
	Latin America & Caribbean	**2.5** w	**2.1** w	**1.8** w	433 t	515 t	699 t		**36.2** w	**23.4** w	**59.3** w	**67.2** w
	Other economies	**1.0** w	**0.9** w	**0.7** w	321 t	345 t	355 t		**25.2** w	**20.2** w	**63.4** w	**63.1** w
	Severely indebted	**2.4** w	**2.1** w	**1.8** w	455 t	546 t	757 t		**36.2** w	**24.3** w	**58.9** w	**66.5** w
	High-income economies	**0.9** w	**0.6** w	**0.5** w	816 t	859 t	915 t		**19.9** w	**16.8** w	**67.2** w	**60.8** w
	OECD members	**0.8** w	**0.6** w	**0.5** w	777 t	814 t	861 t		**19.5** w	**16.7** w	**67.3** w	**60.6** w
	†Other	**2.5** w	**1.8** w	**1.4** w	40 t	45 t	55 t		**27.8** w	**18.9** w	**65.9** w	**64.0** w
102	Ireland	1.2	0.2	0.1	4	4	4	4	26.7	19.6	61.9	64.3
103	†Israel	2.8	1.8	3.3	5	6	8	10	31.2	21.0	59.9	65.5
104	Spain	1.0	0.4	0.2	39	40	40	37	19.8	15.6	67.0	63.4
105	†Singapore	1.6	2.2	1.2	3	3	4	4	23.6	18.1	70.9	61.9
106	†Hong Kong	2.0	1.4	0.8	6	6	7	6	21.0	15.4	70.2	61.4
107	New Zealand	1.3	0.9	0.7	3	4	4	4	22.7	18.7	66.3	62.7
108	Belgium	0.3	0.1	0.1	10	10	10	9	17.9	15.6	67.0	59.6
109	United Kingdom	0.2	0.2	0.2	57	59	61	61	18.9	17.4	65.4	61.3
110	Italy	0.5	0.2	0.1	58	58	55	46	16.4	14.1	68.7	60.4
111	Australia	1.8	1.5	1.4	17	20	23	24	22.1	18.1	67.1	63.0
112	Netherlands	0.9	0.5	0.5	15	16	16	14	17.6	15.6	69.2	59.9
113	Austria	0.3	0.2	0.2	8	8	8	7	17.5	15.5	67.4	60.6
114	France	0.7	0.5	0.4	56	59	63	62	20.1	17.3	66.2	60.5
115	†United Arab Emirates	16.5	4.3	2.2	2	2	3	3	30.8	22.2	67.5	60.7
116	Canada	1.3	1.0	0.8	27	29	32	31	20.9	16.9	67.8	60.7
117	United States	1.0	0.9	0.8	250	270	307	317	21.6	18.1	66.1	61.2
118	Denmark	0.5	0.0	0.0	5	5	5	4	16.9	15.3	67.8	60.2
119	Germany	0.2	0.1	0.1	79	80	78	67	16.2	15.1	68.8	59.2
120	Norway	0.6	0.4	0.4	4	4	5	5	19.0	17.1	64.6	61.0
121	Sweden	0.5	0.3	0.3	9	9	9	9	17.4	17.2	64.6	59.3
122	Japan	1.2	0.6	0.3	124	128	128	114	18.4	15.2	69.7	58.7
123	Finland	0.3	0.4	0.2	5	5	5	5	19.5	16.7	67.2	58.9
124	Switzerland	0.5	0.6	0.4	7	7	7	6	17.0	15.8	68.1	58.3
125	†Kuwait	7.1	4.4	2.9	2	3	4	5	35.6	21.1	63.0	64.9
	World	**2.0** w	**1.7** w	**1.6** w	5,284 t	6,185 t	8,303 t		**32.3** w	**25.1** w	**61.1** w	**64.8** w
	Fuel exporters, excl. former USSR	**3.0** w	**3.3** w	**3.0** w	273 t	367 t	659 t		**44.8** w	**33.9** w	**52.3** w	**61.5** w

a. For the assumptions used in the projections, see the technical notes.   b. Data for Jordan cover the East Bank only.

Table 27. Demography and fertility

		Crude birth rate (per 1,000 population)		Crude death rate (per 1,000 population)		Women of childbearing age as a percentage of all women		Total fertility rate			Assumed year of reaching net reproduction rate of 1	Married women of childbearing age using contraception (percent)[b]
		1965	1990	1965	1990	1965	1990	1965	1990	2000[a]		1988
	Low-income economies	42 *w*	30 *w*	16 *w*	10 *w*	46 *w*	51 *w*	6.3 *w*	3.8 *w*	3.3 *w*		
	China and India	41 *w*	25 *w*	14 *w*	8 *w*	46 *w*	53 *w*	6.3 *w*	3.1 *w*	2.5 *w*		
	Other low-income	46 *w*	38 *w*	21 *w*	13 *w*	45 *w*	47 *w*	6.4 *w*	5.2 *w*	4.6 *w*		
1	Mozambique	49	46	27	18	47	45	6.8	6.4	6.7	2045	..
2	Tanzania	49	48	23	18	45	45	6.6	6.6	6.6	2045	..
3	Ethiopia	43	51	20	18	46	43	5.8	7.5	7.3	2050	..
4	Somalia	50	48	26	18	45	44	6.7	6.8	6.6	2045	..
5	Nepal	46	40	24	14	50	47	6.0	5.7	4.6	2025	*15*
6	Chad	45	44	28	18	47	46	6.0	6.0	6.1	2040	..
7	Bhutan	42	39	23	17	48	48	5.9	5.5	5.4	2035	..
8	Lao PDR	45	47	23	16	47	45	6.1	6.7	6.0	2040	..
9	Malawi	56	54	26	20	46	45	7.8	7.6	7.4	2050	..
10	Bangladesh	47	35	21	14	44	47	6.8	4.6	3.3	2015	*31*
11	Burundi	47	49	24	18	44	46	6.4	6.8	6.6	2045	9
12	Zaire	47	45	21	14	47	45	6.0	6.2	5.6	2035	..
13	Uganda	49	51	19	19	44	43	7.0	7.3	6.6	2045	5
14	Madagascar	47	45	22	15	47	45	6.6	6.3	5.2	2030	..
15	Sierra Leone	48	47	31	22	47	45	6.4	6.5	6.5	2045	..
16	Mali	50	50	27	19	46	45	6.5	7.1	7.0	2050	5
17	Nigeria	51	43	23	14	45	45	6.9	6.0	5.0	2030	..
18	Niger	48	51	29	20	45	44	7.1	7.2	7.3	2055	..
19	Rwanda	52	54	17	18	45	44	7.5	8.3	7.6	2055	..
20	Burkina Faso	48	47	26	18	47	45	6.4	6.5	6.3	2045	..
21	India	45	30	20	11	48	49	6.2	4.0	3.0	2015	45
22	Benin	49	46	24	15	44	44	6.8	6.3	5.2	2035	..
23	China	38	22	10	7	45	56	6.4	2.5	2.1	2000	..
24	Haiti	41	36	21	13	45	48	6.1	4.8	4.2	2035	*10*
25	Kenya	52	45	20	10	41	42	8.0	6.5	5.5	2035	*27*
26	Pakistan	48	42	21	12	43	46	7.0	5.8	4.6	2030	*12*
27	Ghana	47	44	18	13	45	44	6.8	6.2	4.6	2030	*13*
28	Central African Rep.	34	42	24	16	47	46	4.5	5.8	5.3	2035	..
29	Togo	50	48	22	14	46	44	6.5	6.6	5.5	2035	..
30	Zambia	49	49	20	15	46	44	6.6	6.7	6.1	2040	..
31	Guinea	46	48	29	21	45	45	5.9	6.5	6.5	2045	..
32	Sri Lanka	33	20	8	6	47	54	4.9	2.4	2.1	1995	*62*
33	Mauritania	47	48	26	19	47	44	6.5	6.8	6.8	2050	..
34	Lesotho	42	40	18	12	47	45	5.8	5.6	4.5	2025	..
35	Indonesia	43	26	20	9	47	52	5.5	3.1	2.4	2005	*45*
36	Honduras	51	38	17	7	44	46	7.4	5.2	4.1	2025	*41*
37	Egypt, Arab Rep.	43	31	19	10	43	48	6.8	4.0	3.1	2015	38
38	*Afghanistan*	53	..	..	..	..	..	..	..	..	..	..
39	*Cambodia*	44	38	20	15	47	54	6.2	4.5	3.5	2015	..
40	*Liberia*	46	44	20	14	47	44	6.4	6.3	5.2	2035	6
41	*Myanmar*	40	31	18	9	46	50	5.8	3.8	2.9	2010	..
42	*Sudan*	47	44	24	15	46	45	6.7	6.3	5.4	2035	..
43	*Viet Nam*	39	31	18	7	45	48	6.0	3.8	2.9	2010	53
	Middle-income economies	37 *w*	29 *w*	12 *w*	8 *w*	45 *w*	49 *w*	5.4 *w*	3.7 *w*	3.2 *w*		
	Lower-middle-income	38 *w*	30 *w*	13 *w*	9 *w*	45 *w*	49 *w*	5.6 *w*	4.0 *w*	3.4 *w*		
44	Bolivia	46	36	21	10	46	47	6.6	4.8	3.7	2020	*30*
45	Zimbabwe	55	37	17	8	42	47	8.0	4.9	3.4	2015	43
46	Senegal	47	45	23	17	45	44	6.4	6.5	6.3	2045	*12*
47	Philippines	42	29	12	7	44	50	6.8	3.7	2.7	2010	*44*
48	Côte d'Ivoire	52	45	22	12	44	43	7.4	6.7	5.8	2040	..
49	Dominican Rep.	47	27	13	6	43	52	7.2	3.2	2.4	2005	50
50	Papua New Guinea	43	36	20	11	47	48	6.2	5.1	4.0	2020	..
51	Guatemala	46	39	17	8	44	45	6.7	5.4	4.3	2025	*23*
52	Morocco	49	35	18	9	45	48	7.1	4.5	3.4	2020	*36*
53	Cameroon	40	41	20	12	47	43	5.2	5.8	5.3	2035	..
54	Ecuador	45	30	13	7	43	50	6.8	3.7	2.8	2010	*53*
55	Syrian Arab Rep.	48	44	16	7	..	43	7.7	6.5	5.4	2035	..
56	Congo	42	48	18	15	45	43	5.7	6.6	6.3	2045	..
57	El Salvador	46	33	13	8	44	46	6.7	4.2	3.2	2015	*47*
58	Paraguay	41	35	8	6	41	48	6.6	4.6	4.0	2030	48
59	Peru	45	30	16	8	44	50	6.7	3.8	2.8	2010	*46*
60	Jordan[c]	53	43	21	6	45	45	8.0	6.3	5.6	2055	..
61	Colombia	43	24	11	6	43	53	6.5	2.7	2.2	2000	*66*
62	Thailand	41	22	10	7	44	54	6.3	2.5	2.1	1995	*66*
63	Tunisia	44	28	16	7	43	50	7.0	3.6	2.7	2010	50
64	Jamaica	38	24	9	6	42	51	5.7	2.8	2.1	2000	55
65	Turkey	41	28	15	7	45	51	5.7	3.5	2.7	2010	63
66	Romania	15	16	9	11	50	47	1.9	2.2	2.1	1990	..

Note: For data comparability and coverage, see the technical notes.   Figures in italics are for years other than those specified.

		Crude birth rate (per 1,000 population)		Crude death rate (per 1,000 population)		Women of childbearing age as a percentage of all women		Total fertility rate			Assumed year of reaching net reproduction rate of 1	Married women of childbearing age using contraception (percent)[b]
		1965	1990	1965	1990	1965	1990	1965	1990	2000[a]		1988
67	Poland	17	15	7	10	47	48	2.5	2.1	2.1	1990	..
68	Panama	40	24	9	5	44	52	5.7	2.9	2.2	2000	68
69	Costa Rica	45	26	8	4	42	52	6.3	3.1	2.3	2005	..
70	Chile	34	22	11	6	45	53	4.8	2.5	2.1	2000	33
71	Botswana	53	35	19	6	45	44	6.9	4.7	3.1	2015	36
72	Algeria	50	36	18	8	44	46	7.4	5.1	3.7	2020	..
73	Bulgaria	15	13	8	12	51	47	2.1	1.9	1.9	2030	..
74	Mauritius	36	17	8	6	45	56	4.8	1.9	1.8	2030	..
75	Malaysia	40	30	12	5	44	50	6.3	3.8	3.0	2015	..
76	Argentina	23	20	9	9	50	47	3.1	2.8	2.3	2005	..
77	Iran, Islamic Rep.	46	45	18	9	42	46	7.1	6.2	5.6	2060	..
78	Albania	35	25	9	6	44	51	5.4	3.1	2.3	2005	..
79	Angola	49	47	29	19	47	45	6.4	6.5	6.6	2045	..
80	Lebanon	40	..	..	..	..	..	5.9	..	..		..
81	Mongolia	43	35	16	8	46	48	5.9	4.7	3.7	2020	..
82	Namibia	46	42	22	11	46	44	6.1	5.9	4.8	2030	..
83	Nicaragua	49	40	16	7	43	46	7.2	5.3	4.2	2025	..
84	Yemen, Rep.	49	53	27	18	47	43	7.0	7.7	7.5	2055	..
	Upper-middle-income	**35** w	**26** w	**11** w	**7** w	**46** w	**51** w	**5.1** w	**3.4** w	**2.7** w		
85	Mexico	45	27	11	5	43	52	6.7	3.3	2.4	2005	53
86	South Africa	40	33	16	9	46	49	6.1	4.3	3.4	2020	..
87	Venezuela	42	29	8	5	44	51	6.1	3.6	2.7	2010	..
88	Uruguay	21	17	10	10	49	47	2.8	2.3	2.1	1995	..
89	Brazil	39	27	11	7	45	52	5.6	3.2	2.4	2005	65
90	Hungary	13	12	11	13	48	47	1.8	1.8	1.8	2030	73
91	Yugoslavia	21	15	9	9	50	49	2.7	2.0	2.0	2030	..
92	Czechoslovakia	16	14	10	11	46	48	2.4	2.0	2.0	2030	..
93	Gabon	31	42	22	15	48	47	4.1	5.7	6.1	2045	..
94	Trinidad and Tobago	33	24	8	6	46	52	4.3	2.8	2.3	2005	53
95	Portugal	23	12	10	9	48	49	3.1	1.6	1.6	2030	..
96	Korea, Rep.	35	16	11	16	46	58	4.9	1.8	1.8	2030	77
97	Greece	18	11	8	9	51	47	2.3	1.5	1.6	2030	..
98	Saudi Arabia	48	43	20	7	45	42	7.3	7.0	5.9	2040	..
99	Iraq	49	42	18	8	45	44	7.2	6.2	5.1	2030	..
100	Libya	49	43	17	8	45	44	7.4	6.7	5.8	2050	..
101	Oman	50	44	24	6	47	43	7.2	7.0	5.9	2040	..
	Low- and middle-income	**41** w	**30** w	**15** w	**9** w	**46** w	**50** w	**6.1** w	**3.8** w	**3.2** w		
	Sub-Saharan Africa	**48** w	**46** w	**23** w	**16** w	**45** w	**44** w	**6.6** w	**6.5** w	**5.9** w		
	East Asia & Pacific	**39** w	**23** w	**11** w	**7** w	**45** w	**55** w	**6.2** w	**2.7** w	**2.2** w		
	South Asia	**45** w	**32** w	**20** w	**11** w	**47** w	**49** w	**6.3** w	**4.2** w	**3.3** w		
	Europe	**22** w	**19** w	**10** w	**9** w	**48** w	**49** w	**3.1** w	**2.0** w	**2.2** w		
	Middle East & N.Africa	**47** w	**40** w	**20** w	**10** w	**44** w	**46** w	**7.1** w	**5.7** w	**4.8** w		
	Latin America & Caribbean	**39** w	**27** w	**11** w	**7** w	**45** w	**51** w	**5.8** w	**3.3** w	**2.6** w		
	Other economies	**20** w	**18** w	**8** w	**10** w	**47** w	**46** w	**2.7** w	**2.3** w	**2.1** w		
	Severely indebted	**37** w	**28** w	**12** w	**8** w	**46** w	**50** w	**5.5** w	**3.5** w	**2.8** w		
	High-income economies	**19** w	**13** w	**10** w	**9** w	**47** w	**50** w	**2.8** w	**1.7** w	**1.8** w		
	OECD members	**19** w	**13** w	**10** w	**9** w	**47** w	**50** w	**2.7** w	**1.7** w	**1.7** w		
	†Other	**31** w	**17** w	**6** w	**5** w	**45** w	**54** w	**4.6** w	**2.2** w	**2.0** w		
102	Ireland	22	16	12	9	42	49	4.0	2.2	2.1	1990	60
103	†Israel	26	22	6	6	46	49	3.8	2.8	2.3	2005	..
104	Spain	21	11	8	9	49	49	2.9	1.5	1.5	2030	..
105	†Singapore	31	17	6	5	45	60	4.7	1.9	1.9	2030	..
106	†Hong Kong	27	13	6	6	45	56	4.5	1.5	1.5	2030	81
107	New Zealand	23	16	9	8	45	52	3.6	2.0	2.0	2030	..
108	Belgium	17	13	12	11	44	48	2.6	1.6	1.6	2030	81
109	United Kingdom	18	13	12	11	45	48	2.9	1.8	1.9	2030	..
110	Italy	19	10	10	9	48	49	2.7	1.3	1.4	2030	76
111	Australia	20	15	9	7	47	53	3.0	1.9	1.9	2030	76
112	Netherlands	20	12	8	9	47	53	3.0	1.6	1.6	2030	..
113	Austria	18	12	13	11	43	49	2.7	1.5	1.6	2030	80
114	France	18	13	11	10	43	49	2.8	1.8	1.8	2030	..
115	†United Arab Emirates	41	22	14	4	47	47	6.8	4.6	3.6	2020	..
116	Canada	21	14	8	7	47	53	3.1	1.7	1.7	2030	74
117	United States	19	17	9	9	46	52	2.9	1.9	1.9	2030	..
118	Denmark	18	11	10	12	47	51	2.6	1.7	1.6	2030	..
119	Germany	17	11	12	11	45	47	2.5	1.5	1.6	2030	84
120	Norway	18	13	10	10	45	49	2.9	1.8	1.8	2030	..
121	Sweden	16	15	10	12	47	48	2.4	1.9	1.9	2030	56
122	Japan	19	11	7	7	56	50	2.0	1.6	1.6	2030	..
123	Finland	17	13	10	10	48	49	2.4	1.8	1.8	2030	..
124	Switzerland	19	12	10	10	48	50	2.6	1.7	1.7	2030	..
125	†Kuwait	48	25	7	3	45	53	7.4	3.4	2.6	2010	..
	World	**35** w	**26** w	**13** w	**9** w	**46** w	**50** w	**5.1** w	**3.4** w	**3.0** w		
	Fuel exporters, excl. former USSR	**49** w	**42** w	**20** w	**11** w	**44** w	**45** w	**6.9** w	**5.9** w	**5.0** w		

a. For assumptions used in the projections, see the technical notes to Table 26.   b. Figures include women whose husbands practice contraception; see the technical notes.   c. Data for Jordan cover the East Bank only.

Table 28. Health and nutrition

		Population per			Births attended by health staff (percent)	Babies with low birth weight (percent)	Infant mortality rate (per 1,000 live births)		Daily calorie supply (per capita)	
		Physician		Nursing person							
		1965	1984	1965	1984	1985	1985	1965	1990	1965	1989
	Low-income economies	**9,640** w	**5,800** w	**5,980** w	**2,150** w			**124** w	**69** w	**1,975** w	**2,406** w
	China and India	**2,930** w	**1,650** w	**4,420** w	**1,650** w			**114** w	**56** w	**1,966** w	**2,464** w
	Other low-income	**26,500** w	**14,160** w	**9,760** w	**3,540** w			**145** w	**92** w	**1,994** w	**2,298** w
1	Mozambique	18,000	..	5,370	..	28	15	179	137	1,712	1,680
2	Tanzania	21,700	*24,970*	2,100	*5,480*	74	14	138	115	1,831	2,206
3	Ethiopia	70,190	*78,780*	5,970	*5,390*	58	..	165	132	1,853	1,667
4	Somalia	43,810	*19,950*	4,700	*1,900*	2	..	165	126	1,718	1,906
5	Nepal	46,180	30,220	*87,650*	4,680	10	..	171	121	1,889	2,077
6	Chad	72,480	*38,390*	13,610	*3,400*	..	11	183	125	2,395	1,743
7	Bhutan	..	*9,730*	..	..	3	..	171	122	..	..
8	Lao PDR	24,320	*1,360*	4,880	*530*	..	39	148	103	2,135	2,630
9	Malawi	47,320	*11,340*	40,980	..	59	10	200	149	2,259	2,139
10	Bangladesh	8,100	6,390	..	8,530	..	31	144	105	1,970	2,021
11	Burundi	55,910	*21,020*	7,320	*4,380*	12	14	142	107	2,131	1,932
12	Zaire	34,740	*13,540*	..	*1,880*	..	..	141	94	2,187	1,991
13	Uganda	11,080	..	3,120	..	..	10	119	117	2,361	2,153
14	Madagascar	10,620	*9,780*	3,650	..	62	10	201	116	2,447	2,158
15	Sierra Leone	16,840	*13,620*	4,470	*1,090*	25	14	208	147	2,014	1,799
16	Mali	51,510	25,390	3,360	*1,350*	27	17	207	166	1,938	2,314
17	Nigeria	29,530	*6,410*	6,160	*900*	..	25	162	98	2,185	2,312
18	Niger	65,540	*39,670*	6,210	*460*	47	20	180	128	1,996	2,308
19	Rwanda	72,480	*35,090*	7,450	*3,690*	..	17	141	120	1,856	1,971
20	Burkina Faso	73,960	*57,183*	4,150	*1,680*	..	18	190	134	1,882	2,288
21	India	4,880	*2,520*	6,500	*1,700*	33	30	150	92	2,021	2,229
22	Benin	32,390	*15,940*	2,540	*1,750*	34	10	166	113	2,019	2,305
23	China	1,600	1,010	3,000	1,610	..	6	90	29	1,929	2,639
24	Haiti	14,350	*7,140*	13,210	*2,280*	20	17	158	95	2,045	2,013
25	Kenya	13,280	10,050	1,930	..	..	13	112	67	2,208	2,163
26	Pakistan	..	*2,900*	9,910	*4,890*	24	25	149	103	1,773	2,219
27	Ghana	13,740	*20,390*	3,730	*1,660*	73	17	120	85	1,937	2,248
28	Central African Rep.	34,020	..	3,000	..	..	15	157	101	2,055	2,036
29	Togo	23,240	*8,700*	4,990	*1,240*	..	20	153	88	2,454	2,214
30	Zambia	11,380	7,150	5,820	*740*	..	14	121	82	2,072	2,077
31	Guinea	47,050	..	4,110	..	..	18	191	138	2,187	2,132
32	Sri Lanka	5,820	5,520	3,220	1,290	87	28	63	19	2,171	2,277
33	Mauritania	36,530	*11,900*	..	*1,180*	23	10	178	121	1,903	2,685
34	Lesotho	20,060	18,610	4,700	..	28	10	142	93	2,049	2,299
35	Indonesia	31,700	*9,410*	9,490	..	43	14	128	61	1,791	2,750
36	Honduras	5,370	*1,510*	1,530	*670*	50	20	128	64	1,967	2,247
37	Egypt, Arab Rep.	2,300	*770*	2,030	..	24	7	145	66	2,399	3,336
38	*Afghanistan*	15,770	..	24,430	..	..	..	206	..	2,304	..
39	*Cambodia*	22,410	..	3,670	..	..	..	134	117	2,292	2,166
40	*Liberia*	12,560	*9,340*	2,330	*1,370*	89	..	176	136	2,158	2,382
41	*Myanmar*	11,860	3,740	11,370	900	97	16	122	64	1,897	2,440
42	*Sudan*	23,500	10,190	3,360	1,260	20	15	160	102	1,938	1,974
43	*Viet Nam*	..	950	14,250	590	..	18	134	42	2,041	2,233
	Middle-income economies	**3,910** w	**2,250** w	**2,140** w	**970** w			**94** w	**48** w	**2,489** w	**2,860** w
	Lower-middle-income	**5,310** w	**3,000** w	**2,380** w	**1,050** w			**103** w	**51** w	**2,415** w	**2,768** w
44	Bolivia	3,300	*1,530*	3,990	2,470	36	15	160	92	1,868	1,916
45	Zimbabwe	8,010	6,700	990	1,000	69	15	103	49	2,075	2,299
46	Senegal	19,490	..	2,440	*2,030*	..	10	160	81	2,372	2,369
47	Philippines	..	6,570	1,140	2,680	..	18	72	41	1,875	2,375
48	Côte d'Ivoire	20,640	..	2,000	..	20	14	149	95	2,352	2,577
49	Dominican Rep.	1,700	*1,770*	1,640	*1,210*	57	16	110	56	1,834	2,359
50	Papua New Guinea	12,640	6,070	620	880	34	25	140	57	1,996	2,403
51	Guatemala	3,690	*2,180*	8,250	*850*	19	10	112	62	2,026	2,235
52	Morocco	12,120	*4,730*	2,290	*1,050*	..	9	145	67	2,112	3,020
53	Cameroon	26,720	..	5,830	..	..	13	143	88	2,011	2,217
54	Ecuador	3,000	*810*	2,320	*610*	27	10	112	55	2,191	2,531
55	Syrian Arab Rep.	5,400	*1,250*	..	*890*	37	9	114	43	2,177	3,003
56	Congo	14,210	..	950	..	..	12	129	116	2,260	2,590
57	El Salvador	..	*2,830*	1,300	*930*	35	15	120	53	1,853	2,317
58	Paraguay	1,850	*1,460*	1,550	*1,000*	22	6	73	32	2,586	2,757
59	Peru	1,650	*1,040*	900	..	55	9	130	69	2,323	2,186
60	Jordan	2,710	*860*	1,040	*980*	75	7	..	51[a]	2,277	2,634
61	Colombia	2,500	*1,230*	890	*650*	51	15	86	37	2,179	2,598
62	Thailand	7,160	6,290	4,970	710	33	12	88	27	2,138	2,316
63	Tunisia	8,000	2,150	..	370	60	7	145	44	2,217	3,121
64	Jamaica	1,990	2,040	340	490	89	8	49	16	2,232	2,609
65	Turkey	2,900	1,390	..	1,030	78	7	169	60	2,698	3,236
66	Romania	760	570	400	..	99	6	44	27	2,988	3,155

Note: For data comparability and coverage, see the technical notes.   Figures in italics are for years other than those specified.

		Population per				Births attended by health staff (percent)	Babies with low birth weight (percent)	Infant mortality rate (per 1,000 live births)		Daily calorie supply (per capita)	
		Physician		Nursing person							
		1965	1984	1965	1984	1985	1985	1965	1990	1965	1989
67	Poland	800	490	410	190	..	8	42	16	3,292	3,505
68	Panama	2,130	1,000	1,600	390	83	8	56	21	2,241	2,539
69	Costa Rica	2,010	960	630	450	93	9	72	16	2,367	2,808
70	Chile	2,120	1,230	600	370	97	7	98	17	2,581	2,581
71	Botswana	27,450	6,900	17,710	700	52	8	112	38	2,045	2,375
72	Algeria	8,590	2,340	11,770	300		9	154	67	1,701	2,866
73	Bulgaria	600	280	410	160	100	..	31	14	3,443	3,707
74	Mauritius	3,930	1,900	2,030	..	90	9	65	20	2,269	2,887
75	Malaysia	6,200	1,930	1,320	1010	82	9	55	16	2,353	2,774
76	Argentina	600	370	610	980		6	58	29	3,163	3,113
77	Iran, Islamic Rep.	3,890	2,840	4,270	1110		9	152	88	2,060	3,181
78	Albania	2,080	..	540	..		7	87	28	2,374	2,761
79	Angola	13,150	17,750	3,820	1010	15	17	192	130	1,907	1,807
80	Lebanon	1,010	..	2,030	..			56	..	2,485	
81	Mongolia	730	..	320	..	99	10	113	62	2,364	2,479
82	Namibia	..	..	..	..		..	145	100	1,900	1,946
83	Nicaragua	2,560	1,500	1,390	530		15	121	55	2,305	2,265
84	Yemen, Rep.	31,580	..	..	1940			194	124		
	Upper-middle-income	**2,240** w	**940** w	**1,870** w	**870** w			**84** w	**45** w	**2,584** w	**2,987** w
85	Mexico	2,080	..	980	880		15	82	39	2,570	3,052
86	South Africa	2,050	..	490	..		12	124	66	2,759	3,122
87	Venezuela	1,210	700	560	..	82	9	65	34	2,266	2,582
88	Uruguay	880	510	590	..		8	47	21	2,812	2,653
89	Brazil	2,500	1,080	3,100	1210	73	8	104	57	2,417	2,751
90	Hungary	630	310	240	170	99	10	39	15	3,134	3,644
91	Yugoslavia	1,200	550	850	250		7	72	20	3,243	3,634
92	Czechoslovakia	540	280	200	140	100	6	26	12	3,397	3,632
93	Gabon	..	2,790	760	270	92	16	153	97	1,950	2,383
94	Trinidad and Tobago	3,810	940	560	250	90		47	25	2,496	2,853
95	Portugal	1,240	140	1,160	..		8	65	12	2,647	3,495
96	Korea, Rep.	2,680	1,160	2,970	580	65	9	62	17	2,178	2,852
97	Greece	710	350	600	450		6	34	11	3,019	3,825
98	Saudi Arabia	9,400	730	6,060	340	78	6	148	65	1,850	2,874
99	Iraq	5,000	1,740	2,910	1660	50	9	119	65	2,150	2,887
100	Libya	3,860	690	850	..	76	5	138	74	1,875	3,324
101	Oman	23,790	1,700	6,420	390	60	14	191	33		
	Low- and middle-income	**8,170** w	**4,980** w	**5,010** w	**1,850** w			**117** w	**63** w	**2,108** w	**2,523** w
	Sub-Saharan Africa	**33,310** w	**26,670** w	**5,420** w	**2180** w			**157** w	**107** w	**2,074** w	**2,122** w
	East Asia & Pacific	**5,600** w	**2,390** w	**4,130** w	**1,530** w			**95** w	**34** w	**1,939** w	**2,617** w
	South Asia	**6,220** w	**3,460** w	**8,380** w	**2,650** w			**147** w	**93** w	**1,992** w	**2,215** w
	Europe	**1,260** w	**700** w	**510** w	**480** w			**71** w	**30** w	**3,069** w	**3,433** w
	Middle East & N.Africa	**7,740** w	**2,410** w	**6,160** w	**1,800** w			**151** w	**79** w	**2,153** w	**3,011** w
	Latin America & Caribbean	**2,380** w	**1,220** w	**2,100** w	**1,010** w			**94** w	**48** w	**2,445** w	**2,721** w
	Other economies	**500** w	**530** w	**300** w	**290** w			**30** w	**23** w	**3,125** w	**3,327** w
	Severely indebted	**3,140** w	**1,250** w	**2,220** w	**920** w			**93** w	**50** w	**2,569** w	**2,883** w
	High-income economies	**890** w	**470** w	**440** w	**150** w			**24** w	**8** w	**3,091** w	**3,409** w
	OECD members	**880** w	**460** w	**440** w	**150** w			**24** w	**8** w	**3,099** w	**3,417** w
	†Other	**1,660** w	**880** w	**760** w	**210** w			**31** w	**13** w	**2,546** w	**3,072** w
102	Ireland	950	680	170	140		4	25	7	3,605	3,778
103	†Israel	400	350	300	110	99	7	27	10	2,799	3,174
104	Spain	800	320	1,220	260	96		38	8	2,770	3,572
105	†Singapore	1,900	1,410	600	..	100	7	26	7	2,285	3,198
106	†Hong Kong	2,520	1,070	1,250	240		4	27	7	2,486	2,853
107	New Zealand	820	580	570	80	99	5	20	10	3,238	3,362
108	Belgium	700	330	590	..	100	5	24	8		
109	United Kingdom	870	..	200	..	98	7	20	8	3,304	3,149
110	Italy	1,850	230	790	..		7	36	9	3,097	3,504
111	Australia	720	440	150	110	99	6	19	8	3,053	3,216
112	Netherlands	860	450	270	..		4	14	7	3,024	3,151
113	Austria	720	390	350	180		6	28	8	3,244	3,495
114	France	830	320	380	..		5	22	7	3,355	3,465
115	†United Arab Emirates	..	1,020	..	390	96		103	23	2,639	3,309
116	Canada	770	510	190	..	99	6	24	7	3,127	3,482
117	United States	670	470	310	70	100	7	25	9	3,234	3,671
118	Denmark	740	400	190	60		6	19	8	3,420	3,628
119	Germany	640^b	380^b	500^b	230^b		5^b	24	7	3,088^b	3,443^b
120	Norway	790	450	340	60	100	4	17	8	3,036	3,326
121	Sweden	910	390	310	..	100	4	13	6	2,930	2,960
122	Japan	970	660	410	180	100	5	18	5	2,668	2,956
123	Finland	1,300	440	180	60		4	17	6	3,126	3,253
124	Switzerland	710	700	270	..		5	18	7	3,471	3,562
125	†Kuwait	790	640	270	200	99	7	64	14	2,766	3,195
	World	**6,050** w	**4,200** w	**3,700** w	**1,600** w			**91** w	**52** w	**2,383** w	**2,711** w
	Fuel exporters, excl. former USSR	**16,870** w	**4,480** w	**5,440** w	**900** w			**149** w	**84** w	**2,093** w	**2,642** w

a. Data for Jordan cover the East Bank only.   b. Data refer to the Federal Republic of Germany before unification.

Table 29. Education

		Percentage of age group enrolled in education										Primary net enrollment (percent)		Primary pupil-teacher ratio	
		Primary				Secondary				Tertiary (total)					
		Total		Female		Total		Female							
		1965	1989	1965	1989	1965	1989	1965	1989	1965	1989	1975	1989	1965	1989
	Low-income economies	**73 w**	**105 w**	..	**96 w**	**20 w**	**38 w**	..	**31 w**	**2 w**	..	..	..	**37 w**	**38 w**
	China and India	**83 w**	**119 w**	..	**108 w**	**25 w**	**44 w**	..	**35 w**	**2 w**	..	..	..	**35 w**	**39 w**
	Other low-income	**50 w**	**77 w**	**39 w**	**70 w**	**10 w**	**28 w**	**5 w**	**23 w**	**1 w**	**4 w**	..	**68 w**	**43 w**	**38 w**
1	Mozambique	37	68	26	59	3	5	2	4	0	0	..	45	78	..
2	Tanzania	32	63	25	63	2	4	1	4	0	0	..	48	52	33
3	Ethiopia	11	38	6	30	2	15	1	12	0	1	..	28	41	43
4	Somalia	10	..	4	..	2	..	1	..	0	..	16	..	26	..
5	Nepal	20	86	4	57	5	30	2	17	1	6	..	64	29	37
6	Chad	34	57	13	35	1	7	0	3	..	1	..	38	83	67
7	Bhutan	7	26	1	20	0	5		2	..	..	..	..	..	37
8	Lao PDR	40	111	30	98	2	27	1	22	0	2	..	70	37	28
9	Malawi	44	67	32	60	2	4	1	3	0	1	..	50	40	..
10	Bangladesh	49	70	31	64	13	17	3	11	1	4	..	63	45	60
11	Burundi	26	71	15	60	1	4	1	3	0	1	..	51	40	66
12	Zaire	70	78	45	67	5	24	2	16	0	2	..	60	37	..
13	Uganda	67	77	50	..	4	13	2	..	0	1	..	..	35	35
14	Madagascar	65	92	59	90	8	19	5	18	1	4	..	64	71	40
15	Sierra Leone	29	53	21	40	5	18	3	..	0	1	..	..	32	32
16	Mali	24	23	16	17	4	6	2	4	0	..	..	19	46	39
17	Nigeria	32	70	24	63	5	19	3	16	0	3	..	..	33	37
18	Niger	11	28	7	20	1	6	0	4	..	1	..	17	42	41
19	Rwanda	53	69	43	68	2	7	1	6	0	1	..	65	67	57
20	Burkina Faso	12	35	8	27	1	7	1	5	0	1	..	28	47	55
21	India	74	98	57	82	27	43	13	31	5	..	..	42	61
22	Benin	34	65	21	44	3	..	2	..	0	2	..	52	41	35
23	China	89	135	..	128	24	44	..	38	0	2	..	100	30	22
24	Haiti	50	84	44	81	5	19	3	19	0	..	..	44	46	35
25	Kenya	54	94	40	92	4	23	2	19	0	2	88	..	34	33
26	Pakistan	40	38	20	27	12	20	5	12	2	5	..	..	42	41
27	Ghana	69	75	57	67	13	39	7	30	1	2	..	..	32	27
28	Central African Rep.	56	64	28	48	2	11	1	6	..	1	..	46	54	70
29	Togo	55	103	32	80	5	22	2	10	0	3	..	72	50	55
30	Zambia	53	95	46	91	7	20	3	14	..	2	..	80	51	44
31	Guinea	31	34	19	21	5	9	2	5	0	1	..	26	43	38
32	Sri Lanka	93	107	86	106	35	74	35	76	2	4	..	100	..	14
33	Mauritania	13	51	6	42	1	16	0	10	..	3	..	..	20	49
34	Lesotho	94	110	114	119	4	26	4	31	0	4	..	72	57	56
35	Indonesia	72	118	65	115	12	47	7	43	1	..	72	99	41	23
36	Honduras	80	108	79	109	10	..	9	..	1	10	..	..	29	..
37	Egypt, Arab Rep.	75	97	60	89	26	81	15	71	7	20	..	..	39	24
38	*Afghanistan*	16	24	5	16	2	8	1	5	0	1	..	..	53	..
39	*Cambodia*	77	..	56	..	9	..	4	..	1	..	..	..	48	..
40	*Liberia*	41	..	23	..	5	..	3	..	1	3	..	..	32	..
41	*Myanmar*	71	103	65	100	15	24	11	23	1	5	..	..	53	43
42	*Sudan*	29	..	21	..	4	..	2	..	1	3	..	..	48	..
43	*Viet Nam*	..	..	..	..	..	..	..	..	..	..	..	..	..	..
	Middle-income economies	**93 w**	**102 w**	**87 w**	**101 w**	**26 w**	**55 w**	**23 w**	**57 w**	**7 w**	**17 w**	..	**89 w**	**35 w**	**27 w**
	Lower-middle-income	**88 w**	**101 w**	**80 w**	**99 w**	**26 w**	**54 w**	**23 w**	**56 w**	**7 w**	**17 w**	..	**86 w**	**35 w**	**28 w**
44	Bolivia	73	81	60	77	18	34	15	31	5	23	73	83	28	25
45	Zimbabwe	110	125	92	126	6	52	5	42	0	6	..	..	..	38
46	Senegal	40	58	29	49	7	16	3	11	1	3	..	48	43	58
47	Philippines	113	111	111	110	41	73	40	75	19	28	95	99	31	33
48	Côte d'Ivoire	60	..	41	..	6	20	2	12	0	..	..	..	47	..
49	Dominican Rep.	87	95	87	96	12	..	12	..	2	..	..	..	53	47
50	Papua New Guinea	44	73	35	67	4	13	2	10	..	..	..	73	19	32
51	Guatemala	50	79	45	..	8	21	7	..	2	..	53	..	33	35
52	Morocco	57	68	35	55	11	36	5	30	1	11	47	55	39	26
53	Cameroon	94	101	75	93	5	26	2	21	0	3	69	75	47	51
54	Ecuador	91	118	88	117	17	56	16	57	3	25	78	..	37	31
55	Syrian Arab Rep.	78	108	52	102	28	54	13	45	8	20	87	97	36	26
56	Congo	114	..	94	..	10	..	5	..	1	6	..	..	60	64
57	El Salvador	82	78	79	78	17	26	17	26	2	17	..	70	33	40
58	Paraguay	102	106	96	104	13	29	13	30	4	8	83	93	30	25
59	Peru	99	123	90	..	25	67	21	..	8	32	..	95	36	29
60	Jordan	95	..	83	..	38	..	23	..	2	..	..	..	38	28
61	Colombia	84	107	86	108	17	52	16	53	3	14	..	69	36	30
62	Thailand	78	86	74	..	14	28	11	..	2	16	..	..	35	18
63	Tunisia	91	115	65	107	16	44	9	39	2	8	..	95	56	30
64	Jamaica	109	105	106	105	51	61	50	64	3	5	90	99	57	34
65	Turkey	101	112	83	108	16	51	9	39	4	13	..	84	46	30
66	Romania	101	95	100	95	39	88	32	92	10	9	..	..	23	21

Note: For data comparability and coverage, see the technical notes. Figures in italics are for years other than those specified.

		Primary Total 1965	Primary Total 1989	Primary Female 1965	Primary Female 1989	Secondary Total 1965	Secondary Total 1989	Secondary Female 1965	Secondary Female 1989	Tertiary (total) 1965	Tertiary (total) 1989	Primary net enrollment (percent) 1975	Primary net enrollment (percent) 1989	Primary pupil-teacher ratio 1965	Primary pupil-teacher ratio 1989
		Percentage of age group enrolled in education													
67	Poland	104	99	102	99	69	81	69	83	18	20	96	97	28	*16*
68	Panama	102	107	99	105	34	59	36	*63*	7	22	87	90	30	20
69	Costa Rica	106	100	105	99	24	41	25	42	6	27	92	86	27	32
70	Chile	124	100	122	99	34	75	36	78	6	*19*	94	89	52	29
71	Botswana	65	111	71	114	3	37	3	39	. .	3	58	*93*	40	32
72	Algeria	68	94	53	86	7	61	5	53	1	*11*	77	88	43	28
73	Bulgaria	103	97	102	96	54	75	55	76	17	26	96	86	23	16
74	Mauritius	101	103	97	104	26	53	18	53	3	2	82	94	34	24
75	Malaysia	90	96	84	96	28	59	22	59	2	7	. .	. .	29	21
76	Argentina	101	*111*	102	*114*	28	*74*	31	78	14	41	96	. .	20	*19*
77	Iran, Islamic Rep.	63	109	40	101	18	53	11	44	2	7	. .	94	32	24
78	*Albania*	92	99	87	98	33	80	26	73	8	9	. .	. .	27	19
79	*Angola*	39	94	26	. .	5	11	4	. .	0	. .	. .	. .	45	*33*
80	*Lebanon*	106	. .	93	. .	26	. .	20	. .	14	. .	. .	. .	24	. .
81	*Mongolia*	98	98	97	100	66	. .	66	. .	8	. .	. .	. .	32	. .
82	*Namibia*	. .	. .	. .	. .	. .	. .	. .	. .	. .	. .	. .	. .	. .	. .
83	*Nicaragua*	69	*99*	69	*104*	14	*43*	13	*58*	2	8	65	76	34	32
84	*Yemen, Rep.*	13	. .	3	. .	3	. .	1	. .	. .	. .	. .	. .	56	45
	Upper-middle-income	**99 w**	**104 w**	**96 w**	**103 w**	**26 w**	**56 w**	**23 w**	**57 w**	**5 w**	**17 w**	**79 w**	**91 w**	**36 w**	**25 w**
85	Mexico	92	114	90	112	17	53	13	53	4	15	. .	100	47	31
86	South Africa	90	. .	88	. .	15	. .	14	. .	4	. .	. .	. .	34	. .
87	Venezuela	94	*105*	94	*105*	27	*56*	28	62	7	*28*	81	87	34	. .
88	Uruguay	106	*106*	106	*106*	44	77	46	. .	8	*50*	. .	88	31	23
89	Brazil	108	105	108	. .	16	39	16	45	2	11	71	84	28	23
90	Hungary	101	94	100	94	. .	76	. .	77	13	15	. .	92	23	13
91	Yugoslavia	106	95	103	95	65	80	59	79	13	19	. .	. .	31	23
92	Czechoslovakia	99	92	97	93	29	87	35	90	14	18	. .	. .	23	20
93	Gabon	134	. .	122	. .	11	. .	5	. .	. .	4	. .	. .	39	46
94	Trinidad and Tobago	93	97	90	98	36	83	34	84	2	6	87	91	34	28
95	Portugal	84	111	83	108	42	53	34	54	5	18	91	92	32	17
96	Korea, Rep.	101	108	99	109	35	86	25	84	6	38	99	100	62	36
97	Greece	110	*102*	109	*102*	49	97	41	94	10	28	97	*98*	35	22
98	Saudi Arabia	24	76	11	70	4	46	1	39	1	12	42	. .	22	16
99	*Iraq*	74	96	45	87	28	47	14	37	4	14	79	84	22	23
100	*Libya*	78	. .	44	. .	14	. .	4	. .	1	. .	. .	. .	31	. .
101	*Oman*	. .	102	. .	97	. .	48	. .	40	. .	4	32	83	. .	28
	Low- and middle-income	**78 w**	**105 w**	**62 w**	**97 w**	**22 w**	**43 w**	**14 w**	**37 w**	**3 w**	**8 w**	. .	**89 w**	**37 w**	**35 w**
	Sub-Saharan Africa	**41 w**	**69 w**	**31 w**	**61 w**	**4 w**	**18 w**	**2 w**	**14 w**	**0 w**	**2 w**	. .	**47 w**	**43 w**	**40 w**
	East Asia & Pacific	**88 w**	**129 w**	. .	**124 w**	. .	**46 w**	**16 w**	**42 w**	**1 w**	**5 w**	. .	**100 w**	**33 w**	**23 w**
	South Asia	**68 w**	**90 w**	**52 w**	**75 w**	**24 w**	**38 w**	**12 w**	**27 w**	**4 w**	. .	. .	. .	**42 w**	**57 w**
	Europe	**102 w**	**102 w**	**97 w**	**100 w**	**45 w**	**73 w**	**41 w**	**70 w**	**11 w**	**17 w**	. .	**90 w**	**31 w**	**22 w**
	Middle East & N.Africa	**61 w**	**90 w**	**43 w**	**82 w**	**17 w**	**53 w**	**9 w**	**45 w**	**3 w**	**12 w**	. .	**85 w**	**38 w**	**25 w**
	Latin America & Caribbean	**99 w**	**107 w**	**97 w**	**107 w**	**20 w**	**50 w**	**19 w**	**55 w**	**4 w**	**18 w**	. .	**87 w**	**34 w**	**27 w**
	Other economies	**104 w**	**105 w**	**104 w**	**105 w**	**70 w**	**96 w**	**77 w**	**94 w**	**29 w**	**25 w**	. .	**95 w**	**12 w**	**10 w**
	Severely indebted	**96 w**	**105 w**	**92 w**	**100 w**	**25 w**	**52 w**	**24 w**	**54 w**	**6 w**	**18 w**	**79 w**	**88 w**	**33 w**	**25 w**
	High-income economies	**104 w**	**105 w**	**106 w**	**104 w**	**61 w**	**95 w**	**59 w**	**96 w**	**21 w**	**42 w**	**88 w**	**97 w**	**28 w**	**18 w**
	OECD members	**104 w**	**105 w**	**106 w**	**105 w**	**63 w**	**95 w**	**61 w**	**96 w**	**21 w**	**43 w**	**88 w**	**97 w**	**28 w**	**18 w**
	†Other	**99 w**	**103 w**	**98 w**	**102 w**	**39 w**	**77 w**	**33 w**	**79 w**	**11 w**	**24 w**	**93 w**	**96 w**	**27 w**	**22 w**
102	Ireland	108	*101*	108	*101*	51	97	50	102	12	26	91	89	33	28
103	†Israel	95	93	95	95	48	83	51	86	20	*33*	. .	. .	20	19
104	Spain	115	*111*	114	110	38	105	29	111	6	32	100	*100*	34	25
105	†Singapore	105	110	100	109	45	69	41	71	10	. .	100	100	29	26
106	†Hong Kong	103	*105*	99	*104*	29	73	25	75	5	. .	92	. .	29	27
107	New Zealand	106	106	104	105	75	88	74	89	15	41	100	100	22	*19*
108	Belgium	109	*101*	108	*101*	75	99	72	100	15	34	. .	97	21	10
109	United Kingdom	92	107	92	107	66	82	66	84	12	24	97	99	22	12
110	Italy	112	96	110	96	47	78	41	78	11	29	97	. .	28	17
111	Australia	99	106	99	105	62	82	61	83	16	32	98	97	28	. .
112	Netherlands	104	*116*	104	*117*	61	*103*	57	*101*	17	32	92	100	31	17
113	Austria	106	104	105	103	52	82	52	83	9	31	89	93	20	11
114	France	134	113	133	111	56	97	59	100	18	37	98	100	30	16
115	†United Arab Emirates	. .	111	. .	110	. .	64	. .	69	0	9	. .	100	. .	18
116	Canada	105	105	104	105	56	105	55	105	26	66	. .	96	26	16
117	United States	100	. .	. .	. .	83	*109*	67	110	40	*63*	72	. .	29	. .
118	Denmark	98	98	99	98	. .	. .	. .	. .	14	32	. .	. .	11	12
119	Germany	. .	*103*	. .	*104*	. .	97	. .	96	. .	32	. .	88	. .	18
120	Norway	97	98	98	98	64	98	62	101	11	36	100	98	21	16
121	Sweden	95	104	96	104	62	91	60	93	13	31	100	100	20	. .
122	Japan	100	102	100	102	82	96	81	97	13	31	99	100	29	21
123	Finland	92	99	89	99	76	112	80	121	11	43	. .	. .	23	18
124	Switzerland	87	. .	87	. .	37	. .	35	. .	8	26	. .	. .	. .	. .
125	†Kuwait	116	*100*	103	91	52	*90*	43	87	. .	18	68	85	21	*18*
	World	**85 w**	**105 w**	**74 w**	**98 w**	**31 w**	**52 w**	**29 w**	**45 w**	**9 w**	**16 w**	**84 w**	**91 w**	**33 w**	**32 w**
	Fuel exporters, excl. former USSR	**51 w**	**87 w**	**37 w**	**80 w**	**11 w**	**37 w**	**7 w**	**33 w**	**1 w**	**8 w**	**73 w**	**90 w**	**34 w**	**31 w**

Table 30. Income distribution and ICP estimates of GDP

		ICP estimates of GDP per capita[a]			Percentage share of household income, by percentile group of households[b]						
		United States = 100		Current international dollars 1990[c]		Lowest 20 percent	Second quintile	Third quintile	Fourth quintile	Highest 20 percent	Highest 10 percent
		1985	1990[c]		Year						
Low-income economies											
China and India											
Other Low-income											
1	Mozambique	3.0[d]	2.9[d]	620[d]		..	..	..	..	..	..
2	Tanzania	2.6	2.5	540		..	..	..	..	..	..
3	Ethiopia	1.6	1.5	310		..	..	..	..	..	..
4	Somalia	3.1[d]	2.5[d]	540[d]		..	..	..	..	..	..
5	Nepal	4.5[d]	4.4[d]	950[d]		..	..	..	..	..	..
6	Chad	2.4[d]	2.1[d]	440[d]		..	..	..	..	..	..
7	Bhutan	2.1[d]	2.4[d]	520[d]		..	..	..	..	..	..
8	Lao PDR	..	..	..		..	..	..	..	..	..
9	Malawi	3.6	3.1	670		..	..	..	..	..	..
10	Bangladesh	5.0	4.9	1,050	1985–86[e]	10.0	13.7	17.2	21.9	37.2	23.2
11	Burundi	3.0[d]	2.8[d]	600[d]		..	..	..	..	..	..
12	Zaire	5.5[d]	4.4[d]	950[d]		..	..	..	..	..	..
13	Uganda	3.9[d]	3.7[d]	800[d]		..	..	..	..	..	..
14	Madagascar	3.9	3.5	740		..	..	..	..	..	..
15	Sierra Leone	3.0	2.7	580		..	..	..	..	..	..
16	Mali	2.4	2.6	560		..	..	..	..	..	..
17	Nigeria	7.2	6.6	1,420		..	..	..	..	..	..
18	Niger	3.3[d]	2.8[d]	590[d]		..	..	..	..	..	..
19	Rwanda	3.8	2.9	610		..	..	..	..	..	..
20	Burkina Faso	2.8[d]	2.6[d]	560[d]		..	..	..	..	..	..
21	India	4.5	5.4	1,150	1983[e]	8.1	12.3	16.3	22.0	41.4	26.7
22	Benin	6.5	5.3	1,130		..	..	..	..	..	..
23	China	7.6[d]	9.1[d]	1,950[d]		..	..	..	..	..	..
24	Haiti	5.8[d]	4.5[d]	960[d]		..	..	..	..	..	..
25	Kenya	5.3	5.2	1,120		..	..	..	..	..	..
26	Pakistan	8.1	8.3	1,770	1984–85[f]	7.8	11.2	15.0	20.6	45.6	31.3
27	Ghana	8.4[d]	8.1[d]	1,720[d]	1988–89[e]	7.1	11.5	15.9	21.8	43.7	28.5
28	Central African Rep.	5.1[d]	4.2[d]	900[d]		..	..	..	..	..	..
29	Togo	5.4[d]	4.6[d]	990[d]		..	..	..	..	..	..
30	Zambia	4.7	3.8	810		..	..	..	..	..	..
31	Guinea	..	..	..		..	..	..	..	..	..
32	Sri Lanka	11.2	11.1	2,370	1985–86[g]	4.8	8.5	12.1	18.4	56.1	43.0
33	Mauritania	6.4[d]	5.8[d]	1,240[d]		..	..	..	..	..	..
34	Lesotho	7.2[d]	8.0[d]	1,700[d]		..	..	..	..	..	..
35	Indonesia	9.9[h]	11.0	2,350	1987[e]	8.8	12.4	16.0	21.5	41.3	26.5
36	Honduras	8.4[h]	7.5	1,610		..	..	..	..	..	..
37	Egypt, Arab Rep.	15.8	14.5	3,100		..	..	..	..	..	..
38	*Afghanistan*	..	..	..		..	..	..	..	..	..
39	*Cambodia*	..	..	..		..	..	..	..	..	..
40	*Liberia*	8.1[d]	..	..		..	..	..	..	..	..
41	*Myanmar*	..	..	..		..	..	..	..	..	..
42	*Sudan*	6.6[d]	5.5[d]	1,180[d]		..	..	..	..	..	..
43	*Viet Nam*	..	..	..		..	..	..	..	..	..
Middle-income economies											
Lower-middle-income											
44	Bolivia	10.4[h]	8.9	1,910		..	..	..	..	..	..
45	Zimbabwe	9.9	9.2	1,970		..	..	..	..	..	..
46	Senegal	7.0	6.4	1,360		..	..	..	..	..	..
47	Philippines	10.9	10.9	2,320	1985[f]	5.5	9.7	14.8	22.0	48.0	32.1
48	Côte d'Ivoire	10.2	7.2	1,540	1986–87[e]	5.0	8.0	13.1	21.3	52.7	36.3
49	Dominican Rep.	15.0[h]	13.4	2,860		..	..	..	..	..	..
50	Papua New Guinea	8.2[h]	7.0	1,500		..	..	..	..	..	..
51	Guatemala	15.1[h]	13.7	2,920	1979–81	5.5	8.6	12.2	18.7	55.0	40.8
52	Morocco	13.1	12.5	2,670	1984–85[f]	9.8	13.0	16.4	21.4	39.4	25.4
53	Cameroon	14.0	9.5	2,020		..	..	..	..	..	..
54	Ecuador	19.8[h]	17.4	3,720		..	..	..	..	..	..
55	Syrian Arab Rep.	21.6[h]	19.2	4,110		..	..	..	..	..	..
56	Congo	16.4	12.6	2,690		..	..	..	..	..	..
57	El Salvador	9.7[h]	8.8	1,890		..	..	..	..	..	..
58	Paraguay	15.6[h]	14.6	3,120		..	..	..	..	..	..
59	Peru	17.3[h]	12.7	2,720	1985–86[e]	4.4	8.5	13.7	21.5	51.9	35.8
60	Jordan	26.7[d]	20.4[d]	4,530[d]		..	..	..	..	..	..
61	Colombia	22.5[h]	23.2	4,950	1988[g]	4.0	8.7	13.5	20.8	53.0	37.1
62	Thailand	15.9	21.6	4,610		..	..	..	..	..	..
63	Tunisia	19.8	18.6	3,979		..	..	..	..	..	..
64	Jamaica	13.3[h]	14.2	3,030	1988[e]	5.4	9.9	14.4	21.2	49.2	33.4
65	Turkey	21.8	23.5	5,020		..	..	..	..	..	..
66	Romania	40.0	31.7	6,780		..	..	..	..	..	..

Note: For data comparability and coverage, see the technical notes.   Figures in italics are for years other than those specified.

		ICP estimates of GDP per capita[a]			Percentage share of household income, by percentile group of households[b]						
		United States = 100		Current international dollars 1990[c]	Year	Lowest 20 percent	Second quintile	Third quintile	Fourth quintile	Highest 20 percent	Highest 10 percent
		1985	1990[c]								
67	Poland	24.5	21.2	4,530	1987[g]	9.7	14.2	18.0	22.9	35.2	21.0
68	Panama	25.9[h]	19.3	4,120		. .	. .	. .	. .	. .	. .
69	Costa Rica	22.6[h]	22.8	4,870	1986[g]	3.3	8.3	13.2	20.7	54.5	38.8
70	Chile	25.9[h]	29.0	6,190		. .	. .	. .	. .	. .	. .
71	Botswana	16.1	20.1	4,300	1985–86	2.5	6.5	11.8	20.2	59.0	42.8
72	Algeria	27.8[d]	21.9[d]	4,680[d]		. .	. .	. .	. .	. .	. .
73	Bulgaria	41.3[d]	37.0[d]	7,900[d]		. .	. .	. .	. .	. .	. .
74	Mauritius	24.8	30.4	6,500		. .	. .	. .	. .	. .	. .
75	Malaysia	25.0[h]	27.6	5,900	1987[g]	4.6	9.3	13.9	21.2	51.2	34.8
76	Argentina	24.8[h]	21.9	4,680		. .	. .	. .	. .	. .	. .
77	Iran, Islamic Rep.	28.0	20.4	4,360		. .	. .	. .	. .	. .	. .
78	*Albania*	. .	. .	. .		. .	. .	. .	. .	. .	. .
79	*Angola*	. .	. .	. .		. .	. .	. .	. .	. .	. .
80	*Lebanon*	. .	. .	. .		. .	. .	. .	. .	. .	. .
81	*Mongolia*	. .	. .	. .		. .	. .	. .	. .	. .	. .
82	*Namibia*	. .	. .	. .		. .	. .	. .	. .	. .	. .
83	*Nicaragua*	12.6[d]	. .	. .		. .	. .	. .	. .	. .	. .
84	*Yemen, Rep.*	. .	. .	. .		. .	. .	. .	. .	. .	. .
Upper-middle-income											
85	Mexico	31.9[h]	28.0	5,980		. .	. .	. .	. .	. .	. .
86	South Africa	29.8[d]	25.7[d]	5,500[d]		. .	. .	. .	. .	. .	. .
87	Venezuela	35.4[h]	31.6	6,740	1987[g]	4.7	9.2	14.0	21.5	50.6	34.2
88	Uruguay	27.0[h]	28.1	6,000		. .	. .	. .	. .	. .	. .
89	Brazil	24.9[h]	22.4	4,780	1983	2.4	5.7	10.7	18.6	62.6	46.2
90	Hungary	31.2	29.0	6,190	1987–89[g]	10.9	14.8	17.8	22.0	34.5	20.7
91	Yugoslavia	29.2	23.8	5,090	1987[g]	6.1	11.0	16.5	23.7	42.8	26.6
92	Czechoslovakia	. .	. .	. .		. .	. .	. .	. .	. .	. .
93	Gabon	23.8[d]	21.5[d]	4,590[d]		. .	. .	. .	. .	. .	. .
94	Trinidad and Tobago	52.7[d]	39.8[d]	8,510[d]		. .	. .	. .	. .	. .	. .
95	Portugal	33.8	37.2	7,950		. .	. .	. .	. .	. .	. .
96	Korea, Rep.	24.1	33.7	7,190		. .	. .	. .	. .	. .	. .
97	Greece	35.5	34.4	7,340		. .	. .	. .	. .	. .	. .
98	Saudi Arabia	51.9[d]	. .	. .		. .	. .	. .	. .	. .	. .
99	*Iraq*	. .	. .	. .		. .	. .	. .	. .	. .	. .
100	*Libya*	53.1[d]	. .	. .	. .	. .	. .	. .	. .	. .	. .
101	*Oman*	44.2[d]	. .	. .	. .	. .	. .	. .	. .	. .	. .
Low- and middle-income											
Sub-Saharan Africa											
East Asia											
South Asia											
Europe											
Middle East and N. Africa											
Latin America and Caribbean											
Other economies											
Severely indebted											
High-income economies											
OECD members											
†Other											
102	Ireland	40.9	42.7	9,130		. .	. .	. .	. .	. .	. .
103	†Israel	56.7[h]	55.9	11,940	1979	6.0	12.1	17.8	24.5	39.6	23.5
104	Spain	46.0	50.7	10,840	1980–81	6.9	12.5	17.3	23.2	40.0	24.5
105	†Singapore	56.2[d]	69.8[d]	14,920[d]	1982–83	5.1	9.9	14.6	21.4	48.9	33.5
106	†Hong Kong	61.8	76.0	16,230	1980	5.4	10.8	15.2	21.6	47.0	31.3
107	New Zealand	71.1	63.2	13,490	1981–82	5.1	10.8	16.2	23.2	44.7	28.7
108	Belgium	64.7	60.6	12,950	1978–79	7.9	13.7	18.6	23.8	36.0	21.5
109	United Kingdom	66.1	70.0	14,960	1979	5.8	11.5	18.2	25.0	39.5	23.3
110	Italy	65.6	68.1	14,550	1986	6.8	12.0	16.7	23.5	41.0	25.3
111	Australia	76.9	75.1	16,050	1985	4.4	11.1	17.5	24.8	42.2	25.8
112	Netherlands	68.2	68.3	14,600	1983	6.9	13.2	17.9	23.7	38.3	23.0
113	Austria	66.1	69.1	14,750		. .	. .	. .	. .	. .	. .
114	France	69.3	71.2	15,200	1979	6.3	12.1	17.2	23.5	40.8	25.5
115	†United Arab Emirates	99.2[d]	77.7[d]	16,590[d]		. .	. .	. .	. .	. .	. .
116	Canada	92.5	92.0	19,650	1987	5.7	11.8	17.7	24.6	40.2	24.1
117	United States	100.0	100.0	21,360	1985	4.7	11.0	17.4	25.0	41.9	25.0
118	Denmark	74.2	72.0	15,380	1981	5.4	12.0	18.4	25.6	38.6	22.3
119	Germany[i]	73.8	76.3	16,290	1984	6.8	12.7	17.8	24.1	38.7	23.4
120	Norway	84.4	80.6	17,220	1979	6.2	12.8	18.9	25.3	36.7	21.2
121	Sweden	76.9	74.9	16,000	1981	8.0	13.2	17.4	24.5	36.9	20.8
122	Japan	71.6	79.4	16,950	1979	8.7	13.2	17.5	23.1	37.5	22.4
123	Finland	69.5	73.1	15,620	1981	6.3	12.1	18.4	25.5	37.6	21.7
124	Switzerland	100.7[d]	101.6[d]	21,690[d]	1982	5.2	11.7	16.4	22.1	44.6	29.8
125	†Kuwait	91.3[d]	. .	. .		. .	. .	. .	. .	. .	. .
World											
Fuel exporters, excl. former USSR											

a. ICP refers to the United Nations' International Comparison Program, (see the technical notes).   b. These estimates should be treated with caution; see the technical notes for details of different distribution measures.   c. Extrapolated from 1985 figure (see the technical notes).   d. Regression results (see the technical notes).   e. Data refer to per capita expenditure.   f. Data refer to household expenditure.   g. Data refer to per capita income.   h. Extrapolated from earlier ICP exercises.   i. Data refer to the Federal Republic of Germany before unification.

Table 31. Urbanization

		Urban population			Population in capital city as a percentage of		Population in cities of 1 million or more in 1990, as a percentage of			
		As a percentage of total population		Average annual growth rate (percent)			Urban		Total	
		1965	1990	1965-80	1980-90	Urban 1990	Total 1990	1965	1990	1965	1990
Low-income economies		**18** w	**38** w	**3.5** w	**..**	**11** w	**3** w	**41** w	**31** w	**7** w	**9** w
China and India		**18** w	**44** w	**2.9** w	**..**	**3** w	**1** w	**42** w	**29** w	**8** w	**9** w
Other low-income		**16** w	**27** w	**4.7** w	**5.0** w	**26** w	**7** w	**38** w	**35** w	**6** w	**10** w
1	Mozambique	5	27	10.2	10.4	38	10	68	38	3	10
2	Tanzania	5	33	11.3	10.5	21	7	38	18	2	6
3	Ethiopia	8	13	4.9	5.3	29	4	27	30	2	4
4	Somalia	20	36	5.4	5.6	25	9	..	..	..	..
5	Nepal	4	10	6.4	7.3	20	2	..	..	..	..
6	Chad	9	30	8.0	6.5	43	13	..	..	..	..
7	Bhutan	3	5	3.9	5.3	22	1	..	..	..	..
8	Lao PDR	8	19	5.3	6.1	53	10	..	..	..	..
9	Malawi	5	12	7.4	6.2	31	4	..	..	..	..
10	Bangladesh	6	16	6.8	6.2	38	6	50	47	3	8
11	Burundi	2	6	6.9	5.5	82	5	..	..	..	..
12	Zaire	26	40	4.9	4.8	24	9	17	25	5	10
13	Uganda	7	10	4.8	4.4	41	4	..	..	..	..
14	Madagascar	12	25	5.2	6.4	23	6	..	..	..	..
15	Sierra Leone	15	32	5.2	5.3	52	17	..	..	..	..
16	Mali	13	19	4.4	3.7	41	8	..	..	..	..
17	Nigeria	17	35	5.7	6.0	19	7	23	24	4	8
18	Niger	7	20	7.2	7.6	39	8	..	..	..	..
19	Rwanda	3	8	7.5	8.0	54	4	..	..	..	..
20	Burkina Faso	5	9	4.1	5.3	51	5	..	..	..	..
21	India	19	27	3.7	3.7	4	1	32	32	6	9
22	Benin	13	38	8.9	5.1	12	4	..	..	..	..
23	China	18	56	2.3	..	2	1	49	27	9	9
24	Haiti	18	28	3.7	3.7	56	16	47	56	8	16
25	Kenya	9	24	8.1	7.9	26	6	41	27	4	6
26	Pakistan	24	32	4.3	4.6	1	0	44	42	10	13
27	Ghana	26	33	3.2	4.2	22	7	27	22	7	7
28	Central African Rep.	27	47	4.3	4.8	51	24	..	..	..	..
29	Togo	11	26	6.6	6.9	55	14	..	..	..	..
30	Zambia	23	50	6.6	6.2	24	12	..	..	..	..
31	Guinea	12	26	4.9	5.7	89	23	47	88	5	23
32	Sri Lanka	20	21	2.3	1.4	17	4	..	..	..	..
33	Mauritania	9	47	10.6	7.5	83	39	..	..	..	..
34	Lesotho	6	20	7.5	7.0	17	4	..	..	..	..
35	Indonesia	16	31	4.8	5.1	17	5	42	33	7	10
36	Honduras	26	44	5.5	5.4	35	15	..	..	..	..
37	Egypt, Arab Rep.	41	47	2.7	3.1	37	17	53	52	22	24
38	*Afghanistan*	9	..	..	..	..	..	41	..	4	..
39	*Cambodia*	11	12	-0.4	3.8	98	11	..	..	..	..
40	*Liberia*	22	46	6.2	6.1	57	26	..	..	..	..
41	*Myanmar*	21	25	3.2	2.4	32	8	23	32	5	8
42	*Sudan*	13	22	5.9	3.9	35	8	30	35	4	8
43	*Viet Nam*	16	22	3.3	3.4	22	5	37	30	6	7
Middle-income economies		**42** w	**60** w	**3.9** w	**3.4** w	**25** w	**14** w	**41** w	**40** w	**17** w	**25** w
Lower-middle-income		**38** w	**52** w	**3.7** w	**3.6** w	**29** w	**14** w	**39** w	**39** w	**15** w	**21** w
44	Bolivia	40	51	3.2	4.0	34	17	28	33	11	17
45	Zimbabwe	14	28	6.0	5.9	31	9	..	..	..	..
46	Senegal	33	38	3.3	4.0	52	20	40	53	13	20
47	Philippines	32	43	4.0	3.8	32	14	28	32	9	14
48	Côte d'Ivoire	23	40	7.6	4.5	45	18	30	45	7	18
49	Dominican Rep.	35	60	5.2	4.0	52	31	46	51	16	31
50	Papua New Guinea	5	16	8.2	4.5	32	5	..	..	..	..
51	Guatemala	34	39	3.5	3.4	23	9	..	..	..	..
52	Morocco	32	48	4.3	4.3	9	4	39	36	12	17
53	Cameroon	16	41	7.6	5.9	16	7	..	..	..	..
54	Ecuador	37	56	4.7	4.2	22	12	50	49	19	28
55	Syrian Arab Rep.	40	50	4.5	4.4	32	17	58	60	23	30
56	Congo	32	41	3.5	4.7	68	28	..	..	..	..
57	El Salvador	39	44	3.2	2.1	26	11	..	..	..	..
58	Paraguay	36	48	3.8	4.6	47	22	..	..	..	..
59	Peru	52	70	4.3	3.1	41	29	37	41	19	29
60	Jordan[a]	..	61	..	4.1	53	32	33	38	15	26
61	Colombia	54	70	3.6	2.9	21	15	38	39	20	27
62	Thailand	13	23	5.1	4.6	57	13	66	57	8	13
63	Tunisia	40	54	4.0	2.9	37	20	35	37	14	20
64	Jamaica	38	52	2.8	2.4	51	26	..	..	..	..
65	Turkey	34	61	4.1	5.9	8	5	41	35	14	22
66	Romania	38	53	2.9	1.2	18	9	21	18	8	9

Note: For data comparability and coverage, see the technical notes. Figures in italics are for years other than those specified.

		Urban population				Population in capital city as a percentage of		Population in cities of 1 million or more in 1990, as a percentage of			
		As a percentage of total population		Average annual growth rate (percent)		Urban	Total	Urban		Total	
		1965	1990	1965-80	1980-90	1990	1990	1965	1990	1965	1990
67	Poland	50	62	1.9	1.3	9	6	32	28	16	18
68	Panama	44	53	3.4	2.9	37	20	. .	. .	. .	. .
69	Costa Rica	38	47	3.5	3.3	77	36	62	72	24	34
70	Chile	72	86	2.6	2.3	42	36	39	42	28	36
71	Botswana	4	28	12.6	9.9	38	10	. .	. .	. .	. .
72	Algeria	38	52	3.9	4.8	23	12	24	23	9	12
73	Bulgaria	46	68	2.5	1.0	20	13	21	19	10	13
74	Mauritius	37	41	2.5	0.4	36	15	. .	. .	. .	. .
75	Malaysia	26	43	4.6	4.9	22	10	16	22	4	10
76	Argentina	76	86	2.2	1.8	41	36	53	49	40	42
77	Iran, Islamic Rep.	37	57	5.2	5.0	21	12	43	41	16	23
78	Albania	32	35	2.7	2.4	21	7	. .	. .	. .	. .
79	Angola	13	28	6.4	5.8	61	17	49	61	6	17
80	Lebanon	50	. .	4.5	. .	. .	. .	. .	. .	. .	. .
81	Mongolia	42	52	4.0	2.9	42	22	. .	. .	. .	. .
82	Namibia	17	28	4.6	5.3	30	8	. .	. .	. .	. .
83	Nicaragua	43	60	4.6	4.5	44	26	36	44	15	26
84	Yemen, Rep.	11	29	6.6	6.9	11	3	. .	. .	. .	. .
	Upper-middle-income	**47** *w*	**71** *w*	**4.2** *w*	**3.2** *w*	**19** *w*	**14** *w*	**43** *w*	**42** *w*	**20** *w*	**30** *w*
85	Mexico	55	73	4.4	2.9	32	23	41	45	22	32
86	South Africa	47	60	3.2	3.7	11	6	40	30	19	18
87	Venezuela	70	84	4.8	2.8	25	21	34	29	24	27
88	Uruguay	81	86	0.7	0.8	45	39	53	45	43	39
89	Brazil	50	75	4.3	3.4	2	2	48	47	24	35
90	Hungary	43	61	1.9	1.2	33	20	43	33	19	20
91	Yugoslavia	31	56	3.5	2.8	12	7	11	12	3	7
92	Czechoslovakia	51	78	2.4	1.6	11	8	15	11	8	8
93	Gabon	21	46	7.3	6.2	57	26	. .	. .	. .	. .
94	Trinidad and Tobago	30	69	5.6	3.3	12	8	. .	. .	. .	. .
95	Portugal	24	34	1.8	1.9	46	45	44	46	11	16
96	Korea, Rep.	32	72	5.8	3.5	36	26	74	69	24	50
97	Greece	48	63	2.0	1.2	55	34	59	55	28	34
98	Saudi Arabia	39	77	8.5	6.3	17	13	23	29	9	23
99	Iraq	51	71	5.3	4.4	30	21	40	29	20	21
100	Libya	26	70	9.8	6.3	. .	. .	55	65	14	45
101	Oman	4	11	7.5	8.6	41	4	. .	. .	. .	. .
	Low- and middle-income	**24** *w*	**44** *w*	**3.7** *w*	**6.6** *w*	**15** *w*	**6** *w*	**41** *w*	**33** *w*	**10** *w*	**13** *w*
	Sub-Saharan Africa	**14** *w*	**29** *w*	**5.8** *w*	**5.9** *w*	**32** *w*	**9** *w*	**30** *w*	**29** *w*	**4** *w*	**9** *w*
	East Asia & Pacific	**19** *w*	**50** *w*	**3.0** *w*	**12.0** *w*	**9** *w*	**3** *w*	**48** *w*	**30** *w*	**9** *w*	**11** *w*
	South Asia	**18** *w*	**26** *w*	**3.9** *w*	**3.9** *w*	**8** *w*	**2** *w*	**35** *w*	**34** *w*	**6** *w*	**9** *w*
	Europe	**40** *w*	**60** *w*	**2.7** *w*	**2.6** *w*	**15** *w*	**10** *w*	**31** *w*	**27** *w*	**12** *w*	**16** *w*
	Middle East & N.Africa	**35** *w*	**51** *w*	**4.6** *w*	**4.4** *w*	**27** *w*	**13** *w*	**42** *w*	**42** *w*	**15** *w*	**21** *w*
	Latin America & Caribbean	**53** *w*	**71** *w*	**3.9** *w*	**3.0** *w*	**23** *w*	**16** *w*	**44** *w*	**45** *w*	**24** *w*	**33** *w*
	Other economies	**52** *w*	**66** *w*	**2.3** *w*	**1.4** *w*	**6** *w*	**4** *w*	**25** *w*	**23** *w*	**13** *w*	**15** *w*
	Severely indebted	**51** *w*	**69** *w*	**3.8** *w*	**3.0** *w*	**20** *w*	**13** *w*	**41** *w*	**42** *w*	**22** *w*	**29** *w*
	High-income economies	**72** *w*	**77** *w*	**1.3** *w*	**0.8** *w*	**12** *w*	**9** *w*	**38** *w*	**37** *w*	**27** *w*	**29** *w*
	OECD members	**72** *w*	**77** *w*	**1.2** *w*	**0.8** *w*	**11** *w*	**7** *w*	**37** *w*	**36** *w*	**27** *w*	**28** *w*
	†Other	**70** *w*	**79** *w*	**3.2** *w*	**2.2** *w*	**65** *w*	**60** *w*	**73** *w*	**77** *w*	**65** *w*	**73** *w*
102	Ireland	49	57	2.1	0.6	46	26	. .	. .	. .	. .
103	†Israel	81	92	3.5	2.1	12	11	43	45	34	41
104	Spain	61	78	2.2	1.1	17	13	26	28	16	22
105	†Singapore	100	100	1.6	2.2	100	100	100	100	100	100
106	†Hong Kong	89	94	2.1	1.7	100	94	90	99	81	93
107	New Zealand	79	84	1.6	1.0	12	10	. .	. .	. .	. .
108	Belgium	93	97	0.4	0.3	10	10	. .	. .	. .	. .
109	United Kingdom	87	89	0.3	0.2	14	13	33	26	28	23
110	Italy	62	69	1.0	0.6	8	5	42	37	26	25
111	Australia	83	86	2.0	1.5	2	1	60	59	50	51
112	Netherlands	86	89	1.2	0.5	8	7	18	16	16	14
113	Austria	51	58	0.8	0.8	47	27	51	47	26	28
114	France	67	74	1.3	0.6	20	15	30	26	20	19
115	†United Arab Emirates	41	78	23.7	3.9	. .	. .	. .	. .	. .	. .
116	Canada	73	77	1.5	1.1	4	3	37	39	27	30
117	United States	72	75	1.2	1.1	2	1	49	48	35	36
118	Denmark	77	87	1.1	0.4	31	27	38	31	29	27
119	Germany	78	84	0.6	0.5	. .	. .	. .	. .	. .	. .
120	Norway	58	75	1.9	1.0	21	16	. .	. .	. .	. .
121	Sweden	77	84	0.9	0.4	23	19	17	23	13	20
122	Japan	67	77	2.1	0.7	19	15	37	36	25	27
123	Finland	44	60	2.6	0.4	34	20	27	34	12	20
124	Switzerland	53	60	1.0	1.1	7	4	. .	. .	. .	. .
125	†Kuwait	78	96	8.2	5.0	53	50	100	55	78	53
	World	**36** *w*	**50** *w*	**2.6** *w*	**4.5** *w*	**14** *w*	**6** *w*	**39** *w*	**33** *w*	**14** *w*	**16** *w*
	Fuel exporters, excl. former USSR	**30** *w*	**50** *w*	**5.5** *w*	**5.0** *w*	**23** *w*	**12** *w*	**30** *w*	**31** *w*	**10** *w*	**16** *w*

a. Data for Jordan cover the East Bank only.

Table 32. Women in development

		Health and welfare						Education							
		Under-5 mortality rate (per 1,000 live births)		Life expectancy at birth (years)				Maternal mortality (per 100,000 live births)	Percentage of cohort persisting to grade 4				Females per 100 males			
				Female		Male			Female		Male		Primary		Secondary[a]	
		Female 1990	Male 1990	1965	1990	1965	1990	1980	1970	1985	1970	1985	1965	1989	1965	1989
	Low-income economies	**91** w	**98** w	**50** w	**62** w	**48** w	**61** w	..	..	..	..	..	**60** w	**78** w	**40** w	**64** w
	China and India	**69** w	**72** w	**52** w	**66** w	**50** w	**65** w	..	..	..	..	..	**61** w	**78** w	**42** w	**64** w
	Other low-income	**131** w	**145** w	**45** w	**56** w	**44** w	**54** w	..	**65** w	**68** w	**74** w	**74** w	**58** w	**77** w	**34** w	**65** w
1	Mozambique	194	215	39	48	36	45	479[b]	..	..	..	..	56	78	85	54
2	Tanzania	182	203	45	49	41	46	370[b]	82	91	88	90	60	98	33	74
3	Ethiopia	185	205	43	50	42	46	2,000[b]	57	45	56	50	38	64	28	67
4	Somalia	200	223	40	50	37	47	1,100	46	..	51	..	27	..	11	..
5	Nepal	183	175	40	51	41	53	..	..	..	..	..	17	47	17	..
6	Chad	198	221	38	49	35	45	700	..	57	..	63	23	44	6	22
7	Bhutan	183	179	40	47	41	50	..	..	26	..	29	8	59	..	41
8	Lao PDR	159	179	42	51	39	48	..	..	..	..	..	59	77	59	66
9	Malawi	242	255	40	47	38	46	250	55	67	60	71	59	81	40	54
10	Bangladesh	160	142	44	51	45	52	600	..	40	..	37	44	78	14	47
11	Burundi	167	187	44	48	41	45	..	47	85	45	85	42	80	10	57
12	Zaire	143	162	45	54	42	50	800[b]	56	54	65	58	48	73	15	43
13	Uganda	185	206	48	47	46	46	300	..	..	..	..	58	..	30	..
14	Madagascar	160	178	45	52	42	50	300	65	..	63	..	83	95	64	96
15	Sierra Leone	236	261	34	44	31	40	450	..	..	..	..	55	62	37	..
16	Mali	209	238	39	50	37	46	..	52	68	89	75	49	58	30	48
17	Nigeria	152	171	43	54	40	49	1,500	64	..	66	..	63	82	43	75
18	Niger	204	227	38	47	35	44	420[b]	75	..	74	..	46	57	19	42
19	Rwanda	192	213	45	50	42	47	210	63	82	65	81	69	99	37	52
20	Burkina Faso	190	210	40	49	37	46	600	71	87	68	87	48	61	27	48
21	India	121	116	44	58	46	60	500	42	..	45	..	57	69	35	54
22	Benin	155	173	43	52	41	49	1,680[b]	59	..	67	..	44	51	44	..
23	China	29	40	57	71	53	69	44	..	76	..	79	65	85	47	71
24	Haiti	126	144	47	56	44	53	340	..	40	..	40	..	93	44	96
25	Kenya	97	112	50	61	46	57	510[b]	84	77	84	76	57	94	38	70
26	Pakistan	151	145	45	55	47	56	600	56	..	60	..	31	50	27	39
27	Ghana	127	144	49	57	46	53	1,070[b]	77	..	82	..	71	81	34	65
28	Central African Rep.	156	176	41	51	40	48	600	67	67	67	72	34	63	19	38
29	Togo	133	151	44	55	40	52	476[b]	85	80	88	87	42	63	26	31
30	Zambia	123	140	46	52	43	48	110	93	..	99	..	78	91	39	59
31	Guinea	221	245	36	43	34	43	..	..	71	..	81	44	45	19	32
32	Sri Lanka	21	26	64	73	63	69	90	94	97	73	99	86	93	102	105
33	Mauritania	193	215	39	48	36	45	119	..	83	..	83	31	69	11	45
34	Lesotho	125	142	50	57	47	55	..	87	85	70	76	157	122	100	147
35	Indonesia	75	90	45	64	43	60	800	67	83	89	98	82	93	..	82
36	Honduras	70	85	51	67	48	63	82	38	63	35	59	98	98	69	..
37	Egypt, Arab Rep.	95	110	50	62	48	59	500	85	..	93	..	64	81	41	77
38	*Afghanistan*	241	..	..	..	..	..	640	64	..	71	..	17	..	23	..
39	*Cambodia*	161	180	46	52	43	49	..	..	..	..	..	56	..	26	..
40	*Liberia*	168	193	46	56	43	53	173	..	..	..	..	40	..	33	..
41	*Myanmar*	78	94	49	64	46	59	140	39	..	58	..	84	92	57	90
42	*Sudan*	159	178	41	52	39	49	607[b]	..	..	..	..	55	..	30	..
43	*Viet Nam*	46	59	51	69	48	64	110	..	..	..	..	..	..	..	..
	Middle-income economies	**57** w	**68** w	**60** w	**69** w	**56** w	**64** w	..	**78** w	**86** w	**77** w	**90** w	**84** w	**90** w	**83** w	**105** w
	Lower-middle-income	**62** w	**73** w	**58** w	**67** w	**55** w	**63** w	..	**79** w	**87** w	**78** w	**87** w	**78** w	**89** w	**79** w	**109** w
44	Bolivia	109	127	47	62	42	58	480	..	..	..	..	68	89	57	..
45	Zimbabwe	66	78	50	63	46	59	150[b]	74	83	80	83	..	98	..	73
46	Senegal	120	137	42	49	40	46	530[b]	..	91	..	95	57	72	35	51
47	Philippines	45	57	57	66	54	62	80	..	82	..	78	94	94	96	..
48	Côte d'Ivoire	126	144	44	57	40	54	..	77	..	83	..	51	..	19	44
49	Dominican Rep.	68	75	57	69	54	65	56	..	52	..	70	..	98	104	..
50	Papua New Guinea	70	84	44	56	44	54	1,000	76	..	84	..	61	79	27	60
51	Guatemala	76	91	50	66	48	61	110	33	..	73	..	80	..	67	..
52	Morocco	84	99	51	64	48	60	327[b]	78	79	83	82	42	65	31	68
53	Cameroon	117	134	47	59	44	55	303	59	85	58	86	66	85	28	68
54	Ecuador	58	72	57	68	55	64	220	69	..	70	..	91	96	46	91
55	Syrian Arab Rep.	55	67	54	68	51	64	280	92	96	95	97	47	87	28	71
56	Congo	172	185	47	56	41	50	..	86	90	89	98	71	92	29	75
57	El Salvador	63	76	56	68	53	60	74	56	..	56	..	93	98	75	95
58	Paraguay	33	44	67	69	63	65	469	70	75	71	75	88	93	89	104
59	Peru	78	93[c]	52	65	49	61	310	..	..	..	..	82	..	69	..
60	Jordan	62[c]	68[c]	52[c]	69[c]	49[c]	66[c]	..	90	97	92	89	72	93	40	95
61	Colombia	40	49	61	72	57	66	130	57	72	51	68	102	98	57	100
62	Thailand	28	38	58	68	54	63	270	71	..	69	..	89	..	68	97
63	Tunisia	50	63	52	68	51	66	1,000[d]	..	90	..	94	52	83	37	75
64	Jamaica	16	22	67	75	64	71	100	..	..	..	..	99	98	121	..
65	Turkey	73	80	55	69	52	64	207	76	98	81	98	66	89	37	62
66	Romania	23	32	70	73	66	67	180	90	..	89	..	94	95	147	233

Note: For data comparability and coverage, see the technical notes. Figures in italics are for years other than those specified.

		Health and welfare								Education							
		Under-5 mortality rate (per 1,000 live births)		Life expectancy at birth (years)				Maternal mortality (per 100,000 live births)	Percentage of cohort persisting to grade 4				Females per 100 males			
				Female		Male			Female		Male		Primary		Secondary[a]	
		Female 1990	Male 1990	1965	1990	1965	1990	1980	1970	1985	1970	1985	1965	1989	1965	1989
67	Poland	18	23	72	75	66	67	12	99	..	97	..	93	95	217	264
68	Panama	21	29	65	75	62	71	90	97	87	97	86	93	93	100	103
69	Costa Rica	18	22	66	78	63	73	26	93	91	91	90	94	94	110	102
70	Chile	18	23	63	76	57	69	55	86	96	83	97	96	95	106	110
71	Botswana	41	53	49	69	46	65	300	97	94	90	92	129	106	77	109
72	Algeria	83	91	51	66	49	65	129	90	95	95	97	62	81	45	77
73	Bulgaria	14	19	73	76	68	70	22	91	97	100	98	95	93	..	188
74	Mauritius	21	28	63	73	59	67	99	97	98	97	99	90	97	53	98
75	Malaysia	17	22	60	72	56	68	59	..	..	..	..	84	95	..	102
76	Argentina	30	40	69	75	63	68	85	92	..	69	..	97	103	60	172
77	Iran, Islamic Rep.	103	122	52	63	52	63	..	75	89	74	92	46	84	44	71
78	Albania	28	33	67	75	65	70	..	..	..	..	..	87	92	77	121
79	Angola	207	230	37	48	34	44	..	..	..	..	..	49	..	89	..
80	Lebanon	..	..	64	..	60	..	..	..	..	..	..	76	..	..	..
81	Mongolia	76	91	51	64	49	61	140	..	..	..	..	..	..	..	..
82	Namibia	119	140	47	59	44	56	..	48	62	45	55	..	109	..	128
83	Nicaragua	66	80	52	66	49	63	65	48	62	45	55	99	107	69	162
84	Yemen, Rep.	172	191	41	49	39	48	..	..	..	..	..	..	..	..	..
Upper-middle-income		**49** w	**60** w	**62** w	**71** w	**58** w	**65** w	**..**	**76** w	**86** w	**76** w	**95** w	**92** w	**93** w	**88** w	**98** w
85	Mexico	41	51	61	73	58	66	92	..	73	..	94	91	94	53	90
86	South Africa	81	98	54	65	49	59	550[d]	..	..	..	..	99	..	87	..
87	Venezuela	36	45	65	73	61	67	65	84	84	61	87	98	96	109	119
88	Uruguay	22	28	72	77	65	70	56	..	98	..	96	96	95	110	..
89	Brazil	62	75	59	69	55	63	150	56	..	54	..	98	..	93	..
90	Hungary	16	22	72	75	67	67	28	90	97	99	97	94	95	197	198
91	Yugoslavia	25	30	68	76	64	69	27	91	..	99	..	91	94	86	97
92	Czechoslovakia	13	17	73	75	67	68	8	96	97	98	96	93	97	195	133
93	Gabon	148	167	44	55	41	52	124[b]	73	80	78	78	84	98	39	81
94	Trinidad and Tobago	25	34	67	74	63	69	81	78	99	74	96	97	99	107	102
95	Portugal	14	17	68	78	62	72	15	92	..	92	..	95	91	92	99
96	Korea, Rep.	17	24	58	73	55	67	34	96	99	96	99	91	94	59	87
97	Greece	13	15	72	80	69	74	12	97	99	96	99	93	94	86	102
98	Saudi Arabia	72	87	50	66	47	63	52	93	93	91	93	29	84	8	74
99	Iraq	81	89	53	66	51	61	..	84	86	90	92	42	79	29	63
100	Libya	84	100	51	64	48	60	..	92	..	95	..	39	..	13	..
101	Oman	36	46	45	68	43	64	..	82	97	82	100	..	88	..	75
Low- and middle-income		**82** w	**90** w	**52** w	**64** w	**50** w	**62** w	**..**	**61** w	**77** w	**65** w	**81** w	**67** w	**80** w	**52** w	**72** w
Sub-Saharan Africa		**160** w	**179** w	**43** w	**52** w	**41** w	**49** w	**..**	**66** w	**70** w	**69** w	**72** w	**56** w	**78** w	**36** w	**64** w
East Asia & Pacific		**37** w	**48** w	**55** w	**70** w	**52** w	**67** w	**..**	**..**	**78** w	**..**	**82** w	**69** w	**87** w	**50** w	**73** w
South Asia		**124** w	**121** w	**45** w	**58** w	**46** w	**59** w	**..**	**45** w	**..**	**48** w	**..**	**54** w	**68** w	**34** w	**53** w
Europe		**35** w	**40** w	**68** w	**74** w	**63** w	**67** w	**..**	**90** w	**98** w	**93** w	**98** w	**88** w	**93** w	**131** w	**148** w
Middle East & N.Africa		**102** w	**117** w	**49** w	**62** w	**48** w	**60** w	**..**	**81** w	**89** w	**85** w	**92** w	**47** w	**75** w	**34** w	**68** w
Latin America & Caribbean		**52** w	**64** w	**60** w	**71** w	**56** w	**65** w	**..**	**64** w	**75** w	**59** w	**84** w	**95** w	**96** w	**77** w	**110** w
Other economies		**24** w	**32** w	**72** w	**76** w	**65** w	**66** w	**..**	**75** w	**..**	**..**	**..**	**95** w	**96** w	**116** w	**100** w
Severely indebted		**56** w	**67** w	**61** w	**70** w	**57** w	**64** w	**..**	**74** w	**80** w	**71** w	**92** w	**88** w	**91** w	**88** w	**124** w
High-income economies		**9** w	**12** w	**74** w	**80** w	**68** w	**74** w	**..**	**95** w	**97** w	**94** w	**96** w	**94** w	**95** w	**92** w	**100** w
OECD members		**9** w	**11** w	**74** w	**80** w	**68** w	**74** w	**..**	**95** w	**97** w	**94** w	**96** w	**94** w	**95** w	**92** w	**100** w
†Other		**14** w	**18** w	**70** w	**77** w	**65** w	**73** w	**..**	**96** w	**97** w	**96** w	**97** w	**88** w	**93** w	**90** w	**106** w
102	Ireland	8	10	73	77	69	72	7	..	98	..	96	97	95	113	101
103	†Israel	11	15	74	78	71	74	5	96	98	96	98	94	97	127	118
104	Spain	9	12	74	79	69	73	10	76	97	76	96	93	93	70	101
105	†Singapore	7	10	68	77	64	71	11	99	100	99	100	85	90	91	100
106	†Hong Kong	7	10	71	80	64	75	4	94	..	92	..	85	92	72	104
107	New Zealand	10	15	74	79	68	72	..	..	96	..	94	94	95	..	97
108	Belgium	10	12	74	80	68	73	10	..	87	..	85	94	96	85	103
109	United Kingdom	9	12	74	78	68	73	7	..	..	..	..	95	95	94	96
110	Italy	10	12	73	80	68	75	13	..	..	..	..	93	95	80	98
111	Australia	8	11	74	80	68	74	11	77	100	..	98	95	95	92	99
112	Netherlands	8	10	76	80	71	74	5	99	..	96	..	95	98	93	110
113	Austria	9	13	73	80	66	73	11	95	99	92	97	95	95	95	94
114	France	8	10	75	81	68	73	13	97	96	90	99	95	94	108	107
115	†United Arab Emirates	23	32	59	74	56	69	..	97	96	93	94	..	93	0	102
116	Canada	7	9	75	81	69	74	2	95	95	92	93	94	94	94	96
117	United States	10	13	74	80	67	73	9	..	96	..	94	92	..	..	..
118	Denmark	9	11	75	78	70	73	4	98	100	96	100	96	96	104	105
119	Germany	8	11	73	80	67	73	11[e]	97	99	96	97	..	96	..	98
120	Norway	9	11	76	81	71	74	..	99	99	98	..	96	95	95	104
121	Sweden	6	8	76	81	72	75	4	98	..	96	..	96	95	104	108
122	Japan	5	7	73	82	68	76	15	100	100	100	100	96	95	101	99
123	Finland	7	9	73	79	66	73	5	..	99	..	99	90	95	115	111
124	Switzerland	7	9	75	82	69	75	5	94	..	93	..	..	96	..	99
125	†Kuwait	14	20	65	76	61	72	18	96	92	98	93	76	96	63	92
World		**64** w	**70** w	**58** w	**67** w	**55** w	**64** w	**..**	**67** w	**85** w	**70** w	**85** w	**73** w	**83** w	**59** w	**76** w
Fuel exp., excl. former USSR		**117** w	**133** w	**48** w	**60** w	**46** w	**57** w	**..**	**74** w	**89** w	**74** w	**92** w	**59** w	**84** w	**47** w	**77** w

a. See technical notes.   b. Data refer to maternal mortality in hospitals and other medical institutions only.   c. Data for Jordan cover the East Bank only.   d. Community data from rural areas only.   e. Data refer to the Federal Republic of Germany before unification.

Table 33. Forests, protected areas, and water resources

		Forest area (thousands of square kilometers)				Nationally protected areas (1991)			Internal renewable water resources: annual withdrawal (1970–87)				
		Total area 1980		Annual deforestation 1981–85		Area (thousands of square kilometers)	Number	As a percentage of total land area	Total (cubic kilometers)	As a percentage of total water resources	Per capita (cubic meters)		
		Total	Closed	Total	Closed						Total	Domestic	Industrial and agricultural
	Low-income economies												
	China and India												
	Other low-income												
1	Mozambique	154	9	1.2[a]	0.1	0.0	1	0.0	0.8	1	53	13	40
2	Tanzania	420	14	3.0[a]	..	130.0	28	13.8	0.5	1	36	8	28
3	Ethiopia	272	44	0.9	0.1	25.3	11	2.1	2.2	2	48	5	43
4	Somalia	91	15	0.1	0.0	1.8	1	0.3	0.8	7	167	5	162
5	Nepal	21	19	0.8	0.8	11.3	13	8.0	2.7	2	155	6	149
6	Chad	135	5	0.8	..	4.1	2	0.3	0.2	0	35	6	29
7	Bhutan	21	21	0.0	0.0	9.1	5	19.3	0.0	0	15	5	10
8	Lao PDR	136	84	1.3	1.0	0.0	0	0.0	1.0	0	228	18	210
9	Malawi	43	2	1.5	..	10.6	9	8.9	0.2	2	22	7	15
10	Bangladesh	9	9	0.1	0.1	1.0	8	0.7	22.5	1	211	6	205
11	Burundi	0	0	0.0	0.0	0.9	3	3.1	0.1	3	20	7	13
12	Zaire	1,776	1,058	3.7	1.8	85.8	8	3.7	0.7	0	22	13	9
13	Uganda	60	8	0.5	0.1	18.7	32	7.9	0.2	0	20	6	14
14	Madagascar	132	103	1.6	1.5	11.2	37	1.9	16.3	41	1,675	17	1,658
15	Sierra Leone	21	7	0.1	0.1	0.8	2	1.1	0.4	0	99	7	92
16	Mali	73	5	0.4	..	40.1	11	3.2	1.4	2	159	3	156
17	Nigeria	148	60	4.0	3.0	28.7	21	3.1	3.6	1	44	14	30
18	Niger	26	1	0.7	0.0	97.0	6	7.7	0.3	1	44	9	35
19	Rwanda	2	1	0.1	0.0	3.3	2	12.4	0.2	2	23	6	17
20	Burkina Faso	47	3	0.8	0.0	26.4	11	9.6	0.2	1	20	6	14
21	India	640	378	0.5[a]	..	137.7	362	4.2	380.0	18	612	18	594
22	Benin	39	0	0.7	0.0	8.4	2	7.5	0.1	0	26	7	19
23	China	1,150	978	0.0	..	283.6	396	3.0	460.0	16	462	28	434
24	Haiti	0	0	0.0	0.0	0.1	3	0.3	0.0	0	46	11	35
25	Kenya	24	11	0.4	0.2	34.7	36	6.0	1.1	7	48	13	35
26	Pakistan	25	22	0.1	0.1	36.5	53	4.6	153.4	33	2,053	21	2,032
27	Ghana	87	17	0.7	0.2	10.7	8	4.5	0.3	1	35	12	23
28	Central African Rep.	359	36	0.6	0.1	58.6	12	9.4	0.1	0	27	6	21
29	Togo	17	3	0.1	0.0	6.5	11	11.4	0.1	1	40	25	15
30	Zambia	295	30	0.7	0.4	63.6	20	8.5	0.4	0	86	54	32
31	Guinea	107	21	0.9	0.4	1.7	3	0.7	0.7	0	115	12	104
32	Sri Lanka	17	17	0.6	0.6	7.8	43	11.9	6.3	15	503	10	493
33	Mauritania	6	0	0.1	0.0	17.5	4	1.7	0.7	10	473	57	416
34	Lesotho	0	0	..	..	0.1	1	0.2	0.1	1	34	7	27
35	Indonesia	1,169	1,139	10.0[a]	..	192.3	194	10.1	82.0	3	452	9	443
36	Honduras	40	38	0.9	0.9	7.2	35	6.4	1.3	1	508	20	488
37	Egypt, Arab Rep.	0	0	..	..	8.0	13	0.8	56.4	97	1,202	84	1,118
38	*Afghanistan*	12	8	..	..	1.8	5	0.3	26.1	52	1,436	14	1,422
39	*Cambodia*	126	75	0.3	0.3	0.0	0	0.0	0.5	0	69	3	66
40	*Liberia*	20	20	0.5	0.5	1.3	1	1.2	0.1	0	54	15	39
41	*Myanmar*	319	319	6.0[a]	..	1.7	2	0.3	4.0	0	103	7	96
42	*Sudan*	477	7	5.0	0.0	93.6	14	3.7	18.6	14	1,089	11	1,078
43	*Viet Nam*	101	88	2.0[a]	..	9.0	59	2.7	5.1	1	81	11	70
	Middle-income economies												
	Lower-middle-income												
44	Bolivia	668	440	1.2	0.9	98.6	27	9.0	1.2	0	184	18	166
45	Zimbabwe	198	2	0.8	0.0	30.7	25	7.9	1.2	5	129	18	111
46	Senegal	110	2	0.5	..	21.8	10	11.1	1.4	4	201	10	191
47	Philippines	95[b]	95	1.4[a]	1.4[a]	5.7	27	1.9	29.5	9	693	125	568
48	Côte d'Ivoire	98	45	2.6[a]	..	19.9	12	6.2	0.7	1	68	15	53
49	Dominican Rep.	6	6	0.0	0.0	9.6	17	19.8	3.0	15	453	23	430
50	Papua New Guinea	382	342	0.2	0.2	0.3	5	0.1	0.1	0	25	7	18
51	Guatemala	45	44	0.9	0.9	8.3	17	7.7	0.7	1	139	13	126
52	Morocco	32	15	0.1	..	3.6	10	0.8	11.0	37	501	30	471
53	Cameroon	233	165	1.9[a]	1.0[a]	20.3	13	4.3	0.4	0	30	14	16
54	Ecuador	147	143	3.4	3.4	107.5	18	37.9	5.6	2	561	39	522
55	Syrian Arab Rep.	2	1	0.0	..	0.0	0	0.0	3.3	9	449	31	418
56	Congo	213	213	0.2	0.2	13.3	10	3.9	0.0	0	20	12	8
57	El Salvador	1	1	0.1	0.1	0.3	9	1.2	1.0	5	241	17	224
58	Paraguay	197	41	4.5[a]	..	12.0	14	3.0	0.4	0	111	17	94
59	Peru	706	697	2.7	2.7	26.9	20	2.1	6.1	15	294	56	238
60	Jordan	1	0	..	..	1.0	8	1.1	0.4	41	173	50	123
61	Colombia	517	464	8.9	8.2	90.5	41	7.9	5.3	0	179	73	106
62	Thailand	157	92	2.4[a]	1.6[a]	55.1	90	10.7	31.9	18	599	24	575
63	Tunisia	3	2	0.1	..	0.4	7	0.3	2.3	53	325	42	283
64	Jamaica	1	1	0.0	0.0	0.4	2	3.5	0.3	4	157	11	146
65	Turkey	202	89	..	..	2.7	18	0.3	15.6	8	317	76	241
66	Romania	67	63	..	..	10.9	42	4.6	25.4	12	1,144	92	1,052

Note: For data comparability and coverage, see the technical notes. Figures in italics are for years other than those specified. For more extensive coverage and documentation of data on protected areas and water resources, see the Environmental data appendix.

		Forest area (thousands of square kilometers)				Nationally protected areas (1991)			Internal renewable water resources: annual withdrawal (1970-87)				
		Total area 1980		Annual deforestation 1981-85		Area (thousands of square kilometers)	Number	As a percentage of total land area	Total (cubic kilometers)	As a percentage of total water resources	Per capita (cubic meters)		Industrial and agricultural
		Total	Closed	Total	Closed						Total	Domestic	
67	Poland	87	86	..	..	22.4	80	7.2	16.8	30	472	76	396
68	Panama	42	42	0.4	0.4	13.3	16	17.2	1.3	1	744	89	655
69	Costa Rica	18	16	0.4[a]	0.4[a]	6.2	31	12.2	1.4	1	770	31	739
70	Chile	76	76	0.5	..	137.2	66	18.1	16.8	4	1,625	98	1,528
71	Botswana	326	0	0.2	..	100.3	9	17.2	0.1	0	98	5	93
72	Algeria	18	15	0.4	..	127.0	18	5.3	3.0	16	161	35	126
73	Bulgaria	37	33	..	..	2.6	50	2.4	14.2	7	1,600	112	1,488
74	Mauritius	0	0	0.0	0.0	0.0	3	2.2	0.4	16	415	66	349
75	Malaysia	210[b]	210	2.7[a]	..	14.9	51	4.5	9.4	2	765	176	589
76	Argentina	445	445	1.8[a]	..	94.0	115	3.4	27.6	3	1,059	95	964
77	Iran, Islamic Rep.	38	28	0.2	..	75.3	60	4.6	45.4	39	1,362	54	1,308
78	Albania	..	..	..	..	0.4	13	1.5	0.2	1	94	6	88
79	Angola	536	29	0.9	0.4	26.4	6	2.1	0.5	0	43	6	37
80	Lebanon	0	0	0.0	..	0.0	1	0.3	0.8	16	271	30	241
81	Mongolia	95	95	..	..	61.7	15	3.9	0.6	2	272	30	242
82	Namibia	184	..	0.3	..	103.7	11	12.6	0.1	2	79	9	69
83	Nicaragua	45	45	1.2	1.2	3.6	11	2.8	0.9	1	370	93	278
84	Yemen, Rep.	0	0	0.0	..	0.0	0	0.0	1.5	147	127	5	122
Upper-middle-income													
85	Mexico	484	463	10.0[a]	..	100.7	63	5.1	54.2	15	901	54	847
86	South Africa	3	3	..	..	73.9	229	6.1	9.2	18	404	65	339
87	Venezuela	339	319	2.5	1.3	283.1	104	31.0	4.1	0	387	166	221
88	Uruguay	5	5	..	..	0.3	8	0.2	0.6	1	241	14	227
89	Brazil	5,145	3,575	13.8[a,b]	..	215.7	172	2.5	35.0	1	212	91	121
90	Hungary	16	16	..	..	5.8	54	6.2	5.4	5	502	45	457
91	Yugoslavia	105	91	..	..	7.9	62	3.1	8.8	3	393	63	330
92	Czechoslovakia	46	44	..	..	20.6	65	16.1	5.8	6	379	87	292
93	Gabon	206	205	0.2	0.2	10.5	6	3.9	0.1	0	51	37	14
94	Trinidad and Tobago	2	2	0.0	0.0	0.2	7	3.0	0.2	3	149	40	109
95	Portugal	30	26	..	..	5.6	25	6.0	10.5	16	1,062	159	903
96	Korea, Rep.	49	49	..	..	7.6	26	7.6	10.7	17	298	33	265
97	Greece	58	25	..	..	1.0	21	0.8	7.0	12	721	58	663
98	Saudi Arabia	2	0	..	..	212.0	10	9.9	3.6	164	255	115	140
99	Iraq	12	1	..	..	0.0	0	0.0	42.8	43	4,575	137	4,438
100	Libya	2	1	..	..	1.6	3	0.1	2.8	404	623	93	530
101	Oman	0	0	..	..	0.5	2	0.3	0.4	22	561	17	544
Low- and middle-income													
Sub-Saharan Africa													
East Asia													
South Asia													
Europe													
Middle East & N.Africa													
Latin America & Caribbean													
Other economies													
Severely indebted													
High-income economies													
OECD members													
†Other													
102	Ireland	4	3	..	..	0.3	6	0.4	0.8	2	267	43	224
103	†Israel	1	1	..	..	2.1	21	10.0	1.9	88	447	72	375
104	Spain	108	69	..	..	35.0	163	6.9	45.3	41	1,174	141	1,033
105	†Singapore	0	0	..	..	0.0	1	4.4	0.2	32	84	38	46
106	†Hong Kong	..	..	..	..	0.4	12	36.4	..	..	..	..	..
107	New Zealand	95	72	..	..	29.1	152	10.7	1.2	0	379	174	205
108	Belgium	8	7	..	..	0.7	2	2.4	9.0	72	917	101	816
109	United Kingdom	22	20	..	..	46.4	140	18.9	28.4	24	507	101	406
110	Italy	81	64	..	..	20.1	144	6.7	56.2	30	983	138	845
111	Australia	1,067	417	..	..	812.6	746	10.6	17.8	5	1,306	849	457
112	Netherlands	4	3	..	..	3.5	67	9.4	14.5	16	1,023	51	972
113	Austria	38	38	..	..	20.9	178	24.9	3.1	3	417	79	338
114	France	151	139	..	..	53.6	81	9.7	40.0	22	728	116	612
115	†United Arab Emirates	0	0	..	..	0	0	0.0	0.9	300	565	62	503
116	Canada	4,364	2,641	..	..	494.5	426	5.0	42.2	1	1,752	193	1,559
117	United States	2,960	2,096	1.6[a]	..	982.0	972	10.5	467.0	19	2,162	259	1,903
118	Denmark	5	5	..	..	4.1	66	9.5	1.4	11	277	83	194
119	Germany	72[c]	70[c]	..	..	58.6	440	23.6	41.2[c]	26[c]	668[c]	67[c]	601[c]
120	Norway	87	76	..	..	14.9	82	4.6	2.0	0	489	98	391
121	Sweden	278	244	..	..	29.2	195	6.5	4.0	2	479	172	307
122	Japan	253	239	..	..	46.6	684	12.3	107.8	20	923	157	766
123	Finland	232	199	..	..	8.1	35	2.4	3.7	3	774	93	681
124	Switzerland	11	9	..	..	7.5	112	18.2	3.2	6	502	115	387
125	†Kuwait	0	0	..	..	0.3	1	1.7	0.5	..	238	152	86
World													
Fuel exporters, excl. former USSR													

a. Data are for the periods as follows: Tanzania 1989, India 1983–87, Indonesia 1982–90, Myanmar 1984, Viet Nam 1986, Philippines 1981–88, Côte d'Ivoire 1981–86, Cameroon 1976–86, Paraguay 1989–90, Thailand 1985–88, Costa Rica 1973–89, Malaysia 1979–89, Argentina 1980–89, Mexico 1981–83, Brazil (Legal Amazon only) 1989–90, United States 1977–87.   b. See the technical notes for alternative estimates. c. Data refer to the Federal Republic of Germany before unification.

Technical notes

The World Development Indicators provide information on the main features of social and economic development.

The main criterion of country classification is gross national product (GNP) per capita. With the addition of new World Bank member, Albania, the main tables now include country data for 125 economies, listed in ascending order of GNP per capita. Box A.1, showing basic indicators for economies with populations of less than 1 million, covers another fifty-seven economies including, this year, Marshall Islands and the Federated States of Micronesia, former members of the Trust Territory of the Pacific Islands. As only sparse data are available for three additional economies, Cuba, People's Democratic Republic of Korea, and the former Soviet Union, these are not included in the main tables except in summary form under "other economies." Selected data are presented for them in Box A.2. Other changes are outlined in the Introduction.

Considerable effort has been made to standardize the data; nevertheless, statistical methods, coverage, practices, and definitions differ widely among countries. In addition, the statistical systems in many developing economies are still weak, and this affects the availability and reliability of the data. Moreover, cross-country and cross-time comparisons always involve complex technical problems that cannot be fully and unequivocally resolved. The data are drawn from the sources thought to be most authoritative, but many of them are subject to considerable margins of error.

Most social and demographic data from national sources are drawn from regular administrative files, although some come from special surveys or periodic census inquiries. In the case of survey and census data, figures for intermediate years have to be interpolated or otherwise estimated from the base reference statistics. Similarly, because not all data are updated, some figures—especially those relating to current periods—may be extrapolated. Several estimates (for example, life expectancy) are derived from models based on assumptions about recent trends and prevailing conditions. Issues related to the reliability of demographic indicators are reviewed in the U.N.'s *World Population Trends and Policies*. Readers are urged to take these limitations into account in interpreting the indicators, particularly when making comparisons across economies.

To provide long-term trend analysis, facilitate international comparisons and include the effects of changes in intersectoral relative prices, constant price data for most economies are partially rebased to three base years and linked together. The year 1970 is the base year for data from 1960 to 1975, 1980 for 1976 to 1982, and 1987 for 1983 and beyond. These three periods are "chain-linked" to obtain 1987 prices throughout all three periods.

Chain-linking is accomplished for each of the three subperiods by rescaling; this moves the year in which current and constant price versions of the same time series have the same value, without altering the trend of either. Components of GDP are individually rescaled and summed to provide GDP and its subaggregates. In this process, a rescaling deviation may occur between the constant price GDP by industrial origin and the constant price GDP by expenditure. Such rescaling deviations are absorbed under the heading *private consumption, etc.* on the assumption that GDP by industrial origin is a more reliable estimate than GDP by expenditure.

Because private consumption is calculated as a residual, the national accounting identities are maintained. Rebasing does involve incorporating in private consumption whatever statistical discrepancies arise for expenditure. The value added in the services sector also includes a statistical discrepancy, as reported by the original source.

With some exceptions, use of 1987 rather than 1980 values as country weights does not greatly alter the group indexes and growth rates reported here. Most exceptions relate to oil exporters and reflect declining shares of group GNP, trade, and so on from 1980 to 1987. This is most notable for Sub-Saharan Africa, with the dramatic decline in Nigeria's weight. In contrast, changing the base year for country series themselves, as described above, is likely to alter trends significantly. Differences of half a percentage point a year in growth rates could be quite common; larger changes may occur for economies that have undergone significant structural change, such as exporters of fuels.

The summary measures are calculated by simple addition when a variable is expressed in reasonably

Box A.1 Basic indicators for economies with populations of less than 1 million

		Population (thousands) mid-1990	Area (thousands of square kilometers)	GNP per capita[a] Dollars 1990	GNP per capita[a] Average annual growth rate (percent) 1965–90	Average annual rate of inflation[a] (percent) 1965–80	Average annual rate of inflation[a] (percent) 1980–90	Life expectancy at birth (years) 1990	Adult illiteracy (percent) Female 1990	Adult illiteracy (percent) Total 1990
1	Guinea-Bissau	980	36	180	..	..	54.4	39	76	64
2	The Gambia	875	11	260	0.7	8.1	13.8	44	84	73
3	Guyana	798	215	330	−1.3	7.9	25.5	64	5	4
4	Equatorial Guinea	417	28	330	..	..	..	47	63	50
5	São Tomé and Principe	117	1	400	..	..	19.9	67	..	33
6	Maldives	214	b	450	2.8	..	..	62	..	..
7	Comoros	475	2	480	0.4	..	..	55	..	..
8	Solomon Islands	316	29	590	..	7.7	10.0	65	..	..
9	Western Samoa	165	3	730	..	..	9.2	66	..	..
10	Kiribati	70	1	760	..	..	5.5	55	..	..
11	Swaziland	797	17	810	2.2	9.0	11.1	57	..	..
12	Cape Verde	371	4	890	..	..	9.8	66	..	..
13	Tonga	99	1	1,010	..	..	..	67	..	..
14	Vanuatu	151	12	1,100	..	..	4.9	65	..	..
15	St. Vincent	107	b	1,720	2.9	10.9	4.6	70	..	..
16	Fiji	744	18	1,780	1.9	10.3	5.4	65	..	..
17	St. Lucia	150	1	1,900	..	..	4.2	72	..	..
18	Belize	188	23	1,990	2.6	7.1	2.3	68	..	..
19	Grenada	91	b	2,190	..	..	..	70	..	..
20	Dominica	72	1	2,210	1.3	12.6	6.1	75	..	..
21	Suriname	447	163	3,050	1.0	..	6.4	68	5	5
22	St. Kitts and Nevis	40	b	3,330	..	..	6.5	70	..	..
23	Antigua and Barbuda	79	b	4,600	..	..	7.8	74	..	..
24	Seychelles	68	b	4,670	3.2	12.2	3.3	71	..	..
25	Barbados	257	b	6,540	2.3	11.0	5.4	75	..	..
26	Malta	354	b	6,610	7.1	3.5	2.0	73	..	..
27	Cyprus	702	9	8,020	..	..	5.7	77	..	..
28	The Bahamas	255	14	11,420	1.1	6.4	6.0	69	..	..
29	Qatar	439	11	15,860	..	..	..	70	..	..
30	Iceland	255	103	21,400	3.4	26.7	32.8	78	..	..
31	Luxembourg	379	3	28,730	2.3	6.7	4.2	75	..	..
32	*American Samoa*	39	b	c	..	..	..	72	..	..
33	*Andorra*	52	..	c	..	..	..	..	..	..
34	*Aruba*	61	b	d	..	..	..	..	..	..
35	*Bahrain*	503	1	c	..	..	−1.5	69	31	23
36	*Bermuda*	61	b	c	..	8.1	9.1	..	..	..
37	*Brunei*	256	6	c	..	..	−6.9	76	..	..
38	*Channel Islands*	144	..	c	..	..	..	77	..	..
39	*Djibouti*	427	23	e	..	..	..	48	..	..
40	*Faeroe Islands*	48	1	c	..	..	..	..	..	..
41	*Fed. Sts. of Micronesia*	103	1	..	..	..	..	..	..	..
42	*French Guiana*	92	90	d	..	..	..	..	..	..
43	*French Polynesia*	197	4	c	..	..	..	73	..	..
44	*Gibraltar*	31	b	d	..	..	..	..	..	..
45	*Greenland*	57	342	c	..	..	..	..	..	..
46	*Guadeloupe*	387	2	c	..	..	..	74	..	..
47	*Guam*	137	1	c	..	..	..	73	..	..
48	*Isle of Man*	69	..	c	..	..	..	..	..	..
49	*Macao*	459	b	d	..	..	..	72	..	..
50	*Marshall Islands*	34	0	..	..	..	..	..	..	..
51	*Martinique*	360	1	d	..	..	..	76	..	..
52	*Mayotte*	73	..	c	..	..	..	..	..	..
53	*Netherlands Antilles*	189	1	c	..	..	..	77	..	..
54	*New Caledonia*	165	19	d	..	..	..	69	..	..
55	*Puerto Rico*[f]	3530	9	c	..	..	..	76	..	..
56	*Reunion*	593	3	d	..	..	..	72	..	..
57	*Virgin Islands (U.S.)*	110	b	c	2.9	2.3	3.9	74	..	..

Note: Economies in italics are those for which 1990 GNP per capita cannot be calculated; figures in italics are for years other than those specified. a. See the technical note for Table 1. b. Less than 500 square kilometers. c. GNP per capita estimated to be in the high-income range. d. GNP per capita estimated to be in the upper-middle-income range. e. GNP per capita estimated to be in the lower-middle-income range. f. Population is more than 1 million.

Box A.2 Selected indicators for other economies

	Cuba 1965	Cuba 1990	People's Democratic Republic of Korea 1965	People's Democratic Republic of Korea 1990	Former USSR 1965	Former USSR 1990
Population (millions)	8	11	12	22	232	289
Urban population (percentage of total)	58	75	45	60	52	66
Life expectancy at birth (years)	67	76	57	71	69	71
Crude birth rate (per 1,000 population)	34	17	44	22	18	17
Crude death rate (per 1,000 population)	8	6	12	5	7	10
Population per physician	1,150	530	..	420	480	270
Total fertility rate	4.4	1.9	6.5	2.3	2.5	2.3
Infant mortality (per 1,000 live births)	38	12	63	26	28	24
Low birth weight (percent)	..	8	..	..	..	6
Under-5 mortality (per 1,000 live births, female)	..	13	..	27	..	24
Under-5 mortality (per 1,000 live births, male)	..	16	..	36	..	33
Daily calorie supply (per capita)	2,461	3,141	2,039	2,823	3,205	3,386
Food production per capita index (1979–81 = 100)	82	99	73	110	86	112
Female primary education (percentage of female age group)	119	100	..	106	103	105
Total primary education (percentage of total age group)	121	103	..	103	103	105
Area (thousands of square kilometers)	..	111	..	121	..	22,402
Population projected to year 2000 (millions)	..	12	..	25	..	308

Note: For data comparability and coverage, see the technical notes.   Figures in italics are for years other than those specified.

comparable units of account. Economic indicators that do not seem naturally additive are usually combined by a price-weighting scheme. The summary measures for social indicators are weighted by population.

The World Development Indicators, unlike the *World Tables*, provide data for (usually) two reference points rather than annual time series. For summary measures that cover many years, the calculation is based on the same country composition over time and across topics. The World Development Indicators permit group measures to be compiled only if the country data available for a given year account for at least two-thirds of the full group, as defined by the 1987 benchmarks. So long as that criterion is met, noncurrent reporters (and those not providing ample history) are, for years with missing data, assumed to behave like the sample of the group that does provide estimates. Readers should keep in mind that the purpose is to maintain an appropriate relationship across topics, despite myriad problems with country data, and that nothing meaningful can be deduced about behavior at the country level by working back from group indicators. In addition, the weighting process may result in discrepancies between summed subgroup figures and overall totals. This is explained more fully in the introduction to the *World Tables*.

All growth rates shown are calculated from constant price series and, unless otherwise noted, have been computed using the least-squares method. The least-squares growth rate, r, is estimated by fitting a least-squares linear regression trend line to the logarithmic annual values of the variable in the relevant period. More specifically, the regression equation takes the form $\log X_t = a + bt + e_t$, where this is equivalent to the logarithmic transformation of the compound growth rate equation, $X_t = X_o (1 + r)^t$. In these equations, X is the variable, t is time, and $a = \log X_o$ and $b = \log (1 + r)$ are the parameters to be estimated; e is the error term. If b^* is the least-squares estimate of b, then the average annual percentage growth rate, r, is obtained as [antilog (b^*)] − 1 and multiplied by 100 to express it as a percentage.

Table 1. Basic indicators

For basic indicators for economies with populations of less than 1 million, see Box A.1. For selected indicators for three "other economies," see Box A.2.

Population numbers for mid-1990 are World Bank estimates. These are usually projections from the most recent population censuses or surveys; most are from 1980–1990 and, for a few countries, from the 1960s or 1970s. Note that refugees not permanently settled in the country of asylum are generally considered to be part of the population of their country of origin.

The data on *area* are from the Food and Agriculture Organization. Area is the total surface area, measured in square kilometers, comprising land area and inland waters.

GNP per capita figures in U.S. dollars are calculated according to the *World Bank Atlas* method, which is described below.

GNP per capita does not, by itself, constitute or measure welfare or success in development. It does not distinguish between the aims and ultimate uses of a given product, nor does it say whether it merely offsets some natural or other obstacle, or harms or contributes to welfare. For example, GNP is higher in colder countries, where people spend money on heating and warm clothes, than in balmy climates, where people are comfortable wearing light clothes in the open air.

More generally, GNP does not deal adequately with environmental issues, particularly natural resource use. The Bank has joined with others to see how national accounts might provide insights into these issues. The possibility of developing "satellite" accounts is being considered; such accounts could delve into practical and conceptual difficulties, such as assigning a meaningful economic value to resources that markets do not yet perceive as "scarce" and allocating costs that are essentially global within a framework that is inherently national.

GNP measures the total domestic and foreign value added claimed by residents. It comprises GDP (defined in the note for Table 2) plus net factor income from abroad, which is the income residents receive from abroad for factor services (labor and capital) less similar payments made to nonresidents who contributed to the domestic economy.

In estimating GNP per capita, the Bank recognizes that perfect cross-country comparability of GNP per capita estimates cannot be achieved. Beyond the classic, strictly intractable index number problem, two obstacles stand in the way of adequate comparability. One concerns the GNP and population estimates themselves. There are differences in national accounting and demographic reporting systems and in the coverage and reliability of underlying statistical information among various countries. The other obstacle relates to the use of official exchange rates for converting GNP data, expressed in different national currencies, to a common denomination—conventionally the U.S. dollar—to compare them across countries.

Recognizing that these shortcomings affect the comparability of the GNP per capita estimates, the World Bank has introduced several improvements in the estimation procedures. Through its regular review of member countries' national accounts, the Bank systematically evaluates the GNP estimates, fo-

cusing on the coverage and concepts employed and, where appropriate, making adjustments to improve comparability. As part of the review, Bank staff estimates of GNP (and sometimes of population) may be developed for the most recent period.

The World Bank also systematically assesses the appropriateness of official exchange rates as conversion factors. An alternative conversion factor is used (and reported in the *World Tables*) when the official exchange rate is judged to diverge by an exceptionally large margin from the rate effectively applied to foreign transactions. This applies to only a small number of countries. For all other countries the Bank calculates GNP per capita using the *Atlas* method.

The *Atlas* conversion factor for any year is the average of a country's exchange rate for that year and its exchange rates for the two preceding years, after adjusting them for differences in relative inflation between the country and the United States. This three-year average smooths fluctuations in prices and exchange rates for each country. The resulting GNP in U.S. dollars is divided by the midyear population for the latest of the three years to derive GNP per capita.

Some sixty low- and middle-income economies have suffered declining real GNP per capita in constant prices during the 1980s. In addition, significant currency and terms of trade fluctuations have affected relative income levels. For this reason the levels and ranking of GNP per capita estimates, calculated by the *Atlas* method, have sometimes changed in ways not necessarily related to the relative domestic growth performance of the economies.

The following formulas describe the procedures for computing the conversion factor for year t:

$$(e^{*}_{t-2,t}) = \frac{1}{3} \left[e_{t-2} \left(\frac{P_t}{P_{t-2}} \middle| \frac{P_t^{\$}}{P_{t-2}^{\$}} \right) + e_{t-1} \left(\frac{P_t}{P_{t-1}} \middle| \frac{P_t^{\$}}{P_{t-1}^{\$}} \right) + e_t \right]$$

and for calculating per capita GNP in U.S. dollars for year t:

$$(Y_t^{\$}) = (Y_t | N_t \div e^{*}_{t-2,t})$$

where

Y_t = current GNP (local currency) for year t
P_t = GNP deflator for year t
e_t = average annual exchange rate (local currency to the U.S. dollar) for year t
N_t = midyear population for year t
$P_t^{\$}$ = U.S. GNP deflator for year t.

Because of problems associated with the availability of comparable data and the determination of conversion factors, information on GNP per capita is not shown for some economies.

The use of official exchange rates to convert national currency figures to U.S. dollars does not reflect the relative domestic purchasing powers of currencies. The United Nations International Comparison

Program (ICP) has developed measures of real GDP on an internationally comparable scale, using purchasing power parities (PPPs) instead of exchange rates as conversion factors. Table 30 shows the most recent ICP estimates. Information on the ICP has been published in four studies corresponding to the first four phases; and in separate reports for Phase V, published by the Economic Commission for Europe (ECE), the Economic and Social Commission for Asia and the Pacific (ESCAP), the European Communities (EC), and the Organization for Economic Cooperation and Development (OECD).

The ICP figures reported in Table 30 are preliminary and may be revised. The United Nations and its regional economic commissions, as well as other international agencies, such as the EC, the OECD, and the World Bank, are working to improve the methodology and to extend annual purchasing power comparisons to all countries. However, exchange rates remain the only generally available means of converting GNP from national currencies to U.S. dollars.

The *average annual rate of inflation* is measured by the growth rate of the GDP implicit deflator for each of the periods shown. The GDP deflator is first calculated by dividing, for each year of the period, the value of GDP at current values by the value of GDP at constant values, both in national currency. The least-squares method is then used to calculate the growth rate of the GDP deflator for the period. This measure of inflation, like any other, has limitations. For some purposes, however, it is used as an indicator of inflation because it is the most broadly based measure, showing annual price movements for all goods and services produced in an economy.

Life expectancy at birth indicates the number of years a newborn infant would live if prevailing patterns of mortality at the time of its birth were to stay the same throughout its life. Data are World Bank estimates based on data from the U.N. Population Division, the U.N. Statistical Office, and national statistical offices.

Adult illiteracy is defined here as the proportion of the population over the age of fifteen who cannot, with understanding, read and write a short, simple statement on their everyday life. This is only one of three widely accepted definitions, and its application is subject to qualifiers in a number of countries. The data are from the illiteracy estimates and projections prepared in 1989 by Unesco. More recent information and a modified model have been used, therefore the data for 1990 are not strictly consistent with those published in last year's indicators.

The summary measures for GNP per capita, life expectancy, and adult illiteracy in this table are weighted by population. Those for average annual rates of inflation are weighted by the 1987 share of country GDP valued in current U.S. dollars.

Tables 2 and 3. Growth and structure of production

Most of the definitions used are those of the *U.N. System of National Accounts* (SNA), Series F, No. 2, Revision 3. Estimates are obtained from national sources, sometimes reaching the World Bank through other international agencies but more often collected during World Bank staff missions.

World Bank staff review the quality of national accounts data and in some instances, through mission work or technical assistance, help adjust national series. Because of the sometimes limited capabilities of statistical offices and basic data problems, strict international comparability cannot be achieved, especially in economic activities that are difficult to measure, such as parallel market transactions, the informal sector, or subsistence agriculture.

GDP measures the total output of goods and services for final use produced by residents and nonresidents, regardless of the allocation to domestic and foreign claims. It is calculated without making deductions for depreciation of "manmade" assets or depletion and degradation of natural resources. Although SNA envisages estimates of GDP by industrial origin to be at producer prices, many countries still report such details at factor cost. International comparability of the estimates is affected by differing country practices in valuation systems for reporting value added by production sectors. As a partial solution, GDP estimates are shown at purchaser values if the components are on this basis, and such instances are footnoted. However, for a few countries in Tables 2 and 3, GDP at purchaser values has been replaced by GDP at factor cost.

The figures for GDP are dollar values converted from domestic currencies using single-year official exchange rates. For a few countries where the official exchange rate does not reflect the rate effectively applied to actual foreign exchange transactions, an alternative conversion factor is used (and reported in the *World Tables*). Note that Table 3 does not use the three-year averaging technique applied to GNP per capita in Table 1.

Agriculture covers forestry, hunting, and fishing as well as agriculture. In developing countries with high levels of subsistence farming, much agricultural production is either not exchanged or not exchanged for money. This increases the difficulty of measuring the contribution of agriculture to GDP and reduces the reliability and comparability of such numbers.

Industry comprises value added in mining; manufacturing (also reported as a separate subgroup); construction; and electricity, water, and gas. Value added in all other branches of economic activity, including imputed bank service charges, import duties, and any statistical discrepancies noted by national compilers, are categorized as *services, etc.*

Partially rebased, chain-linked 1987 series in domestic currencies, as explained at the beginning of the technical notes, are used to compute the growth rates in Table 2. The sectoral shares of GDP in Table 3 are based on current price series.

In calculating the summary measures for each indicator in Table 2, partially rebased constant 1987 U.S. dollar values for each economy are calculated for each year of the periods covered; the values are aggregated across countries for each year; and the least-squares procedure is used to compute the growth rates. The average sectoral percentage shares in Table 3 are computed from group aggregates of sectoral GDP in current U.S. dollars.

Table 4. Agriculture and food

The basic data for *value added in agriculture* are from the World Bank's national accounts series at current prices in national currencies. Value added in current prices in national currencies is converted to U.S. dollars by applying the single-year conversion procedure, as described in the technical note for Tables 2 and 3.

The figures for the remainder of this table are from the Food and Agriculture Organization (FAO). *Cereal imports* are measured in grain equivalents and defined as comprising all cereals in the *Standard International Trade Classification* (SITC), Revision 2, Groups 041–046. *Food aid in cereals* covers wheat and flour, bulgur, rice, coarse grains, and the cereal component of blended foods. The figures are not directly comparable because of reporting and timing differences. Cereal imports are based on calendar-year data reported by recipient countries, and food aid in cereals is based on data for crop years reported by donors and international organizations, including the International Wheat Council and the World Food Programme. Furthermore, food aid information from donors may not correspond to actual receipts by beneficiaries during a given period because of delays in transportation and recording, or because aid is sometimes not reported to the FAO or other relevant international organizations. Food aid imports may also not show up in customs records. The earliest available food aid data are for 1974. The time reference for food aid is the crop year, July to June.

Fertilizer consumption measures the plant nutrients used in relation to arable land. Fertilizer products cover nitrogenous, potash, and phosphate fertilizers (which include ground rock phosphate). Arable land is defined as land under temporary crops (double-cropped areas are counted once), temporary meadows for mowing or pastures, land under market or kitchen gardens, and land temporarily fallow or lying idle, as well as land under permanent crops. The time reference for fertilizer consumption is the crop year, July to June.

The *average index of food production per capita* shows the average annual quantity of food produced per capita in 1988–90 in relation to the average produced annually in 1979–81. The estimates are derived by dividing the quantity of food production by the total population. For this index food is defined as comprising nuts, pulses, fruits, cereals, vegetables, sugar cane, sugar beet, starchy roots, edible oils, livestock, and livestock products. Quantities of food production are measured net of animal feed, seeds for use in agriculture, and food lost in processing and distribution.

The summary measures for fertilizer consumption are weighted by total arable land area; the summary measures for food production are weighted by population.

Table 5. Commercial energy

The data on energy are primarily from U.N. sources. They refer to commercial forms of primary energy—petroleum and natural gas liquids, natural gas, solid fuels (coal, lignite, and so on), and primary electricity (nuclear, geothermal, and hydroelectric power)—all converted into oil equivalents. Figures on liquid fuel consumption include petroleum derivatives that have been consumed in nonenergy uses. For converting primary electricity into oil equivalents, a notional thermal efficiency of 34 percent has been assumed. The use of firewood, dried animal excrement, and other traditional fuels, although substantial in some developing countries, is not taken into account because reliable and comprehensive data are not available.

Energy imports refer to the dollar value of energy imports—Section 3 in the *Standard International Trade Classification*, Revision 1—and are expressed as a percentage of earnings from merchandise exports. Because data on energy imports do not permit a distinction between petroleum imports for fuel and those for use in the petrochemicals industry, these percentages may overestimate the dependence on imported energy.

The summary measures of energy production and consumption are computed by aggregating the respective volumes for each of the years covered by the periods and then applying the least-squares growth rate procedure. For energy consumption per capita, population weights are used to compute summary measures for the specified years.

The summary measures of energy imports as a percentage of merchandise exports are computed from group aggregates for energy imports and merchandise exports in current dollars.

Table 6. Structure of manufacturing

The basic data for *value added in manufacturing* are from the World Bank's national accounts series at current prices in national currencies. Value added in current prices in national currencies is converted to U.S. dollars by applying the single-year conversion procedure, as described in the technical note for Tables 2 and 3.

The data for *distribution of manufacturing value added* among industries are provided by the United Nations Industrial Development Organization (UNIDO), and distribution calculations are from national currencies in current prices.

The classification of manufacturing industries is in accordance with the U.N.'s *International Standard Industrial Classification of All Economic Activities* (ISIC), Revision 2. *Food, beverages, and tobacco* comprise ISIC Division 31; *textiles and clothing*, Division 32; *machinery and transport equipment*, Major Groups 382–84; and *chemicals*, Major Groups 351 and 352. *Other* comprises wood and related products (Division 33), paper and related products (Division 34), petroleum and related products (Major Groups 353–56), basic metals and mineral products (Divisions 36 and 37), fabricated metal products and professional goods (Major Groups 381 and 385), and other industries (Major Group 390). When data for textiles, machinery, or chemicals are shown as not available, they are also included in *other*.

Summary measures for value added in manufacturing are totals calculated by the aggregation method noted at the beginning of the technical notes.

Table 7. Manufacturing earnings and output

Four indicators are shown—two relate to real earnings per employee, one to labor's share in total value added generated, and one to labor productivity in the manufacturing sector. The indicators are based on data from the United Nations Industrial Development Organization (UNIDO), although the deflators are from other sources, as explained below.

Earnings per employee are in constant prices and are derived by deflating nominal earnings per employee by the country's consumer price index (CPI). The CPI is from the International Monetary Fund's *International Financial Statistics. Total earnings as a percentage of value added* are derived by dividing total earnings of employees by value added in current prices to show labor's share in income generated in the manufacturing sector. *Gross output per employee* is in constant prices and is presented as an index of overall labor productivity in manufacturing with 1980 as the base year. To derive this indicator, UNIDO data on gross output per employee in current prices are adjusted using the implicit deflators for value added in manufacturing or in industry, taken from the World Bank's national accounts data files.

To improve cross-country comparability, UNIDO

has, where possible, standardized the coverage of establishments to those with five or more employees.

The concepts and definitions are in accordance with the *International Recommendations for Industrial Statistics*, published by the United Nations. Earnings (wages and salaries) cover all remuneration to employees paid by the employer during the year. The payments include (a) all regular and overtime cash payments and bonuses and cost of living allowances; (b) wages and salaries paid during vacation and sick leave; (c) taxes and social insurance contributions and the like, payable by the employees and deducted by the employer; and (d) payments in kind.

The term "employees" in this table combines two categories defined by the U.N., regular employees and persons engaged. Together these groups comprise regular employees, working proprietors, active business partners, and unpaid family workers; they exclude homeworkers. The data refer to the average number of employees working during the year.

"Value added" is defined as the current value of gross output less the current cost of (a) materials, fuels, and other supplies consumed, (b) contract and commission work done by others, (c) repair and maintenance work done by others, and (d) goods shipped in the same condition as received.

The value of gross output is estimated on the basis of either production or shipments. On the production basis it consists of (a) the value of all products of the establishment, (b) the value of industrial services rendered to others, (c) the value of goods shipped in the same condition as received, (d) the value of electricity sold, and (e) the net change in the value of work-in-progress between the beginning and the end of the reference period. In the case of estimates compiled on a shipment basis, the net change between the beginning and the end of the reference period in the value of stocks of finished goods is also included.

Tables 8 and 9. Growth of consumption and investment; structure of demand

GDP is defined in the note for Tables 2 and 3, but for these two tables it is in purchaser values.

General government consumption includes all current expenditure for purchases of goods and services by all levels of government. Capital expenditure on national defense and security is regarded as consumption expenditure.

Private consumption, etc., is the market value of all goods and services, including durable products (such as cars, washing machines, and home computers) purchased or received as income in kind by households and nonprofit institutions. It excludes purchases of dwellings but includes imputed rent for owner-occupied dwellings (see the note for Table 10 for details). In practice, it includes any statistical discrepancy in the use of resources. At constant prices, it also includes the rescaling deviation from partial rebasing, which is explained at the beginning of the technical notes.

Gross domestic investment consists of outlays on additions to the fixed assets of the economy plus net changes in the level of inventories.

Gross domestic savings are calculated by deducting total consumption from GDP.

Exports of goods and nonfactor services represent the value of all goods and nonfactor services provided to the rest of the world; they include merchandise, freight, insurance, travel, and other nonfactor services. The value of factor services, such as investment income, interest, and labor income, is excluded. Current transfers are also excluded.

The *resource balance* is the difference between exports of goods and nonfactor services and imports of goods and nonfactor services.

Partially rebased 1987 series in constant domestic currency units are used to compute the indicators in Table 8. Distribution of GDP in Table 9 is calculated from national accounts series in current domestic currency units.

The summary measures are calculated by the method explained in the note for Tables 2 and 3.

Table 10. Structure of consumption

Percentage shares of selected items in total household consumption expenditure are computed from details of GDP (expenditure at national market prices) defined in the U.N.'s *System of National Accounts* (SNA), mostly as collected from the International Comparison Program (ICP) Phases IV (1980) and V (1985). For countries not covered by the ICP, less detailed national accounts estimates are included, where available, in order to present a general idea of the broad structure of consumption. The data cover eighty-four countries (including Bank staff estimates for China) and refer to the most recent estimates, generally for 1980 and 1985. Where they refer to other years, the figures are shown in italics. *Consumption* here refers to private (nongovernment) consumption as defined in the SNA and in the notes for Tables 2 and 3, 4, and 9, except that education and medical care comprise government as well as private outlays. This ICP concept of "enhanced consumption" reflects who uses rather than who pays for consumption goods, and it improves international comparability because it is less sensitive to differing national practices regarding the financing of health and education services.

Cereals and tubers, a major subitem of *food*, comprise the main staple products: rice, flour, bread, all other cereals and cereal preparations, potatoes, yams, and other tubers. For high-income OECD members, however, this subitem does not include tubers. *Gross rents, fuel and power* consist of actual and imputed rents and repair and maintenance charges, as well as the subitem *fuel and power* (for heating, lighting, cooking, air conditioning, and so forth). Note that this item excludes energy used for transport (rarely reported to be more than 1 percent of total consumption in low- and middle-income economies). As mentioned, *medical care* and *education* include government as well as private consumption expenditure. *Transport and communication* also includes the purchase of *automobiles*, which are reported as a subitem. *Other consumption*, the residual group, includes beverages and tobacco, nondurable household goods and household services, recreational services, and services (including meals) supplied by hotels and restaurants; carry-out food is recorded here. It also includes the separately reported subitem *other consumer durables*, comprising household appliances, furniture, floor coverings, recreational equipment, and watches and jewelry.

Estimating the structure of consumption is one of the weakest aspects of national accounting in low- and middle-income economies. The structure is estimated through household expenditure surveys and similar survey techniques. It therefore shares any bias inherent in the sample frame. Since, conceptually, expenditure is not identical to consumption, other apparent discrepancies occur, and data for some countries should be treated with caution. For example, some countries limit surveys to urban areas or, even more narrowly, to capital cities. This tends to produce lower than average shares for food and high shares for transport and communication, gross rents, fuel and power, and other consumption. Controlled food prices and incomplete national accounting for subsistence activities also contribute to low food shares.

Table 11. Central government expenditure

The data on central government finance in Tables 11 and 12 are from the IMF *Government Finance Statistics Yearbook* (1990) and IMF data files. The accounts of each country are reported using the system of common definitions and classifications found in the IMF *Manual on Government Finance Statistics* (1986).

For complete and authoritative explanations of concepts, definitions, and data sources, see these IMF sources. The commentary that follows is intended mainly to place these data in the context of the broad range of indicators reported in this edition.

The shares of *total expenditure* and *current revenue* by category are calculated from series in national currencies. Because of differences in coverage of available data, the individual components of central government expenditure and current revenue shown in these tables may not be strictly comparable across all economies.

Moreover, inadequate statistical coverage of state, provincial, and local governments dictates the use of central government data; this may seriously understate or distort the statistical portrayal of the allocation of resources for various purposes, especially in countries where lower levels of government have considerable autonomy and are responsible for many economic and social services. In addition, "central government" can mean either of two accounting concepts: consolidated or budgetary. For most countries, central government finance data have been consolidated into one overall account, but for others only the budgetary central government accounts are available. Since all central government units are not always included in the budgetary accounts, the overall picture of central government activities is usually incomplete. Countries reporting budgetary data are footnoted.

Consequently, the data presented, especially those for education and health, are not comparable across countries. In many economies, private health and education services are substantial; in others, public services represent the major component of total expenditure but may be financed by lower levels of government. Caution should therefore be exercised in using the data for cross-country comparisons. Central government expenditure comprises the expenditure by all government offices, departments, establishments, and other bodies that are agencies or instruments of the central authority of a country. It includes both current and capital (development) expenditure.

Defense comprises all expenditure, whether by defense or other departments, on the maintenance of military forces, including the purchase of military supplies and equipment, construction, recruiting, and training. Also in this category are closely related items such as military aid programs. Defense does not include expenditure on public order and safety, which are classified separately.

Education comprises expenditure on the provision, management, inspection, and support of preprimary, primary, and secondary schools; of universities and colleges; and of vocational, technical, and other training institutions. Also included is expenditure on the general administration and regulation of the education system; on research into its objectives, organization, administration, and methods; and on such subsidiary services as transport, school meals, and school medical and dental services. Note that Table 10 provides an alternative measure of expenditure on education, private as well as public, relative to household consumption.

Health covers public expenditure on hospitals, maternity and dental centers, and clinics with a major medical component; on national health and medical insurance schemes; and on family planning and preventive care. Note that Table 10 also provides a measure of expenditure on medical care, private as well as public, relative to household consumption.

Housing, amenities; social security and welfare cover expenditure on housing (excluding interest subsidies, which are usually classified with "other") such as income-related schemes; on provision and support of housing and slum-clearance activities; on community development; and on sanitation services. These categories also cover compensation for loss of income to the sick and temporarily disabled; payments to the elderly, the permanently disabled, and the unemployed; family, maternity, and child allowances; and the cost of welfare services, such as care of the aged, the disabled, and children. Many expenditures relevant to environmental defense, such as pollution abatement, water supply, sanitary affairs, and refuse collection, are included indistinguishably in this category.

Economic services comprise expenditure associated with the regulation, support, and more efficient operation of business; economic development; redress of regional imbalances; and creation of employment opportunities. Research, trade promotion, geological surveys, and inspection and regulation of particular industry groups are among the activities included.

Other covers interest payments and items not included elsewhere; for a few economies it also includes amounts that could not be allocated to other components (or adjustments from accrual to cash accounts).

Total expenditure is more narrowly defined than the measure of general government consumption given in Table 9 because it excludes consumption expenditure by state and local governments. At the same time, central government expenditure is more broadly defined because it includes government's gross domestic investment and transfer payments.

Overall surplus/deficit is defined as current and capital revenue and official grants received, less total expenditure and lending minus repayments.

Table 12. Central government current revenue

Information on data sources and comparability is given in the note for Table 11. Current revenue by source is expressed as a percentage of *total current revenue*, which is the sum of tax revenue and nontax revenue and is calculated from national currencies.

Tax revenue comprises compulsory, unrequited, nonrepayable receipts for public purposes. It includes interest collected on tax arrears and penalties collected on nonpayment or late payment of taxes and is shown net of refunds and other corrective transactions. *Taxes on income, profit, and capital gains* are taxes levied on the actual or presumptive net income of individuals, on the profits of enterprises, and on capital gains, whether realized on land sales, securities, or other assets. Intragovernmental payments are eliminated in consolidation. *Social security contributions* include employers' and employees' social security contributions as well as those of self-employed and unemployed persons. *Domestic taxes on goods and services* include general sales and turnover or value added taxes, selective excises on goods, selective taxes on services, taxes on the use of goods or property, and profits of fiscal monopolies. *Taxes on international trade and transactions* include import duties, export duties, profits of export or import monopolies, exchange profits, and exchange taxes. *Other taxes* include employers' payroll or labor taxes, taxes on property, and taxes not allocable to other categories. They may include negative values that are adjustments, for instance, for taxes collected on behalf of state and local governments and not allocable to individual tax categories.

Nontax revenue comprises receipts that are not a compulsory nonrepayable payment for public purposes, such as fines, administrative fees, or entrepreneurial income from government ownership of property. Proceeds of grants and borrowing, funds arising from the repayment of previous lending by governments, incurrence of liabilities, and proceeds from the sale of capital assets are not included.

Table 13. Money and interest rates

The data on monetary holdings are based on the IMF's *International Financial Statistics* (IFS). *Monetary holdings, broadly defined,* comprise the monetary and quasi-monetary liabilities of a country's financial institutions to residents but not to the central government. For most countries, monetary holdings are the sum of money (IFS line 34) and quasi-money (IFS line 35). Money comprises the economy's means of payment: currency outside banks and demand deposits. Quasi-money comprises time and savings deposits and similar bank accounts that the issuer will readily exchange for money. Where nonmonetary financial institutions are important issuers of quasi-monetary liabilities, these are also included in the measure of monetary holdings.

The growth rates for monetary holdings are calculated from year-end figures, while the average of the year-end figures for the specified year and the previous year is used for the ratio of monetary holdings to GDP.

The *nominal interest rates of banks*, also from IFS, represent the rates paid by commercial or similar banks to holders of their quasi-monetary liabilities (deposit rate) and charged by the banks on loans to prime customers (lending rate). The data are, however, of limited international comparability, partly because coverage and definitions vary and partly because countries differ in the scope available to banks for adjusting interest rates to reflect market conditions.

Because interest rates (and growth rates for monetary holdings) are expressed in nominal terms, much of the variation among countries stems from differences in inflation. For easy reference, the Table 1 indicator of recent inflation is repeated in this table.

Table 14. Growth of merchandise trade

The main data source for current trade values is the U.N. Commodity Trade (Comtrade) data file supplemented by World Bank estimates. The statistics on merchandise trade are based on countries' customs returns.

Merchandise *exports* and *imports*, with some exceptions, cover international movements of goods across customs borders; trade in services is not included. Exports are valued f.o.b. (free on board) and imports c.i.f. (cost, insurance, and freight) unless otherwise specified in the foregoing sources. These values are in current dollars.

The growth rates of merchandise exports and imports are based on constant price data, which are obtained from export or import value data as deflated by the corresponding price index. The World Bank uses its own price indexes, which are based on international prices for primary commodities and unit value indexes for manufactures. These price indexes are country-specific and disaggregated by broad commodity groups. This ensures consistency between data for a group of countries and those for individual countries. Such consistency will increase as the World Bank continues to improve its trade price indexes for an increasing number of countries. These growth rates can differ from those derived from national practices because national price indexes may use different base years and weighting procedures from those used by the World Bank.

The *terms of trade*, or the net barter terms of trade, measure the relative movement of export prices against that of import prices. Calculated as the ratio of a country's index of average export prices to its average import price index, this indicator shows changes over a base year in the level of export prices as a percentage of import prices. The terms of trade index numbers are shown for 1985 and 1990, where 1987 = 100. The price indexes are from the source cited above for the growth rates of exports and imports.

The summary measures for the growth rates are calculated by aggregating the 1987 constant U.S. dollar price series for each year and then applying the least-squares growth rate procedure for the periods shown.

Tables 15 and 16. Structure of merchandise imports and exports

The shares in these tables are derived from trade values in current dollars reported in the U.N. trade data system and the U.N.'s *Yearbook of International Trade Statistics*, supplemented by World Bank estimates, as explained in the technical note for Table 14.

Merchandise *exports* and *imports* are also defined in that note.

The categorization of exports and imports follows the *Standard International Trade Classification* (SITC), Series M, No. 34, Revision 1. For some countries, data for certain commodity categories are unavailable and the full breakdown cannot be shown.

In Table 15, *food* commodities are those in SITC Sections 0, 1, and 4 and Division 22 (food and live animals, beverages, oils and fats, and oilseeds and nuts) excluding Division 12, tobacco, which is included in *other primary commodities*; thus the data are not strictly comparable with those published last year, particularly if tobacco is a major import item. *Fuels* are the commodities in SITC Section 3 (mineral fuels, and lubricants and related materials). *Other primary commodities* comprise SITC Section 2 (crude materials, excluding fuels), less Division 22 (oilseeds and nuts), plus Division 12 (tobacco) and Division 68 (nonferrous metals). *Machinery and transport equipment* are the commodities in SITC Section 7. *Other manufactures*, calculated residually from the total value of manufactured imports, represent SITC Sections 5 through 9, less Section 7 and Division 68.

In Table 16, *fuels, minerals, and metals* are the commodities in SITC Section 3 (mineral fuels, and lubricants and related materials), Divisions 27 and 28 (minerals and crude fertilizers, and metalliferous ores), and Division 68 (nonferrous metals). *Other primary commodities* comprise SITC Sections 0, 1, 2, and 4 (food and live animals, beverages and tobacco, inedible crude materials, oils, fats, and waxes), less Divisions 27 and 28. *Machinery and transport equipment* are the commodities in SITC Section 7. *Other manufactures* represent SITC Sections 5 through 9, less Section 7 and Division 68. *Textiles and clothing*, representing SITC Divisions 65 and 84 (textiles, yarns, fabrics, and clothing), are a subgroup of *other manufactures*.

The summary measures in Table 15 are weighted by total merchandise imports of individual countries in current dollars; those in Table 16 by total merchandise exports of individual countries in current dollars. (See the technical note for Table 14.)

Table 17. OECD imports of manufactured goods: origin and composition

The data are from the United Nations, reported by high-income OECD economies, which are the OECD members excluding Greece, Portugal, and Turkey.

The table reports the value of *imports of manufactures* of high-income OECD countries by the economy of origin, and the composition of such imports by major manufactured product groups.

The table replaces one in past editions on the origin and destination of manufactured exports, which was based on exports reported by individual economies. Since there was a lag of several years in reporting by many developing economies, estimates based on various sources were used to fill the gaps. Until these estimates can be improved, the current table, based on up-to-date and consistent but less comprehensive data, is included instead. Manufactured imports of the predominant markets from individual economies are the best available proxy of the magnitude and composition of the manufactured exports of these economies to all destinations taken together.

Manufactured goods are the commodities in the *Standard International Trade Classification* (SITC), Revision 1, Sections 5 through 9 (chemical and related products, basic manufactures, manufactured articles, machinery and transport equipment, and other manufactured articles and goods not elsewhere classified), excluding Division 68 (nonferrous metals). This definition is somewhat broader than the one used to define exporters of manufactures.

The major manufactured product groups reported are defined as follows: *textiles and clothing* (SITC Sections 65 and 84), *chemicals* (SITC Section 5), *electrical machinery and electronics* (SITC Section 72), *transport equipment* (SITC Section 73), and *others*, defined as the residual. SITC Revision 1 data are used for the year 1970, whereas the equivalent data in Revision 2 are used for the year 1990.

Table 18. Balance of payments and reserves

The statistics for this table are mostly as reported by the IMF but do include recent estimates by World Bank staff and, in rare instances, the Bank's own coverage or classification adjustments to enhance international comparability. Values in this table are in U.S. dollars converted at current exchange rates.

The *current account balance after official transfers* is the difference between (a) exports of goods and services (factor and nonfactor) as well as inflows of unrequited transfers (private and official) and (b) imports of goods and services as well as all unrequited transfers to the rest of the world.

The current account balance before official transfers is the current account balance that treats net official unrequited transfers as akin to official capital movements. The difference between the two balance of payments measures is essentially foreign aid in the form of grants, technical assistance, and food aid, which, for most developing countries, tends to make current account deficits smaller than the financing requirement.

Net workers' remittances cover payments and receipts of income by migrants who are employed or expect to be employed for more than a year in their new economy, where they are considered residents. These remittances are classified as private unrequited transfers and are included in the balance of payments current account balance, whereas those derived from shorter-term stays are included in services as labor income. The distinction accords with internationally agreed guidelines, but many developing countries classify workers' remittances as a factor income receipt (hence, a component of GNP). The World Bank adheres to international guidelines in defining GNP and, therefore, may differ from national practices.

Gross international reserves comprise holdings of monetary gold, special drawing rights (SDRs), the reserve position of members in the IMF, and holdings of foreign exchange under the control of monetary authorities. The data on holdings of international reserves are from IMF data files. The gold component of these reserves is valued throughout at year-end (December 31) London prices: that is, $37.37 an ounce in 1970 and $385.00 an ounce in 1990. The reserve levels for 1970 and 1990 refer to the end of the year indicated and are in current dollars at prevailing exchange rates. Because of differences in the definition of international reserves, in the valuation of gold, and in reserve management practices, the levels of reserve holdings published in national sources do not have strictly comparable significance. Reserve holdings at the end of 1990 are also expressed in terms of the number of months of imports of goods and services they could pay for.

The summary measures are computed from group aggregates for gross international reserves and total imports of goods and services in current dollars.

Table 19. Official development assistance from OECD and OPEC members

Official development assistance (ODA) consists of net disbursements of loans and grants made on concessional financial terms by official agencies of the members of the Development Assistance Committee (DAC) of the Organization for Economic Cooperation and Development (OECD) and members of the Organization of Petroleum Exporting Countries (OPEC) to promote economic development and welfare. Although this definition is meant to exclude purely military assistance, the borderline is sometimes blurred; the definition used by the country of origin usually prevails. ODA also includes the value of technical cooperation and assistance. All data shown are supplied by the OECD, and all U.S. dollar values are converted at official exchange rates.

Total net flows are net disbursements to developing countries and multilateral institutions. The disbursements to multilateral institutions are now reported for all DAC members on the basis of the date of issue of notes; some DAC members previously reported on the basis of the date of encashment. *Total net bilateral flows to low-income economies* exclude unallocated bilateral flows and all disbursements to multilateral institutions.

The nominal values shown in the summary for ODA from high-income OECD countries are converted at 1987 prices using the dollar GDP deflator. This deflator is based on price increases in OECD countries (excluding Greece, Portugal, and Turkey) measured in dollars. It takes into account the parity changes between the dollar and national currencies. For example, when the dollar depreciates, price changes measured in national currencies have to be adjusted upward by the amount of the depreciation to obtain price changes in dollars.

The table, in addition to showing totals for OPEC, shows totals for the Organization of Arab Petroleum Exporting Countries (OAPEC). The donor members of OAPEC are Algeria, Iraq, Kuwait, Libya, Qatar, Saudi Arabia, and United Arab Emirates. ODA data for OPEC and OAPEC are also obtained from the OECD.

Table 20. Official development assistance: receipts

Net disbursements of ODA from all sources consist of loans and grants made on concessional financial terms by all bilateral official agencies and multilateral sources to promote economic development and welfare. They include the value of technical cooperation and assistance. The disbursements shown in this table are not strictly comparable with those shown in Table 19 since the receipts are from all sources; disbursements in Table 19 refer only to those made by high-income members of the OECD and members of OPEC. Net disbursements equal gross disbursements less payments to the originators of aid for amortization of past aid receipts. Net disbursements of ODA are shown per capita and as a percentage of GNP.

The summary measures of per capita ODA are computed from group aggregates for population and for ODA. Summary measures for ODA as a percentage of GNP are computed from group totals for ODA and for GNP in current U.S. dollars.

Table 21. Total external debt

The data on debt in this and successive tables are from the World Bank Debtor Reporting System, supplemented by World Bank estimates. That system is concerned solely with developing economies and does not collect data on external debt for other groups of borrowers or from economies that are not members of the World Bank. The dollar figures on debt shown in Tables 21 through 25 are in U.S. dollars converted at official exchange rates.

The data on debt include private nonguaranteed debt reported by twenty-six developing countries and complete or partial estimates for an additional twenty-one others that do not report but for which this type of debt is known to be significant.

Public loans are the external obligations of public debtors, including the national government, its agencies, and autonomous public bodies. *Publicly guaranteed loans* are the external obligations of private debtors that are guaranteed for repayment by a public entity. These two categories are aggregated in the tables. *Private nonguaranteed loans* are the external obligations of private debtors that are not guaranteed for repayment by a public entity.

Use of IMF credit denotes repurchase obligations to the IMF for all uses of IMF resources, excluding those resulting from drawings in the reserve tranche. It is shown for the end of the year specified. It comprises purchases outstanding under the credit tranches, including enlarged access resources, and all special facilities (the buffer stock, compensatory financing, extended fund, and oil facilities), Trust Fund loans, and operations under the enhanced structural adjustment facilities. Use of IMF credit outstanding at year-end (a stock) is converted to U.S. dollars at the dollar-SDR exchange rate in effect at year-end.

Short-term debt is debt with an original maturity of one year or less. Available data permit no distinctions between public and private nonguaranteed short-term debt.

Total external debt is defined for the purpose of this Report as the sum of public, publicly guaranteed, and private nonguaranteed long-term debt, use of IMF credit, and short-term debt.

Table 22. Flow of public and private external capital

Data on disbursements, repayment of principal (amortization), and payment of interest are for public, publicly guaranteed, and private nonguaranteed long-term loans.

Disbursements are drawings on long-term loan commitments during the year specified.

Repayment of principal is the actual amount of principal (amortization) paid in foreign currency, goods, or services in the year specified.

Interest payments are actual amounts of interest paid in foreign currency, goods, or services in the year specified.

Table 23. Aggregate net resource flows and net transfers

Net flows on long-term debt are disbursements less the repayment of principal on public, publicly guaranteed, and private nonguaranteed long-term debt. *Official grants* are transfers made by an official agency in cash or in kind in respect of which no legal debt is incurred by the recipient. Data on official grants exclude grants for technical assistance.

Net foreign direct investment is defined as investment that is made to acquire a lasting interest (usually 10 percent of the voting stock) in an enterprise operating in a country other than that of the investor (defined according to residency), the investor's purpose being an effective voice in the management of the enterprise. *Aggregate net resource flows* are the sum of net flows on long-term debt (excluding IMF) plus official grants (excluding technical assistance) and net foreign direct investment. *Aggregate net transfers* are equal to aggregate net resource flows minus interest payments on long-term loans and remittance of all profits.

Table 24. Total external debt ratios

Total external debt as a percentage of exports of goods and services represents public, publicly guaranteed, private nonguaranteed long-term debt, use of IMF credit, and short-term debt drawn at year-end, net of repayments of principal and write-offs. Throughout this table, goods and services include workers' remittances. For estimating *total external debt as a percentage of GNP*, the debt figures are converted into U.S. dollars from currencies of repayment at year-end official exchange rates. GNP is converted from national currencies to U.S. dollars by applying the conversion procedure described in the technical note for Tables 2 and 3.

Total debt service as a percentage of goods and services is the sum of principal repayments and interest payments on total external debt (as defined in the note for Table 21). It is one of several conventional measures used to assess a country's ability to service debt.

Interest payments as a percentage of exports of goods and services are actual payments made on total external debt.

The summary measures are weighted by exports of goods and services in current dollars and by GNP in current dollars, respectively.

Table 25. Terms of external public borrowing

Commitments refer to the public and publicly guaranteed loans for which contracts were signed in the year specified. They are reported in currencies of repayment and converted into U.S. dollars at average annual official exchange rates.

Figures for *interest rates, maturities,* and *grace periods* are averages weighted by the amounts of the loans. Interest is the major charge levied on a loan and is usually computed on the amount of principal drawn and outstanding. The maturity of a loan is the interval between the agreement date, when a loan agreement is signed or bonds are issued, and the date of final repayment of principal. The grace period is the interval between the agreement date and the date of the first repayment of principal.

Public loans with variable interest rates, as a percentage of public debt, refer to interest rates that float with movements in a key market rate; for example, the London interbank offered rate (LIBOR) or the U.S. prime rate. This column shows the borrower's exposure to changes in international interest rates.

The summary measures in this table are weighted by the amounts of the loans.

Table 26. Population growth and projections

Population growth rates are period averages calculated from midyear populations.

Population estimates for mid-1990 and estimates of fertility and mortality are made by the World Bank from data provided by the U.N. Population Division, the U.N. Statistical Office, and country statistical offices. Estimates take into account the results of the latest population censuses, which in some cases are neither recent nor accurate. Note that refugees not permanently settled in the country of asylum are generally considered to be part of the population of their country of origin.

The projections of population for 2000, 2025, and the year in which the population will eventually become stationary (see definition below) are made for each economy separately. Information on total population by age and sex, fertility, mortality, and international migration is projected on the basis of generalized assumptions until the population becomes stationary.

A stationary population is one in which age- and sex-specific mortality rates have not changed over a long period, and during which fertility rates have remained at replacement level; that is, when the net

reproduction rate (defined in the note for Table 27) equals 1. In such a population, the birth rate is constant and equal to the death rate, the age structure is constant, and the growth rate is zero.

Population projections are made age cohort by age cohort. Mortality, fertility, and migration are projected separately, and the results are applied iteratively to the 1985 base-year age structure. For the projection period 1985 to 2005, the changes in mortality are country specific: increments in life expectancy and decrements in infant mortality are based on previous trends for each country. When female secondary school enrollment is high, mortality is assumed to decline more quickly. Infant mortality is projected separately from adult mortality. Note that the data reflect the potentially significant impact of the human immunodeficiency virus (HIV) epidemic.

Projected fertility rates are also based on previous trends. For countries in which fertility has started to decline (termed "fertility transition"), this trend is assumed to continue. It has been observed that no country where the population has a life expectancy of less than 50 years has experienced a fertility decline; for these countries fertility transition is delayed, and then the average decline of the group of countries in fertility transition is applied. Countries with below-replacement fertility are assumed to have constant total fertility rates until 1995–2000 and then to regain replacement level by 2030.

International migration rates are based on past and present trends in migration flows and migration policy. Among the sources consulted are estimates and projections made by national statistical offices, international agencies, and research institutions. Because of the uncertainty of future migration trends, it is assumed in the projections that net migration rates will reach zero by 2025.

The estimates of the size of the stationary population are very long-term projections. They are included only to show the implications of recent fertility and mortality trends on the basis of generalized assumptions. A fuller description of the methods and assumptions used to calculate the estimates is contained in the forthcoming, 1992–93 edition of *World Population Projections*.

Table 27. Demography and fertility

The *crude birth rate* and *crude death rate* indicate respectively the number of live births and deaths occurring per thousand population in a year. They come from the sources mentioned in the note to Table 26.

Women of childbearing age are those from age 15 to 49.

The *total fertility rate* represents the number of children that would be born to a woman if she were to live to the end of her childbearing years and bear children at each age in accordance with prevailing age-specific fertility rates. The rates given are from the sources mentioned in the note for Table 26.

The *net reproduction rate* (NRR), which measures the number of daughters a newborn girl will bear during her lifetime, assuming fixed age-specific fertility and mortality rates, reflects the extent to which a cohort of newborn girls will reproduce themselves. An NRR of 1 indicates that fertility is at replacement level: at this rate women will bear, on average, only enough daughters to replace themselves in the population. As with the size of the stationary population, the assumed year of reaching replacement-level fertility is speculative and should not be regarded as a prediction.

Married women of childbearing age using contraception are women who are practicing, or whose husbands are practicing, any form of contraception. Contraceptive usage is generally measured for women age 15 to 49. A few countries use measures relating to other age groups, especially 15 to 44.

Data are mainly derived from demographic and health surveys, contraceptive prevalence surveys, World Bank country data, and Mauldin and Segal's article "Prevalence of Contraceptive Use: Trends and Issues" in volume 19 of *Studies in Family Planning* (1988). For a few countries for which no survey data are available, and for several African countries, program statistics are used. Program statistics may understate contraceptive prevalence because they do not measure use of methods such as rhythm, withdrawal, or abstinence, nor use of contraceptives not obtained through the official family planning program. The data refer to rates prevailing in a variety of years, generally not more than two years before the year specified in the table.

All summary measures are country data weighted by each country's share in the aggregate population.

Table 28. Health and nutrition

The estimates of *population per physician* and *per nursing person* are derived from World Health Organization (WHO) data and are supplemented by data obtained directly by the World Bank from national sources. The data refer to a variety of years, generally no more than two years before the year specified. The figure for physicians, in addition to the total number of registered practitioners in the country, includes medical assistants whose medical training is less than that of qualified physicians but who nevertheless dispense similar medical services, including simple operations. Nursing persons include graduate, practical, assistant, and auxiliary nurses, as well as paraprofessional personnel such as health workers,

first aid workers, traditional birth attendants, and so on. The inclusion of auxiliary and paraprofessional personnel provides more realistic estimates of available nursing care. Because definitions of doctors and nursing personnel vary—and because the data shown are for a variety of years—the data for these two indicators are not strictly comparable across countries.

Data on *births attended by health staff* show the percentage of births recorded where a recognized health service worker was in attendance. The data are from WHO, supplemented by UNICEF data. They are based on national sources, derived mostly from official community reports and hospital records; some reflect only births in hospitals and other medical institutions. Sometimes smaller private and rural hospitals are excluded, and sometimes even relatively primitive local facilities are included. The coverage is therefore not always comprehensive, and the figures should be treated with extreme caution.

Babies with low birth weight are children born weighing less than 2,500 grams. Low birth weight is frequently associated with maternal malnutrition and tends to raise the risk of infant mortality and lead to poor growth in infancy and childhood, thus increasing the incidence of other forms of retarded development. The figures are derived from both WHO and UNICEF sources and are based on national data. The data are not strictly comparable across countries since they are compiled from a combination of surveys and administrative records that may not have representative national coverage.

The *infant mortality rate* is the number of infants who die before reaching one year of age, per thousand live births in a given year. The data are from the U.N. publication *Mortality of Children under Age 5: Projections, 1950–2025* as well as from the World Bank.

The *daily calorie supply (per capita)* is calculated by dividing the calorie equivalent of the food supplies in an economy by the population. Food supplies comprise domestic production, imports less exports, and changes in stocks; they exclude animal feed, seeds for use in agriculture, and food lost in processing and distribution. These estimates are from the Food and Agriculture Organization.

The summary measures in this table are country figures weighted by each country's share in the aggregate population.

Table 29. Education

The data in this table refer to a variety of years, generally not more than two years distant from those specified; however, figures for females sometimes refer to a year earlier than that for overall totals. The data are mostly from Unesco.

Primary school enrollment data are estimates of children of all ages enrolled in primary school. Figures are expressed as the ratio of pupils to the population of school-age children. Although many countries consider primary school age to be 6 to 11 years, others do not. For some countries with universal primary education, the gross enrollment ratios may exceed 100 percent because some pupils are younger or older than the country's standard primary school age.

The data on *secondary* school enrollment are calculated in the same manner, but again the definition of secondary school age differs among countries. It is most commonly considered to be 12 to 17 years. Late entry of more mature students as well as repetition and the phenomenon of "bunching" in final grades can influence these ratios.

The *tertiary* enrollment ratio is calculated by dividing the number of pupils enrolled in all post-secondary schools and universities by the population in the 20–24 age group. Pupils attending vocational schools, adult education programs, two-year community colleges, and distance education centers (primarily correspondence courses) are included. The distribution of pupils across these different types of institutions varies among countries. The youth population—that is, 20 to 24 years—has been adopted by Unesco as the denominator since it represents an average tertiary level cohort even though people above and below this age group may be registered in tertiary institutions.

Primary net enrollment is the percentage of school-age children who are enrolled in school. Unlike gross enrollment, the net ratios correspond to the country's primary-school age group. This indicator gives a much clearer idea of how many children in the age group are actually enrolled in school, without the number being inflated by over- (or under-) age children.

The *primary pupil-teacher ratio* is the number of pupils enrolled in school in a country, divided by the number of teachers in the education system.

The summary measures in this table are country enrollment rates weighted by each country's share in the aggregate population.

Table 30. Income distribution and ICP estimates of GDP

The first three columns of this table contain the results of the U.N. International Comparisons Program (ICP), this year combined with World Bank staff estimates for countries not covered in the most recent ICP study, Phase V for 1985. The rest of the table reports distribution of income or expenditure accruing to percentile groups of households ranked by to-

tal household income, per capita income, or expenditure.

The 1985 indexed figures on GDP per capita (US=100) are presented in the first column. They include: (i) preliminary results of ICP Phase V for 1985; (ii) the latest available results from either ICP Phase III for 1975 or Phase IV for 1980 extrapolated to 1985 for countries that participated in only the earlier phases; and (iii) estimates obtained by regression for countries that did not participate in any of the phases. Economies whose 1985 figures are extrapolated from earlier work or imputed by regression are footnoted accordingly.

The blend of actual, extrapolated and regression-based 1985 figures underlying the first column is extrapolated to 1990 using World Bank estimates of real per capita GDP growth and expressed as an index (US=100) in the second column. These are converted to 1990 "international dollars" in the third column by scaling all results up by the U.S. inflation rate between 1985 and 1990. The adjustment does not take account of changes in the terms of trade.

ICP recasts traditional national accounts through special price collections and disaggregation of GDP by expenditure components. ICP details are prepared by national statistical offices, and the results are coordinated by the U.N. Statistical Office (UNSO) with support from other international agencies, particularly the Statistical Office of the European Communities (Eurostat) and the Organization for Economic Cooperation and Development (OECD). The World Bank, the Economic Commission for Europe (ECE), and the Economic and Social Commission for Asia and the Pacific (ESCAP) also contribute to this exercise. A total of sixty-four countries participated in ICP Phase V, and preliminary results are now available for fifty-seven. For one country (Nepal), total GDP data were not available, and comparisons were made for consumption only. Luxembourg and Swaziland, two economies with populations under 1 million (for which Table 1 indicators are reported, in Box A.1), have participated in ICP; their 1985 results, as a percentage of the U.S. results, are 81.3 and 13.6, respectively. More comprehensive ICP results for 1985 (including several Caribbean countries) are expected to be available in 1992. The figures given here are subject to change and should be regarded as indicative only.

The "international dollar" (I$) has the same purchasing power over total GDP as the U.S. dollar in a given year, but purchasing power over subaggregates is determined by average international prices at that level rather than by U.S. relative prices. These dollar values, which are different from the dollar values of GNP or GDP shown in Tables 1 and 3 (see the technical notes for these tables), are obtained by special conversion factors designed to equalize the purchasing powers of currencies in the respective countries. This conversion factor, commonly known as the Purchasing Power Parity (PPP), is defined as the number of units of a country's currency required to buy the same amounts of goods and services in the domestic market as one dollar would buy in the United States. The computation involves deriving implicit quantities from national accounts expenditure data and specially collected price data, and then revaluing the implicit quantities in each country at a single set of average prices. The average price index thus equalizes dollar prices in every country so that cross-country comparisons of GDP based on them reflect differences in quantities of goods and services free of price-level differentials. This procedure is designed to bring cross-country comparisons in line with cross-time real value comparisons that are based on constant price series.

The ICP Phase V figures presented here are the results of a two-step exercise. Countries within a region or group such as the OECD are first compared using their own group average prices. Next, since group average prices may differ from each other, making the countries belonging to different groups not comparable, the group prices are adjusted to make them comparable at the world level. The adjustments, done by UNSO, are based on price differentials observed in a network of ''link'' countries representing each group. However, the linking is done in a manner that retains in the world comparison the relative levels of GDP observed in the group comparisons, called ''fixity.''

The two-step process was adopted because the relative GDP levels and rankings of two countries may change when more countries are brought into the comparison. It was felt that this should not be allowed to happen within geographic regions; that is, that the relationship of, say, Ghana and Senegal should not be affected by the prices prevailing in the United States. Thus overall GDP per capita levels are calculated at ''regional'' prices and then linked together. The linking is done by revaluing GDPs of all the countries at average ''world'' prices and reallocating the new regional totals on the basis of each country's share in the original comparison.

Such a method does not permit the comparison of more detailed quantities (such as food consumption). Hence these subaggregates and more detailed expenditure categories are calculated using world prices. These quantities are indeed comparable internationally, but they do not add up to the indicated GDPs because they are calculated at a different set of prices.

Some countries belong to several regional groups. A few of the groups have priority; others are equal.

Thus fixity is always maintained between members of the European Communities, even within the OECD and world comparison. For Austria and Finland, however, the bilateral relationship that prevails within the OECD comparison is also the one used within the global comparison. But a significantly different relationship (based on Central European prices) prevails in the comparison within that group, and this is the relationship presented in the separate publication of the European comparison.

To derive ICP-based 1985 figures for countries that are yet to participate in any ICP survey, an estimating equation is first obtained by fitting the following regression to 1985 data:

$$\ln (r) = .5726 \ln (\text{ATLAS}) + .3466 \ln (\text{ENROL}) + .3865;$$
$$\quad\quad (.0319) \quad\quad\quad (.0540) \quad\quad\quad\quad (.1579)$$
$$\text{RMSE} = .2240; \text{ Adj.R-Sq} = .9523; \text{ N}=76$$

where all variables and estimated values are expressed as US=100;

r = ICP estimates of per capita GDP converted to U.S. dollars by PPP, the array of r consisting of all 1985 actual ICP values and extrapolations of the latest available ICP numbers for countries that participated in the 1980 or 1975 exercise but not in 1985;
ATLAS = per capita GNP estimated by the *Atlas* method;
ENROL = secondary school enrollment; and
RMSE = root mean squared error.

ATLAS and ENROL are used as rough proxies of inter-country wage differentials for unskilled and skilled human capital, respectively. Following Isenman (see Paul Isenman, ''Inter-Country Comparisons of 'Real' (PPP) Incomes: Revised Estimates and Unresolved Questions,'' in *World Development*, 1980, vol. 8, pp. 61–72), the rationale adopted here is that ICP and conventional estimates of GDP differ mainly because wage differences persist among nations due to constraints on the international mobility of labor. A technical paper providing fuller explanation is available on request. For further details on ICP procedures, readers may consult the ICP Phase IV report, *World Comparisons of Purchasing Power and Real Product for 1980* (New York: United Nations, 1986).

The income distribution data cover rural and urban areas for all countries. The data refer to different years between 1979 and 1989 and are drawn from a variety of sources. These include the Economic Commission for Latin America and the Caribbean, the Luxembourg Income Study, the OECD, the U.N.'s *National Accounts Statistics: Compendium of Income Distribution Statistics, 1985*, the World Bank, and national sources. Data for many countries have been updated, and some of the income distribution data previously published have been deleted because they refer to years long past.

In many countries the collection of income distribution data is not systematically organized or integrated with the official statistical system. The data are derived from surveys designed for other purposes, most often consumer expenditure surveys, that also collect information on income. These surveys use a variety of income concepts and sample designs, and in many cases their geographic coverage is too limited to provide reliable nationwide estimates of income distribution. Although the data presented here represent the best available estimates, they do not avoid all these problems and should be interpreted with caution.

Similarly, the scope of the indicator is limited for certain countries, and data for other countries are not fully comparable. Because households vary in size, a distribution in which households are ranked according to per capita household income, rather than according to total household income, is superior for many purposes. The distinction is important because households with low per capita incomes frequently are large households, whose total income may be high, whereas many households with low household incomes may be small households with high per capita income. Information on the distribution of per capita household income exists for only a few countries and is infrequently updated. Where possible, distributions are ranked according to per capita income; more often they are ranked by household income, with others ranked by per capita expenditure or household expenditure. Since the size of household is likely to be small for low-income households (for instance, single-person households and couples without children), the distribution of household income may overstate the income inequality. Also, since household savings tend to increase faster as income levels increase, the distribution of expenditure is inclined to understate the income inequality. The World Bank's Living Standards Measurement Study and the Social Dimensions of Adjustment project (the latter covering Sub-Saharan African countries) are assisting a few countries in improving their collection and analysis of data on income distribution.

Table 31. Urbanization

Data on urban population and agglomeration in large cities are from the U.N.'s *World Urbanization Prospects,* supplemented by data from the World Bank. The growth rates of urban population are calculated from the World Bank's population estimates; the estimates of urban population shares are calculated from both sources just cited.

Because the estimates in this table are based on different national definitions of what is urban, cross-country comparisons should be made with caution.

The summary measures for urban population as a percentage of total population are calculated from country percentages weighted by each country's share in the aggregate population; the other summary measures in this table are weighted in the same fashion, using urban population.

Table 32. Women in development

This table provides some basic indicators disaggregated to show differences between the sexes that illustrate the condition of women in society. The measures reflect the demographic status of women and their access to health and education services. Statistical anomalies become even more apparent when social indicators are analyzed by gender, because reporting systems are often weak in areas related specifically to women. Indicators drawn from censuses and surveys, such as those on population, tend to be about as reliable for women as for men; but indicators based largely on administrative records, such as maternal and infant mortality, are less reliable. More resources are now being devoted to developing better information on these topics, but the reliability of data, even in the series shown, still varies significantly.

The *under-5 mortality rate* shows the probability of a newborn baby dying before reaching age 5. The rates are derived from life tables based on estimated current life expectancy at birth and on infant mortality rates. In general, throughout the world more males are born than females. Under good nutritional and health conditions and in times of peace, male children under 5 have a higher death rate than females. These columns show that female-male differences in the risk of dying by age 5 vary substantially. In industrial market economies, female babies have a 23 percent lower risk of dying by age 5 than male babies; the risk of dying by age 5 is actually higher for females than for males in some lower-income economies. This suggests differential treatment of males and females with respect to food and medical care.

Such discrimination particularly affects very young girls, who may get a smaller share of scarce food or receive less prompt costly medical attention. This pattern of discrimination is not uniformly associated with development. There are low- and middle-income countries (and regions within countries) where the risk of dying by age 5 for females relative to males approximates the pattern found in industrial countries. In many other countries, however, the numbers starkly demonstrate the need to associate women more closely with development. The health and welfare indicators in both Table 28 and in this table's maternal mortality column draw attention, in particular, to the conditions associated with childbearing.

This activity still carries the highest risk of death for women of reproductive age in developing countries. The indicators reflect, but do not measure, both the availability of health services for women and the general welfare and nutritional status of mothers.

Life expectancy at birth is defined in the note to Table 1.

Maternal mortality refers to the number of female deaths that occur during childbirth per 100,000 live births. Because deaths during childbirth are defined more widely in some countries to include complications of pregnancy or the period after childbirth, or of abortion, and because many pregnant women die from lack of suitable health care, maternal mortality is difficult to measure consistently and reliably across countries. The data in these two series are drawn from diverse national sources and collected by the World Health Organization (WHO), although many national administrative systems are weak and do not record vital events in a systematic way. The data are derived mostly from official community reports and hospital records, and some reflect only deaths in hospitals and other medical institutions. Sometimes smaller private and rural hospitals are excluded, and sometimes even relatively primitive local facilities are included. The coverage is therefore not always comprehensive, and the figures should be treated with extreme caution.

Clearly, many maternal deaths go unrecorded, particularly in countries with remote rural populations; this accounts for some of the very low numbers shown in the table, especially for several African countries. Moreover, it is not clear whether an increase in the number of mothers in hospital reflects more extensive medical care for women or more complications in pregnancy and childbirth because of poor nutrition, for instance. (Table 28 shows data on low birth weight.)

These time series attempt to bring together readily available information not always presented in international publications. WHO warns that there are inevitably gaps in the series, and it has invited countries to provide more comprehensive figures. They are reproduced here, from the 1986 WHO publication *Maternal Mortality Rates*, supplemented by the UNICEF publication *The State of the World's Children 1989*, as part of the international effort to highlight data in this field. The data refer to any year from 1977 to 1984.

The *education* indicators, based on Unesco sources, show the extent to which females have equal access to schooling.

Percentage of cohort persisting to grade 4 is the percentage of children starting primary school in 1970 and 1985, respectively, who continued to the fourth grade by 1973 and 1988. Figures in italics represent

earlier or later cohorts. The data are based on enrollment records. The slightly higher persistence ratios for females in some African countries may indicate male participation in activities such as animal herding.

All things being equal, and opportunities being the same, the ratios for *females per 100 males* should be close to 100. However, inequalities may cause the ratios to move in different directions. For example, the number of females per 100 males will rise at secondary school level if male attendance declines more rapidly in the final grades because of males' greater job opportunities, conscription into the army, or migration in search of work. In addition, since the numbers in these columns refer mainly to general secondary education, they do not capture those (mostly males) enrolled in technical and vocational schools or in full-time apprenticeships, as in Eastern Europe.

All summary measures are country data weighted by each country's share in the aggregate population.

Table 33. Forests, protected areas, and water resources

This table on natural resources represents a step toward including environmental data in the assessment of development and the planning of economic strategies. It provides a partial picture of the status of forests, the extent of areas protected for conservation or other environmentally related purposes, and the availability and use of fresh water. The data reported here are drawn from the most authoritative sources available. Perhaps even more than other data in this Report, however, these data should be used with caution. Although they accurately characterize major differences in resources and uses among countries, true comparability is limited because of variation in data collection, statistical methods, definitions, and government resources.

No conceptual framework has yet been agreed upon that integrates natural resource and traditional economic data. Nor are the measures shown in this table intended to be final indicators of natural resource wealth, environmental health, or resource depletion. They have been chosen because they are available for most countries, are testable, and reflect some general conditions of the environment.

The *total area* of forest refers to the total natural stands of woody vegetation in which trees predominate. These estimates are derived from country statistics assembled by the Food and Agriculture Organization (FAO) in 1980. Some of them are based on more recent inventories or satellite-based assessments performed during the 1980s. In 1992 the FAO will complete and publish an assessment of world forest extent and health that should modify some of these estimates substantially. The total area of *closed* forest refers to those forest areas where trees cover a high proportion of the ground and there is no continuous ground cover. Closed forest, for members of the Economic Commission for Europe (ECE), however, is defined as those forest areas where tree crowns cover more than 20 percent of the area. These natural stands do not include tree plantations. More recent estimates of total forest cover are available for some countries. Total forest area in the Philippines was estimated to be between 68,000 and 71,000 square kilometers in 1987. The most recent estimate for Malaysia is 185,000 square kilometers.

Total annual deforestation refers to both closed and open forest. Open forest is defined as at least a 10 percent tree cover with a continuous ground cover. In the ECE countries, open forest has 5–20 percent crown cover or a mixture of bush and stunted trees. Deforestation is defined as the permanent conversion of forest land to other uses, including pasture, shifting cultivation, mechanized agriculture, or infrastructure development. Deforested areas do not include areas logged but intended for regeneration, nor areas degraded by fuelwood gathering, acid precipitation, or forest fires. In temperate industrialized countries the permanent conversion of remaining forest to other uses is relatively rare. Assessments of annual deforestation, both in open and closed forest, are difficult to make and are usually undertaken as special studies. The estimates shown here for 1981–85 were calculated in 1980, projecting the rate of deforestation during the first five years of the decade. Figures in italics are estimates from other periods and are based on more recent or better assessments than those used in the 1980 projections.

Special note should be taken of Brazil—the country with the world's largest tropical closed forest—which now undertakes annual deforestation assessments. The estimate of deforestation in Brazil is the most recent. Brazil is unique in having several assessments of forest extent and deforestation that use a common methodology based on images from Landsat satellites. Closed forest deforestation in the Legal Amazon of Brazil during 1990 is estimated at 13,800 square kilometers, down from the 17,900 square kilometers estimated in 1989. Between 1978 and 1988, deforestation in this region averaged about 21,000 square kilometers, having peaked in 1987 and declined greatly thereafter. By 1990, cumulative deforestation (both recent and historical) within the Legal Amazon totaled 415,000 square kilometers. Deforestation outside the Legal Amazon also occurs, but there is much less information on its extent. A 1980 estimate, that open forest deforestation in Brazil totaled about 10,500 square kilometers, is the most recent available.

Nationally protected areas are areas of at least 1,000 hectares that fall into one of five management categories: scientific reserves and strict nature reserves; national parks of national or international significance (not materially affected by human activity); natural monuments and natural landscapes with some unique aspects; managed nature reserves and wildlife sanctuaries; and protected landscapes and seascapes (which may include cultural landscapes). This table does not include sites protected only under local or provincial law or areas where consumptive uses of wildlife are allowed. These data are subject to variations in definition and in reporting to the organizations, such as the World Conservation Monitoring Centre, that compile and disseminate these data.

Internal renewable water withdrawal data are subject to variation in collection and estimation methods but accurately show the magnitude of water use in both total and per capita terms. These data, however, also hide what can be significant variation in total renewable water resources from one year to another. They also fail to distinguish the variation in water availability within a country both seasonally and geographically. Because freshwater resources are based on long-term averages, their estimation explicitly excludes decade-long cycles of wet and dry. These data are compiled from national, international, and professional publications from a variety of years. In the absence of other measures, estimates of sectoral withdrawals are modeled when necessary (based on information on industry, irrigation practices, livestock populations, crop mix, and precipitation). Data from small countries and arid regions are thought less reliable than those from large countries and more humid zones. These data do not include fresh water created by desalination plants.

Annual withdrawal refers to the average annual flows of rivers and underground waters that are derived from precipitation falling within the country. The *total* withdrawn and the *percentage* withdrawn of the total renewable resource are both reported in this table. The total water withdrawn for use can exceed the total renewable resource of a country for two reasons. Water might be withdrawn from a lake or river shared with another country, or it might be withdrawn from an aquifer that is not part of the renewable cycle. *Domestic* use includes drinking water, municipal use or supply, and uses for public services, commercial establishments, and homes. Direct withdrawals for *industrial* use, including withdrawals for cooling thermoelectric plants, are combined in the final column of this table with withdrawals for *agriculture* (irrigation and livestock production). Per capita water withdrawal is calculated by dividing a country's total withdrawal by its population in the year that withdrawal estimates are available.

Data sources

Production and domestic absorption	U.N. Department of International Economic and Social Affairs. Various years. *Statistical Yearbook*. New York. ———. Various years. *Energy Statistics Yearbook*. Statistical Papers, series J. New York. U.N. International Comparison Program Phases IV (1980) and V (1985) reports, and data from ECE, ESCAP, Eurostat, OECD, and U.N. FAO, IMF, UNIDO, and World Bank data; national sources.
Fiscal and monetary accounts	International Monetary Fund. *Government Finance Statistics Yearbook*. Vol. 11. Washington, D.C. ———. Various years. *International Financial Statistics*. Washington, D.C. U.N. Department of International Economic and Social Affairs. Various years. *World Energy Supplies*. Statistical Papers, series J. New York. IMF data.
Core international transactions	International Monetary Fund. Various years. *International Financial Statistics*. Washington, D.C. U.N. Conference on Trade and Development. Various years. *Handbook of International Trade and Development Statistics*. Geneva. U.N. Department of International Economic and Social Affairs. Various years. *Monthly Bulletin of Statistics*. New York. ———. Various years. *Yearbook of International Trade Statistics*. New York. FAO, IMF, U.N., and World Bank data.
External finance	Organisation for Economic Co-operation and Development. Various years. *Development Co-operation*. Paris. ———. 1988. *Geographical Distribution of Financial Flows to Developing Countries*. Paris. IMF, OECD, and World Bank data; World Bank Debtor Reporting System.
Human resources	Eduard Bos, Patience W. Stephens, and My T. Vu. *World Population Projections, 1992–93 Edition* (forthcoming). Baltimore, Md.: Johns Hopkins University Press. Institute for Resource Development/Westinghouse. 1987. *Child Survival: Risks and the Road to Health*. Columbia, Md. Mauldin, W. Parker, and Holden J. Segal. 1988. ''Prevalence of Contraceptive Use: Trends and Issues.'' *Studies in Family Planning* 19, 6: 335–53. Sivard, Ruth. 1985. *Women—A World Survey*. Washington, D.C.: World Priorities. U.N. Department of International Economic and Social Affairs. Various years. *Demographic Yearbook*. New York. ———. Various years. *Population and Vital Statistics Report*. New York. ———. Various years. *Statistical Yearbook*. New York. ———. 1989. *Levels and Trends of Contraceptive Use as Assessed in 1988*. New York. ———. 1988. *Mortality of Children under Age 5: Projections 1950–2025*. New York. ———. 1991. *World Urbanization Prospects 1991*. New York. ———. 1991. *World Population Prospects: 1990*. New York. U.N. Educational Scientific and Cultural Organization. Various years. *Statistical Yearbook*. Paris. ———. 1988. *Compendium of Statistics on Illiteracy*. Paris. UNICEF. 1989. *The State of the World's Children 1989*. Oxford: Oxford University Press. World Health Organization. Various years. *World Health Statistics Annual*. Geneva. ———. 1986. *Maternal Mortality Rates: A Tabulation of Available Information*, 2nd edition. Geneva. ———. Various years. *World Health Statistics Report*. Geneva. World Resources Institute. 1990. *World Resources 1990–91*. New York. FAO and World Bank data.

Classification of economies

Part 1 Classification of economies by income and region

Income group	Subgroup	Sub-Saharan Africa		Asia		Europe and Central Asia		Middle East and North Africa		
		East and Southern Africa	West Africa	East Asia and Pacific	South Asia	Eastern Europe and Central Asia	Rest of Europe	Middle East	North Africa	Americas
Low-income	Large			China	India					
	Small	Burundi Comoros Ethiopia Kenya Lesotho Madagascar Malawi Mozambique Rwanda Somalia Sudan Tanzania Uganda Zaire Zambia	Benin Burkina Faso Central African Rep. Chad Equatorial Guinea Gambia, The Ghana Guinea Guinea-Bissau Liberia Mali Mauritania Niger Nigeria São Tomé and Principe Sierra Leone Togo	Cambodia Indonesia Lao PDR Solomon Islands Viet Nam	Bangladesh Bhutan Maldives Myanmar Nepal Pakistan Sri Lanka			Afghanistan	Egypt, Arab Rep.	Guyana Haiti Honduras
Middle-income	Lower	Angola Botswana Djibouti Mauritius Namibia Swaziland Zimbabwe	Cameroon Cape Verde Congo, Rep. Côte d'Ivoire Senegal	Fiji Kiribati Korea, Dem. Rep.[a] Malaysia Mongolia Papua New Guinea Philippines Thailand Tonga Vanuatu Western Samoa		Albania[a] Bulgaria Poland Romania	Turkey	Iran, Islamic Rep. Jordan Lebanon Syrian Arab Rep. Yemen, Rep.	Algeria Morocco Tunisia	Argentina Belize Bolivia Chile Colombia Costa Rica Cuba[a] Dominica Dominican Rep. Ecuador El Salvador Grenada Guatemala Jamaica Nicaragua Panama Paraguay Peru St. Lucia St. Vincent
	Upper	Reunion Seychelles South Africa	Gabon	American Samoa Guam Korea, Rep. Macao New Caledonia Pacific Is., Trust Terr.		Czechoslovakia Hungary Former USSR[a] Yugoslavia	Gibraltar Greece Isle of Man Malta Portugal	Bahrain Iraq Oman Saudi Arabia	Libya	Antigua and Barbuda Barbados Brazil French Guiana Guadeloupe Martinique Mexico Netherlands Antilles Puerto Rico St. Kitts and Nevis Suriname Trinidad and Tobago Uruguay Venezuela
No. of low- & middle-income economies 145		25	23	23	8	8	6	10	5	37

(Continues on the following page.)

(continued)

Income group	Subgroup	Sub-Saharan Africa — East and Southern Africa	West Africa	Asia — East Asia and Pacific	South Asia	Europe and Central Asia — Eastern Europe and Central Asia	Rest of Europe	Middle East and North Africa — Middle East	North Africa	Americas
High-income	OECD countries			Australia Japan New Zealand			Austria Belgium Denmark Finland France Germany Iceland Ireland Italy Luxembourg Netherlands Norway Spain Sweden Switzerland United Kingdom			Canada United States
	Non-OECD countries	Mayotte		Brunei French Polynesia Hong Kong Singapore OAE[b]			Andorra Channel Islands Cyprus Faeroe Islands Greenland	Israel Kuwait Qatar United Arab Emirates		Aruba Bahamas Bermuda Virgin Islands (US)

Note: Economies with populations of less than 30,000 are not included.
a. Not included in regional measures because of data limitations.
b. Other Asian economies—Taiwan, China.

Definitions of groups

Part 1

Income group: The economies are divided according to 1990 GNP per capita, calculated using the *World Bank Atlas* method. The groups are: low-income, $610 or less; lower-middle-income, $611–2,465; upper-middle-income, $2,466–$7,619; and high-income, $7,620 or more.

Subgroup: Low-income economies are further divided by size, and high-income by membership of OECD.

Region: Economies are divided into five major regions and eight additional subregions.

Part 2

Major export category: Major exports are those that account for 50 percent or more of total exports from one category, in the period 1987–89. The categories are: nonfuel primary (SITC 0, 1, 2, and 4, plus 68), fuels (SITC 3), manufactures (SITC 5 to 9, minus 68) and services (factor and nonfactor service receipts plus workers' remittances). If no single category accounts for 50 percent or more of total exports, that economy is classified as *diversified*.

Indebtedness: Standard World Bank definitions of severe and moderate indebtedness, averaged over three years (1988–90) are used to classify economies in this table. *Severely-indebted* means three of four key ratios are above critical levels: debt to GNP (50 percent), debt to exports of goods and services (275 percent), accrued debt service to exports (30 percent), and accrued interest to exports (20 percent). *Moderately indebted* means three of the four key ratios exceed 60 percent of, but do not reach, the critical levels. *Less indebted economies* and those not covered in the World Bank Debtor Reporting System are also listed.

Part 2 Classification of economies by major export category and indebtedness

	Low- and middle-income						High-income non-OECD	High-income OECD
	More indebted economies							
	Low-income		Middle-income					
Group	Severely indebted	Moderately indebted	Severely indebted	Moderately indebted	Less indebted economies	Debtor Reporting System	High-income non-OECD	High-income OECD
Exporters of manufactures			Bulgaria Poland	Hungary	China Czechoslovakia Korea, Rep. Lebanon Romania	Korea, Dem. Rep.[a] Macao New Caledonia	French Polynesia Hong Kong Israel Singapore OAE[b]	Canada Finland Germany Ireland Italy Japan Sweden Switzerland
Exporters of nonfuel primary products	Burundi Equatorial Guinea Ethiopia Ghana Guinea Guinea-Bissau Guyana Honduras Liberia Madagascar Malawi Mauritania Myanmar Niger São Tomé and Principe Somalia Sudan Tanzania Uganda Zaire Zambia	Rwanda Togo	Argentina Côte d'Ivoire Nicaragua	Chile Costa Rica Guatemala	Bhutan Botswana Chad Papua New Guinea Paraguay Solomon Islands St. Vincent Swaziland Zimbabwe	Afghanistan Albania[a] American Samoa Cuba[a] French Guiana Guadeloupe Guam Mongolia Namibia Reunion Suriname Viet Nam	Faeroe Islands Greenland	Iceland New Zealand
Exporters of fuels (mainly oil)	Nigeria		Algeria Congo, Rep. Venezuela	Angola Gabon	Iran, Islamic Rep. Oman Trinidad and Tobago	Gibraltar Iraq Libya Saudi Arabia Former USSR[a]	Brunei Qatar United Arab Emirates	
Exporters of services	Egypt, Arab Rep.	Benin		Dominican Republic Jamaica Jordan Yemen, Rep.	Burkina Faso Cape Verde Djibouti Fiji Grenada Haiti Lesotho Maldives Malta Nepal Panama Seychelles St. Kitts and Nevis St. Lucia Tonga Vanuatu Western Samoa	Antigua and Barbuda Barbados Cambodia Greece Kiribati Martinique Netherlands Antilles	Bahamas Bermuda Cyprus Aruba	United Kingdom
Diversified exporters[c]	Kenya Mozambique Sierra Leone	Bangladesh Central African Rep. Comoros India Indonesia Mali Pakistan Sri Lanka	Bolivia Brazil Ecuador Mexico Morocco Peru Syrian Arab Rep.	Cameroon Colombia El Salvador Philippines Senegal Turkey Uruguay	Belize Dominica Gambia, The Lao PDR Malaysia Mauritius Portugal Thailand Tunisia Yugoslavia	Bahrain South Africa	Kuwait	Australia Austria Belgium Denmark France Luxembourg Netherlands Norway Spain United States
No. of economies 178	26	11	15	17	44	29	15	21

Note: Economies with populations of less than 30,000 are not included.
a. Not included in regional measures because of data limitations. b. Other Asian economies—Taiwan, China.
c. Economies in which no single export category accounts for more than 50 percent of total exports.